The
INTERNATIONAL CRITICAL COMMENTARY
on the Holy Scriptures of the Old and New Testaments

GENERAL EDITORS:

S. R. DRIVER
Regius Professor of Hebrew, University of Oxford

A. PLUMMER
Master of University College, University of Durham

C. A. BRIGGS
*Edward Robinson Professor of Biblical Theology,
Union Theological Seminary, New York*

THE FIRST EPISTLE OF ST PAUL
TO THE CORINTHIANS

THE INTERNATIONAL CRITICAL COMMENTARY

A CRITICAL AND EXEGETICAL COMMENTARY

ON THE

FIRST EPISTLE OF ST PAUL TO THE CORINTHIANS

Right Rev. ARCHIBALD ROBERTSON, D.D., LL.D.

AND

Rev. ALFRED PLUMMER, M.A., D.D.

A CRITICAL AND EXEGETICAL COMMENTARY

THE FIRST EPISTLE OF ST PAUL TO THE CORINTHIANS

BY

The Right Rev. ARCHIBALD ROBERTSON, D.D., LL.D.

Bishop of Exeter
Principal of King's College, London
Formerly Principal of Bishop Hatfield's Hall, Durham
Honorary Fellow of Trinity College, Oxford

AND

The Rev. ALFRED PLUMMER, M.A., D.D.

Master of University College, Durham
Formerly Fellow and Tutor of Trinity College, Oxford

T. & T. CLARK LIMITED, 59 GEORGE STREET

PRINTED IN THE U.K. BY PAGE BROS (NORWICH) LTD

FOR

T. & T. CLARK LTD, EDINBURGH

0 567 05027 0

Latest impression 1986

PREFACE

MORE than fourteen years ago I promised to Dr. Plummer, Editor of the "International Critical Commentary," an edition of this Epistle, of which I had the detailed knowledge gained by some years of teaching. Almost immediately, however, a change of work imposed upon me new duties in the course of which my predominant interests were claimed, in part by administrative work which curtailed opportunities for study or writing, in part by studies other than exegetical.

I had hoped that in my present position this diversion of time and attention would prove less exacting; but the very opposite has been the case. Accordingly my task in preparing for publication the work of past years upon the Epistle has suffered from sad lack of continuity, and has not, with the exception of a few sections, been carried beyond its earlier chapters.

That the Commentary appears, when it does and as it does, is due to the extraordinary kindness of my old friend, tutor at Oxford, and colleague at Durham, Dr. Plummer. His generous patience as Editor is beyond any recognition I can express: he has, moreover, supplied my shortcomings by taking upon his shoulders the greater part of the work. Of the Introduction, also, he has written important sections; the Index is entirely his work.

While, however, a reader versed in documentary criticism may be tempted to assign each *nuance* to its several source, we desire each to accept general responsibility as contributors, while to Dr. Plummer falls that of Editor and, I may add, the main share of whatever merit the volume may possess.

It is hoped that amidst the exceptional number of excellent commentaries which the importance of the First Epistle to the Corinthians has called forth, the present volume may yet, with God's blessing, have a usefulness of its own to students of St Paul.

A. EXON:

Exeter,
Conversion of St Paul,
1911.

CONTENTS

INTRODUCTION

---

§ I. CORINTH.

WHAT we know from other sources respecting Corinth in St Paul's day harmonizes well with the impression which we receive from 1 Corinthians. The extinction of the *totius Graeciae lumen*, as Cicero (*Pro lege Manil.* 5) calls the old Greek city of Corinth, by the Roman consul L. Mummius Achaicus, 146 B.C., was only temporary. Exactly a century later Julius Caesar founded a new city on the old site as *Colonia Julia Corinthus.** The rebuilding was a measure of military precaution, and little was done to show that there was any wish to revive the glories of Greece (Finlay, *Greece under the Romans*, p. 67). The inhabitants of the new city were not Greeks but Italians, Caesar's veterans and freedmen. The descendants of the inhabitants who had survived the destruction of the old city did not return to the home of their parents, and Greeks generally were for a time somewhat shy of taking up their abode in the new city. Plutarch, who was still a boy when St Paul was in Greece, seems hardly to have regarded the new Corinth as a Greek town. Festus says that the colonists were called *Corinthienses*, to distinguish them from the old *Corinthii*. But such distinctions do not seem to have been maintained. By the time that St Paul visited the city there were plenty of Greeks among the inhabitants, the current language was in the main Greek, and the descendants of the first Italian colonists had become to a large extent Hellenized.

The mercantile prosperity, which had won for the old city such epithets as ἀφνειός (Hom. *Il.* ii. 570; Pind. Fragg. 87, 244), εὐδαίμων (Hdt. iii. 52), and ὄλβια (Pind. *Ol.* xiii. 4; Thuc. i. 13), and which during the century of desolation had in some degree passed to Delos, was quickly recovered by the new city, because it was the result of an extraordinarily advantageous position, which remained unchanged. Corinth, both old and new, was situated

---

* Other titles found on coins and in inscriptions are *Laus Juli Corinthus* and *Colonia Julia Corinthus Augusta*.

on the 'bridge' or causeway between two seas; πόντου γέφυρ'
ἀκάμαντος (Pind. *Nem.* vi. 67), γέφυραν ποντιάδα πρὸ Κορίνθου
τειχέων (*Isth.* iii. 35). Like Ephesus, it was both on the main commercial route between East and West and also at a point at which
various side-routes met the main one. The merchandise which
came to its markets, and which passed through it on its way to
other places, was enormous; and those who passed through it
commonly stayed awhile for business or pleasure. "This
bimaris Corinthus was a natural halting-place on the journey
between Rome and the East, as we see in the case of S. Paul
and his companions, and of Hegesippus (Eus. *H.E.* iv. 22). So
also it is called the περίπατος or 'lounge' of Greece" (Lightfoot,
S. Clement of Rome, ii. pp. 9, 10). The rhetorician Aristeides
calls it "a palace of Poseidon"; it was rather the market-place
or the Vanity Fair of Greece, and even of the Empire.

It added greatly to its importance, and doubtless to its
prosperity, that Corinth was the metropolis of the Roman
province of Achaia, and the seat of the Roman proconsul
(Acts xviii. 12). In more than one particular it became the
leading city in Greece. It was proud of its political priority,
proud of its commercial supremacy, proud also of its mental
activity and acuteness, although in this last particular it was
surpassed, and perhaps greatly surpassed, by Athens. It may
have been for this very reason that Athens was one of the last
Hellenic cities to be converted to Christianity. But just as the
leaders of thought there saw nothing sublime or convincing in
the doctrine which St Paul taught (Acts xvii. 18, 32), so the
political ruler at Corinth failed to see that the question which
he quite rightly refused to decide as a Roman magistrate, was
the crucial question of the age (Acts xviii. 14–16). Neither
Gallio nor any other political leader in Greece saw that the
Apostle was the man of the future. They made the common
mistake of men of the world, who are apt to think that the
world which they know so well is the whole world (Renan,
S. Paul, p. 225).

In yet another particular Corinth was first in Hellas. The
old city had been the most licentious city in Greece, and
perhaps the most licentious city in the Empire. As numerous
expressions and a variety of well-known passages testify, the
name of Corinth had been a by-word for the grossest profligacy,
especially in connexion with the worship of Aphrodite Pande-
mos.* Aphrodite was worshipped elsewhere in Hellas, but

---

* Κορινθιάζεσθαι, Κορινθία κόρη, Κορ. παῖς : οὐ παντὸς ἀνδρὸς ἐς Κόρινθον
ἔσθ' ὁ πλοῦς, a proverb which Horace (*Ep.* I. xvii. 36) reproduces, *non cuivis
homini contingit adire Corinthum.* Other references in Renan, p. 213, and
Farrar, *St Paul*, i. pp. 557 f.

nowhere else do we find the ἱερόδουλοι as a permanent element in the worship, and in old Corinth there had been a thousand of these. Such worship was not Greek but Oriental, an importation from the cult of the Phoenician Astarte; but it is not certain that this worship of Aphrodite had been revived in all its former monstrosity in the new city. Pausanias, who visited Corinth about a century later than St Paul, found it rich in temples and idols of various kinds, Greek and foreign; but he calls the temple of Aphrodite a ναίδιον (VIII. vi. 21): see Bachmann, p. 5. It is therefore possible that we ought not to quote the thousand ἱερόδουλοι in the temple of Aphrodite on Acrocorinthus as evidence of the immorality of Corinth in St Paul's day. Nevertheless, even if that pestilent element had been reduced in the new city, there is enough evidence to show that Corinth still deserved a very evil reputation; and the letters which St Paul wrote to the Church there, and from Corinth to other Churches, tell us a good deal.

It may be doubted whether the notorious immorality of Corinth had anything to do with St Paul's selecting it as a sphere of missionary work. It was the fact of its being an imperial and cosmopolitan centre that attracted him. The march of the Empire must everywhere be followed by the march of the Gospel. The Empire had raised Corinth from the death which the ravages of its own legions had inflicted and had made it a centre of government and of trade. The Gospel must raise Corinth from the death of heathenism and make it a centre for the diffusion of discipline and truth. In few other places were the leading elements of the Empire so well represented as in Corinth: it was at once Roman, Oriental, and Greek. The Oriental element was seen, not only in its religion, but also in the number of Asiatics who settled in it or frequently visited it for purposes of commerce. Kenchreae is said to have been chiefly Oriental in population. Among these settlers from the East were many Jews,* who were always attracted to mercantile centres; and the number of them must have been considerably increased when the edict of Claudius expelled the Jews from Rome (Acts xviii. 2; Suet. *Claud.* 25). In short, Corinth was the Empire in miniature;—the Empire reduced to a single State, but with some of the worst features of heathenism intensified, as Rom. i. 21–32, which was written in Corinth, plainly shows. Any one who could make his voice heard in Corinth was addressing a cosmopolitan and representative audience, many of whom would be sure to go elsewhere, and

---

* Philo, *Leg. ad Gai.* 36; cf. Justin, *Try.* 1. It is unfortunate that neither the edict of Claudius nor the proconsulship of Gallio can be dated with accuracy.

might carry with them what they had heard. We need not wonder that St Paul thought it worth while to go there, and (after receiving encouragement from the Lord, Acts xviii. 9) to remain there a year and a half. Nor need we wonder that, having succeeded in finding the 'people' (λαός) whom the Lord had already marked as His own, like a new Israel (Acts xviii. 10), and having succeeded in planting a Church there, he afterwards felt the keenest interest in its welfare and the deepest anxiety respecting it.

It was from Athens that St Paul came to Corinth, and the transition has been compared to that of passing from residence in Oxford to residence in London; that ought to mean from the old unreformed Oxford, the home of lost causes and of expiring philosophies, to the London of our own age. The difference in miles between Oxford and London is greater than that between Athens and Corinth; but, in St Paul's day, the difference in social and intellectual environment was perhaps greater than that which has distinguished the two English cities in any age. The Apostle's work in the two Greek cities was part of his great work of adapting Christianity to civilized Europe. In Athens he met with opposition and contempt (Acts xvii. 18, 32),* and he came on to Corinth in much depression and fear (1 Cor. ii. 3); and not until he had been encouraged by the heavenly vision and the experience of considerable success did he think that he would be justified in remaining at Corinth instead of returning to the more hopeful field in Macedonia. During the year and a half that he was there he probably made missionary excursions in the neighbourhood, and with success: 2 Corinthians is addressed 'unto the Church of God which is at Corinth, with all the saints which are in the whole of Achaia.'

So far as we know, he was the first Christian who ever entered that city; he was certainly the first to preach the Gospel there. This he claims for himself with great earnestness (iii. 6, 10, iv. 15), and he could not have made such a claim, if those whom he was addressing knew that it was not true. Some think that Aquila and Priscilla were Christians before they reached Corinth. But if that was so, St Luke would probably have known it, and would have mentioned the fact; for their being of the same belief would have been a stronger reason for the Apostle's taking up his abode with them than their being of the same trade, τὸ ὁμότεχνον (Acts xviii. 3).† On the other

---

* This attitude continued long after the Apostle's departure. For a century or two Athens was perhaps the chief seat of opposition to the Gospel.

† It is possible that this is one of the beloved physician's medical words. Doctors are said to have spoken of one another as ὁμότεχνοι (Hobart, *Med. Lang. of St Luke*, p. 239).

hand, if they were converted by St Paul in Corinth, would not either he or St Luke have mentioned so important a success, and would not they be among those whom he baptized himself? If they were already Christians, it may easily have been from them that he learnt so much about the individual Christians who are mentioned in Rom. xvi. The Apostle's most important Jewish convert that is known to us is Crispus, the ruler of the Corinthian synagogue (Acts xviii. 8; 1 Cor. i. 14). Titius or Titus Justus may have been his first success among the Roman proselytes (Acts xviii. 7; Ramsay, *St Paul the Traveller*, p. 256), or he may have been a Gentile holding allegiance to the synagogue, but not a circumcised proselyte (Zahn, *Intr. to N.T.*, i. p. 266). Acts xviii. 7 means that the Apostle taught in his house, instead of in the synagogue; not that he left the house of Aquila and Priscilla to live with Titus Justus.* About Stephanas (1 Cor. xvi. 15, i. 16) we are doubly in doubt, whether he was a Gentile or a Jew, and whether he was converted and baptized in Athens or in Corinth. He was probably a Gentile; that he was a Corinthian convert is commonly assumed, but it is by no means certain.

A newly created city, with a very mixed population of Italians, Greeks, Orientals, and adventurers from all parts, and without any aristocracy or old families, was likely to be democratic and impatient of control; and conversion to Christianity would not at once, if at all, put an end to this independent spirit. Certainly there was plenty of it when St Paul wrote. We find evidence of it in the claim of each convert to choose his own leader (i. 10–iv. 21), in the attempt of women to be as free as men in the congregation (xi. 5–15, xiv. 34, 35), and in the desire of those who had spiritual gifts to exhibit them in public without regard to other Christians (xii., xiv.).

Of the evils which are common in a community whose chief aim is commercial success, and whose social distinctions are mainly those of wealth, we have traces in the litigation about property in heathen courts (vi. 1–11), in the repeated mention of the πλεονέκτης as a common kind of offender (v. 10, 11, vi. 10), and in the disgraceful conduct of the wealthy at the Lord's Supper (xi. 17–34).

The conceited self-satisfaction of the Corinthians as to their intellectual superiority is indicated by ironical hints and serious warnings as to the possession of γνῶσις (viii. 1, 7, 10, 11,

---

* Justus, as a surname for Jews or proselytes, meant (like δίκαιος in Luke i. 6) 'careful in the observance of the Law.' It was common in the case of Jews (Acts i. 23; Col. iv. 11). Josephus had a son so called, and he tells us of another Justus who wrote about the Jewish war (*Vita*, 1, 9, 65). It is said to be frequent in Jewish inscriptions.

xiii. 2, 8) and σοφία (i. 17, iii. 19), by the long section which
treats of the false and the true wisdom (i. 18–iii. 4), and by the
repeated rebukes of their inflated self-complacency (iv. 6, 18, 19,
v. 2, viii. 1; cf. xiii. 4).

But the feature in the new city which has made the deepest
mark on the Epistle is its abysmal immorality. There is not
only the condemnation of the Corinthians' attitude towards the
monstrous case of incest (v. 1–13) and the solemn warning
against thinking lightly of sins of the flesh (vi. 12–20), but also
the nature of the reply to the Corinthians' letter (vii. 1–xi. 1).
The whole treatment of their marriage-problems and of the right
behaviour with regard to idol-meats is influenced by the thought
of the manifold and ceaseless temptations to impurity with which
the new converts to Christianity were surrounded, and which
made such an expression as 'the Church of God which is at
Corinth' (i. 2), as Bengel says, *laetum et ingens paradoxon*. And
the majority of the converts—probably the very large majority—
had been heathen (xii. 2), and therefore had been accustomed
to think lightly of abominations from which converts from
Judaism had always been free. Anxiety about these Gentile
Christians is conspicuous throughout the First Epistle; but at
the time when the Second was written, especially the last four
chapters, it was Jewish Christians that were giving him most
trouble. In short, Corinth, as we know it from other sources,
is clearly reflected in the letter before us.

That what we know about Corinth and the Apostle from
Acts is reflected in the letter will be seen when it is examined
in detail; and it is clear that the writer of Acts does not derive
his information from the letter, for he tells us much more than
the letter does. As Schleiermacher pointed out long ago, the
personal details at the beginning and end of 1 and 2 Corinthians
supplement and illuminate what is told in Acts, and it is clear
that each writer takes his own line independently of the other
(Bachmann, p. 12).

§ II. AUTHENTICITY.

It is not necessary to spend much time upon the discussion
of this question. Both the external and the internal evidence
for the Pauline authorship are so strong that those who attempt
to show that the Apostle was not the writer succeed chiefly in
proving their own incompetence as critics. Subjective criticism
of a highly speculative kind does not merit many detailed
replies, when it is in opposition to abundant evidence of the
most solid character. The captious objections which have been

urged against one or other, or even against all four, of the great Epistles of St Paul, by Bruno Bauer (1850–1852), and more recently by Loman, Pierson, Naber, Edwin Johnson, Meyboom, van Manen, Rudolf Steck, and others, have been sufficiently answered by Kuenen, Scholten, Schmiedel, Zahn, Gloël, Wrede, and Lindemann; and the English reader will find all that he needs on the subject in Knowling, *The Witness of the Epistles*, ch. iii., or in *The Testimony of St Paul to Christ*, lect. xxiv. and *passim* (see Index). But the student of 1 Corinthians can spend his time better than in perusing replies to utterly untenable objections. More than sixty years ago, F. C. Baur said of the four chief Epistles, that "they bear so incontestably the character of Pauline originality, that there is no conceivable ground for the assertion of critical doubts in their case" (*Paulus*, Stuttg. 1845, ii. *Einleit.*, Eng. tr. i. p. 246). And with regard to the arguments which have been urged against these Epistles since Baur's day, we may adopt the verdict of Schmiedel, who, after examining a number of these objections, concludes thus: "In a word, until better reasons are produced, one may really trust oneself to the conviction that one has before one writings of Paul" (*Hand-Commentar zum N.T.*, II. i. p. 51).

The external evidence in support of Pauline authorship in the fullest sense is abundant and unbroken from the first century down to our own day. It begins, at the latest, with a formal appeal to 1 Corinthians as "the letter of the blessed Paul, the Apostle" by Clement of Rome about A.D. 95 (*Cor.* 47), the earliest example in literature of a New Testament writer being quoted by name. And it is possible that we have still earlier evidence than that. In the Epistle of Barnabas iv. 11 we have words which seem to recall 1 Cor. iii. 1, 16, 18; and in the *Didache* x. 6 we have μαρὰν ἀθά, enforcing a warning, as in 1 Cor. xvi. 22. But in neither case do the words *prove* acquaintance with our Epistle; and, moreover, the date of these two documents is uncertain: some would place both of them later than 95 A.D. It is quite certain that Ignatius and Polycarp knew 1 Corinthians, and it is highly probable that Hermas did. "Ignatius must have known this Epistle almost by heart. Although there are no *quotations* (in the strictest sense, with mention of the source), echoes of its language and thought pervade the whole of his writings in such a manner as to leave no doubt whatever that he was acquainted with the First Epistle to the Corinthians" (*The N.T. in the Apostolic Fathers*, 1905, p. 67). We find in the Epistles of Ignatius what seem to be echoes of 1 Cor. i. 7, 10, 18, 20, 24, 30, ii. 10, 14, iii. 1, 2, 10–15, 16, iv. 1, 4, v. 7, vi. 9, 10, 15, vii. 10, 22, 29, ix. 15, 27, x. 16, 17, xii. 12, xv. 8–10, 45, 47, 58, xvi. 18; and a number of these, being quite beyond dispute, give increase of probability to the rest. In Polycarp there are seven such echoes, two of which (to 1 Cor. vi. 2, 9) are quite certain, and a third (to xiii. 13) highly probable. In the first of these (Pol. xi. 2), Paul is mentioned, but not this Epistle. The passage in Hermas (*Mand.* iv. 4) resembles 1 Cor. vii. 39, 40 so closely that reminiscence is more probable than mere coincidence. Justin Martyr, about A.D. 147, quotes from 1 Cor. xi. 19 (*Try.* 35), and Athenagoras, about A.D. 177, quotes part of xv. 55 as κατὰ τὸν ἀπόστολον (*De Res. Mort.* 18). In Irenaeus there are more than 60 quotations; in Clement of Alexandria, more than 130; in Tertullian, more than 400, counting verses separately. Basilides certainly knew it, and Marcion admitted it to his very select canon. This brief statement by no means exhausts all the evidence of the two centuries subsequent to the writing of the Epistle, but it is sufficient to show how substantial the external evidence is.

The internal evidence is equally satisfactory. The document, in spite of its varied contents, is harmonious in character and language. It is evidently the product of a strong and original mind, and is altogether worthy of an Apostle. When tested by comparison with other writings of St Paul, or with Acts, or with other writings in the N.T., we find so many coincidences, most of which must be undesigned, that we feel confident that neither invention, nor mere chance, nor these two combined, would be a sufficient explanation. The only hypothesis that will explain these coincidences is that we are dealing with a genuine letter of the Apostle of the Gentiles. And it has already been pointed out how well the contents of the letter harmonize with what we know of Corinth during the lifetime of St Paul.

The *integrity* of 1 Corinthians has been questioned with as much boldness as its authenticity, and with as little success. On quite insufficient, and (in some cases) trifling, or even absurd, grounds, some sections, verses, and parts of verses, have been suspected of being interpolations, *e.g.* xi. 16, 19 b, 23–28, xii. 2, 13, parts of xiv. 5 and 10, and the whole of 13, xv. 23–28, 45. The reasons for suspecting smaller portions are commonly better than those for suspecting longer ones, but none are sufficient to warrant rejection. Here and there we are in doubt about a word, as Χριστοῦ (i. 8), Ἰησοῦ (iv. 17), ἡμῶν (v. 4), and τὰ ἔθνη (x. 20), but there is probably no verse or whole clause that is an interpolation. Others again have conjectured that our Epistle is made up of portions of two, or even three, letters, laid together in strata; and this conjecture is sometimes combined with the hypothesis that portions of the letter alluded to in v. 9 are imbedded in our 1 Corinthians. Thus, iii. 10–23, vii. 17–24, ix. 1–x. 22, x. 25–30, xiv. 34–36, xv. 1–55, are supposed to be

fragments of this first letter. An hypothesis of this kind
naturally involves the supposition that there are a number of
interpolations which have been made in order to cement the
fragments of the different letters together. These wild conjectures may safely be disregarded. There is no trace of them
in any of the four great Uncial MSS. which contain the whole
Epistle (ℵ A B D), or in any Version. We have seen that
Ignatius shows acquaintance with every chapter, with the possible
exception of viii., xi., xiii., xiv. Irenaeus quotes from every
chapter, excepting iv., xiv., and xvi. Tertullian goes through it
to the end of xv. (*Adv. Marc.* v. 5–10), and he quotes from xvi.
The Epistle reads quite intelligibly and smoothly as we have it;
and it does not follow that, because it would read still more
smoothly if this or that passage were ejected, therefore the
Epistle was not written as it has come down to us. As Jülicher
remarks, "what is convenient is not always right." * Till better
reasons are produced for rearranging it, or for rejecting parts of
it, we may be content to read it as being still in the form in
which the Apostle dictated it.

§ III. Occasion and Plan.

The *Occasion* of 1 Corinthians is patent from the Epistle
itself. Two things induced St Paul to write. (1) During his
long stay at Ephesus the Corinthians had written to him, asking
certain questions, and perhaps also mentioning certain things as
grievances. (2) Information of a very disquieting kind respecting the condition of the Corinthian Church had reached the
Apostle from various sources. Apparently, the latter was the
stronger reason of the two; but either of them, even without
the other, would have caused him to write.

Since his departure from Corinth, after spending eighteen
months in founding a Church there, a great deal had happened
in the young community. The accomplished Alexandrian Jew
Apollos, 'mighty in the Scriptures,' who had been well instructed
in Christianity by Priscilla and Aquila (Acts xviii. 24, 26) at
Ephesus, came and began to preach the Gospel, following (but,
seemingly, with greater display of eloquence) in the footsteps of
St Paul. Other teachers, less friendly to the Apostle, and with
leanings towards Judaism, also began to work. In a short time
the infant Church was split into parties, each party claiming this
or that teacher as its leader, but, in each case, without the
chosen leader giving any encouragement to this partizanship

* Recent Introductions to the N.T. (Holtzmann, Jülicher, Gregory, Barth,
Weiss, Zahn) treat the integrity of 1 Corinthians as certain.

(i. 10, 11). It is usual to attribute these dissensions to that love of faction which is so conspicuous in all Greek history, and which was the ruin of so many Greek states ; and no doubt there is truth in this suggestion. But we must remember that Corinth at this time was scarcely half Greek. The greater part of the population consisted of the children and grandchildren of Italian colonists, who were still only imperfectly Hellenized, supplemented by numerous Orientals, who were perhaps scarcely Hellenized at all. The purely Greek element in the population was probably quite the smallest of the three. Nevertheless, it was the element which was moulding the other two, and therefore Greek love of faction may well have had something to do with the parties which so quickly sprang up in the new Corinthian Church. But at any other prosperous city on the Mediterranean, either in Italy or in Gaul, we should probably have had the same result. In these cities, with their mobile, eager, and excitable populations, crazes of some kind are not only a common feature, but almost a social necessity. There must be something or somebody to rave about, and either to applaud or to denounce, in order to give zest to life. And this craving naturally generates cliques and parties, consisting of those who approve, and those who disapprove, of some new pursuits or persons. The pursuits or the persons may be of quite trifling importance. That matters little : what is wanted is something to dispute about and take sides about. As Renan says (*St Paul*, p. 374), let there be two preachers, or two doctors, in one of the small towns in Southern Europe, and at once the inhabitants take sides as to which is the better of the two. The two preachers, or the two doctors, may be on the best of terms : that in no way hinders their names from being made a party-cry and the signal for vehement dissensions.

After a stay of a year and six months, St Paul crossed from Corinth to Ephesus with Priscilla and Aquila, and went on without them to Jerusalem (Acts xviii. 11, 18, 19, 21). Thence he went to Galatia, and returned in the autumn to Ephesus. The year in which this took place may be 50, or 52, or 54 A.D. Excepting the winter months, intercourse between Corinth and Ephesus was always frequent, and in favourable weather the crossing might be made in a week, or even less. It was natural, therefore, that the Apostle during his three years at Ephesus should receive frequent news of his converts in Corinth. We know of only one definite source of information, namely, members of the household of a lady named Chloe (i. 11), who brought news about the factions and possibly other troubles : but no doubt there were other persons who came with tidings from Corinth. Those who were entrusted with the letter from the Corinthians to the Apostle (see on xvi. 17) would tell him a great deal. Apollos, now at Ephesus (xvi. 12), would do the same. The condition of things which Chloe's people reported was of so disturbing a nature that the Apostle at once wrote to deal with the matter, and he at the same time answered the questions which the Corinthians had raised in their letter. As will be seen from the Plan given below, these two reasons for writing, namely, reports of serious evils at Corinth, and questions asked by the converts themselves, cover nearly all, if not quite all, of what we find in our Epistle. There may, however, be a few topics which were not prompted by either of them, but are the spontaneous outcome of the Apostle's anxious thoughts about the Corinthian Church. See *Ency. Brit.*, 11th ed., art. 'Bible,' p. 873; art. 'Corinthians,' pp. 151 f.

It is quite certain that our 1 Corinthians is not the first letter which the Apostle wrote to the Church of Corinth; and it is probable that the earlier letter (v. 9) is wholly lost. Some critics, however, think that part of it survives in 2 Cor. vi. 14–vii. 1, an hypothesis which has not found very many supporters. The question of there being yet another letter, which was written between the writing of our two Epistles, and which probably survives, almost in its entirety, in 2 Cor. x. 1–xiii. 10, is a question which belongs to the Introduction to that Epistle, and need not be discussed here.

But there is another question, in which both Epistles are involved. Fortunately nothing that is of great importance in either Epistle depends upon the solution of it, for no solution finds anything approaching to general assent. It has only an indirect connexion with the occasion and plan of our Epistle; but this will be a convenient place for discussing it. It relates to the hypothesis of a *second visit* of St Paul to Corinth, a visit which was very brief, painful, and unsatisfactory, and which (perhaps because of its distressing character) is not recorded in Acts. Did any such visit take place during the Apostle's three years at Ephesus? If so, did it take place before or after the sending of 1 Corinthians? We have thus three possibilities with regard to this second visit of St Paul to Corinth, which was so unlike the first in being short, miserable, and without any good results. (1) It took place before 1 Corinthians was written. (2) It took place after that Epistle was written. (3) It never took place at all. Each one of these hypotheses involves one in difficulties, and yet one of them must be true.

Let us take (3) first. If that could be shown to be correct, there would be no need to discuss either of the other two.

As has already been pointed out, the silence of Acts is in no way surprising, especially when we remember how much of the life of St Paul (2 Cor. xi. 23–28) is left unrecorded by St Luke. If the silence of Acts is regarded as an objection, it is more than counter-balanced by the antecedent probability that, during his three years' stay in Ephesus, the Apostle would visit the Corinthians again. The voyage was a very easy one. It was St Paul's practice in missionary work to go over the ground a second time (Acts xv. 36, 41, xviii. 23); and the intense interest in the condition of the Corinthian Church which these two Epistles exhibit renders it somewhat unlikely that the writer of them would spend three years within a week's sail of Corinth, without paying the Church another visit.

But these *a priori* considerations are accompanied by direct evidence of a substantial kind. The passages which are quoted in support of the hypothesis of a second visit are 1 Cor. xvi. 7; 2 Cor. ii. 1, xii. 14, 21, xiii. 1, 2. We may at once set aside 1 Cor. xvi. 7 (see note there): the verse harmonizes well with the hypothesis of a second visit, but is not evidence that any such visit took place. 2 Cor. xii. 21 is stronger: it is intelligible, if no visit of a distressing character had previously been paid; but it is still more intelligible, if such a visit had been paid; 'lest, when I come, my God should again humble me before you.' 2 Cor. ii. 1 is at least as strong: 'For I determined for myself this, not again in sorrow to come to you.' 'Again in sorrow' comes first with emphasis, and the most natural explanation is that he has visited them ἐν λύπῃ once, and that he decided that he would not make the experiment a second time. It is incredible that he regarded his first visit, in which he founded the Church, as a visit paid ἐν λύπῃ. Therefore the painful visit must have been a second one. Yet it is possible to avoid this conclusion by separating 'again' from 'in sorrow,' which is next to it, and confining it to 'come,' which is remote from it. This construction, if possible, is not very probable.

But it is the remaining texts, 2 Cor. xii. 14, xiii. 1, 2, which are so strong, especially xiii. 2: 'Behold, this is the third time I am ready to come to you'—'This is the third time I am coming to you. . . . I have said before, and I do say before, as when I was present the second time, so now being absent, to those who were in sin before, and to all the rest,' etc. It is difficult to think that the Apostle is referring to *intentions* to come, or *willingness* to come, and not to an actual visit; or again that he is counting a letter as a visit. That is possible, but it is not natural. Again, the preposition in τοῖς προημαρτηκόσιν is more naturally explained as meaning 'who were in sin before my second visit' than 'before their conversion.' Wieseler (*Chronologie*, p. 232) considers that these passages render the assumption of a second visit to Corinth indispensable (*nothwendig*). Conybeare and Howson (ch. **xv.** *sub init.*) maintain that 'this visit is proved' by these passages. Lightfoot (*Biblical Essays*, p. 274) says : "There are passages in the Epistles (*e.g.* 2 Cor. xii. 14, xiii. 1, 2) which seem inexplicable under any other hypothesis, except that of a second visit—the difficulty consisting not so much in the words themselves, as in their relation to their context." Schmiedel (*Hand. Comm.* ii. 1, p. 68) finds it hard to understand how any one can reject the hypothesis ; *die Leugnung der Zwischenreise ist schwer verständlich* ; and he goes carefully through the evidence. Sanday (*Ency. Bibl.* i. 903) says : "The supposition that the second visit was only contemplated, not paid, appears to be excluded by 2 Cor. xiii. 2." Equally strong on the same side are Alford, J. H. Bernard (*Expositor's Grk. Test.*), Jülicher (*Introd. to N.T.* p. 31), Massie (*Century Bible*), G. H. Rendall (*Epp. to the Corr.* p. 31), Waite (*Speaker's Comm.*) ; and with them agree Bleek,* Findlay, Osiander, D. Walker, and others to be mentioned below. On the other hand, Baur, de Wette, Edwards, Heinrici, Hilgenfeld, Paley, Renan, Scholten, Stanley, Zahn, and others, follow Beza, Grotius, and Estius in questioning or denying this second visit of St Paul to Corinth. Ramsay (*St Paul the Traveller*, p. 275) thinks that, if it took place at all, it was from Philippi rather than Ephesus. Bachmann, the latest commentator on 2 Corinthians (Leipzig, 1909, p. 105), thinks that only an over-refined and artificial criticism can question it. We may perhaps regard the evidence for this visit as something short of proof; but it is manifest, both from the evidence itself, and also from the weighty names of those who regard it as conclusive, that we are not justified in treating the supposed visit as so improbable that there is no need to consider whether it took place before or after the writing of our Epistle.†

Many modern writers place it between 1 and 2 Corinthians, and connect it with the letter written 'out of much affliction and anguish of heart with many tears' (2 Cor. ii. 4). The visit was paid ἐν λύπῃ. The Apostle had to deal with serious evils, was perhaps crippled by illness, and failed to put a stop to them. After returning defeated to Ephesus, he wrote the sorrowful letter. This hypothesis is attractive, but it is very difficult to bring it into harmony with the Apostle's varying plans and the Corinthians' charges of fickleness (2 Cor. i. 15–24). But, in any case, if this second visit was paid after 1 Corinthians was written, the commentator on that Epistle need not do more than mention it. See *Ency. Brit.*, 11th ed., vii. p. 152.

---

* Bleek is said to have been the first to show how many indications of a second visit are to be found (*Stud. Krit.* p. 625, 1830).

† For the arguments against the supposed visit see the section on the Date of this Epistle.

But the majority of modern writers, including Alford, J. H Bernard, Bleek, Billroth, Credner, Hausrath, Hofmann, Holsten, Klöpper, Meyer, Neander, Olshausen, Otto, Reuss, Rückert, Sanday, Schenkel, Schmiedel, Waite, and B. Weiss follow Chrysostom in placing the second visit *before* 1 Corinthians. Some place it before the letter mentioned in 1 Cor. v. 9. This has decided advantages. The lost letter of v. 9 may have alluded to the painful visit and treated it in such a way as to render any further reference to it unnecessary. This might account for the silence of 1 Corinthians respecting the visit. Even if the visit be placed after the lost letter, its painful character would account for the silence about it in our Epistle. Some think that the Epistle is not silent, and that iv. 18 refers to this visit: 'As if, however, I were not coming to see you, some got puffed up.' But this cannot refer to a visit that is paid, as if it meant, 'You thought that I was not coming, and I did come.' It refers to a visit that is contemplated, as the next verse shows: 'Come, however, I shall quickly to see you.'

The following tentative scheme gives the events which led up to the writing of our Epistle:—

(1) St Paul leaves Corinth with Aquila and Priscilla and finally settles at Ephesus.

(2) Apollos continues the work of the Apostle at Corinth.

(3) Other teachers arrive, hostile to the Apostle, and Apollos leaves.

(4) St Paul pays a short visit to Corinth to combat this hostility and other evils, and fails.

(5) He writes the letter mentioned in 1 Cor. v. 9.

(6) Bad news arrives from Corinth brought by members of Chloe's *familia*, perhaps also by the bearers of the Corinthians' letter, and by Apollos.

The Apostle at once writes 1 Corinthians.

The *Plan* of the Epistle is very clear. One is seldom in doubt as to where a section begins and ends, or as to what the subject is. There are occasional digressions, or what seem to be such, as the statement of the great Principle of Forbearance (ix. 1–27), or the Hymn in praise of Love (xiii.), but their connexion with the main argument of the section in which they occur is easily seen. The question which cannot be answered with absolute certainty is not a very important one. We cannot be quite sure how much of the Epistle is a reply to questions asked by the Corinthians in their letter to the Apostle. Certainly the discussion of various problems about Marriage (vii. 1–40) is such, as is shown by the opening words, περὶ δὲ ὧν ἐγράψατε: and almost certainly the question about partaking of Idol-meats (viii. 1–xi. 1) was raised by the Corinthians, περὶ δὲ τῶν εἰδωλοθύτων. The difficulty was a real one and of frequent occurrence ; and, as the Apostle does not refer to teaching already given to them on the subject, they would be likely to consult him, all the more so as there seem to have been widely divergent opinions among themselves about the question. It is not impossible that other sections which begin in a similar way are references to the Corinthian letter, περὶ δὲ τῶν πνευματικῶν (xii. 1), περὶ δὲ τῆς λογίας τῆς εἰς τοὺς ἁγίους (xvi. 1), and περὶ δὲ Ἀπολλὼ τοῦ ἀδελφοῦ (xvi. 12). But most of the expressions which look like quotations from the Corinthian letter occur in the sections about Marriage and Idol-meats ; e.g. καλὸν ἀνθρώπῳ γυναικὸς μὴ ἅπτεσθαι (vii. 1), πάντες γνῶσιν ἔχομεν (viii. 1), πάντα ἔξεστιν (x. 23). The directions about Spiritual Gifts and the Collection for the Saints may have been prompted by information which the Apostle received by word of mouth. What is said about Apollos (xvi. 12) must have come from Apollos himself ; but the Corinthians may have asked for his return to them.

According to the arrangement adopted, the Epistle has four main divisions, without counting either the Introduction or the Conclusion.

Epistolary Introduction, i. 1-9.

> A. *The Apostolic Salutation*, i. 1-3.
>
> B. *Preamble of Thanksgiving and Hope*, i. 4-9.

I. Urgent Matters for Blame, i. 10-vi. 20.

> A. *The Dissensions* (Σχίσματα), i. 10-iv. 21.
>> The Facts, i. 10-17.
>> The False Wisdom and the True, i. 18-iii. 4.
>> The False Wisdom, i. 18-ii. 5.
>> The True Wisdom, ii. 6-iii. 4.
>>> The True Wisdom described, ii. 6-13.
>>> The Spiritual and the animal Characters, ii. 14-iii. 4.
>> The True Conception of the Christian Pastorate, iii. 5-iv. 21.
>>> General Definition, iii. 5-9.
>>> The Builders, iii. 10-15
>>> The Temple, iii. 16, 17.
>>> Warning against a mere 'human' Estimate of the Pastoral Office, iii. 18-iv. 5.
>>> Personal Application ; Conclusion of the subject of the Dissensions, iv. 6-21.
>
> B. *Absence of Moral Discipline ; the Case of Incest*, v. 1-13.

Consequences of accepting the Resurrection of Christ, xv. 20–28.
Arguments from Experience, xv. 29–34.

C. *Answers to Objections: the Body of the Risen*, xv. 35–58.
The Answers of Nature and of Scripture, xv. 35–49.
Victory over Death, xv. 50–57.
Practical Result, xv. 58.

Practical and Personal; the Conclusion, xvi. 1–24.

The Collection for the Poor at Jerusalem, xvi. 1–4.
The Apostle's Intended Visit to Corinth, xvi. 5–9.
Timothy and Apollos commended, xvi. 10–12.
Exhortation, xvi. 13, 14.
Directions about Stephanas and others, xvi. 15–18.
Concluding Salutations, Warning, and Benediction, xvi. 19–24.

No Epistle tells us so much about the life of a primitive local Church; and 2 Corinthians, although it tells us a great deal about the Apostle himself, does not tell us much more about the organization of the Church of Corinth. Evidently, there is an immense amount, and that of the highest interest, which neither Epistle reveals. Each of them suggests questions which neither of them answers; and it is very disappointing to turn to Acts, and to find that to the whole of this subject St Luke devotes less than twenty verses. But the instructiveness of 1 Corinthians is independent of a knowledge of the historical facts which it does not reveal.

§ IV. Place and Date.

The place where the Epistle was written was clearly Ephesus (xvi. 8), where the Apostle was remaining until the following Pentecost. This is recognized by Euthal *praef.* ἀπὸ ἐφέσου τῆς Ἀσίας, also by B^3 P in their subscriptions. The subscriptions of D^b K L d^{corr} Euthal. *cod.* all agree in giving 'Philippi' or 'Philippi in Macedonia' as the place of writing, a careless inference from xvi. 5, which occurs also in the Syrr. Copt. Goth. Versions, in later cursives, and in the Textus Receptus.

St Paul is at Ephesus in Acts xviii. 19–21, but the data of this

Epistle (xvi. 5–8) are quite irreconcilable with its having been written during this short visit. It must therefore belong to some part of St Paul's unbroken residence at Ephesus for three years (Acts xx. 18, τὸν πάντα χρόνον: 31, τριετίαν νύκτα καὶ ἡμέραν), which falls within the middle or Aegean period of his ministry. The first, or Antiochean period extends from Acts xi. 25–xviii. 23, when Antioch finally ceases to be his headquarters. The Aegean period ends with his last journey to Jerusalem and arrest there (xxi. 15). This begins the third period, that of the Imprisonments, which carries us to the close of the Acts. Our Epistle accordingly falls within the limits of Acts xix. 21–xx. 1. We have to consider the probable date of the events there described, and the relation to them of the data of our Epistle.

The present writer discussed these questions fully in Hastings, *DB*. art. 'Corinthians,' without the advantage of having seen the art. 'Chronology,' by Mr. C. H. Turner, in the same volume, or Harnack's *Chronologie d. Altchristlichen Literatur*, which appeared very shortly after. The artt. 'Felix,' 'Festus,' were written immediately upon the appearance of Harnack's volume, that on 'Aretas' previously. This chapter does not aim at being a full dissertation on the chronology of the period. For this, reference must be made to all the above articles; Mr. Turner's discussion is monumental, and placed the entire question on a new and possibly final basis.

The general scheme of dates for St Paul's life as covered by the Acts lies between two points which can be approximately determined, namely, his escape from Damascus under Aretas (Acts ix. 25; 2 Cor. xi. 32, 33) not long (ἡμέρας τινάς, Acts ix. 19) after his conversion, and the arrival of Festus as procurator of Judaea (Acts xxiv. 27) in succession to Felix. The latter date fixes the beginning of the διετία ὅλη of Acts xxviii. 30; the close of the latter, again, gives the interval available, before the Apostle's martyrdom shortly after the fire of Rome (64 A.D.), for the events presupposed in the Epistles to Timothy and Titus.

Aretas to the Apostolic Council.

The importance of the Aretas date, which Harnack fails to deal with satisfactorily, is that Damascus is shown by its coins to have been under the Empire as late as 34 A.D., and that it is practically certain that it remained so till the death of Tiberius, March 37 A.D. This latter year, then, is the earliest possible date for St Paul's escape, and his conversion must be placed at earliest in 35 or 36.

From this date we reckon that of the first visit of St Paul

(as a Christian) to Jerusalem, three years after his conversion
(Gal. i. 18), *i.e.* in 37–38, and of the Apostolic Council (Acts xv. ;
Gal. ii. ; the evidence for the identity of reference in these two
chapters is decisive), fourteen years from the conversion
(Gal. ii. 1). (The possibility that the fourteen years are
reckoned from the first visit must be recognized, but the
probability is, as Turner shows, the other way; and the
addition of three years to our reckoning will involve insuperable difficulty in the later chronology.)   This carries us to 49,
whether we add 14 to 35, or—as usual in antiquity, reckoning
both years in—13 to 36.   This result—49 A.D. for the Apostolic
Council—agrees with the other data.   The pause in the Acts
(xii. 24, the imperfects summing up the character of the period),
after the death of Agrippa I., which took place in 44 (see Turner,
p. 416 b), covers the return of Barnabas and Saul from their
visit to Jerusalem to relieve the sufferers from the famine.   This
famine cannot be placed earlier than 46 A.D. (Turner); supposing
this to have been the year of the visit of Barnabas and Saul
to Jerusalem, their departure (Acts xiii. 3) on the missionary
journey to Cyprus, etc., cannot have taken place till after the
winter 46–47 ; the whole journey must have lasted quite eighteen
months.   We thus get the autumn of 48 for the return to
Antioch (xiv. 26); and the χρόνον οὐκ ὀλίγον (*v.* 28) spent there
carries us over the winter, giving a date in the first half of 49,
probably the feast of Pentecost (May 24), for the meeting with
the assembled Apostles at Jerusalem.   This date, therefore,
appears to satisfy all the conditions.

Apostolic Council to the end of Residence at Ephesus.

Assuming its validity, the sequence of the narrative in the
Acts permits us to place the departure of St Paul from Antioch
over Mount Taurus 'after some days' (Acts xv. 36–41) in
September 49, his arrival at Philippi in the summer, and at
Corinth in the autumn, of 50.   The eighteen months (xviii. 11)
of his stay there would end about the Passover (April 2–9) of
52.   By Pentecost he is at Jerusalem, and by midsummer at
Antioch.   Here, then, closes the Antiochene period (44–52) of
his ministry.   Antioch is no longer a suitable headquarters,
Corinth, Philippi, Ephesus claim him, and he transfers his field
of work to the region of the Aegean.   His final visit to Antioch
appears to be not long (xviii. 23, χρόνον τινά) : if he left it about
August, his journey to Ephesus, unmarked by any recorded
episode, would be over before midwinter, say by December 52.
The τριετία (see above) of his residence there cannot, then,

have ended before 55; the 'three months' of xix. 8 and the 'two years' of *v.* 10 carry us to about March of that year: the remainder of the τριετία (which may not have been quite complete) is occupied by the episodes of the sons of Sceva, the mission of Timothy and Erastus (xix. 22), and the riot in the theatre. Whether this permits St Paul to leave Ephesus for Corinth soon after Pentecost 55 (1 Cor. xvi. 8), or compels us to allow till Pentecost 56, cannot be decided until we have considered the second main date, namely, that of the procuratorship of Festus.

From Festus back to 1 Corinthians.

That Felix became procurator of Judaea in 52 A.D. may be taken as fairly established (Hastings, *DB.* artt. 'Felix,' and 'Chronology,' p. 418). The arrival of Festus is placed by Eusebius in his Chronicle in the year Sept. 56–Sept. 57; that of Albinus, his successor, in 61–62. The latter date is probably correct. But the crowded incidents set down by Josephus to the reign of Felix, coupled with the paucity of events ascribed by him to that of Festus, suggest that Felix's tenure of office was long compared with that of Festus (the πολλὰ ἔτη of Acts xxiv. 10 cannot be confidently pressed in confirmation of this). We cannot, moreover, be sure that Eusebius was guided by more than conjecture as to the date of Felix's recall. His brother Pallas, whose influence with Nero (according to Josephus) averted his condemnation, was removed from office in 55, certainly before Felix's recall; but the circumstances of his retirement favour the supposition that he retained influence with the Emperor for some time afterwards. It is not improbable, therefore, that Felix was recalled in 57–58. St Paul's arrest, two years before the recall of Felix (Acts xxiv. 27), would then fall in the year Sept. 55–Sept. 56, *i.e.* at Pentecost (Acts xx. 16) 56 (for the details see Turner in Hastings, *DB.* art. 'Chronology,' pp. 418, 419).

We have, then, for the events of Acts xix. 21–xxiv. 27, the interval from about March 55 to Pentecost (?) 58, or till Pentecost 56 for the remainder of St Paul's stay at Ephesus, the journey from Ephesus to Corinth, the three months spent there, the journey to Philippi, the voyage thence to Troas, Tyre, and Caesarea, and arrival at Jerusalem. This absolutely precludes any extension of St Paul's stay at Ephesus until 56. The Pentecost of 1 Cor. xvi. 8 must be that of 55, unless indeed we can bring down the recall of Felix till 58–59, which though by no means impossible, has the balance of probability against it. Still more considerable is the balance of likelihood against 60 or even 61 as the date for Felix's recall, and 58 or 59 for St Paul's arrest. The former date, 58, must be given up, and St. Paul's arrest dated at latest in 57, more probably in 56.

Resultant Scheme.

Accordingly from Aretas to Festus, that is from St Paul's escape from Damascus to the end of his imprisonment at Caesarea, we have at most 22 years (37–59), more probably only 21. It is evident that the time allowed above for the successive events of the Antiochene and Aegean periods of his ministry, which has throughout been taken at a reasonable minimum, completely fills the chronological framework supplied by the prior dates. The narrative of St Paul's ministry in the Acts, in other words, is continuously consecutive. While giving fuller detail to some parts of the story than to others, it leaves no space of time unaccounted for; the limits of date at either end forbid the supposition of any such unrecorded period. Unless we are—contrary to all the indications of this part of the book—to ignore the Acts as an untrustworthy source, we have in the Acts and Epistles combined a coherent and chronologically tenable scheme of the main events in St Paul's life for these vitally important 21 years. It must be added that the minor points of contact with the general chronology,—the proconsulships of Sergius Paulus and of Gallio, the expulsion of the Jews from Rome by Claudius, the marriage of Drusilla to Felix,—fit without difficulty into the scheme, and that no ascertainable date refuses to do so. For these points, omitted here in order to emphasize the fundamental data, the reader must consult Mr. Turner's article and the other authorities referred to below.

We may therefore safely date our Epistle towards the close of St Paul's residence at Ephesus, and in the earlier months of the year 55.

Bearing of St Paul's movements on the question of Date.

The date of the previous letter referred to in v. 9 can only be matter of inference. Seeing that the Apostle corrects a possible mistake as to its meaning, it was probably of somewhat recent date. There is every antecedent likelihood that letters passed not infrequently between the Apostle at Ephesus and his converts across the Aegean (see Hastings, *DB*. artt. '1 Corinthians,' § 6, and '2 Corinthians,' § 4 g). But the language of our Epistle is difficult, or impossible, to reconcile with the supposition that the Apostle's Ephesian sojourn had been broken into by a visit to Corinth. "There is not a single trace" of it

(Weizsäcker, *Apost. Zeitalter*, pp. 277, 300). The case for such a visit is entirely based on supposed references to it in 2 Cor.; these references at any rate show that this visit, if paid at any time, was of a painful character (ἐν λύπῃ, 2 Cor. ii. 1). If, then, such a visit had been paid before 1 Corinthians was written, to what was this λύπη due? Not to the σχίσματα, of which St Paul knew only from Chloe's people (i. 11). Not to the πορνεία, nor to the disorders at the Lord's Supper, of which, he expressly tells us, he knew by report only (v. 1, xi. 18). Not to the litigiousness, nor to the denials of the Resurrection, of both of which he speaks with indignant surprise. If a distressing visit had preceded our Epistle, the painful occasion of it was dead and buried when St Paul wrote, and St Paul's references to it (clearly as a recent sore) in 2 Corinthians become inexplicable. Certainly when our Epistle was written a painful visit (ἐν ῥάβδῳ, iv. 21) was before the Apostle's mind as a possible necessity. But there is no πάλιν, no hint that there had already been a passage of the kind. On the contrary, some gainsayers were sceptical as to his coming at all; there is, in fact, nothing to set against the clear inference from 1 Cor. ii. 1 sqq., that St Paul's first stay at Corinth had so far been his one visit there. So far, in fact, as our Epistle is concerned, the idea of a previous second visit is uncalled for, to say the very least. If 2 Corinthians necessitates the assumption of such a visit,* it must be inserted before that Epistle and after our present letter. But the question whether such necessity exists depends on the possibility of reconciling the visit with the data as a whole. (On this aspect of the matter the present writer would refer to Hastings, *DB*. vol. i. pp. 492–5, §§ 4, 5.) The most ingenious method of saving the 'painful' visit has a direct bearing on the date of our Epistle. Recognizing the conclusive force of the objections to placing the visit before our letter, Dr J. H. Kennedy (*The Second and Third Epistles to the Corinthians*, Methuen, 1900) places this Epistle before the Pentecost of the year *previous* to St Paul's departure from Ephesus, distinguishes Timothy's mission to Corinth (1 Cor iv. 17, xvi. 10) from his (later) mission with Erastus 'to Macedonia' (Acts xix. 22), makes our Epistle the *prelude* to the painful visit (xvi. 5), and breaks up the Second Epistle so as to obtain a scheme into which that visit will fit. 1 Corinthians would then be dated (in accordance with the chronology adopted above) *before Pentecost* 54.

But, interesting and ingenious as is Dr. Kennedy's discussion, the close correspondence of ch. xvi. 3–6 with the facts of Acts xx. 1–3—the journey through Macedonia to Corinth, the winter spent there, the start for Jerusalem with the brethren—makes

---

* See the previous section, pp. xxi–xxiv.

the divorce of the two passages very harsh and improbable. In our Epistle the plan actually followed is already planned; its abandonment and resumption follow rapidly, as described in 2 Corinthians, and it seems impossible to doubt that our Epistle was written with the immediate prospect (not of the painful visit but) of the visit actually recorded in Acts xx. 3 ; *i.e.* in the spring of 55.

The following table gives the schemes adopted by Harnack in his *Chronologie* (supra), Turner (*DB.* as above); Ramsay, *St Paul the Traveller* and *Expositor*, 1896, p. 336, *A fixed date*, etc.; Lightfoot, *Biblical Essays*, pp. 216–233; Wieseler, *Chronologie d. Apost. Zeitalters* (Eng. tr.); Lewin, *Fasti Sacri.* See also Blass, *Acta Apostolorum*, 1895, pp. 21–24; Kennedy (as above). See also *Ency. Brit.*, 11th ed., III. pp. 891 f., VII. p. 151.

	Harnack.	Turner.	Ramsay.	Lightfoot.	Wieseler.	Lewin.
The Crucifixion .	29 or 30	29	30	...	30	33
Conversion of St Paul .	30	35 or 36	32	34	40	37
First visit to Jerusalem	33	38	34	37	43	39
Second visit to Jerusalem . . .	...	46	45	45	45	44
First missionary journey . . .	45	**47**	46 or 47	48	45–57	45
Third visit to Jerusalem ; the Apostolic Council . . .	47	49	50	51	50	49
Second missionary journey . . .	47	49	50	51	50	49
Corinth reached late in	48	50	51	52	52	52
Epistles to the Thessalonians . . .	48–50	50–52	51–53	52–53	52–53	52
Fourth visit to Jerusalem . . .	50	52	53	54	54	53
Return to Antioch .	50	52	53	54	54	53
Third missionary journey . . .	50	52	53	54	54	54
In Ephesus ; 1 Corinthians . . .	50–53	52–55	53–56	54–57	54–57	54–57
In Macedonia ; 2 Corinthians . . .	53	55	56	57	57	57
In Corinth ; Epistle to Romans . . .	53, 54	55, 56	56, 57	57, 58	57, 58	57, 58
Fifth visit to Jerusalem ; arrest . . .	54	56	57	58	58	58

§ V. Doctrine.

The First Epistle to the Corinthians is not, like that to the Romans, a doctrinal treatise; nor is it, like Galatians, the document of a crisis involving far-reaching doctrinal consequences. It deals with the practical questions affecting the life of a Church founded by the writer: one great doctrinal issue, arising out of circumstances at Corinth (xv. 12), is directly treated; but doctrine is, generally speaking, implied or referred to rather than enforced. Yet, none the less, the doctrinal importance and instructiveness of the letter can hardly be overrated. In its alternations of light and shadow it vividly reproduces the life of a typical Gentile-Christian community, seething with the interaction of the new life and the inherited character, with the beginnings of that age-long warfare of man's higher and lower self which forms the under-current of Christian history in all ages.

The Apostle recalls to first principles every matter which engages his attention; at every point his convictions, as one who had learned from Christ Himself, are brought to bear upon the question before him, though it may be one of minor detail. At the least touch the latent forces of fundamental Faith break out into action.

First of all, we must take note of *the Apostle's relation to Christ.* He is 'a called Apostle of Jesus Christ' (i. 1), and asserts this claim in the face of those who call it in question (ix. 3). He rests it, firstly, on having 'seen Jesus our Lord' (ix. 1), clearly at his Conversion; secondly, on the fruits of his Apostle-ship, which the Corinthians, whom he had begotten in the Lord (iii. 6 sqq., iv. 15, see notes on these passages), should be the last to question (ix. 2). This constituted his answer to critics (ix. 3). As far, then, as authority was concerned, he claimed to have it directly from Christ, without human source or channel (as in Gal. i. 1, 12). But this did not imply independence of the tradition common to the Apostles in regard to the facts of the Lord's life, death, and Resurrection. In regard to the Institu-tion of the Lord's Supper (see below), the words παρέλαβον ἀπὸ τοῦ Κυρίου have been taken as asserting the contrary. But they do not necessarily, nor in the view of the present writer probably, imply more than that the Lord was the source (ἀπό) of the παράδοσις. The circumstantial details here, as in the case of the appearances after the Resurrection, would most naturally come through those who had witnessed them (xv. 1–10), in common with whom St Paul handed on what had been handed on to him. So again in dealing with marriage, he is careful to distinguish between the reported teaching of the Lord and what he gives as his own judgment, founded, it is true, upon fidelity to the Spirit of Christ (vii. 10, 12, 25, 40).

The passages in question have an important bearing upon St Paul's knowledge in detail of the earthly life, ministry, and words of Christ. It is not uncommonly inferred from his nearly exclusive insistence upon the incarnation, passion, death and Resurrection of our Lord that he either knew or cared to know nothing of the historical Jesus (2 Cor. v. 16; 1 Cor. ii. 2).* But the appeal of ch. vii. 10, 25 is a warning that the inference from silence is precarious here. The *pre-existence* of Christ is clearly taught in xv. 45–48.† That St Paul taught pre-existence only— as distinct from the Divinity of Christ (His pre-existence *in the Unity of the Godhead*),—was the view of Baur, followed in substance by Pfleiderer (*Paulinism*, Eng. tr. i. 139 sqq.), Schmiedel, *in loc.*, and many others. It is bound up with the old Tübingen theory which restricts the Pauline *homologumena* to 1 and 2 Corinthians, Romans, and Galatians. If we are allowed to combine the thoughts of Phil. ii. 5 sqq., and Col. i. 15–18, ii. 9, with 1 Cor. xv., it becomes impossible to do justice to the whole thought of St Paul by the conception of an ἄνθρωπος ἐξ οὐρανοῦ (xv. 47), pre-existent *in the Divine Idea* only. The fundamental position of Christ 'and that crucified' (ii. 2; cf. iii. 10, 11) in the Apostle's preaching is only intelligible in connexion with His cosmic function as Mediator (viii. 6, δι' οὗ τὰ πάντα) which again stands closely related with the thought expanded in Col. i. 15 f. In a word, it is now admitted that, according to St Paul, Christ, as the Mediator between God and man, stood at the centre of the Gospel. Whether this equally applies to the teaching of Christ Himself, as recorded in the Gospels, or whether, on the contrary, the teaching of Christ is reducible to the two heads of the Fatherhood of God and the Brotherhood of Man, without any proclamation of Himself as the Mediator of the former, as Harnack in *Das Wesen des Christentums* and other recent writers have contended, is a question worthy of most careful inquiry, but not in this place.‡ It belongs to the study of the history and doctrine of the Gospels.

---

* That this is an erroneous inference is shown by Fletcher, *The Conversion of St Paul*, pp. 55–57; by Cohu, *St Paul in the Light of Modern Research*, pp. 110–116; by Jülicher, *Paulus u. Jesus*, pp. 54–56.

† See also what is implied in 'the rock *was* Christ'; note on x. 4: and Swete, *The Ascended Christ*, pp. 61, 111, 157.

‡ That there is no such essential difference between the teaching of Christ and the teaching of St Paul as Wrede (*Paulus*, 1905) has contended, is urged by Kölbing (*Die geistige Einwirkung der Person Jesu auf Paulus*, 1906) and A. Meyer (*Wer hat das Christentum begründet, Jesus oder Paulus*, 1907), no less than by more conservative scholars. See A. E. Garvie, *The Christian Certainty*, pp. 399 f.

The Epistle contains not only the clearly-cut doctrines of the death of Christ for our sins and of His *Resurrection from the dead on the Third Day*, but the equally clear assertion that these doctrines were not only the elements of St Paul's own teaching, but were taught by him in common with the older Apostles (xv. 1–11). The doctrine which is mainly in question here is that of the Resurrection of the dead, of which the fifteenth chapter of the Epistle is the classical exposition. St Paul is meeting the denial by some (τινές) of the Corinthians that there is a resurrection of the dead. The persons in question, who were most probably the representatives, not of Sadducaism, but of vague Greek opinion influenced perhaps by popular Epicurean ideas, did not deny the Resurrection of Jesus Christ. Their assent to it must, however, have become otiose. To the Resurrection of Christ, then, St Paul appeals in refutation of the opinion he has to combat. After reminding them that they had learned from him, as a fundamental truth, the fact of the Resurrection of Christ from the dead, attested by many appearances to the Apostles, and by the appearance to himself at his conversion, he proceeds to establish the link between this primary truth and that of the Resurrection of the dead in Christ. The relation between the two is that of antecedent and consequent,—of cause and effect. If the consequent is denied the antecedent is overthrown (*vv.* 12–19), and with it the whole foundation of the Christian hope of eternal life. But Christ has risen, and mankind has in Him a new source of life, as in Adam it had its source of death. The consummation of life in Christ is then traced out in bold, mysterious touches (*vv.* 23–28). First Christ Himself; then, at the Parousia, those that are Christ's; then the End. The End embraces the redelivery by Him of the Kingdom to His Father: the Kingdom is mediatorial and has for its purpose the subjugation of the enemies, death last of them all. All things, other than God, are to be subjected to the Son; when this is accomplished, the redelivery,—the subjection of the Son Himself,—takes effect, 'that God may be all in all.'

On this climax of the history of the Universe, it must suffice to point out that St Paul clearly does not mean that the personal being of the Son will have an end; but that the Kingdom of Christ, so far as it can be distinguished from the Kingdom of God, will then be merged in the latter. St Paul here gathers up the threads of all previous eschatological thought; the Messiah, the enemies, the warfare of Life and Death, the return of Christ to earth, and the final destiny of the saints. It is important to notice that he contemplates no earthly reign of the Christ after His Return. The quickening of the saints 'at His Coming' immediately ushers in 'the End,' the redelivery, the close of the

Mediatorial Kingdom. This is in harmony with the earlier teaching of the Apostle in 1 and 2 Thessalonians, and there is nothing in any of his Epistles out of harmony with it. But the thought of the *early* Return of Christ (*v.* 51) is already less prominent. The 'time is short' (vii. 29), but instead of 'we that are alive,' it is now 'we shall not all sleep.' This is borne out by 2 Cor. v. 3, where the possibility that the great change will find us in the body (οὐ γυμνοί) is still contemplated, but only as a possibility. The remainder (*vv.* 35 sqq.) of the chapter brings out St Paul's characteristic doctrine of the Resurrection body. This is in direct contrast with the crude conceptions current among the Pharisees, according to which the bodies of the saints were thought of as passing underground from their graves to the place of resurrection, and there rising in the same condition in which death found them.

St Paul, on the other hand, contrasts the mortal (φθαρτόν) or animal (ψυχικόν) body with the risen or spiritual body. The former is ἐπίγειον, χοϊκόν, and 'cannot inherit the kingdom of God.' It will be the same individual body (ἡμᾶς, vi. 14; see Rom. viii. 12), but yet not the same; it will be quickened, changed (*v.* 51), will put on incorruption, immortality; it (the same body) is 'sown' as an earthly body, but will be raised a spiritual body.

This change is in virtue of our membership of Christ, and is the working-out of the same Divine power, first exerted in the raising of Christ Himself, and finally extended to all His members (cf. Phil. iii. 21; 1 Cor. vi. 14; Rom. viii. 19, 21, 23). It follows that the Apostle conceived of the risen Body of Christ Himself as 'a spiritual body'; not that He brought His human body from heaven, but that His heavenly personality (xv. 47) at last, through His Resurrection, the work of the Father's Power (Rom. vi. 4), constituted Him, as the 'last Adam,' 'quickening spirit' (xv. 45), and the source of quickening to all His members. His body is now, therefore, a glorious body (Phil. iii. 21), and the incorruption which His members inherit is the direct effect of their union with the Body of Christ (xv. 48 sq.).

The whole horizon of this passage is limited, therefore, to the resurrection of the just. It is the κεκοιμημένοι (a term exclusively reserved for the dead in Christ) that are in view throughout: the whole argument turns upon the quickening, in Christ (xv. 22, 23), of those who belong to Him. As to the resurrection of the wicked, which St Paul certainly believed (ix. 24, 27; Rom. xiv. 10, 12; cf. Acts xxiv. 15), deep silence reigns in the whole of ch. xv.

The Resurrection of Christ, then, occupies the central place in St Paul's doctrine of the Christian Life, both here and here-after, just as the doctrine of His Death for our sins is the foundation of our whole relation to God as reconciled sinners. The Resurrection not only supplies the indispensable proof of the real significance of the Cross; it is the source of our life as members of Christ, and the guarantee of our hope in Him.

Of the *Person of Christ*, our Epistle implies much more than it expressly lays down. Christ was the whole of his Gospel (ii. 2); He is 'the Lord' (cf. Rom. x. 13), 'through whom are all things, and we through Him' (viii. 6); He satisfies all the needs of man, mental, moral, and religious (i. 30), and union with Him is the sphere of the whole life and work (xv. 58) of the Christian, of his social relations (vii. 22, 39), and of the activities of the Christian Church (v. 4, xii. 5, 12) as a body.

The doctrine of *grace*, so prominent in other Epistles of this group, is for the most part felt rather than expressly handled in our Epistle. The passing reference in xv. 56 (ἡ δὲ δύναμις τῆς ἁμαρτίας ὁ νόμος) may be compared with that in ix. 20, 21, where he explains that the Christian, though not ὑπὸ νόμον, is not ἄνομος Θεοῦ but ἔννομος Χριστοῦ (for which see Rom. viii. 2). It may be noted that a passage in this Epistle (iv. 7, τί δὲ ἔχεις ὃ οὐκ ἔλαβες) turned the entire course of Augustine's thought upon the efficacy of Divine grace, with momentous consequences to the Church (Aug. *de div. quaest. ad Simplic.* i.; cf. *Retract.* II. i. 1; *de don. Persev.* 52).

On the *Christian Life*, our Epistle is an inexhaustible mine of suggestion.* With regard to personal life, it may be noted that the ascetic instinct which has ever tended to assert itself in the Christian Church finds its first utterance here (vii. 1, 25, 40, θέλω, νομίζω ὅτι καλόν, etc.), as representing the Apostle's own mind, but coupled with solemn and lofty insistence (οὐκ ἐγὼ ἀλλὰ ὁ κύριος) on the obligations of married life. His 'ascetic' counsels rest on the simple ground of the higher expediency. This latter principle (τὸ σύμφορον) is the keynote of the Ethics of our Epistle. The 'world' (vii. 31),—all, that is, which fills human life, its joys, sorrows, interests, ties, possessions, opportunities,—is to the Christian but means to a supreme end, in which the highest good of the individual converges with the highest good of his neighbour and of all (x. 24). Free in his sole responsibility to God (iii. 21, ii. 15, x. 23), the Spiritual Man limits his own freedom (vi. 12, ix. 19), in order to the building up of others and the discipline of self (ix. 24–27). The supreme good, to which all else is subordinated, is 'partaking of the Gospel' (ix. 23), *i.e.* of the benefit the Gospel declares, namely,

* See A. B. D. Alexander, *The Ethics of St Paul*, esp. pp. 115–125, 231, 237–256, 293–297; Stalker, *The Ethic of Jesus*, pp. 175, 351.

the unspeakable blessedness which God has granted to them that love Him (ii. 9, 12),—begun in grace (i. 4) here, consummated in glory (ii. 7, xv. 43) hereafter. To analyse this conception further would carry us beyond the horizon of this Epistle (cf. Rom. iii. 23, viii. 18, etc. etc.); but it may be noted that there is a close correlation between the glory of God (x. 31) as the objective standard of action, and the glory of God in sharing which our chief happiness is finally to consist; also that the *summum bonum*, thus conceived, is no object of merely self-regarding desire : to desire it is to desire that all for whom Christ died may be led to its attainment. This principle of the "higher expediency" determines the treatment of the ethical problems which occur in the Epistle : the treatment of the body, matrimony, the eating of εἰδωλόθυτα;—and again, the use and abuse of spiritual gifts. But in its application to the latter, it is, as it were, transformed to its highest personal embodiment in the passion of Christian Love. The higher expediency lays down the duty of subordinating self to others, the lower self to the higher, things temporal to things eternal. Love is the inward state (correlative with Faith) in which this subordination has become an imperative instinct, raising the whole life to victory over the world. Such is the positive side of St Paul's Ethics, according to which an act may be 'lawful,' while yet the Christian will choose in preference what is 'expedient' (vi. 12, x. 23; cf. ix. 24–27), gaining, at the cost of forbearance, spiritual freedom for himself, and the good of others. Such are the Ethics of 'grace' as distinct from 'law' (Rom. vi. 14). But many Christians are under law (iii. 1 sqq.) rather than under grace : they need stern warning against sin, and of such warnings the Epistle is full (vi. 9, 10, viii. 12, x. 12–14, xi. 27, xv. 34, xvi. 22). The charter of Christian liberty (ii. 15) is for the spiritual person : emancipation from the law (xv. 56; cf. Rom. vii. 24–viii. 2) comes, not by indulgence (vi. 12), but by self-conquest (ix. 21, 26 sq.).

Not less instructive is our Epistle as to the *Collective Work of the Church.* No other book of the N.T., in fact, reflects so richly the life of the Christian body as it then was, and the principles which guided it (see Weizsäcker, *Apost. Zeitalter*, pp. 575–605). We note especially the development of *discipline*, of *organization*, and of *worship*.

As to *Discipline*, the classical passage is v. 1 sqq. ; here St Paul describes, not what had been done by the community, but what they ought to have done in dealing with a flagrant case of immorality. The congregation are met together ; the Apostle himself, in spirit, is in their midst ; the power of the Lord Jesus is present. In the name of the Lord Jesus they expel the offender, 'delivering him to Satan for the destruction of his flesh,

that his spirit may be saved in the day of the Lord.' Here we
have the beginning of ecclesiastical censures, to be inflicted by the
community as a whole. The physical suffering entailed (cf. ch.
xi. 30; Acts v. 1 sqq.) is assumed to be terrible (ὅλεθρος), but
is inherently temporal and remedial. The community would
naturally have the power, upon repentance shown, to restore the
culprit to fellowship (2 Cor. ii. 6, 10, although the case there in
question is probably a different one). Such an assembly as St
Paul here conceives would *a fortiori* be competent to dispose of
any matters of personal rights or wrongs which might arise among
members (vi. 1, 2, 5, v. 12), without recourse to heathen
magistrates (ἄδικοι, vi. 1); for St Paul, who regards submission
to the magistrate in regard to the criminal law as a duty (Rom.
xiii. 1 sqq.), dissuades Christians from invoking the heathen
courts to settle quarrels, which are, moreover, wholly out of
place among brethren.

The *Organization* of the Corinthian Church is evidently still
at an early stage. There is no mention of bishops, presbyters,
or deacons: next after Apostles, prophets and teachers are
named, in remarkable agreement with the reference in Acts xiii.
1. Moreover, if we compare the list in 1 Cor. xii. 28 sqq. with
those of Rom. xii. 6–8 and of Eph. iv. 11, the coincidence is too
close to be accidental. The following table gives the three lists
in synoptic form :—

1. ἀπόστολοι (Cor., Eph.).
2. προφῆται (Cor., Eph. ; προφητεία, Rom.).
   [εὐαγγελισταί (Eph.)
   ποιμένες (Eph.).
   διακονία (Rom.).]

3. διδάσκαλοι (1 Cor., Eph.); διδάσκων (Rom.). Then follow
παρακαλῶν (Rom.), δυνάμεις, ἰάματα, and ἀντιλήμψεις (1 Cor.),
μεταδιδούς (Rom.) ; κυβερνήσεις (1 Cor.), προιστάμενος (Rom.),
ἐλεῶν (Rom.), γένη γλωσσῶν (1 Cor.).

There is clearly no systematic order throughout, nor can we
take the lists as statistical. The variations are due to the unstudied spontaneity with which in each passage the enumeration
is made. All the more significant is it, therefore, that 'prophets'
(after 'Apostles' in our Epistle and Ephesians) take the highest
rank in all three lists, while 'teachers,' who rank very high in
all three lists, *are the only other term common to all*. In our list
(ch. xii.) the three 'orders' of Apostles, prophets, teachers, are the
only ones expressly ranked as 'first, second, third.' Whether
'Apostles' include, as in Rom. xvi. 7 and perhaps Gal. i. 19, an
indefinite number, or are confined to the Twelve and (ch. ix. 1)
St Paul himself, our Epistle does not clearly indicate (not even

in ch. xv. 7). The office of prophet is not strictly limited to a
class, but potentially belongs to all (ch. xiv. 30–32). That
presbyters, here as elsewhere (Phil. i. 1 ; Acts xiv. 23, xx. 17,
etc.), had been appointed by the Apostle, would be antecedently
likely, but there is no reference to any such permanent officers
in this, nor in the second, Epistle, not even in places where (as
in v. 1 sqq., vi. 1 sqq., xiv. 32 sq.) the context would suggest the
mention of responsible officers.   The low place in the list
occupied by administrative gifts (κυβερνήσεις, cf. προιστάμενος
in Rom.) seems to imply that administrative offices are still
voluntarily undertaken ; so in xvi. 15 the household of Stephanas
have a claim to deference (cf. 1 Thess. v. 12), but on the ground
of their *voluntary* devotion to the διακονία (ἔταξαν ἑαυτούς).
The work begun by St Paul at Corinth was carried on by
successors (Apollos alone is named, iii. 6), who 'water' where
he had 'planted,' 'build upon' the Stone which he had 'laid':
they are παιδαγωγοί, while he remains the one 'Father' in
Christ.   The Epistle, however, refers to them only in passing,
and in no way defines their status.   Probably they are to be
classed with the prophets and teachers of ch. xii. 28 (cf. Acts
xiii. 1).   Church organization, like public worship, was possibly
reserved for further regulation (xi. 34).

Public Worship is the subject of a long section of the Epistle,
in which the veiling of women, the Eucharist, and the use and
abuse of spiritual gifts are the topics in turn immediately dealt
with (xi. 2–xiv.).   The assembly for worship is the ἐκκλησία
(xi. 18), a term in which the O.T. idea of the 'congregation,'
and the Greek democratic idea of the mass-meeting of the
citizens, find a point of convergence.   At some ἐκκλησίαι out-
siders (ἰδιῶται, probably unbaptized persons, corresponding to
the 'devout Greeks' at a synagogue) might be present (xiv. 16, 23),
or even heathens pure and simple (ἄπιστοι) ; yet this would be
not at the κυριακὸν δεῖπνον, but at a more mixed assembly (ὅλη,
xiv. 23).   That the assemblies εἰς τὸ φαγεῖν (xi. 33) were distinct
and periodical was apparently the case in Pliny's time (see
Weizsäcker, *Apost. Zeitalter*, 568 f.).   The 'Amen' was in use as
the response to prayer or praise (xiv. 16).   It would be hasty
to conclude from xi. 2 sqq. that women might, without St Paul's
disapproval, under certain conditions, pray or prophesy in
public : they very likely had done so at Corinth, but St Paul,
while for the present concentrating his censure upon their doing
so with unveiled head, had in reserve the total prohibition
which he later on lays down (xiv. 34).   Otherwise, the liberty of
prophesying belonged to all ; the utterance was to be tested
(xiv. 29), but the test was the character of the utterance itself
(xii. 1 sq.) rather than the *status* of the speaker.   Prayer and

praise, ἐν γλώσσῃ (see Hastings, *DB.* art. 'Tongues'), was a marked feature of public worship at Corinth, but St Paul insists on its inferiority to prophecy. Sunday is mentioned as the day against which alms were to be set apart; we may infer from this that it was the usual day for the principal ἐκκλησία (see above). The purpose of this assembly was to break the bread, and drink the cup, of the Lord.

In xi. 17–34 we have the *locus classicus* for the Eucharist of the Apostolic age. It has been argued that we have here a stage in the development of the sacred Rite anterior to, and differing materially from, what is described by Justin, *Apol.* i. § 56; the difference consisting in the previous consecration of the elements, in Justin's account, by the προεστώς, and reception by the communicants at his hands. At Corinth, on the other hand, (*vv.* 21, 33) an abuse existed in that 'each taketh before other his own supper,' so that the meal lost its character as 'a Lord's Supper.' If the 'consecration' (so it is argued) were already at this time an essential part of the service, the abuse in question could not have occurred; or at any rate St Paul's remedy would have been 'wait for the consecration' and not 'wait for one another' (*v.* 33). But, in the line of development, the Corinthian Eucharist comes between the original institution, as described by St Paul and by the Evangelists, and the Eucharist of Justin.* In all the N.T. accounts of the Institution, the acts and words of Christ, and His delivery of the bread and cup after consecration to those present, are recorded, and form the central point. The argument under notice assumes that this central feature has disappeared at the second, or Corinthian, stage of development, to reappear in the third, namely Justin's. This assumption is incredible. In carrying out the command τοῦτο ποιεῖτε, 'do this,' we cannot believe that at Corinth, or anywhere else, what Christ was recorded to have done was just the feature to be omitted.

> Quod in caena Christus *gessit*
> *Faciendum* hoc expressit

is an accurate expression of the characteristic which from the first differentiated the Common Meal into the Christian εὐχαριστία. The words 'do this' were certainly part of the 'tradition' handed on by St Paul at Corinth (see below); and had it been *left undone*, the Apostle would not have failed to notice it. Further, the argument for the absence, at Corinth, of the acts of consecration, assumes erroneously that 'the *Lord's Supper*' in *v.* 20 "can be no other than the bread and the cup of the Lord in *v.* 27"

* See A. W. F. Blunt, *The Apologies of Justin Martyr*, 1911, pp. xxxix-xliv, 98–101.

(Beet, *in loc.*). This assumption is a reaction from the ana-chronism of introducing the 'Agape' of later times in explanation of this passage. (The name Agape, see *Dict. of Chr. Antiq. s.v.*, is occasionally used for the Eucharist, but more properly for the Common Meal from which the Eucharist had been wholly separated.) The Lord's Supper (so named only here in N.T.) is not the Eucharist proper, still less the Agape, *but the entire re-enactment of the Last Supper*, with the Eucharistic acts occurring in the course of it, as they do in the paschal meal recorded in the Synoptic Gospels.* In the early Church the name 'Lord's Supper' was not the earliest, nor the commonest, name for the Eucharist. It was primarily (though not quite exclusively) applied to the annual re-enactment of the Last Supper which survived after the Agape had first been separated from the Eucharist and then had gradually dropped out of use (*Dict. of Chr. Antiq.* art. 'Lord's Supper'). In any case 'the Lord's Supper' at Corinth would be already in progress when the Eucharistic Bread and Cup were blessed. St Paul's censure (ἕκαστος γὰρ προλαμβάνει, *v.* 21), and his remedy (ἐκδέχεσθε, *v.* 33), relate to the supper which was over before (μετὰ τὸ δειπνῆσαι, *v.* 25) the blessing of the Cup, and was doubtless (see note on xi. 23, 27) well advanced when the Eucharistic Bread was broken: what he blames and what he enjoins are alike compatible with the supposition that the procedure of the Last Supper was closely adhered to at Corinth. Whose duty it was to 'preside' (as did the head of the family at the Passover, our Lord at the Last Supper, and the προεστώς in Justin's time) we do not know, but it may be taken as certain that some one did so. In *v.* 34, Εἴ τις πεινᾷ κ.τ.λ., we notice the first step towards the segregation of the Eucharistic acts proper from the joint meal in which they were still, as it were, embedded. The Supper, if the direction of *v.* 34 was observed, would cease to have its original character of a meal to satisfy hunger (still traceable in *Did.* x. 1, μετὰ τὸ ἐμπλησ-θῆναι); it dropped out of use in connexion with the Eucharist, except in so far as it left traces in the ritual. As a separate, non-Eucharistic sacred meal (*Dict. of Chr. Antiq.* art. 'Agape') it survived for a time. This separation of the Eucharist from the Supper, of which we here trace the origin only, was a step towards the shifting of the former, later than any N.T. evidence, to the "ante-lucan" hour which had become usual in Pliny's time.

The question of St Paul's relation to the Eucharistic Institution, which only indirectly touches the doctrine of this Epistle, must be briefly noticed here. In their account of the

---

* Dr. E. Baumgartner contends that in 1 Cor. we have a description of the Agape alone, without the Eucharist (*Eucharistie und Agape im Urchris-tentum*, 1909). But see Cohu, *St Paul*, pp. 303 f.

Last Supper the two first Gospels stand by themselves over against St Luke and St Paul in mentioning no command to repeat our Lord's action. St Luke's account, again, in the Western text (which is more trustworthy in its omissions than in its other variations), records simply the blessing *first* of the Cup, then of the Bread, with no command to repeat the action : what follows (Luke xxii. 19, 20, τὸ ὑπὲρ ὑμῶν ... ἐκχυνόμενον) is (if with WH. we adopt the Western Text) an importation from 1 Cor. xi. 24, 25. St Paul then, as compared with the Gospel record, stands alone in recording our Saviour's command to 'do this in remembrance of Me.' Whence did he receive it? His answer is that he 'received' (the whole account) '*from the Lord*' (v. 23). This may mean 'by direct revelation,' or may (as certainly in xv. 3) mean 'received,' as he handed it on, orally, the Lord being here mentioned as the ultimate (ἀπό) authority for the Rite. It has been argued, on the assumption that St Paul claims direct revelation to himself as the authority for the Christian Eucharist, that this claim is the *sole source* of any idea that the Last Supper (or rather the Eucharistic action) was ordered to be repeated, that St Paul first caused it to be so celebrated, and that the authority of the Institution hangs upon a vision or revelation claimed by St Paul. Further, it is suggested that the vision in question was largely coloured by the mysteries celebrated at Eleusis, near Athens and not far from Corinth (so P. Gardner, *The Origin of the Lord's Supper,* 1903).

The narrative of the Institution in the two first Gospels, though they record no express command to repeat it, renders the last-named suggestion somewhat gratuitous. Our Lord was keeping an annual feast, and His disciples certainly at that time expected to keep it in future: in view of this fact, of the references in the Acts of the Apostles (ii. 42, xx. 7) to the repetition of the Supper, and of its thoroughly Hebraic and Palestinian antecedents (cf. Bickell, *Messe und Pascha*; Anrich, *Antike Mysterienwesen*, p. 127), it is much more probable that St Paul is here the representative of a common tradition than the author of an institution traceable to himself alone. The whole tone of the passage, in which their 'coming together to eat' is not inculcated but taken for granted, supports this view against any hypothesis of a practice initiated by the Apostle himself. See also Andersen, *D. Abendmahl in d. ersten 2 Jahrhund.* 1906).

The doctrine of the Eucharist presupposed in our Epistle is simple, but, so far as it goes, very definite. The Bread and the Cup are a partaking (κοινωνία) of the Lord's Body and Blood (x. 16, xi. 27); and to eat 'or' (v. 27 ; 'and,' v. 29) drink unworthily, 'not discerning the Body' (v. 29), is to 'eat and drink judgment' to oneself. The Body is clearly the body. not merely of the Church, but 'of the Lord'; the latter words, added in later copies, are a correct gloss. The interpretation of our Lord's words here implied takes us at any rate beyond any 'Zwinglian' view of sacramental reception. The reception is, moreover, in commemoration (ἀνάμνησις) of the Lord, and is a proclaiming (καταγγέλλειν) of the Lord's Death 'till He come.' We see in these words and in ch. x. 15–18 the relation of the Eucharist to sacrificial conceptions. To St Paul, the Death of Christ (ch. v. 7, ἐτύθη) is the Christian sacrifice. To it the Eucharist is primarily and directly related. In ch. x. St. Paul (in order to drive home his warning against joining in any *ceremonial* eating of εἰδωλόθυτα) insists, with appeal to Jewish and to Christian rites, that to partake of what is sacrificed is to become a party to the sacrificial act (and so to enter upon that fellowship of the worshipper with the deity which sacrifice aims at establishing or maintaining). It follows, then, that St Paul thinks of the Eucharist as the act by which Christians, collectively and individually, make (as it were) the Sacrifice of the Cross their own act, 'appropriate' it, maintain and deepen their fellowship with God through Christ. The Christian Passover, once for all slain (v. 7), is eaten at every Eucharist. This is an essential agreement with the statements, closely identical in substance, by which Chrysostom (*Hom. in Hebr.* xvii.) and Augustine (*c. Faust.* xx. 18) independently justify the term 'sacrifice' as applied to the Eucharist.

Baptism is frequently referred to in our Epistle (i. 13–16, x. 2, xii. 13; cf. vi. 11), but the doctrinal reference in each case is indirect. The ἀπελούσασθε of vi. 11 ('ye washed them away from yourselves') must be compared with Acts ii. 38, xxii. 16, and Rom. vi. 3, 4. There can be little doubt that the reference of vi. 11 at least includes baptism; comparing then the ἐν τῷ πνεύματι there with xii. 13, ἐν ἑνὶ πνεύματι, we see how closely associated was baptism with the Holy Spirit as its sphere and its underlying power (Tit. iii. 5). It must not be forgotten that St Paul's readers had been baptized as adults. This fact, and the sharp contrast between the old heathen life and the new life entered upon at baptism, brought out very strongly the significance of the Rite.

The *Doctrine of the Holy Spirit*, as regards the *Personality* of the Spirit, comes out in xii. 11, καθὼς βούλεται; while in ch. ii. 11, where the relation of the Spirit to God is seen to be not less intimate than that of man's spirit to man, we have the *Divinity* of the Spirit unmistakably taught. The Spirit is "the self-conscious life" of God,—but not an impersonal function of God. The gift of the Spirit, accordingly, constitutes the man, in whom the Spirit dwells, a Temple of God (iii. 16). There is the indwelling of the Spirit, common to all members of Christ, the instrument of the sanctification which is to be attained by all ; and there is also the special energy of the Spirit, different in different persons, which equips them for some special service as members of the one body (xii.). So St Paul himself, "incidentally and with great reserve," claims the guidance of the Spirit of God for Himself (vii. 40). The inspiration of the prophet is not such as to supersede self-control (xiv. 32), as it did in the superficially similar phenomena of heathen ecstasy (xii. 2, 3). (See on this subject Swete, *The Holy Spirit in the New Testament*, pp. 176–192.)

§ VI. CHARACTERISTICS, STYLE, AND LANGUAGE.

The general characteristics of St Paul's style, especially in his letters of the Aegean period, are of course markedly present in this Epistle. But it lacks the systematic sequence of marshalled argument so conspicuous in the Epistle to the Romans ; it is more personal than that Epistle, while yet the feeling is not so high-wrought as it is in Galatians and in the Second Epistle. But warmth of affection, as well as warmth of remonstrance and censure, characterize the Epistle throughout. The two Epistles to the Corinthians and that to the Galatians stand, in respect of direct personal appeal, in a class by themselves among St Paul's Epistles. Philippians is equally personal, but there everything speaks of mutual confidence and sympathy, unclouded by any reproach or suspicion. The three Epistles to the Corinthians and the Galatians are not less sympathetic, but the sympathy is combined with anxious solicitude, and alternates with indignant remonstrance. The earlier letters to the Thessalonians, again, presuppose an altogether simpler relation between the Apostle and his converts : his solicitude for them is directed to the inevitable and human perils—instability, overwrought expectation of the last things, moral weakness—incident to sincere but very recent converts from heathenism.

In our Epistle and its two companions the personal situation is more complicated and precarious : a definite disturbing cause is at work ; the Apostle himself is challenged and is on the defensive ; the personal question has far-reaching correlatives, which touch the foundations of the Gospel.

In our Epistle these phenomena are less acutely present than in the other two. The doctrinal issue, which in Galatians stirs the Apostle to the depths, is felt rather than apparent (xv. 56, vii. 18, 19) ; the personal question is more prominent (iv. 3, ix.

ɪ, 3, etc.), but less so than in Galatians, far less so than in the Second Epistle.

In our Epistle the Apostle, in asserting and defending his Apostolic status and mission, never for a moment vacates his position of unquestionable authority, nor betrays a doubt as to his readers' acceptance of it.

One great general characteristic of our Epistle is the firmness of touch with which St Paul handles the varied matters that come before him, carrying back each question, as it comes up for treatment, to large first principles. The petty σχίσματα at Corinth are viewed ɪn the light of the essential character of the Gospel and of the Gospel ministry, the moral disorders in the light of membership of Christ who has bought us all for Himself, the question of marriage, or meats offered to idols, or the exercise of spiritual gifts, from the point of view of "the higher expediency," that is to say, of the subordination of the temporal to the eternal. And where a commandment of the Lord is on record, whether in the sphere of morality (vii.) or of positive ordinance (xi.), its authority claims unquestioning obedience.

In discussing spiritual gifts, the instinct of "the higher expediency" is sublimated into the principle, or rather passion, of Christian charity or love, and its exposition rises to a height of inspired eloquence which would alone suffice to give our Epistle a place of pre-eminence among the Epistles of the New Testament. Side by side with this marvellous passage we must place the rising tide of climax upon climax in ch. xv. The first climax is the emphatic close in v. 11 of the fundamental assertions which go before. Then, after the sombre earnestness of vv. 12–20, the Resurrection and its sequel are enforced in a passage of growing intensity culminating in the close of v. 28. Then a lull (vv. 29–34), and in v. 35 we begin the final ascent, which reaches its height in v. 55, the 'full close' of vv. 56–58 forming a peroration of restful confidence.

In these passages there is no sign of rhetorical artifice, but the glow of ardent conviction, gaining the very summit of effect, because effect is the last thing thought of. 'Sincerity' of style, the note of Pauline utterance, is as conspicuous in these towering heights as in his simplest salutations, his most matter-of-fact directions on practical subjects. For the rest, this Epistle exhibits all the characteristics of St Paul's style, especially as we have it in the four letters of the Aegean period of his ministry, his period of intensest controversy. Equipped with a language hardly adequate to the rich variety and subtlety of his thought or to the intensity of his feeling, he is ever struggling to express more than he actually says ; the logical sequence is broken by the intrusion of new ideas, feeling supersedes grammar and

forbids the completion of a clause (*e.g.* ix. 15). The scope of
the Epistle, practical direction rather than theological argument,
explains the absence of the characteristic ἄρα οὖν so common in
Romans ; generally, in fact, the argument here is less abstruse,
and is comparatively easy to follow (see below). But it is not
always in the form that we should expect in a modern writer.
In x. 30, for example, he asks, 'Why do I incur blame for that for
which I give thanks ?'—meaning, 'Why give thanks for what
involves me in blame ?'—just as in Rom. vii. 16, where he means
that 'if *I hate what I do*, I (by hating it) assent to the law,' he
similarly inverts the ideas, saying, 'If *I do what I hate*,' etc.
At times, again, he assumes a connexion of ideas obvious perhaps
to his readers, but no longer so to the modern reader, as in xi. 10
(διὰ τοὺς ἀγγέλους). The same consideration to some extent
applies to his enigmatic reference (xv. 29) to the practice of
'baptizing for the dead.' It may be added that the mention of
such a practice with no word of blame does not, in view of St
Paul's style, justify the inference that he sanctioned or approved
it. He is so engrossed in his immediate point—that the Resurrection is presupposed by the whole life of the Christian community,
that he does not turn aside to parry any wrong inference that
might be drawn from his words. Similarly, in viii. 10 he insists on
the bad example to the weak of taking part in a sacrificial feast,
as if the action were in itself indifferent, whereas we learn later
on (x. 14 and following) that the act is *per se* idolatrous. Or
again, in xi. 5, from the prohibition against a woman prophesying
unveiled, it has been inferred that she might do so if properly
veiled, whereas in xiv. 34 we find this entirely disallowed. It is,
in fact, St Paul's manner to hold a prohibition as it were in
reserve, producing it when the occasion demands it.

The language of this Epistle, as of St Paul generally, is the
Greek of a Hellenist Jew ; not necessarily of one who thought
in Hebrew but spoke in Greek, but rather of a Jew of the Dis-
persion, accustomed to use the Greek of the Jewish community
of his native city, and conversant with the Old Testament
Scriptures in their Greek version. His studies under Gamaliel
had doubtless been wholly Hebraic, and he could speak fluently
in the Aramaic dialect of Palestine (Acts xxii.). But once only,
in this Epistle at least, does he certainly go behind the LXX
to the Hebrew (iii. 19). His language is not 'literary' Greek ;
he shows little sign of knowledge of Greek authors, except in
current quotations [the language of Rom. ii. 14, 15 has close
points of contact with Aristotle, gained perhaps indirectly
through the Greek schools of Tarsus]; even the quotation
(xv. 33) from Menander's *Thais* is without the elision necessary
to scansion. We miss the subtle play of mood, versatile com-

mand of particles, and artistic structure of periods, that characterize classical Greek (see Weiss, *Introd. to N.T.* § 16. 7).

The extent to which St Paul's thought has been influenced by Greek thought has been sometimes exaggerated. But the influence of Hellenism in shaping the forms in which he expressed his thought can be clearly traced in some cases. We can see that he becomes gradually familiar with certain *philosophical terms*. None of the following are found in the Epistles to the Thessalonians: γνῶσις, σοφία, σύνεσις, συνείδησις, σχῆμα, all of which are found in 1 Corinthians and later Epistles. The following also are not found in the Epistles to the Thessalonians, but are found in one or more of the Epistles which are later than 1 Corinthians: αἴσθησις, διάνοια, Θειότης, μορφή, ὄρεξις. Perhaps ἀκρασία and ἰδιώτης ought to be added to the first group, and ἀκρατής to the second. In his essay on "St Paul and Seneca," Lightfoot has shown what parallels there are between expressions in the Pauline Epistles and expressions which were in use among the Stoics. The meaning may be very different, but there is a similarity which is perhaps not wholly accidental in the wording (see notes on iii. 21, iv. 8, vi. 7, 19, vii. 20, 31, 33, 35, viii. 4, ix. 25, xii. 14, xiii. 4).

We may perhaps assign the *argumentative form*, into which so much of St Paul's language is thrown, to the influence of Hellenism. In this he is very different from other N.T. writers who did not come so decidedly under Greek influence. Every one who has tried knows how difficult it is to make an analysis of the Epistles of St James and of St John. Perhaps no one has succeeded in making an analysis of either which convinced other students that the supposed sequence of thought was really in the writer's mind. But there is little difference of opinion as to the analysis of St Paul's Epistles. And not only is the sequence of thought in most cases clear, but the separate arguments which constitute the sequence are clear also. They may not always seem to be convincing, but they can be put into logical shape, with premiss and conclusion. Such a method of teaching is much more Western than Oriental, much more Greek than Jewish.

The following is a list of words peculiar to 1 *Corinthians in N.T.*†

ἄγαμος, vii. 8, 11, 32, 34; * ἀγενής, i. 28; * ἀδάπανος, ix. 18; * ἀδήλως, ix. 26; αἴνιγμα, xiii. 12; ἀκατακάλυπτος, xi. 5, 13; ἄκων, ix. 17; * ἀμετακίνητος, xv. 58; ἀνάξιος, vi. 2; ἀναξίως,

† An asterisk indicates that the word is not found in the LXX.

xi. 27; ἀνδρίζομαι, xvi. 13; ἀντίλημψις, xii. 28; * ἀπελεύθερος,
vii. 22; * ἀπερισπάστως, vii. 35; ἀπόδειξις, ii. 4; ἀρχιτέκτων,
iii. 10; ἀστατέω, iv. 11; ἀσχημονέω, vii. 36, xiii. 5; ἀσχήμων,
xii. 23; ἄτομος, xv. 52; αὐλός, xiv. 7; * Ἀχαϊκός, xvi. 17; ἄψυχος,
xiv. 7; βρόχος, vii. 35; γεώργιον, iii. 9; * γυμνιτεύω, iv. 11;
διαίρεσις, xii. 4, 5, 6; ?* διερμηνευτής, xiv. 28; διόπερ, viii. 13,
x. 14; * δουλαγωγέω, ix. 27; δράσσομαι, iii. 19; δυσφημέω, iv. 13;
ἐγκρατεύομαι, vii. 9, ix. 25; εἰδώλιον, viii. 10; ἐκνήφω, xv. 34;
ἔκτρωμα, xv. 8; * ἐνέργημα, xii. 6, 10; * ἐνκοπή, ix. 12; ἐντροπή,
vi. 5, xv. 34; ἐξαίρω, v. 13; ἑορτάζω, v. 8; ἐπιθανάτιος, iv. 9;
ἐπιθυμητής, x. 6; ἐπισπάομαι, vii. 18; ἑρμηνία, xii. 10, xiv. 26;
?* ἑρμηνευτής, xiv. 28; ἑτερόγλωσσος, xiv. 21; * εὐπάρεδρος, vii.
35; εὔσημος, xiv. 9; εὐσχημοσύνη, xii. 23; ἦθος, xv. 33; ἠχέω,
xiii. 1; * θηριομαχέω, xv. 32; ἴαμα, xii. 9, 28, 30; * ἱερόθυτος,
x. 28; καλάμη, iii. 12; κατακαλύπτομαι, ix. 6, 7; καταστρώννυμαι,
x. 5; καταχράομαι, vii. 31, ix. 18; ?* κημόω, ix. 9; * κομάω, xi.
14, 15; κόμη, xi. 15; κυβέρνησις, xii. 28; κύμβαλον, xiii. 1;
* λογία, xvi. 1, 2; λοίδορος, v. 11, vi. 10; λύσις, vii. 27; * μάκ-
ελλον, x. 25; μέθυσος, v. 11, vi. 10; μήτιγε, vi. 3; μωρία, i. 18,
21, 23, ii. 14, iii. 19; νή, xv. 31; * νηπιάζω, xiv. 20; * ὀλοθρευτής,
x. 10; ὁμιλία, xv. 33; * ὄσφρησις, xii. 17; παίζω, x. 7; παραμυθία, xiv. 3; παρεδρεύειν (ix. 13); πάροδος, xvi. 7; * πιθός, ii. 4;
περικάθαρμα, iv. 13; περίψημα, iv. 13; * περπερεύομαι, xiii. 4;
πτηνά, xv. 39; * πυκτεύω, ix. 27; ῥιπή, xv. 52; σύμφορον, vii. 35,
x. 33; σύμφωνος, vii. 5; συγγνώμη, vii. 6; * συνζητητής, i. 20;
συνμερίζομαι, ix. 13; τάγμα, xv. 23; * τυπικῶς, x. 11; * ὑπέρακμος,
vii. 36; φιλόνεικος, xi. 16; φρήν, xiv. 20; χοϊκός, xv. 47, 48, 49;
* χρηστεύομαι, xiii. 4; * ὡσπερεί, xv. 8.

None of these words (nearly 100 in all) occur anywhere else
in N.T. But a few of them are doubtful, owing to uncertainty
of text; and a few of them occur in quotations, and therefore
are no evidence of St Paul's vocabulary, e.g. ἦθος, ὁμιλία, δράσσομαι, ἐξαίρω.

The number of words which are found in this Epistle and
elsewhere in N.T., but not in any of the other Pauline Epistles,†
is still larger; and the extent of these two lists warns us to be
cautious when we use vocabulary as an argument with regard
to authorship. Statistics with regard to 1 Corinthians are all
the more valuable, both because of the length of the Epistle,
and also because the authorship is certain on quite other grounds.
Putting the two lists together, we have nearly 220 words in
1 Corinthians, which are not found in any other of the Pauline
Epistles. A fact of that kind puts us on our guard against
giving great weight to the argument that Ephesians, or Colossians,

† It is assumed here that the Pastoral Epistles (but not the Epistle to the
Hebrews) were written by St Paul.

or the Pastoral Epistles, cannot have been written by the Apostle, because of the large number of words in each of them which do not occur in any other letter written by him. There are far more important tests.†

Words peculiar to 1 Corinthians in the Pauline Epistles.

ἀγνωσία, xv. 34 ; ἀγοράζω, vi. 20, vii. 23, 30 ; ἄδηλος, xiv. 8 ; ἄζυμος, v. 7, 8 ; ἀκρασία, vii. 5 ; ἀλαλάζω, xiii. 1 ; ἀμέριμνος, vii. 32 ; ἀμπελών, ix. 7 ; ἀνακρίνω, ten times ; ἀνάμνησις, xi. 24, 25 ; ἀποφέρω, xvi. 3 ; ἀργύριον, iii. 12 ; ἀροτριάω, ix. 10 ; ἅρπαξ, v. 10, 11, vi. 10 ; ἄρρωστος, xi. 30 ; ἀστήρ, xv. 41 ; ἄτιμος, iv. 10, xii. 23 ; αὐλέομαι, xiv. 7 ; αὔριον, xv. 32 ; γαμίζω, vii. 38 ; δειπνέω, xi. 25 ; δεῖπνον, xi. 20, 21 ; διαιρέω, xii. 12 ; διδακτός, ii. 13 ; διερμηνεύω, xii. 30, xiv. 5, 13, 27 ; δώδεκα, xv. 5 ; ἐάω, x. 13 ; εἰδωλόθυτος, viii. 1, 4, 7, 10, x. 19 ; εἴκοσι, x. 8 ; ἔκβασις, x. 13 ; ἐκπειράζω, x. 9 ; ἐλεεινός, xv. 19 ; ἔννομος, ix. 21 ; ἔνοχος, xi. 27 ; ἔξεστιν, vi. 12, xii. 4 ; ἐξουσιάζω, vi. 12, vii. 4 ; ἐπάνω, xv. 16 ; ἐπιβάλλω, vii. 35 ; ἐπίκειμαι, ix. 16 ; ἔσοπτρον, xiii. 12 ; εὐγενής, i. 26 ; * εὐκαιρέω, xvi. 12 ; εὐσχήμων, vii. 35, xii. 24 ; θάπτω, xv. 4 ; θέατρον, iv. 9 ; θύω, v. 7, x. 20 ; ἱερόν, ix. 13 ; ἰχθύς, xv. 39 ; καίω, xiii. 3 ; κατακαίω, iii. 15 ; κατάκειμαι, viii. 10 ; καταμένω, xvi. 6 ; κιθάρα, xiv. 7 ; κιθαρίζω, xiv. 7 ; κινδυνεύω, xv. 30 ; κλάω, x. 16, xi. 24 ; κόκκος, xv. 37 ; κορέννυμαι, iv. 8 ; κτῆνος, xv. 39 ; κυριακός, xi. 20 ; μαίνομαι, xiv. 23 ; μαλακός, vi. 9 ; μηνύω, x. 28 ; μοιχός, vi. 9 ; μολύνω, viii. 7 ; μυρίος, iv. 15, xiv. 19 ; νῖκος, xv. 54, 55, 57 ; ξυράομαι, xi. 5, 6 ; ὅλως, v. 1, vi. 7, xv. 29 ; ὁσάκις, xi. 25, 26 ; οὐαί, ix. 16 ; οὐδέποτε, xiii. 8 ; ὄφελος, xv. 32 ; παράγω, vii. 31 ; παροξύνομαι, xiii. 5 ; πάσχα, v. 7 ; πεντακόσιοι, xv. 6 ; πεντηκοστή, xvi. 8 ; περιβόλαιον, xi. 15 ; περιτίθημι, xii. 23 ; πλεῖστος, xiv. 27 ; πνευματικῶς, ii. 13, 14 ; ποιμαίνω, ix. 7 ; ποίμνη, ix. 7 ; πόλεμος, xiv. 8 ; πόμα, x. 4 ; πορνεύω, vi. 18, x. 8 ; πόρνη, vi. 15, 16 ; ποτήριον, eight times ; προσκυνέω, xiv. 25 ; προφητεύω, eleven times ; πωλέω, x. 25 ; ῥάβδος, iv. 21 ; σαλπίζω, xv. 52 ; σελήνη, xv. 41 ; στάδιον, ix. 24 ; συμβαίνω, x. 11 ; συνάγω, v. 4 ; συνεῖδον, iv. 4 ; συνέρχομαι, seven times ; συνετός, i. 19 ; συνήθεια, viii. 7, xi. 16 ; συνστέλλω, vii. 29 ; * σχίσμα, i. 10, xi. 18, xii. 25 ; σχολάζω, vii. 5 ; τήρησις, vii. 19 ; τίμιος, iii. 12 ; τοίνυν, ix. 26 ; ὑπηρέτης, iv. 1 ; * ὑπωπιάζω, ix. 27 ; φυτεύω, iii. 6, 7, 8, ix. 7 ; χαλκός, xiii. 1 ; χόρτος, iii. 12 ; ψευδομάρτυς, xv. 15 ; ψυχικός, ii. 14, xv. 44, 46.

There are a few words which are common to this Epistle and one or more of the Pastoral Epistles, but are found nowhere

† As Schmiedel says about 1 Thessalonians : *Begnügt man sich nicht mit mechanischem Zählen, alphabetischem Aufreihen und dem fast werthlosen Achten auf die* ἅπαξ λεγόμενα.

else in N.T. These are, ἀθανασία, xv. 53, 54; ἀλοάω, ix. 9, 10 (in a quotation); ἐκκαθαίρω, v. 7; * συνβασιλεύω, iv. 8; ὑπεροχή, ii. 1. There are a good many more which are common to this Epistle and one or more of the Pastoral Epistles, and which are found elsewhere in N.T., although not in other Epistles of St Paul. But these are of less importance, although all links between the Pastoral Epistles and the unquestionably genuine Epistles are of value.

Phrases peculiar to 1 Corinthians in N.T.

ἡ σοφία τοῦ κόσμου, i. 20, iii. 18.
οἱ ἄρχοντες τοῦ αἰῶνος τούτου, ii. 6, 8.
πρὸ τῶν αἰώνων, ii. 7.
τὸ πνεῦμα τοῦ κόσμου, ii. 12.
Θεοῦ συνεργοί, iii. 9.
τοῦτο δέ φημι, vii. 29, xv. 50; cf. x. 15, 19.
Ἰησοῦν τὸν κύριον ἡμῶν ἑόρακα, ix. 1; cf. John xx. 25.
τὸ ποτήριον τῆς εὐλογίας, x. 16.
ποτήριον Κυρίου, x. 21.
κυριακὸν δεῖπνον, xi. 20.
εἰς τὴν ἐμὴν ἀνάμνησιν, xi. 24, 25: ? Luke xxii. 19.
τὸ ποτήριον τοῦ κυρίου, xi. 27.
εἰ τύχοι, xiv. 10, xv. 37; cf. τυχόν, xvi. 6.
τὸ πλεῖστον, xiv. 27.
ἐν ἀτόμῳ, ἐν ῥιπῇ ὀφθαλμοῦ, xv. 52.
Μαρὰν ἀθά, xvi. 22.

Quotations from the O.T.

The essay on the subject in Sanday and Headlam, *Romans*, pp. 302–307, should be consulted; also Swete, *Introduction to the O.T. in Greek*, pp. 381–405. The number of quotations in 1 Corinthians is about thirty, and none of the Epistles has so many, excepting Romans and Hebrews; and none quotes from so many different books, excepting Romans. In 1 Corinthians, eleven different books are quoted; Isaiah about eight times, Psalms four or five times, Deuteronomy four times, Genesis four, Exodus two or three, Numbers once or twice, Zechariah once or twice; Job, Jeremiah, Hosea, Malachi, once each. In several cases the quotation resembles more than one passage in the O.T., and we cannot be sure which passage the Apostle has in ʌis mind. In other cases there is a conflation of two passages, both of which are clearly in his mind. Consequently, exact numbers cannot always be given. All the quotations are short, and it is probable that all of them were made from memory.

There are no long citations, such as we have in Hebrews, which no doubt were in most cases copied.

If, with Swete, we may count as direct quotations those which (though not announced by a formula, such as καθὼς γέγραπται) appear from the context to be intended as quotations, or agree *verbatim* with some context in the O.T., then at least half the quotations in 1 Corinthians are direct.* They are—

i. 19 = Isa. xxix. 14	x. 7 = Exod. xxxii. 6
i. 31 = Jer. ix. 24	x. 26 = Ps. xxiv. 1
(1 Sam. ii. 10)	
ii. 9 = Isa. lxiv. 4 (?)	xiv. 21 = Isa. xxviii. 11 f.
ii. 16 = Isa. xl. 13	xv. 27 = Ps. viii. 6, 7
iii. 19 = Job v. 13	xv. 32 = Isa. xxii. 13
iii. 20 = Ps. xciv. 11	xv. 45 = Gen. ii. 7
vi. 16 = Gen. ii. 24	xv. 54 = Isa. xxv. 8
ix. 9 = Deut. xxv. 4	xv. 55 = Hos. xiii. 14

Out of these thirty quotations from the O.T., about twenty-five are in exact or substantial agreement with the LXX, and this is in accordance with evidence derived from the other Epistles. Sometimes the variations from the LXX bring the citation closer to the Hebrew, as if the Apostle were consciously or unconsciously guided by the Hebrew in diverging from the LXX, *e.g.* in xv. 54 = Isa. xxv. 8. Sometimes he seems to make changes in order to produce a wording more suitable for his argument, *e.g.* in iii. 20 = Ps. xciv. 11, where he substitutes σοφῶν for ἀνθρώπων, or in i. 19 = Isa. xxix. 14, where he substitutes ἀθετήσω for κρύψω (cf. Ps. xxxiii. 10).

The quotations which are in agreement with the LXX are these—

vi. 16 = Gen. ii. 24	x. 21 = Mal. i. 7, 12
ix. 9 = Deut. xxv. 4	x. 26 = Ps. xxiv. 1
x. 7 = Exod. xxxii. 6	xv. 32 = Isa. xxii. 13
x. 20 = Deut. xxxii. 17	xv. 45 = Gen. ii. 7.

In the following instances there is substantial agreement with the LXX, the difference in some cases being slight :—

i. 19 = Isa. xxix. 14	x. 22 = Deut. xxxii. 21
i. 31 = Jer. ix. 24	xi. 7 = Gen. v. 1
ii. 16 = Isa. xl. 13	xi. 25 = Exod. xxiv. 8 ;
	Zech. ix. 11
iii. 20 = Ps. xciv. 11	xiii. 5 = Zech. viii. 17
v. 7 = Exod. xii. 21	xv. 25 = Ps. cx. 1
v. 13 = Deut. xvii. 7, xxi. 21,	xv. 27 = Ps. viii. 6
xxii. 24	
x. 5 = Num. xiv. 16	xv. 47 = Gen. ii. 7
x. 6 = Num. xi. 34, 4	xv. 55 = Hos. xiii. 14

---

* The large number of direct quotations shows that it is not correct to say that, in teaching at Corinth, the Apostle left the O.T. foundation of the Gospel more or less in the background : see esp. xv. 3, 4, v. 7.

Perhaps under the same head should be placed—

ii. 9 = Isa. lxiv. 4, lxv. 17 ; and xiv. 21 = Isa. xxviii. 11.

But in both of these there is divergence from both the Hebrew and the LXX.

In a few cases he seems to show a preference for the Hebrew, or possibly for some version not known to us.

i. 20 = Isa. xix. 11 f., xxxiii. 18   xiv. 25 = Isa. xlv. 14
iii. 19 = Job v. 13   xv. 54 = Isa. xxv. 8

In xv. 57, τῷ δὲ Θεῷ χάρις τῷ διδόντι ἡμῖν τὸ νῖκος resembles 2 Macc. x. 38, εὐλόγουν τῷ Κυρίῳ τῷ τὸ νῖκος αὐτοῖς διδόντι, but this is probably an accidental coincidence.

§ VII. The Text of the First Epistle to the Corinthians.

The problem of textual criticism—the historical problem of establishing, as nearly as possible, the earliest ascertainable form of the text—exists for all N.T. books under very similar conditions. The great wealth of material, the early divergence of readings which can be more or less grouped into classes constituting types of text, and then the practical super-session of divergent types by an eclectic text which became dominant and which is represented in the greater number of later MSS.,—these are the general phenomena. But the different collections of N.T. books—the Gospels, Acts, Catholic Epistles, Pauline Epistles, Apocalypse—have each of them special histories and their textual phenomena special features. Our Epistle shares the special phenomena of the Pauline collection, and in this collection it has some distinctive features of its own.

GENERAL FEATURES.

During the first century or so after they were written, the books of the N.T. were copied with more freedom and less exactness than was afterwards the case. With the exception of some readings, probably editorial in character, distinctive of the 'Syrian' text (practically the *Textus Receptus*), nearly all the various readings in the N.T. originated in this early period. In a very few cases, readings, which cannot have been original, are traceable to so early a date, antecedent to all ascertainable divergence of texts, that the original readings displaced by them have not survived. These are the cases of "primitive corruption," where conjecture is needed to restore the original text. These cases are rare in the entire N.T., and very rare in the Pauline Epistles. In our Epistle there is only one probable example, namely, xii. 2 ὅτε, where ποτέ, not preserved in any document, was very likely written by St. Paul (see note *in loc.*).

WESTERN TEXT.

Apart from such rare cases, the early freedom of copying has bequeathed to us a congeries of readings amongst which we distinguish a large class which, while probably (and in many cases certainly) not original, yet remount to an antiquity higher than that of any extant version, and which are as a whole common to the Greek text embodied in many early MSS., and to the early versions, especially the Old Latin. To these readings the collective term 'Western' is applied. It is probably a misnomer, but is too firmly rooted in current use to be conveniently discarded. This class of readings, or type of text, is the centre of many interesting problems, especially as regards the Lucan books.

ALEXANDRIAN READINGS.

There is also a body of readings not assignable to this type but nevertheless of very early origin ; these readings are of a kind apparently due to editorial revision rather than to transcriptional licence, while yet they are not, on transcriptional grounds, likely to belong to the original text. These readings, mainly preserved in texts of Egyptian provenance, have been referred by Westcott and Hort to the textual labours of the Alexandrians. This limited group, although its substantive existence has been questioned (*e.g.* by Salmon), is due probably to a true factor in the history of the text.

THE PAULINE EPISTLES.

(1) *Syrian Readings.*

In the Pauline Epistles, the first task of criticism is to distinguish readings which, whether adopted or not in the 'Syrian' or 'received' text, are in their origin pre-Syrian. Such readings will be preserved in one or more of the great uncials ℵ A B C D G, of the important cursives 17, 67**, in the older witnesses for the Old Latin text, in one of the Egyptian Versions, or by certain* quotation in some Christian writer before

---

* Quotations in patristic texts are liable, both in MS. transmission and in

250 A.D. The chances of a genuine pre-Syrian reading, *not preserved in any of the above sources*, lingering in any later MSS. or authorities, is so slight as to be negligible.

RESIDUAL EARLY TEXT.

Having eliminated distinctively 'Syrian' readings, we are still confronted with great diversity of text, and with the task of classifying the material. We have to identify readings distinctively 'Western,' and to segregate from the residue such readings as may prove assignable to Alexandrian recension; the ultimate residuary readings, or 'neutral' text, will, with very rare exceptions, represent the earliest form of the text that can by any historical process be ascertained. This, the most important problem, is also the most difficult, as we are dealing with a period (before 250 A.D.) anterior to the date of any existing document. The question is,—In what extant authorities do we find a text approximately free from traces of the causes of variation noted above: early liberties with the text in copying, and Alexandrian attempts at its restoration?

Briefly, we need in the Pauline Epistles, for readings independent of the 'Western' text, the support of ℵ or B. Readings confined to D E F G, the Old Latin, or patristic quotations (apart from Alexandria), are probably 'Western.' The distinctively Alexandrian readings will be attested by ℵ A C P, some cursives, Alexandrian Fathers, and Egyptian Versions. But these authorities do not *ipso facto* prove the Alexandrian character of a reading, which is matter for delicate and discriminating determination. It must be added that the readings classed as Alexandrian are neither many nor, as a rule, important. The purely Alexandrian type of text is an entity small in bulk, as compared with the 'Western.'

As a result of the above lines of inquiry, we find that in the Pauline Epistles, as elsewhere, B is the most constant single representative of the 'Neutral' type of text; but it has, in these Epistles only, an occasional tendency to incorporate 'Western' readings, akin to those of G. ℵ, on the other hand, which in the N.T. generally bears more traces than B of mixture of (pre-Syrian) texts, is freer from such traces in the Pauline Epistles than elsewhere. Of other MSS. of the Pauline Epistles, neutral readings are most abundant in A C P 17, and in the second hand of 67. See E. A. Hutton, *An Atlas of Textual Criticism*, pp. 43 f.

print, to assimilation to the received text; we must rely only on critically edited patristic texts.

Authorities for this Epistle.

The First Epistle to the Corinthians is preserved in the following main documents :—

Greek Uncial MSS.

ℵ (Fourth century.) The Sinaitic MS., now at St Petersburg, the only MS. containing the whole N.T.

A (Fifth century.) The Codex Alexandrinus; now at the British Museum.

B (Fourth century.) The Vatican MS.

C (Fifth century.) The Codex Ephraem, a Palimpsest; now at Paris. Lacks vii. 18 ἐν ἀκροβυστίᾳ–ix. 6 τοῦ μὴ ἐργάζεσθαι: xiii. 8 παύσονται–xv. 40 ἀλλὰ ἕτερα.

D (Sixth century.) Codex Claromontanus; now at Paris. A Graeco-Latin MS. xiv. 13 διὸ ὁ λαλῶν–22 σημεῖον ἐστίν is supplied by a later but ancient hand. Many subsequent hands (sixth to ninth centuries) have corrected the MS. (see Gregory, *Prolegomena*, pp. 418–422).

E (Ninth century.) At St Petersburg. A copy of D, and unimportant.

F (Late ninth century.) Codex Augiensis (from Reichenau), now at Trin. Coll. Cambr. Probably a copy of G; in any case, secondary to G, from which it very rarely varies (see Gregory, p. 429).

Fᵃ (Seventh century.) Coisl. i. ; at Paris. A MS. of Gen.-Kings, containing N.T. passages added by the scribes as marginal notes, including 1 Cor. vii. 39, xi. 29.

G (Late ninth century.) The Codex Börnerianus; at Dresden. Interlined with the Latin (in minuscules). Lacks 1 Cor. iii. 8–16, vi. 7–14 (as F).

H (Sixth century.) Coisl. 202. At Paris (the part containing x. 22–29, xi. 9–16). An important witness, but unhappily seldom available. The MS. is scattered in seven different libraries, having been employed for bindings.

Iᵃ (Fifth century.) Codex Muralti vi. At St Petersburg. Contains xv. 53 τοῦτο–xvi. 9 ἀνέῳ.

K (Ninth century.) Codex S. Synod. xcviii. Lacks i. 1–vi. 13 ταύτην καί: viii. 7 τινὲς δὲ–viii. 11 ἀπέθανεν.

L (Ninth century.) Codex Angelicus. At Rome.

M (Ninth century.) Harl. 5913*; at the British Museum. Contains xv. 52 σαλπίσει to the end of xvi. The MS. also contains fragments of 2 Corinthians and (in some leaves now at Hamburg) of Hebrews.

P (Ninth century.) Porfirianus Chiovensis. A palimpsest
acquired in the East by Porphyrius Bishop of Kiew.
Lacks vii. 15 ὑμᾶς ὁ Θεός–17 περιπάτει : xii. 23 τοῦ
σώματος–xiii. 5 οὐ λογί– : xiv. 23 ἤ ἄπιστοι–39 τὸ λαλεῖν μή.
A good type of text in St Paul's Epistles.

Φ (Fifth century.) [Papyrus] Porfirianus Chiovensis. Contains
i. 17 ογου ινα μη–συνζητητ (20) ; vi. 13 τι· ο Θεος–15 ματ
[α υμων μελη]Χ[ριστο]υ, vi. 16–18 (fragmentary), vii. 3–14
(fragmentary). The only papyrus uncial MS. of the N.T.

Ψ (Eighth or ninth century.) Codex Athous Laurae, 172
(or B 52).

S (Same date.) Codex Athous Laurae. Contains i. 1–v. 8,
xiii. 8 εἴτε δὲ προφ–xvi. 24.

ב (Fifth century.) Vatic. Gr. 2061. Contains iv. 4–vi. 16,
xii. 23–xiv. 21, xv. 3–xvi. 1. A palimpsest, from Rossano,
perhaps originally from Constantinople. Its readings are
not yet available.

It will be seen that א A B L Ψ contain the whole Epistle,
C D F G K P nearly the whole, while Fᵃ H I² M Q S ב contain
but small portions. The oldest MSS. are א B of the fourth century,
A C I² Q ב of the fifth, and D H of the sixth. Marks of punctuation are very few in א A B C D H ; they are more frequent in G.
(On the punctuation see Scrivener (ed. 4), vol. i. p. 48 ; Gregory,
vol. iii. pp. 111–115.)

Cursive MSS.

The Epistles of St Paul are to be found in some 480 cursives,
of which we mention only one or two as of special interest.

17. (Ev. 33, Act 13. Ninth century.) At Paris (Nat. Gr. 14).
See Westcott and Hort, *Introd.* §§ 211, 212.

37. (Ev. 69, Act 31, Apoc. 14. Fifteenth century.) The well-
known Leicester codex. Contains a good text.

47. Bodleian. Roe 16. (Eleventh century.)

67. (Act 66, Apoc. 34. Eleventh century.) At Vienna. The
marginal corrections (67**) embody very early readings,
akin to those of M (*supra*). See Westcott and Hort,
Introd. § 212.

Versions.

The OLD LATIN of this Epistle is transmitted in the Graeco-
Latin uncials D E F G, the Latin of which is cited as d e f g.
d has a text independent of D, but in places adapted to it ;
e approximates more to the Vulgate ; g is a Vulgate text *except
in Romans and* 1 *Corinthians*, where it is based on the Old Latin,

f a Vulgate text with Old Latin admixture. The Greek text of each of these MSS. has to some extent influenced the Latin.

The Epistle is also contained in

x (Ninth century.) Bodleian; Laud. Lat. 108, E. 67, a thrice-corrected text, having much in common with d.

m (Ninth century.) At Rome; the *Speculum pseudo-Augustinianum.*

r (Sixth century.) The Freisingen MS., now at Munich. The two last named contain fragments only.

On the Vulgate, Egyptian (Bohairic or Coptic and Thebaic or Sahidic),* Syriac, Armenian, and Gothic, reference may be made to Sanday and Headlam, *Romans*, p. lxvi sq. As to the Syriac, it should be noted that the later (or Harclean) Syriac has some more ancient readings (Westcott and Hort, *Introd.* p. 156 sq.); we have not, for St Paul's Epistles, any Syriac version older than the Peshito. Also, the high antiquity formerly claimed for the Peshito was founded mainly upon the quotations from it in St Ephraem; but these now prove to be untrustworthy, being due to assimilation in the printed text of this Father.

ILLUSTRATIVE READINGS.

We will now consider some readings (taken at hazard except as regards their generally interesting character), which will illustrate the mutual relations of the documents for the text of this Epistle. We omit all reference to E and F, as being secondary (as mentioned above) to D and G respectively.

It must be remembered that the documents, while furnishing merely the external credentials of a reading, have already been subjected to a classification on the basis of innumerable readings as to which no serious doubt exists; the combination of external evidence as to antiquity with 'internal' evidence (*i.e.* considerations of transcriptional probability, and of latent—as opposed to superficial—inferiority) has reached a result in which modern critical editors are as a rule agreed. Those MSS. or groups of MSS., which are most frequently ranged in support of the undoubtedly right readings, are naturally deserving of special consideration where the reading is *prima facie* less certain.†

Such a group is ℵ B. These two fourth-century MSS., although in part written by one hand, are copied from quite

---

* On the so-called Bashmuric version and its kindred, see Scrivener, *Introd.* (ed. 4), vol. ii. pp. 101–106, 140.

† The readings discussed below are treated independently of the notes on the several passages; in a few cases the view taken differs from that expressed in the notes.

distinct originals. The text of ℵ has clearly been affected by influences foreign to anything in the ancestry of B. The text of their common ancestor must have been of the very highest antiquity, and the test of many indisputable passages shows also that its antiquity must have been antiquity of type, not of date only. Apart from the small classes of 'primitive corruptions' and of 'Western non-interpolations,' the combinations ℵ B can only be set aside on the most cogent grounds; our Epistle contains few, if any, passages where such grounds can be shown.

Typical Syrian Readings.

In such passages as (1) vi. 20, where C³ Dᵇᶜ K L P, Syrr., Chrys. add the words which follow ὑμῶν, we have a typical 'Syrian' reading, and the shorter text is supported by ℵ B in common with the vast preponderance of MSS. and versions. A similar example is (2) the inversion of Θεός and Κύριος, in vii. 17, in K L, the later Syriac, and later Greek Fathers. This was probably due to the desire to place Θεός first in order, overlooking the decisive fact that κέκληκεν calls for Θεός rather than ὁ Κύριος (v. 15 and elsewhere). In (3) iii. 4 σαρκικοί, (4) viii. 2 εἰδέναι for ἐγνωκέναι, ἔγνωκε for ἔγνω, the case is the same,—ℵ B, with an ample host of allies, ranged against a text which gained later currency but which lacks early attestation.

Typical Western Readings.

The case is somewhat different in the next instances to be mentioned, where the reading unsupported by ℵ B has some early currency, mainly 'Western' in character. Such cases are (5) iii. 1 σαρκίνοις, ℵ A B C D* 17, 67**, Clem. Orig., where Dᶜ G L P, Clem. Orig. (in other places) read σαρκικοῖς. Here the latter reading may be classed as 'Western'; but P, which supports it, joins the great uncials in (6) v. 3 in support of σαρκικοί against D* and G, which have σαρκινοι. The latter reading is purely 'Western'; P elsewhere (see below) frequently represents a non-Western text.

Affinities of P.

An example of this is (7) viii. 7 where we have ℵ A B P 17, 67**, and the Egyptian and Aethiopic Versions supporting συνηθείᾳ against the 'Western and Syrian' συνειδήσει. The same holds good of (8) xii. 2 ὅτε (see note there). Another passage where P joins ℵ B (and 17) against a Western reading (adopted

in the Syrian text) is (9) ix. 2 μου τῆς, where D G K L (and
Latin MSS., *apostolatus mei*) have τῆς ἐμῆς (A omits this
verse).

One more interesting example of this class of variants is the
ternary variation in vii. 29, which it is worth while to set out in
full—

(10) vii. 29 ἐστίν τὸ λοιπόν, ℵ A B D*ᵇ P 17 Copt. Syr. Arm.,
        Eus. (in one place) Ephr. Bas. Euthal. (D omits
        τό.)
        τὸ λοιπὸν ἐστίν, Dᶜ K L, Eus. (another place) Chrys.
        ἐστίν λοιπὸν ἐστίν, G 67** , d e f g m Vulg., Orig. Tert.
        Hieron. Aug.

The attestation of the first reading clearly outweighs that of
either of the other two. The second is clearly a 'Syrian'
reading, the third as clearly 'Western,' D here preserving
the non-Western reading, and P once more siding, against the
Western reading, with ℵ B. This, however, is not always the
case. In (11) xvi. 23 the omission of Χριστοῦ, ℵ B 17, f, some
MSS. of Vulg. Goth., Thdt., is probably right, though ℵᶜ A C D
G K L M P, e g, some MSS. of Vulg., the versions generally, and
most patristic quotations, follow the tendency to insert it (so far
more natural than its omission, if found). But the insertion (in
view of the combination ℵᶜ A C L P, Euthal.) may be 'Alexandrian' rather than 'Western.'

Possible Alexandrian Readings.

So far our instances (with the possible exception of the last)
have been cases of the excellence of the text supported by the
combination ℵ B.

We will next consider some few possible examples of 'Alexandrian' editing.

(12) iv. 6 (add after γέγραπται) φρονεῖν, ℵ C Dᶜ L P Syrr. Copt.
        Arm. Goth., Greek Fathers, Euthal.
        om. ℵ A B D* G, Latin MSS. and Vulg., Orig.
        Latin Fathers.

This is certainly an addition not 'Western,' but pre-Syrian.
It corresponds with the character assigned by WH. to the
Alexandrian touches.

(13) ix. 9 κημώσεις, B* D* G, Chrys. Thdt.
        φιμώσεις, ℵ A B³ C D² ᵃⁿᵈ ³ K L P al. omn., Orig.
        Chrys. Euthal.

This is the first example we have taken of B differing from ℵ, and *prima facie* this might seem a clear case of the slight 'Western' element present in B, in St Paul's Epistles. But the Alexandrian witnesses are ranged on the side opposed to B, and we must remember that φιμώσεις is in the LXX source of the quotation, and the assimilation of the text to its original would be more natural, as a correction, than the introduction of a variant. (The versions of course are neutral here.)

(14) xv. 51 πάντες μέν, ℵ A C² Dᶜ G K L P, f g Vulg. Copt. Syr.ᵖᵒˢ Ephr. (?) Greek Fathers, Euthal.
     (om. μέν) B C* D*, d e Arm. Aeth. Syr.ᵖʳⁱ Greek MSS. known to Jerome.

The μέν, if (as probable) not genuine, illustrates once more the significance of the combination ℵ A L P, Euthal.; it has the character of an Alexandrian touch. But it seems to have been read by both Ephraem in the East and Tertullian in the West.

(15) x. 9 Χριστόν, D G K L, Vulg. Syr.ᵖʳⁱ ᵉᵗ ᵖᵒˢᵗ ᵗˣᵗ Copt., Marcion Iren. Chrys., etc.
     Κύριον, ℵ B C P 17, etc., Syr.ᵖᵒˢᵗ ᵐᵍ Copt.ᶜᵒᵈ Arm. Aeth., Dam., etc.
     Θεόν, A, Euthal.

There is no question but that Χριστόν is of inferior and Western attestation. Θεόν looks like, and may possibly be, an Alexandrian correction (assimilation to Ps. lxxvii. 18, LXX).

(16) ix. 15 οὐδείς, ℵ* B D* 17, d e Sah. Basm., and early Latin Fathers.
     οὐθείς μή, A.
     τις, G. 26.
     ἵνα τις, ℵᶜ C Dᵇ ᶜ K L P, f Vulg., many Greek and Latin Fathers.

(All MSS. except K read κενώσει here, the later cursives only reading κενώσῃ with most late Greek Fathers.)

The reading ἵνα τις, adopted by the Syrian text, is apparently pre-Syrian in origin; it lacks the full Alexandrian attestation, but on the other hand it bears every mark of an editorial touch. If pre-Syrian, it is Alexandrian rather than Western.

(17) xi. 24 κλώμενον, ℵᶜ C³ Dᵇ ᶜ G K L P, d e g Syr., Euthal. Greek Fathers (θρυπτόμ. D*).
     om. ℵ* A B C 17, 67**, Ath. Cyr. Fulg. (expressly).
     tradetur, f Vulg., Cypr.

Here P sides with the Western witnesses in what is clearly a
'Western' interpolation (cf. Gal. i. 18, ii. 14 πέτρος).

The two last cases are on opposite sides of the border line
which distinguishes readings of the Alexandrian type from other
inferior, but pre-Syrian, readings.

Western Element in B.

We will next give an example or two of the 'Western'
element in B (see above on ix. 9)—

(18) ii. 1   μυστήριον, ℵ* A C Copt. (Boh.), Amb. Aug. Ambrst.,
              etc.
              μαρτύριον, ℵᶜ B D G L P, Latin and other verss., Cyr.-
              Alex.

This is a doubtful case, as the readings hang somewhat evenly
in the balance, and the attestation of μαρτ. is perhaps not exclusively Western.   But if WH. are right in preferring μυστ.,
B may here betray Western admixture.   The reading is one of
the least certain in this Epistle.

(19) xi. 19 (post ἵνα) καί, B D 37 71, d e Vulg. Sah., Ambrst.
             (om. καί) ℵ A C Dᵇᶜ G K L P f g, Syr. Copt. Arm.,
             Orig. Epiph. Euthal. Chrys., etc.

Tertullian, Cyprian, and Jerome apparently are to be counted
on the side of omission, as well as G.   But the reading of B,
which is of little intrinsic probability, is clearly 'Western' in its
other attestation.

(20) xv. 14 (after πίστις) ὑμῶν, ℵ A Dᵇᶜ G K L P, d e f g Vulg.
             verss.
             ἡμῶν, B D* 17 67**, Sah. Basm. Goth.

The bulk of the Western authorities are here against B ; the
latter probably preserves a very ancient, but not original, reading,
possibly an early itacism (see below on xv. 49).

(21) In xiv. 38 the reading of B ἀγνοείτω, supported by the
         correctors of ℵ A D, and by K L, Syr. Arm. Aeth., Orig.
         against ℵ* A* D* G*, Basm. and the Latin Versions, with
         Orig. in one place, is no doubt correct, as also in xv. 51
         where οὐ has been transferred to stand after the second
         πάντες in ℵ C G 17.   B here has the support of P as well
         as K L and Greek MSS. known to Jerome.

In (22) x. 20, omission of τὰ ἔθνη, B has Western support only ;
    but the case is probably one of 'Western non-interpolation.'

Singular Readings of B.

There remain to be noticed a few singular or sub-singular readings of B which may not impossibly be right in some cases.

(23) xiii. 4 (after ζηλοῖ) ἡ ἀγαπή, ℵ A C D G K L, d e g m Syr., Orig. Cyr. Cypr.
  om. B 17, etc., f Vulg. Copt. Arm. By no means improbable.

(24) viii. 8 περισσευόμεθα, B, Orig. (all the rest—ομεν). But for the quotation in Orig., which shows the reading to be very ancient, we might have set it down to the scribe of B. The same is true of

(25) xiii. 5 τὸ μὴ ἑαυτῆς B, Clem.^paed. The rest, including Clem.^strom, have τὰ ἑαυτῆς. The latter is probably right, but the reference in Clem*paed*. shows that the variant is of high antiquity.

(26) xv. 49 φορέσομεν, B 46, Arm. Aeth., Thdt. and a few Fathers. The weight of evidence, and transcriptional probability, is here wholly on the side of ℵ and all other MSS. against B.

The above examples (13, 14, 18–26) show that where ℵ and B are ranged against one another it is necessary to deal with each case on its evidential merits, but that B is rarely to be set aside without hesitation.

Combined Witness of ℵ B in disputed Readings.

We will lastly take some passages where ℵ and B are again at one, and probably right, though they are less clear than those mentioned at the outset.

(27) xiii. 3 καυχήσωμαι, ℵ A B 17, Boh., Ephr. Hieron. (and Greek MSS. known to him).
  καυθήσωμαι, C K, d e f g m Vulg. verss., Orig. Ephr. Meth. Chrys., etc.
  καυθήσομαι, D G L, Bas. Euthal. Cyr. Max.

The latter reading is Western in its attestation, while καυχ. has the important indirect (but quite clear) support of Clem.-Rom. 55, a witness of exceptional antiquity. Transcriptional probability is, moreover, on the side of καυχήσωμαι.

(28) vii. 34 (before μεμέρισται) καί, ℵ A B D* P 17, 67, f Vulg. Syr.^post Copt., Euthal and Early Fathers.
  om. D^c G K L, d e g m, Chrys. Thdt. Dam. Amb. Ambrst. Hieron.

There can be no doubt that this omission is 'Western' and 'Syrian.'

(29) vii. 34 (after μεμέρ.) καί, ℵ A B Dᵃ G K L P, d e g Vulg., Meth.
Eus., etc.
om. D*, some copies of Vulg., Latin Fathers.

The omission is here purely Western and of limited range.

(30) vii. 34 (after γυνή) ἡ ἄγαμος, ℵ A B (C is lacking) P 17, Vulg
Copt., Euthal. Hieron. (and Gk. MSS. known to).
om. D G K L, d e f g m fuld. Syr. Arm. Aeth., Meth

This omission again is clearly 'Western.'

(31) vii. 34 (after παρθένος) ἡ ἄγαμος, ℵ A D G K L, d e f g fuld.
Syr. Arm. Aeth., Bas. Latin Fathers.
om. B P, several mss. Vulg. Copt. Basm., Eus.
Hieron. (with reasons).

Reviewing as a whole the evidence (28–31) bearing upon this verse, the καί both before and after μεμέρισται must be admitted as thoroughly attested. The omission of ἡ ἄγαμος after ἡ γυνή is inferior in attestation to its presence (additionally attested by ℵ A) in both places. This latter reading, again, is clearly not original, but conflate; its support by ℵ A, Euthal. may point to an Alexandrian origin. Jerome, on the evidence before him, believed the reading ἡ γ. ἡ ἄγ. καὶ ἡ παρθ. to be what St Paul actually wrote—*apostolica veritas*. Moreover, the apparent difficulty of this reading explains the early transference of ἡ ἄγαμος from after γυνή to follow παρθένος. [The 'unmarried woman' is generic, including widows; the virgin (under control) is the special case whose treatment is in question.] Μεμέρισται, both in number and in sense, fits ill with what follows it. The question of punctuation, as to which the MSS. give no help, must follow that of text. The crucial points, on which ℵ B are agreed, are the καί in both places and the genuineness of ἡ ἄγ. after ἡ γυνή.

Our last example shall be the ἀμήν, xvi. 24.

(32) xvi. 24 ἀμήν, ℵ A C D K L P, d e vg^clem verss., Chrys. Thdt
Dam.
om. B M 17, f g r fuld. tol., Euthal. Ambrst.
G has γενεθήτω· γενεθήτω (*sic*).

The MSS. support ἀμήν conclusively at the end of Galatians, Rom. xvi. 27, and at the end of Jude. Elsewhere, in view of the strong liturgical instinct to add it where possible, the witness of even a few MSS. is enough to displace it. The other leading

uncials, in varying combinations, add it at the end of most of the
Epistles, and some MSS. in every case. It is noteworthy that
(except in Galatians, Romans, Jude) B, wherever it is available,
is the one constant witness against this interpolation. The one
exception to this in the whole N.T. is at the close of St Luke's
Gospel, where the ἀμήν must be a very early addition.

Our Epistle, to judge by the external evidence, was in wide
circulation long before the "Apostolus" was circulated as a
collection of letters; certainly we have earlier and wider traces of
its use than we have of that of the companion Epistle. It must
accordingly have been copied many times before it was included
in a comprehensive roll or codex. The wonder is that the text
has suffered so little in transmission; one possibility of primitive
corruption (xii. 2) is, for an Epistle of this length, slight indeed.

§ VIII. COMMENTARIES.

These are very numerous, and a long list will be found in
Meyer. See also the Bibliography in the 2nd ed. of Smith's
Dictionary of the Bible, i. pp. 656, 658; Hastings, *DB.* i. p. 491,
iii. p. 731; *Ency. Bibl.* i. 907. In the selection given below, an
asterisk indicates that the work is in some way important, a dagger,
that valuable information respecting the commentator is to be
found in Sanday and Headlam on *Romans* in this series, pp.
xcviii.–cix.

Patristic and Scholastic: Greek.

*† Origen (d. 253). Some fragments have come down to
us in Cramer's *Catena*, vol. v. (Oxf. 1844), in the *Philocalia*
(J. Arm. Robinson, Camb. 1893); additional fragments of great
interest are given in the new and valuable recension by Claude
Jenkins in the *Journal of Theological Studies*, January, April,
July, and October 1908; and C. H. Turner comments on these,
January 1909.

*† Chrysostom (d. 407). The Homilies on 1 and 2 Corin-
thians are considered the best examples of his teaching.‡ They
show admirable judgment, but sometimes two or more interpretations are welded together in a rhetorical comment. He generally
illuminates what he touches.

*† Theodoret (d. 457). Migne, *P.G.* lxxxii. He follows
Chrysostom closely, but is sometimes more definite and pointed.

*† Theophylact (d. after 1118). Migne, *P.G.* cxxv. He follows

‡ They have been translated in the Oxford Library of the Fathers.

the Greek Fathers and is better than nearly all Latin commentators of that date.

Oecumenius (Bp. of Tricca, end of tenth century).   Migne,
P.G. cxviii., cxix.   The relation of his excerpts to those of Theophylact is greatly in need of further examination.

Patristic and Scholastic: Latin.

† Ambrosiaster or Pseudo-Ambrosius.   He is the unknown
author of the earliest commentary on all the Pauline Epistles
that has come down to us.   He is now commonly identified
either with Decimius Hilarianus Hilarius, governor of Africa in
377, praetorian prefect in Italy in 396, or with the Ursinian
Isaac, a convert from Judaism (C. H. Turner, *Journal of Theological Studies*, April 1906).   His importance lies in the Latin
text used by him, which " must be at least as old as 370 . . . it
is at least coeval with our oldest complete manuscripts of the
Greek Bible, and thus presupposes a Greek text anterior to
them."   Ambrosiaster's text of the Pauline Epistles is " equivalent
to a complete fourth century pre-Vulgate Latin codex of these
epistles " (Souter, *A Study of Ambrosiaster*, p. 196).

† Pelagius.   Migne, *P.L.* xxx.   Probably written before 410.

Pseudo-Primasius.   Migne, *P.L.* lxviii.   A revision of
Pelagius made by a pupil or pupils of Cassiodorus.

Bede (d. 735).   Mainly a *catena* from Augustine.

* Atto Vercellensis.   Migne, *P.L.* cxxxiv. Bishop of Vercelli
in Piedmont in the tenth century.   Depends on his predecessors,
but thinks for himself.

* Herveius Burgidolensis (d. 1149).   Migne, *P.L.* clxxxi.   A
Benedictine of Bourg-Dieu or Bourg-Deols in Berry.   One of
the best of mediaeval commentators for strength and sobriety.
He and Atto often agree, and neither seems to be much used by
modern writers.

Peter Lombard (d. 1160).

† Thomas Aquinas (d. 1274).

Modern Latin.

Faber Stapulensis, Paris, 1512.

Cajetan, Venice, 1531.

† Erasmus, Desiderius (d. 1536).

*† Calvin, John.   Quite the strongest of the Reformers as a
commentator, clear-headed and scholarly, but too fond of finding
arguments against Rome.   His work on the Pauline Epistles
ranges from 1539 to 1551.

† Beza, Theodore (d. 1605), Paris, 1594.

Cornelius a Lapide, Antwerp, 1614.   Roman (Jesuit).
* Estius, Douay, 1614.   Roman (sober and valuable).
† Grotius, Amsterdam, 1644–1646.
*† Bengel, Tübingen, 1742 ; 3rd ed. London, 1862.   Fore most in Scriptural insight and pithy expression.
*† Wetstein, Amsterdam, 1751, 1752.   Rich in illustration.

English.

† H. Hammond, London, 1653, "The father of English commentators."   'Historical.'
† John Locke, London, 1705–1707.   'Historical.'
Edward Burton, Oxford, 1831.
T. W. Peile, Rivingtons, 1853.
C. Hodge, New York, 1857.   Calvinist.
† C. Wordsworth, Rivingtons, 4th ed. 1866.
* F. W. Robertson, Smith & Elder, 5th ed. 1867.
*† H. Alford, Rivingtons, 6th ed. 1871.
P. J. Gloag, Edinburgh, 1874.
* A. P. Stanley, Murray, 4th ed. 1876.   Picturesque and suggestive, but not so strong in scholarship.
T. T. Shore in *Ellicott's Commentary*, n.d.
J. J. Lias in the *Cambridge Greek Testament*, 1879.
* T. S. Evans in the *Speaker's Commentary*, 1881.   Rich in exact scholarship and original thought, but sometimes eccentric in results.
D. Brown in *Schaff's Commentary*, 1882.
F. W. Farrar in the *Pulpit Commentary*, 1883.
*† J. A. Beet, Hodder, 2nd ed. 1884.   Wesleyan.
* T. C. Edwards, Hamilton Adams, 1885.   Very helpful.
* C. J. Ellicott, Longmans, 1887.   Minute and strong in grammatical exegesis.   Perhaps the best English Commentary on the Greek text (but misses Evans' best points).
W. Kay (posthumous), 1887.   Scholarly, but slight.
Marcus Dods in the *Expositor's Bible*.
* J. B. Lightfoot (posthumous), Notes on i.–vii. 1895. Important.
* G. G. Findlay in the *Expositor's Greek Testament*, Hodder, 1900.   Thorough grasp of Pauline thought.
* J. Massie in the *Century Bible*, n.d.
W. M. Ramsay, Historical Commentary in the *Expositor*, 6th series.

New Translations into English.

The Twentieth Century New Testament, Part II., Marshall, 1900.

INTRODUCTION lxix

R. F. Weymouth, *The N.T. in Modern Speech*, Clarke, 2nd ed. 1905.

A. S. Way, *The Letters of St Paul*, Macmillan, 2nd ed. 1906.

* W. G Rutherford (posthumous), *Thessalonians and Corinthians*, Macmillan, 1908.

German.

Billroth, 1833 ; Eng. tr., Edinburgh, 1837.

Rückert, Leipzig, 1836.

Olshausen, 1840 ; Eng. tr., Edinburgh, 1855.

J. E. Osiander, Stuttgart, 1849.

*† De Wette, Leipzig, 3rd ed. 1855.

G. H. A. Ewald, Göttingen, 1857.

Neander, Berlin, 1859.

* Heinrici, *Das Erste Sendschreiben*, etc., 1880.

*† Meyer, 5th ed. 1870 ; Eng. tr., Edinburgh, 1877. Re-edited by B. Weiss, and again by * Heinrici, 1896 and 1900; again by J. Weiss, 1910.

Maier, Freiburg, 1857. Roman.

Kling, in Lange's *Bibelwerk*, 1861 ; Eng. tr., Edinburgh, 1869.

Schnedermann, in Strack and Zöckler, 1887.

H. Lang, in Schmidt & Holzendorff ; Eng. tr., London, 1883. Thin.

* Schmiedel, Freiburg, i. B., 1892. Condensed, exact, and exacting.

* B. Weiss, Leipzig, 2nd ed. 1902. Brief, but helpful. Eng. tr., New York and London, 1906; less useful than the original. Also his * *Textkritik d. paul. Briefe* (xiv. 3 of *Texte und Untersuchungen*), 1896.

* P. Bachmann, in Zahn's *Kommentar*, Leipzig, 1910.

Also Schäfer, 1903 ; Bousset, 1906 ; Lietzmann, 1907 ; Schlatter, 1908.

French.

E. Reuss, Paris, 1874–80.

*† F. Godet, Paris, 1886 ; Eng. tr., Edinburgh, 1888. Strong in exegesis, but weak in criticism.

General.

The literature on the life and writings of St Paul is enormous, and is increasing rapidly. Some of the works which are helpful and are very accessible are mentioned here.

Conybeare and Howson, *Life and Epistles of St Paul.*
Farrar, *Life and Work of St. Paul.*
Lewin, *Life and Epistles of St Paul*; *Fasti Sacri.*
R. J. Knowling, *The Witness of the Epistles*, 1892; *The Testimony of St Paul to Christ*, 1905.
J. B. Lightfoot, *Biblical Essays.*
Hort, *Judaistic Christianity*; *The Christian Ecclesia.*
H. St J. Thackeray, *The Relation of St Paul to Contemporary Jewish Thought*, 1900.
Ramsay, *St Paul the Traveller*, 1902; *Pauline and other Studies*, 1906.
Ropes, *The Apostolic Age*, 1906.
Weinel, *St Paul, the Man and his Work*, Eng. tr 1906.
Pfleiderer, *Paulinism*, Eng. tr. 1877.
Du Bose, *The Gospel according to St Paul*, 1907.
W. E. Chadwick, *The Pastoral Teaching of St Paul*, 1907.
A. T. Robertson, *Epochs in the Life of St Paul*, 1909.
Cohu, *St Paul in the Light of Modern Research*, 1911.
Baur, *Paulus* (ed. 2), 1866 (still worth consulting in spite of views now obsolete).
Holsten, *Das Evangelium des Paulus*, 1880; *Einleitung in die Korintherbriefe*, 1901.
Räbiger, *Kristische Untersuchungen über 1 and 2 Kor.*, 1886.
Weizsäcker, *Apost. Zeitalter*, 1886.
Holtzmann, *Einleitung in das N.T.*, 1892.
Jülicher, *Einleitung in das N.T.*, 1894; Eng. tr. 1904.
Krenkel, *Beiträge z. Aufhellung d. Geschichte und d. Briefe d. Apostels Paulus*, 1895.
Zahn, *Einleitung in das N.T.*, Eng. tr. 1909.
Hastings, *DB.*, articles ,'Baptism'; 'Lord's Supper'; 'Paul the Apostle'; 'Resurrection'; 'Tongues, Gift of'; 'Greek Patristic Commentaries on the Pauline Epistles' (vol. v.).
Ency. Bibl., articles, 'Baptism'; Eucharist'; 'Spiritual Gifts.'
Ency. Brit. (11th ed., Dec. 1910), articles, 'Apologetics' (p. 193), 'Apostle,' 'Atonement' (pp. 875 f.), 'Baptism' (pp. 368 f.), 'Christianity' (pp. 284 f.), 'Church History' (pp. 334 f.), 'Corinthians,' 'Eschatology' (pp. 762 f.), 'Eucharist.'
The apocryphal letters between St Paul and the Corinthians have been edited by Harnack in his *Geschichte d. altchrist. Litteratur*, 1897, and also in Lietzmann's excellent *Materials for the use of Theological Lecturers and Students*, 1905. See also Moffatt, *Intr. to the Lit. of the N.T.* (pp. 129 f.).

THE FIRST
EPISTLE TO THE CORINTHIANS

◆

I. 1-3. THE APOSTOLIC SALUTATION.

Paul, a divinely chosen Apostle, and Sosthenes our brother, give Christian greeting to the Corinthian Church, itself also divinely called.

[1] Paul, an Apostle called by divine summons equally with the Twelve, and Sosthenes whom ye know, [2] give greeting to the body of Corinthian Christians, who have been consecrated to God in Christ, called out of the mass of mankind into the inner society of the Church to which so many other Christian worshippers belong. [3] May the free and unmerited favour of God, and the peace which comes from reconciliation with Him, be yours! May God Himself, our Heavenly Father, and the Lord Jesus Messiah, grant them to you!

The Salutation is in the usual three parts: the sender (*v. 1*), the addressees (*v. 2*), and the greeting (*v. 3*).

1. κλητός. Elsewhere only Rom. i. 1. As all are called to be ἅγιοι, so Paul is called to be an Apostle: see on *v. 2*, and note the same parallelism, Rom. i. 1, 6. In O.T. the idea of κλῆσις is often connected with prophets.*

διὰ θελήματος Θεοῦ. As in 2 Cor., Eph., Col., 2 Tim.; expanded, with emphasis on his divine call to the exclusion of any human source or channel, in Gal. i. 1. *Sua ipsius voluntate nunquam P. factus esset apostolus* (Beng.). *Per quod tangit etiam illos, quos neque Christus miserat, neque per voluntatem Dei*

* Cf. Isa. vi. 8, 9; Jer. i. 4, 5. See W. E. Chadwick. *The Pastoral Teaching of St Paul.* p. 76.

praedicabant (Herveius Burgidolensis), viz., the self-constituted teachers, the false apostles.

Σωσθένης. He was not necessarily the amanuensis, for Tertius (Rom. xvi. 22) does not appear in the Salutation. In Gal. i. 1, a number of unnamed persons are associated with the Apostle. Nor need this Sosthenes be the Corinthian Jew (Acts xviii. 17) who was the chief of the synagogue (superseding Crispus the convert?) and perhaps leader of the complaint before Gallio.* If the two are identical, S. himself had (1) subsequently become a Christian, (2) migrated from Corinth to Ephesus.

ὁ ἀδελφός. A Christian: xvi. 12; 2 Cor. i. 1; Col. i. 1; Philem. 1; Rom. xvi. 23; Heb. xiii. 23. The article implies that he was well known to some Corinthians. Deissmann (*Bible Studies*, pp. 87, 142) has shown that ἀδελφοί was used of members of religious bodies long before Christians adopted it in this sense. It is remarkable that Apollos is not named as joining in sending the letter (xvi. 12).

> A D E omit κλητός. Χριστοῦ Ἰησοῦ (B D E F G 17, Am.) is to be preferred to Ἰησοῦ Χρ. (א A L P, Syrr. Copt. Arm. Aeth.): see note on Rom. i. 1. Contrast *vv*. 1, 2, 4 with 3, 7, 8, 9, 10, where Κύριος is added.

2. τῇ ἐκκλησίᾳ τοῦ Θεοῦ. The genitive is possessive: x. 32, xi. 16, 22, xv. 9; 2 Cor. i. 1; Gal. i. 13; etc. Cf. Deut. xviii. 16, xxiii. 1; etc. As Chrysostom remarks, the expression is at once a protest against party-spirit; 'the Church of God,' not of any one individual.

τῇ οὔσῃ. See Acts xiii. 1.

ἡγιασμένοις ἐν Χρ. Ἰ. The plural in apposition to the collective singular throws a passing emphasis upon the individual responsibility of those who had been consecrated in baptism (vi. 11) as members of Christ. The perfect participle indicates a fixed state.

κλητοῖς ἁγίοις. Called by God (Gal. i. 6; Rom. viii. 30, ix. 24; etc.) to the Christian society through the preaching of the Gospel (Rom. x. 14; 2 Thess. ii. 14). See note on Rom. i. 7 and separate note on ἅγιοι; also Chadwick, *Pastoral Teaching*, pp. 96, 98. The active καλεῖν is never used of the human instrument, but only of God or Christ. *Admonet Corinthios majestatis ipsorum* (Beng.).

σὺν πᾶσι. This is generally connected simply with τῇ ἐκκλησίᾳ, as if St Paul were addressing the Corinthian Church along with all other Christians. But this little suits the in-

---

* Chrysostom identifies Sosthenes with Crispus, and assumes that he was beaten for having become a Christian. Both conjectures are very improbable. That he headed the deputation to Gallio is very probable, and that he is the Corinthian Jew is also very probable.

dividual character of this Epistle, which (much more than
Romans, for example) deals with the special circumstances of
one particular Church. It is therefore better, with Heinrici,
to connect the words with κλητοῖς ἁγίοις (contrast 2 Cor. i. 1).
Euthymius Zigabenus takes it so. St Paul is not making his
Epistle 'Catholic,' nor is he "greeting the whole Church in
Spirit," but he is commending to the Corinthians the fact that
their call is not for themselves alone, but into the unity of the
Christian brotherhood, a thought specially necessary for them.
See xiv. 36. Throughout the Epistle it is the Corinthians alone
that are addressed, not all Christendom.

τοῖς ἐπικαλουμένοις. This goes back to Joel ii. 32, and
involves the thought of faith, the common bond of all. See
Rom. x. 12, 13. Here, as there, St Paul significantly brings in
the worship of Christ under the O.T. formula for worship addressed to the LORD God of Israel. To be a believer is to
worship Christ.

ἐν παντὶ τόπῳ. Cf. 2 Cor. i. 1b; but it is hardly possible to
read into the present expression the limitation to Achaia. This
consideration confirms the view taken above of the force of σὺν
πᾶσι κ.τ.λ., in spite of the parallels given by Lightfoot of Clem.
ad Cor. 65, and the Ep. of the Church of Smyrna on the death
of Polycarp, καὶ πάσαις ταῖς κατὰ πάντα τόπον τῆς ἁγίας καὶ καθο-
λικῆς ἐκκλησίας παροικίαις. Cf. 2 Cor. ii. 14; 1 Thess. i. 8.

αὐτῶν καὶ ἡμῶν. Connected either with τόπῳ or with
Κυρίου. The latter (AV., RV.) would be by way of epanorthosis; 'our Lord'—rather 'theirs and ours.' In itself ἡμῶν is
general enough to need no such epanorthosis: but the thought
of the claim (v. 13) of some, to possess Christ for themselves
alone, might explain this addition. The connexion with τόπῳ
(Vulg. in omni loco ipsorum et nostro) is somewhat pointless, in
spite of the various attempts to supply a point by referring it
either to Achaia and Corinth, or to Ephesus and Corinth, or to
Corinth and the whole world, or to the Petrine and the Pauline
Churches, etc. etc. He may mean that the home of his converts is his home; cf. Rom. xvi. 13.

BD* E F G place τῇ οὔσῃ ἐν Κορίνθῳ after ἡγιασμένοις ἐν Χρ. Ἰησοῦ.
אּ A D² L P, Vulg. Syrr. Copt. Arm. Aeth. place it before. A omits
Χριστοῦ. אּ³ A* D³ E L P, Arm. Aeth. insert τε after αὐτῶν, probably for
the sake of smoothness. Such insertions are frequent both in MSS. and
versions.

3. χάρις ὑμῖν καὶ εἰρήνη. This is St Paul's usual greeting,
the Greek χαίρειν combined with the Hebrew *Shalom*, and both
with a deepened meaning. In 1 and 2 Tim., and in 2 John 3,
ἔλεος is added after χάρις. St James has the laconic and
secular χαίρειν (cf. Acts xv. 23). St Jude has ἔλεος ὑμῖν καὶ

εἰρήνη καὶ ἀγάπη. In 1 and 2 Pet. we have χάρις ὑμῖν καὶ εἰρήνη, as here. The fact that 'grace and peace' or 'grace, mercy, and peace' is found in St Paul, St Peter, and St John, is some evidence "that we have here the earliest Christian password or *symbolum*. Grace is the source, peace the consummation" (Edwards). The favour of God leads naturally to peace of mind. Enmity to God has ceased, and reconciliation has followed. *Quae gratia a non offenso ? Quae pax a non rebellato ?* asks Tertullian (*Adv. Marc.* v. 5). See on Rom. i. 5 and 7. In Dan. iii. 31 [98] we have as a salutation, εἰρήνη ὑμῖν πληθυνθείη. See J. A. Robinson, *Ephesians*, pp. 221–226. In 2 Macc. i. 1 we have χαίρειν . . . εἰρήνην ἀγαθήν, and in the Apoc. of Baruch lxxviii. 2, "mercy and peace." Such greetings are not primarily Christian.

I. 4–9. PREAMBLE OF THANKSGIVING AND HOPE.

I thank God continually for your present spiritual condition. Christ will strengthen you to the end according to Divine assurance.

⁴ I never cease thanking God, because of the favours which He bestowed upon you through your union with Christ Jesus, ⁵ whereby as immanent in Him ye received riches of every kind, in every form of inspired utterance and every form of spiritual illumination, for the giving and receiving of instruction. ⁶ These gifts ye received in exact proportion to the completeness with which our testimony to the Messiah was brought home to your hearts and firmly established there; ⁷ so that (as we may hope from this guarantee) there is not a single gift of grace in which you find yourselves to be behind other Churches, while you are loyally and patiently waiting for the hour when our Lord Jesus Christ shall be revealed. ⁸ And this hour you need not dread, for our Lord Himself, who has done so much for you hitherto, will also unto the very end keep you secure against such accusations as would be fatal in the Day of our Lord Jesus Christ. ⁹ This is a sure and certain hope: for it was God, who cannot prove false, who Himself called you into fellowship with His Son and in His Son, Jesus Christ our Lord ; and God will assuredly do His part to make this calling effective.

This Thanksgiving is a conciliatory prelude to the whole Epistle, not directed to a section only (*v.* 12), nor ironical (!), nor studiously indefinite (Hofm.), but a measured and earnest encomium of their general state of grace (Acts xviii. 10), with special stress on their *intellectual* gifts, and preparing the way for candid dealing with their inconsistencies.

4. εὐχαριστῶ. Sosthenes seems to be at once forgotten ; this important letter is the Apostle's own, and his alone : contrast εὐχαριστοῦμεν, 1 Thess. i. 2 ; ὥσπερ οὖν πατὴρ ἐπὶ υἱοῖς εὐχαριστεῖ ὅτ᾽ ἂν ὑγιαίνωσιν, τὸν αὐτὸν τρόπον ὅτ᾽ ἂν βλέπῃ διδάσκαλος τοὺς ἀκροατὰς πλουτοῦντας λόγῳ σοφίας, εὐχαριστεῖ πάντοτε περὶ αὐτῶν (Orig.). With this Thanksgiving compare that in 2 Macc. ix. 20 (AV.). See also Deissmann, *Light from the Anc. East*, p. 168. St Paul's εὐχαριστῶ is uttered in full earnest : there is no irony, as some think. In the sense of thanksgiving, the verb belongs to Hellenistic rather than to class. Grk. (Lightfoot on 1 Thess. i. 2): πάντοτε as in 1 Thess. i. 2 ; 2 Thess. i. 3.

τῇ χάριτι τ. Θ. τ. δοθείσῃ. Special gifts of grace are viewed as incidental to, or presupposing, a state of grace, *i.e.*, the state of one living under the influence of, and governed by, the redemption and reconciliation of man effected by Jesus Christ ; more briefly, 'the grace of our Lord Jesus Christ' (2 Cor. viii. 9 ; cf. ὑπὸ χάριν, Rom. vi. 14). The aorists (δοθείσῃ . . . ἐπλουτίσθητε . . . ἐβεβαιώθη) sum up their history as a Christian community from their baptism to the time of his writing.

τῷ Θεῷ μου (ℵ¹ A C D E F G L P, Latt. Syr. Copt. Arm.) ; ℵ* B, Aeth. omit μου. A* and some other authorities omit τοῦ Θεοῦ after χάριτι.

5. ὅτι ἐν παντί. Cf. 2 Cor. viii. 7, ὥσπερ ἐν παντὶ περισσεύετε πίστει καὶ λόγῳ καὶ γνώσει. The two passages, though doubtless addressed to different situations, bring out strikingly by their common points the stronger side of Corinthian Christianity, λόγος and γνῶσις, both true gifts of the Spirit (xii. 8), although each has its abuse or caricature (i. 17–iv. 20 and viii. 1 f.).* Λόγος is the gift of speech, not chiefly, nor specially, as manifested in the Tongues (which are quite distinct in xii. 8 f.), but closely related to the teacher's work. It was the gift of Apollos (Acts xviii. 24). The λόγος σοφίας is the gift of the Spirit, while σοφία λόγου—cultivating expression at the expense of matter (*v.* 17)—is the gift of the mere rhetorician, courting the applause (*vanum et inane σοφῶς* !) of the ordinary Greek audience. St Paul, according to his chief opponent at Corinth, was wanting in this gift (2 Cor. x. 10, ὁ λόγος ἐξουθενημένος) : *his* oratorical power was founded in deep conviction (*v.* 18, ii. 4, iv. 20).

---

* St Paul does not hesitate to treat γνῶσις as a divine gift (xii. 8, xiii. 2, xiv. 6), and this use is very rare in N.T., except in his Epistles and in 2 Pet. When St John wrote, the word had worse associations. This is the earliest use of it in N.T. In the Sapiential Books of O.T. it is very frequent.

St Paul "loses sight for a moment of the irregularities which had disfigured the Church at Corinth, while he remembers the spiritual blessings which they had enjoyed. After all deductions made for these irregularities, the Christian community at Corinth must have presented as a whole a marvellous contrast to their heathen fellow-citizens,—a contrast which might fairly be represented as one of light and darkness" (Lightfoot). This Epistle contains no indication of the disloyalty to the Apostle which we trace in 2 Cor., especially in x.–xiii.

πάσῃ γνώσει. See 2 Cor. xi. 6, where St Paul claims for himself eminence in the true γνῶσις, and also 1 Cor. viii. 1 f.

6. καθώς. It introduces, not a mere parallel or illustration, but rather an explanation of what precedes : 'inasmuch as'; *v.* 7 ; John xiii. 34, xvii. 2. But 1 Thess. i. 5 (quoted by Lightfoot) is less strong.

τὸ μαρτύριον τοῦ Χρ. 'The witness borne [by our preaching] to Christ'; *genitivus objecti.* Cf. xv. 15. Origen takes it of the witness borne by the Scriptures to Christ, and also of the witness borne *by* Christ, who is the ἀρχίμαρτυς through His death.

ἐβεβαιώθη. Either (1) was established *durably* (βεβαιώσει, *v.* 8) in or among you (Meyer); or (2) was verified and established by its influence on your character (2 Cor. iii. 2); or (3) was brought home to your deepest conviction as true by the witness of the Spirit (ii. 4).* This last is the best sense.

B* F G, Arm. have τοῦ Θεοῦ for τοῦ Χριστοῦ.

7. ὥστε ὑμᾶς μὴ ὑστερεῖσθαι. With the infin., ὥστε points to a *contemplated* result ; with the indic., to the result as a fact (2 Cor. v. 16; Gal. ii. 13). What follows, then, is a statement of what was *to be looked for* in the Corinthians as the effect of the grace (*v.* 4) of God given to them in Christ; and there was evidently much in their spiritual condition which corresponded to this (xi. 2; Acts xviii. 10).

ὑστερεῖσθαι. 'Feel yourselves inferior'; middle, as in xii. 24. The active or passive is more suitable for expressing the bare fact (2 Cor. xi. 5), or physical want (2 Cor. xi. 9; Phil. iv. 12); while the middle, more passive than the active and more active than the passive, is applicable to persons rather than things, and to feelings rather than to external facts. The prodigal began to *realize* his state of want (ὑστερεῖσθαι, Luke xv. 14), while the young questioner appealed to an external standard (τί ἔτι ὑστερῶ; Matt. xix. 20).

χαρίσματι. Cf. Rom. i. 11, where it is in context with στηριχθῆναι, as here with βεβαιωθῆναι. Philo uses the word

* Deissmann (*Bible Studies*, p. 104 f.) thinks that the meaning of "a legal guarantee," which βεβαίωσις has in papyri, lies at the basis of the expression.

of divine gifts (*De alleg. leg.* iii. 24), and in N.T., excepting
1 Pet. iv. 10, it is peculiar to Paul. It is used by him (1) of
God's gift of salvation through Christ, Rom. v. 15, vi. 23;
(2) of any special grace or mercy, vii. 7; 2 Cor. i. 11; and
(3) of special equipments or miraculous gifts, as that of healing,
xii. 9; cf. xii. 4; Rom. xii. 6. Here it is by no means to be
restricted to (3), but includes (2), for the immediate context,
especially v. 8, dwells on gifts flowing from a state of grace.

ἀπεκδεχομένους. As in Rom. viii. 19. For the sense cf.
Col. iii. 3 f.; 1 Pet. i. 7; 1 John iii. 2, 3; and see Μαρὰν ἀθά,
xvi. 22. In this reference, of waiting for the Advent, the word
is always used of faithful Christians (Gal. v. 5; Phil. iii. 20;
Heb. ix. 28).* *Character Christiani veri vel falsi revelationem
Christi vel expectare vel horrere* (Beng.).

ἀποκάλυψιν. See Rom. viii. 19; 1 Pet. i. 13. Quite needlessly, Michelsen suspects the verse of being a gloss.

8. ὃς καὶ βεβαιώσει. Origen asks, τίς βεβαιοῖ; and answers,
Χριστὸς Ἰησοῦς. The ὅς refers to τοῦ Κυρίου ἡμ. Ἰ. Χρ.; certainly not, as Beng. and others, to Θεός in v. 4. This remote
reference is not made probable by the words ἐν τῇ ἡμέρᾳ τ. Κ.
ἡμ. Ἰ. Χρ. instead of simply ἐν τῇ ἡμ. αὐτοῦ. We have Christ's
name ten times in the first ten verses, and the solemn repetition
of the sacred name, instead of the simple pronoun, is quite in
St Paul's manner; v. 3, 4; 2 Cor. i. 5; 2 Tim. i. 18. Cf. Gen.
xix. 24, which is sometimes wrongly interpreted as implying a
distinction of Persons. The καί points to correspondence 'on
His part,' answering to ἐβεβαιώθη, ἀπεκδεχομένους, in vv. 6, 7.

βεβαιώσει. Cf. 2 Cor. i. 21, and, for the thought, Rom.
xvi. 25; 1 Thess. iii. 13, v. 24. If they fail, it will not be His
fault.

ἕως τέλους. The sense is intenser than in 2 Cor. i. 13;
cf. εἰς ἐκείνην τὴν ἡμέραν (2 Tim. i. 12). *Mortis dies est unicuique dies adventus Domini* (Herv.).†

ἀνεγκλήτους. 'Unimpeachable,' for none will have the right
to impeach (Rom. viii. 33; Col. i. 22, 28). The word implies,
not actual freedom from sins, but yet a state of spiritual renewal
(ii. 12 f.; Phil. i. 10; 2 Cor. v. 17; Rom. viii. 1). This pro-
leptic construction of the accusative is found in 1 Thess. iii. 13,
v. 23; Phil. iii. 21. Connect ἐν τῇ ἡμέρᾳ with ἀνεγκλήτους.

---

* "As though that were the highest gift of all; as if that attitude of expectation were the highest posture that can be attained here by the Christian"
(F. W. Robertson).

† The doctrine of the approach of the end is constantly in the Apostle's
thoughts: iii. 13, iv. 5, vi. 2, 3, vii. 29, xi. 26, xv. 51, xvi. 22. We have ἕως
τέλους in 2 Cor. i. 13 with the same meaning as here, and in 1 Thess. ii. 16
the more common εἰς τέλος with a different meaning. See Abbott, *Johannine
Grammar*, 2322.

ἐν τῇ ἡμέρᾳ (א A B C L P, Syrr. Copt. Arm. Aeth.) rather than ἐν τῇ παρουσίᾳ (D E F G, Ambrst.).   B omits Χριστοῦ.

9. The confident hope expressed in *v.* 8 rests upon the faithfulness of God (x. 13 ; 1 Thess. v. 24; Rom. viii. 30; Phil. i. 6) who had been the agent, as well as the source, of their call. With δι᾽ οὗ cf. Heb. ii. 10, and also ἐξ αὐτοῦ καὶ δι᾽ αὐτοῦ καὶ εἰς αὐτὸν τὰ πάντα, Rom. xi. 36. Διά with genitive can be applied either to Christ or to the Father,* but ἐξ οὗ would not be applied by St Paul to Christ. "Wherever God the Father and Christ are mentioned together, origination is ascribed to the Father and mediation to Christ" (Lightfoot, who refers especially to viii. 6). By St Paul, as by St John (vi. 44), the calling is specifically ascribed to the Father.

εἰς κοινωνίαν. This fellowship (Rom. viii. 17 ; Phil. iii. 10 f.) exists now and extends to eternity : it is effected by and in the Spirit (Rom. viii. 9 f.) ; hence κοινωνία (τοῦ) πνεύματος (2 Cor. xiii. 13 ; Phil. ii. 1). *Vocati estis in societatem non modo apostolorum vel angelorum, sed etiam Filii ejus J. C. Domini nostri* (Herv.). The genitive τοῦ υἱοῦ is objective, and "the κοινωνία τοῦ υἱοῦ αὐτοῦ is co-extensive with the βασιλεία τοῦ Θεοῦ" (Lightfoot).

D* F G (not d f g) have ὑφ᾽ οὗ instead of δι᾽ οὗ.

After this preamble, in which the true keynote of St Paul's feeling towards his Corinthian readers is once for all struck, he goes on at once to the main matters of censure, arising, not from their letter to him (vii. 1), but from what he has heard from other sources. In the preamble we have to notice the solemn impression which is made by the frequent repetition of 'Christ Jesus' or 'our Lord Jesus Christ.' Only once (*v.* 5) have we αὐτός instead of the Name. And in the beginning of the next section the Apostle repeats the full title once more, as if he could not repeat it too often (Bachmann).

I. 10–VI. 20. URGENT MATTERS FOR CENSURE.

I. 10–IV. 21. THE DISSENSIONS (Σχίσματα).

10–17. *Do be united. I have been informed that there are contentions among you productive of party spirit. It was against this very thing that I so rarely baptized.*

¹⁰ But I entreat you, Brothers, by the dear name of our Lord Jesus Christ, into fellowship with whom you were called by

* See Basil, *De Spiritu,* v. 10.

God Himself, do be unanimous in professing your beliefs, and
do not be split up into parties. Let complete unity be restored
both in your ways of thinking and in your ultimate convictions,
so that all have one creed. ¹¹ I do not say this without good
reason: for it is quite clear to me, from what I was told by
members of Chloe's household, that there are contentions and
wranglings among you. ¹² What I mean is this; that there is
hardly one among you who has not got some party-cry of his
own; such as, " I for my part stand by Paul," " And I for my
part stand by Kephas," " And I stand by Apollos," " And I stand
by Christ." ¹³ Do you really think that Christ has been given to
any party as its separate share? Was it Paul who was crucified
for you? Or was it to allegiance to Paul that you pledged
yourselves when you were baptized? ¹⁴ Seeing that you thus
misuse my name, I thank God that not one of you was baptized
by me, excepting Crispus, the ruler of the synagogue, and my
personal friend Gaius. ¹⁵ So that God has prevented any one
from saying that it was to allegiance to me that you were pledged
in baptism. ¹⁶ Yes, I did baptize the household of Stephanas,
my first converts in Achaia. Besides these, to the best of my
knowledge, I baptized no one. ¹⁷ For Christ did not make me
His Apostle to baptize, but to proclaim His Glad-tidings :—and
I did this with no studied rhetoric, so that the Cross of Christ
might prevail by its own inherent power.

In these verses (10–17) we have the facts of the case. The
Apostle begins with an exhortation to avoid dissensions (*v.* 10),
then proceeds to describe (11, 12) and to show the impropriety
of (13–17) their actual dissensions. *Quorum prius salutem narra-
verat, postmodum vulnera patefecit* (Herv.).

10. παρακαλῶ δέ. ' But (in contrast to what I wish to think,
and do think, of you) I earnestly beg.' Παρακαλεῖν, like
παραιτέομαι (Acts xxv. 11), suggests an aim at *changing* the mind,
whether from sorrow to joy (consolation), or severity to mercy
(entreaty), or wrong desire to right (admonition or exhortation).
The last is the sense here. The word is used more than a
hundred times in N.T.

ἀδελφοί. Used in affectionate earnestness, especially when
something painful has to be said (vii. 29, x. 1, xiv. 20, etc.). It
probably implies personal acquaintance with many of those who
are thus addressed : hence its absence from Ephesians and
Colossians.

διὰ τοῦ ὀνόματος. We should have expected the accusative,
'for the sake of the Name.' The genitive makes the Name the
instrument of the appeal (Rom. xii. 1, xv. 30; 2 Cor. x. 1):
cf. ἐν ὀνόματι, 2 Thes. iii. 6. It is not an adjuration, but is
similar to διὰ τ. κυρίου Ἰησοῦ (1 Thess. iv. 2). This appeal to the
one Name is an indirect condemnation of the various party-
names.

ἵνα. This defines the *purport* rather than the purpose of
the command or request, as in Matt. iv. 3, εἰπὸν ἵνα οἱ λίθοι οὗτοι
ἄρτοι γένωνται.

τὸ αὐτὸ λέγητε. The expression is taken from Greek political
life, meaning 'be at peace' or (as here) 'make up differences.'
So Arist. *Pol.* III. iii. 3, Βοιωτοὶ δὲ καὶ Μεγαρῆς τὸ αὐτὸ λέγοντες
ἡσύχαζον, and other examples given by Lightfoot *ad loc.* Cf. τὸ
αὐτὸ φρονεῖν (Rom. xv. 15 ; Phil. ii. 2), and see Deissmann, *Bible
Studies*, p. 256. The πάντες comes last with emphasis. St Paul
is urging, not unison, but harmony. For his knowledge of Greek
writers see xv. 34 ; Rom. ii. 14 ; Acts xvii. 28.

μὴ ᾖ. 'That there may not be,' as there actually are: he
does not say γένηται.

σχίσματα. Not 'schisms,' but 'dissensions' (John vii. 43,
ix. 16), 'clefts,' 'splits'; the opposite of τὸ αὐτὸ λέγητε πάντες.

κατηρτισμένοι. The word is suggestive of fitting together
what is broken or rent (Matt. iv. 21). It is used in surgery for
setting a joint (Galen), and in Greek politics for *composing
factions* (Hdt. v. 28). See reff. in Lightfoot on 1 Thess. iii. 10.
Cf. 2 Cor. xiii. 11 ; Gal. vi. 1 ; Heb. xiii. 21 : *apte et congruenter
inter se compingere* (Calv.).

νοΐ . . . γνώμῃ. Νοῦς is 'temper' or 'frame of mind,'
which is *changed* in μετάνοια and is *kindly* in εὔνοια, while γνώμη
is 'judgment' on this or that point. He is urging them to give
up, not erroneous beliefs, but party-spirit.

11. ἐδηλώθη. Not 'was reported,' but 'was made (only too)
evident.' The verb implies that he was unable to doubt the
unwelcome statement. In papyri it is used of official evidence.
For ἀδελφοί see on *v.* 10.

ὑπὸ τῶν Χλόης. This probably means 'by slaves belonging
to Chloe's household.' She may have been an Ephesian lady
with some Christian slaves who had visited Corinth. Had they
belonged to Corinth, to mention them as St Paul's informants
might have made mischief (Heinrici). The name Chloe was
an epithet of Demeter, and probably (like Phoebe, Hermes,
Nereus, Rom. xvi. 1, 14, 15) she was of the freedman class
(see Lightfoot, *ad loc.*). She is mentioned as a person known
to the Corinthians. There is no reason to suppose that she

was herself a Christian, or that the persons named in xvi. 17 were members of her household. Evidence is wanting.

ἔριδες. More unseemly than σχίσματα, although not necessarily so serious. Nevertheless, not σχίσματα, unless crystallized into αἱρέσεις, but ἔριδες, are named as 'works of the flesh' in Gal. v. 19, 20, or in the catalogues of vices, Rom. i. 29–31; 2 Cor. xii. 20; 1 Tim. vi. 4. The divisions became noisy.

12. λέγω δὲ τοῦτο. 'Now I mean this': but perhaps the force of the δέ is best given by having no conjunction in English; 'I mean this.' The τοῦτο refers to what follows, as in vii. 29, xv. 50, whereas in vii. 35 it refers to what precedes, like αὕτη in ix. 3.

ἕκαστος. This must not be pressed, any more than in xiv. 26, to mean that there were no exceptions. No doubt there were Corinthians who joined none of the four parties. It is to be remembered that all these party watchwords are on one level, and all are in the same category of blame. Championship for any one leader against another leader was wrong. St Paul has no partiality for those who claim himself, nor any respect for those who claim Christ, as their special leader. Indeed, he seems to condemn these two classes with special severity. The former exalt Paul too highly, the latter bring Christ too low: but all four are alike wrong. That, if such a spirit showed itself in Corinth at all, Paul, the planter, builder, and father of the community, would have a following, would be inevitable. And Apollos had watered (Acts xviii. 27, 28), and had tutored Paul's children in Christ. His brilliancy and Alexandrian modes of thought and expression readily lent themselves to any tendency to form a party, who would exalt these gifts at the expense of Paul's studied plainness. "The difference between Apollos and St Paul seems to be not so much a difference of views as in the mode of stating those views: the eloquence of St Paul was rough and burning; that of Apollos was more refined and polished" (F. W. Robertson).*

Κηφᾶ. Excepting Gal. ii. 7, 8, St Paul always speaks of Κηφᾶς, never of Πέτρος. He was unquestionably friendly to St Paul (Gal. ii. 7–9; and vv. 11–14 reveal no difference of doctrine between them). But among the Jewish or 'devout Greek' converts at Corinth there might well be some who would willingly defer to any who professed, with however little authority (Acts xv. 24), to speak in the name of the leader of the Twelve. "His conduct at Antioch had given them all the handle that they needed to pit Peter against Paul" (A. T.

---

* It is a skilful stroke that the offender's own words are quoted, and each appears as bearing witness against himself. What each glories in becomes his own condemnation; ἐκ τοῦ στόματός σου.

Robertson, *Epochs in the Life of Paul*, p. 187). There is no evidence, not even in ix. 5, that Peter had ever visited Corinth. It is remarkable that, even among Jewish Christians, the Greek 'Peter' seems to have driven the original 'Kephas' (John i. 43) out of use.

Χριστοῦ. The 'Christ' party may be explained in the light of 2 Cor. x. 7, 10, 11, and possibly xi. 4, 23 (compare xi. 4 with Gal. i. 6), where there seems to be a reference to a prominent opponent of St Paul, whose activity belongs to the situation which is distinctive of 2 Cor. From these passages we gather that, when 2 Cor. was written, there was a section at Corinth, following a leader who was, at least for a time, in actual rebellion against St Paul. This section claimed, in contrast to him, to belong to Christ, which was virtually a claim that Christ belonged to them and not to him ; and this claim seems to have been connected with a criterion of genuine Apostleship, namely, to have known Christ in the flesh, *i.e.* during His life on earth. Doubtless the situation in 2 Cor. goes beyond that which is presupposed in this Epistle. But ἐγὼ δὲ Χριστοῦ here must not be divorced from the clearer indications there. Those who used the watchword 'of Christ' were probably more advanced Judaizers than those who used the name of Kephas, to whom they stood related, as did the anti-Pauline Palestinian party (Acts xxi. 20, 21) to Kephas himself. The 'parties' at Corinth, therefore, are the local results of streams of influence which show themselves at work elsewhere in the N.T. We may distinguish them respectively as St Paul and his Gospel, Hellenistic intellectualism (Apollos), conciliatory conservatism, or 'the Gospel of the circumcision' (Kephas), and 'zealots for the Law,' hostile to the Apostleship of St Paul. These last were the exclusive party.* See Deissmann, *Light from the Anc. East*, p. 382.

We need not, therefore, consider seriously such considerations as that ἐγὼ δὲ Χριστοῦ was the cry of *all three* parties (Räbiger, misinterpreting μεμέρισται) ; or that St Paul *approves* this cry (Chrysostom, appealing to iii. 22, 23) ; or that it is St Paul's own reply to the others ; or that it represents a 'James' party (in which case, why is James not mentioned ?) ; or that it marks those who carried protest against party so far as to form a party on that basis. In iii. 23 St Paul says ὑμεῖς δὲ Χριστοῦ most truly and from his heart ; that is true of *all* :

---

* The conjecture that the original reading was ἐγὼ δὲ Κρίσπου is not very intelligent. Could Crispus have been made the rival of Paul, Apollos, and Peter? Could Clement of Rome have failed to mention the Crispus party, if there had been one? He mentions the other three. And see *vv.* 13 and 14.

what he censures here is its exclusive appropriation by *some*. To say, with special emphasis, '*I* am of Christ,' is virtually to say that Christ is mine and not yours.

In Acts xviii. 24 and xix. 1, ℵ, Copt. have 'Apelles,' while D in xviii. 24 has 'Apollonius.' The reading 'Apelles' seems to be Egyptian, and goes back to Origen, who asks whether Apollos can be the same as the Apelles of Rom. xvi. 10.

For a history of the controversies about the four parties, see Bachmann, pp. 58–63.

13. μεμέρισται. The clauses are all interrogative, and are meant for the refutation of all. 'Does Christ belong to a section? Is Paul your saviour? Was it in his name that you were admitted into the Church?' The probable meaning of μεμέρισται is 'has been apportioned,' *i.e.* given to some one as his separate share (vii. 17; Rom. xii. 3; Heb. vii. 2). This suggestion has been brilliantly supported by Evans. To say, 'Is Christ divided?' implying a *negative* answer, gives very little point. Lightfoot suggests that an *affirmative* answer is implied; 'Christ has been and is divided *only too truly*.' But this impairs the spring and homogeneity of the three questions, giving the first an affirmative, and the other two a negative answer. It amounts to making the first clause a plain statement; 'In that case the Body of Christ has been divided.' *Dividitur corpus, cum membra dissentiunt* (Primasius). *Si membra divisa sunt, et totum corpus* (Atto Vercellensis). This meaning is hardly so good as the other.

μὴ Παῦλος ἐσταυρώθη κ.τ.λ. To say ἐγὼ Παύλου would imply this. To be a slave is ἄλλου εἶναι, another person's property (Arist. *Pol.* I.). A Christian belongs to Christ (iii. 23), and he therefore may call himself δοῦλος Ἰησοῦ Χριστοῦ, as St Paul often does (Rom. i. 1, etc.): but he may not be the δοῦλος of any human leader (vii. 23; cf. iii. 21; 2 Cor. xi. 20). St Paul shows his characteristic tact in taking himself, rather than Apollos or Kephas, to illustrate the Corinthian error. Cf. ix. 8, 9, xii. 29, 30.

εἰς τὸ ὄνομα. He takes the strongest of the three expressions: the εἰς (Matt. xxviii. 19; Acts viii. 16, xix. 5) is stronger than ἐπί (Acts ii. 38, *v.l.*) or ἐν (Acts x. 48). '*Into* the name' implies entrance into fellowship and allegiance, such as exists between the Redeemer and the redeemed. Cf. the figure in x. 2, and see note there. St Paul deeply resents modes of expression which seem to make him the rival of Christ. *Non vult a sponsa amari pro sponso* (Herv.). At the Crucifixion we were bought by Christ; in baptism we accepted Him as Lord and Master: *crux et baptismus nos Christo asserit* (Beng.). "The guilt of these partizans did not lie in holding views

differing from each other: it was not so much in saying 'this
is the truth,' as it was in saying 'this is *not* the truth.' The
guilt of schism is when each party, instead of expressing fully
his own truth, attacks others, and denies that others are in
the Truth at all" (F. W. Robertson). See Deissmann, *Bible
Studies*, pp. 146, 196; *Light from the Anc. East*, p. 123.

It is difficult to decide between ὑπὲρ ὑμῶν (א A C D² E F G L P, *pro
vobis* Vulg.) and περὶ ὑμῶν (B D*). The former would be more likely to
be substituted for the latter, as most usual, than *vice versa*. But περί is
quite in place, in view of its sacrificial associations. See note on Rom.
viii. 3.

14. εὐχαριστῶ. A quasi-ironical turn; 'What difficulties I
have unconsciously escaped.'

Κρίσπον. One of the first converts (Acts xviii. 8).* Ruler
of the synagogue.

Γάϊον. Probably the host of St Paul 'and of the whole
Church' at Corinth (Rom. xvi. 23), but probably not the
hospitable Gaius of 3 John 5, 6. This common Roman *prae-
nomen* belongs probably to five distinct persons in the N.T.
The Greek preserves the correct Latin form, which is sometimes
written *Caius*, because the same character originally stood in
Latin for both G and C. Crispus, 'curly,' is a *cognomen*.

After εὐχαριστῶ, א³ A C D E F G L P, Vulg. add τῷ Θεῷ, while A 17,
Syrr. Copt. Arm. add τῷ Θεῷ μου—a very natural gloss. א* B 67,
Chrys. omit.

15. ἵνα μή τις εἴπῃ. The ἵνα points to the *tendency* of
such an action on the Apostle's part among those who had
proved themselves capable of such low views: compare ἵνα
in Rom. xi. 11; John ix. 2. Their making such a statement
was "a result viewed as possible by St Paul" (Evans, who calls
this use of ἵνα "subjectively ecbatic"). Thus the sense comes
very near to that of ὥστε with the infinitive (*v.* 7). In N.T.,
ἵνα never introduces a result as an objective fact, but its strictly
final or telic force shows signs of giving way (*v.* 10),—a first
step towards its vague use in mod. Grk. as a mere sign of
the infinitive. Those who strive to preserve its strictly telic
sense in passages like this (as Winer, Meyer, and others) have
recourse to the so-called Hebraic teleological instinct of referring everything, however mechanically, to over-ruling Providence.
In vii. 29, if 'the time is cut short,' this was done with the

* "Most of the names of Corinthian Christians indicate either a Roman
or a servile origin (*e.g.* Gaius, Crispus, Fortunatus, Achaicus, xvi. 17;
Tertius, Rom. xvi. 22; Quartus, Rom. xvi. 23; Justus, Acts xviii. 7)" (*Ency.
Bibl.* 898). It was because of the importance of such converts that the
Apostle baptized Crispus and Gaius himself. We do not know whether Gaius
was Jew or Gentile; but the opposition of the Jews in Corinth to St Paul
was so bitter that probably most of his first converts were heathen.

providential intention 'that those who have wives should be as those who have none': and in John ix. 2 the sense would be that 'if this man sinned or his parents,' the reason was that Providence purposed that he should be born blind. While refusing to follow such artificial paradoxes of exegesis, we may fully admit that *Providentia Dei regnat saepe in rebus quarum ratio postea cognoscitur.*

ἐβαπτίσθητε (אABC*, Vulg. Copt. Arm.) rather than ἐβάπτισα (C⁰DEFGLP). RV. corrects AV.

16. ἐβάπτισα δὲ καί. A correction which came into his mind as he dictated:—on reflexion, he can remember no other case. Possibly his amanuensis reminded him of Stephanas.

Στεφανᾶ. The name is a syncopated form, like Apollos, Demas, Lucas, Hermas, etc. It would seem that Stephanas was an earlier convert even than Crispus (xvi. 15). 'Achaia' technically included Athens, and Stephanas may himself have been converted there with the ἕτεροι of Acts xvii. 34; but his household clearly belongs to Corinth, and they, not the head only, are the 'first-fruits of Achaia,' which may therefore be used in a narrower sense.

λοιπόν. The neut. sing. acc. (of respect) used adverbially; *quod superest* (Vulg. *caeterum*): τὸ λοιπόν is slightly stronger. See Lightfoot on Phil. iii. 1 and on 1 Thess. iv. 1. Cf. iv. 2; 2 Cor. xiii. 11. St Paul forestalls possible objection.

17. οὐ γὰρ ἀπέστειλέν με. This verse marks the transition to the discussion of principle which lies at the root of these σχίσματα, viz. the false idea of σοφία entertained by the Corinthians. The Apostle did not as a rule baptize by his own hand, but by ὑπηρέται. Perhaps other Apostles did the same (Acts x. 48). See John iv. 1, 2 for our Lord's practice. Baptizing required no special, personal gifts, as preaching did. Baptism is not disparaged by this; but baptism presupposes that the great charge, to preach the Gospel,* has been fulfilled; Matt. xxviii. 19; Luke xxiv. 47; [Mark] xvi. 15: and, with special reference to St Paul, ix. 16, 17; Acts ix. 15, 20, xxii. 15, 21, xxvi. 16. Ἀπέστειλεν = 'sent as His ἀπόστολος.'

οὐκ ἐν σοφίᾳ λόγου. See note on *v.* 5. Preaching was St Paul's great work, but his aim was not that of the professional rhetorician. Here he rejects the standard by which an age of rhetoric judged a speaker. The Corinthians were judging by

---

* The translation of εὐαγγελίζεσθαι varies even in RV.; here, 'preach the gospel'; Acts xiii. 32, xiv. 15, 'bring good tidings'; Acts xv. 35, Gal. i. 16, 23, 'preach'; 1 Pet. i. 25, 'preach good tidings.'

The old explanation, that missionary preaching requires a special gift, whereas baptizing can be performed by any one, is probably right.

externals. The fault would conspicuously apply, no doubt, to
those who 'ran after' Apollos. But the indictment is not
limited to that party. All alike were externalists, lacking a
sense for depth in simplicity, and thus easily falling a prey to
superficialities both in the matter and in the manner of teaching.
L'évangile n'est pas une sagesse, c'est un salut (Godet).

ἵνα μὴ κενωθῇ. To clothe the Gospel in σοφία λόγου was to
impair its substance: κενοῦν, cf. ix. 15; Rom. iv. 14; 2 Cor. ix.
3, and εἰς κενόν, Gal. ii. 2; Phil. ii. 16. In this he glances at the
Apollos party.

I. 18–III. 4. THE FALSE WISDOM AND THE TRUE.

(i) I. 18–II. 5. The False Wisdom.

*18–31. The message of the Cross is foolishness to the
wonder-seeking Jew and to the wisdom-seeking Greek: but
to us, who have tried it, it is God's power and God's wisdom.
Consider your own case, how God has chosen the simple and
weak in preference to the wise and strong, that all glorying
might be in Him alone.*

[18] To those who are on the broad way that leadeth to destruction, the message of the Cross of course is foolishness; but to
those who are in the way of salvation, as we feel that we are, it
manifests the power of God. [19] For it stands written in Scripture,
I will destroy the wisdom of the wise, and the discernment of
the discerning I will set at nought. [20] What, in God's sight, is
the Greek philosopher? What, in God's sight, is the Jewish
Rabbi? What, be he Jew or Gentile, is the skilful disputer of
this evil age? Did not God make foolish and futile the profane
wisdom of the non-Christian world? [21] For when, in the providence of God, the world, in spite of all its boasted intellect and
philosophy, failed to attain to a real knowledge of God, it was
God's good pleasure, by means of the proclaimed Glad-tidings,
which the world regarded as foolishness, to save those who have
faith in Him. [22] The truth of this is evident. Jews have no
real knowledge of the God whom they worship, for they are
always asking for miracles; nor Greeks either, for they ask for a
philosophy of religion: [23] but we proclaim a Messiah who has
been crucified, to Jews a revolting idea, and to Greeks an absurd
one. [24] But to those who really accept God's call. both Jews

and Greeks, this crucified Messiah is the supreme manifestation of God's power and God's wisdom. ²⁵ For what the Greek regards as the unwisdom of God is wiser than mankind, and what the Jew regards as the impotency of God is stronger than mankind.

²⁶ For consider, Brothers, the circumstances of your own call. Very few of you were wise, as men count wisdom, very few were of great influence, very few were of high birth. ²⁷ Quite the contrary. It was the unwisdom of the world which God specially selected, in order to put the wise people to shame by succeeding where they had failed; and it was the uninfluential agencies of the world which God specially selected, in order to put its strength to shame, by triumphing where that strength had been vanquished; ²⁸ and it was the low-born and despised agencies which God specially selected, yes, actual nonentities, in order to bring to nought things that are real enough. ²⁹ He thus secured that no human being should have anything to boast of before God. ³⁰ But as regards you, on the other hand, it is by His will and bounty that ye have your being by adoption in Christ Jesus, who became for us wisdom manifested from God,—wisdom which stands for both righteousness and sanctification, yes, and redemption as well. ³¹ God did all this, in order that each might take as his guiding principle what stands written in Scripture, He that glorieth, let him glory in the Lord.

The Gospel in its essence makes no appeal to appreciation based on mere externalism. Divine Wisdom is not to be gauged by human cleverness (18–25). The history and composition of the Corinthian Church is a refutation of human pretensions by Divine Power (26–29), which, in the Person of Christ, satisfies the deeper needs and capacities of man (30, 31).

18. ὁ λόγος. In contrast, not to λόγος σοφίας (v. 5, ii. 6), but to σοφία λόγου (v. 17); the preaching of a crucified Saviour.

The AV. spoils the contrast by rendering 'the wisdom of *words*' and 'the *preaching* of the Cross.' The use of σοφία in these two chapters should be compared with the ἅγιον πνεῦμα in the Book of Wisdom (i. 5, ix. 17), πνεῦμα σοφίας (vii. 7), etc. St Paul had possibly read the book. We have in Wisdom the opposition between the σῶμα and the πνεῦμα or ψυχή or σοφία (i. 4, ii. 3, ix. 15).

τοῦ σταυροῦ. "This expression shows clearly the stress

which St Paul laid on the death of Christ, not merely as a great moral spectacle, and so the crowning point of a life of self-renunciation, but as in itself the ordained instrument of salvation" (Lightfoot).   Cf. Ign. *Eph.* 18.

τοῖς μὲν ἀπολλυμένοις.   'For them who are perishing' (*dativus commodi*), not 'In the opinion of those who are perishing' (Chrys.).   Compare carefully 2 Cor. ii. 16, iv. 3 ; 2 Thess. ii. 10. The verb (John iii. 16) is St Paul's standing expression for the destiny of the wicked (xv. 18).   The force of the present tense is 'axiomatic,' of that which is certain, whether past, present, or future : ἀπὸ τοῦ τέλους τὰς κατηγορίας τιθείς (Theodoret).   The idea of *predestination* to destruction is quite remote from this context : St Paul simply assigns those who reject and those who receive 'the Word of the Cross' to the two classes corresponding to the issues of faith and unbelief ; and he does not define 'perishing.'   It is rash to say that he means annihilation ; still more rash to say that he means endless torment.   Eternal loss or exclusion may be meant.

μωρία.   See on *v.* 21 and 2 Cor. iv. 3.

τοῖς δὲ σωζομένοις.   It is not quite adequate to render this 'to those who are in course of being saved.'   Salvation is the certain result (xv. 2) of a certain relation to God, which relation is a thing of the present.   This relation had a beginning (Rom, viii. 24), is a fact now (Eph. ii. 5, 8), and characterizes our present state (Acts ii. 47) ; but its inalienable confirmation belongs to the final adoption or ἀπολύτρωσις (Rom. viii. 23 ; cf. Eph. iv. 30).   Meanwhile there is great need for watchful steadfastness, lest, by falling away, we lose our filial relation to God.   Consider x. 12, ix. 27 ; Gal. v. 4 ; Matt. xxiv. 13.

ἡμῖν.   'As we have good cause to know.'   The addition of the pronoun throws a touch of personal warmth into this side of the statement : 'you and I can witness to that.'*

δύναμις Θεοῦ ἐστίν.   See Rom. i. 16.   Not merely 'a demonstration of God's power,' nor '*a* power of God,' but 'God's power.'   The contrast between δύναμις (not σοφία) Θεοῦ and μωρια belongs to the very core of St Paul's teaching (ii. 4 ; cf. iv. 20).   Wisdom can carry *conviction*, but to *save*,—to give illumination, penitence, sanctification, love, peace, and hope to a human soul,—needs power, and divine power.

19. γέγραπται γάρ.   Proof of what is stated in *v.* 18, *i.e.* as regards the failure of worldly cleverness in dealing with the things of God.   By γέγραπται, used absolutely, St Paul always means

---

* Both Irenaeus (I. iii. 5) and Marcion (Tert. *Marc.* v. 5) omit the ἡμῖν, and Marcion seems to have read δύναμις καὶ σοφία Θεοῦ ἐστίν.   To omit the ἡμῖν is to omit a characteristic touch ; and to insert καὶ σοφία rather spoils the point.

the O.T. Scriptures; *v.* 31, ii. 9, iii. 19, x. 7, xv. 45; Rom. ι 17, ii. 24, iii. 4, 10, etc.

ἀπολῶ τὴν σοφίαν. From Isa. xxix. 14 (LXX), substituting ἀθετήσω for κρύψω, in accordance with St Paul's usual freedom of citation.* The Prophet, referring to the failure of worldly statesmanship in Judah in face of the judgment of the Assyrian invasion, states a principle which the Apostle seizes and applies. Possibly ἀθετήσω comes from Ps. xxxiii. 10.

σύνεσιν. Worldly common sense (Matt. xi. 25). It has its place in the mind that is informed by the Spirit of God (Col. i. 9), and the absence of it is a calamity (Rom. i. 21, 31). On σύνεσις and σοφία see Arist. *Eth. Nic.* VI. vii. 10.

ἀθετήσω. The verb is post-classical, frequent in Polybius and LXX. Its etymological sense is not 'destroy,' but 'set aside' or 'set at nought,' and this meaning satisfies the present passage and the use in N.T. generally.

20. ποῦ σοφός; A very free citation from the general sense of Isa. xxxiii. 18 (cf. xix. 12): St Paul adapts the wording to his immediate purpose. The original passage refers to the time following on the disappearance of the Assyrian conqueror, with his staff of clerks, accountants, and takers of inventories, who registered the details of the spoil of a captured city. On the tablet of Shalmaneser in the Assyrian Gallery of the British Museum there is a surprisingly exact picture of the scene described by Isaiah. The marvellous disappearance of the invading host was to Isaiah a signal vindication of Jehovah's power and care, and also a refutation, not so much of the conqueror's 'scribes,' as of the worldly counsellors at Jerusalem, who had first thought to meet the invader by an alliance with Egypt, or other methods of statecraft, and had then relapsed into demoralized despair. St Paul's use of the passage, therefore, although very free, is not alien to its historical setting. See further on ii. 9 respecting examples of free quotation. For ποῦ; see xv. 55; Rom. iii. 27. The question is asked in a triumphant tone.†

The 'wise' is a category more suitable to the Gentile (*v.* 22), the 'scribe' to the Jew, while the 'disputer' no doubt suits Greeks, but suits Jews equally well (Acts vi. 9, ix. 29, xxviii. 29). This allotment of the terms is adopted by Clement of Alexandria and by Theodoret, and is more probable than that of Meyer and

---

* He quotes from Isa. xxix. in Col. ii. 21 and Rom. ix. 20. Our Lord quotes from it Matt. xi. 5, xv. 8 f.

† He may have in his mind Isa. xix. 12, ποῦ εἰσιν νῦν οἱ σοφοὶ σου ; and Isa. xxxiii. 18, ποῦ εἰσιν οἱ γραμματικοί ; ποῦ εἰσι οἱ συμβουλεύοντες ; Nowhere else in N.T., outside Gospels and Acts, does γραμματεύς occur. Bachmann shows that there is a parallel between the situation in Isaiah and the situation here ; but τοῦ αἰῶνος τούτου goes beyond the former.

Ellicott, which makes σοφός generic, while γραμματεύς is applied
to the Jew, and συνζητητής to the Greek. But it is unlikely
that St Paul is here making an exact classification, or means any
one of the terms to be applied to Jew or Gentile exclusively.

συνζητητής. A ἅπαξ λεγόμενον, excepting Ign. *Eph.* 18, from
this passage.

τοῦ αἰῶνος τούτου. This is certainly applicable to Jews (see on
ii. 8), but not to them exclusively (Gal. i. 4; Rom. xii. 2). The
phrase is rabbinical, denoting the time before the Messianic age
or 'age to come' (Luke xviii. 30, xx. 35). *This* αἰών, the state of
things now present, including the ethical and social conditions
which are as yet unchanged by the coming of Christ, is fleeting
(vii. 31), and is saturated with low motives and irreligion (ii. 6;
2 Cor. iv. 4; Eph. ii. 2). As αἰών, "by metonymy of the
container for the contained," denotes the things existing in time,
in short the world, ὁ αἰὼν οὗτος may be rendered 'this world';
hujus saeculi quod totum est extra sphaeram verbi crucis (Beng.).
See Grimm-Thayer *s.v.* αἰών, and the references at the end of the
article; also Trench, *Syn.* § lix. The genitive belongs to all
three nouns.

οὐχὶ ἐμώρανεν; *Nonne stultam fecit* (Vulg.), *infatuavit* (Tertull.
and Beza). Cf. Rom. i. 22, 23, and Isa. xix. 11, xliv. 25, 33.
The passage in Romans is an expansion of the thought here.
God not only showed the futility of the world's wisdom, but
frustrated it by leaving it to work out its own results, and still
more by the power of the Cross, effecting what human wisdom
could not do,—not even under the Law (Rom. viii. 3).

τοῦ κόσμου. Practically synonymous with τοῦ αἰῶνος τούτου
(ii. 12, iii. 18, 19): but we do not find ὁ κόσμος ὁ μέλλων, for
κόσμος is simply the *existing* universe, and is not always referred
to with censure (v. 10; John iii. 16).*

After κόσμου, אᵃ Cᵃ Dᵃ E F G L, Vulg. Syrr. Copt. add τούτου.
א* A B C* D* P 17, Orig. omit. It is doubtless an insertion from the
previous clause.

21. ἐπειδὴ γάρ. Introduces, as the main thought, God's
refutation of the world's wisdom by means of what the world
holds to be folly, viz. the word of the Cross, thus explaining
(γάρ) what was stated in *vv.* 19, 20. But this main thought
presupposes (ἐπειδή) the self-stultification of the world's wisdom
in the providence of God.

ἐν τῇ σοφίᾳ τοῦ Θεοῦ. This is taken by Chrysostom and
others (*e.g.* Edwards, Ellicott) as God's wisdom displayed in His

---

* St Paul uses κόσμος nearly fifty times, and very often in 1 and 2 Cor.
With him the use of the word in an ethical sense, of what in the main is evil,
is not rare (ii. 12, iii. 19, v. 10, xi. 32). See Hobhouse, *Bampton Lectures*,
pp. 352 f.

works (Rom. i. 20; Acts xiv. 17), by which (ἐν quasi-instrumental) the world ought to have attained to a knowledge of Him. But this sense of σοφία would be harsh and abrupt; and the order of the words is against this interpretation, as is also the context (ἐμώρανεν, εὐδόκησεν ὁ Θεός). 'The wisdom of God' is here God's wise dealing with mankind in the history of religion, especially in permitting them to be ignorant (Acts xvii. 30; Rom. xi. 32; cf. Acts xiv. 16; Rom. i. 24).   So Alford, Findlay, Evans, Lightfoot.

οὐκ ἔγνω.   This applies to Jew as well as to Greek, although not in the same manner and degree. "The Pharisee, no less than the Greek philosopher, had a σοφία of his own, which stood between his heart and the knowledge of God" (Lightfoot).   See Rom. x. 2.   The world's wisdom failed, the Divine 'foolishness' succeeded.

εὐδόκησεν.   Connects directly with γάρ.   The word belongs to late Greek: Rom. xv. 26; Gal. i. 15; Col. i. 19.

διὰ τῆς μωρίας τοῦ κηρύγματος.   Cf. Isa. xxviii. 9–13.   Κήρυγμα (Matt. xii. 41) differs from κήρυξις as the aorist does from the present or imperfect: it denotes the action, not in process, but completed, or viewed as a whole. It denotes, not 'the thing preached' (RV. marg.), but 'the proclamation' itself (ii. 4; 2 Tim. iv. 17); and here it stands practically for 'the word of the Cross' (v. 18), or the Gospel, but with a slight emphasis upon the presentation. Κηρύσσειν, which in earlier Greek meant 'to herald,' passes into its N.T. and Christian use by the fact that the 'Good-tidings' proclaimed by Christ and His Apostles was the germ of all Christian teaching (Matt. iii. 1, iv. 17). 'The foolishness of preaching' is a bold oxymoron (cf. v. 25), presupposing and interpreting v. 18.   In N.T., μωρία is peculiar to 1 Cor. (18, 23, ii. 14, iii. 19).

τοὺς πιστεύοντας.   With emphasis at the end of the sentence, solving the paradox of God's will to work salvation for man through 'foolishness.'   The habit of faith (pres. part.), and not cleverness, is the power by which salvation is appropriated (Rom. i. 17, iii. 25).   He does not say τοὺς πιστεύσαντας, which might mean that to have once believed was enough.

22. ἐπειδή. This looks forward to v. 23, to which v. 22 is a kind of protasis: 'Since—while Jews and Gentiles alike demand something which suits their unsympathetic limitations—we, on the other hand, preach,' etc. The two verses explain, with reference to the psychology of the religious world at that time, what has been said generally in vv. 18, 21. The repeated καί brackets (Rom. iii. 9) the typical Greek with the typical Jew, as the leading examples, in the world in which St Paul's readers lived, of

the ἀπολλύμενοι, the κόσμος and its wisdom.   In a similar way
the opposed sects of Epicureans and Stoics are bracketed by St
Luke (Acts xvii.) as belonging, for his purpose, to one category.
By the absence of the article (not '*the* Jews,' '*the* Greeks,' as
in AV.) the terms connote characteristic attributes rather than
denote the individuals.   There were many exceptions, as the
N.T. shows.

σημεῖα αἰτοῦσιν.   Matt. xii. 38, xvi. 4; John iv. 48.   The
Jewish mind was matter-of-fact and crudely concrete.   "Hebrew
idiom makes everything as concrete as possible" (R. H. Kennett).
There were certain wonders specified as to be worked by the
Messiah when He came, and these they 'asked for' importun-
ately and precisely.   The Greek restlessly felt after something
which could dazzle his ingenious speculative turn, and he passed
by anything which failed to satisfy intellectual curiosity (Acts
xvii. 18, 21, 32).*   Lightfoot points to the difference between
the arguments used by Justin in his Apologies addressed to
Gentiles, and those used by him in his controversy with Trypho
the Jew.†   See Deissmann, *Light from the Anc. East*, p. 393.

The AV. has 'require *a* sign.'   L, Arm. have σημεῖον.   Beyond question
σημεῖα (א A B C D, etc.) must be read: 'ask for signs' is right.   B. Weiss
prefers σημεῖον.‡

23. Χριστὸν ἐσταυρωμένον.   'A crucified Messiah' (ii. 2;
Gal. iii. 1).   'We preach a Christ crucified' (RV. marg.), the
very point at which the argument with a Jew encountered a wall
of prejudice (Acts xxvi. 23, εἰ παθητὸς ὁ Χριστός.   Cf. Gal. ii. 21,
v. 11).   The Jews demanded a victorious Christ, heralded by
σημεῖα, who would restore the glories of the kingdom of David
and Solomon.   To the Jew the Cross was the sufficient and
decisive refutation (Matt. xxvii. 42; cf. Luke xxiv. 21) of the
claim that Jesus was the Christ.   To the first preachers of Christ,
the Cross was the atonement for sin (xv. 3, 11).   On this subject
the Jew had to unlearn before he could learn; and so also, in
a different way, had the Greek.   Both had to learn the divine
character of humility.   Christ was not preached as a conqueror
to please the one, nor as a philosopher to please the other: He
was preached as the crucified Nazarene.

ἔθνεσιν δὲ μωρίαν.   The heathen, prepared to weigh the '*pros
and cons*' of a new *system*, lacked the presuppositions which
might have prepared the Jew for simple faith in the Christ.   To
him, the Gospel presented no *prima facie* case; it was unmean-

---

* *Graios, qui vera requirunt* (Lucr. i. 641).

† See also *Biblical Essays*, pp. 150 f., and Edwards *ad loc.*

‡ Yet he interprets it in a plural sense.   Eichhorn more consistently interprets it of a worldly Messiah, Mosheim of a miraculous deliverance of Jesus
from crucifixion.

ing, not even plausible: he was not, like the Jew, bent on
righteousness (Rom. ix. 30–x. 3). Compare Cicero's horror of
crucifixion (*Pro Rabir.* 5), Lucian's reference to our Saviour
(*De mort. Peregr.* 13) as τὸν ἀνεσκολοπισμένον ἐκεῖνον σοφιστήν,
and the well-known caricature, found on the Palatine, of a slave
bowing down to a crucified figure with an ass's head, inscribed
Ἀλεξάμενος θεον σεβεται.

A few authorities (C³ D³, Clem-Alex.) have Ἕλλησι instead of ἔθνεσιν.
Orig. seems to have both readings.

24. αὐτοῖς corresponds to ἡμῖν in *v.* 18, as τοῖς κλητοῖς to τοῖς
σωζομένοις: 'to the actual believers' in contrast to other Jews
and Gentiles.   The pronoun is an appeal to personal experience,
as against objections *ab extra.*

Χριστόν.   This implies the repetition of ἐσταυρωμένον.   It is
in the Cross that God's power (Rom i. 16) and wisdom (*v.* 30,
below) come into operation for the salvation of man.   God's
power and wisdom show themselves in a way which is not in
accordance with men's *a priori* standards: they altogether tran-
scend such standards.

Whether St Paul is here touching directly the line of thought
which is expressed in the prologue to the Fourth Gospel is very
doubtful.   He may be said to do so indirectly, in so far as the
doctrine of the work of Christ involves that of His Person (Col.
i. 17–20, ii. 9).*

25. τὸ μωρὸν τοῦ Θεοῦ.   Either, 'a foolish thing on God's
part' (such as a crucified Messiah), or, better, 'the foolishness of
God' (AV.), in a somewhat rhetorical sense, not to be pressed.
God's wisdom, at its lowest, is wiser than men, and God's power,
at its weakest, is stronger than men.   It is quite possible to
treat the construction as a condensed comparison; 'than men's
wisdom,' 'than men's power' (Matt. v. 20; John v. 36).   So
Lightfoot, Conybeare and Howson, etc.   *Infirmitas Christi
magna victoria est* (Primasius).   *Victus vicit mortem, quam nullus
gigas evasit* (Herv.).   *Mortem, quam reges, gigantes, et principes
superare non poterant, ipse moriendo vicit* (Atto).

Throughout the above passage (17–25) we may note the
close sequence of explanatory conjunctions, γάρ (18, 19, 21),
ἐπειδή (22), ὅτι (25).   Without pretending to seize every nuance

---

* "This means that Christ stands for God's wisdom upon earth, and exercises God's power among men.   Such a view implies a very close relation
with the Godhead.   But it should also be noted that this is still connected in
St Paul's mind with the Mission that has been laid upon Jesus, rather than
regarded as the outcome of His essential nature" (Durell, *The Self-Revelation
of our Lord*, p. 150).   On the order of the words Bengel remarks that we
recognize God's power before we recognize His wisdom.

of transition, or to call the Apostle to stringent account for every conjunction that he uses, the connexion of the successive clauses may be made fairly plain by following it in the order of thought. The γάρ and ὅτι, going from effect to cause, present the sequence in reverse order.   In following the order of thought, however, we must not forget that proof is sometimes from broad principles, sometimes from particular facts.   The order works out somewhat as follows :—

The Divine Power and Wisdom, at their seeming lowest, are far above man's highest (25); for this reason (22–24) our Gospel —a poor thing in the eyes of men, is, to those who know it, the Power and Wisdom of God.   This exemplifies (21) the truth underlying the history of the world, that man's wisdom is convicted of failure by the simplicity of the truth as declared by God.   This is how God, now as of old, turns to folly the wisdom of the wise (19, 20), a principle which explains the opposite look which the 'word of the Cross' has to the ἀπολλύμενοι and the σωζόμενοι (18): and that is why (17) my mission is to preach οὐκ ἐν σοφίᾳ λόγου.

As a chain of explanatory statements, the argument might have gone straight from *v.* 18 to *v.* 22; but St Paul would not omit a twofold appeal, most characteristic of his mind, to Scripture (19, 20), and to the religious history of mankind (21), the latter being exhibited as a verification of the other.

> Texts vary considerably as to the position of ἐστίν in the first clause of *v.* 25, and also in the second clause.   In the second, א* B 17 omit ἐστίν, and it is probably an interpolation from the first.

26. βλέπετε γάρ.   An unanswerable *argumentum ad hominem*, clinching the result of the above passage, especially the comprehensive principle of *v.* 25.   The verb is imperative (RV.), not indicative (AV.), and governs τὴν κλῆσιν directly.   It is needless subtlety to make τ. κλ. an accusative of respect, 'Behold—with reference to your call—how that not many,' etc.

τὴν κλῆσιν ὑμῶν.   'Summon before your mind's eye what took place then; note the ranks from which one by one you were summoned into the society of God's people; very few come from the educated, influential, or well-connected class.'   With κλῆσις compare κλητοί, *vv.* 2, 24: it refers, not so much to the external call, or even to the internal call of God, as to the conversion which presupposes the latter: πάντων ἀνθρώπων κεκλημένων οἱ ὑπακοῦσαι βουληθέντες κλητοὶ ὠνομάσθησαν (Clem. Alex. *Strom.* I. p. 314).   See on vii. 20, and Westcott on Eph. i. 18.

ἀδελφοί. As in *v.* 10, the affectionate address softens what
might give pain.

ὅτι οὐ πολλοί. A substantival clause, in apposition to κλῆσιν
as the part to the whole: they are to 'behold their calling,'
specially noting these facts which characterized it. From 'not
many' we may assume that in each case there were *some*: but
x. 5 warns us against interpreting οὐ πολλοί as meaning more
than 'very few.'

κατὰ σάρκα. This applies to δυνατοί and εὐγενεῖς as well as to
σοφοί. Each of the three terms is capable of a higher sense,
as εὐγενεῖς in Acts xvii. 11; each may be taken either (1) as a
predicate, 'not many of the called were wise,' etc.; or (2) as
belonging to the subject, the predicate being understood, 'not
many wise *had part therein*'; or (3) like (2), but with a different
predicate, 'not many wise *were called*' (AV., RV.). The last is
best.

Some of the converts were persons of culture and position;
Dionysius at Athens (Acts xvii. 34), Erastus at Corinth (Rom.
xvi. 23), the ladies at Thessalonica and Beroea (Acts xvii. 4, 12).
But the names known to us (xvi. 17; Rom. xvi.) are mostly
suggestive of slaves or freedmen. Lightfoot refers to Just. *Apol.*
ii. 9; Orig. *Cels.* ii. 79.*

27. τὰ μωρά. Cf. Matt. xi. 25. The gender lends force to the
paradox: τοὺς σοφούς leads us to expect τοὺς ἰσχυρούς, κ.τ.λ., but
the contrast of genders is not kept up in the other cases.

ἐξελέξατο. The verb is the correlative of κλῆσις (26), but
here, as in many other places, it brings in the idea of choice for
a particular end. Thus, of the choosing of Matthias, of Stephen,
of St Paul as a σκεῦος ἐκλογῆς, of St Peter to admit the first
Gentiles (Acts xv. 7). The emphatic threefold ἐξελέξατο ὁ Θεός
prepares the way for *v.* 31. See iv. 7 and Eph. ii. 8. The
Church, like the Apostle (2 Cor. xii. 10), was strong in weakness.

28. ἐξουθενημένα. See on vi. 4; also 2 Cor. x. 10. Ἀγενής
here only.

καὶ τὰ μὴ ὄντα. 'Yea things that are not.' The omission of
the καί (א* A C* D* F G 17) gives force to the (then) "studi-

---

* A century later it was a common reproach that Christianity was a
religion of the vulgar, and Apologists were content to imitate St Paul and
glory in the fact, rather than deny it. But the charge became steadily less
and less true. In Pliny's famous letter to Trajan, he speaks of *multi omnis
ordinis* being Christians. See Harnack, *Mission and Expansion of Christianity*, bk. iv. ch. 2; Lightfoot, *Clement*, I. p. 30. Celsus, who urges this
reproach, would not have written a serious treatise against the faith, if people
of culture and position were not beginning to adopt it. See Glover, *Conflict
of Religions in the Roman Empire*, ch. 9.

ously unconnected" and hyperbolical τὰ μὴ ὄντα : but the καί
(א³ B C³ D³ E L P, Vulg. Syrr. Copt. Arm. Aeth.) is quite in St
Paul's style. The μή does not mean '*supposed* not to exist,' but
'non-existent,' μή with participles being much more common
than οὐ.

καταργήσῃ. The verb means 'to reduce a person or thing to
ineffectiveness,' 'to render *workless* or inoperative,' and so 'to
bring to nought.' It is thus a stronger word than καταισχύνῃ,
and is substituted for it to match the antithesis between ὄντα
and μὴ ὄντα. It is very frequent in this group of the Pauline
Epistles. Elsewhere it is rare (2 Thess. ii. 8; 2 Tim. i. 10;
Luke xiii. 7 ; Heb. ii. 14); only four times in LXX, and very rare
in Greek authors. Cf. κενωθῇ, *v.* 17, and κενώσει, ix. 15.

Instead of τὰ ἀγενῆ τοῦ κόσμου, Marcion (Tert. Marc. v. 5, *inhonesta et
minima*) seems to have read τὰ ἀγενῆ καὶ τὰ ἐλάχιστα.

29. ὅπως μὴ καυχήσηται πᾶσα σάρξ. For the construction see
Rom. iii. 20; Acts x. 14. The negative coheres with the verb,
not with πᾶσα: in xv. 39 (οὐ πᾶσα σάρξ) the negative coheres
with πᾶσα. Πᾶσα σάρξ is a well-known Hebraism (Acts ii. 17),
meaning here the human race apart from the Spirit; 'that all
mankind should abstain from glorying before God.'*

ἐνώπιον τοῦ Θεοῦ. Another Hebraic phrase. *Non coram illo
sed in illo gloriari possumus* (Beng.).

'In His presence' (AV.) comes from the false reading ἐνώπιον αὐτοῦ
(C, Vulg. Syrr.). The true reading (א A B C³ D E F G L P, Copt. Aeth.)
is a forcible contrast to πᾶσα σάρξ.

30. ἐξ αὐτοῦ δὲ ὑμεῖς ἐστέ. 'But *ye* (in emphatic contrast) are
His children' (another contrast). This is their true dignity, and
the δέ shows how different their case is from that of those just
mentioned. The wise, the strong, the well-born, etc. may boast
of what seems to distinguish them from others, *but* it is the
Christian who really has solid ground for glorying. Some would
translate 'But it proceeds from Him that ye are in Christ Jesus,'
i.e. 'your being Christians is His doing.' But in that case ὑμεῖς
ἐστε (note the accentuation) is hard to explain: the pronoun is
superfluous: we should expect simply ἐν Χριστῷ Ἰησοῦ ἐστε.
Moreover, the sense given to ἐξ αὐτοῦ is hard to justify. It is
far more probable that we ought to read ὑμεῖς ἐστέ (WH., Lightfoot, Ellicott) and not ὑμεῖς ἐστε (T.R.). The meaning will then
be, 'But from *Him* ye have *your* being in Christ Jesus.' The

---

* Renan (*S. Paul*, p. 233) gives καυχάομαι as an instance of the way in
which a word gets a hold on the Apostle's mind so that he keeps on repeating
it : *un mot l'obsède ; il le ramène dans une page à tout propos* ; not for want
of vocabulary but because he cares so much more about his meaning than his
style (v. 17). "f. *v.* 31, iii. 21, iv. 7, v. 6, ix. 15, 16, xv. 31.

addition of ἐν Χρ. 'Ι. shows that more is meant than being His offspring in the sense of Acts xvii. 28. 'By adoption in Christ you are among things that really exist, although you may be counted as nonentities : in this there is room for glorying' (iv. 7; Eph. ii. 8 f.). This is the interpretation of the Greek Fathers, probably from a sense of the idiom, and not from bias of any kind.*

ὃς ἐγενήθη. This shows what the previous words involve. Not 'who is made' (AV.), nor 'who was made' (RV.), but 'who became' by His coming into the world and by what He accomplished for us. He showed the highest that God could show to man (v. 18, ii. 7), and opened the way to the knowledge of God through reconciliation with Him.

σοφία ἡμῖν. This is the central idea, in contrast with the false σοφία in the context, and it is expanded in the terms which follow. For the dative see vv. 18, 24.

ἀπὸ Θεοῦ. The words justify ἐξ αὐτοῦ and qualify ἐγενήθη . . . ἡμῖν, not σοφία only. The ἀπό points to the source of *ultimate* derivation. See Lightfoot on 1 Thess. ii. 6.

δικαιοσύνη τε καὶ . . . ἀπολύτρωσις. The terms, linked into one group by the conjunctions, are in apposition to σοφία and define it (RV. marg.) : the four terms are not co-ordinate (AV., RV.).† Lightfoot suggests, on not very convincing grounds, that τε καί serve to connect specially δικαιοσύνη and ἁγιασμός, leaving ἀπολύτρωσις "rather by itself." The close connexion between δικ. and ἁγ. is, of course, evident (Rom. vi. 19), δικ. being used by St Paul of the moral state founded upon and flowing from, faith in Christ (Rom. x. 4, 10, vi. 13; Gal. v. 5; Phil. iii. 9), and ἁγ. being used of the same state viewed as progress towards perfect holiness (v. 2; 1 Thess. iv. 3–7). By 'righteousness' he does not mean 'justification': that is presupposed and included. 'Righteousness' is the character of the justified man in its practical working. This good life of the pardoned sinner is to be distinguished from (a) God's righteousness (Rom. iii. 26, by which we explain Rom. i. 17), and from (b) Righteousness in the abstract sense of a right relation between persons (Acts x. 35, xxiv. 25).

καὶ ἀπολύτρωσις. Placed last for emphasis, as being the foundation of all else that we have in Christ (Rom. v. 9, 10, viii. 32 ; cf. iii. 24). Others explain the order by reference to the thought of *final* or completed redemption (Luke xxi. 28 ; Eph.

---

* See Deissmann, *Die neutestamentliche Formel "in Christo Jesu."* Chrysostom remarks how St Paul keeps "nailing them to the Name of Christ."

† It was probably in order to co-ordinate all four that L, Vulg. Syrr. Copt. Arm. have ἡμῖν before σοφία.

i. 14, iv. 30). *Redemptio primum Christi donum est quod inchoatur in nobis, et ultimum perficitur* (Calv.). The former is better, but it does not exclude the latter.

31. ἵνα καθὼς γέγραπται. Cf. ii. 9. We have here a case either of broken construction, a direct being substituted for a dependent clause (ix. 15), or of ellipse, a verb like γένηται being understood (iv. 6, xi. 24 ; 2 Thess. ii. 3 ; Gal. i. 20, etc.).

ὁ καυχώμενος. A free quotation, combining the LXX of Jer. ix. 23, 24 with 1 Sam. ii. 10, which resembles it. Jer. ix. 23, 24 runs, μὴ καυχάσθω ὁ σοφὸς ἐν τῇ σοφίᾳ αὐτοῦ καὶ μὴ καυχάσθω ὁ ἰσχυρὸς ἐν τῇ ἰσχύϊ αὐτοῦ καὶ μὴ καυχάσθω ὁ πλούσιος ἐν τῷ πλούτῳ αὐτοῦ, ἀλλ' ἢ ἐν τούτῳ κ α υ χ ά σ θ ω ὁ κ α υ χ ώ μ ε ν ο ς, συνιεῖν καὶ γινώσκειν ὅτι ἐγώ εἰμι Κύριος ὁ ποιῶν ἔλεος. In 1 Sam. ii. 10 we have δυνατός and δυνάμει for ἰσχυρός and ἰσχύϊ with the ending, γινώσκειν τὸν Κύριον καὶ ποιεῖν κρίμα καὶ δικαιοσύνην ἐν μέσῳ τῆς γῆς. The occurrence of 'the wise' and 'the strong' and 'the rich' (as in *v.* 26 here) makes the quotation very apt.

Clement of Rome (*Cor.* 13) quotes the same passage, but ends thus ; ἀλλ' ἢ ὁ καυχώμενος ἐν Κυρίῳ καυχάσθω τοῦ ἐκζητεῖν αὐτὸν καὶ ποιεῖν κρίμα καὶ δικαιοσύνην, thus approximating to St Paul's quotation. Probably he quotes the LXX and unconsciously assimilates his quotation to St Paul's. Lightfoot suggests that both the Apostle and Clement may have had a Greek version of 1 Sam. which differed from the LXX. For a false 'glorying in God' see Rom. ii. 17, and for a true glorying, Ecclus. xxxix. 8, l. 20.

Bachmann remarks that this is one of the remarkable quotations in which, by a free development of O.T. ideas and expressions, Christ takes the place of Jehovah ; and he quotes as other instances in Paul, ii. 16, x. 22 ; 2 Cor. x. 17 ; Phil. ii. 11 ; Rom. x. 13. Hort's remarks on 1 Pet. ii. 3, where ὁ Κύριος in Ps. xxxiv. 8 is transferred by the Apostle to Christ, will fit this and other passages. "It would be rash, however, to conclude that he meant to identify Jehovah with Christ. No such identification can be clearly made out in the N.T. St Peter is not here making a formal quotation, but merely borrowing O.T. language, and applying it in his own manner. His use, though different from that of the Psalm, is not at variance with it, for it is through the χρηστότης of the Son that the χρηστότης of the Father is clearly made known to Christians." The Father is glorified in the Son (John xiv. 13), and therefore language about glorifying the Father may, without irreverence, be transferred to the Son; but the transfer to Christ would have been irreverent if St Paul had not believed that Jesus was what He claimed to be.

Deissmann (*New Light on the N.T.*, p. 7) remarks that the

testimony of St Paul at the close of this chapter, "as to the origin of his congregations in the lower class of the great towns, is one of the most important historical witnesses to Primitive Christianity." See also, *Light from the Anc. East*, pp. 7, 14, 60, 142.

II. 1–5. The False Wisdom (*continued*).

So I came to you and preached, not a beautiful philosophy, but a crucified Christ.   I was a feeble, timid speaker ; and it was not my eloquence, but the power of God, that converted you.

¹And (in accordance with this principle of glory only in the Lord) when I first came to Corinth, Brothers, it was as quite an ordinary person (so far as any pre-eminence in speech or wisdom is concerned) that I proclaimed to you the testimony of God's love for you.   ²For I did not care to know, still less to preach, anything whatever beyond Jesus Christ; and what I preached about Him was that He was crucified.   ³And, as I say, it was in weakness and timidity and painful nervousness that I paid my visit to you : ⁴and my speech to you and my message to you were not conveyed in the persuasive words which earthly wisdom adopts.   No, their cogency came from God's Spirit and God's power ; ⁵for God intended that your faith should rest on His power, and not on the wisdom of man.

1. κἀγώ.   'And I, accordingly.'   The καί emphasizes the Apostle's consistency with the principles and facts laid down in i. 18–31, especially in 27–31.   His first preaching at Corinth eschewed the false σοφία, and conformed to the essential character of the Gospel.   The negative side comes first (*vv.* 1, 2).

ἐλθών.   At the time of his first visit (Acts xviii. 1 f.).   We have an analogous reference, 1 Thess. i. 5, ii. 1.

ἀδελφοί.   The rebuke latent in this reminder, and the affectionate memories of his first ministry to souls at Corinth (iv. 15), combine to explain this address (i. 10, 26).

ἦλθον.   The repetition, ἐλθὼν πρὸς ὑμᾶς . . . ἦλθον, instead of ἦλθον πρὸς ὑμᾶς, is not a case of broken construction, still less a Hebraism.   It gives solemn clearness and directness to St Paul's appeal to their beginnings as a Christian body.

καθ' ὑπεροχήν.   Most commentators connect the words with καταγγέλλων rather than ἦλθον.   Compare κατὰ κράτος (Acts xix. 20), καθ' ὑπερβολήν (1 Cor. xii. 31).   Elsewhere in N.T. ὑπεροχή

occurs only 1 Tim. ii. 2 ; cf. ὑπερέχειν, Rom. xiii. 1, etc. 'Pre-
eminence' is an exact equivalent.

λόγου ἢ σοφίας. See on i. 5, 17.

καταγγέλλων. The tense marks, not the purpose of the visit,
for which the future would be suitable, but the way in which the
visit was occupied. The aorists sum it up as a whole. Lightfoot
suggests that ἀγγέλλειν after verbs of mission or arrival (Acts xv.
27) is commonly in the *present* participle, as meaning 'to *bear*,
rather than to deliver, tidings.' But this does not always suit
καταγγέλλειν in N.T.; see xi. 26; Acts iv. 2; Rom. i. 8; Phil. i. 17;
and ἀγγέλλειν, uncompounded, occurs only John xx. 18, with
ἀπαγγ. as *v.l.*

μαρτύριον. 'He spoke in plain and simple language, as became a witness' (Lightfoot). *Testimonium simpliciter dicendum
est : nec eloquentia nec subtilitate ingenii opus est, quae testem sus-
pectum potius reddit* (Wetstein). Cf. xv. 15; 2 Thess. i. 10;
1 Tim. ii. 6; 2 Tim. i. 8. The first reference is decisive as to
the meaning here.

τοῦ Θεοῦ. *genitivus objecti* as in i. 6. The testimony is the
message of God's love to mankind declared in the saving work
of Christ (Rom. v. 8; John iii. 16); it is therefore a μαρτύριον
τ. Θεοῦ as well as a μαρτ. τ. Χριστοῦ. There is, of course, a
witness *from* God (1 John v. 9), but the present connexion is
with the Apostolic message about God and His Christ.

μαρτύριον (א³ B D E F G L P, Vulg. Sah. Aeth. Arm. AV. RV. marg.)
is probably to be preferred to μυστήριον (א* A C, Copt. RV.).   WH.
prefer the latter; but it may owe its origin to *v.* 7. On the other hand,
μαρτ. may come from i. 6.

2. οὐ γὰρ ἔκρινα τι εἰδέναι. 'Not only did I not speak of,
but I had no thought for, anything else.' Cf. Acts xviii. 5, συνεί-
χετο τῷ λόγῳ, 'he became engrossed in the word.' For κρίνειν
of a personal resolve see vii. 37; Rom. xiv. 13; 2 Cor. ii. 1.
Does the οὐ connect directly with ἔκρινα or with τι εἰδέναι, as
in AV., RV. ? The latter is attractive on account of its incisive-
ness; 'I deliberately refused to know anything.' But it assumes
that οὐκ ἔκρινα = ἔκρινα οὐ, on the familiar analogy of οὐ φημί.
Apparently there is no authority for this use of οὐκ ἔκρινα: οὐκ ἐῶ,
as Lightfoot points out, is not strictly analogous. Accordingly,
we must preserve the connexion suitable to the order of the
words; 'I did not think fit to know anything.' He did not
regard it as his business to know more. Ellicott remarks that
"the meaning is practically the same": but we must not give to
a satisfactory meaning the support of unsatisfactory grammar.

τι εἰδέναι. Not quite in the sense of ἐγνωκέναι τι (viii. 2),
'to know something,' as Evans here. In that case εἰ μή would
mean 'but only.' But τι simply means 'anything' whatever.

'Ιησοῦν Χριστόν. As in i. 1; contrast i. 23. In the Epistles
of this date, Χριστός still designates primarily the Office; 'Jesus,
the Anointed One, and that (not as King in His glory, but)—
crucified.'

καὶ τοῦτον ἐσταυρωμένον. The force of καὶ τοῦτον is definitely
to specify the point on which, in preaching Jesus Christ, stress
was laid (ὁ λόγος τ. σταυροῦ, i. 18), the effect being that of a
climax. The Apostle regards the Person and Work of Jesus
the Messiah as comprising in essence the whole Gospel, and
the Crucifixion, which with him involves the Resurrection, as
the turning-point of any preaching of his work. This most vital
point must not be forgotten when considering vv. 6 f. below.

τι εἰδέναι (B C P 17) is to be preferred to εἰδέναι τι (אA D² F G L).
D² L ins. τοῦ before εἰδέναι τι.

3. κἀγώ. He now gives the positive side—in what fashion he
did come (3–5). As in v. 1, the ἐγώ is emphatic; but here the
emphasis is one of contrast. 'Although I was the vehicle of
God's power (i. 18, ii. 4, 5), I not only eschewed all affectation
of cleverness or grandiloquence, but I went to the opposite
extreme of diffidence and nervous self-effacement. Others in my
place might have been bolder, but I personally was as I say.'
Or else we may take *v.* 3 as beginning again at the same point
as *v.* 1; as if the Apostle had been interrupted after dictating
v. 2, and had then begun afresh. Lightfoot regards κἀγώ as
simply an emphatic repetition, citing Juvenal i. 15, 16, *Et nos
ergo manum ferulae subduximus, et nos Consilium dedimus
Sullae.*

ἐν ἀσθενείᾳ. Cf. 2 Cor. xi. 29, xii. 10. The sense is general,
but may include his unimpressive presence (2 Cor. x. 10) and
shyness in venturing unaccompanied into strange surroundings
(cf. Acts xvii. 15, xviii. 5), coupled with anxiety as to the tidings
which Timothy and Silvanus might bring (cf. 2 Cor. ii. 13).
There was also the thought of the appalling wickedness of
Corinth, of his poor success at Athens, and of the deadly hostility
of the Jews to the infant Church of Thessalonica (Acts xvii. 5,
13). Possibly the malady which had led to his first preaching
in Galatia (Gal. iv. 13) was upon him once more. If this was
epilepsy, or malarial fever (Ramsay), it might well be the recurrent
trouble which he calls a 'thorn for the flesh' (2 Cor. xii. 7).

ἐν φόβῳ καὶ ἐν τρόμῳ πολλῷ. We have φόβος and τρόμος combined in 2 Cor. vii. 15; Phil. ii. 12; Eph. vi. 5. The physical
manifestation of distress is a climax. St Paul rarely broke new
ground without companions, and to face new hearers required
an effort for which he had to brace himself. But it was not the
Gospel which he had to preach that made him tremble: he was

'not ashamed' of that (Rom. i. 16). Nor was it fear of personal danger. It was rather "a trembling anxiety to perform a duty." In Eph. vi. 5, slaves are told to obey their masters μετὰ φόβου κ. τρόμου, which means with that conscientious anxiety that is opposed to ὀφθαλμοδουλία (Conybeare and Howson).* No other N.T. writer has this combination of φόβος and τρόμος. Some MSS. omit the second ἐν.

ἐγενόμην πρὸς ὑμᾶς. These words are probably to be taken together, exactly as in xvi. 10; 'I was with you.' The sense of becoming in the verb, and of movement in the preposition, is attenuated. 'My visit to you was in weakness,' preserves both the shade of meaning and the force of the tense. Cf. 2 John 12; 1 Thess. ii. 7, 10.

4. καὶ ὁ λόγος μου. See on i. 5, 17. Various explanations have been given of the difference between λόγος and κήρυγμα, and it is clear that to make the former 'private conversation,' and the latter ' public preaching,' is not satisfactory. Nor is the one the delivery of the message and the other the substance of it: see on i. 21. More probably, ὁ λόγος looks back to i. 18, and means the Gospel which the Apostle preached, while κήρυγμα is the act of proclamation, viewed, not as a process (κήρυξις), but as a whole. Cf. 2 Tim. iv. 17.

οὐκ ἐν πιθοῖς σοφίας λόγοις. The singular word πιθός or πειθός, which is found nowhere else, is the equivalent of the classical πιθανός, which Josephus (Ant. VIII. ix. 1) uses of the plausible words of the lying prophet of 1 Kings xiii. The only exact parallel to πιθός or πειθός from πείθω is φιδός or φειδός from φείδομαι, and in both cases the spelling with a diphthong seems to be incorrect (WH. App. p. 153). The rarity of the word has produced confusion in the text. Some cursives and Latin witnesses support a reading which is found in Origen and in Eus. Praep. Evang. i. 3., ἐν πειθοῖ [ἀνθρωπίνης] σοφίας λόγων, in persuasione sapientiae [humanae] verbi, or sermones for sermonis; where πειθοῖ is the dat. of πειθώ. From this, ἐν πειθοῖ σοφίας has been conjectured as the original reading; but the evidence of ℵ A B C D E L P for ἐν πιθοῖς or πειθοῖς is decisive; † and while σοφίας λόγοις almost certainly is genuine, ἀνθρωπίνης almost certainly is not, except as interpretation.

The meaning is that the false σοφία, the cleverness of the rhetorician, which the Apostle is disclaiming and combating

---

* Three times in Acts (xviii. 9, xxiii. 11, xxvii. 24) St Paul receives encouragement from the Lord. There was something in his temperament which needed this. In Corinth the vision assured him that his work was approved and would succeed. He not only might work, he must do so (ix. 16).

† It is remarkable that the word has not been adopted by ecclesiastical writers.

throughout this passage, was specially directed to the art of
persuasion : cf. πιθανολογία (Col. ii. 4).

ἀποδείξει. Not elsewhere in N.T. It has two very different
meanings : (1) 'display' or 'showing off' (cf. iv. 9 and Luke
i. 80), and (2) 'demonstration' in the sense of 'stringent proof.'
The latter is the meaning here. Aristotle distinguishes it from
συλλογισμός. The latter proves that a certain conclusion follows
from given premises, which may or may not be true. In ἀπόδειξις the premises are known to be true, and therefore the
conclusion is not only logical, but certainly true. In *Eth. Nic.*
I. iii. 4 we are told that to demand rigid demonstrations (ἀπο-
δείξεις) from a rhetorician is as unreasonable as to allow a
mathematician to deal in mere plausibilities. Cf. Plato *Phaed.*
77 C. *Theaet.* 162 E.* St Paul is not dealing with scientific
certainty : but he claims that the certitude of religious truth
to the believer in the Gospel is as complete and as 'objective'
—equal in degree, though different in kind—as the certitude of
scientific truth to the scientific mind. Mere human σοφία may
dazzle and overwhelm and seem to be unanswerable, but *assensum
constringit non res* ; it does not penetrate to those depths of the
soul which are the seat of the decisions of a lifetime. The
Stoics used ἀπόδειξις in this sense.

πνεύματος καὶ δυνάμεως. See on i. 18. The demonstration
is that which is wrought by God's power, especially His power
to save man and give a new direction to his life. As it is all
from God, why make a party-hero of the human instrument?
Some Greek Fathers suppose that miracle-working power is
meant, which is an idea remote from the context. Origen
refers πνεύματος to the O.T. prophecies, and δυνάμεως to the
N.T. miracles, thus approximating to the merely philosophic
sense of ἀπόδειξις. And if δυνάμεως means God's power, πνεύματος will mean His Spirit, the Holy Spirit. The article is
omitted as in *v.* 13 (cf. Gal. v. 16 and Phil. ii. 1 with 2 Cor.
xiii. 13). See Ellicott *ad loc.* The genitives are either subjective, 'demonstration proceeding from and wrought by the
Spirit and power of God,' or qualifying, 'demonstration consisting in the spirit and power of God,' as distinct from persuasion produced by mere cleverness. The sense of πνεύματος
is well given by Theophylact : ἀρρήτῳ τινὶ τρόπῳ πίστιν ἐνεποίει
τοῖς ἀκούουσιν. For the general sense see 1 Thess. i. 5 and
ii. 13 ; 'our Gospel came not in word only, but also in power
and in the Holy Spirit'; and 'ye accepted it not as the word
of men, but, as it is in truth, the word of God, which also

---

* In papyri, ἀπόδειξις is used of official evidence or proof. Bachmann
quotes ; ἀπόδειξιν δοὺς τοῦ ἐπίστασθαι ἱερατικὰ γράμματα (Tebt. Pap. ii. 291,
41).

worketh in you that believe.' St Paul's appeal is to the strong conviction and deep practical power of the Gospel. Not that strong conviction is incompatible with error: there is such a thing as ἐνέργεια πλάνης, causing men to believe what is false (2 Thess. ii. 11); but the false σοφία engenders no depth of conviction. Lightfoot quotes Longinus, who describes St Paul as πρῶτον . . . προϊστάμενον δόγματος ἀναποδείκτου — meaning philosophic proof, whereas St Paul is asserting a proof different in kind. "It was moral, not verbal [nor scientific] demonstration at which he aimed." This epistle is proof of that.

ἀνθρωπίνης (ℵ° A C L P, Copt. AV.) before σοφίας is rejected by all editors.

5. ἵνα. This expresses, either the purpose of God, in so ordering the Apostle's preaching (Theodoret), or that of the Apostle himself. The latter suits the ἔκρινα of *v.* 2; but the former best matches the thought of *v.* 4, and may be preferred (Meyer, Ellicott). The verse is co-ordinate with i. 31, but rises to a higher plane, for πίστις is more intimately Christian than the καύχησις of the O.T. quotation.

μὴ ᾖ ἐν σοφίᾳ ἀνθρώπων. The preposition marks the medium or sphere in which faith has its root: cf. ἐν τούτῳ πιστεύομεν (John xvi. 30). We often express the same idea by 'depend on' rather than by 'rooted in'; 'that your faith may not depend upon wisdom of men, but upon power of God.' What depends upon a clever argument is at the mercy of a cleverer argument. Faith, which is at its root personal trust, springs from the vital contact of human personality with divine. Its affirmations are no mere abstract statements, but comprise the experience of personal deliverance; οἶδα γὰρ ᾧ πεπίστευκα (2 Tim. i. 12). Here the negative statement is emphasized.

(ii.) II. 6–III. 4. The True Wisdom.

II. 6–13.   *The True Wisdom described.*

To mature Christians we Apostles preach the Divine Wisdom, which God has revealed to us by His Spirit.

⁶Not that as preachers of the Gospel we ignore wisdom: when we are among those whose faith is ripe, we impart it. But it is not a wisdom that is possessed by this age; no, nor yet by the leaders of this age, whose influence is destined soon to decline. ⁷On the contrary, what we impart is the Wisdom of God, a mystery hitherto kept secret, which God ordained from before all time for our eternal salvation. ⁸Of

this wisdom no one of the leaders of this age has ever acquired knowledge, for if any had done so, they would never have crucified the Lord whose essential attribute is glory. ⁹ But, so far from any of them knowing this wisdom, what stands written in Scripture is exactly true about them, Things which eye saw not, and ear heard not, and which entered not into the heart of man,—whatsoever things God prepared for them that love Him. ¹⁰ But to us, who are preachers of His Gospel, God has unveiled these mysteries through the operation of His Spirit; for His Spirit can explore all things, even the deep mysteries of the Divine Nature and Will. ¹¹ We can understand this a little from our own experience. What human being knows the inmost thoughts of a man, except the man's own spirit within him? Just so no one has attained to knowledge of the inmost thoughts of God, except God's own Spirit. ¹² Yet what we received was not the spirit which animates and guides the non-Christian world, but its opposite, the Spirit which proceeds from God, given to us that we may appreciate the benefits lavished upon us by God. ¹³ And what He has revealed to us we teach, not in choice words taught by the rhetoric of the schools, but in words taught by the Spirit, matching spiritual truth with spiritual language.

6. Σοφίαν δὲ λαλοῦμεν. The germ of the following passage is in i. 24, 30: Christ crucified is to the κλητοί the wisdom of God. This is the guiding thought to be borne in mind in discussing St Paul's conception of the true wisdom.* There are two points respecting λαλοῦμεν. Firstly, St Paul includes others with himself, not only his immediate fellow workers, but the Apostolic body as a whole (xv. 11). Secondly, the verb means simply 'utter': it must not be pressed to denote a kind of utterance distinct from λόγος and κήρυγμα (*v.* 4), such as private conversation.

ἐν τοῖς τελείοις. It is just possible that there is here an allusion to the technical language of mystical initiation; but, if so, it is quite subordinate. By τέλειοι St Paul means the mature or full-grown Christians, as contrasted with νήπιοι (iii. 1).† The word is used again xiv. 20; Phil. iii. 15; Eph. iv. 13. Those who had attained to the fulness of Christian experience

---

* See ch. x. in Chadwick, *Pastoral Teaching*, pp. 356 f., and note the emphatic position of σοφίαν.

† This sense is frequent in papyri and elsewhere. 'Initiated' would be τετελεσμένοι.

would know that his teaching was really philosophy of the highest kind. The ἐν means, not merely 'in the opinion of,' but literally 'among,' *in consessu*; 'in such a circle' the Apostle utters true wisdom.

It is quite clear that St Paul distinguishes two classes of hearers, and that both of them are distinct from the ἀπολλύμενοι of i. 18, or the Jews and Greeks of i. 22, 23. On the one hand, there are the τέλειοι, whom he calls lower down πνευματικοί (*v.* 13–iii. 1); on the other hand, there is the anomalous class of σάρκινοι, who are babes in Christ. Ideally, all Christians, as such, are πνευματικοί (xii. 31; Gal. iii. 2, 5; Rom. viii. 9, 15, 26). But practically, many Christians need to be treated as (ὡς, iii. 1), and to all intents are, σάρκινοι, νήπιοι, ψυχικοί (*v.* 14), even σαρκικοί (iii. 3). The work of the Apostle has as its aim the raising of all such imperfect Christians to the normal and ideal standard; ἵνα παραστήσωμεν πάντα ἄνθρωπον τέλειον ἐν Χριστῷ (Col. i. 28, where see Lightfoot). St Paul's thought, therefore, seems to be radically different from that which is ascribed to Pythagoras, who is said to have divided his disciples into τέλειοι and νήπιοι. It is certainly different from that of the Gnostics, who erected a strong barrier between the initiated (τέλειοι) and the average Christians (ψυχικοί). There are clear traces of this Gnostic distinction between esoteric and exoteric Christians in the school of Alexandria (Eus. *H.E.* v. xi.), and a residual distinction survives in the ecclesiastical instinct of later times (Ritschl, *Fides Implicita*). The vital difference is this: St Paul, with all true teachers, recognizes the principle of gradations. He does not expect the beginner at once to equal the Christian of ripe experience; nor does he expect the Gospel to level all the innumerable diversities of mental and moral capacity (viii. 7, xii. 12–27; Rom. xiv.). But, although gradations of classes among Christians must be allowed, there must be no differences of *caste*. The 'wisdom' is open to all; and all, in their several ways, are capable of it, and are to be trained to receive it. So far as the Church, in any region or in any age, is content to leave any class in permanent nonage, reserving spiritual understanding for any caste, learned, or official, or other,—so far the Apostolic charge has been left unfulfilled and the Apostolic ideal has been abandoned.

The δέ is explanatory and corrective; 'Now by wisdom I mean, not,' etc.

τοῦ αἰῶνος τούτου.   See on i. 20.

οὐδὲ τῶν ἀρχόντων.   It is quite evident from *v.* 8 that the ἄρχοντες are those who took part in the Crucifixion of the Lord of Glory. They, therefore, primarily include the rulers of the

Jews. Peter says, καὶ νῦν, ἀδελφοί, οἶδα ὅτι κατὰ ἄγνοιαν ἐπράξατε, ὥσπερ καὶ οἱ ἄρχοντες ὑμῶν (Acts iii. 17); and if St Luke is responsible for the *form* in which this speech is reported, the words may be regarded as the earliest commentary on our passage. But Pilate also was a party to the crime: and 'the rulers of this dispensation' includes all, as well ecclesiastical as civil.

Some Fathers and early writers, from Marcion (Tert. *Marc.* v. 6) downwards, understand the ἄρχοντες τοῦ αἰῶνος τούτου to mean *demons*: cf. κοσμοκράτορας τοῦ σκότους τοῦ αἰῶνος τούτου (Eph. vi. 12). Perhaps this idea exists already in Ignatius; ἔλαθεν τὸν ἄρχοντα [τ. αἰῶνος] τούτου . . . ὁ θάνατος τοῦ Κυρίου. See Thackeray, *The Relation of St Paul to Contemporary Jewish Thought*, pp. 156 f., 230 n. But this interpretation is wholly incompatible with *v.* 8, as also is the very perverse suggestion of Schmiedel that St Paul refers to *Angels*, whose rule over certain departments in God's government of the world belongs only to this dispensation, and ceases with it (καταργουμένων), and who are unable to see into the mysteries of redemption (Gal. iii. 19; 1 Pet. i. 12). See Abbott, *The Son of Man*, p. 5.

τῶν καταργουμένων. See on i. 28. The force of the present tense is 'axiomatic.' These rulers and their function belong to the sphere of πρόσκαιρα (vii. 31 ; 2 Cor. iv. 18), and are destined to vanish in the dawn of the Kingdom of God. So far as the Kingdom is come, they are gone. Yet they have their place and function in relation to the world in which we have our present station and duties (vii. 20, 24, 31), until all 'pass away into nothingness.'

7. ἀλλὰ λαλοῦμεν. The verb is repeated for emphasis with the fully adversative ἀλλά (Rom. viii. 15; Phil. iv. 17); 'But what we *do* utter is,' etc.

Θεοῦ σοφίαν. The Θεοῦ is very emphatic, as the context demands, and nearly every uncial has the words in this order. To read σοφίαν Θεοῦ (L) mars the sense.

ἐν μυστηρίῳ. We may connect this with λαλοῦμεν, to characterize the manner of communication, as we say, 'to speak *in* a whisper,' or to characterize its effect—'while declaring a mystery.' *Or* we may connect with σοφίαν: and this is better, in spite of the absence of τήν before ἐν μυστηρίῳ (see Lightfoot on 1 Thess. i. 1). The 'wisdom' is ἐν μυστηρίῳ, because it has been for so long a secret, although now made known to all who can receive it, the ἅγιοι (Col. i. 26) and κλητοί.

Assuming that μαρτύριον is the right reading in *v.* 1, we have here almost the earliest use of μυστήριον in N.T. (2 Thess. ii. 7 is the earliest). See J. A. Robinson, *Ephesians*, pp. 234-240, for a full discussion of the use of the word in N.T., also Westcott, *Ephesians*, pp. 180–182.

τὴν ἀποκεκρυμμένην. For the sense see Eph. iii. 5; Col. i. 26; Rom. xvi. 25. The words are explanatory of ἐν μυστηρίῳ. The wisdom of God had been hidden even from prophets and saints (Luke x. 24), until the fulness of time: now it is made manifest. But it remains hidden from those who are not prepared to receive it; *e.g.* from Jews (2 Cor. iii. 14) and the ἀπολλύμενοι generally (2 Cor. iv. 3–6). This contrast is followed up in *vv.* 8–16.

ἣν προώρισεν ὁ Θεός. To be taken directly with the words that follow, without supplying ἀποκαλύψαι or any similar link. The 'wisdom' is 'Christ crucified' (i. 18–24), fore-ordained by God (Acts iv. 28; Eph. iii. 11) for the salvation of men. It was no afterthought or change of plan, as Theodoret remarks, but was fore-ordained ἄνωθεν καὶ ἐξ ἀρχῆς.

εἰς δόξαν ἡμῶν. Our *eternal* glory, or complete *salvation* (2 Cor. iv. 17; Rom. viii. 18, 21, etc.). From meaning 'opinion,' and hence 'public repute,' 'praise,' or 'honour,' δόξα acquires in many passages the peculiarly Biblical sense of 'splendour,' 'brightness,' 'glory.' This 'glory' is used sometimes of physical splendour, sometimes of special 'excellence' and 'pre-eminency'; or again of 'majesty,' denoting the unique glory of God, the sum-total either of His incommunicable attributes, or of those which belong to Christ. In reference to Christ, the glory may be either that of His pre-incarnate existence in the Godhead, or of His exaltation through Death and Resurrection, at God's right hand.

It is on this sense of the word that is based its eschatological sense, denoting the final state of the redeemed. Excepting Heb. ii. 10 and 1 Pet. v. 1, this eschatological sense is almost peculiar to St Paul and is characteristic of him (xv. 43; 1 Thess. ii. 12; 2 Thess. ii. 14; Rom. v. 2; Phil. iii. 21, etc.). This state of the redeemed, closely corresponding to 'the Kingdom of God,' is called 'the glory of God,' because as God's adopted sons they share in the glory of the exalted Christ, which consists in fellowship with God. This 'glory' may be said to be enjoyed in this life in so far as we are partakers of the Spirit who is the 'earnest' (ἀρραβών) of our full inheritance (2 Cor. i. 22, v. 5; Eph. i. 14; cf. Rom. viii. 23). But the eschatological sense is primary and determinant in the class of passages to which the present text belongs, and this fact is of importance.

What is the wisdom of which the Apostle is speaking? Does he mean a special and esoteric doctrine reserved for a select body of the initiated (τέλειοι)? Or does he mean the Gospel, 'the word of the Cross,' as it is apprehended, not by babes in

Christ, but by Christians of full growth? Some weighty considerations suggest the former view, which is adopted by Clement,
Origen, Meyer, and others; especially the clear distinction made
in iii. 1, 2 between the γάλα and the βρῶμα, coupled with the
right meaning of ἐν in v. 6. On the other hand, the frequent
assertions (i. 18, 24, 30) that Christ crucified is the Power and
Wisdom of God, coupled with the fact that this Wisdom was
'fore-ordained for our salvation' (see also σῶσαι in i. 21), seem
to demand the equation of the wisdom uttered by the Apostle
with the μωρία τοῦ κηρύγματος, and the equation of Θεοῦ σοφίαν
in ii. 7 with Θεοῦ σοφίαν in i. 24 (cf. i. 30). These considerations seem to be decisive. With Heinrici, Edwards, and others,
we conclude that St Paul's 'wisdom' is the Gospel, simply.
With this Chrysostom agrees; σοφίαν λέγει τὸ κήρυγμα καὶ τὸν
τρόπον τῆς σωτηρίας, τὸ διὰ τοῦ σταυροῦ σωθῆναι· τελείους δὲ τοὺς
πεπιστευκότας.

But the γάλα and the βρῶμα of iii. 2, and the distinction
between τέλειοι and νήπιοι ἐν Χριστῷ, must be satisfied. The
τέλειοι are able to follow the 'unsearchable riches of Christ' and
'manifold wisdom of God' (Eph. iii. 8, 10) into regions of
spiritual insight, and into questions of practical import, to which
νήπιοι cannot at present rise. But they may rise, and with
proper nurture and experience will rise. There is no bar to
their progress.

The 'wisdom of God,' therefore, comprises primarily Christ
and Him crucified; the preparation for Christ as regards Jew and
Gentile; the great mystery of the call of the Gentiles and the apparent rejection of the Jews; the justification of man and the
principles of the Christian life; and (the thought dominant in the
immediate context) the consummation of Christ's work in the δόξα
ἡμῶν. The Epistle to the Romans, which is an unfolding of the
thought of 1 Cor. i. 24–31, is St Paul's completest utterance of this
wisdom. It is βρῶμα, while our Epistle is occupied with things
answering to γάλα, although we see how the latter naturally leads
on into the range of deeper problems (xiii., xv.). But there is
no thought here, or in Romans, or anywhere in St Paul's writings,
of a *disciplina arcani* or body of esoteric doctrine. The βρῶμα
is meant for all, and all are expected to grow into fitness for it
(see Lightfoot on Col. i. 26 f.); and the form of the Gospel (ii. 2)
contains the whole of it in germ.

8. ἦν οὐδεὶς ... ἔγνωκεν. The ἦν must refer to σοφίαν, 'which
wisdom none of the rulers of this world hath discerned.'

εἰ γάρ. Parenthetical confirmation of the previous statement.
'Had they discerned, as they did not, they would not have crucified, as they did.' It is manifest from this that the ἄρχοντες are

neither demons nor angels, but the rulers who took part in crucifying the Christ.

τὸν Κύριον τῆς δόξῆς. Cf. Jas. ii. 1; Eph. i. 17; Acts vii. 2; also Ps. xxiv. 7; Heb. ix. 5. The genitive is qualifying, but the attributive force is strongly emphatic, bringing out the contrast between the indignity of the Cross (Heb. xii. 2) and the majesty of the Victim (Luke xxii. 69, xxiii. 43).*

9. ἀλλά. 'On the contrary (so far from any, even among the great ones of this world, knowing this wisdom, the event was) just as it stands written.' There is no difficulty in understanding γέγονεν, or some such word, with καθὼς γέγραπται. But the construction can be explained otherwise, and perhaps better. See below, and on i. 19.

ἃ ὀφθαλμὸς οὐκ εἶδεν. The relative is co-ordinate with ἥν in v. 8, refers to σοφία, and therefore is *indirectly* governed by λαλοῦμεν in v. 7 (so Heinrici, Meyer, Schmiedel). It might (so Evans) be governed by ἀπεκάλυψεν, if we read ἡμῖν δέ and take v. 10 as an apodosis. But this is awkward, especially as ἃ does not precede καθὼς γέγραπται. The only grammatical irregularity which it is necessary to acknowledge is that ἃ serves first as an accusative governed by εἶδεν and ἤκουσεν, then as nominative to ἀνέβη, and once more in apposition to ὅσα (or ἃ) in the accusative. Such an anacoluthon is not at all violent.

ἐπὶ καρδίαν . . . οὐκ ἀνέβη. Cf. Acts vii. 23; Isa. lxv. 17; Jer. iii. 16, etc. 'Heart' in the Bible includes the mind, as here, Rom. i. 21, x. 6, etc.

ὅσα. In richness and scale they exceed sense and thought (John xiv. 2).

ἡτοίμασεν. Here only does St Paul use the verb of God. When it is so used, it refers to the blessings of *final glory*, with (Luke ii. 31) or without (Matt. xx. 23, xxv. 34; Mark x. 40; Heb. xi. 16) including present grace; or else to the miseries of *final punishment* (Matt. xxv. 41). See note on δόξα, v. 7. The analogy of N.T. language, and the dominant thought of the context here, compel us to find the primary reference in the consummation of final blessedness. See Aug. *De catech. rud.* 27; *Const. Apost.* VII. xxxii. 2; with Irenaeus, Cyprian, Clement of Alexandria and Origen. This does not exclude, but rather carries with it, the thought of 'present insight into Divine things' (Edwards). See on v. 10, and last note on v. 7.

---

* *Crux servorum supplicium. Eo Dominum gloriae affecerunt* (Beng.). "The levity of philosophers in rejecting the cross was only surpassed by the stupidity of politicians in inflicting it " (Findlay). The placing of τ. κ. τ. δόξης between οὐκ ἄν and the verb throws emphasis on the words; 'they would never have crucified *the Lord of Glory*': cf. Heb. iv. 8, viii. 7 (Abbot, *Johannine Gr.*, 2566).

τοῖς ἀγαπῶσιν αὐτόν. See Rom. viii. 28–30. Clement of Rome (*Cor.* 34), in quoting this passage, restores τοῖς ὑπομένουσιν from Isa. lxiv. 4 in place of τοῖς ἀγαπῶσιν. This seems to show that he regards the καθὼς γέγραπται as introducing a quotation from Isaiah.

We ought possibly to read ὅσα ἡτοίμασεν with A B C, Clem-Rom. But ἃ ἡτοίμασεν is strongly supported (א D E F G L P, Clem-Alex. Orig. Polyc-Mart.). Vulg. has *quae* with d e f g r.

The much debated question of the source of St Paul's quotation must be solved within the limits imposed by his use of καθὼς γέγραπται. See on i. 19 and 31. The Apostle unquestionably intends to quote Canonical Scripture. Either, then, he actually does so, or he unintentionally (Meyer) slips into a citation from some other source. The only passages of the O.T. which come into consideration are three from Isaiah. (1) lxiv. 4, ἀπὸ τοῦ αἰῶνος οὐκ ἠκούσαμεν οὐδὲ οἱ ὀφθαλμοὶ ἡμῶν εἶδον Θεὸν πλὴν σοῦ καὶ τὰ ἔργα σοῦ, ἃ ποιήσεις τοῖς ὑπομένουσιν ἔλεον (Heb. 'From eternity they have not heard, they have not hearkened, neither hath eye seen, a God save Thee, who shall do gloriously for him that awaiteth Him'). (2) lxv. 17, καὶ οὐ μὴ ἐπέλθῃ αὐτῶν ἐπὶ τὴν καρδίαν (observe the context). Also (3) lii. 15, as quoted Rom. xv. 21, a passage very slightly to the purpose. The first of these three passages is the one that is nearest to the present quotation. Its general sense is, 'The only living God, who, from the beginning of the world, has proved Himself to be such by helping all who trust in His mercy, is Jehovah'; and it must be admitted that, although germane, it is not very close to St Paul's meaning here. But we must remember that St Paul quotes with great freedom, often compounding different passages and altering words to suit his purpose. Consider the quotations in i. 19, 20, 31, and in Rom. ix. 27, 29, and especially in Rom. ix. 33, x. 6, 8, 15. Freedom of quotation is a *vera causa*; and if there are degrees of freedom, an extreme point will be found somewhere. With the possible exception of the doubtful case in Eph. v. 14, it is probable that we reach an extreme point here. This view is confirmed by the fact that Clement of Rome, in the earliest extant quotation from our present passage, goes back to the LXX of Isa. lxiv. 4, which is evidence that he regarded that to be the source of St Paul's quotation. At the very least, it proves that Clement felt that there was resemblance between 1 Cor. ii. 9 and Isa. lxiv. 4.

Of other solutions, the most popular has been that of Origen (*in Matt.* xxvii. 9); *in nullo regulari libro hoc positum invenitur, nisi in Secretis Eliae Prophetae.* Origen was followed by others, but was warmly contradicted by Jerome (*in Esai.* lxiv. 4: see also *Prol. in Gen.* ix. and *Ep.* lvii. [ci.] 7), who nevertheless allows that the passage occurs not only in the Apocalypse of Elias, but also in the Ascension of Esaias. This, however, by no means proves that the Apostle quotes from either book ; for the writers of those books may both of them be quoting from him. Indeed, it is fairly certain that this is true of the Apocalypse of Elias ; unless we reject the testimony of Epiphanius (*Haer.* xlii.), who says that this Apocalypse also contains the passage in Eph. v. 14, which (if St Paul quotes it without adaptation) is certainly from a Christian source. And there is no good reason for doubting the statement of Epiphanius. The Apocalypse of Elias, if it existed at all before St Paul's time, would be sure to be edited by Christian copyists, who, as in the case of many other apocalyptic writings, inserted quotations from N.T. books, especially from passages like the present one. The Ascension of Esaias, as quoted by Epiphanius (lxvii. 3), was certainly Christianized, for it contained allusions to the Holy Trinity. It is probably identical with the Ascension and Vision of Isaiah, published by Laurence in an Ethiopic, and by Gieseler in a Latin, version. The latter (xi. 34) contains our passage, and was doubtless the one known to Jerome ; the Ethiopic, though Christian, does not contain it. See Tisserant, *Ascension d'Isaie*, p. 211.

On the whole, therefore, we have decisive ground for regard ing our passage as the source whence these Christian or Christianized *apocrypha* derived their quotation, and not *vice versa*. Still more strongly does this hold good of the paradox of " oversanguine liturgiologists" (Lightfoot), who would see in our passage a quotation from the Liturgy of St James, a document of the Gentile Church of Aelia far later than Hadrian, and full of quotations from the N.T.*

Resch, also over-sanguine, claims the passage for his collection of *Agrapha*, or lost Sayings of our Lord, but on no grounds which call for discussion here.

Without, therefore, denying that St Paul, like other N.T. writers, might quote a non-canonical book, we conclude with Clement of Rome and Jerome, that he meant to quote, and actually does quote—very freely and with reminiscence of lxv. 17 —from Isa. lxiv. 4. He may, as Origen saw, be quoting from a lost Greek version which was textually nearer to our passage than the Septuagint is, but such an hypothesis is at best only a guess, and, in view of St Paul's habitual freedom, it is not a very helpful guess.

The above view, which is substantially that of the majority of modern commentators, including Ellicott, Edwards, and Lightfoot

* Lightfoot, *S. Clement of Rome*, I. pp. 389 f., II. pp. 106 f. ; Hammond, *Liturgies Eastern and Western*, p. x. Neither Origen nor Jerome know of any liturgical source.

(to whose note this discussion has special obligations) is rejected by Meyer-Heinr., Schmiedel, and some others, who think that St Paul, perhaps *per incuriam*, quotes one of the apocryphal writings referred to above. It has been shown already that this hypothesis is untenable. For further discussion, see Lightfoot, *S. Clement of Rome*, I. p. 390, and on Clem. Rom. *Cor.* 34; Resch, *Agrapha*, pp. 102, 154, 281; Thackeray, *St Paul and Contemporary Jewish Thought*, pp. 240 f. On the seemingly hostile reference of Hegesippus to this verse, see Lightfoot's last note *in loc.*

These two verses (9, 10) give a far higher idea of the future revelation than is found in Jewish apocalyptic writings, which deal rather with marvels than with the unveiling of spiritual truth. See Hastings, *DB.* iv. pp. 186, 187; Schürer, *J.P.*, II. iii. pp. 129–132; *Ency. Bib.* i. 210.

10. ἡμῖν γάρ. Reason why we can utter things hidden from eye, ear, and mind of man : 'Because to *us* God, through the Spirit, unveiled them,' or, 'For to *us* they were revealed by God through the Spirit.' The ἡμῖν follows hard upon and interprets τοῖς ἀγαπῶσιν αὐτόν, just as ἡμῖν on τοῖς σωζομένοις (i. 18): cf. ἡμῖν in i. 30 and ἡμῶν in ii. 7. The ἡμῖν is in emphatic contrast to 'the rulers of this world' who do not know (*v.* 8). God reveals His glory, through His Spirit, to those for whom it is prepared. See note on *v.* 7; also Eph. i. 14, 17; 2 Cor. i. 22.

If δέ be read instead of γάρ, we must either adopt the awkward construction of ἃ ὀφθαλμός κ.τ.λ. advocated by Evans and rejected above, or else, with Ellicott, make δέ introduce a second and supplementary contrast (co-ordinate with, but more general than, that introduced by ἀλλά in *v.* 9) to the ignorance of the ἄρχοντες in *v.* 8. On the whole, the "latent inferiority" of the reading δέ is fairly clear.

ἀπεκάλυψεν. The aorist points to a definite time when the revelation took place, viz. to the entry of the Gospel into the world.* Compare the aorists in Col. i. 26; Eph. iii. 5.

τὸ γὰρ πνεῦμα. Explanatory of διὰ τοῦ πνεύματος. The σωζό-μενοι and the ἀγαπῶντες τὸν Θεόν possess the Spirit, who has, and gives access to, the secrets of God.

ἐραυνᾷ. The Alexandrian form of ἐρευνᾷ (T.R.). The word does not here mean 'searcheth in order to know,' any more than it means this when it is said that God searches the heart of man (Rom. viii. 27; Rev. ii. 23; Ps. cxxxix. 1). It expresses "the

---

* Is it true that "revelation is distinguished from ordinary spiritual influences by its *suddenness*"? May there not be a gradual unveiling? Revelation implies that, without special aid from God, the truth in question would not have been discovered. Human ability and research would not have sufficed.

activity of divine knowledge" (Edwards); or rather, it expresses
the activity of the Spirit in throwing His light upon the deep
things of God, for those in whom He dwells. *Scrutatur omnia,
non quia nescit, ut inveniat, sed quia nihil relinquit quod nesciat*
(Atto).   For the form see Gregory, *Prolegomena* to Tisch.,
p. 81.

τὰ βάθη.   Cf. 'Ω βάθος πλούτου καὶ σοφίας καὶ γνώσεως Θεοῦ
(Rom. xi. 33), and contrast τὰ βαθέα τοῦ Σατανᾶ, ὡς λέγουσιν (Rev.
ii. 24).*

ἡμῖν γάρ (B and several cursives, Sah. Copt., Clem-Alex. Bas.) seems to
be preferable to ἡμῖν δέ (אACDEFGLP, Vulg. Syrr. Arm. Aeth.,
Orig.), but the external evidence for the latter is very strong.   Certainly
ἀπεκάλυψεν ὁ Θεός (אABCDEFGP, Vulg. Copt. Arm. Aeth.) is
preferable to ὁ Θεὸς ἀπ. (L, Sah. Orig.).   After πνεύματος, אᵃDEFGL,
Vulg. Syrr. Sah. Arm. Aeth. AV. add αὐτοῦ. א* ABC, Copt. RV. omit.

11. τίς γὰρ οἶδεν ἀνθρώπων.   This verse, taken as a whole,
confirms the second clause of *v.* 10, and thereby further explains
the words διὰ τοῦ πνεύματος.   The words ἀνθρώπων and ἀνθρώπου,
repeated, are emphatic, the argument being *a minori ad majus.*
Even a human being has within him secrets of his own, which
no human being whatever can penetrate, but only his own spirit.
How much more is this true of God!   The language here
recalls Prov. xx. 27, φῶς Κυρίου πνοὴ ἀνθρώπων, ὃς ἐραυνᾷ ταμεῖα
κοιλίας.   Cf. Jer. xvii. 9, 10.   The question does not mean that
nothing about God can be known; it means that what is known
is known through His Spirit (*v.* 10).

τὰ τοῦ ἀνθρώπου.   The personal memories, reflexions, motives,
etc., of any individual human being; all the thoughts of which
he is conscious (iv. 4).

τὸ πνεῦμα τοῦ ἀνθρ. τὸ ἐν αὐτῷ.   The word πνεῦμα is here used,
as in v. 5, vii. 34; 2 Cor. vii. 1; 1 Thess. v. 23, in the purely
psychological sense, to denote an element in the natural constitution of every human being.   This sense, if we carefully
separate all passages where it may stand for the spirit of man as
touched by the Spirit of God, is not very frequent in Paul.   See
below on *v.* 14 for the relation of πνεῦμα to ψυχή.

οὕτως καὶ κ.τ.λ.   It is here that the whole weight of the statement lies.

ἔγνωκεν.   This seems to be purposely substituted for the
weaker and more general οἶδεν.   For the contrast between the
two see 2 Cor. v. 16; 1 John ii. 29.   "The ἔγνωκεν seems to
place τὰ τοῦ Θεοῦ a degree more out of reach than οἶδεν does τὰ
τοῦ ἀνθρώπου" (Lightfoot, whose note, with its illustrations from
1 John, should be consulted).   This passage is a *locus classicus*

* Clem. Rom. (*Cor.* 40) has προδήλων οὖν ἡμῖν ὄντων τούτων, καὶ ἐγκεκυ-
φότες εἰς τὰ βάθη τῆς θείας γνώσεως.

for the Divinity, as Rom. viii. 26, 27 is for the Personality, of the Holy Spirit.

εἰ μή. 'But only,' as in Gal. i. 7, and (probably) i. 19; cf. ii. 16.

τὸ πνεῦμα τοῦ Θεοῦ. St Paul does not add τὸ ἐν αὐτῷ, which would have suggested a closer analogy between the relation of man's spirit to man and that of God's Spirit to God than the argument requires, and than the Apostle would hold to exist.

A 17, Ath. Cyr-Alex. omit ἀνθρώπων. F G omit the second τοῦ ἀνθρώπου. F G have ἔγνω, while L has οἶδεν, for ἔγνωκεν (א A B C D E P, Vulg. *cognovit*).

12. ἡμεῖς δέ. See on ἡμῖν in v. 10: 'we Christians.'

οὐ τὸ πνεῦμα τοῦ κόσμου . . . ἀλλά. An interjected negative clause, added to give more force to the positive statement that follows, as in Rom. viii. 15. What does St Paul mean by 'the spirit of the world'?

(1) Meyer, Evans, Edwards, and others understand it of Satan, or the spirit of Satan, the κόσμος being "a system of organized evil, with its own principles and its own laws" (Evans): see Eph. ii. 2, vi. 11; John xii. 31; 1 John iv. 3, v. 19; and possibly 2 Cor. iv. 4. But this goes beyond the requirements of the passage: indeed, it seems to go beyond the analogy of N.T. language, in which κόσμος has not *per se* a bad sense. Nor is 'the wisdom of the world' Satanical. It is human, not divine; but it is evil only in so far as 'the flesh' is sinful: *i.e.* it is not inherently evil, but only when ruled by sin, instead of being subjected to the Spirit. See Gifford's discussion of the subject in his *Comm. on Romans*, viii. 15.

(2) Heinrici, Lightfoot, and others understand of the temper of the world, "the spirit of human wisdom, of the world as alienated from God": *non sumus instituti sapientia mundi* (Est.). On this view it is practically identical with the ἀνθρωπίνη σοφία of *v.* 13, and homogeneous with the φρόνημα τῆς σαρκός of Rom. viii. 6, 7: indeed, it may be said to be identical with it in substance, though not in aspect. In both places in this verse, therefore, πνεῦμα would be impersonal, and *almost* attributive, as in Rom. viii. 15; but there the absence of the article makes a difference. Compare the πνεῦμα ἕτερον ὃ οὐκ ἐλάβετε in 2 Cor. xi. 4. On the whole, this second explanation of 'the spirit of the world' seems to be the better.

ἐλάβομεν. Like ἀπεκάλυψεν (*v.* 10), this aorist refers to a definite time when the gift was received. "St Paul regards the gift as ideally summed up when he and they were ideally included in the Christian Church, though it is true that the Spirit is received constantly" (Lightfoot). Cf. xii. 13.

τὸ πνεῦμα τὸ ἐκ τοῦ Θεοῦ. The gift rather than the Person of the Spirit, although here, as not infrequently in Paul, the distinction between the Personal Spirit of God (*v.* 11), dwelling in man (Rom. viii. 11), and the spirit (in the sense of the higher element of man's nature), inhabited and quickened by the Holy Spirit, is subtle and difficult to fix with accuracy. The Person is in the gift, and the activity of the recipient is the work of the Divine Indweller.

ἵνα εἰδῶμεν. This is the result to which *vv.* 10–12 lead up. The words reproduce, under a different aspect, the thought in ἡμῖν ἀπεκάλυψεν ὁ Θεός, and give the foundation for *v.* 13, ἃ καὶ λαλοῦμεν.

τὰ . . . χαρισθέντα ἡμῖν. The same blessings appear successively as δόξαν ἡμῶν (*v.* 7), ὅσα ἡτοίμασεν κ.τ.λ. (*v.* 9), and τὰ χαρισθέντα (*v.* 12). The last perhaps includes "a little more of present reference" (Ellicott). The connexion of thought in the passage may be shown by treating *vv.* 11 and 12 as expanding the thought of *v.* 10 into a kind of syllogism ;—major premiss, None knows the things of God, but only the Spirit of God ; minor premiss, We received the Spirit which is of God ; conclusion, So that we know what is given us by God. The possession of the gift of the Spirit of God is a sort of middle term which enables the Apostle to claim the power to know, and to utter, the deep things of God.

After τοῦ κόσμου, D E F G, Vulg. Copt. Arm. add τούτου. אABCLP, Syrr. Aeth. omit.

13. ἃ καὶ λαλοῦμεν. This is the dominant verb of the whole passage (*vv.* 6, 7 : see notes on ἥν, *v.* 8, ἃ and ὅσα, *v.* 9). The καί emphasizes the justification, furnished by the preceding verses, for the claim made ; 'Which are the very things that we do utter.' The present passage is the personal application of the foregoing, as *vv.* 1–5 are of i. 18–31.

διδακτοῖς ἀνθρωπίνης σοφίας. 'Taught by man's wisdom.' We have similar genitives in John vi. 45, διδακτοὶ Θεοῦ, and in Matt. xxv. 34, εὐλογημένοι τοῦ πατρός. In class. Grk. the construction is found only in poets ; κείνης διδακτά (Soph. *Elect.* 343), διδακταῖς ἀνθρώπων ἀρεταῖς (Pind. *Ol.* ix. 152). Cf. i. 17.

διδακτοῖς πνεύματος. See on *v.* 4, where, as here and 1 Thess. i. 5, πνεῦμα has no article. The Apostle is not claiming verbal inspiration ; but *verba rem sequuntur* (Wetstein). Cf. Luke xxi. 15 ; Jer. i. 9. *Sapientia est scaturigo sermonum* (Beng.). Bentley, Kuenen, etc. conjecture ἐν ἀδιδάκτοις πνεύματος.

πνευματικοῖς πνευματικὰ συγκρίνοντες. Two questions arise here, on the answer to which the interpretation of the words depends,—the gender of πνευματικοῖς, and the meaning of συν·

κρίνειν.   The latter is used by St Paul only here and 2 Cor. x. 12,
where it means 'to compare.'   This is a late use, frequent from
Aristotle onwards, but out of place here, although adopted in
both AV. and RV. text.   Its classical meaning is 'to join
fitly,' 'compound,' 'combine' (RV. marg.).   In the LXX it has
the meaning 'to interpret,' but only in the case of dreams
(Gen. xl. 8, 16, 22, xli. 12, 15; Judg. vii. 15; Dan. v. 12,
vii. 15, 16).   We have, therefore, the following possibilities to
consider :—
 (1) Taking πνευματικοῖς as neuter ;—either,
      (a) Combining spiritual things (the words) with spiritual
            things (the subject matter) ; or,
      (β) Interpreting (explaining) spiritual things by spiritual
            things.
This (β) may be understood in a variety of ways ;—
      Interpreting O.T. types by N.T. doctrines.
      Interpreting spiritual truths by spiritual language.
      Interpreting spiritual truths by spiritual faculties.
Of these three, the first is very improbable ; the third is
substantially the explanation adopted by Luther ; *und richten
geistliche Sachen geistlich.*
 (2) Taking πνευματικοῖς as masculine ;—either,
      (γ) Suiting (matching) spiritual matter to spiritual
            hearers ; or,
      (δ) Interpreting spiritual truths to spiritual hearers.
In favour of taking πνευματικοῖς as neuter may be urged the
superior epigrammatic point of keeping the same gender for both
terms, and the naturalness of πνευματικοῖς being brought into
close relation with the συν- in συνκρίνοντες.   These considerations are of weight, and the resultant sense is good and relevant,
whether we adopt (a) or the third form of (β).   As Theodore
of Mopsuestia puts it, διὰ τῶν τοῦ πνεύματος ἀποδείξεων τὴν τοῦ
πνεύματος διδασκαλίαν πιστούμεθα.
On the other hand, in favour of taking πνευματικοῖς as masculine, there is its markedly emphatic position, as if to prepare the
way for the contrast with ψυχικός which immediately follows, and
which now becomes the Apostle's main thought.   This consideration perhaps turns the scale in favour of taking πνευματικοῖς as
'spiritual *persons*.'   Of the two explanations under this head, one
would unhesitatingly prefer (δ), were not the use of συνκρίνειν in
the sense of 'interpret' confined elsewhere to the case of dreams.
This objection is not fatal, but it is enough to leave us in doubt
whether St Paul had this meaning in his mind.   The other
alternative (γ) has the advantage of being a little less remote
from the Apostle's only other use of the word.   In either case,
taking πν. as masculine, we have the Apostle coming back "full

circle" to the thought of *v.* 6, ἐν τοῖς τελείοις, which now receives
its necessary justification.

Before concluding the discussion of the true wisdom, the
Apostle glances at those who are, and those who are not, fitted
to receive it.

After πνεύματος, Dˢ E L P, Aeth. AV. add ἁγίου. ℵ A B C Dˢ F G 17,
Vulg. RV. omit.

II. 14-III. 4. THE SPIRITUAL AND THE ANIMAL CHARACTERS.

*Only the spiritual man can receive the true wisdom.
You Corinthians cannot receive it, for your dissensions show
that you are not spiritual.*

¹⁴ Now the man whose interests are purely material has no
mind to receive what the Spirit of God has to impart to him : it
is all foolishness to him, and he is incapable of understanding it,
because it requires a spiritual eye to see its true value. ¹⁵ But
the spiritual man sees the true value of everything, yet his own
true value is seen by no one who is not spiritual like himself.
¹⁶ For what human being ever knew the thoughts of the Lord
God, so as to be able to instruct and guide Him ?   But those of
us who are spiritual do share the thoughts of Christ.

iii. ¹ And I, Brothers, acting on this principle, have not been
able to treat you as spiritual persons, but as mere creatures of
flesh and blood, as still only babes in the Christian course.
² I gave you quite elementary teaching, and not the more solid
truths of the Gospel, for these ye were not yet strong enough
to digest. ⁸ So far from being so then, not even now are ye
strong enough, for ye are still mere beginners.   For so long as
jealousy and contention prevail among you, are you not mere
tyros, behaving no better than the mass of mankind?   ⁴ For
when one cries, I for my part stand by Paul, and another, I by
Apollos, are you anything better than men who are still
uninfluenced by the Spirit of God?

14. ψυχικὸς δὲ ἄνθρωπος. This is in sharpest contrast to
πνευματικοῖς (*v.* 13), for ψυχικός means 'animal' (*animalis homo*,
Vulg.) in the etymological sense, and nearly so in the ordinary
sense : see xv. 44, 46 ; Jas. iii. 15 ; Jude 19 (ψυχικοὶ πνεῦμα οὐκ

ἔχοντες).* The term is not necessarily based upon a supposed 'trichotomous' psychology, as inferred by Apollinaris and others from τὸ πνεῦμα καὶ ἡ ψυχὴ καὶ τὸ σῶμα in Thess. v. 23 (see Lightfoot's note). It is based rather upon the conception of ψυχή as the mere correlative of organic life. Aristotle defines it as πρώτη ἐντελέχεια σώματος φυσικοῦ ὀργανικοῦ. In man, this comprises πνεῦμα in the merely psychological sense (note on v. 11), but not necessarily in the sense referred to above (note on v. 12). See, however, v. 5; Phil. i. 27; Eph. vi. 17; Col. iii. 23; 1 Pet. iv. 6. In Luke i. 46, ψυχή and πνεῦμα seem to be synonymous. The ψυχή ranges with νοῦς (Rom. vii. 23, 35; Col. ii. 18), in one sense contrasted with σάρξ, but like σάρξ in its inability to rise to practical godliness, unless aided by the πνεῦμα. We may say that ψυχή is the 'energy' or correlative of σάρξ.

Although, therefore, ψυχή is not used in N.T. in a bad sense, to distinguish the animal from the spiritual principle in the human soul, yet ψυχικός is used of a man whose motives do not rise above the level of merely human needs and aspirations. The ψυχικός is the 'unrenewed' man, the 'natural' man (AV., RV.), as distinct from the man who is actuated by the Spirit. The word is thus practically another name for the σαρκικός (iii. 1, 3). See J. A. F. Gregg on Wisd. ix. 15.

οὐ δέχεται. Not 'is incapable of receiving,' but 'does not accept,' i.e. he rejects, refuses. Δέχεσθαι = 'to accept,' 'to take willingly' (2 Cor. viii. 17; 1 Thess. i. 6, etc.).

ὅτι πνευματικῶς ἀνακρίνεται. The nature of the process is beyond him; it requires characteristics which he does not possess. The verb is used frequently by St Paul in this Epistle, but not elsewhere. It is one of the 103 N.T. words which are found only in Paul and Luke (Hawkins, Hor. Syn. p 190). Here it means 'judge of,' 'sift,' as in Acts xvii. 11 of the liberal-minded Beroeans, who sifted the Scriptures, to get at the truth : Dan. Sus. 13, 48, 51.

15. ὁ δὲ πνευματικός. The man in whom πνεῦμα has its rightful predominance, which it gains by being informed by, and united with, the Spirit of God, and in no other way. Man as man is a spiritual being, but only some men are actually spiritual ; just as man is a rational being, but only some men are actually rational. Natural capacity and actual realization are not the same thing.

ἀνακρίνει μὲν πάντα. 'He judges of everything,' 'sifts every-

* Cf. Juvenal (xv. 147 f.), Mundi Principio indulsit communis conditor illis Tantum animas, nobis animum quoque. See Chadwick, Pastoral Teaching, p. 153.

thing,' 1 Thess. v. 21 ; Phil. i. 10 ; contrast Rom. ii. 18. The whole Epistle exemplifies this principle in St Paul's person (vii. 25, viii. 1, x. 14, xi. 1, etc.). Aristotle, in defining virtue, comes back to the judgment formed by the mature character : ὡς ἂν ὁ φρόνιμος ὁρίσειεν (*Eth. Nic.* II. vi. 15). ' Judgeth ' (AV., RV.) does not quite give the meaning of what is expressed here : ' examines ' is nearer to it.

αὐτὸς δὲ ὑπ' οὐδενὸς ἀνακρίνεται. This perhaps means ' by no non-spiritual person ' (cf. 1 John iv. 1). It does not mean that the spiritual man is above criticism (iv. 3, 4, xiv. 32 ; Rom. xiv. 4). St Paul is not asserting the principle of Protagoras, that the individual judgment is for each man the criterion of truth ; πάντων μέτρον ἄνθρωπος, τῶν μὲν ὄντων ὡς ἐστί τῶν δὲ μὴ ὄντων ὡς οὐκ ἐστί. He is asserting, with Bishop Butler, the supremacy of conscience, and the right and duty of personal judgment. But it is the spiritual man who has this vantage-ground. The text has been perverted in more than one direction ; on the one hand, as an excuse for the licence of persons whose conduct has stamped them as unspiritual, *e.g.* the Anabaptists of Münster ; on the other, as a ground for the irresponsibility of ecclesiastical despotism in the mediæval Papacy, *e.g.* by Boniface VIII. in the Bull *Unam sanctam*, and by Cornelius à Lapide on this passage. The principle laid down by St Paul gives no support to either anarchy or tyranny ; it is the very basis of lawful authority, both civil and religious ; all the more so, because it supplies the principle of authority with the necessary corrective.

ἀνακρίνεται. ' Is judged of,' ' subjected to examination.' See on iv. 3, 4, 5, ix. 3, x. 25, 27 ; also on Luke xxiii. 14. Ἀνά-κρισις (Acts xxv. 26) was a legal term at Athens for a preliminary investigation, preparatory to the actual κρίσις, which for St Paul would have its analogue in ' the day ' (iv. 5). Lightfoot gives examples of the way in which the Apostle delights to accumulate compounds of κρίνω (iv. 3, vi. 1-6, xi. 29-32 ; 2 Cor. x. 12 ; Rom. ii. 1). By playing on words he sometimes illuminates great truths or important personal experiences.

א* omits the whole of this verse. A C D* F G omit μέν after ἀνακρίνει πάντα (א¹ B D² E F G L) is to be preferred to τὰ πάντα (A C D* P).

16. τίς γὰρ ἔγνω. Proof of what has just been claimed for the πνευματικός : he has direct converse with a source of light which is not to be superseded by any merely external norm. The quotation (τίς . . . αὐτόν) is from the LXX of Isa. xl. 13, adapted by the omission of the middle clause, καὶ τίς αὐτοῦ σύνβουλος ἐγένετο ; This clause is retained in Rom. xi. 34, while ὃς συνβιβάσει αὐτόν is omitted. The aorist (ἔγνω) belongs to

the quotation, and must not be pressed as having any special force here; 'hath known' (AV., RV.). On the other hand, the immediate transition from νοῦν Κυρίου to νοῦν Χριστοῦ as equivalent is full of deep significance. Cf. Wisd. ix. 13; Ecclus. i. 6; Job xxxvi. 22, 23, 26; and see on Rom. x. 12, 13.

νοῦν Κυρίου. The νοῦν (LXX) corresponds to the Hebrew for πνεῦμα in the original. In God, νοῦς and πνεῦμα are identical (see, as to man, on *v.* 14), but not in aspect, νοῦς being suitable to denote the Divine knowledge or counsel, πνεῦμα the Divine action, either in creation or in grace.

ὃς συνβιβάσει αὐτόν. The relative refers to σύνβουλος in Isa. xl. 13. As St Paul omits the clause containing σύνβουλος, the ὃς is left without any proper construction. But it finds a kind of antecedent in τίς; 'Who hath known . . . that he should instruct' (RV.). Συνβιβάζειν occurs several times in N.T. in its classical meanings of 'join together,' 'conclude,' 'prove'; but in Biblical Greek, though not in classical, it has also the meaning of 'instruct.' Thus in Acts xix. 33, where the true reading (א A B E) seems to be συνεβίβασαν Ἀλέξανδρον, Alexander is 'primed' with a defence of the Jews, for which he cannot get a hearing. This meaning of 'instruct' is frequent in LXX. In class. Grk. we should have ἐνβιβάζειν.

ἡμεῖς δὲ νοῦν Χριστοῦ ἔχομεν. We have this by the agency of the Spirit of God; and the mind of the Spirit of God is known to the Searcher of hearts (Rom. viii. 27). The mind of Christ is the correlative of His Spirit, which is the Spirit of God (Rom. viii. 9; Gal. iv. 6), and this mind belongs to those who are His by virtue of their vital union with Him (Gal. ii. 20, 21, iii. 27; Phil. i. 8; Rom. xiii. 14). The thought is that of *v.* 12 in another form: see also vii. 40; and 2 Cor. xiii. 3, τοῦ ἐν ἐμοὶ λαλοῦντος Χριστοῦ. The emphatic ἡμεῖς (see on i. 18, 23, 30, ii. 10, 12) serves to associate all πνευματικοί with the Apostle, and also all his readers, so far as they are, as they ought to be, among οἱ σωζόμενοι (i. 18).

We ought probably to prefer Χριστοῦ (א A C D³ E L P, Vulg. Syrr. Copt. Arm., Orig.) to Κυρίου (B D* F G, Aug. Ambrst.). Χριστοῦ would be likely to be altered to conform with the previous Κυρίου.

III. 1–4. In following to its application his contrast between the spiritual and the animal character, the Apostle is led back to his main subject, the σχίσματα. These dissensions show which type of character predominates among his readers. The passage corresponds to ii. 13 (see note there), and forms its negative counterpart, prepared for by the contrast (ii. 13–16) between the spiritual and the animal man.

Κἀγώ, ἀδελφοί.   See on i. 10 and ii. 1.

ὡς πνευματικοῖς.   Ideally, all Christians are πνευματικοί (xii. 3, 13; Gal. iv. 3–7): but by no means all the Corinthians were such in fact.*   Along with the heathen, they are in the category of ψυχικοί or σαρκικοί, but they are not on a level with the heathen. They are babes in character, but 'babes *in Christ*'; and, apart from the special matters for blame, there are many healthy features in their condition (i. 4–9, xi. 2).

ἀλλ' ὡς σαρκίνοις.   The word is chosen deliberately, and it expresses a shade of meaning different from σαρκικός, placing the state of the Corinthians under a distinct aspect.   The termination -ινος denotes a *material* relation, while -ικος denotes an *ethical* or dynamic relation, to the idea involved in the root.   In 2 Cor. iii. 3 the tables are *made* of stone, the hearts are *made* of flesh (see note on ἀνθρώπινος, iv. 3).   Accordingly, σαρκίνος means 'of flesh and blood,' what a man cannot help being, but a state to be subordinated to the higher law of the Spirit, and enriched and elevated by it.   We are all σαρκίνοι (ζῶ ἐν σαρκί, Gal. ii. 20), but we are not to live κατὰ σάρκα (xv. 50; Rom. viii. 12; 2 Cor. x. 2, 3).   The state of the νήπιος is not culpable *in itself*, but it becomes culpable if unduly prolonged (xiii. 11, xiv. 20).

There are two other views respecting σαρκίνος which may be mentioned, but seem to be alien to the sense.   Meyer holds that the word means 'wholly of flesh,' without any influence of the spirit (John iii. 6).   In the σαρκικός, although the flesh still has the upper hand, yet there is some counteracting influence of the spirit.   This view makes the state of the σαρκικός an advance upon that of the σαρκίνος, and is really an inversion of the true sense.   Evans regards σαρκίνος as a term free from *any* reproach. It is "the first moral state after conversion, in a figure borrowed from an infant, which to outward view is little more than a living lump of dimpled flesh, with few signs of intelligence."   This is an exaggeration of the true sense.   Cf. Arist. *Eth. Nic.* III. ix. 2.

σαρκίνοις (א A B C* D* 17) is the original reading, of which σαρκικοῖς (D³ E F G L P) is obviously a correction.

2.   γάλα ὑμᾶς ἐπότισα, οὐ βρῶμα.   Cf. Heb. v. 12, where στερεὰ τροφή takes the place of βρῶμα.   The verb governs both substantives by a very natural zeugma: it takes a double accusative, and the passive has the accusative of the thing (xii. 13).   The γάλα is described ii. 2, the βρῶμα, ii. 6–13, and the distinction corresponds to the method necessarily adopted by every skilful teacher. The wise teacher proves himself to be such by his ability to impart, in the most elementary grade, what is really fundamental

* Cf. γενώμεθα πνευματικοί, γενώμεθα ναὸς τέλειος τῷ Θεῷ (Ep. of Barn. iv. 11), a possible reminiscence of this and *v.* 16.

and educative—what is simple, and yet gives insight into the full instruction that is to follow. The 'milk,' or ὁ τῆς ἀρχῆς τοῦ Χριστοῦ λόγος (Heb. vi. 1), would be more practical than doctrinal (as ii. 2), and would tell of 'temperance and righteousness and judgment to come' before communicating the foundation-truths as to the person and work of Christ. Christ Himself begins in this way; 'Thou knowest the commandments'; 'Repent ye, for the kingdom of God is at hand.' The metaphor was current among the Rabbis, and occurs in Philo (see Lightfoot's note). The aorist ἐπότισα refers to a definite period, evidently that which began with the ἦλθον of ii. 1, viz. the eighteen months of Acts xviii. 11.

οὔπω γὰρ ἐδύνασθε. 'For ye had not yet the power.' The verb is used absolutely, as in x. 13.* This use is not rare in LXX, and is found in Plato, Xenophon, etc. The tense indicates a process. This process was one of growth, but the growth was too slow.

D E F G L, Arm. Aeth. AV. insert καί before οὐ βρῶμα. ℵ A B C P, Vulg. Copt. RV. omit.

3. ἀλλ' οὐδὲ ἔτι νῦν δύνασθε. The new verse (but hardly a new paragraph) should begin here (WH.). B omits ἔτι, but the omission may be accidental. It adds force to the rebuke, but for that reason might have been inserted. The external evidence justifies its retention. The ἀλλά has its strongest 'ascensive' force; 'Nay, but not yet even now have ye the power' (vi. 8; 2 Cor. i. 9; Gal. ii. 3). The impression made by this passage, especially when combined with vv. 6, 10, ii. 1, and ἀκούεται in v. 1, is that St Paul had as yet paid only one visit to Corinth. The ἄρτι in xvi. 7 does not necessarily suggest a hasty visit already paid. The second visit of a painful character, which seems to be implied in 2 Cor. xiii., may have been paid *after* this letter was written. Those who think it was paid *before* this letter, explain the silence about it throughout this letter by supposing that it was not only painful, but very short.

ὅπου γὰρ ἐν ὑμῖν. The adverb of place acquires the force of a conditional particle in classical authors as here: cf. Clem. Rom. *Cor.* 43. In Tudor English, 'where' is sometimes used for 'whereas.' But here the notion of place, corresponding to ἐν ὑμῖν, is not quite lost; 'seeing that envy and strife find place among you.' Cf. ἔνι in Gal. iii. 28.

ζῆλος καὶ ἔρις. Strife is the outward result of envious feeling: Gal. v. 20; Clem. Rom. *Cor.* 3. There is place in Christian ethics for honourable emulation (Gal. iv. 18), but ζῆλος without

* Irenaeus (IV. xxxviii. 2) has οὐδὲ γὰρ ἠδύνασθε βαστάζειν (from John xvi. 12), and his translator has *nondum enim poteratis escam percipere.*

qualification, though ranked high by Aristotle* (*Rhet.* ii. 11), is placed by the Apostle among 'works of the flesh.' Lightfoot gives other instances of differences in estimation between heathen and Christian ethics.

οὐχὶ σαρκικοί ἐστε; See above on σαρκίνοι, and cf. ix. 11 ; Rom. xv. 27. Here, as in 2 Cor. i. 12, σαρκικοί means 'conformable to and governed by the flesh,' actuated by low motives, above which they ought by this time to have risen.

κατὰ ἄνθρωπον περιπατεῖτε. 'Walk on a merely human level' (xv. 32 ; Gal. i. 11, iii. 15; Rom. iii. 5): contrast κατὰ Θεόν (2 Cor. vii. 9–11 ; Rom. viii. 27). This level cannot be distinguished from that of the ψυχικὸς ἄνθρωπος (ii. 14). Περιπατεῖν, of manner of life, is frequent in Paul and 2 and 3 John, while other writers more often have ἀναστρέφειν and ἀναστροφή: cf. ὀρθοδοποῦν (Gal. ii. 14), πορεύεσθαι (Luke i. 6, viii. 14) and see vii. 17. Cf. Jn. xii. 35.

D* F G have σαρκίνοι for σαρκικοί. D E F G L, Syrr. AV. add καὶ διχοστασίαι after ἔρις. א A B C P, Vulg. Copt. Arm. Aeth. RV. omit. See Iren. IV. xxxviii. 2.

4. ὅταν γὰρ λέγῃ τις. 'For whenever one saith': each such utterance is one more verification (γάρ) of the indictment.† Cf. the construction in xv. 27.

ἐγὼ μέν . . . ἕτερος δέ. The μέν and the δέ correspond logically, although not grammatically. St Paul mentions only himself and Apollos by name (cf. iv. 6), because he can less invidiously use these names as the point of departure for the coming analysis of the conception of the Christian Pastorate (iii. 5–iv. 5).

οὐκ ἄνθρωποί ἐστε; 'Are ye not mere human creatures?' They did not rise above a purely human level. The expression is the negative equivalent of σαρκικοί in the parallel clause,— negative, because implying the lack, not only of spirituality, but even of manliness. The lack of spirituality is implied in the whole context, the lack of manliness in the word itself, which classical writers contrast with ἀνήρ. In xvi. 13 this contrast is implied in ἀνδρίζεσθε. See Ps. xlix. 2 and Isa. ii. 9 for a similar contrast in Hebrew. The Corinthians were ἄνθρωποι in failing to rise to the higher range of motives; and they were σαρκικοί in

* He contrasts it with envy, which is always bad and springs from a mean character ; whereas the man who is moved by emulation is conscious of being capable of higher things. Wetstein distinguishes thus ; ζῆλος *cogitatione*, ἔρις *verbis*, διχοστασίαι *opere*.

† Abbott renders, 'In the very moment of saying'; by uttering a party-cry he stamps himself as carnal ; so also in xiv. 26 (*Johan. Gr.* 2534). There is here nothing inconsistent with i. 5–7. There he thanks God for the gifts with which He had enriched the Corinthians. Here he blames them for the poor results.

allowing themselves to be swayed by the lower range, a range which they ought (ἔτι γάρ) to have left behind as a relic of heathenism (vi. 11, xii. 2).

"In all periods of great social activity, when society becomes observant of its own progress, there is a tendency to exalt the persons and means by which it progresses. Hence, in turn, kings, statesmen, parliaments, and then education, science, machinery and the press, have had their hero-worship. Here, at Corinth, was a new phase, 'minister-worship.' No marvel, in an age when the mere political progress of the Race was felt to be inferior to the spiritual salvation of the Individual, and to the purification of the Society, that ministers, the particular organs by which this was carried on, should assume in men's eyes peculiar importance, and the special gifts of Paul or Apollos be extravagantly honoured. No marvel either, that round the more prominent of these, partizans should gather" (F. W. Robertson). Origen says that, if the partizans of Paul or Apollos are mere ἄνθρωποι, then, if you are a partizan of some vastly inferior person, δῆλον ὅτι οὐκέτι οὐδὲ ἄνθρωπος εἶ, ἀλλὰ καὶ χεῖρον ἢ ἄνθρωπος. You may perhaps be addressed as γεννήματα ἐχιδνῶν, if you have such base preferences. Bachmann remarks that, although the present generation has centuries of Christian experience behind it, it can often be as capricious, one-sided, wrong-headed, and petty as any Corinthians in its judgments on its spiritual teachers and their utterances.

We should read οὐκ (א* A B C 17) rather than the more emphatic, and in this Epistle specially common οὐχί (D E F G L P), which is genuine in *v.* 3, i. 20, v. 12, vi. 7, etc. And we should read ἄνθρωποι (א* A B C D E F G 17, Vulg. Copt. Aeth. RV.) rather than σαρκικοί (א³ LP, Syrr. AV.). ἀνθρώπινοι (iv. 3, x. 13) is pure conjecture.

We now reach another main section of this sub-division (i. 10–iv. 21) of the First Part (i. 10–vi. 20) of the Epistle. St Paul has hitherto (i. 17–iii. 4) been dealing with the false and the true conception of σοφία, in relation to Christian Teaching. He now passes to the Teacher.

III. 5–IV. 21. THE TRUE CONCEPTION OF THE CHRISTIAN PASTORATE.

Personal Application of the foregoing, and Conclusion of the subject of the Dissensions (iv. 6–21).

III. 5–9. General Definition of the Christian Pastorate.

Teachers are mere instruments in the hands of God, who alone produces the good results.

⁵ What is there really in either Apollos or me? We are not heads of parties, and we are not the authors or the objects of your faith. We are just servants, through whose instrumentality you received the faith, according to the grace which the Lord gave to each of you. ⁶ It was my work to plant the faith in you, Apollos nourished it; but it was God who, all the time, was causing it to grow. ⁷ So then, neither the planter counts for anything at all, nor the nourisher, but only He who caused it to grow, viz. God. ⁸ Now the planter and the nourisher are in one class, equals in aim and spirit; and yet each will receive his own special wage according to his own special responsibility and toil. ⁹ God is the other class; for it is God who allows us a share in His work; it is God's field (as we have seen) that ye are; it is God's building (as we shall now see) that ye are.

The Apostle has shown that the dissensions are rooted, firstly, in a misconception of the Gospel message, akin, in most cases, to that of the Greeks, who seek wisdom in the low sense of cleverness, and akin, in other cases, to that of the Jews, who are ever seeking for a sign. He goes on to trace the dissensions to a second cause, viz. a perverted view of the office and function of the Christian ministry. First, however, he lays down the true character of that ministry.

5. τί οὖν ἐστίν; A question, Socratic in form, leading up naturally to a definition, and thus checking shallow conceit (*v.* 18, iv. 6) by probing the idea underlying its glib use of words. 'What *is* Apollos? *i.e.* What is his essential office and function? How is he to be 'accounted of'? (iv. 1). The two names are mentioned three times, and each time the order is changed, perhaps intentionally, to lead up to ἕν εἰσιν (*v.* 8). The οὖν follows naturally upon the mention of Apollos in *v.* 4, but marks also a transition to a question raised by the whole matter under discussion,—a new question, and a question of the first rank.

διάκονοι. The word is used here in its primary and general

sense of 'servant.'* It connotes *active* service (see note on
ὑπηρέτης in iv. 1) and is probably from a root akin to διώκω (cf.
'pursuivant'). See Hort, *Christian Ecclesia*, pp. 202 f.

δι' ὧν ἐπιστεύσατε. *Per quos, non in quos* (Beng.). The aorist
points back to the time of their conversion (cf. xv. 2 ; Rom. xiii.
11), but it sums up their whole career as Christians.

καὶ ἑκάστῳ ὡς ὁ Κύριος ἔδωκεν. As in vii. 17 ; Rom. xii. 3.
The construction is condensed for ἕκαστος ὡς ὁ Κ. ἔδωκεν αὐτῷ
It may be understood either of the measure of faith given by the
Lord to each believer, or of the measure of success granted by Him
to each διάκονος. Rom. xii. 3 favours the former, but perhaps
ὁ Θεὸς ηὔξανεν favours the latter. We have ἕκαστος five times in
vv. 5–13. God deals separately with each individual soul: cf.
iv. 5, vii. 17, 20, 24, xii. 7, 11. And whatever success there is
to receive a reward (*v.* 8) is really His ; *Deus coronat dona sua,
non merita nostra* (Augustine). It is clear from the frequent
mention of Θεός in what follows that ὁ Κύριος means God, and it
seems to be in marked antithesis to διάκονοι.

We should read τί in both places (א* A B 17, Vulg. d e f g Aeth. RV.),
rather than τίς (C D E F G L P, Syrr. Copt. Arm. AV.). D² L, Syrr. Arm.
Aeth. place Παῦλος first and Ἀπολλώς second, an obvious correction, to
agree with *vv.* 4 and 6. D E F G L, Vulg. Arm. Copt. omit ἐστιν after
τ. δέ. D² L P, Syrr. AV. insert ἀλλ' ἤ before διάκονοι. א A B C D* E F G,
Vulg. Copt. Arm. RV. omit.

6. ἐγὼ ἐφύτευσα κ.τ.λ. St Paul expands the previous statement. Faith, whether initial or progressive, is the work of God
alone, although He uses men as His instruments. Note
the significant change from aorists to imperfect. The aorists
sum up, as wholes, the initial work of Paul (Acts xviii. 1–18) and
the fostering ministry of Apollos (Acts xviii. 24–xix. 1): the
imperfect indicates what was going on *throughout*; God was all
along causing the increase (Acts xiv. 27, xvi. 14).† *Sine hoc
incremento granum a primo sationis momento esset instar lapilli :
ex incremento statim fides germinat* (Beng.). See Chadwick,
Pastoral Teaching, p. 183.

7. ἐστιν τί. 'Is something,' *est aliquid*, Vulg. (cf. Acts v. 36 ;
Gal. ii. 6, vi. 3) ; so Evans ; *quiddam, atque adeo, quia solus, omnia*
(Beng.). Or, ἐστίν τι, 'is anything' (AV., RV.).

*Nos mercenarii sumus, alienis ferramentis operamur, nihil
debetur nobis, nisi merces laboris nostri, quia de accepto talento
operamur* (Primasius).

---

* "There is no evidence that at this time διακονία or διακονεῖν had an
exclusively official sense " (Westcott on Eph. iv. 12) ; cf. Heb. vi. 10.
† Latin and English Versions ignore the change of tense ; and the difference
between human activities, which come and go, and divine action, which goes
on for ever, is lost.

ἀλλ᾽ ὁ αὐξάνων Θεός. The strongly adversative ἀλλά implies the opposite of what has just been stated; 'but God who giveth the increase *is everything.*' See on vii. 19, and cf. Gal. vi. 15. To refer ἐπότισεν and ὁ ποτίζων to Baptism, as some of the Fathers do, is to exhibit a strange misappreciation of the context. See Lightfoot's note. Θεός is placed last with emphasis; 'but the giver of the increase—God.'

ἕν εἰσιν. Are in one category, as fellow-workers; consequently it is monstrous to set them against one another as rivals. As contrasted with God, they are all of one value, just nothing. But that does not mean that each, when compared with the other, is exactly equal in His sight. The other side of the truth is introduced with δέ.

ἕκαστος δέ. 'Yet each has his own responsibility and work, and each shall receive his proper reward.' The repeated ἴδιον marks the separate responsibility, correcting a possible misapprehension of the meaning of ἕν: *congruens iteratio, antitheton ad 'unum'* (Beng.). The latter point is drawn out more fully in *vv.* 10 f.

9. Θεοῦ γάρ. The γάρ refers to the first half, not the second, of *v.* 8. The workers are in one category, because they are Θεοῦ συνεργοί. The verse contains the dominant thought of the whole passage, gathering up the gist of *vv.* 5–7. Hence the emphatic threefold Θεοῦ. The Gospel is the power of God (i. 18), and those who are entrusted with it are to be thought of, not as rival members of a rhetorical profession, but as bearers of a divine message charged with divine power.

Θεοῦ συνεργοί. This remarkable expression occurs nowhere else: the nearest to it is 2 Cor. vi. 1; the true text of 1 Thess. iii. 2 is probably διάκονον, not συνεργόν.* It is not quite clear what it means. Either, 'fellow-workers with one another in God's service'; or, 'fellow-workers with God.' Evans decides for the former, because "the logic of the sentence loudly demands it." So also Heinrici and others. But although God does all, yet human instrumentality in a sense co-operates (ὅσα ἐποίησεν ὁ Θεὸς μετ᾽ αὐτῶν, Acts xiv. 27), and St Paul admits this aspect of the matter in ἡ χάρις τοῦ Θεοῦ σὺν ἐμοί, xv. 10, and in συνεργοῦντες, 2 Cor. vi. 1. This seems to turn the scale in favour of the more simple and natural translation, 'fellow-workers with God.'† Compare τοὺς συνεργούς μου ἐν Χριστῷ Ἰησοῦ (Rom. xvi. 3), which

---

* In LXX συνεργός is very rare; 2 Mac. viii. 7, xiv. 5, of favourable opportunities.

† *Dei enim sumus adjutores* (Vulg.); *Etenim Dei sumus administri* (Beza); *Denn wir sind Gottes Mitarbeiter* (Luth.). In such constructions, συναιχμάλωτός μου, σύνδουλοι αὐτοῦ, συνέκδημος ἡμῶν, the συν- commonly refers to the person in the genitive: but see ix. 23.

appears to show how St Paul would have expressed the former meaning, had he meant it.

Θεοῦ γεώργιον, Θεοῦ οἰκοδομή. The one metaphor has been employed in *vv.* 6–8, the other is to be developed in *vv.* 10 f. St Paul uses three metaphors to express the respective relations of himself and of other teachers to the Corinthian Church. He is planter (6), founder (10), and father (iv. 15). Apollos and the rest are waterers, after-builders, and tutors. The metaphor of building is a favourite one with the Apostle. On the different meanings of οἰκοδομή, which correspond fairly closely to the different meanings of 'building,' see J. A. Robinson, *Ephesians*, pp. 70, 164 : it occurs often in the Pauline Epistles, especially in the sense of 'edification,' a sense which Lightfoot traces to the Apostle's metaphor of the building of the Church. Here it is fairly certain that γεώργιον does not mean the 'tilled land' (RV. marg.), but the 'husbandry' (AV., RV.) or 'tillage' (AV. marg.) that results in tilled land, and that therefore οἰκοδομή does not mean the edifice, but the building-process which results in an edifice. The word γεώργιον is rather frequent in Proverbs; elsewhere in LXX it is rare, and it is found nowhere else in N.T. In the Greek addition to what is said about the ant (Prov. vi. 7) we are told that it is without its knowing anything of tillage (ἐκείνῳ γεωργίου μὴ ὑπάρχοντος) that it provides its food in summer. Again, in the Greek addition to the aphorisms on a foolish man (Prov. ix. 12), we are told that he wanders from the tracks of his own husbandry (τοὺς ἄξονας τοῦ ἰδίου γεωργίου πεπλάνηται). In Ecclus. xxvii. 6 it is said that the 'cultivation of a tree' (γεώργιον ξύλου) is shown by its fruit. The meaning here, therefore, is that the Corinthians exhibit God's operations in spiritual husbandry and spiritual architecture; *Dei agricultura estis, Dei aedificatio estis* (Vulg.).* It is chiefly in 1 and 2 Cor., Rom., and Eph. that the metaphor of building is found. See also Acts ix. 31, xx. 32; Jude 20; 1 Pet. ii. 5, with Hort's note on the last passage. In Jer. xviii. 9, xxiv. 6, and Ezek. xxxvi. 9, 10 we have the metaphors of building and planting combined.

III. 10–15. The Builders.

I have laid the only possible foundation. Let those who build on it remember that their work will be severely tested at the Last Day.

¹⁰ As to the grace which God gave me to found Churches, I have, with the aims of an expert master-builder, laid a foundation

* Augustine (*De cat. rud.* 21) rightly omits the first *estis.*

for the edifice; it is for some one else to build upon it. But, whoever he may be, let him be careful as to the materials with which he builds thereon. ¹¹ For, as regards the foundation, there is no room for question: no one can lay any other beside the one which is already laid, which of course is Jesus Christ. ¹² But those who build upon this foundation may use either good or bad material; they may use gold, silver, and sumptuous stones, or they may use wood, hay, and straw. But each builder's good or bad work is certain to be made manifest in the end. For the Day of Judgment will disclose it, because that Day is revealed in fire; and the fire is the thing that will assuredly test each builder's work and will show of what character it is. ¹⁴ If any man's work—the superstructure which he has erected—shall stand the ordeal, he will receive a reward. ¹⁵ If any man's work shall be burnt to the ground, he will lose it, though he himself shall be saved from destruction, but like one who has passed through fire.

St Paul follows up the building-metaphor, first (v. 10) distinguishing his part from that of others, and then (11–15) dwelling on the responsibility of those who build after him.

10. Κατὰ τὴν χάριν κ.τ.λ. The necessary prelude to a reference to his own distinctive work (cf. vii. 25). The 'grace' is not that of Apostleship in general, but that specially granted to St Paul, which led him to the particular work of founding new Churches, and not building on another man's foundation (Rom. xv. 19, 20).

ὡς σοφὸς ἀρχιτέκτων. The same expression is found in LXX of Isa. iii. 3, and σόφος is frequent of the skilled workmen who erected and adorned the Tabernacle (Exod. xxxv. 10, 25, xxxvi. 1, 4, 8). It means *peritus*. Aristotle (*Eth. Nic.* vi. vii. 1) says that the first notion of σοφία is, that, when applied to each particular art, it is skill; Phidias is a skilled sculptor.* See Lightfoot *ad loc.* 'Αρχιτέκτων occurs nowhere else in N.T.

θεμέλιον ἔθηκα. The aorist, like ἐφύτευσα (v. 6), refers to the time of his visit (ἦλθον, ii. 1): θεμέλιον is an adjective (*sc.* λίθον), but becomes a neuter substantive in late Greek. In the plural

---

* This use of σοφός is more common in poets than in prose writers. When σοφός became usual of philosophical wisdom, δεινός took its place in the sense of skilful. Herodotus (v. xxiii. 3) uses both words of the clever and shrewd Histiaeus. Plato (*Politicus* 259) defines the ἀρχιτέκτων, as distinct from an ἐργαστικός, as one who contributes knowledge, but not manual labour. Tertullian (*Adv. Marc.* v. 6) interprets it here as *depalator disciplinae divinae*, one who stakes out the boundaries.

we may have either gender; οἱ θεμέλιοι (Heb. xi. 10, Rev. xxi. 14, 19), or τὰ θεμέλια (Acts xvi. 26 and often in LXX). No architect can build without *some* foundation, and no expert will build without a *sure* foundation. Cf. Eph. ii. 20.

ἄλλος δέ. The reference is not specially to Apollos : ' The superstructure I leave to others.' But they all must build, according to the rule that follows, *thoughtfully*, not according to individual caprice.

πῶς ἐποικοδομεῖ. Refers specially, although not exclusively, to the choice of materials (*vv.* 12, 13). The edifice, throughout, is the Church, not the fabric of doctrine ; but ἐποικοδομεῖν refers to the teaching—both form and substance—which forms the Church, or rather forms the character of its members (Gal. iv. 19).

ἔθηκα (א* A B C* 17) is to be preferred to τέθεικα (א³ C³ D E) or τεθηκα (L P). D omits the second δέ. There is no need to conjecture ἐποικοδόμη for the second ἐποικοδομεῖ (all MSS). In vii. 32 the balance of evidence is strongly in favour of πῶς ἀρέσῃ.

11. θεμέλιον γάρ. A cautionary premiss to *v.* 12, which continues the thought of the previous clause : ' Let each man look to it how he builds upon this foundation, because, although (I grant, nay, I insist) none can lay *any foundation* παρὰ τὸν κείμενον, yet the superstructure is a matter of separate and grave responsibility.' Θεμέλιον stands first for emphasis. There *can* be but one fundamental Gospel (Gal. i. 6, 7), the foundation lies there, and the site is already occupied. By whom is the foundation laid? Obviously (*v.* 10), by St Paul, when he preached Christ at Corinth (ii. 2). This is the *historical* reference of the words ; but behind the laying of the stone at Corinth, or wherever else the Church may be founded, there is the eternal laying of the foundation-stone by God, the ' only wise ' architect of the Church. See Evans.

Compare the use of κειμένη of the city that is already there, and τιθέασιν of the lamp which has to be placed (Matt. v. 14, 15).

ὅς ἐστιν Ἰησοῦς Χριστός. Both name and title are in place, and neither of them alone would have seemed quite satisfying. see on ii. 2. He is the foundation of all Christian life, faith, and hope.[*] In Eph. ii. 20 He is the chief corner-stone, ἀκρογωνιαῖος, the basis of unity: cf. Acts iv. 11. It is only by admitting some inconsistency of language that the truth can be at all adequately expressed. There is inconsistency even if we leave Eph. ii. 20 out of account. He has just said that he laid the foundation in a skilful way. Now he says that it was lying there ready for him, and that no other foundation is possible. Each statement, in its own proper sense, is true ; and we need

[*] See Lock, *St Paul, the Master-Builder*, pp. 69 f.

both in order to get near to the truth. As in Gal. i. 8, παρά
means 'besides,' not 'contrary to,' 'at variance with.'

Ἰησοῦς Χριστός (א A B L P Sah. Copt. Arm. Aeth.) rather than Χριστός
Ἰησοῦς (C³ D E, Vulg.).   Several cursives have Ἰησοῦς ὁ Χρ.

12. εἰ δέ τις κ.τ.λ. The various kinds of superstructure
represent various degrees of inferiority in the *ministry* of the
'after-builders,' *i.e.* according as they make, or fail to make, a
lasting contribution to the structure. With regard to the whole
passage, three things are to be noted :

(1) The metaphor is not to be pressed too rigidly by seeking
to identify each term with some detail in the building. This
Grotius does in the following way : *proponit ergo nobis domum
cujus parietes sunt ex marmore, columnae partim ex auro partim
ex argento, trabes ex ligno, fastigium vero ex stramine et culmo ;*
all which is very frigid.* The materials are enumerated with
a rapid and vivid *asyndeton,* which drives each point sharply
and firmly home.

(2) The 'wood, hay, stubble' do not represent teaching that
is intentionally disloyal or false (αὐτὸς δὲ σωθήσεται), but such
as is merely inferior.

(3) The imagery alternates between the suggestion of teaching
as moulding persons, and the suggestion of persons as moulded
by teaching (Evans), so that it is irrelevant to ask whether the
materials enumerated are to be understood of the fruits of
doctrine, such as different moral *qualities* (Theodoret), or of
worthy and unworthy *Christians.* The two meanings run into
one another, for the qualities must be exhibited in the lives of
persons. We have a similar combination of two lines of thought
in the interpretation of the parable of the Sower. There the
seed is said to be sown, and the soil is said to be sown, and in
the interpretation these two meanings are mingled. Yet the
interpretation is clear enough.

χρυσίον, ἀργύριον. As distinct from χρυσός and ἄργυρος,
which indicate the metals in any condition, these diminutives
are commonly used of gold and silver *made* into something, such
as money or utensils ; as when by 'gold' we mean gold coins,
or by 'silver' mean silver coins or plate (Acts iii. 6, xx. 33).
But this is not a fixed rule. See Matt. xxiii. 16 and Gen. ii. 11.

λίθους τιμίους. Either 'costly stones,' such as marble or
granite, suitable for building, or 'precious stones,' suitable for
ornamentation. Isa. liv. 11, 12 and Rev. xxi. 18, 19, combined

---

* It is perhaps worse than frigid. Obviously, it would be unskilful to
use both sets of material in the same building ; Origen regards ξύλα as worse
than χόρτος, and χόρτος than καλάμη, which can hardly be right. See Chase,
Chrysostom, pp. 186, 187.

with the immediate context ('gold and silver'), point to the latter meaning. It is internal decoration that is indicated.

χόρτον, καλάμην. Either of these might mean straw or dried grass for mixing with clay, as in Exod. v. 12, καλάμην εἰς ἄχυρα, 'stubble instead of straw'; and either might mean material for thatching. *Romuleoque recens horrebat regia culmo* (Virg. *Aen.* viii. 654). Luther's contemptuous expression respecting the Epistle of St James as a 'right strawy epistle' was made in allusion to this passage. Nowhere else in N.T. does καλάμη occur.

After ἐπὶ τ. θεμέλιον, ℵ³ C³ D E L P, Vulg. AV. add τοῦτον. ℵ* A B C*, Sah. Aeth. RV. omit. We ought probably to read χρυσίον (ℵ B) and ἀργύριον (ℵ B C) rather than χρυσόν and ἄργυρον (A D E L P). B, Aeth. insert καί after χρυσίον.

13. ἑκάστου τὸ ἔργον. These words sum up the alternatives, standing in apposition to the substantival clause, εἰ δέ τις . . . καλάμην. Individual responsibility is again insisted upon : we have ἕκαστος four times in *vv.* 8–13.

ἡ γὰρ ἡμέρα δηλώσει. 'The Day' (as in 1 Thess. v. 4; Rom. xiii. 12; Heb. x. 25), without the addition of Κυρίου (1 Thess. v. 2) or of κρίσεως (Matt. xii. 36) or of ἐκείνη (2 Thess. i. 10; 2 Tim. i. 12, 18, iv. 8), means the Day of Judgment. This is clear from iv. 3, 5, *ubi ex intervallo, ut solet, clarius loquitur* (Beng.). The expression 'Day of the Lord' comes from the O.T. (Isa. ii. 12; Jer. xlvi. 10; Ezek. vii. 10, etc.), and perhaps its original meaning was simply a definite period of time. But with this was often associated the idea of day as opposed to night: 'the Day' would be a time of light, when what had hitherto been hidden or unknown would be revealed. So here. And here the fire which illuminates is also a fire which *burns*, and thus *tests* the solidity of that which it touches. What is sound survives, what is worthless is consumed.

ἐν πυρὶ ἀποκαλύπτεται. The nominative is neither τὸ ἔργον nor ὁ Κύριος, but ἡ ἡμέρα. 'The Day' is (to be) revealed in fire (2 Thess. i. 7, 8, ii. 8; Dan. vii. 9 f.; Mal. iv. 1). This is a common use of the present tense, to indicate that a coming event is so certain that it may be spoken of as already here. The predicted revelation is sure to take place. See on ἀποκαλύπτεται in Luke xvii. 30, Lightfoot on 1 Thess. v. 2, and Hort on 1 Pet. i. 7, 13.

St Paul is not intending to describe the details of Christ's Second Coming, but is figuratively stating, what he states without figure in iv. 5, that at that crisis the real worth of each man's work will be searchingly tested. This test he figures as the fire of the Second Advent, wrapping the whole building round, and reducing all its worthless material to ashes. The fire, therefore, is regarded more as a testing than as an illuminating agent, as *tentatio tribulationis* (August. *Enchir.* 68), which by its destructive power makes manifest the enduring power of all that it touches. There is no thought in the passage of a penal, or disciplinary, or purgative purpose; nor again is there the remotest reference to the state of the soul between death and judgment. *Hic locus ignem purgatorium non modo non fovet sed plane extinguit, nam in novissimo demum die ignis probabit. . . . Ergo ignis purgatorius non praecedit* (Beng.). The ἐν suggests that fire is the element in which the revelation takes place. At the Parousia Christ is to appear ἐν πυρὶ φλογός (2 Thess. i. 8) or ἐν φλογὶ πυρός (Is. lxvi. 15). In the Apocalypse of Baruch (xlviii. 39) we have, "A fire will consume their thoughts, and in flame will the meditations of their reins be *tried*; for the Judge will come and will not tarry." But elsewhere in that book (xliv. 15, lix. 2, etc.) the fire is to consume the wicked, a thought of which there is no trace here. There are no wicked, but only unskilful builders; all build, although some build unwisely, upon Christ.

καὶ ἑκάστου. Still under the ὅτι. It is better to regard τὸ ἔργον as the acc. governed by δοκιμάσει, with αὐτό as pleonastic, than as the nom. to ἐστιν. A pleonastic pronoun is found with good authority in Matt. ix. 27 ; Luke xvii. 7 ; and elsewhere : but the readings are sometimes uncertain. To take αὐτο with πῦρ, 'the fire itself,' has not much point. In all three verses (13, 14, 15), τὸ ἔργον refers, not to a man's personal character, good or bad, but simply to his work *as a builder* (12).

ℵ D E L, Vulg. Sah. Copt. Arm. Aeth. omit αὐτό, but we ought probably to read it with A B C P 17 and other cursives.

14. μενεῖ. It is doubtful, and not very important, whether we should accent this word as a future, to agree with κατακαήσεται and other verbs which are future, or μένει, as a present, which harmonizes better with the idea of permanence : cf. μένει in xiii. 13.

μισθόν. Compare *v.* 8 and Matt. xx. 8 : in ix. 17, 18 the reference is quite different. The nature of the reward is not stated, but it is certainly not eternal salvation, which may be won by those whose work perishes (*v.* 15). Something corresponding to the 'ten cities' and 'five cities' in the parable may be meant ; opportunities of higher service.

15. κατακαήσεται. This later form is found as a *v.l.* (AL) in 2 Pet. iii. 10, where it is probably a correction of the puzzling εὑρεθήσεται (ℵ B K P). In Rev. xviii. 8 the more classical κατακανθήσεται is found. The burning of Corinth by Mummius may have suggested this metaphor.

ζημιωθήσεται. It does not much matter whether we regard this as indefinite, 'He shall suffer loss' (AV., RV.), *detrimentum patietur* (Vulg.), *damnum faciet* (Beza), or understand τὸν μισθόν from *v.* 14, 'He shall be mulcted of the expected reward.' In Exod. xxi. 22 we have ἐπιζήμιον ζημιωθήσεται. The αὐτός is in favour of the latter.

αὐτὸς δὲ σωθήσεται. The αὐτός is in contrast to the μισθός: the reward will be lost, but the worker himself will be saved. If ζημιωθήσεται is regarded as indefinite, then αὐτός may be in contrast to the ἔργον: the man's bad work will perish, but that does not involve his perdition. The σωθήσεται can hardly refer to anything else than eternal salvation, which he has not forfeited by his bad workmanship: he has built on the true foundation. Salvation is not the μισθός, and so it may be gained when all μισθός is lost. But it may also be lost as well as the μισθός. The Apostle does not mean that every teacher who takes Christ as the basis of his teaching will necessarily be saved: his meaning is that a very faulty teacher may be saved, and 'will be saved, if at all, so as through fire.' See Augustine, *De Civ. Dei*, xxi. 21, 26.

οὕτως δὲ ὡς διὰ πυρός. 'But only as one passing through fire is saved': a quasi-proverbial expression, indicative of a narrow escape from a great peril, as 'a firebrand pluckt out of the fire' (Amos iv. 11; Zech. iii. 2). It is used here with special reference to the fire which tests the whole work (*v.* 13). The διά is local rather than instrumental. The fire is so rapid in its effects that the workman has to rush *through* it to reach safety: cf. δι' ὕδατος (1 Pet. iii. 20), and διήλθομεν διὰ πυρὸς καὶ ὕδατος (Ps. lxvi. 12). To explain σωθήσεται διὰ πυρός as meaning 'shall be kept alive in the midst of hell-fire' is untenable translation and monstrous exegesis. Such a sense is quite inadmissible for σωθήσεται and incompatible with οὕτως ὡς. Moreover, the fire in *v.* 13 is the fire alluded to, and that fire cannot be Gehenna. Atto of Vercelli thinks that this passage is one of the 'things hard to be understood' alluded to in 2 Pet. iii. 16. Augustine (*Enchir.* 68) says that the Christian who 'cares for the things of the Lord' (vii. 32) is the man who builds with 'gold, silver, and precious stones,' while he who 'cares for the things of the world, how he may please his wife' (vii. 33), builds with 'wood, hay, stubble.'

III. 16–17. The Temple.

St Paul now passes away from the builders to the Temple. The section is linked with *vv.* 10–15 both by the opening words, which imply some connexion, and by the word ναός, which is

doubtless suggested by the 'building' of *vv.* 9 f. (cf. Eph.
ii. 20–22). On the other hand, it is quite certain that there is
a change of subject : αὐτὸς σωθήσεται (*v.* 15) and φθερεῖ τοῦτον ὁ
Θεός are contradictory propositions, and they cannot be made
to apply to the same person, for φθείρειν cannot be attenuated
to an equivalent for ζημιοῦν (*v.* 15).

The subject of the σχίσματα still occupies the Apostle's mind,
and he seems to be thinking of their ultimate tendency. By
giving rein to the flesh (*v.* 3) they tend to banish the Holy
Spirit, and so to destroy the Temple constituted by His presence.

16. Οὐκ οἴδατε; Frequent in this Epistle, and twice in
Romans ; also Jas. iv. 4. As in v. 6, vi. 16, 19, the question
implies a rebuke. The Corinthians are so carnal that they
have never grasped, or have failed to retain, so fundamental a
doctrine as that of the indwelling of the Spirit.*

ναὸς Θεοῦ ἐστε. Not 'a temple of God,' but ' God's Temple.'
There is but one Temple, embodied equally truly in the whole
Church, in the local Church, and in the individual Christian ;
the local Church is meant here. As a metaphor for the Divine
indwelling, the ναός, which contained the Holy of Holies, is more
suitable than ἱερόν, which included the whole of the sacred enclosure (vi. 19 ; 2 Cor. vi. 16; Eph. ii. 21). To converts from
heathenism the ναός might suggest the *cella* in which the image
of the god was placed. It is one of the paradoxes of the Christian
Church that there is only one ναὸς Θεοῦ and yet each Christian
is a ναός : *simul omnes unum templum et singula templa sumus,
quia non est Deus in omnibus quam in singulis major* (Herv.).
Ναός is from ναίειν, 'to dwell.'

καὶ τὸ πνεῦμα. The καί is epexegetic. Both Gentile and Jew
might speak of their ναὸς Θεοῦ, but, while the pagan temple was
inhabited by an *image* of a god, and the Jewish by a *symbol* of
the Divine Presence (Shekinah), the Christian temple is inhabited
by the *Spirit* of God Himself.

ἐν ὑμῖν οἰκεῖ. 'In you hath His dwelling-place.' In Luke
xi. 51 we have οἶκος, where, in the parallel passage in Matt.
xxiii. 35, we have ναός. Τότε οὖν μάλιστα ἐσόμεθα ναὸς Θεοῦ, ἐὰν
χωρητικοὺς ἑαυτοὺς κατασκευάσωμεν τοῦ Πνεύματος τοῦ Θεοῦ (Orig.).

---

* On the very insufficient ground that Kephas is not mentioned in *vv.* 5
and 6, but is mentioned in *v.* 22, Zahn regards *vv.* 16–20 as directed against
the Kephas party. He says that St Paul knows more than he writes about
this faction, and fears more than he knows (*Introd. to N.T.* i. pp. 288 f.).

See on *v.* 1 for the resemblance to Ep. of Barn. iv. 11. Ignatius (*Eph.*
15) has πάντα οὖν ποιῶμεν, ὡς αὐτοῦ ἐν ἡμῖν κατοικοῦντος, ἵνα ὦμεν αὐτοῦ ναοὶ
καὶ αὐτὸς ἐν ἡμῖν Θεός.

It is not easy to decide between ἐν ὑμῖν οἰκεῖ (B P 17) and οἰκεῖ ἐν ὑμῖν (אACDEFGL, Vulg.). The former is more forcible, placing the 'permanent dwelling' last, with emphasis.

17. εἴ τις ... φθείρει ... φθερεῖ. The AV. greatly mars the effect by translating the verb first 'defile' and then 'destroy.' The same verb is purposely used to show the just working of the *lex talionis* in this case: one destruction is requited by another destruction. The destroyers of the Temple are those who banish the Spirit, an issue to which the dissensions were at least tending. Here the reference is to unchristian faction, which destroyed, by dividing, the unity of the Church: a building shattered into separate parts is a ruin. In vi. 19 the thought is of uncleanness in the strict sense. But all sin is a defiling of the Temple and is destructive of its consecrated state.* We have a similar play on words to express a similar resemblance between sin and its punishment in Rom. i. 28; καθὼς οὐκ ἐδοκίμασαν τὸν Θεὸν ἔχειν ἐν ἐπιγνώσει, παρέδωκεν αὐτοὺς ὁ Θεὸς εἰς ἀδόκιμον νοῦν. And there is a still closer parallel in Rev. xi. 18; διαφθεῖραι τοὺς διαφθείροντας τὴν γῆν. Neither φθείρειν nor διαφθείρειν are commonly used of God's judgments, for which the more usual verb is ἀπολλύειν or ἀπολλύναι: but both here and in Rev. xi. 18 φθείρειν or διαφθείρειν is preferred, because of its double meaning, 'corrupt' and 'destroy.' The sinner destroys by corrupting what is holy and good, and for this God destroys him. We have φθείρειν in the sense of corrupt, xv. 33; 2 Cor. xi. 3; Rev. xix. 2.

φθερεῖ τοῦτον ὁ Θεός. The Vulgate, like the AV., ignores the telling repetition of the same verb: *si quis autem templum Dei violaverit, disperdet illum Deus.* Tertullian (*Adv. Marc.* v. 6) preserves it: *si templum Dei quis vitiaverit, vitiabitur, utique a Deo templi;* and more literally (*De Pudic.* 16, 18) *vitiabit illum Deus.* But neither φθερεῖ here, nor ὄλεθρος in 1 Thess. v. 3, nor ὄλεθρον αἰώνιον in 2 Thess. i. 9, must be pressed to mean annihilation (see on v. 5). Nor, on the other hand, must it be watered down to mean mere physical punishment (cf. xi. 30). The exact meaning is nowhere revealed in Scripture; but terrible ruin and eternal loss of some kind seems to be meant. See Beet's careful examination of these and kindred words, *The Last Things*, pp. 122 f.

ἅγιός ἐστιν. It is 'holy,' and therefore not to be tampered with without grave danger. Both the Tabernacle and the Temple are frequently called ἅγιος, and in the instinct of archaic religion in the O.T. the idea of danger was included in that of

---

* This is a third case, quite different from the two cases in *vv* 14, 15. A good superstructure wins a reward for the builder. A bad superstructure perishes but the builder is rescued. But he who, instead of adding to the edifice, ruins what has been built, will himself meet with ruin.

'holiness.' See Gray on Num. iv. 5, 15, 19, 20, and Kirk patrick on 1 Sam. vi. 20 and 2 Sam. vi. 7; and cf. Lev. x. 6, xvi. 2, 13.

οἵτινές ἐστε ὑμεῖς. It has been doubted whether ναός or ἅγιος is the antecedent of οἵτινες, but the former is probably right : 'which temple ye are' (AV., RV.).* The relative is attracted into the plural of ὑμεῖς. Edwards quotes, τὸν οὐρανόν, οὓς δὴ πόλους καλοῦσιν (Plato, *Crat.* 405). The meaning seems to be, ' The temple of God is holy ; ye are the temple of God ; therefore ye must guard against what violates your consecration.' As distinct from the simple relative, οἵτινες commonly carries with it the idea of category, of belonging to a class ; 'and this is what ye are,' 'and such are ye': cf. Gal. v. 19, where the construction :s parallel.

Φθερεῖ (א A B C, d e f g Vulg.) rather than φθείρει (D E F G L P, Am.) where the difference between Greek and Latin in bilingual MSS. is remark- able : see on iv. 2.   τοῦτον (א B C L P) rather than αὐτόν (A D E F G).

III. 18–IV. 5. Warning against a mere 'Human' Estimate of the Pastoral Office.

Let no one profane God's Temple by taking on himself to set up party teachers in it. Regard us teachers as simply Christ's stewards.

[18] I am not raising baseless alarms ; the danger of a false estimate of oneself is grave. It may easily happen that a man imagines that he is wise in his intercourse with you, with the wisdom of the non-Christian world. Let him become simple enough to accept Christ crucified, which is the way to become really wise. [19] For this world's wisdom is foolishness in God's sight, as it stands written in Scripture, Who taketh the wise in their own craftiness; [20] and in another passage, The Lord knoweth the thoughts of the wise that they are vain. [21] If this is so, it is quite wrong for any one to plume himself on the men whom he sets up as leaders. For yours is no party-heritage ; it is universal. [22] Paul, Apollos, Kephas, the world, life, death, whatever is, and whatever is to be, all of it belongs to you ; [23] but you—you belong to no human leader; you belong to Christ, and Christ to God. Between you and God there is no human leader.

* We find the same thought, on a lower level, even in such a writer as Ovid (*Epp. ex Ponto*, II. i. 34) ; *quae templum pectore semper habet.*

IV. [1] The right way of regarding Apollos, myself, and other teachers, is that we are officers under Christ, commissioned to dispense the truths which His Father has revealed to us in Him, just as stewards dispense their masters' goods. [2] Here, furthermore, you must notice that all stewards are required to prove their fidelity. [3] But, as regards myself, it is a matter of small moment that my fidelity should be scrutinized and judged by you or by any human court. Yet that does not mean that I constitute myself as my own judge. [4] My judgments on myself would be inconclusive. For it may be the case that I have no consciousness of wrong-doing, and yet that this does not prove that I am guiltless. My conscience may be at fault. The only competent judge of my fidelity is the Lord Christ. [5] That being so, cease to anticipate His decision with your own premature judgments. Wait for the Coming of the Judge. It is He who will both illumine the facts that are now hidden in darkness, and also make manifest the real motives of human conduct: and then whatever praise is due will come to each faithful steward direct from God. That will be absolutely final.

The Apostle sums up his 'case' against the σχίσματα, combining the results of his exposure of the false 'wisdom,' with its correlative conceit, and of his exposition of the Pastoral Office (18–23). He concludes by a warning against their readiness to form judgments, from a mundane standpoint, upon those whose function makes them amenable only to the judgment of the Day of the Lord.

18. Μηδεὶς ἑαυτὸν ἐξαπατάτω. A solemn rebuke, similar to that of μὴ πλανᾶσθε in vi. 9, xv. 33, and Gal. vi. 7, and even more emphatic than that which is implied in οὐκ οἴδατε (v. 16). He intimates that the danger of sacrilege and of its heavy penalty (vv. 16, 17) is not so remote as some of the Corinthians may think. Shallow conceit may lead to disloyal tampering with the people of Christ. That there is a *sacrilegious* tendency in faction is illustrated by Gal. v. 7–12, vi. 12, 13; 2 Cor. xi. 3, 4, 13–15, 20; and the situation alluded to in Galatians may have been in the Apostle's mind when he wrote the words that are before us —words which have a double connexion, viz. with vv. 16, 17, and with the following section. St Paul is fond of compounds with ἐκ: v. 7, 13, vi. 14, xv. 34.

εἴ τις δοκεῖ σοφὸς εἶναι. Not, 'seemeth to be wise' (AV.), *videtur sapiens esse* (Vulg.); but, 'thinketh that he is wise' (RV.),

sibi videtur esse sapiens (Beza). He considers himself an acute
man of the world, quite able to decide for himself whether Paul,
or Apollos, or Kephas is the right person to follow in matters of
religion. We have the same use of δοκεῖ in viii. 2, x. 12, xiv. 37.
Excepting Jas. i. 26, εἴ τις δοκεῖ is peculiar to Paul ; and there
the AV. makes the same mistake as here, in translating 'seem'
instead of 'think.' Here ἐξαπατάτω, and there ἀπατῶν, may be
regarded as decisive. It is the man's *self-deceit* that is criticized
in both cases : his estimate is all wrong. See J. B. Mayor on
Jas. i. 26. It is perhaps not accidental that the Apostle says εἴ
τις . . . ἐν ὑμῖν, and not εἴ τις ὑμῶν. The warning suggests that
the self-styled σοφός is among them, but not that he is one of
themselves : the wrong-headed teacher has come from elsewhere.

ἐν ὑμῖν ἐν τῷ αἰῶνι τούτῳ. We might put a comma after ἐν
ὑμῖν, for the two expressions are in contrast ; 'in your circle,'
which has the heavenly wisdom and ought to be quite different
from what is 'in this world' and has only mundane wisdom.
The latter is out of place in a Christian society (i. 20, 22, ii. 6, 8).
Epictetus (*Enchir.* 18) warns us against thinking ourselves wise
when *others* think us to be such ; μηδὲν βούλου δοκεῖν ἐπίστασθαι·
κἂν δόξῃς τισιν εἶναί τις, ἀπίστει σεαυτῷ.

Cyprian (*Test.* iii. 69, *De bono patient.* 2) takes ἐν τῷ αἰῶνι τούτῳ with
μωρὸς γενέσθω : *mundo huic stultus fiat.* So also does Origen (*Cels.* i. 13 ;
Philoc. 18) ; and also Luther : *der werde ein Narr in dieser Welt.* This
makes good sense ; 'If any man thinks himself wise in relation to you
Christians, let him become a fool in relation to this world' : but it is not
the right sense. It is σοφός, not μωρός, that is qualified by ἐν τῷ αἰῶνι τ. :
'If any man thinks himself wise in your circle—I mean, of course, with this
world's wisdom.' From ἐν ὑμῖν, 'in a Christian Church,' it might have
been supposed that he meant the true wisdom, and he adds ἐν τ. αἰ. τ. to
avoid misunderstanding.

μωρὸς γενέσθω. 'Let him drop his false wisdom,' the conceit
that he has about himself : i. 18–20, 23, ii. 14.

ἵνα γένηται σοφός. So as to be brought 'unto all riches of
the full assurance of understanding, unto full knowledge of the
mystery of God, even Christ' (Col. ii. 3).*

19. He explains the paradox of the last verse by stating the
principle already established, i. 21, ii. 6.

παρὰ τῷ Θεῷ. 'Before God' as judge ; Rom. ii. 13, xii. 16 ;
Acts xxvi. 8. Although μωρός is common in N.T. and LXX,
μωρία occurs, in N.T., only in these three chapters ; and, in
LXX, only in Ecclus. xx. 31, xli. 15.

ὁ δρασσόμενος κ.τ.λ. From Job v. 13 ; a quotation independent of the LXX, and perhaps somewhat nearer to the

* Cf. Οὐαὶ οἱ συνετοὶ ἑαυτοῖς καὶ ἐνώπιον ἑαυτῶν ἐπιστήμονες : Barnabas
(iv. 11) quotes these words as γραφή.

original Hebrew. Job is quoted rarely in N.T., and chiefly by St Paul; and both here and in Rom. xi. 35, and in no other quotation, he varies considerably from the LXX. Like ὁ ποιῶν in Heb. i. 7, ὁ δρασσόμενος here is left without any verb. It expresses the strong grasp or 'grip' which God has upon the slippery cleverness of the wicked: cf. Ecclus. xxvi. 7, where it is said of an evil wife, ὁ κρατῶν αὐτῆς ὡς ὁ δρασσόμενος σκορπίου: and Ecclus. xxxiv. (xxxi.) 2, the man who has his mind upon dreams is ὡς δρασσόμενος σκιᾶς. The words in Ps. ii. 12 which are mistranslated 'Kiss the Son' are rendered in the LXX, δράξασθε παιδείας, 'Lay hold on instruction.' The verb occurs nowhere else in N.T., and in the LXX of Job v. 13 we have ὁ καταλαμβάνων.

πανουργία. 'Versatile cleverness,' 'readiness for anything' in order to gain one's own ends. 'Craftiness,' like *astutia* (Vulg.), emphasizes the cunning which πανουργία often implies. The LXX has ἐν φρονήσει, a word which commonly has a good meaning, while πανουργία almost always has a bad one, although not always in the LXX, *e.g.* Prov. i. 4, viii. 5. The adjective πανοῦργος is more often used in a better sense, and in the LXX is used with φρόνιμος to translate the same Hebrew word. Perhaps 'cleverness' would be better here than 'craftiness' (AV., RV.). See notes on Luke xx. 23; Eph. iv. 14.

20. Κύριος γινώσκει. From Ps. xciv. 11, and another instance (i. 20) of St Paul's freedom in quoting: the LXX, following the Hebrew, has ἀνθρώπων, where he (to make the citation more in point) has σοφῶν. But the Psalm contrasts the designs of men with the designs of God, and therefore the idea of σοφός is in the context.

διαλογισμούς. In the LXX the word is used of the thoughts of God (Ps. xl. 6, xcii. 5). When used of men, the word often, but not always, has a bad sense, as here, especially of questioning or opposing the ways of God (Ps. lvi. 5; Luke v. 22, vi. 8; Rom. i. 21; Jas. ii. 4).

21. ὥστε μηδεὶς καυχάσθω. Conclusion from *vv.* 18–20. The connexion presupposes an affinity between conceit in one's *own* wisdom and a readiness to make over much of a human leader. The latter implies much confidence in one's own estimate of the leader. Consequently, the spirit of party has in it a subtle element of shallow arrogance. We have ὥστε, 'so then,' with an imperative, iv. 5, x. 12, xi. 33, xiv. 39, xv. 58. Outside this argumentative and practical Epistle the combination is not very common; very rare, except in Paul. It seems to involve an abrupt change from the *oratio obliqua* to the *oratio recta*. It marks the transition from explanation to exhortation.

ἐν ἀνθρώποις. To 'glory in men' is the opposite of 'glorying in the Lord' (i. 31). The Apostle is referring to their wrong-headed estimation of himself, Apollos, and others (as in iv. 6), not to party-leaders boasting of their large following. Leaders might glory in the patience and faith of their disciples (2 Thess. i. 4), but not in that as any credit to the leaders themselves. All partizan laudation is wrong.

πάντα γὰρ ὑμῶν ἐστίν. 'You say, I belong to Paul, or, I belong to Apollos. So far from that being true, it is Paul and Apollos who belong to you, for *all* things belong to you.' Instead of contenting himself with saying 'We are yours,' he asserts that and a very great deal more; not merely πάντες, 'all servants of God,' but πάντα, 'all God's creatures,' belong to them. Yet his aim is, not merely to proclaim how wide their heritage is, but to show them that they have got the facts by the wrong end. They want to make him a chieftain; he is really their servant. The Church is not the property of Apostles; Apostles are ministers of the Church. *Quia omnia vestra sunt, nolite in singulis gloriari; nolite speciales vobis magistros defendere, quoniam omnibus utimini* (Atto). *Omnia propter sanctos creata sunt, tanquam nihil habentes et omnia possidentes* (Primasius).

The thought is profound and far-reaching. The believer in God through Christ is a member of Christ and shares in His universal lordship, all things being subservient to the Kingdom of God, and therefore to his eternal welfare (vii. 31; Rom. viii. 28; John xvi. 33; 1 John v. 4, 5), as means to an end. The Christian loses this birthright by treating the world or its interests as ends in themselves, *i.e.* by becoming enslaved to persons (vii. 23; 2 Cor. xi. 20) or things (vi. 12; Phil. iii. 19). Without God, we should be the sport of circumstances, and 'the world' would crush us, if not in 'life,' at least in 'death.' As it is, all these things alike 'are ours.' We meet them as members of Christ, rooted in God's love (Rom. viii. 37). The Corinthians, by boasting in men, were forgetting, and thereby imperilling, their prerogative in Christ. There is perhaps a touch of Stoic language in these verses; see on iv. 8. Origen points out that the Greeks had a saying, Πάντα τοῦ σοφοῦ ἐστίν, but St Paul was the first to say, Πάντα τοῦ ἁγίου ἐστίν.

22. εἴτε . . . εἴτε . . . εἴτε. The enumeration, rising in a climax, is characteristic of St Paul (Rom. viii. 38): the πάντα is first expanded and then repeated. We might have expected a third triplet, *past*, present, and future; but the past is not ours in the sense in which the present and future are. We had no part in shaping it, and cannot change it. In the first triplet, he places himself first, *i.e.* at the bottom of the climax.

εἴτε κόσμος. The transition from Kephas to the κόσμος is, as Bengel remarks, rather *repentinus saltus*, and made, he thinks, with a touch of impatience, lest the enumeration should become too extended. But perhaps alliteration has something to do with it. This Bengel spoils, by substituting 'Peter' for 'Kephas.' The 'world' is here used in a neutral sense, without ethical significance, the world we live in, the physical universe.

εἴτε ζωὴ εἴτε θάνατος. If κόσμος is the physical universe, it is probable that ζωή and θάνατος mean physical life and death. They sum up all that man instinctively clings to or instinctively dreads. From life and death in this general sense we pass easily to ἐνεστῶτα. It is by life in the world that eternal life can be won, and death is the portal to eternal life. In Rom. viii. 38 death is mentioned before life, and ἐνεστῶτα and μέλλοντα do not close the series.

εἴτε ἐνεστῶτα εἴτε μέλλοντα. These also ought probably to be confined in meaning to the things of this life. They include the whole of existing circumstances and all that lies before us to the moment of death. All these things 'are yours,' *i.e.* work together for your good. It is possible that μέλλοντα includes the life beyond the grave; but the series, as a whole, reads more consistently, if each member of it is regarded as referring to human experience in this world.

For ὑμῶν, ὑμεῖς, B and one or two cursives read ἡμῶν, ἡμεῖς. After ὑμῶν, D² E L, f g Vulg. Syrr. Copt. Arm. add ἐστίν.

23. ὑμεῖς δὲ Χριστοῦ. These words complete the rebuke of those who said that they belonged to Paul, etc. They belonged to no one but Christ, and they all alike belonged to Him. While all things were theirs, they were not their own (vi. 20, vii. 23), and none of them had any greater share in Christ than the rest (i. 13). Christians, with all their immense privileges, are not the ultimate owners of anything. There is only one real Owner, God. On the analogy between Χριστοῦ here and Καίσαρος = "belonging to the Emperor" in papyri see Deissmann, *Light from the Anc. East*, p. 382. Cf. xv. 23; Gal. iii. 29, v. 24.

Χριστὸς δὲ Θεοῦ. Not quite the same in meaning as Luke ix. 20, xxiii. 35; Acts iii. 18; Rev. xii. 10. In all those passages we have ὁ Χριστὸς τοῦ Θεοῦ or αὐτοῦ. Here Χριστός is more of a proper name. The thought of the Christian's lordship over the world has all its meaning in that of his being a son of God through Christ (Rom. viii. 16, 17). This passage is one of the few in which St Paul expresses his conception of the relation of Christ to God (see on ii. 16). Christ, although ἐν μορφῇ Θεοῦ ὑπάρχων (Phil. ii. 6, where see Lightfoot and Vincent), is so derivatively (Col. i. 15, where see Lightfoot and Abbott): His glory in His risen and exalted state is given by God (Phil. ii. 9; cf. Rom. vi. 10), and in the end is to be merged in God (see on xv. 28). Theodoret says here, οὐχ ὡς κτίσμα Θεοῦ, ἀλλ᾽ ὡς υἱὸς τοῦ Θεοῦ. There is no need to suppose, with some of the Fathers and later writers, that St Paul is here speaking of our Lord's human nature exclusively; there is no thought of separating the two natures; he is speaking of 'Christ,' the Divine Mediator in His relation to His Father and to His 'many brethren.' See many admirable remarks in Sanday, *Ancient and Modern Christologies*, on the doctrine of Two Natures in Christ, pp. 37, 50, 52, 90, 165, and especially p. 173; see also Edwards' and Stanley's notes *ad loc.*

IV. 1. Οὕτως ἡμᾶς λογιζέσθω. The thought of iii. 5 is resumed, and the reproof of the tendency to 'glory in men' is completed by a positive direction as to the right attitude towards the pastors of the Church. The Corinthians must regard them *ut ministros Christi, non ut aequales Christo* (Primasius). The οὕτως probably refers to what follows, as in iii. 15, ix. 26. The ἡμᾶς certainly refers to all who are charged with the ministry of the New Testament or Covenant (2 Cor. iii. 6). But we get good sense if we make οὕτως refer to what precedes; 'Remembering that we and everything else are yours, as you are Christ's, let a man take account of us as men who are ministers of Christ.' This throws a certain amount of emphasis on ἡμᾶς, the emphasis being removed from οὕτως: but ἡμᾶς may receive emphasis, for it is the attitude of the Corinthians towards the Apostle and other teachers that is in question.

ἄνθρωπος. Almost equivalent to τις (xi. 28), but a *gravior dicendi formula.* This use is rare in class. Grk.

ὑπηρέτας. Substituted for διάκονοι in iii. 5. The word originally denoted those who row (ἐρέσσειν) in the lower tier of a trireme, and then came to mean those who do anything under another, and hence simply 'underlings.'* In the Church, St Luke (i. 2) applies it to any service of the word; later it was used almost technically of sub-deacons. See on Luke iv. 20, and Suicer, *s.v.* St Paul uses the word nowhere else.

οἰκονόμους. The οἰκονόμος (οἶκος and νέμειν) was the responsible head of the establishment, assigning to each slave his duties and entrusted with the administration of the stores. He was a slave in relation to his master (Luke xii. 42), but the ἐπίτροπος or overseer (Matt. xx. 8) in relation to the workmen (see on Luke

---

* St Paul is probably not thinking of the derivation; 'Christ is the pilot; we are rowers under Him.' By Χριστοῦ he may mean 'not of any earthly master.'

xii. 42 and xvi. 1 ; in the latter place, the οἰκονόμος seems to be a freeman).   God is the Master (iii. 23) of the Christian household (1 Tim. iii. 15), and the stores entrusted to His stewards are the 'mysteries of God.'   These mysteries are the truths which the stewards are commissioned to teach (see on ii. 7).   Between the Master and the stewards stands the Son (xv. 25 ; Heb. iii. 6), whose underlings the stewards are.   See on οἰκονομίαν in Eph. i. 10 and Col. i. 25.

2. ὧδε.   'Here,' *i.e.* 'on earth and in human life,' or perhaps 'in these circumstances.'   See on i. 16 for λοιπόν.

ζητεῖται κ.τ.λ.   The AV. cannot be improved upon ; 'It is required in stewards that a man be found faithful.'   See on i. 10 for this use of ἵνα : the attempts to maintain its full 'telic' force here are too clumsy to deserve discussion : see further on v. 2, and compare εὑρεθῇ in 1 Pet. i. 7.

πιστός.   Cf. Luke xii. 42, xvi. 10 ; Num. xii. 7 ; 1 Sam. xxii. 14 : the meaning is 'trustworthy.'   To be an οἰκονόμος is not enough.*

ὧδε (א A B C D* F G P 17, e Vulg.) rather than ὃ δέ (D³ E L).   In Luke xvi. 25 there is a similar corruption in some texts.   ζητεῖται (B L, d e f g Vulg. Copt. Syrr.) rather than ζητεῖτε (א A C D P and F G -ητε).   Here, as in φθερεῖ (iii. 17), d e f g support the better reading against D E F G.   Lachmann takes ὧδε at the end of *v.* 1,—an improbable arrangement.

3. ἐμοὶ δέ.   The δέ implies contrast to something understood, such as 'I do not claim to be irresponsible ; inquiry will have to be made as to whether I am faithful ; but (δέ) the authority to which I bow is not yours, nor that of any human tribunal, but God's.'

εἰς ἐλάχιστόν ἐστιν.   'It amounts to very little,' 'it counts for a very small matter.'   Cf. εἰς οὐδὲν λογισθῆναι (Acts xix. 27).   He does not say that it counts for nothing.   "I have often wondered how it is that every man sets less value on his own opinion of himself than on the opinion of others.   So much more respect have we to what our neighbours think of us than to what we think of ourselves" (M. Aurelius, xii. 4).

ἵνα ἀνακριθῶ.   'To be judged of,' or 'to be put on my trial,' or 'to pass your tribunal' (see on ii. 14, 15).   The verb is neutral, and suggests neither a favourable nor an unfavourable verdict.   The dominant thought here, as in ii. 14, 15, is the competency of the tribunal.   The clause is almost equivalent to a simple infinitive, the ἵνα defining the purport of a possible volition, whether of, for, or against what is named.   He does

* Chadwick, *The Pastoral Teaching of St Paul*, p. 164 f.   He does not say 'be judged trustworthy,' but 'be found actually to be so.'   In 1 Pet. iv. 10 every Christian is a steward.

not mean that the Corinthians had thought of formally trying
him, but that he cares little for what public opinion may decide
about him.

ἡ ὑπὸ ἀνθρωπίνης ἡμέρας.   The phrase is in contrast to ἡ
ἡμέρα (iii. 13), which means the Day of the Lord, the Lord's
Judgment-Day.   That is the tribunal which the Apostle recognizes; a *human* tribunal he does not care to satisfy.   He may
have had in his mind the use of a word equivalent to 'day' in
the sense of a 'court,' which is found in Hebrew and in other
languages.*   'Daysman' in Job ix. 33 means 'arbitrator' or
'umpire': compare *diem dicere alicui*.   From *dies* comes *dieta* =
'diet'; and hence, in German, *Tag* = 'diet,' as in *Reichstag*,
Landtag.   'Man's judgment' (AV., RV.) gives the sense sufficiently.   Jerome is probably wrong in suggesting that the
expression is a 'Cilicism,' one of St Paul's provincialisms.
*Humanus dies dicitur in quo judicant homines, quia erit et dies
Domini, in quo judicabit et Dominus* (Herv.).   Atto says much
the same.

ἀλλ' οὐδὲ ἐμαυτὸν ἀνακρίνω.   'Nay, even my own verdict
upon my conduct, with the knowledge which I have of its
motives, is but a human judgment, incompetent definitely to
condemn (1 John iii. 20), and still more incompetent to acquit.' †
"We cannot fail to mark the contrast between this avowal of
inability to judge oneself and the claim made in ch. ii. on
behalf of the spiritual man, who judges all things.   Self-know-
ledge is more difficult than revealed truth" (Edwards): Ps.
xix. 12.

4. οὐδὲν γὰρ ἐμαυτῷ σύνοιδα.   'For (supposing that) I know
nothing against myself,' 'Suppose that I am not conscious of
any wrong-doing on my part.'   The Apostle is not stating a fact,
but an hypothesis; he was conscious of many faults; yet, even
if he were not aware of any, that would not acquit him.   Nowhere else in N.T. is the verb used *in this sense* (see Acts v. 2,
xii. 12, xiv. 6): it means to 'share knowledge,' and here to
'know about oneself' what is unknown to others.   It expresses
conscience in the *recording* sense.   As conscience can condemn
more surely than it can acquit, the word, when used absolutely,
has more frequently a bad sense, and hence comes to mean to
'be conscious of guilt': *nil conscire sibi, nulla pallescere culpa*

---

* Aesch. *in Ctes.* p. 587; Εἰς τρία μέρη διαιρεῖται ἡ ἡμέρα, ὅταν εἰσίῃ
γραφὴ παρανόμων εἰς τὸ δικαστήριον, where ἡ ἡμέρα means the time of the
trial.

† We might have expected ἀλλ' οὐδὲ αὐτὸς ἐμαυτὸν ἀνακρίνω, but the
meaning is clear.   He does not base his refusal to pass judgment on himself
on the difficulty of being impartial.   Such a judgment, however impartial and
just, could not be final, and therefore would be futile.

(Hor. *Ep.* i. i. 61) illustrates the same kind of meaning in the Latin equivalent. See on ἢ καί, Rom. ii. 15. The archaic 'I know nothing *by* myself' (AV.) has caused the words to be seriously misunderstood. In sixteenth-century English 'by' might mean 'against,' and means 'against' here. Latimer says, "Sometimes I say more *by* him than I am able to prove; this is slandering" (i. 518). Jonson, in the *Silent Woman*, "An intelligent woman, if she know *by* herself the least defect, will be most curious to hide it" (iv. 1), which is close to the use here. T. L. O. Davies (*Bible Words*, p. 81) gives these and other examples.*

ἀλλ' οὐκ ἐν τούτῳ. 'Nevertheless, not hereby,' 'But yet not in this fact,' 'not therefore.' This ἐν τούτῳ is frequent in St John, especially in the First Epistle and in connexion with γινώσκειν (John xiii. 35; 1 John ii. 3, 5, iii. 16, 19, 24, iv. 2, 13, v. 2), but also with other verbs (John xv. 8, xvi. 30). The οὐκ is placed away from its verb with special emphasis; *sed non in hoc* (Vulg.), *non per hoc* (Beza). Without difference of meaning, Ignatius (*Rom.* 5) has ἀλλ' οὐ π α ρ ὰ τοῦτο δεδικαίωμαι.

δεδικαίωμαι. 'Am I acquitted.' The word is used in a general sense, not in its technical theological sense. To introduce the latter here (Meyer, Beet, etc.) is to miss the drift of the passage, which deals, not with the question as to how man is justified in God's sight, but with the question as to who is *competent to sit in judgment* on a man's work or life. St Paul is not dealing with the question of his own personal 'justification by faith,' as though he said 'I am justified not by this, but in some other way': he is saying in the first person, what would apply equally to any one else, that an unaccusing conscience does not *per se* mean absence of guilt.

ὁ δὲ ἀνακρίνων με Κύριός ἐστιν. 'But he that judgeth me is the Lord,' *i.e.* Christ, as the next verse shows. The δέ goes back to οὐδὲ ἐμαυτὸν ἀνακρίνω, what intervenes being a parenthesis; 'not I myself, but our Lord, is the judge.'

5. ὥστε. With the imperative (see on iii. 21), 'So then.'

μή τι κρίνετε. 'Cease to pass any judgment,' or 'Make a practice of passing no judgment' (pres. imper.). The τι is a cognate accusative, such as we have in John vii. 24. 'As far as I am concerned, you may judge as you please, it is indifferent to me; but, as Christians, you should beware of passing any judgment on any one, until the Judge of all has made all things clear. All anticipation is vain.'

πρὸ καιροῦ. 'Before the fitting time,' or 'the appointed

---

* The use is perhaps not yet extinct in Yorkshire. "I know nothing *by* him" might still be heard for "I know nothing against him."

time,' when οἱ ἅγιοι τὸν κόσμον κρινοῦσιν (vi. 2). Καιρός has
no exact equivalent in English, French, or German. Cf. Matt.
viii. 29.

ἕως ἂν ἔλθῃ. The addition or omission of ἄν after ἕως in the
N.T. is somewhat irregular, and this fact precludes any sure
generalization as to particular shades of meaning. In later
Greek the force of ἄν is weakened, and therefore the difference
between its presence and absence is lessened. Here, not the
coming, but the time of it, is doubtful; 'till the Advent, whenever that may be.' See Milligan on 2 Thess. ii. 7, where there
is no ἄν, and Edwards here. In Rev. ii. 25, ἄχρι οὗ ἂν ἥξω, it is
doubtful whether ἥξω is fut. indic. or aor. subj. At the Day of
Judgment they will take part in judging (vi. 2, 3), with all the
facts before them.

ὃς καὶ φωτίσει. 'Who shall both throw light upon,' 'shall
illumine,' *lucem inferet in* (Beng.). But the difference between
'bringing light to' and 'bringing to light' is not great. The καί
is probably 'both,' not 'also'; but if 'also,' the meaning is, 'will
come to judge and also will illumine,' which is less probable.
Φωτίζω points to the *source* of the revelation.

τὰ κρυπτὰ τοῦ σκότους. *Abscondita tenebrarum* (Vulg.); *occulta
tenebrarum* = *res tenebris occultatas* (Beza). The genitive may be
possessive or characterizing, 'the hidden things which darkness
holds,' or 'the hidden things whose nature is dark.' The point
is, not that what will be revealed is morally bad, although that
may be suggested, but that hitherto they have been quite secret,
hidden, it may be, from the person's own conscience.

καὶ φανερώσει. Two things are necessary for an unerring
judgment of human actions,—a complete knowledge of the facts,
and full insight into the motives. These the Lord will apply
when He comes; and to attempt to judge men without these
indispensable qualifications is futile arrogance. Φανερόω points
to the *result* of the revelation.

καὶ τότε ὁ ἔπαινος. 'And *then*, and not till then, *the* measure of
praise that is due will come to each from God.' 'He will have
his praise' (RV.), what rightly belongs to him, which may be
little or none, and will be very different from the praise of
partizans here. We have the same thought in 2 Cor. x. 18;
Rom. ii. 29; and Clem. Rom. reproduces it, *Cor.* 30. Compare
μισθός, iii. 14, and ὁ μισθός, Rom. iv. 4, and see Hort on 1 Pet.
i. 7, p. 43.

ἀπὸ τοῦ Θεοῦ. At the end, with emphasis; the award is final,
as ἀπό intimates; there is no further court of appeal: and it is
from God that Christ has authority to judge the world (John
v. 27). Cf. 2 Esdr. xvi. 62–65. With ἑκάστῳ compare the fivefold
ἕκαστος in iii. 5–13.

D E F G, Aug. omit the ὅς before καί. D omits the τοῦ before Θεοῦ. The conjecture of ὑπό for ἀπό before τοῦ Θεοῦ has no probability of being right. Christ is the ὡρισμένος ὑπὸ τοῦ Θεοῦ κριτής (Acts x. 42) : cf. μέλλει κρίνειν τὴν οἰκουμένην ἐν ἀνδρὶ ᾧ ὥρισεν (Acts xvii. 31) : so that the judgments pronounced by Christ are ἀπὸ τοῦ Θεοῦ.

IV. 6–21. Personal Application of the foregoing Passage (III. 5–IV. 5), and Close of the Subject of the Dissensions.

My aim in all this is to correct party-spirit and conceit. Do compare your self-glorification with the humiliations of your teachers. This admonition comes from a father whom you ought to imitate. I really am coming to you. Is it to be in severity or in gentleness?

⁶ These comments I have modified in form, so as to apply to myself and Apollos, without including others, for you certainly have made party-leaders of him and me. And I have done this for your sakes, not ours, in order that by us as examples you may learn the meaning of the words, Go not beyond what is written ; in short, to keep any one of you from speaking boastfully in favour of the one teacher to the disparagement of the other. ⁷ For, my friend, who gives you the right to prefer one man to another and proclaim Paul and Apollos as leaders? And what ability do you possess that was not given to you by God? You must allow that you had it as a gift from Him. Then why do you boast as if you had the credit of acquiring it? ⁸ No doubt you Corinthians are already in perfect felicity ; already you are quite rich ; without waiting for us poor teachers, you have come to your kingdom! And I would to God that you had come to the Kingdom, that we also might be there with you! But we are far from that happy condition. For it seems to me that God has exhibited us His Apostles last of all, as men doomed to death are the last spectacle in a triumphal procession : for a spectacle we are become to the universe, to the whole amphitheatre of angels and men. ¹⁰ We poor simpletons go on with the foolishness of preaching Christ, while you in your relation to Him are men of sagacity. We feel our weakness ; you are so strong as to stand alone. You have the glory, and we the contempt. ¹¹ Up to this very moment we go hungry, thirsty, and scantily clothed ; we get plenty of hard blows and

have no proper home; [12] and we have to work hard with our
hands to earn our daily bread. Men revile us, and we bless
them ; they persecute us, and we are patient; they slander us,
and we merely deprecate. [13] We have been treated as the scum
of the earth, the refuse of society, and are treated so still.

[14] I am not writing in this tone to put you to shame : you are
my dearly loved children, and I am showing you where you are
wrong. [15] For you may have any number of instructors in Christ,
yet you have not more than one father : for in Christ Jesus it was
I, and no one else, who begat you through the Glad-tidings
which I brought you. [16] I have, therefore, the right to beseech
you to follow my steps. [17] And because I wish you to follow my
example, I have sent Timothy to you ; for he also is a child of
mine, dearly loved as you are, loyal and trusty in the Lord, and
he will bring back to your remembrance the simple and lowly
ways which I have as a Christian teacher, not only at Corinth,
but everywhere and in every Church. [18] Some of you boastfully
declared that my sending Timothy meant that I did not dare to
come myself; so they would do as they pleased. [19] But I do
mean to come, and that soon, to you, if the Lord pleases ; and
I will then take cognizance, not of what these inflated boasters
say, but of what they can do. Have they any spiritual power ?
[20] For the Kingdom of God is not a thing of words, but of
spiritual power. [21] Which is it to be then ? Am I to come to
you rod in hand, or in love and a spirit of gentleness ?

After a brief, plain statement of his purpose (6, 7) in the
preceding exposition of the Pastoral Office, the Apostle severely
rebukes the inflated glorying of his readers (8–13), and then, in
a more tender strain (14–16), but still not without sternness
(17–21), explains the mission of Timothy, the precursor of his
own intended visit.

6. Ταῦτα δέ. ' Now these things,' viz. the whole of the
remarks from iii. 5 onwards, the δέ introducing the conclusion
and application of the whole.

ἀδελφοί. As in i. 10, iii. 1.

μετεσχημάτισα. ' I put differently,' ' transferred by a figure ' ;
lit. ' altered the arrangement ' (σχῆμα). The Apostle means
that he used the names of Apollos and himself to illustrate a
principle which might, but for reasons of tact, have been more
obviously illustrated by other names. In LXX the verb is
found once (4 Mac. ix. 22), in N.T. in Paul only; of false

apostles fashioning themselves into Apostles of Christ, like Satan fashioning himself into an angel of light (2 Cor. xi. 13–15); and of the glorious change of our body of humiliation (Phil. iii. 21). The meaning here is different from both these, and the difference of meaning in the three passages turns upon the implied sense of σχῆμα in each case. See Lightfoot *ad loc.* and also on Phil. ii. 7 and iii. 21; Trench, *Syn.* § LXX.; Hastings, *DB.* II. p. 7. In the present passage there seems to be a reference to the *rhetorical* sense of σχῆμα (=*figura*) to denote a *veiled allusion*. The meaning here will be, 'I have transferred these warnings to myself and Apollos for the purpose of a covert allusion, and that for your sakes, that in our persons you may get instruction.' The μετασχημι ιτισμός, therefore, consists in putting forward the names of those not really responsible for the στάσεις instead of the names of others who were more to blame.*

ἐν ἡμῖν μάθητε. 'May learn in us as an object-lesson,' 'in our case may learn.' They could read between the lines.

τὸ μὴ ὑπὲρ ἃ γέγραπται. The article, as often, has almost the effect of inverted commas; 'the principle' or 'the lesson'— "Never go beyond," etc. The maxim is given in an elliptical form without any verb, as in *ne sutor ultra crepidam*: cf. v. 1, xi. 24; 2 Pet. ii. 22. Here, as elsewhere, some texts insert a verb in order to smooth the ellipse. By ἃ γέγραπται the Apostle means passages of Scripture such as those which he has quoted, i. 19, 31, iii. 19, 20. It is possible that there was a maxim of this kind current among the Jews, like μηδὲν ἄγαν among the Greeks. It is strange that any one should suppose that ἃ γέγραπται can refer to what St Paul himself has written or intends to write, or to the commands of our Lord.† It was perhaps a Rabbinical maxim.

ἵνα μὴ κ.τ.λ. This second ἵνα introduces the consequence expected from μάθητε, and so the ultimate purpose of μετεσχημάτισα, viz. to avoid all sectarian divisions. The proposal to take ἵνα in the local sense of 'where,' 'in which case,' '*wobei*,' may be safely dismissed. Even in class. Grk. this sense of ἵνα is chiefly poetical, and it is quite out of keeping with N.T. usage and with the context here. It is less easy to be certain whether φυσιοῦσθε is the present indicative, which would be very irregular after ἵνα, or an irregularly contracted subjunctive. Gal. iv. 17 is the only *certain* instance in N.T. of ἵνα with the

---

* That there was no jealousy or rivalry between St Paul and Apollos is clear from iii. 6, 8–10, xvi. 12. It is possible that it was the factious conduct of his partizans that drove Apollos from Corinth (Renan, *S. Paul*, p. 375).

† Rudolf Steck would refer this to Rom. xii. 3; an extraordinary conjecture.

present indicative; but some of the best editors admit it in John xvii. 3; Tit. ii. 4; 1 John v. 20. The double ἵνα is Pauline; Gal. iii. 14, iv. 5.

The sense is an expansion of 'glorying in men' (iii. 21): party-spirit, essentially egoist, cries up one leader at the expense of another leader. Some take ἑνός and ἑτέρου, not as leaders, but as members, of the respective parties. This is not the probable meaning. To cry up a favourite leader of your own choosing is to betray an inflated self-conceit. See on *v.* 18. With εἰς ὑπὲρ τοῦ ἑνός may be contrasted οἰκοδομεῖτε εἰς τὸν ἕνα (1 Thess. v. 11), where the opposite cause and effect are indicated, the union, which results from mutual edification. Here ὑπέρ means 'on behalf of' or 'in favour of.' We have a similar use of ὑπέρ and κατά in Rom. viii. 31. See Blass, § 45. 2.

For ἐν ἡμῖν, D 17, Copt. read ἐν ὑμῖν. ὑπὲρ ἃ (ℵ A B C P 17) is to be preferred to ὑπὲρ ὅ (D E F G L). After γέγραπται, ℵ³ D³ L P, Syrr. Copt. Arm. AV. insert φρονεῖν to avoid the ellipse: ℵ* A B D* E F G, Vulg. RV. omit. Some editors propose to omit τὸ μὴ ὑπὲρ ἃ γέγραπται as a marginal gloss. The sentence is intelligible without these words, but a gloss would have taken some other form. The φρονεῖν may come from Rom. xii. 3.

7. τίς γάρ σε διακρίνει; The γάρ introduces a reason why such conceit is out of place; 'For who sees anything special in you?' The verb has a variety of meanings (see Acts xv. 9 and on συνκρίνειν in ii. 13), and these meanings are linked by the idea of 'separate' in one sense or another: here it means to distinguish favourably from others. 'Who gives you the right to exalt one and depress another? No one has given you such a right: then do you claim it is an inherent right?' *Tu, qui amplius te accepisse gloriaris, quis te ab eo qui minus accepit separavit, nisi is qui tibi dedit quod alteri non dedit?* (Atto).

τί δὲ ἔχεις ὃ οὐκ ἔλαβες. The δέ adds another home-thrust, another searching question. 'Let us grant that you have some superiority. Is it inherent? You know that you have nothing but what you have received. Your good things were all of them *given* to you.' Origen suggests that the question may mean, 'Why do you pretend to have a gift which you have not received from God?' But he prefers the usual interpretation. The question is a favourite one with Cyril of Alexandria, who quotes it nine times in his commentary on St John.

εἰ δὲ καὶ ἔλαβες. 'But if thou *didst* receive it.' The καί throws an emphasis on ἔλαβες, and εἰ καί represents the insistence on what is fact (2 Cor. iv. 3, v. 16, xii. 11), while καὶ εἰ represents an assumed possibility; but it is not certain that this distinction always holds good in Paul.

It has been urged that the usual interpretation of ἔλαβες as

'received from God, the Giver of all good gifts' is not suitable
to the context; and that the Apostle means that such Christian
wisdom as the Corinthians possessed was not their own making,
but came to them through ministry of their teachers. But, after
iii. 5–7, 21 (cf. xii. 6, xv. 10), St Paul would not be likely to make
any such claim. The main point is, 'whatever superiority you
may have is not your own product, it was a gift'; and St Paul
was much more likely to mean that it was God's gift, than anything derived from himself and Apollos.

The question which he asks strikes deeper than the immediate
purpose of this passage. It is memorable in the history of
theology for the revolution which it brought about in the
doctrine of Grace. In A.D. 396, in the first work which he
wrote as a bishop, Augustine tells us: "To solve this question
we laboured hard in the cause of the freedom of man's will, but
the Grace of God won the day," and he adds that this text was
decisive (*Retract.* II. i. 1; see also *De divers. quaest. ad Simplici-
anum,* i.). Ten years before the challenge of Pelagius, the study
of St Paul's writings, and especially of this verse and of Rom.
ix. 16, had crystallized in his mind the distinctively Augustinian
doctrines of man's total depravity, of irresistible grace, and of
absolute predestination.

The fundamental thought here is that the teachers, about
whom the Corinthians 'gloried,' were but ministers of what was
the gift of God. The boasting temper implied forgetfulness of
this fact. It treated the teachers as exhibitors of rhetorical skill,
and as ministering to the *taste* of a critical audience, which was
entitled to class the teachers according to the preferences of this
or that hearer. Ἔλαβες here coincides with ἐπιστεύσατε in iii. 5.

8. The Apostle now directly attacks the self-esteem of his
readers in a tone of grave irony. 'You may well sit in judgment
upon us, from your position of advanced perfection, whence you
can watch us struggling painfully to the heights which you have
already scaled.' *Haec verba per ironiam dicta sunt: non enim
sunt affirmantis, sed indignantis, et commoti animi. Illos quippe
regnare, saturatos et divites factos, in quibus superius diversa vitia
et plures errores redarguit* (Atto). It spoils the irony of the
assumed concession to take the three clauses which follow as
questions (WH.). That the three argumentative questions
should be followed by three satirical affirmations is full of point.
Six consecutive questions would be wearisome and somewhat
flat.

ἤδη κεκορεσμένοι ἐστέ, ἤδη ἐπλουτήσατε, χωρὶς ἡμῶν ἐβασιλεύσατε.
The RV. might have given each of the three clauses a note
of exclamation. Some give one to the last, and it covers the

other two. It is evident that the three verbs form a climax, and
the last gives the key to the allusion. These highly blessed
Corinthians are already in the Kingdom of God, enjoying its
banquets, its treasures, and its thrones. The verbs stand for
the satisfaction of all desires in the Messianic Kingdom
(Luke xxii. 29, 30 ; 1 Thess. ii. 12 ; 2 Tim. ii. 12). The attitude
of the πεφυσιωμένοι amounted to a claim to be already in
possession of all that this Kingdom was to bring. They have
got a private millennium of their own. Like the ἤδη in the two
first clauses, χωρὶς ἡμῶν is emphatic. 'Without us, who taught
you all that you know of the Gospel, and who are still labouring
to enter the Kingdom, you are as Kings in the Kingdom.'
'Without us' does not mean 'without our aid,' but 'without our
company.' The contrast is between the fancied beatitude of the
Corinthians and the actual condition of the Apostles. The
Corinthians pose as perfected saints ; their teachers are still very
far indeed from perfection.*

In πλουτεῖν and βασιλεύειν we have a coincidence with the
language of the Stoics, as in iii. 21. There πάντα ὑμῶν ἐστίν has
parallels in Zeno and Seneca; *emittere hanc dei vocem, Haec
omnia mea sunt* (*De Benef.* VII. ii. 3). But, whether or no
St Paul is consciously using Stoic expressions, there is no
resemblance in meaning. The thought of victory over the
world by incorporation into Christ is far removed from that of
independence of the world through personal αὐτάρκεια. Here
again we have the difference between the true and the false
σοφία.

καὶ ὄφελόν γε ἐβασιλεύσατε. In this late Greek this un-
augmented second aorist has become a mere particle, an
exclamation to express a wish as to what might have happened,
but has not, or what might happen, but is not expected. Hence
it is followed by the indicative without ἄν. In LXX it is often
followed by the aorist, as here, especially in the phrase ὄφελον
ἀπεθάνομεν. In 2 Cor. xi. 1 and Gal. v. 12, as here, the wish
has a touch of irony. The γέ emphasizes the wish ; 'As far as
my feelings are concerned, would that your imaginary royalty
were real, for then our hard lot would be at an end.'

ἵνα . . . συνβασιλεύσωμεν. In ironical contrast to χωρὶς
ἡμῶν. 'You seem to have arrived at the goal far in front of us

---

* Chrysostom points out that "piety is insatiable." A Christian can
never be satisfied with his condition ; and for those who were as yet scarcely
beginners to suppose that they had reached the end, was childish.
Bachmann quotes the well-known Logion preserved by Clement of
Alexandria (704 ed. Potter, and found in a somewhat different form in
Oxyrhynchus papyri ; οὐ παύσεται ὁ ζητῶν ἕως ἂν εὕρῃ, εὑρὼν δὲ θαμβήσεται,
θαμβηθεὶς δὲ βασιλεύσει, βασιλεύσας δὲ ἐπαναπαύεται. See Deissmann, *Light,*
p. xiii.

poor teachers : indeed I wish that it were so, so that we might hope
to follow and share your triumph.' The only other place in
N.T. in which συνβασιλεύειν occurs is 2 Tim. ii. 12, where it is
used of reigning with Christ.

9. δοκῶ γάρ, ὁ Θεός . . . ἀπέδειξεν. 'For it seems to me,
God has set forth us, the Apostles, as last.' There is a great
pageant in which the Apostles form the ignominious finale, consisting of doomed men, who will have to fight in the arena till
they are killed. St Paul is thinking chiefly of himself; but, to
avoid the appearance of egoism, he associates himself with other
Apostles. Perhaps ἀπέδειξεν is used in a technical sense ; 'placed
upon the scene,' 'made a show of,' 'exhibited'; or, possibly,
'nominated,' 'proclaimed,' as if being doomed men was an
office or distinction : cf. ἐδέοντο ἀποδεῖξαί τινα αὐτῶν βασιλέα
(Joseph. *Ant.* vi. iii. 3). This latter meaning increases the
irony of the passage. In 2 Thess. ii. 4, ἀποδεικνύντα seems to
be used in this sense.

ὡς ἐπιθανατίους. The adjective occurs nowhere else in N.T. ;
but in LXX of Bel and the Dragon 31 it is used of the condemned conspirators who were thrown to the lions, two at a time,
daily ; τῶν ἐπιθανατίων σώματα δύο. Dionysius of Halicarnassus
(*A.R.* vii. 35), about B.C. 8, uses it of those who were thrown
from the Tarpeian rock. Tertullian (*De Pudic.* 14) translates it
here, *veluti bestiarios*, which is giving it too limited a meaning.
Cf. ἐθηριομάχησα, xv. 32. *Spectandos proposuit, ut morti addictos*
(Beza).*

ὅτι θέατρον ἐγενήθημεν. 'Seeing that we are become a
spectacle' ; explaining ' exhibited (or ' nominated ') us as doomed
men.' Here θέατρον = θέαμα : the place of seeing easily comes
to be substituted for what is seen there, and also for οἱ θεαταί, as
we say ' the house' for the audience or spectators. Cf. θεατριζό-
μενοι, *spectaculum facti* (Vulg. both there and here), Heb. x. 33.

τῷ κόσμῳ. 'The intelligent universe,' which is immediately
specified by the two anarthrous substantives which follow :
angels and men make up the κόσμος to which the Apostles are
a spectacle. See on xiii. 1. It is perhaps true to say that,
wherever angels are mentioned in N.T., good angels are always
meant, unless something is added in the context to intimate the
contrary, as in Matt. xxv. 41 ; 2 Cor. xii. 7 ; Rev. xii. 7, 9, etc.
Godet remarks here that of course *les mauvais ne sont pas exclus*,
and this is also the opinion of Augustine and Herveius.

---

* The Epistle contains a number of illustrations taken from heathen life ;
here and vii. 31, the theatre ; the idol-feasts, viii. 10, x. 20 ; racing and
boxing in the games, with a crown as a prize, ix. 24–27 ; the syssitia, x. 27 ;
the fighting with wild beasts, xv. 32.

Strangely enough, Atto supposes that St Paul means evil angels only. The Apostle thinks of the ἄγγελοι as wondering spectators of the vicissitudes of the Church militant here on earth (cf. Eph. iii. 19; 1 Pet. i. 12). Origen thinks of them as drawn to the strange sight of a man still clothed in flesh wrestling with principalities and powers, etc.

After δοκῶ γάρ, ℵ³ B³ D E L P add ὅτι : ℵ* A B* C D* F G omit.

10. ἡμεῖς μωροὶ . . . ὑμεῖς δὲ φρόνιμοι. *Est increpatio cum ironia* (Herv.). The three antitheses refer respectively to teaching, demeanour, and worldly position. The Apostles were 'fools on account of Christ' (2 Cor. iv. 11; Phil. iii. 7), because it was owing to their preaching Christ that the world regarded them as crazy (i. 23; Acts xxvi. 24). The Corinthians were 'wise in Christ,' because they maintained that as Christians they had great powers of discernment and possessed the true wisdom; διά in servos, ἐν in consortes convenit (Beng.): ταῦτα λέγων εἰρωνικῶς προέτρεπεν αὐτοὺς γενέσθαι φρονίμους ἐν Χριστῷ (Orig.). Cf. x. 15.

ὑμεῖς ἔνδοξοι, ἡμεῖς δὲ ἄτιμοι. The order is here inverted, not merely to avoid monotony, but in order to append to ἡμεῖς ἄτιμοι the clauses which expand it. Chiasmus is common in these Epistles (iii. 17, viii. 13, xiii. 2; 2 Cor. iv. 3, vi. 8, ix. 6, x. 12, etc.). Ἔνδοξος is one of the 103 words which are found only in Paul and Luke in N.T. (Hawkins, *Hor. Syn.* p. 191).

11. ἄχρι τῆς ἄρτι ὥρας. Their ἀτιμία is without respite, and is unbroken, up to the moment of writing. This is emphatically restated at the end of *v.* 13: privation, humiliation, and uttez contempt is their continual lot.

γυμνιτεύομεν. 'We are scantily clothed'; ἐν ψύχει καὶ γυμνό-τητι (2 Cor. xi. 27). The word generally means 'to go light-armed' (Plut., Dio. Cass.); it occurs nowhere else in N.T. or LXX, Cf. Jas. ii. 15, where γυμνός means 'scantily clad.'

κολαφιζόμεθα. 'We are buffeted,' 'are struck with the fist.' The verb is late, and probably colloquial (1 Pet. ii. 20; Mark xiv. 65; Matt. xxvi. 67). The substantive κόλαφος is said to be Doric = Attic κόνδυλος. The verb is possibly chosen rather than δέρειν (ix. 26; 2 Cor. xi. 20), or τύπτειν (Acts xxiii. 2), or ὑπωπιά-ζειν (ix. 26, 27), or κονδυλίζειν (Amos ii. 7; Mal. iii. 5), to mark the treatment of a *slave: velut servi; adeo non regnamus* (Beng.). Seneca, in the last section of the *Apocolocyntosis*, says that Caesar successfully claimed a man as his slave after producing witnesses who had seen the man beaten by Caesar *flagris, ferulis, colaphis.* In 2 Cor. xii. 7 the verb is used of the ἄγγελος Σατανᾶ, 'buffeting' the Apostle.

ἀστατοῦμεν. 'Are homeless,' 'have not where to lay our

head' (Matt. viii. 20; Luke ix. 58).   The verb occurs nowhere else in N.T. or LXX, but is used by Aquila for ἄστεγος in Isa. lviii. 7.   It certainly does not mean *instabiles sumus* (Vulg.), but *nusquam habemus sedem* (Primasius).   The Apostles *fugabantur ab infidelibus de loco in locum* (Atto); ἐλαυνόμεθα γάρ (Chrys.). Their life had no repose; they were vagrants, and were stigmatized as such.

γυμνιτεύομεν is accepted by all editors, L alone reading γυμνητεύομεν. Gregory, *Prolegomena* to Tisch., p. 81.

12. κοπιῶμεν ἐργ. τ. ἰδίαις χερσίν.   Again and again he mentions this (ix. 6; 2 Cor. xi. 7; 1 Thess. ii. 9; 2 Thess. iii. 8; cf. Acts xviii. 3, xx. 34).   See Knowling on Acts xviii. 3, Deissmann, *Light*, p. 317, and Ramsay, *St Paul*, pp. 34–36.   He had worked for his own living when he was at Corinth, and he was doing this at Ephesus at the time of writing.   He must maintain his independence.   *Graviter peccat, et libertatem arguendi amittit, qui ab eo aliquid accipit, qui propterea tribuit ne redarguat* (Atto). The plural may be rhetorical, but it probably includes other teachers who did the like.   Greeks despised manual labour; St Paul glories in it.

λοιδορούμενοι εὐλογοῦμεν, διωκόμενοι ἀνεχόμεθα.   He is perhaps not definitely alluding to the Lord's commands (Matt. v. 44; Luke vi. 27), but he is under their influence.   Here again, Greek prejudice would be against him.   In the preliminary induction which Aristotle (*Anal. Post.* II. xii. 21) makes for the definition of μεγαλοψυχία, he asks what it is that such μεγαλόψυχοι as Achilles, Ajax, and Alcibiades have in common, and answers, τὸ μὴ ἀνέχεσθαι ὑβριζόμενοι.   In his full description (*Eth. Nic.* IV. iii. 17, 30), of the high-minded man, he says that he πάμπαν ὀλιγωρήσει the contempt of others, and that he is not μνησίκακος; but this is because he is conscious that he never deserves ill, and because he does not care to bear anything, good or ill (and least of all ill), long in mind.   Just as the Greek would think that the Apostle's working with his own hands stamped him as βάναυσος, so he would regard his manner of receiving abuse and injury as fatal to his being accounted μεγαλόψυχος; he must be an abject person.

13. δυσφημούμενοι.   In 1 Mac. vii. 41 the verb is used of the insults of Rabshakeh as the envoy of Sennacherib, but it is not found elsewhere in N.T.

παρακαλοῦμεν.   'We deprecate,' *obsecramus* (Vulg.).   The verb is very frequent in N.T., with many shades of meaning, radiating from the idea of 'calling to one's side' in order to speak privately, to gain support.   Hence such meanings as 'exhort,' 'entreat,' 'instruct,' 'comfort.'   'Exhort' is certainly

not the meaning here, as if insulting language was requited with
a sermon ; yet Origen and Basil seem to take it so.   To give the
soft answer that turns away wrath (Prov. xv. 1) may be right, but
it is not a common meaning of παρακαλεῖν. Tyndale and other
early versions have 'we pray,' which again is not the meaning, if
'pray' means 'pray to God.'*

ὡς περικαθάρματα. The uncompounded κάθαρμα is more
common in both the senses which the two forms of the word
have in common.   These are (1) 'sweepings,' rubbish, and, (2)
as in Prov. xxi. 18, 'scapegoats,' *i.e.* victims, *piacula, lustramina*,
used as *expiationis pretium*, to avert the wrath of the gods.   At
Athens, in times of plague or similar visitations, certain outcasts
were flung into the sea with the formula, περίψημα ἡμῶν γένου
(Suidas), to expiate the pollution of the community.   These were
worthless persons, and hence the close connexion between the
two meanings.   Demosthenes, in the *De Corona*, addresses
Aeschines, ὦ κάθαρμα, as a term of the deepest insult.   It is not
quite certain which of the two meanings is right here ; nor does
the coupling with περίψημα settle the matter, for that word also
is used in two similar senses.   Godet distinguishes the two words
by saying that περικαθάρματα are the dust that is swept up from
a floor and περίψημα the dirt that is rubbed or scraped off an
object.   Neither word occurs elsewhere in N.T.   On the whole,
it is probable that neither word has here the meaning of 'scapegoat' or 'ransom' (ἀπολύτρωσις): and in Tobit v. 18 περίψημα
is probably 'refuse' (AV., RV.).   See Lightfoot on περίψημα
(Ign. *Eph.* 8), and Heinichen on Eus. *H.E.* vii. xxii. 7, *Melet.*
xv. p. 710, who shows that in the third century περίψημά σου
had become a term of formal compliment, 'your humble and
devoted servant.'   See *Ep. Barn.* 4, 6.

τοῦ κόσμου . . . πάντων. Whatever the meaning of the two
words, these genitives give them the widest sweep, and πάντων is
neuter (AV., RV.), unless the meaning of 'scapegoat' is given
to περίψημα.†

δυσφημούμενοι (א* A C P 17) rather than βλασφημούμενοι (א B D E F
G L).   The internal evidence turns the scale.   It is more probable that
the unusual δυσφ. would be changed to the common βλασφ. than *vice
versa*.

14. Οὐκ ἐντρέπων ὑμᾶς.   The severity of tone ends as abruptly
as it began (*v.* 8).   *Aspera blandis mitigat, ut salutaris medicus.*

* Plato (*Crito* 49) puts into the mouth of Socrates ; "We ought not to
retaliate or render evil for evil to any one, whatever evil we may have suffered
from him. . . . Warding off evil by evil is never right."   But returning good
for evil goes far beyond that.
† Tertullian and the Vulgate transliterate, *peripsema* ; Beza has *sordes,*
Luther *Fegopfer* (*Auswurf*).

These sudden changes of tone are much more common in Paul than in other N.T. writers. The section that follows (14–21), with its mingled tenderness and sternness—both alike truly paternal, forms a worthy colophon to the whole discussion of the σχίσματα. The root-meaning of ἐντρέπειν is perhaps 'to turn in,' and so to make a person 'hang his head,' as a sign, either of reverence (Matt. xxi. 37; Luke xviii. 2, 4; Heb. xii. 9) or of shame, as here (cf. ἐντροπή, vi. 5, xv. 34). In these senses it is frequent in late writers, in LXX, and in Paul. The participle expresses the spirit in which the Apostle writes ; 'not as shaming you,' 'not as making you abashed.' What he had written might well 'make them hang their heads,' but to effect that was not his purpose in writing; he wrote to bring home to their hearts a solemn fatherly warning.

νουθετῶν. The duty of a parent, as appears from Eph. vi. 4.* Excepting in a speech of St Paul (Acts xx. 31), νουθετεῖν and νουθεσία do not occur in N.T. outside the Epistles of St Paul, and they cover all four groups. Νουθετεῖν, 'to put in mind,' has always a touch of sternness, if not of blame ; 'to admonish,' or 'warn.' We have νουθετεῖν τοὺς κακῶς πράσσοντας (Aesch. Pr. 264), and νουθετεῖν κονδύλοις (Aristoph. Vesp. 254). Plato (Gorg. 479a) combines it with κολάζειν. See Abbott on Eph. vi. 4 and Col. i. 28.

νουθετῶν (א A C P 17, RV.) rather than νουθετῶ (B D E F G L, Vulg. AV.) ; but the evidence is not decisive. Lachm. and Treg. prefer νουθετῶ.

15. ἐὰν γάρ. The reason for his taking on himself this duty ; 'If, as time goes on, ye should have in turn an indefinite number of tutors in Christ, yet ye *will* never *have had* but one father.' The conditional clause, with a pres. subjunct. and ἄν, in the protasis implies futurity as regards the apodosis. As there is but one planting and one laying of the foundation-stone (iii. 6, 10), so the child can have but one father.

παιδαγωγοὺς . . . ἐν Χριστῷ. The words are closely connected. Without ἐν Χριστῷ to qualify it, παιδαγωγούς would have been too abrupt, if not too disparaging. There is no hint that they have already had too many. The παιδαγωγός (Gal. iii. 24) was not a teacher, but the trusty slave who acted as tutor or guardian and escorted them to and from school, and in general *took care* of those whom the father had *begotten*.† He might be

* Cf. τούτους ὡς πατὴρ νουθετῶν ἐδοκίμασας (Wisd. xi. 10), and νουθετήσει δίκαιον ὡς υἱὸν ἀγαπήσεως (Pss. Sol. xiii. 8). Excepting Timothy (v. 17 ; 2 Tim. i. 2), St Paul nowhere else calls any one τέκνον ἀγαπητόν. *Spiritualis paternitas singularem necessitudinem et affectionem conjunctam habet, prae omni alia propinquitate* (Beng.).

† See Ramsay, *Galatians*, p. 383 ; Smith, *Dict. of Ant.* ii. p. 307. The same usage is found in papyri.

more capable, and even more affectionate, than the father, but he could never become father. The frequent ἐν Χριστῷ gives "the ideal sphere of action" (Ellicott).*

ἀλλ' οὐ πολλοὺς πατέρας. 'Still (viii. 7) not many fathers.' The verb to be understood must be future, for the possibility of μυρίοι παιδαγωγοί is future : 'however many these may be, yet ye will not have (or, have had) many fathers.'

ἐν γὰρ Χριστῷ 'I. The whole process, first and last, is ἐν Χριστῷ.† That was the sphere, while the Gospel was the means (διὰ τοῦ εὐαγγ.). The two pronouns, ἐγὼ ὑμᾶς, are in emphatic proximity; 'whoever may have been the parent of other Churches, it was I who in Christ begat you.' The thought is that of ἐγὼ ἐφύτευσα (iii. 6) and of θεμέλιον ἔθηκα (iii. 10), while the παιδαγωγοί are those who water the plant, or build the superstructure.

16. παρακαλῶ οὖν. 'Therefore, as having the right to do so, I call upon my children to take after their father.' *Si filii estis, debitum honorem debetis impendere patri, et imitatores existere* (Atto). Cf. 1 Thess. i. 6, 7, ii. 7, 11.

μιμηταί μου γίνεσθε. 'Show yourselves imitators of me'; 'by your conduct prove your parentage.' Here and xi. 1 (see note there), 'imitators' rather than 'followers' (AV.). The context shows the special points of assimilation, viz. humility and self-sacrifice (*vv.* 10–13). In Phil. iii. 17 we have συνμιμηταί. The charge is not given in a spirit of self-confidence. He has received the charge to lead them, and he is bound to set an example for them to follow, but he takes no credit for the pattern (xi. 1).

17. Διὰ τοῦτο. 'Because I desire you to prove imitators of me, I sent Timothy, a real son of mine in the Lord, to allay the contrary spirit among you.' Timothy had probably already left Ephesus (Acts xix. 22), but was at work in Macedonia, and would arrive at Corinth later than this letter (Hastings, *DB.* i. p. 483). It is not stated in Acts that Corinth was Timothy's ultimate destination, but we are told that the Corinthian Erastus (Rom. xvi. 23) was his companion on the mission. It is not clear whether ἔπεμψα is the ordinary aorist, 'I sent' or 'have sent,' or the epistolary aorist, 'I send.' Deissmann, *Light*, p. 157.

τέκνον. 'Child' in the same sense as ἐγέννησα (*v.* 15). St Paul had converted him (Acts xvi. 1), on his visit to Lystra (Acts xiv. 7; cf. 1 Tim. i. 2, 18; 2 Tim. i. 2). This ἀγαπητὸν καὶ πιστὸν τέκνον was fittingly sent to remind children who were equally beloved, but were not equally faithful, of their duties towards the Apostle who was the parent of both. The first

* Findlay quotes *Sanhedrin*, f. xix 2 ; "Whoever teaches the son of his friend the Law, it is as if he had begotten him."

† See Deissmann, *Die neutestamentliche Formel "in Christo Jesu."*

ὅς gives the relation of Timothy to the Apostle, the second his relation to the Corinthians; ὁ ἀδελφός (2 Cor. i. 1) gives his relation to all Christians. His sparing this beloved child was proof of his love for them; 1 Thess. iii. 1, 2.

ἀναμνήσει. λήθην δὲ αὐτῶν ὁ λόγος κατηγορεῖ (Orig.). They had forgotten much of what St Paul had taught them in person· εἰ κατέχετε (xv. 2).

τὰς ὁδούς μου. The real Apostle had been superseded in their imagination by an imaginary Paul, the leader of a party. His 'ways' are indicated i. 17, ii. 1–5, iv. 11–13, ix. 15, 22, 27.

καθὼς πανταχοῦ ἐν πάσῃ ἐκ. 'Exactly as everywhere in every Church.' There is a general consistency in the Apostle's teaching, and Timothy will not impose any special demands upon the Corinthians, but will only bring them into line with what St Paul teaches everywhere. This is one of several passages which remind the Corinthians that they are only members of a much greater whole (see on i. 2). They are not the whole Church, and they are not the most perfect members. On the other hand, no more is required of them than is required of other Christians.

After διὰ τοῦτο, ℵ A P 17 add αὐτό: ℵ* B C D E F G L omit.   μου τέκνον (ℵ A B C P 17) rather than τέκνον μου (D E F G L).   After ἐν Χριστῷ, D* F G add Ἰησοῦ: A B D³ E L P omit.

18. Ὡς μὴ ἐρχομένου δέ μου. Some of them boastfully gave out; 'Timothy is coming in his place; Paul himself will not come.' The δέ marks the contrast between this false report and the true purpose of Timothy's mission.

ἐφυσιώθησάν τινες. *Vitium Corinthiis frequens, inflatio* (Beng.); v. 6, 19, v. 2, viii. 1.* The tense is the natural one to use, for St Paul is speaking of definite facts that had been reported to him. He cannot use the present tense, for he is ignorant of the state of things at the time of writing. But by using the aorist he does not imply that the evil is a thing of the past, and therefore 'are puffed up' (AV., RV.), *inflati sunt* (Vulg.), may be justified. There is nothing to show whether he knew who the τινες were (cf. xv. 12; Gal. i. 7). Origen suggests that ὁ θεσπέσιος Παῦλος does not mention any one, because he foresaw that the offenders would repent, and there was therefore no need to expose them. They are probably connected with the more definite and acrimonious opponents of 2 Cor. x. 1, 7, 10, xi. 4, where a leader, who is not in view in this Epistle, has come on the scene.

19. ἐλεύσομαι δὲ ταχέως. He intends remaining at Ephesus

* The verb is peculiar to Paul in N.T., and (excepting Col. ii. 18) is peculiar to this Epistle.

till Pentecost (xvi. 8). His plans, and changes of plan, and the charges made against him about his proposed visit, are discussed in 2 Cor. i. 15, 16, 23.

ἐὰν ὁ Κύριος θελήσῃ. A solemn touch; cf. xvi. 7; Jas. iv. 15. It is impossible, and not very important, to decide whether ὁ Κύριος means our Lord or the Father. Our Lord has just been mentioned; on the other hand, in connexion with θέλειν or θέλημα, God is commonly meant. We have a similar doubt 1 Thess. iii. 12.

γνώσομαι οὐ τ. λόγον . . . ἀλλὰ τ. δύναμιν. 'Their words I shall ignore; they proceed from persons whose heads are turned with conceit; but their power I shall put to the proof.' This, as Godet remarks, is the language of a judge who is about to conduct a trial. 'The power' certainly does not mean that of working miracles (Chrys.); but rather that of winning men over to a Christian life. In ii. 4, 5 we had the antithesis between λόγος and δύναμις in a different form.

For τῶν πεφυσιωμένων, L has τὸν πεφυσιόμενον: some cursives and Origen support the reading, but no editors adopt it. Before these words F inserts αὐτῶν.

20. ἡ βασιλεία τ. Θεοῦ. This expression has three meanings in the Pauline Epistles: (1) the future Kingdom of God, when God is 'all in all' (xv. 28); akin to this (2) the mediatorial reign of Christ, which is the Kingdom of God in process of development; and so, as here (and see Rom. xiv. 17), we have (3) the inward reality which underlies the external life, activities, and institutions of the Church, in and through which the Kingdom of Christ is realizing itself. In the externals of Church life, 'word' counts for something, but 'power' alone is of account in the sight of God.* By 'power' is meant spiritual power: see on ii. 5.

21. ἐν ῥάβδῳ. Exactly as in 1 Sam. xvii. 43, σὺ ἔρχῃ ἐπ' ἐμὲ ἐν ῥάβδῳ καὶ λίθοις; and 2 Sam. vii. 14, ἐλέγξω αὐτὸν ἐν ῥαβδῳ καὶ ἐν ἀφαῖς: where the ἐν means 'accompanied by' or 'provided with.' Cf. Heb. ix. 25, ἐν αἵματι ἀλλοτρίῳ. 'To lift up his hand with a sling-stone,' ἐπᾶραι χεῖρα ἐν λίθῳ σφενδόνης (Ecclus. xlvii. 5). Abbott (*Johan. Gr.* 2332) gives examples from papyri. The idea of environment easily passes into that of equipment. Cf. Stat. *Theb.* iv. 221, *Gravi metuendus in hasta*; and Ennius, *levesque sequuntur in hasta.* The rod is that of spiritual rebuke and discipline; cf. οὐ φείσομαι (2 Cor. xiii. 3). It is strange that any one should contend, even for controversial purposes, such as defence of the temporal power, that a literal

* See *Regnum Dei*, the Bampton Lectures for 1901, pp. 47–61, in which St Paul's views of the Kingdom are examined in detail.

rod is meant. But cf. Tarquini, *Juris eccles. inst.* p. 41, 19th ed. An allusion to the lictor's rod is not likely.*

ἔλθω. Deliberative subjunctive; 'Am I to come?' It is possible to make the verb dependent upon θέλετε, but it is more forcible to keep it independent (AV., RV.). Cf. ἐπιμένωμεν τῇ ἁμαρτίᾳ; (Rom. vi. 1).

ἐν ἀγάπῃ. The preposition here is inevitably ἐν, and it was probably the antithesis with ἐν ἀγάπῃ that led to the expression ἐν ῥάβδῳ here, just as the bear-skin led to Virgil's *Horridus in jaculis*, the rest of the line being *et pelle Libystidis ursae* (*Aen.* v. 37).

πνεύματί τε πραΰτητος. *Either* 'the Spirit of meekness.' *i.e.* the Holy Spirit, manifested in one of His special gifts or fruits (Gal. v. 23), *or* 'a spirit of meekness,' *i.e.* a disposition of that character (cf. 2 Cor. iv. 13). The latter would be inspired by the Holy Spirit (Rom. viii. 5). The absence of the article is in favour of the latter here. Contrast τὸ πνεῦμα τῆς ἀληθείας (John xiv. 17, xvi. 13) with πνεῦμα σοφίας (Eph. i. 17), and see J. A. Robinson, *Ephesians*, pp. 38, 39, and the note on πνεῦμα ἁγιωσύνης (Rom. i. 4). Had the Apostle meant the Holy Spirit, he would probably have written ἐν τῷ πν. τῆς πρ. By πραΰτης is meant the opposite of 'harshness' or 'rudeness.' Trench, *Syn.* §§ xlii., xliii., xcii.; Westcott on Eph. iv. 2.

πραΰτητος (A B C 17) rather than πραότητος (א D E F G P). In Gal. v. 23, א joins A B C in favour of πραΰτης. In Eph. iv. 2, א B C 17 support πραΰτης, in 2 Cor. x. 1, א B F G P 17 do so, in Col. iii. 12, א A B C P 17. Lachmann, following Oecumenius and Calvin, makes iv. 21 the beginning of a new paragraph: it is a sharp, decisive dismissal of the subject of the σχίσματα.

V. 1–13. ABSENCE OF MORAL DISCIPLINE.

There is a case of gross immorality among you, and your attitude towards it is distressing. Have no fellowship with such offenders.

¹ It is actually notorious among you that there is a case of unchastity of a revolting character, a character so revolting as not to occur even among the heathen, that a man should have his step-mother as his concubine. ² And you, with this monstrous crime among you, have gone on in your inflated self-complacency, when you ought rather to have been overwhelmed with grief,

* This has been suggested by Dr. E. Hicks, *Roman Law in the N.T.* p. 182. But the rod as a metaphor for correction is common enough (Job ix. 34, xxi. 9; Ps. lxxxix. 32; Isa. x. 5, etc.).

that it should have become necessary that the person who was guilty of this dreadful offence should be removed from your midst.   ³ As for my view of it, there must be no uncertainty. Although absent in body yet present in spirit, I have already pronounced the sentence, which I should have pronounced had I been present, on the man who has perpetrated this enormity. ⁴ In the Name of our Lord Jesus, when you are all assembled in solemn congregation and my spirit is with you armed with the effectual power of our Lord Jesus, ⁵ I have given sentence that such an offender is to be handed over to Satan for the destruction by suffering of the flesh in which he has sinned, so that his spirit may be saved in the Day of the Lord.   ⁶ Your glorying is not at all to your credit.   Do you really not know that a very little leaven affects the whole lump of dough?   ⁷ You must entirely cleanse away the old leaven, if you are to be (as, of course, as Christians you are) as free from leaven as a new lump of dough.   You are bound to make this new start for many reasons ; and above all, because Christ, our spotless Paschal Lamb, has been sacrificed, and therefore everything which corrupts must be put away.   ⁸ Consequently we should keep our feast, not with leaven from our old lives, nor yet with leaven of vice and wickedness, but with bread free from all leaven, the bread of unsullied innocence and truth.

⁹ I said to you in my letter that you were not to keep company with fornicators.   ¹⁰ I did not exactly mean that you were to shun all the fornicators of the non-Christian world, any more than all the cheats, or extortioners, or idolaters.   That would mean that you would have to go out of the world altogether.   ¹¹ What I meant was, that you were not to keep company with any one who bears the sacred name of Christian and yet is given to fornication, or cheating, or idolatry, or abusive language, or hard drinking, or extortion ;—with such a man you must not even share a meal.   ¹² Of course I did not refer to those who are not Christians ; for what right have I to sit in judgment on them?   I confine my judgments to those who are in the Church.   ¹³ Do not you do the same?   Those who are outside it we leave to God's judgment.   Only one practical conclusion is possible.   Remove the wicked person from among you.

The Apostle now comes to the second count of his indictment. It is not merely that a particularly flagrant case of immorality has occurred. That this should happen at all is bad enough. But what makes it far worse is the way in which it is taken by the community. Their morbid and frivolous self-conceit is untroubled. They have shown no sign of proper feeling: still less have they dealt with the case, as they ought to have done, by prompt expulsion (*vv.* 1–5). In view of the infectiousness of such evil, they ought to eliminate it, as leaven from a Jewish house at the Passover (6, 7); for the life of the Christian community is a spiritual Passover (8). His previous warning has been misunderstood. It means that for grave and scandalous sins a Christian must be made to suffer by isolation; and this, in the case in question, must be drastically enforced (9–13).

The passage is linked to the section dealing with the σχίσματα by the spiritual disorder (τὸ φυσιωθῆναι) which, according to St Paul's diagnosis, lies at the root of both evils. Inordinate attention to external differences, and indifference to vital questions of morality, are both of them the outcome of self-satisfied frivolity. But the passage is more obviously linked with ch. vi., and especially with the subject of πορνεία which occupies its last portion (vi. 12–20).

This indictment, following upon iv. 21 without any connecting particle, bursts upon the readers like a thunder-clap.

1. Ὅλως. Not 'commonly' (AV.), but 'actually' (RV.). The word means 'altogether,' 'most assuredly,' 'incontrovertibly'; or, with a negative, 'at all.' Such a thing *ought not* to be heard of *at all* (exactly as in vi. 7; cf. xv. 29), and it is matter of common talk: ὅλως *nulla debebat in vobis audiri scortatio; at auditur* ὅλως (Beng.).

ἀκούεται ἐν ὑμῖν. The ἐν ὑμῖν grammatically localizes the report, but in effect it localizes the offence: it was among them that the rumour was circulating, because in their midst the sin was found: 'unchastity is reported [as existing] among you.' The report may have reached the Apostle through the same channel as that which brought information about the factions (i. 11), or through Stephanas (xvi. 17). The weight of the Apostle's censure falls, not upon the talk about the crime within the community, but upon its occurrence, and the failure to deal with it.

πορνεία. Illicit sexual intercourse in general. In Rev. xix 2, as in class. Grk., it means prostitution: in Matt. v. 32, xix. 9

it is equivalent to μοιχεία, from which it is distinguished Matt.
xv. 19 and Mark vii. 21 : cf. Hos. iii. 3 ; Ecclus. xxiii. 23, where
we have ἐν πορνείᾳ ἐμοιχεύθη.

καὶ τοιαύτη. 'And of so monstrous a character as does not
exist even among the heathen.' The οὐδέ intensifies ἐν τοῖς
ἔθνεσιν, and ἀκούεται is not to be understood : 'is not so much
as named among the Gentiles' (AV.) is wrong, based on a
wrong reading. Cf. *novum crimen et ante hunc diem inauditum*
(Cic. *Pro Lig.* i. 1) ; and *scelus incredibile et praeter hanc unam in
hac vita inauditum* (*In Cluent.* 6), of Sassia's marriage with her
son-in-law, Melinus.*

ὥστε γυναῖκά τινα τοῦ πατρὸς ἔχειν. The placing of τινα
between γυναῖκα and πατρός throws emphasis on to these two
words (Blass, *Gr.* § 80, 2). Chrysostom suggests that St Paul
uses γυναῖκα του πατρός rather than μητρυιάν in order to emphasize
the enormity. More probably, he chooses the language of
Lev. xviii. 8. The Talmud prescribes stoning for this crime.
Cf. Amos ii. 7; Lev. xviii. 8. The woman was clearly not the
mother of the offender, and probably (although the use of
πορνεία rather than μοιχεία does not prove this) she was not, at
the time, the wife of the offender's father. She may have been
divorced, for divorce was very common, or her husband may
have been dead. There is little doubt that 2 Cor. vii. 12
refers to a different matter, and that ὁ ἀδικηθείς there is not the
offender's father, but Timothy or the Apostle himself. As
St Paul here censures the male offender only, the woman was
probably a heathen, upon whom he pronounces no judgment
(*v.* 12). The ἔχειν implies a permanent union of some kind,
but perhaps not a formal marriage : cf. John **iv.** 18. Origen
speaks of it as a marriage (γάμος), and ἔχω is used of marriage in
vii. 2 ; Matt. xiv. 4, etc. In the lowest classes of Roman society
the *legal* line between marriage and concubinage was not sharply
defined.

After ἔθνεσιν, אᵌ L P, Syrr. AV. add ὀνομάζεται : א* A B C D E F G
17, Vulg. Copt. Arm. Aeth. omit.

2. καὶ ὑμεῖς. The pronoun is emphatic ; 'you, among whom
this enormity has taken place and is notorious, you are puffed
up.' He does not mean that they were puffed up *because* of this
outrage, as if it were a fine assertion of Christian freedom, but
in spite of it. It ought to have humbled them to the dust, and
yet they still retained their self-satisfied complacency. WH.,
Tisch., Treg. and RV. marg. make this verse interrogative ; 'Are
ye puffed up? Did ye not rather mourn?' But the words are

* There is also the case of Callias, who married his wife's mother.
Andocides (B.C. 400), in his speech on the mysteries, asks whether among
ₜne Greeks such a thing had ever been done before.

more impressive as the statement of an amazing and shocking fact: οὐχί is not always interrogative (x. 29; Luke xii. 51, xiii. 3, 5, xvi. 30; John ix. 9, xiii. 10, 11). Their morbid self-importance, which made them so intolerant of petty wrongs (vi. 7), made them very tolerant of deep disgrace.

ἐπενθήσατε. 'Mourned,' as if for one who was dead.

ἵνα αρθῇ. The ἵνα indicates, not the purpose of the mourning, but the *result* of it, *contemplated* as its normal effect (see on i. 15). A proper Christian instinct would have led them to have expelled the guilty person in irrepressible horror at his conduct.

ὁ τὸ ἔργον τοῦτο πράξας. *Qui hoc facinus patravit* (Beza). The language is purposely vague, but the context suggests a bad meaning: πράξας (not ποιήσας) indicates a moral point of view. The attitude of the Corinthian Christians towards such conduct is probably to be accounted for by traditional Corinthian laxity.* It is said that the Rabbis evaded the Mosaic prohibitions of such unions (Lev. xx. 11 ; Deut. xxii. 30) in the case of prose-lytes. A proselyte made an entirely new start in life and cut off all his former relationships ; therefore incest, in his case, was impossible, for he had no relations, near or distant. It is not likely that this evasion of the Mosaic Law, if already in exist-ence, was known to the Corinthians and had influenced them.

L has ἐξαρθῇ for ἀρθῇ (א A B C D E F G P); and B D E F G L P have ποιήσας for πράξας (א A C 17, and other cursives). It is not easy to decide in this latter case, and editors are divided. Compare 2 Cor. xii. 21 ; Rom. i. 32, ii. 1–3.

3. ἐγὼ μὲν γάρ. 'For *I*,' with much emphasis on the pronoun, which is in contrast to the preceding ὑμεῖς : 'my feelings about it are very different from yours.' The γάρ introduces the justifi-cation of ἵνα ἀρθῇ, showing what expulsion involves. St Paul does not mean that, as the Corinthians have not excommunicated the offender, he must inflict a graver penalty : this would be punishing the offender for what was the fault of his fellows. He is explaining what he has just said about their failing to remove the man. No δέ follows the μέν : the contrast which μέν marks is with what goes before (*v.* 2), not with anything that is to follow. The correlation of μὲν . . . δέ is much less common in N.T. than in class. Grk. In some books μέν does not occur, and in several cases it has no δέ as here : 1 Thess. ii. 18 ; Rom. vii. 12, x. 1, etc. See Blass, *Gr.* § 77. 12.

ἀπὼν τῷ σώματι. 'Although absent in the body.' Again a contrast : 'you, who are on the spot, do nothing ; I, who am far away, and might excuse myself on that account, take very serious action.' Origen compares Elisha (2 Kings v. 26).

* What Augustine says of Carthage was still more true of Corinth : *circumstrepebat me undique sartago flagitiosorum amorum* (*Conf.* iii. 1).

τῷ πνεύματι. 'His own spirit,' as in *v.* 4 : cf. *v.* 5 and ii. 11.
In Col. ii. 5 we have a similar utterance, but there σάρξ takes
the place of σῶμα. It is the highest constituent element in
man's nature, and his point of contact with the Spirit of God.

ἤδη κέκρικα ὡς παρὼν τὸν κ.τ.λ. *Either,* 'have already, as if
I were present, judged the man'; *or,* 'have already, as if I were
present, decided with regard to the man'; *or,* 'have already
come to a decision, as if I were present: with regard to the
man,' etc. In the last case, which is perhaps the best, τὸν . . .
κατεργασάμενον is governed by παραδοῦναι and is repeated in τὸν
τοιοῦτον.*

Before ἀπών, D³ E F G L, AV. insert ὡς : ℵ A B C D* P 17, Vulg.
Copt. Aeth. RV. omit.

4. ἐν τῷ ὀνόματι κ.τ.λ. Here we have choice of four constructions. *Either,* take ἐν τῷ ὀνόματι with συναχθέντων and σὺν
τῇ δυνάμει with παραδοῦναι, *or* both with συναχθέντων, *or* both
with παραδοῦναι, *or* ἐν τῷ ὀνόμ. with παραδοῦναι and σὺν τῇ δυν.
with συναχθέντων. If the order of the words is regarded as
decisive, the first of these will seem to be most natural, and
it yields good sense. Lightfoot adopts it. The Greek commentators mostly prefer the second construction, but neither it
nor the third is as probable as the first and the fourth. It is
not likely that either συναχθέντων or παραδοῦναι is meant to have
both qualifications, while the other has none. The fourth construction is the best of the four. The solemn opening, ἐν τῷ
ὀνόματι τοῦ Κυρίου Ἰησοῦ, placed first with emphasis, belongs to
the main verb, the verb which introduces the sentence that is
pronounced upon the offender, while σὺν τῇ δυνάμει τ. Κ. ἡμῶν Ἰ.
supplies a coefficient that is essential to the competency of the
tribunal. The opening words prepare us for a sentence of grave
import, but we are kept in suspense as to what the sentence will
be, until the conditions which are to give it validity are described.
Graviter suspensa manet et vibrat oratio (Beng.). We translate,
therefore ; 'With regard to the man who has thus perpetrated
the deed, In the name of our Lord Jesus Christ—you being
assembled and *my* spirit with the power of our Lord Jesus Christ
—to deliver such an one to Satan.' The τὸν τοιοῦτον is not
rendered superfluous by the preceding τὸν . . . κατεργασάμενον :
it intimates that the Apostle is prepared to deal in a similar way
with any similar offender.

* Evans thinks that ὡς παρών does not mean '*as if* I were present in the
body,' but 'as being *really* present in the spirit.' His spirit had at times
exceptional power of insight into the state of a church at a distance : οὐκ ὡς
ἀπόστολος ἀλλ' ὡς προφήτης εἶπεν (Orig.).

After ὀνόματι τ. Κυρίου, B D E F G L P have ἡμῶν, and it is probably genuine, but ℵ A and other witnesses omit, and it might easily be inserted from the next clause. P and some other witnesses omit the second ἡμῶν. After first Ἰησοῦ, ℵ D³ E F G L P, Vulg. Syrr. add Χριστοῦ : A B D*, Am. omit. After second Ἰησοῦ, D³ F L add Χριστοῦ : ℵ A B D* P, Vulg. omit, AV. inserts 'Christ' in both places ; RV. omits in both.

5. παραδοῦναι τ. τ. τῷ Σατανᾷ. This means solemn expulsion from the Church and relegation of the culprit to the region outside the commonwealth and covenant (Eph. ii. 11, 12), where Satan holds sway. We have the same expression 1 Tim. i. 20. It describes a severer aspect of the punishment which is termed αἴρειν ἐκ μέσου (v. 2) and ἐξαίρειν ἐξ ὑμῶν (v. 13). Satan is the ἄρχων τοῦ κόσμου τούτου (John xii. 31, xvi. 11), and the offender is sent back to his domain ; *ut qui auctor fuerat ad vitium nequitiae, ipse flagellum fieret disciplinae* (Herv.). St Paul calls Satan 'the *god* of this age' (2 Cor. iv. 4), an expression which occurs nowhere else ; and a Christian, who through his own wickedness forfeits the security of being a member of Christ in His Church, becomes, like the heathen, exposed to the malignity of Satan (1 John v. 19) to an extent that Christians cannot be.

εἰς ὄλεθρον τῆς σαρκός. There is no need to choose between the two interpretations which have been put upon this expression, for they are not mutually exclusive and both are true. The sinner was handed over to Satan for the 'mortification of the flesh,' *i.e.* to destroy his sinful lusts ; τὸ φρόνημα τῆς σαρκός is Origen's interpretation. This meaning is right, for the punishment was inflicted with a remedial purpose, both in this case and in that of 1 Tim. i. 20 : and the interpretation is in harmony with the frequent Pauline sense of σάρξ (Rom. viii. 13 and Col. iii. 5), as distinct from σῶμα. But so strong a word as ὄλεθρος implies more than this. 'Unto destruction of the flesh' includes physical suffering, such as follows spiritual judgment on sin (xi. 30 ; Acts v. 1 f., xiii. 11).* The Apostle calls his own 'thorn for the flesh' an ἄγγελος Σατανᾶ (2 Cor. xii. 7 ; cf. Luke xiii. 16). We have the same idea in Job, where Jehovah says to Satan, Ἰδοὺ παραδίδωμί σοι αὐτόν (ii. 6). And in the book of Jubilees (x. 2) demons first lead astray, and then blind and kill, the grandchildren of Noah. Afterwards Noah is taught by angels how to rescue his offspring from the demons. See Thackeray, *St Paul and Contemporary Jewish Thought*, p. 171. Here the punishment is for the good, not only of the community, but also of the offender, upon whom the suffering inflicted by Satan would have a healing effect.

ἵνα τὸ πνεῦμα. The purpose of the suffering is not mere

* Renan, Godet, and Goudge regard the expression as meaning sentence of death by a wasting sickness. Expulsion is not mentioned here ; hence the sharp command in *v.* 13.

destruction; it is remedial, ἵνα σωθῇ. Cf. αὐτὸς σωθήσεται (iii. 15). Here τὸ πνεῦμα, as the seat of personality, is suggested by the context instead of αὐτός.* As in 2 Cor. vii. 1, τὸ πνεῦμα is used in contrast to ἡ σάρξ, and as the chief and distinctive factor in the constitution of man, but as not *per se* distinctive of a state of grace. Strong measures may be needed in order to secure its salvation. See Abbott, *The Son of Man*, pp. 482, 791.

ἐν τῇ ἡμέρᾳ τ. Κυρίου. i. 8; 2 Cor. i. 14; 1 Thess. v. 2, etc. It is sometimes assumed that, while the Corinthian Church was competent, by itself, to *expel* an offender (*v*. 2), it was by virtue of the extraordinary power given to St Paul as an Apostle that the delivery to Satan was inflicted. There is nothing in the passage to prove this; and the γάρ in *v*. 3 rather points the other way. Why should St Paul inflict a more severe punishment than that which the Corinthian Church ought to have inflicted? †

It is still more often assumed that the sequel of this case is referred to in 2 Cor. ii. 5–11, vii. 12. It is inferred from these passages that the Corinthian Church held a meeting such as the Apostle prescribes in this chapter, and by a majority (2 Cor. ii. 6) passed the sentence of expulsion, whereupon the offender was led to repentance; and that the Corinthians then awaited the Apostle's permission to remit the sentence, which permission he gives (2 Cor. ii. 10). This view, however, is founded on two assumptions, one of which is open to serious question, and the other to question which is so serious as to be almost fatal. The view assumes that 2 Cor. i.–ix. was written soon after 1 Cor. which is very doubtful. It also assumes that 2 Cor. ii. 5–11 and vii. 12 refer to this case of incest, which is very difficult to believe. 2 Cor. vii. 12 certainly refers to the same case as 2 Cor. ii. 5–11, and the language in vii. 12 is so utterly unsuitable to the case of incest that it is scarcely credible that it can refer to it. See Hastings, *DB*. i. p. 493, iii. p. 711, and iv. p. 768; G. H. Rendall, *The Epistles to the Corinthians*, pp. 63, 71; Goudge, p. 41; Plummer on 2 Cor. vii. 12.

***

F has αὐτόν for τὸν τοιοῦτον. After τοῦ Κυρίου, ℵ L add Ἰησοῦ, D adds Ἰησοῦ Χριστοῦ, A F M add ἡμῶν Ἰησοῦ Χριστοῦ: B has simply τοῦ Κυρίου, which may be the original reading, but τοῦ Κυρίου Ἰησοῦ is not improbable; so AV., RV., WH. marg.

---

* ἀπὸ τοῦ κρείττονος ὀνομάσας ὅλου τοῦ ἀνθρώπου σωτηρίαν (Orig.). There was no need to add the ψυχή and the σῶμα. The penalty is for the good of the community as well as of the offender. A shepherd, says Origen, must drive out a tainted sheep that would infect the flock.

† The resemblance of this passage to various forms of magic spells and curses is sometimes pointed out. The fundamental difference is this, that all such spells and curses aim at serious evil to the persons against whom they are directed. The Apostle aims at the rescue of the offender from perdition Moreover, he desires to rescue the Corinthian Church from grave peril.

6. Οὐ καλὸν τὸ καύχημα ὑμῶν. 'Not seemly is your boast':
it is ill-timed, and it is discreditable to all who share in it.*
Where a revolting crime is bringing disgrace and peril to the
community, there can be no place for boasting. St Paul does
not mean that the *subject* of their glorying, the thing they glory
in (*e.g.* their enlightenment, or their liberty) is not good; but
that in such distressing circumstances overt glorying is very
unsuitable. As Evans elaborately points out, καύχημα is not
materies gloriandi, but *gloriatio* (Beza, Beng.), or (more accurately) *gloriatio facta*, boasting uttered.† So also in 2 Cor.
v. 12.

μικρὰ ζύμη. The μικρά comes first with emphasis, and hence
implies an argument *a fortiori*: if even a *little* leaven is so
powerful, if even one unsatisfactory feature may have a septic
influence in a community, how much more must a scandal of
this magnitude infect the whole life of the Church. The simile
of leaven is frequent in the N.T. See Gal. v. 9. Here the
stress of the argument lies less in the evil example of the offender
than in the fact that toleration of this conduct implies con-
currence (Rom. i. 32) and debases the standard of moral
judgment and instinct. To be indifferent to grave misbehaviour
is to become partly responsible for it. A subtle atmosphere,
in which evil readily springs up and is diffused, is the result.
The leaven that was infecting the Corinthian Church was a
vitiated public opinion. Cf. 2 Thess. iii. 6; also the charge of
Germanicus to his soldiers as to their treatment of insubordinate
comrades: *discedite a contactu, ac dividite turbidos* (Tac. *Ann.*
i. 43).

Both here and in Gal. v. 9 we find the reading δολοῖ for ζυμοῖ in D
with *corrumpit* in Vulg. and other Latin texts.

7. ἐκκαθάρατε τὴν π. ζύμην. A sharp, summary appeal: 'Rid
yourselves of these infected and infectious remains of your
unconverted past,' even as a Jewish household, in preparation
for the Passover, purges the house of all leaven (Exod. xii. 15 f.,
xiii. 7). This was understood as a symbol of moral purification,
and the search for leaven as symbolizing infectious evil was
scrupulously minute, *e.g.* with candles to look into corners and
mouse-holes for crumbs of leavened bread. Zeph. i. 12 was
supposed to imply this. The penalty for eating leavened bread

---

* Some Latin texts omit the negative, making the statement sarcastic
(Lucif. Ambrst. and MSS. known to Augustine). The οὐ may easily have
been lost owing to the preceding Κυρίου or Χριστοῦ.

† If he had meant *materies gloriandi*, he would probably have said that
they had none, οὐκ ἔχετε καύχημα. Like οὐκ ἐπαινῶ (xi. 17, 22), οὐ καλόν
is a reproachful litotes.

during the feast was scourging. On compounds with ἐκ see on
iii. 18, and cf. 2 Tim. ii. 21.

τὴν παλαιὰν ζύμην. It was their acquiescing in the scandal
which revealed the presence of a remnant of heathen corruption. The summons to thoroughly purge away all sinful taints
cuts deep into the corporate and individual conscience. Each
knows the plague-spot in himself. The verb occurs again
2 Tim. ii. 21, and nowhere else in N.T.; also Deut. xxvi. 13.
With παλαιάν here cf. παλαιὸς ἄνθρωπος, Rom. vi. 6; Eph. iv. 22;
Col. iii. 9. Ignatius (*Magn.* 10) says, ὑπέρθεσθε οὖν τὴν κακὴν
ζύμην τὴν παλαιωθεῖσαν καὶ ἐνοξίσασαν. By the evil leaven which
has become stale and sour he means Judaism. Note the οὖν.

ἵνα ἦτε νέον φύραμα. 'That you may be a new lump of
dough,' *i.e.* may make a new start in sanctification free from
old and evil influence.* Cf. οἶνον νέον (Matt. ix. 17), and see
Trench, *Syn.* § 60. There is only one φύραμα, only one body
of Christians, just as there is only one loaf (x. 17). See on
Luke xii. 1 for the evil associations connected with leaven:
γέγονεν ἐκ φθορᾶς αὐτὴ καὶ φθείρει τὸ φύραμα (Plutarch). See
Hastings, *DB.* III. p. 90.

καθώς ἐστε ἄζυμοι. This is the proper, the ideal condition
of all Christians. 'Ye *are* unleavened, having been baptized
and made a καινὴ κτίσις in Christ (2 Cor. v. 17; Eph. iv. 24;
Col. iii. 10), and are becoming in fact what you are in principle
and by profession' (vi. 11). St Paul habitually idealizes,
speaking to Christians as if they were Christians in the fullest
sense, thus exemplifying Kant's maxim that you should treat a
man as if he were what you would wish him to be.

It is utterly wrong to take ἄζυμοι literally; 'ye are without
leaven,' because (it is assumed) they were at that moment
keeping the Passover. (1) In the literal sense, ἄζυμος is used
of things, not of persons. (2) The Corinthian Church consisted
almost entirely of Gentile Christians. (3) The remark would
have no point in this context. But the imagery in this passage
suggests, though it does not prove, that St Paul was writing
at or near the Passover season (cf. xvi. 8). See Deissmann,
Light, p. 333.

καὶ γὰρ τὸ πάσχα ἡμῶν ἐτύθη. Directly, this is the reason
for the preceding statement; 'You are ἄζυμοι, purified from the
leaven of your old self, by virtue of the death of your Saviour.'
Indirectly and more broadly, this is a reason for the practical
summons at the beginning of the verse: 'It is high time for

* The Vulgate has the curious rendering, *ut sitis nova conspersio.* This
rare substantive is found, with the same unexpected meaning, twice in
Tertullian (*Marcion.* iv. 24, *Valent.* 31), in the sense of a lump of dough,
and once in Irenaeus (v. xiv. 2), probably as a translation of φύραμα.

you to purge out the old leaven; for the Lamb is already slain and your house is not yet fully cleansed: you are late!' See Deut. xvi. 6; Mark xiv. 12; Luke xxii. 7.* The ἡμῶν serves to link the Christian antitype to the Jewish type.

Χριστός. 'Even Christ'; last for emphasis, like ὁ κρίνων (Rom. ii. 1) and ὁ πατριάρχης (Heb. vii. 4). The force of the Apostle's appeal is in any case obvious, but it gains somewhat in point if we suppose him to have in mind the tradition which is embodied in the Fourth Gospel, that Christ was crucified on the 14th Nisan, the day appointed for the slaying of the paschal lamb. We may say that the Pauline tradition, like the Johannine, makes the Death of Christ, rather than the Last Supper, the antitype of the Passover, but we can hardly claim St Paul as a definite witness for the 14th Nisan.† On this difficult subject see Sanday, *Outlines of the Life of Christ*, p. 146; Hastings, *DB.* I. p. 411, *DCG.* II. 5; and the literature there quoted.

Nor, again, can this passage be claimed as evidence for the Christian observance of Easter, although such observance would probably be coeval with that of the Lord's Day. As in Mark xiv. 12; Luke xxii. 7, 11; John xviii. 28, πάσχα is here used of the paschal lamb, not, as commonly, of the paschal supper or of the paschal octave.

ἐκκαθάρατε without connecting particle (א* A B D E F G, Vulg. Copt. RV.) rather than ἐκκαθάρατε οὖν (א³ C L P, Aeth. AV.). On still stronger evidence, ὑπὲρ ὑμῶν must be omitted after τὸ πάσχα ὑμῶν. Cursives have ἐθύθη for ἐτύθη. Did Ignatius (see above) have οὖν in his text?

8. ὥστε. With cohortative subjunctive as with imperative, see on iii. 21.

ἑορτάζωμεν. "Our passover-feast is not for a week, but for a life-time" (Godet), ὅτι πᾶς ὁ χρόνος ἑορτῆς ἐστι καιρὸς τοῖς Χριστιανοῖς (Chrys.). The verb occurs nowhere else in N.T., but is frequent in LXX. Ἰησοῦς ὁ Χριστός ἐστιν ἡ νέα ζύμη (Orig.).

ἐν ζύμῃ. See on iv. 21 for this use of ἐν.

κακίας καὶ πονηρίας. Trench, *Syn.* § 11, makes κακία the vicious principle, πονηρία its outward exercise. It is doubtful whether this is correct. In LXX both words are used indifferently to translate the same Hebrew words, which shows that to Hellenists they conveyed ideas not widely distinct. In the Vulgate both *malitia* and *nequitia* are used to translate both words, *malitia* being used most often for κακία, and *nequitia* for πονηρία, for which *iniquitas* also is used. 'Malice' may trans-

---

* In Mark xiv. 12 the AV. has '*kill* the Passover,' with 'sacrifice' in the margin; in Luke xxii. 7, 'kill,' without any alternative; here 'sacrifice,' with 'slay' in the margin: the R.V. has 'sacrifice' in all three places.

† On the general relation between the two traditions see J. Kaftan, *Jesus u. Paulus*, pp. 59–69.

late κακία in most places in the N.T., but not in Matt. vi. 34,
where Vulg. has *malitia* (!), nor in Acts viii. 22, where it has
nequitia. It is noteworthy that *pravitas* is not used for either
word. Luke xi. 39 shows that πονηρία may mean thoughts or
purposes of wickedness; cf. Mark vii. 22. The genitives are
genitives of apposition.

ἀζύμοις. Perhaps 'unleavened bread' (AV., RV.) is right,
with reference to the unleavened cakes eaten at the Passover;
ἑπτὰ ἡμέρας ἄζυμα ἔδεσθε (Exod. xii. 15). But ἄζυμα is very
indefinite; 'unleavened elements.' Origen refers this to i. 2.

εἰλικρινίας. The word is a *crux* as regards etymology, but
it seems to mean 'transparency,' 'limpid purity,' and hence
'ingenuousness.'

ἀληθείας. In its wider sense, 'rectitude,' 'integrity'; cf.
xiii. 6; Eph. v. 9; John iii. 21.*

ἑορτάζωμεν (‫א‬ B C F G L, d e Vulg.) rather than ἑορτάζομεν (A D E P).
For πονηρίας F has πορνείας.

9. Ἔγραψα ὑμῖν ἐν τῇ ἐπιστολῇ. Pursuing the main purpose
of the passage, viz. to rebuke their indifference respecting moral
scandal, the Apostle corrects a possible misapprehension of his
former directions; or at any rate he shows how what he said
before would apply in cases more likely to occur than the one
which has just been discussed. 'I wrote to you in my letter,'
in the letter which was well known to the Corinthians, a letter
earlier than our 1 Corinthians and now lost. It is true that
ἔγραψα might be an 'epistolary aorist' (Gal. vi. 11; 1 John ii. 14)
referring to the letter then being written. But ἐν τῇ ἐπιστολῇ
(cf. 2 Cor. vii. 8) must refer to another letter. Rom. xvi. 22;
Col. iv. 16; 1 Thess. v. 27 are all retrospective, being parts of
a postscript. In *this* letter he has not given any direction
about not keeping company with fornicators; for a summons
to expel a member who has contracted an incestuous union
cannot be regarded as a charge not to associate with fornicators.
It is evident that here, as in 2 Cor. x. 9 f., he is making reference
to an earlier letter which has not been preserved. So also Atto;
non in hac epistola sed altera: and Herveius; *in alia jam epistola*.
Some think that 2 Cor. vi. 14–vii. 1 may be part of the letter
in question. See notes there and Introduction to 2 Corinthians
in the Cambridge Greek Testament. Stanley gives two spurious

* It is possible that these two words are meant to prepare for what
follows. Perhaps the Apostle saw that there had been some shuffling and
evasion about the injunction in the former letter. They said that they did
not understand it, and made that an excuse for ignoring it. How St Paul
heard of the misinterpretation of his earlier letter we are not told. Zahn
suggests the Corinthians' letter, of which he finds traces even before vii. 1
(*Introd. to N.T.* p. 261).

letters, one from, the other to, St Paul, which are not of much
interest, but which have imposed upon the Armenian Church
(Appendix, p. 591 f.).*

μὴ συναναμίγνυσθαι.   Lit. 'not to mix yourselves up together
with': *ne commisceamini* (Vulg.).   This expressive combination
of two prepositions with the verb occurs again in a similar connexion 2 Thess. iii. 14; also in the A text of Hos. vii. 8.   Cf.
2 Thess. iii. 6.

10.   οὐ πάντως.   'Not altogether,' 'not absolutely,' 'not in
all circumstances.'   It limits the prohibition of intercourse with
fornicators, which does not apply in the case of fornicators who
are outside the Christian community.   The Apostle is not
repeating the prohibition in another form, which would have
required μή, as before.   The οὐ = 'not, I mean,' or 'I do not
mean.'   The meaning is quite clear.

τοῦ κόσμου τούτου.   'Of the non-Christian world.'

ἢ τοῖς πλεονέκταις.   'Or' here is equivalent to our 'any
more than.'

τοῖς πλεονέκταις καὶ ἅρπαξιν.   These form a single class,
coupled by the single article and the καί, and separated from
each of the other classes by ἤ.   This class is that of the
absolutely selfish, who covet and sometimes seize more than
their just share of things.   They exhibit that *amor sui* which is
the note of 'this world,' and which usurps the place of *amor
Dei*, until πλεονεξία becomes a form of idolatry (Eph. v. 5).

εἰδωλολάτραις.   In the literal sense; x. 14; 1 John v. 21.
This is the first appearance of the word (Rev. xxi. 8, xxii. 15),
which may have been coined by St Paul.   In Eph. v. 5 it is used
in a figurative sense of a worshipper of Mammon.   The triplet
of vices here consists of those which characterize non-Christian
civilization; lax morality, greed, and superstition.   The last, in
some form or other, is the inevitable substitute for spiritual
religion.

ἐπεὶ ὠφείλετε ἄρα.   'Since in that case you would have to';
cf. vii. 14.   Ἐπεί implies a protasis, which is suppressed by an
easy ellipse; 'since, were it not so, then,' etc.   Ἄρα introduces
a subjective sequence, while οὖν introduces an objective one.
Ὠφείλετε is in an apodosis, where the idiomatic imperfect marks

---

* There is little doubt that a number of the Apostle's letters have perished,
especially those which he wrote in the early part of his career, when his
authority was less clearly established, and the value of his words less understood ; 2 Thess. ii. 2, iii. 17.   See Renan, *S. Paul*, p. 234.

Ramsay points out the resemblance between this passage (9–13) and
2 Thessalonians, which guards against misconception of his teaching that
nad arisen owing to the strong emphasis which he had laid on the coming of
the Kingdom (*Pauline Studies*, p. 36).

the consequence of a state of things that is supposed not to exist; and the ἄν which is usual in such an apodosis is commonly omitted with such verbs as ὠφείλετε, ἔδει, καλὸν ἦν, etc.

ἐκ τοῦ κόσμου ἐξελθεῖν. This for most people is impossible; but at Corinth in St Paul's day it was well for Christians to see as little of the heathen world as was possible. In x. 27 he does not forbid the presence of Christians at private entertainments given by heathen, but he implies that they ought not to wish to go to them.

οὐ πάντως (א* A B C D* E F G 17, Vulg.) rather than καὶ οὐ πάντως א³ D³ L P, Arm. Aeth.). The 'yet' in AV. seems to represent καί. καὶ ἅρπαξιν (א* A B C D* F G P 17, Aeth.) rather than ἤ ἅρπαξιν (א³ D³ E L, Vulg. Syrr. Copt. Arm.), an alteration to conform to ἤ on each side. AV. has 'or,' RV. 'and.' ὠφείλετε (א A B* C D E F G L 17, Latt.) rather than ὀφείλετε (B³ P, Chrys. Thdrt.), another mistaken correction, the force of the imperfect not being seen.

11. νῦν δὲ ἔγραψα. 'But, as it is, I wrote' (RV. marg.), not 'But now I write' (RV.). The latter is grammatically possible and makes good sense, but it is unlikely that ἔγραψα is in *v.* 9 historical, of an earlier letter, and here epistolary, of the present letter. The νῦν is logical, not temporal, 'now you see,' 'now you understand' that the earlier letter meant something different. Had the Apostle meant the νῦν to be temporal and the verb to refer to the present letter, he would have written γράφω, as in iv. 14. He has stated what the earlier letter did not mean (οὐ πάντως), and he now very naturally states what it did mean.*

ἐάν . . . ᾖ. The form of protasis covers all cases that may come to light: see on iv. 15. Almost all editors prefer ᾖ to ἤ before πόρνος.

ὀνομαζόμενος. 'Any who bears the name of a brother,' though he has forfeited the right to it. He is called a brother, but he really is a πόρνος or, etc. Some early interpreters take ὀνομαζόμενος with what follows; 'if any brother be called a whoremonger,' or 'be a notorious whoremonger.' The latter would require ὀνομαστός, and we should have ἀδελφός τις rather than τις ἀδελφός. Evidently ἀδελφός and ὀνομαζόμενος are to be taken together. He is called a Christian, and he really is a disgrace to the name; that is a reason for shunning him. But if he is a Christian and is called some bad name, that is not a reason for shunning him: the bad name may be a slander.

πλεονέκτης. There is no good ground for supposing that, either here, or in *v.* 10, or anywhere else, πλεονέκτης means 'sensual' (see on Eph. iv. 19). The desire which it implies is the desire for possessions, greed, grasping after what does not belong to one.

* Abbott, *Johan. Gr.* 2691, gives other examples.

εἰδωλολάτρης. Stanley would give this word also the meaning of 'sensual.' But there is no improbability in Corinthian converts being tainted with idolatry. Origen says that in his time the plea that idolatry was a matter of indifference was common among Christians serving in the army. Modern experience teaches that it is very difficult to extinguish idolatrous practices among converts, and Chrysostom may be right in suggesting that the Apostle inserts 'idolater' in his list as a preparation for what he is about to say on the subject (viii. 10, x. 7, 14 f.). The Corinthians were evidently very lax.

λοίδορος. Origen notes with what very evil people the λοίδο-ρος is classed: ἡλίκοις κακοῖς τὸν λοίδορον συνηρίθμησεν. The word occurs vi. 10, and in LXX in Proverbs and Ecclus., but nowhere else. Chrysostom (on vi. 10) says that many in his day blamed the Apostle for putting λοίδοροι and μέθυσοι into such company. Matt. v. 21, 22; 1 Pet. iii. 9.

μέθυσος. Rom. xiii. 13. In Attic writers applied to women, men being called μεθυστικοί, παροινικοί, or παροίνιοι. Cf. ὀργὴ μεγάλη γυνὴ μέθυσος (Ecclus. xxvi. 8); but elsewhere in LXX it is used of men (Ecclus. xix. 1; Prov. xxiii. 21, xxvi. 9). It some-times means 'intoxicated' rather than 'given to drink.' The μέθυσος and the λοίδορος are additions to the first list.

μηδὲ συνεσθίειν. An emphatic intimation of what he means by μὴ συναναμίγνυσθαι. Cf. Luke xv. 2; Gal. ii. 12. The Apostle is not thinking of Holy Communion, in which case the μηδέ would be quite out of place: he is thinking of social meals; 'Do not invite him to your house or accept his invitations.' But, as Theodoret points out, a prohibition of this kind would lead to the exclusion of the offender from the Lord's Table. Great caution is required in applying the Apostle's prohibition to modern circumstances, which are commonly not parallel. The object here, as in 2 John 10, is twofold: to prevent the spread of evil, and to bring offenders to see the error of their ways. In any case, what St Paul adds in giving a similar injunction must not be forgotten; καὶ μὴ ὡς ἐχθρὸν ἡγεῖσθε, ἀλλὰ νουθετεῖτε ὡς ἀδελφόν (2 Thess. iii. 15). Clement of Rome (Cor. 14) says of the ringleaders of the schism, χρηστευσώμεθα αὐτοῖς κατὰ τὴν εὐσπλαγχνίαν καὶ γλυκύτητα τοῦ ποιήσαντος ἡμᾶς, perhaps 'n reference to Matt. v. 45, 48.

νῦν (אᵇ A B Dˢ E F G L P) rather than νυνὶ (א* C D* D²): the more emphatic form might seem to be more suitable. Vulg. Syrr. Copt. Aeth. Goth. support ᾖ against ἤ before πόρνος. For μηδέ, A has μή and F has μήτε.

12. τί γάρ μοι τοὺς ἔξω κρίνειν; 'For what business of mine is it to judge those that are outside?' Quid enim mihi (Vulg.); Ad quid mihi (Tert.); Quid mea interest (Beza). Gives the

reason why they ought never to have supposed that he ordered
them to shun the company of heathen who were fornicators: the
meaning given in *v.* 11 is the only possible meaning.   The phrase
τοὺς ἔξω (1 Thess. iv. 12; Col. iv. 5) is of Jewish origin.   Jews
applied it to Gentiles; our Lord applies it to Jews who are not
His disciples (Mark iv. 11); St Paul applies it to non-Christians,
whether Jews or Gentiles.   In 1 Tim. iii. 7, where he speaks of
non-Christians judging Christians, he uses οἱ ἔξωθεν.   The
expression states a fact, without any insinuation of censure.
How could they suppose that he claimed jurisdiction over heathen
and placed a stigma upon them for heathen behaviour?   Epictetus
(*Enchir.* 47) tells those who are continent not to be severe upon
those who are not, or to claim any superiority.

οὐχὶ τοὺς ἔσω ὑμεῖς κρίνετε; τοὺς ἔσω and ὑμεῖς are in emphatic
juxtaposition: 'Is it not those that are *within* that *you* judge?
They are *your* sphere of jurisdiction.'   The present tense is
'axiomatic,' stating what is normal.   The proposal to put a
colon at οὐχί and make κρίνετε an imperative ('No; judge ye
those who are within') is unintelligible.   Οὐχί is not an answer to
τί; and the sentence is much less telling as a command than as
a question.   Οὐχί is one of the words which are far more common
in Paul and Luke than elsewhere in N.T.

13. ὁ Θεὸς κρίνει.   The verb is certainly to be accented as a
present: it states the normal attribute of God.   And the sentence
is probably categorical; 'But them that are without God judgeth.'
This is more forcible than to bring it under the interrogative
οὐχί; 'Is it not the case that you judge those who are within,
while God judges those who are without?'   But WH. and
Bachmann adopt the latter.

ἐξάρατε τὸν πονηρόν.   A quotation from Deut. xvii. 7, bringing
to a sharp practical conclusion the discussion about the treatment of πορνεία, and at the same time giving a final rebuke to
them for their indifference about the case of incest.   The offender
must be at once expelled.   Origen adds that we must not be
content with expelling the evil man from our society; we must
take care to expel the evil one (τὸν πονηρόν) from our hearts.   Note
the double ἐξ: the riddance must be complete.   See on iii. 18.

Vulg. Arm. Copt. Aeth. take κρινει as a future.   ἐξάρατε (ℵ A B C D*
F G P, Vulg.) rather than καὶ ἐξαρεῖτε (D³ E L), or καὶ ἐξάρατε (17).   The
verb occurs nowhere else in N.T., but is very frequent in LXX.

VI. 1-11. LITIGATION BEFORE HEATHEN COURTS.

The Apostle passes on to a third matter for censure, and in
discussing it he first treats of the evil and its evil occasion (1–8)

and then, in preparation for what is to follow, points out that all unrighteousness is a survival from a bad past which the Corinthians ought to have left behind them (9–11).

1–8. The Evil and its Evil Occasion.

How can you dare to go to law with one another in heathen caurts ?   If there must be suits, let Christian judge Christian.

[1] The subject of judging brings me to another matter.   Is it possible that, when one of you has a dispute with a fellow-Christian, he takes upon himself to bring the dispute before a heathen tribunal, instead of bringing it before believers.   [2] Or is it that you do not know that, at the Last Day, believers will sit with Christ to judge the world?   And if the world is to be judged hereafter at your bar, are you incompetent to serve in the pettiest tribunals?   [3] Do not you know that we are to sit in judgment on angels?   After that, one need hardly mention things of daily life.   [4] If, then, you have questions of daily life to be decided, do you really take heathens, who are of no account to those who are in the Church, and set them to judge you?   [5] It is to move you to shame that I am speaking like this.   Have things come to such a pass that, among the whole of you, there is not a single person who is competent to arbitrate between one Christian and another, but that, on the contrary, Christian goes to law with Christian, and that too before unbelievers?   [7] Nay, at the very outset, there is a terrible defect in your Christianity that you have lawsuits at all with one another.   Why not rather accept injury?   Why not rather submit to being deprived?   But, so far from enduring wrong, what you do is this; you wrong and deprive other people, and those people your fellow-Christians.

The subject of going to law before heathen tribunals is linked to the subject discussed in the previous chapter by the reference to the question of *judgment* (v. 12, 13).*   The moral sense of a Christian community, which ought to make itself felt in judging offenders within its own circle, ought still more to suffice for

* There may be another link.   In v. 10, 11 St Paul twice brackets the πόρνος with the πλεονέκτης, and he now passes from the one to the other.   It was *desire to have more than one had a right to* (πλεονεξία) which led to this litigation in heathen courts.   See on Eph. iv. 19.

settling disputes among its members, without recourse to heathen courts, whose judges stand presumably on a lower ethical level than Christians. But there is no real argumentative connexion with the preceding section. The Apostle has finished two points in his indictment, and he now passes on to another.

The Apostle's principles with regard to secular and heathen magistrates are perfectly consistent. In Rom. xiii. he inculcates the attitude of a good citizen, which is not only obedience to law, but the recognition of the magistrate as God's minister. This carries with it submission to the law as administered by the courts, and acceptance of the authority of the courts in criminal cases. St Paul had had experience of the protection of Roman Justice (Acts xviii. 12 f., xxv. 16), and he himself appealed to Caesar. But to *invoke* the courts to decide disputes *between Christians* was quite another matter; and he lays it down here that to do so is a confession of the failure of that justice which ought to reign in the Christian Society. 'Obey the criminal courts, but do not go out of your way to invoke the civil courts,' is a fair, if rough, summary of his teaching.

1. Τολμᾷ τις ὑμῶν. We know nothing of the facts, but it is clear from *v.* 8 that the Apostle has no merely isolated case in view: τολμᾷ *grandi verbo notatur laesa majestas Christianorum* (Beng.); Rom. xv. 18. The word is an argument in itself; 'How can you dare, endure, bring yourself to?'

πρᾶγμα. In the forensic sense; 'a cause for trial,' 'a case,' Joseph. *Ant.* XIV. x. 7.

τὸν ἕτερον. Not 'another' (AV.), but 'his neighbour' (RV.), 'his fellow' (x. 24, xiv. 17; Rom. ii. 1; Gal. vi. 4).

κρίνεσθαι. Middle; 'go to law,' 'seek for judgment' Cf. κριθῆναι (Matt. v. 40; Eccles. vi. 10). The question comes with increased force after v. 12, 13. 'It is no business of ours to judge the heathen: and are we to ask them to judge us?'

ἐπὶ τῶν ἀδίκων. 'Before the unrighteous.'* The term is not meant to imply that there was small chance of getting justice in a heathen court; St Paul's own experience had taught him otherwise. The term reflects, not on Roman tribunals, but on the pagan world to which they belonged. He perhaps chose the word rather than ἀπίστων, in order to suggest the paradox of seeking justice among the unjust. The Rabbis taught that Jews must not carry their cases before Gentiles, and we may be sure

---

* Augustine (*De doct. Christ.* iv. 18) seems to have read ὑπὸ τ. ἀδ. He has, *judicari ab iniquis et non apud sanctos.* Vulg. has *apud* with both words, as also has Augustine, *Enchir. ad Laurent.* 78.

that it was in the Greek majority at Corinth, and not in the
Jewish minority, that this evil prevailed.* Greeks were fond οι
litigation, φιλοδικοί (Arist. *Rhet.* II. xxiii. 23), and as there were
no Christian courts they must enter heathen tribunals if they
wanted to go to law. See Edwards. For ἐπί see 2 Cor. vii. 14 ;
Mark xiii. 9 ; Acts xxv. 9.

καὶ οὐχὶ ἐπὶ τῶν ἁγίων.   He does not mean that Christian
courts ought to be instituted, but that Christian disputants should
submit to Christian arbitration.

2. ἤ οὐκ οἴδατε.   Such conduct was incompatible with principles which ought to be familiar to them.   He first asks, 'How
can you be so presumptuous?'   Then, on the supposition
that this is not the cause of their error, he asks, 'How can
you be so ignorant?'   The ἤ introduces an alternative explanation.   The formula οὐκ οἴδατε occurs five times in this chapter
(2, 3, 9, 16, 19 ; cf. 2 Cor. xiii. 5, etc.).

οἱ ἅγιοι τὸν κόσμον κρινοῦσιν.   Here, no doubt, the verb should
be accented as a future ; contrast v. 13.   It is in the Messianic
Kingdom that the saints will share in Christ's reign over the
created universe.   'Judge' does not here mean 'condemn,' and
the world' does not mean 'the evil world.'   It is only from the
context, as in Acts xiii. 27, that κρίνειν sometimes becomes
equivalent to κατακρίνειν, and ὁ κόσμος frequently is used without
any idea of moral, *i.e.* immoral quality ; cf. iii. 22.   Indeed, it is
not clear that κρινοῦσιν here means 'will pronounce judgment
upon' ; it is perhaps used in the Hebraic sense of 'ruling.'   So
also in Matt. xix. 28.   This sense is frequent in Judges (iii. 10,
x. 2, 3, xii. 9, 11, 13, 14, etc.).   Wisd. iii. 8 is parallel ; 'They
shall judge the nations and have dominion over the peoples' ;
also Ecclus. iv. 15.   St Paul may have known the Book of
Wisdom.   Cf. the Book of Enoch (cviii. 12), "I will bring forth
clad in shining light those who have loved My holy Name, and
I will seat each on the throne of his honour."   The saints are to
share in the final perfection of the Messianic reign of Christ.
They themselves are to appear before the Judge (Rom. xiv. 10 ;
2 Tim. iv. 1) and are then to share His glory (iv. 8 ; Rom. viii. 17 ;
Dan. vii. 22 ; Rev. ii. 26, 27, iii. 21, xx. 4).   The Apostle's
eschatology (xv. 21–24) supplies him with the thought of these
verses.   He is certainly not thinking of the time when *earthly*
tribunals will be filled with Christian judges.†

καὶ εἰ ἐν ὑμῖν κρίνεται ὁ κ.   The καί adds a further question,

---

* To bring a lawsuit before a court of idolaters was regarded as blas-
phemy against the Law.

† Polycarp quotes the question, 'Know we not that the saints shall judge
the world?' as the doctrine of Paul (*Phil.* 11).

and presses home the bearing of the preceding question. The
ἐν ὑμῖν is less easy to explain; 'among you,' 'in your court,' 'in
your jurisdiction,' may be the meaning. Or we may fall back
on the instrumental use of ἐν. Like κρίνετε in v. 12, κρίνεται
expresses what is normal. 'The heathen are to be judged by
you; they are in your jurisdiction. How incongruous that you
should ask to be judged by them!'

ἀνάξιοί ἐστε κριτηρίων ἐλαχίστων. 'Are ye unworthy of the
smallest tribunals?' So in RV. marg. Cf. Jas. ii. 6; Judg.
v. 10; Dan. vii. 10, 26; Susann. 49: also μὴ ἐρχέσθω ἐπὶ
κριτήριον ἐθνικόν (*Apost. Const.* ii. 45). In papyri, οἱ ἐπὶ τῶν
κριτηρίων means those who preside in tribunals. The meaning
'case' or 'cause' is insufficiently supported. Ἀνάξιος is found
nowhere else in N.T.

D³ E L, AV. omit ἤ before οὐκ οἴδατε.

3. The thought of *v.* 2 is repeated and expanded. To say
that Christians will judge angels restates 'will judge the world'
in an extreme form, for the sake of sharpening the contrast.
Ἄγγελοι are the highest order of beings under God, yet they are
creatures and are part of the κόσμος. But the members of
Christ are to be crowned with glory and honour (Ps. viii. 6), and
are to share in His regal exaltation, which exceeds any angelic
dignity. He 'judges,' *i.e.* rules over, angels, and the saints
share in that rule. The words may mean that the saints are to
be His assessors in the Day of Judgment, that angels will then
be judged, and that the saints will take part in sentencing them.
If so, this must refer to fallen angels, for it is difficult to believe
that St Paul held that all angels, good and bad, will be judged
hereafter. But he gives no epithet to angels here, because it is
not needed for his argument; indeed, to have said 'fallen angels,'
or 'evil angels,' would rather have marred his argument. As
Evans rightly insists, it is the *exalted nature* of angels that is the
Apostle's point. 'You are to judge the world. Nay, you are to
judge, not only men, but angels. Are you unable to settle petty
disputes among yourselves?' St Paul's purpose is to emphasize
the *augustness* of the 'judging' to which members of Christ are
called.* To press the statement in such a way as to raise the
question of the exact nature, scope, or details, of the judgment
of angels, is to go altogether beyond the Apostle's purpose.
Thackeray (*St Paul and Contemporary Jewish Thought,* pp. 152 f.)
has shown from Jude 6, Wisd. iii. 8, and Enoch xiii.–xvi. that

---

* Godet remarks that *Paul ne veut pas désigner tels ou tels anges; il veut
réveiller dans l'église le sentiment de sa compétence et de sa dignité, en lui
rappelant que des êtres d'une nature aussi élevée seront un jour soumis à sa
jurisdiction.* See also Milligan on 1 Thess. iii. 13, and Findlay here.

there is nothing in this unique statement to which a Jew of that day would not have subscribed. See Abbott, *The Son of Man*, p. 213.

μήτιγε βιωτικά. The γε strengthens the force of the μήτι, which is that of a condensed question; 'need I so much as mention?' *Nedum quae ad hujus vitae usum pertinent* (Beza): *quanto magis saecularia*. The clause may be regarded as part of the preceding question (WH.), or as a separate question (AV., RV.), or as an appended remark, 'to say nothing at all of things of this life' (Ellicott). The adjective occurs Luke xxi. 34, but is not found in LXX, nor earlier than Aristotle. Following the well-known difference in N.T. between βίος and ζωή (see on Luke viii. 43), βιωτικά means questions relating to our life on earth on its merely human side, or to the resources of life, such as food, clothing, property, etc. Philo (*Vit. Mos.* iii. 18), πρὸς τὰς βιωτικὰς χρείας ὑπηρετεῖν. See Trench, *Syn.* § xxvii.; Cremer, *Lex.* p. 272; Lightfoot on Ign. *Rom.* vii. 3.

Μήτιγε is written by different editors as one word, or as two (μήτι γε), or as three. Tregelles is perhaps alone in writing μή τι γε.

4. βιωτικὰ κριτήρια. 'Tribunals dealing with worldly matters.' The adj. is repeated with emphasis, which is increased by its being placed first. That is the surprising thing, that Christians should have βιωτικά that require litigation.

μὲν οὖν. 'Nay but,' or 'Nay rather.' The force of the words is *either* to emphasize the cumulative scandal of having such cases at all and of bringing them ἐπὶ τῶν ἀδίκων, *or* (if καθίζετε is imperative) to advise an alternative course to that described in *v.* 2.

ἐὰν ἔχητε. This form of protasis (cf. iv. 15) requires a future or its equivalent in the apodosis. Here we have an equivalent, whether we take καθίζετε as imperative or interrogative. 'If you must have such things as courts to deal with these petty matters, then set,' etc.; or 'do you set?'—'Is that your way of dealing with the matter?' It is intolerably forced to put a comma after κριτήρια, make it an *accus. pendens*, and take ἐὰν ἔχητε with τοὺς ἐξουθενημένους.

τοὺς ἐξουθενημένους ἐν τῇ ἐκκλησίᾳ. If καθίζετε is imperative, then these words mean 'those in the Church who are held of no account,' *i.e.* the least esteemed of the Christians. The Apostle sarcastically tells them that, so far from there being any excuse for resorting to heathen tribunals, any selection of the simplest among themselves would be competent to settle their disputes about trifles. Let the insignificant decide what is insignificant.

If καθίζετε is indicative and the sentence interrogative, then these words mean, 'those who, in the Church, are held of no account,' viz. the ἄδικοι of *v.* 1.   The meaning is the same if the sentence is categorical.

Both constructions are possible, and both make good sense. Alford, Edwards, Ellicott, Evans, and Lightfoot give strong reasons for preferring the imperative, as AV.   In this they follow a strong body of authorities ; the Vulgate, Peshito, Coptic, and Armenian, Chrysostom, Theodoret, Augustine, Beza, Calvin, Estius, Bengel, and Wetstein.   To mention only one of the arguments used ;—it does seem improbable that St Paul would call heathen magistrates 'those who, in the Church, are held ot no account.'   He has, it is true, spoken of the heathen in general (not the magistrates in particular) as ἄδικοι : but here he is speaking of those who preside in the heathen tribunals.   And if he wanted to speak disparagingly of them, is 'those whom Christians despise' a likely phrase for him to use?   The Vulgate renders, *contemptibiles qui sunt in ecclesia, illos constituite ad judicandum* ; but the Greek means *contemptos* rather than *contemptibiles*.   Augustine also has *contemptibiles*, but he renders τούτους καθίζετε, *hos collocate.**

Nevertheless, Tischendorf, WH. and the Revisers support a considerable number of commentators, from Luther to Schmiedel, in punctuating the sentence as a question.   It is urged that the Apostle, after the reminder of *vv.* 2, 3, returns to the question of *v.* 1 ; 'Will they, by going outside their own body for justice, confess themselves, the appointed judges of angels, to be unfit to decide the pettiest arbitrations?' †

We must be content to leave the question open.   The general sense is clear.   The Corinthians were doing a shameful thing in going to heathen civil courts to settle disputes between Christians.

πρὸς ἐντροπὴν ὑμῖν λέγω.   'I say this to move you to shame'; see on iv. 14.   As in xv. 34, the words refer to what precedes, and they suit either of the interpretations given above, either the sarcastic command or the reproachful question ; but they suit the latter somewhat better.   Only here, and xv. 34 does ἐντροπή occur in N.T., but it is not rare in the Psalms.

5. οὕτως οὐκ ἔνι κ.τ.λ.   'Is there such a total lack among you of any wise person' that you are thus obliged to go outside?

* It is evident that καθίζετε is a word which is more suitable for constitut-ing simple Christians as arbitrators than for adopting heathen magistrates, already appointed, as judges of Christians.

† There is yet another way, suggested by J. C. K. Hofmann and accepted by Findlay ; 'Well then, as for secular tribunals—if you have men that are made of no account in the Church, set these on the bench !' The punctuation does not seem to be very probable.

With the use of τούτους here we may compare τούτους in xvi. 3 and τοῦτον in 2 Thess. iii. 14.

Or, 'So is there not found among you one wise person?' The
οὔτως refers to the condition of things in the Corinthian Church:
Chrys., τοσαύτη σπάνις ἀνδρῶν συνετῶν παρ' ὑμῖν; it is now
commonly admitted that ἔνι "is not a contraction from ἔνεστι, but
the preposition ἐν or ἐνί, strengthened by a vigorous accent, like
ἔπι, πάρα, and used with an ellipse of the substantive verb"
(Lightfoot on Gal. iii. 28; J. B. Mayor on Jas. i. 17): translate,
therefore, 'is not found.'

διακρῖναι ἀνὰ μέσον τοῦ ἀδελφοῦ αὐτοῦ. A highly condensed
sentence; 'to decide between his fellow-Christian' meaning 'to
act as arbitrator between one fellow-Christian and another.' We
want ἀνὰ μέσον ἀδελφοῦ καὶ τοῦ ἀδ. αὐτοῦ, like ἀνὰ μέσον ἐμοῦ καὶ
σοῦ (Gen. xxiii. 15). J. H. Moulton (*Gr.* p. 99) suspects a
corruption in the text, but dictation may account for the ab-
breviation: τῶν ἀδελφῶν αὐτοῦ is the simplest conjecture. The
compound preposition ἀνὰ μέσον is frequent in papyri. As the
Lord had directed (Matt. xviii. 17), the aggrieved brother ought
to 'tell it to the Church.'*

Both here and in xv. 34 there is difference of reading between λέγω and
λαλῶ. Here λέγω (א D E F G L P) is to be preferred to λαλῶ (B, with C
doubtful). ἔνι (א B C L P) rather than ἐστιν (D E F G). οὐδεὶς σοφός
(א B C 17, Copt.) rather than οὐδὲ εἷς σοφός (F G P) or σοφὸς οὐδὲ εἷς (D³ L)
or σοφός without οὐδὲ εἷς or οὐδείς (D* E, Aeth.). For τοῦ ἀδελφοῦ some
editors conjecture τῶν ἀδελφῶν.

6. ἀλλὰ ἀδελφὸς κ.τ.λ. We have the same doubt as that
respecting μήτιγε βιωτικά (*v.* 3). This verse may be a continuation of the preceding question (WH., RV.), or a separate
question (AV.), or an appended statement (Ellicott). In the
last case, ἀλλά is 'Nay,' 'On the contrary.'

καὶ τοῦτο. This is the climax. That there should be disputes about βιωτικά is bad; that Christian should go to law
with Christian is worse; that Christians should do this before
unbelievers is worst of all. It is a scandal before the heathen
world. Cf. καὶ τοῦτο (Rom. xiii. 11; 3 John 5) and the more
classical καὶ ταῦτα (Heb. xi. 12), of which Wetstein gives
numerous examples.

7. ἤδη μὲν οὖν. 'Nay, verily there is at once,' 'there is to
begin with, without going any further': μὲν οὖν, separate, as in
v. 4, and with no δέ to answer to the μέν.

ὅλως. 'Altogether,' *i.e.* no matter what the tribunal may be:
or 'generally,' 'under any circumstances,' *i.e.* no matter what
the result may be.

ἥττημα. 'A falling short' of spiritual attainment, or of

* Cicero (*Ad Fam.* ix. 25) writes to Papirius Paetus, *Noli pati litigare
fratres, et judiciis turpibus conflictari.*

Christian blessings, 'a defect' (RV.), or possibly 'a defeat.
They have been worsted in the spiritual fight. Origen here
contrasts ἡττᾶσθαι with νικᾶν.* Cf. Isa. xxxi. 8, οἱ δὲ νεανίσκοι
ἔσονται εἰς ἥττημα. In Rom. xi. 12 the meaning seems to be
'defeat' (see note there), and these are the only passages in the
Bible in which the word occurs. See Field, *Otium Norvic.*
iii. 97.

κρίματα. Elsewhere in N.T. the word means 'decrees' or
'judgments,' but here it is almost equivalent to κριτήρια (*v.* 4):
'matters for judgment,' 'lawsuits.'

μεθ' ἑαυτῶν. Literally, 'with your own selves.' It is possible that this use of μεθ' ἑαυτῶν for μετ' ἀλλήλων is deliberate,
in order to show that in bringing a suit against a fellow-Christian
they were bringing a suit against themselves, so close was the
relationship. The solidarity of the Church made such conduct
suicidal. But the substitution occurs where no such idea can be
understood (Mark xvi. 3).

There are passages in M. Aurelius which are very much in
harmony with these verses. He argues that men are kinsmen,
and that all wrong-doing is the result of ignorance. Those who
know better must be patient with those who know not what
they do in being insolent and malicious. "But I, who have
seen the nature of the good that it is beautiful, and of the bad
that it is base (αἰσχρόν), and the nature of him that does the
wrong, that it is akin to me, not so much by community of
blood and seed as by community of intelligence and divine
endowment,—I can neither be injured by any of them, for no
one can fix on me what is base; nor can I be angry with one
who is my kinsman, nor feel hatred against him" (ii. 1). "On
every occasion a man should say, This comes from God : this
is from one of the same tribe and family and society, but from
one who does not know what befits his nature. But I know ;
therefore I treat him according to the natural law of fellowship
with kindness and justice" (iii. 11). "With what are you so
displeased? with the badness of men? Consider the decision,
that rational beings exist for one another, and that to be patient
is a part of righteousness, and that men do wrong against their
will" (iv. 3).

ἀδικεῖσθε, ἀποστερεῖσθε. 'Endure wrong,' 'endure depriva-
tion.' The verbs are middle, not passive.

---

* He says that the man who accepts injury without retaliating νενίκηκεν,
while the man who brings an action against a fellow-Christian ἡττᾶται. He
is worsted, has lost his cause, by the very fact of entering a law-court. Similarly, Clem. Alex. *Strom.* vii. 14, which is a commentary on this section ;
"To say then that the wronged man goes to law before the wrongdoers is
nothing else than to say that he desires to retaliate and wishes to do wrong
to the second in return, which is likewise to do wrong also himself."

ἤδη μὲν οὖν (אᵇ A B C Dᵇ E L P, Aeth.); omit οὖν (א* D* 17, Vulg. Copt. Arm.). The οὖν is probably genuine. A omits ὅλως. The ἐν before ὑμῖν has very little authority; *est in vobis* (Vulg.).

8. ἀλλὰ ὑμεῖς. 'Whereas *you*, on the contrary.' The emphatic pronoun contrasts their conduct with what is fitting. 'Not content with refusing to *endure* wrong (and as Christians you ought to be ready to endure it), you yourselves *inflict* it, and that on fellow-Christians';—a climax of unchristian conduct. Matt. v. 39–41 teaches far otherwise; and the substance of the Sermon on the Mount would be known to them. The sentence is not part of the preceding question.*

D transposes ἀδικεῖτε and ἀποστερεῖτε. For τοῦτο, L, Arm., Chrys., Thdrt. have ταῦτα, perhaps to cover the two verbs.

9–11. Unrighteousness in all its forms is a survival from a bad past, which the Corinthians ought to have left behind them.

Evil-doers, such as some of you were, cannot enter the Kingdom.

⁹ Is this wilfulness on your part, or is it that you do not know that wrong-doers will have no share in the Kingdom? Do not be led astray by false teachers. No fornicator, idolater, adulterer, sensualist, sodomite, ¹⁰ thief, cheat, drunkard, reviler, or extortioner will have any share in God's Kingdom. ¹¹ And of such vile sort some of you once were. But you washed your pollutions away, you were made holy, you were made righteous, by sharing in the Name of our Lord Jesus Christ and in the gift of the Spirit of God.

These three verses conclude the subject of *vv.* 1–8 by an appeal to wider principles, and thus prepare the way for the fourth matter of censure (12–20). The connexion with *vv.* 1–8 is definite, although not close. The Corinthians have shown themselves ἄδικοι, in the narrower sense of 'unjust,' by their conduct to one another (ἀδικεῖτε, *v.* 8). They need, however, to be reminded that ἀδικία in any sense (see note below) excludes a man from the heritage of God's Kingdom. The Apostle goes on to specify several forms of ἀδικία which they ought to have abandoned, and finally returns to the subject of πορνεία.

* It is remarkable that in six verses we have four cases in which there is doubt whether the sentence is interrogative or not; *vv.* 3, 4, 6, 8. In this last case the interrogative is very improbable. See also on **v. 13.**

9. ἢ οὐκ οἴδατε. See *vv.* 2 and 19. There is an alternative implied. '[Is it from a reckless determination to do as they please regardless of the consequences,] or is it from real ignorance of the consequences?' In either case their error is disastrous.

ἄδικοι. The word is suggested by the previous ἀδικεῖτε, and this should be marked in translation ; 'ye do wrong' . . . 'wrongdoers shall not inherit.' No English version preserves the connexion ; nor does the Vulgate, *injuriam facitis . . . iniqui :* but Beza does so, *injuriam facitis . . . injustos.* Now the word takes a wider meaning ; it is wrongdoing of any kind, and not the special kind of being unjust in matters of personal rights, that is meant ; and here the Apostle passes to a more comprehensive survey of the spiritual state of his readers, and also to a sterner tone : εἰς ἀπειλὴν κατακλείει τὴν παραίνεσιν (Chrys.). The evil that he has now to deal with is the danger of *Gentile licentiousness.*

Θεοῦ βασιλείαν. When St Paul uses the shorter form, 'God's Kingdom' (*v.* 10, xv. 50 ; Gal. v. 21), instead of the more usual ἡ βας. τοῦ Θ. (iv. 20 ; Rom. xiv. 17 ; 2 Thess. i. 5 ; cf. Eph. v. 5), he elsewhere writes βας. Θεοῦ. Here Θεοῦ is placed first, in order to bring ἄδικοι and Θεοῦ into emphatic contrast by juxtaposition : '*wrong*-doers' are manifestly out of place in '*God's* Kingdom.' Cf. πρόσωπον Θεὸς ἀνθρώπου οὐ λαμβάνει (Gal. ii. 6). 'To inherit the Kingdom of God' is a Jewish thought, in allusion to the promise given to Abraham ; but St Paul, in accordance with his doctrine of grace, enlarges and spiritualizes the idea of inheritance. He reminds the Corinthians that, although all Christians are heirs, yet heirs may be disinherited. They may disqualify themselves. In iv. 20, the Kingdom is regarded as present. Here and xv. 50 it is regarded as future. It is both : see J. Kaftan, *Jesus u. Paulus*, p. 24 ; Dalman, *Words*, p. 125 ; Abbott, *The Son of Man*, p. 576.

Μὴ πλανᾶσθε. See on Luke xxi. 8. The verb is passive, 'Do not be led astray,' and implies fundamental error.* The revisers sometimes correct the 'deceived' of AV. to 'led astray,' but here and xv. 33 they retain 'deceived.' The charge is a sharper repetition of ἢ οὐκ οἴδατε. Some Jews held that the belief in one God sufficed without holiness of life. Judaizers may have been teaching in Corinth that faith sufficed.†

* Origen illustrates thus ; "Let no one lead you astray with persuasive words, saying that God is merciful, kind, and loving, and ready to forgive sins."

† Duchesne thinks that there is nothing in 1 or 2 Corinthians "to lead to the conclusion that the Apostle's rivals had introduced Judaizing tendencies in Corinth" (*Early Hist of the Chr. Church*, p. 23). That can hardly be maintained respecting 2 *Corinthians*, and is very disputable about this Epistle.

The order of the ten kinds of offenders is unstudied. He enumerates sins which were prevalent at Corinth just as they occur to him. Of the first five, three (and perhaps four) deal with sinners against purity, while the fifth, 'idolaters,' were frequently sinners of the same kind. Of the last five, three are sinners against personal property or rights, such as are censured in *v.* 8. All of them are in apposition to ἄδικοι, an apposition which would seem quite natural to Greeks, who were accustomed to regard δικαιοσύνη as the sum-total of virtues (Arist. *Eth. Nic.* v. i. 15), and therefore ἀδικία as the sum-total of vices (*ibid.* § 19: see on Luke xiii. 27). Several of these forms of evil are dealt with in this Epistle (*vv.* 13–18, v. 1, 11, viii. 10, x. 14, etc.): cf. Rom. i. 27 and iii. 13; Gal. v. 19, 20; 1 Tim. i. 10.*

For Θεοῦ βασιλείαν, L, d e f Vulg. have the more usual βασ. Θεοῦ. D* has οὐδέ throughout *vv.* 9, 10. οὐ μέθυσοι (א A C P 17) rather than οὔτε μέθ. (B D³ E L). L P insert οὐ before κληρονομήσουσιν at the end of *v.* 10.

11. καὶ ταῦτά τινες ἦτε. 'And such dreadful things as these *some* of you *were*.' While the neuter indicates a horror of what has been mentioned, the τινες and the tense lighten the sad statement. Not all of them, not even many, but only some, are said to have been guilty; and it is all a thing of the past. Cf. ἦτε in Rom. vi. 17.

ἀλλά. The threefold 'But' emphasizes strongly the contrast between their present state and their past, and the consequent demand which their changed moral condition makes upon them.

ἀπελούσασθε. Neither 'ye are washed' (AV.), nor 'ye were washed' (RV.), nor 'ye washed yourselves' (RV. marg.), but 'ye washed them away from you,' 'ye washed away your sins'; exactly as in Acts xxii. 16, the only other place in N.T. in which the compound verb occurs; ἀναστὰς βάπτισαι καὶ ἀπόλουσαι τὰς ἁμαρτίας σου. Their seeking baptism was their own act, and they entered the water as voluntary agents, just as St Paul did. Cf. 2 Tim. ii. 21.

ἡγιάσθητε, ἐδικαιώθητε. The repetitions of the aorist show that these verbs refer to the same event as ἀπελούσασθε. The

---

* There is a manifest reproduction of *vv.* 9, 10 in Ign. *Eph.* 16; also in Ep. of Polycarp, 5. On the general sense of the two verses see Sanday on St Paul's Equivalent for the Kingdom of Heaven, *JTS.* July 1900, pp. 481 f.

Aristot. (*Eth. Nic.* VII. iv. 4) says that people are called μαλακοί in reference to the same things as they are called ἀκόλαστοι, viz. περὶ τὰς σωματικὰς ἀπολαύσεις: Plato (*Rep.* viii. 556 B) πρὸς ἡδονάς τε καὶ λύπας. Origen here gives the word a darker meaning. See Deissmann, *Light*, p. 150. He gives a striking illustration of the list of vices here and elsewhere, derived from counters in an ancient game. Each counter had the name of a vice or a virtue on it; and in the specimens in museums the vices greatly preponderate (pp. 320 f.).

crisis, of which their baptism was the concrete embodiment, had marked their transition from the rule of self to the service of God (consecration), and from the condition of guilty sinners to that of pardoned children of God (justification). Neither of the verbs here is to be taken in the technical theological sense which each of them sometimes bears : cf. ἅγιοι (i. 2) and ἡγίασται (vii. 14). Here ἐδικαιώθητε forms a kind of climax, completing the contrast with ἄδικοι (v. 9). The new life is viewed here as implicit in the first decisive turn to Christ, which again was inseparably connected with their baptism. Cf. Rom. vi. 7.

ἐν τῷ ὀνόματι τ. κ. ʼI. Χρ.   As in Acts ii. 38, x. 48; cf. εἰς τὸ ὄν., Acts viii. 16, xix. 5.   Matt. xxviii. 19 is the only passage in which the Trinitarian form is found. See Hastings, *DB.* 1. p. 241 f. This passage is remarkable as being an approach to the Trinitarian form, for ἐν τῷ Πνεύματι is coupled with 'in the Name of the Lord Jesus Christ,' and τοῦ Θεοῦ is added ; so that God, and the Lord Jesus Christ, and the Spirit are all mentioned. But it is doubtful whether this verse can be taken as evidence of a baptismal formula. Godet certainly goes too far in claiming it as *implying* the use of the threefold Name (see on Matt. xxviii. 19). But it is right to take ἐν τῷ ὀνόματι κ.τ.λ. with all three verbs. Cf. "saved in His Name" (Enoch, xlviii. 7).

B C P 17, Vulg. Copt. Arm. Aeth. insert ἡμῶν after τοῦ Κυρίου : ℵ A D E L omit. It is not easy to decide. ℵ B C D* E P, Vulg. Copt. Arm. Aeth. insert Χριστοῦ after ʼΙησοῦ : A D³ L omit. The word is probably genuine. In both cases the evidence of C is not clear : there is space for the word, but it is not legible.

VI. 12-20. THE SUBJECT OF FORNICATION IN THE LIGHT OF FIRST PRINCIPLES.

Christian freedom is not licentiousness.   Our bodies were not made for unchastity.   The body is a temple of the Spirit.

¹² Perhaps I may have said to you at some time ; In all things I can do as I like. Very possibly. But not all things that I may do do me good. In all things I can do as I like, but I shall never allow anything to do as it likes with me.   ¹³ I am not going to let myself be the slave of appetite. It is true that the stomach and food were made for one another. Yet they were not made to last for ever : the God who made them will put an end to both. But it is not true that the body was made for fornication. The body is there to serve the Lord, and the

Lord is there to have the body for His service: ¹⁴ and as God raised Him from the dead, so will He also raise us up by His own power. ¹⁵ Is it that you do not know that your bodies are members of Christ? Shall I then take away from Christ members which are His and make them members of a harlot? Away with so dreadful a thought! ¹⁶ Or is it that you do not know that the union of a man with his harlot makes the two to be one body? I am not exaggerating; for the Scripture says, The two shall become one flesh. ¹⁷ But the union of a man with the Lord makes the two to be one spirit. ¹⁸ Do not stop to parley with fornication: turn and fly. In the case of no other sin is such grievous injury done to the body as in this case: the fornicator sins against his own body. ¹⁹ Does that statement surprise you? Do you not know that your body is a temple of the Holy Spirit, who makes His home in you, being sent for that very purpose from God? And, what is more, you are not your own property, but God's. He paid a high price for you. Surely you are bound to use to His glory the body which He has bought.

12–20. St Paul now passes to a fourth matter for censure. He has already taken occasion, in connexion with a specially flagrant case of πορνεία, to blame the lack of moral discipline in the community. He now takes up the subject of πορνεία generally, dealing with it in the light of first principles. The sin was prevalent at Corinth (*v.* 9, vii. 2; 2 Cor. xii. 21), and was virtually condoned by public opinion in Greece and in Rome. Moreover, the Apostle's own teaching as to Christian liberty (Rom. v. 20, vi. 14) had been perverted and caricatured, not only by opponents (Rom. iii. 8), but also by some 'emancipated' Christians at Corinth itself. The latter had made it an excuse for licence. He proceeds now to show the real meaning and scope of Christian liberty, and in so doing sets forth the Christian doctrine of the body as destined for eternal union with Christ.

12. πάντα μοι ἔξεστιν. These are St Paul's own words (see on x. 23). They may have been current among the Corinthians as a trite maxim. If so, the Apostle here adopts them as his own, adding the considerations which limit their scope. More probably they were words he had used, which were well known as his, and which had been misused by persons whom he now proceeds to warn. Of course, πάντα is not absolute in extent:

no sane person would maintain that it was meant to cover such
things as πορνεία and justify πανουργία. It covers, however, a very
great deal, viz. the whole of that wide range of things which are
not wrong *per se*. But within this wide range of things which
are indifferent, and therefore permissible, there are many things
which become wrong, and therefore not permissible, in view of
principles which are now to be explained.

μοι ἔξεστιν. *Saepe Paulus prima persona singulari eloquitur,
quae vim habent gnomes ; in hac praesertim epistola*, v. 15, vii. 7,
viii. 13, x. 23, 29, 30, xiv. 11 (Beng.). The saying applies to
all Christians. On its import see J. Kaftan, *Jesus u. Paulus*,
pp. 51, 52.

ἀλλ' οὐ πάντα συμφέρει. Liberty is limited by the law of the
higher expediency, *i.e.* by reference to the moral or religious life
of all those who are concerned, viz. the agent and those whom
his conduct may influence. In this first point the Apostle is
possibly thinking chiefly of the people influenced.* We have no
longer any right to do what in itself is innocent, when our doing
it will have a bad effect on others. Our liberty is abused when
our use of it causes grave scandal.

οὐκ ἐγὼ ἐξουσιασθήσομαι ὑπό τινος. This is the second point ;
really included in the higher law of expediency, but requiring to
be stated separately, in order to show that the agent, quite apart
from those whom his conduct may influence, has to be considered. What effect will his action have upon himself? We
have no longer any right to do what in itself is innocent, when
experience has proved that our doing it has a bad effect on ourselves. Our liberty is abused when our use of it weakens our
character and lessens our power of self-control. St Paul says
that, for his part, he 'will *not* be brought under the power of
anything.' The οὐκ is emphatic, and the ἐγώ slightly so, but
very slightly : the ἐγώ is rendered almost necessary by the preceding μοι. We must beware of using liberty in such a way as
to *lose* it, *e.g.* in becoming slaves to a habit respecting things
which in themselves are lawful. The τινος is neuter, being one
of the πάντα.

The verb ἐξουσιάζειν is chosen because of its close connexion
with ἔξεστι through ἐξουσία : it is frequent in LXX, especially in
Ecclesiastes ; in N.T., vii. 4 and Luke xxii. 25.† This play on
words cannot be reproduced exactly in English ; perhaps 'I can
make free with all things, but I shall *not* let anything make free

* In x. 23 f., where St Paul again twice quotes his own πάντα μοι ἔξεστιν,
he is certainly thinking chiefly of the people influenced.

† Nowhere else does the passive occur. But in late Greek the rule that
only verbs which have an accusative can be used in the passive is not observed.
See Lightfoot on δογματίζεσθε (Col. ii. 20).

with me' may serve to show the kind of thought: *mihi res non me rebus submittere conor*.

These two verses (12, 13) are a kind of preface to the subject of πορνεία, to show that it is not one of those things which may or may not be lawful according to circumstances. It is in all circumstances wholly outside the scope of Christian liberty, however that liberty may be defined. 'While many things are lawful, and become wrong only if indulged (like the appetite for food) to an extent that is harmful to ourselves or to others, fornication is not a legitimate use of the body, but a gross abuse of it, being destructive of the purpose for which the body really exists.'

13. τὰ βρώματα . . . τοῖς βρώμασιν. It is quite possible that some of the Corinthians confused what the Apostle here so clearly distinguishes, the appetite for food and the craving for sensual indulgence. "We have traces of this gross moral confusion in the Apostolic Letter (Acts xv. 23–29), where things wholly diverse are combined, as directions about meats to be avoided and a prohibition of fornication" (Lightfoot). The Apostles, who framed these regulations, did not regard them as on the same plane, but the heathen, for whom they were framed, did. St Paul makes the distinction luminously clear. Not only are meats made for the belly, but the belly, which is essential to physical existence, is made for meats, and cannot exist without them. There is absolute correlation between the two, as long as earthly life lasts : but no longer, for both of them will eventually be done away. When the σῶμα ceases to be ψυχικόν and becomes πνευματικόν (xv. 44), neither the βρώματα nor the κοιλία will have any further function, and therefore 'God will bring to nought' both of them.

τὸ δὲ σῶμα οὐ τῇ πορνείᾳ. No such relation exists between the σῶμα and πορνεία as between the κοιλία and βρώματα. The supposed parallel breaks down in two essential particulars. (1) The σῶμα was not made for πορνεία, but for the Lord, in order to be a member of Christ, who lived and died to redeem it. (2) The σῶμα is not, like the κοιλία, to be brought to nought, but to be transformed and glorified (Phil. iii. 21). 'The 'body' is contrasted with 'flesh and blood' (xv. 37, 50), and the κοιλία belongs to the latter, and has only a temporal purpose, whereas the 'body' has an eternal purpose. So far, therefore, from πορνεία standing to the body in the same relation as meats to the belly, it fatally conflicts with the body's essential destiny, which is membership with Christ.

It is possible that in selecting the relation between appetite and food as a contrast to πορνεία St Paul is indirectly discouraging Judaistic distinctions of meats, or ascetic prohibitions of flesh and wine. No kind of food is forbidden to the Christian. But even if there had been no Judaizers at work in Corinth, and no tendency towards asceticism, he would probably have selected the relation between βρώματα and κοιλία for his purpose. The argument is still used, "If I may gratify one bodily appetite, why may I not gratify another? *Naturalia non sunt turpia. Omnia munda mundis.*"

καὶ ὁ Κύριος τῷ σώματι. A startling assertion of perfect correlation : *quanta dignatio !* (Beng.). The Son of God, 'sent in the likeness of sinful flesh,' has His purpose and destiny, viz. to dwell in and glorify the body (Rom. viii. 23) which is united with Him through the Spirit (*v.* 17); and it is lawful to say that He is for it as well as it for Him.

14. ὁ δὲ Θεός. This is parallel to ὁ δὲ Θεός in *v.* 13, and puts the contrast between the two cases in a very marked way. In the case of the κοιλία, and the βρώματα to which it is related, God will reduce both of them to nothingness. In the case of the σῶμα, and the Κύριος to which it is related, God has raised the Κύριος, and will raise up the σῶμα of every one who is a member of Him. The contrast between the two cases is complete. On the other hand, the close relationship between the Lord and all true Christians is shown by the doubled conjunction ; καὶ τὸν Κύριον . . . καὶ ἡμᾶς. See Sanday (*The Life of Christ in Recent Research,* p. 132) on the view that it was St Paul who deified Christ.

The change from the simple (ἤγειρεν) to the compound verb (ἐξεγερεῖ) has perhaps little meaning. In late Greek, compounds do not always have any additional force, and the difference is not greater than that between 'raise' and 'raise up.' The compound may be used to mark the future raising as not less sure than the one which is past, and it is well to mark the difference, as RV. does. AV., with 'raise up' for both, ignores the change, as does Vulg., *suscitavit . . . suscitabit,* and Iren. int. (v. vi. 2). The compound occurs only here and Rom. ix. 17 in N.T.; in LXX it is very frequent. See on ἐξαπατάτω, iii. 18.

διὰ τῆς δυνάμεως αὐτοῦ. This may qualify both verbs, but is more appropriate to ἐξεγερεῖ. There was need to remind the Corinthians of God's power, in order to confirm their belief in their own future resurrection (xv. 12); but no one who believed that Christ had been raised needed to be reminded of that : cf. Matt. xxii. 29. It is worth observing that St Paul does not take any account of 'the quick' who will not need to be raised. Contrast xv. 51 ; 1 Thess. iv. 15 f.; Rom. viii. 11.

ἐξεγερεῖ (א C D³ E K L, Vulg. Syrr. Copt. Aeth.) is probably to be preferred to ἐξεγείρει (A D* Q, d e *suscitat*), or to ἐξήγειρεν (B, Am. *suscitavit*). ἐξεγειρεῖ (P) may be regarded as supporting either of the first two, of which ἐξεγείρει may be safely set aside. It is possible that B has preserved the original reading, for no intelligent copyist would alter ἐξεγερεῖ into ἐξήγειρεν, but an unintelligent one might assimilate the second verb to the first. If ἐξήγειρεν is regarded as original it may be explained as referring to spiritual resurrection to newness of life, or possibly as referring to our resurrection as comprised potentially in that of Christ : ' God both raised the Lord and (by so doing) raised up us.' But it is unlikely that the Apostle would have obscured the certainty of the future resurrection of the body by using language which would have encouraged Hymenæus and Philetus (2 Tim. ii. 17, 18). *Qui dominum suscitavit, et nos suscitabit* (Tert. *Marc.* v. 7).

15. οὐκ οἴδατε κ.τ.λ. He presses home the principle that 'the body is for the Lord.' By virtue of that principle every Christian, and every one of his members, is a member of Christ. The higher heathen view was that man's body is in common with the brutes, τὸ σῶμα κοινὸν πρὸς τὰ ζῶα, and only his reason and intelligence in common with the gods (Epict. *Dissert.* i. iii. 1); but the Christian view is τὸ σῶμα μέλος τοῦ Χριστοῦ.* Epictetus speaks of both God and gods, and in popular language calls God 'Zeus.' In this chapter he speaks of God as the father of men and gods; but, at the best, he falls far short of Christian Theism. The Christian view, which first appears here, is developed in another connexion in xii. and in Rom. xii. See also Eph. iv. 15, 16, v. 30.

ἄρας οὖν. The AV. misses a point in translating, 'Shall I then *take* the members of Christ?' The RV. has, 'Shall I then take *away* the members of Christ?' Αἴρειν is not simply, 'to take,' which is λαμβάνειν, but either 'to take up,' 'raise' (Acts xxvii. 17), or 'to take away' (v. 2; Eph. iv. 31; Col. ii. 14; and nowhere else in Paul). The verb is very common in Gospels and Acts; elsewhere rare in N.T. The Apostle assumes that union with a harlot, unlike union with a lawful wife, robs Christ of members which belong to Him. Union with Christ attaches to our body through the spirit (v. 17), and sin is apostasy from the spiritual union with Christ. This is true of all sin, but πορνεία is a peculiarly direct blow at the principle τὸ σῶμα τῷ Κυρίῳ. *Quantum flagitium est, corpus nostrum a sacra illa conjunctione abreptum ad res Christo indignas transferri* (Calv.). As Augustine remarks (*De Civ. Dei* xxi. 25), "they cannot be at once the members of Christ and the members of a harlot."

ποιήσω. It is impossible and unimportant to decide whether ποιήσω is deliberative subjunctive ('Am I to take away . . . and make?') or future indicative ('Shall I take away?' etc.). The two aorists would mark two aspects, simultaneous in effect, of one and the same act. But the future harmonizes better with μὴ γένοιτο. AV., RV., Alford, Edwards, Ellicott, B. Weiss prefer the future.

* Origen says, μέλη τότε γίνεται Χριστοῦ, ὅτε πάντα κατὰ τὸν αὐτοῦ λόγον κινοῦμεν.

μὴ γένοιτο. Like οὐκ οἴδατε, this expression of strong dissent is frequent in this group of the Pauline Epistles (Romans, ten times; Galatians, twice; and here). Elsewhere in N.T., Luke xx. 16. It is rare in LXX, and never stands as an independent sentence: Gen. xliv. 7, 17; Josh. xxii. 29, xxiv. 16; 1 Kings xx. [xxi.] 3. It is one of several translations of the same Hebrew, another of which is ἴλεως (1 Chron. xi. 19; 2 Sam. xx. 20; Matt. xvi. 22). Neither μὴ γένοιτο nor ἴλεως is confined to Jewish and Christian writings: the former is frequent in Arrian, the latter is found in inscriptions. In Hom. *Od.* vii. 316 we have μὴ τοῦτο φίλον Διὶ πατρὶ γένοιτο, of detaining Ulysses against his wish. Cf. *Di meliora.* Here it expresses horror.

After τὰ σώματα there is the common confusion between ὑμῶν (א³ B C D E F G K L P, Latt.) and ἡμῶν (א* A). ἄρα (P and a few cursives) or ἢ ἄρα (F G) cannot be regarded as more probable than ἄρας (א A B C D E, etc.); yet Baljon adopts it: ἄρας has much force, not only in marking the grievous wrong done to Christ, but also in showing the voluntary, and even deliberate, character of the act.

16. ἢ οὐκ οἴδατε. Again (*v.* 2) we have this reproachful question. The Apostle proceeds to corroborate the ποιήσω πόρνης μέλη of *v.* 15.

ὁ κολλώμενος. The word may come from προσκολλᾶσθαι in Gen. ii. 24, as in Eph. v. 31, or possibly from Ecclus. xix. 2, ὁ κολλώμενος πόρναις τολμηρότερος ἔσται. Both the simple and the compound verb are frequent in LXX; in N.T. the compound is very rare. In both, only the passive, with reflective sense, is found. In N.T. the usual construction is the simple dat., as here. In LXX the constr. varies greatly, and there (2 Kings xviii. 6; cf. Ecclus. ii. 3) we have κολλᾶσθαι τῷ Κυρίῳ, as here, to express loyal and permanent adherence, resulting in complete spiritual union. This is placed in marked contrast to the temporary physical union which is so monstrous. The verb is frequent in *Ep. Barnabas* (ix. 9, x. 11, xix. 2, 6, xx. 2).

ἔσονται γάρ, φησίν, οἱ δύο εἰς σ. μ. The subject to be understood with φησίν must always depend upon the context. The word may introduce the objection of an opponent (2 Cor. **x.** 10). In Heb. viii. 5 we must understand 'God.' Here we may do the same, or (what amounts to the same) supply ἡ γραφή. The εἴπῃ in xv. 27, and the λέγει in 2 Cor. vi. 2, and Gal. iii. 16, and Eph. iv. 8, are similar. In each case there is divine authority for the statement. The quotation is direct from the LXX, which has οἱ δύο, as in Matt. xix. 5; Mark x. 8; Eph. v. 31, although it is not in the original. For εἶναι εἰς = γίνεσθαι there is perhaps no exact parallel in N.T., although the expression is frequent; xiv. 22; 2 Cor. vi. 18: Eph. i. 12; Heb. i. 5, viii. 10; etc. In most of these cases εἰς may mean 'to serve as.' It is manifest that here no distinction is to be drawn between σῶμα and σάρξ.

18. φεύγετε τὴν πορνείαν. 'Do not stop to dispute about it: make a practice (pres. imperat.) of flying at once.' So also of idolatry, which was so closely allied with impurity, x. 14. The asyndeton marks the urgency. Cf. 1 Thess. iv. 3.

πᾶν ἁμάρτημα κ.τ.λ. The difficulty of this passage lies in the distinction drawn between ἐκτὸς τ. σώματος, the predicate of 'every sin that a man doeth,' and εἰς τ. ἴδιον σῶμα, as marking the distinctive sin of the fornicator. Commentators differ greatly as to the explanation of ἐκτὸς τ. σώματος, which is the specially difficult expression. But the general meaning of vv. 13b–18 is plain. The body has an eternal destiny, τὸ σῶμα τῷ Κυρίῳ. Fornication takes the body away from the Lord and robs it of its glorious future, of which the presence of the Spirit is the present guarantee (cf. Rom. viii. 9–11). In v. 18 we have the sharply cut practical issue, 'Flee fornication.' Clearly the words that follow are meant to strengthen the *severitas cum fastidio* of the abrupt imperative : they are not an anti-climax. Any exegesis which fails to satisfy this elementary requirement may be set aside ; and for this reason the explanations of Evans, Meyer, and Heinrici may be passed over.

It is obvious that ἐκτός and εἰς are related as opposites. The meaning of either will help to determine the meaning of the other ; and the meaning of εἰς τ. ἴδιον σῶμα ἁμαρτάνει is fairly certain. For ἁμαρτάνειν εἰς, by the common usage of secular and Biblical Greek, means 'to sin *against*.' It cannot mean 'sin *in*,' or 'sin *by means of*,' or '*involve in* sin.' What then does 'to sin against one's own body' mean? The axiom, τὸ σῶμα τῷ Κυρίῳ, καὶ ὁ Κύριος τῷ σώματι, answers this question. To sin against one's own body is to defraud it of its part in Christ, to cut it off from its eternal destiny. This is what fornication does in a unique degree.* While fornication is εἰς τὸ ἴδιον σ., other sins are ἐκτὸς τοῦ σ. The one phrase is the opposite of the other. What St Paul asserts of fornication he denies of every other sin.

In what sense does he deny of all other sins that they are sins against a man's own body? If pressed and made absolute, the denial becomes a paradox. He has just told us (vv. 9, 10) that

---

* Alford puts a similar view somewhat differently. The Apostle's assertion "is *strictly true*. Drunkenness and gluttony are sins done *in* and *by* the body, and are sins *by abuse of* the body, but they are *introduced from without*, sinful in their *effect*, which effect it is each man's duty to foresee and avoid. But fornication is the *alienating that body which is the Lord's, and making it a harlot's body* ; it is not an *effect on* their body from participation of things without, but a *contradiction of the truth* of the body, wrought *within itself*."

there are many sins which exclude their doer from the Kingdom, and which therefore deprive the body of its future life in Christ. Obviously, he is here speaking relatively, and by way of comparison. All other sins are ἐκτὸς τοῦ σ., in the sense that they do not, as directly as fornication does, alienate the body from Christ, its Life and its Goal.

This explanation gains in clearness if we compare the words of our Lord (Matt. xii. 31), πᾶσα ἁμαρτία καὶ βλασφημία ἀφεθήσεται τοῖς ἀνθρώποις· ἡ δὲ τοῦ Πνεύματος βλασφημία οὐκ ἀφεθήσεται, κ.τ.λ. There too the language may be comparative. We know abundantly from Scripture that there is forgiveness for every sin, if rightly sought. In the first clause the Saviour does not proclaim an absolute indiscriminate amnesty for every other sin: any sin, unrepented and unabsolved, is an αἰώνιον ἁμάρτημα (Mark iii. 29). Neither clause is to be pressed beyond its purpose to an absolute sense. But sin against the Spirit is so incomparably less pardonable than any other, that, by comparison with it, they may be regarded as venial. He who sins against the Spirit is erecting a barrier, insuperable to a unique degree, against his own forgiveness. In like manner, the words ἐκτὸς τοῦ σ. ἐστι are not absolutely nor unconditionally predicated of 'every sin which a man doeth':* they merely assert that other sins "stop short of the baleful import of sensual sin" with its direct onslaught on the dominant principle, τὸ σῶμα τῷ Κυρίῳ. Cf. Hos. vi. 6, 'I will have mercy, and not sacrifice,' which does not mean that sacrifice is forbidden, but that mercy is greatly superior. Luke x. 20, xiv. 12, 13, xxiii. 28 are similar. Cf. ix. 10, x. 24, 33.

19. ἢ οὐκ οἴδατε. 'Or, if you cannot see that unchastity is a sin against your own body, are you ignorant that the body of each of you is a sanctuary (John ii. 21) of the Holy Spirit (Rom. viii. 11; 2 Cor. vi. 16; 2 Tim. i. 14)?' What in iii. 16 he stated of the Christian community as a whole, he here states of every member of it. In each case he appeals to facts which ought to be well known, as in vv. 2, 3, 9, 15, 16, v. 6, ix. 13, 24; Rom. vi. 19, xi. 2. Excepting Jas. iv. 4, the expression is peculiar to these Epistles. Note the emphatic position of ἁγίου: 'it is a Spirit that is *holy* that is in you.' In the temple of Aphrodite at Corinth, πορνεία was regarded as *consecration*: the Corinthians are here told that it is a monstrous *desecration* (Findlay). Epictetus (*Dis.* ii. 8) says, "Wretch, you are carrying God with you, and you know it not. Do you think I mean some god of silver or gold? You carry Him within yourself, and perceive not that you are polluting Him by impure thoughts and dirty deeds."

* On ἐάν in relative sentences see Deissmann, *Bible Studies*, pp. 201 f.

οὗ ἔχετε ἀπὸ Θ. The relative is attracted out of its own case, as often. Not content with emphasizing 'holy,' he gives further emphasis to the preceding plea by pointing out that the indwelling Spirit is a gift direct from God Himself. Such a Spirit cannot dwell in a polluted sanctuary. *Ep. of Barnabas* iv. 11, vi. 15.

For τὸ σῶμα, A²L 17, Copt. Arm. have τὰ σώματα, and Vulg. has *membra*.

καὶ οὐκ ἐστὲ ἑαυτῶν· 'I spoke of *your* body; but in truth the body is not your own to do as you please with it, any more than the Spirit is your own. You have no right of property in either case. Indeed, your whole personality is not your own property, for God bought you with the life-blood of His Son.' Acts xx. 28; Rom. xiv. 8. Epictetus again has a remarkable parallel; "If you were a statue of Phidias, you would think both of yourself and of the artist, and you would try to do nothing unworthy of him who made you, or of yourself. But now, because Zeus has made you, for this reason you do not care how you shall appear. And yet, is the artist in the one case like the artist in the other? or the work in the one case like the other?" See Long's translation and notes, i. pp. 156, 157, 288.

20. ἠγοράσθητε γὰρ τιμῆς. This 'buying with a price,' which causes a change of ownership, is a different metaphor from 'paying a ransom' (λύτρον, ἀντίλυτρον: λύτρωσις, ἀπολύτρωσις), which causes freedom. There is no need to state the price; οὐκ ἀργυρίῳ ἢ χρυσίῳ, ἀλλὰ τιμίῳ αἵματι (1 Pet. i. 19, where see Hort). The Vulgate has *pretio* only in vii. 23, but here has *pretio magno*, and the epithet weakens the effect. And there is no person from whom we are 'bought' (Abbott, *The Son of Man*, p. 702).

δοξάσατε δὴ τ. Θ. ἐν τ. σώματι ὑμ. As in *v.* 18, we have a sharp practical injunction which carries us a great deal further, and this same injunction is given in still more comprehensive terms to close the question about partaking of idol-meats (x. 31). Habitually to keep the body free from unchastity is imperative; but we must do more than that. Seeing that we belong, not to ourselves, but to God, we must use the body, in which He has placed His Spirit, to His glory. This verse goes far beyond the negative injunction in *v.* 18, and hence the δή enforcing the imperative, as in Acts xiii. 2; Luke ii. 15; Judith xiii. 11, Ἀνοίξατε, ἀνοίξατε δὴ τὴν πύλην: Hom. *Od.* xx. 18, Τέτλαθι δή, κραδίη. The 'Therefore' of AV. and RV. is not quite right; 'therefore' would be οὖν, as in x. 31: '*Be sure* to glorify,' '*I urge you* to glorify' is the force of the particle used here.

ℵ*, d e Copt. omit δή. Vulg., Tert. Cypr. Lucif. Ambrst. have *glorificate* (or *clarificate*) *et portate* (or *tollite*) *deum* (or *dominum*) *in corpore vestro*. Lightfoot suggests that *portate* (or *tollite*) may have arisen from a reading ἄραγε (Matt. vii. 20, xvii. 26 ; Acts xvii. 27 ?) which was confused with ἄρατε. Marcion read δοξάσατε ἄρατε τὸν Θεόν, which may be mere dittography, or from ἄρα δέ = ἄρα δή (Nestle, p. 307). Methodius read ἄρά γε δοξάσατε, omitting δή. Chrys. seems to have read δοξάσατε δὴ ἄρα τὸν Θεόν.

The addition καὶ ἐν τῷ πνεύματι ὑμῶν ἅτινά ἐστιν τοῦ Θεοῦ (C³ D² D³ K L P, Syrr. AV.) is rejected by all editors. The words are wanting in all the best witnesses and are not required for the argument. The Apostle is concerned with the sanctity of the body : the spirit is beside the mark. Lightfoot thinks that this may possibly be a liturgical insertion, like that of the doxology to the Lord's Prayer (Matt. vi. 13) and the baptismal formula (Acts viii. 37). But the words do not occur in any liturgy that is known to us, and the addition may be due to a wish to make the conclusion less abrupt and more complete.

VII. 1-40. MARRIAGE AND ITS PROBLEMS.

We here begin the second main division of the Epistle, if the Introduction (i. 1–9) is not counted. The Apostle, in a preamble (1–7), points out that marriage is a contract, and the normal relations must be maintained, unless both parties agree to suspend them. Ideally, celibacy may be better, but that is not for every one. Then (8–40) he gives advice to different classes. *Superius* (v., vi.) *locutus fuerat de illicitis ; nunc vero* (vii.) *loquitur de licitis* (Atto).

VII. 1–7. Celibacy is Good, but Marriage is Natural.

As you ask me, I prefer my own unmarried condition ; but for most of you it is safer to marry, and let husband and wife observe conjugal duty to one another.

¹ But now, as to the questions raised in your letter to me. Continence, as you suggest, is doubtless an excellent thing. ² But this ideal state is not for every one, and, as temptation is inevitable, and abounds at Corinth, the right remedy is that each man should have a wife of his own, and each woman a husband of her own. ³ And the marriage should be complete, each side always rendering to the other what is due. ⁴ A married woman cannot do as she likes respecting her own person ; it is her husband's. And in the same manner his rights are limited by hers. ⁵ Abandon the attempt to combine celibacy with

matrimony. When both agree to it, continence for a limited
time may be a good thing, if you have the intention of devoting
yourselves the better to prayer, and then coming together again.
If the time is not limited, you will be giving Satan a permanent
opportunity of using your incontinence to your ruin. ⁶ But I
give this advice rather by way of permission and indulgence
than of injunction and command. ⁷ Still, my own personal
preference would be that all men should remain unmarried, as I
do myself. But people differ, and God's gifts differ, and each
must act as God's gift directs him.

It is clear from the words with which this section opens that
the discussion of the questions which were raised in the letter
sent by the Corinthians begins here. In the remaining chapters
(vii.–xvi.) we cannot always be sure whether he is referring to
their letter or writing independently of it: but in the first six
chapters there are no answers to questions asked by them.
With regard to the questions discussed here, it is likely enough
that every one of them had been asked in the letter. The
Apostle does not write a tract on marriage; it would, no doubt,
have been different if he had done so. He takes, without much
logical arrangement, and perhaps just in the order in which they
had been put to him, certain points which, as we can see, might
easily have caused practical difficulty in such a Church as that
of Corinth.* In so licentious a city some may easily have
urged that the only safe thing to do was to abstain from the
company of women altogether, γυναικὸς μὴ ἅπτεσθαι, like those
condemned in 1 Tim. iv. 3. Or they may have maintained that
at any rate second marriages were wrong, and that separation
from a heathen partner was necessary. Our Lord's words
(Matt. xix. 11, 12), if they were known to the Corinthians, might
easily give rise to the belief that marriage was to be discouraged.
Quite certainly, some forms of heathen philosophy taught this,
and asceticism was in the air before the Gospel was preached.
In any case, it is unlikely that disparagement of marriage was a
special tenet of any one of the four *parties* at Corinth. No one
has conjectured this of the Apollos party: but for different
and very unconvincing reasons different commentators have
attributed this tenet to one or other of the three parties. Still,

* On Nietzsche's attack on St Paul, as a man of vicious life, see Weinel,
St Paul, pp. 85–93.

some persons at Corinth *had* raised the question, "Is marriage to be allowed?" They had *not* raised the question, "Is marriage to be obligatory?" See *Journ. of Th. St.*, July 1901, pp. 527–538.

1. Περὶ δὲ ὧν ἐγράψατε. An elliptical expression (such as is common enough) for περὶ τούτων, ἅ, or περὶ τούτων, περὶ ὧν: cf. Luke ix. 36; John vii. 31. Bachmann quotes from papyri, περὶ ὧν ἔγραψας, μελήσει μοι. Note that there is no μοι after ἔγραψας, and there is probably no μοι here : אB C 17, Am. RV. omit. The δέ is perhaps merely transitional; but it may intimate that the subject now to be discussed is in opposition to the one which has just been dismissed. He is passing from what is always wrong to what is generally lawful. It is putting too much meaning into the plural verb to say that we may infer from it that the letter was written in the name of the whole Church. It is probable that it was so written; but even if it came from only a few of the members, the Apostle would have to use the plural. There is nothing to show that the words which follow are a quotation from the letter, but they express what seems to have been the tone of it. Having in the two previous chapters warned the Corinthians against the danger of Gentile licentiousness, he here makes a stand against a spirit of *Gentile asceticism.*

καλὸν ἀνθρώπῳ γυναικὸς μὴ ἅπτεσθαι. 'For a man,' he does not say 'for a husband' (ἀνδρί). A single life is not wrong; on the contrary, it is laudable, καλόν. This he repeats *vv.* 8 and 26; cf. *v.* 6, ix. 15; Gal. iv. 18. He is not dissuading from marriage or full married life ; he is contending that celibacy may be good.* For those who can bear it, it may be a bracing discipline (ix. 24, 27): but not all can bear it. For ἅπτεσθαι see Gen. xx. 6 ; Prov. vi. 29 ; and cf. *virgo intacta.*

2. διὰ δὲ τὰς πορνείας. The plural (Matt. xv. 19 ; Mark vii. 21) refers to the notoriously frequent cases at Corinth. Atto paraphrases '*Neque enim ita volo prohibere licita, ut per illicita errent,*' and adds, *Nota quia non dicitur, propter propaginem filiorum, sed propter fornicationem.* To Christians who believed that the end of the world was very near, the necessity of pre-

---

* Orthodox Jews were opposed to celibacy, regarding marriage as a duty ; but there were some who agreed with St Paul. "Why should I marry?" asked Rabbi ben Azai : "I am in love with the law. Let others see to the prolongation of the human race" (Renan, p. 397). **The second half of Ps. cxx. 7 gives the common view.**

serving the human race from extinction would not have seemed a very strong argument. This passage is sometimes criticized as a very low view of marriage. But the Apostle is not discussing the characteristics of the ideal married life ; he is answering questions put to him by Christians who had to live in such a city as Corinth. In a society so full of temptations, he advises marriage, not as the lesser of two evils, but as a necessary safeguard against evil. So far from marriage being wrong, as some Corinthians were thinking, it was for very many people a duty. The man who wrote Eph. v. 22, 23, 32, 33 had no low view of marriage.

ἕκαστος . . . ἑκάστη. This forbids polygamy, which was advocated by some Jewish teachers.

τὴν ἑαυτοῦ γυναῖκα . . . τὸν ἴδιον ἄνδρα. The Apostle seems always to use ἑαυτοῦ, ἑαυτῶν, or αὐτοῦ (Eph. v. 28, 31, 33) of a man's relation to his wife, but ἴδιος (xiv. 35 ; Eph. v. 22 ; Tit. ii. 5) of a woman's to her husband (1 Thess. iv. 4 is doubtful). Does this show that he regarded the husband as the owner and the wife as being owned? Rom. xiv. 4 somewhat encourages this. But the difference between ἑαυτοῦ and ἴδιος was becoming blurred: see J. H. Moulton, *Gr.* i. pp. 87 f. ; Deissmann, *Bible Studies*, pp. 122 f. A few texts omit καὶ ἑκάστη κ.τ.λ.

ἐχέτω. 'Have,' not 'keep,' as is clear from the use of ἀνθρώπῳ and not ἀνδρί in *v.* 1, where we should have had τῆς γυναικός and not γυναικός, if married people were under consideration. In *vv.* 12, 13, ἔχει cannot mean 'keeps,' and ἐχέτω does not mean that married people are to continue to live together, but that unmarried people are to marry. The imperative is hortatory, not merely permissive.

3. τῇ γυναικὶ ὁ ἀνήρ. Here he is speaking of married persons, and therefore γυναικί has the article, and we have ἀνήρ and not ἄνθρωπος.

τὴν ὀφειλήν. Not found in LXX, but frequent in papyri in the common sense of debt (Matt. xviii. 32 ; Rom. xiii. 7). See Deissmann, *Bible Studies*, p. 221.

ἀποδιδότω. Present imperative : the mutual recognition of conjugal rights is the normal condition, and it is not the conferring of a favour (διδότω), but the payment of a debt (ἀποδιδότω). Cf. the change from δοῦναι (the questioners' view) to ἀπόδοτε (Christ's correction) in Matt. xxii. 17, 21.

τὴν ὀφειλήν (‫א‬ A B C D E F G P Q 17, Vulg. Copt. Arm. Aeth.) is to be preferred to τὴν ὀφειλημένην εὔνοιαν (KL, Syrr.), or τ. ὀφ. τιμήν (Chrys.), or τ. ὀφ. τιμὴν καὶ εὔνοιαν (40), which may have been euphemisms adopted in public reading. Or they may be ascetic periphrases to obscure the plain meaning of τ. ὀφειλήν. Cf. Rom. xiii. 7.
A, Copt. Arm. omit δέ before καί.

4. ἡ γυνή. It is probably not in order to mark the equality of the sexes that the order is changed : the wife is here mentioned first because she has just been mentioned in the previous verse. Equality between the sexes is indicated by using the same expression respecting both, thus correcting Jewish and Gentile ideas about women.

τοῦ ἰδίου σώματος οὐκ ἐξουσιάζει. The words involve, as Bengel points out, *elegans paradoxon*. How can it be one's own if one cannot do as one likes with it? See on vi. 12. But in wedlock separate ownership of the person ceases. Neither party can say to the other, 'Is it not lawful for me (ἔξεστίν μοι) to do what I will with mine own?' (Matt. xx. 15). By pointing out that the aim is to be, not self-gratification, but the fulfilment of a duty which each owes to the other, St Paul partly anticipates the criticism mentioned above. He raises the matter from the physical level to the moral.

5. μὴ ἀποστερεῖτε. After what has been stated it is evident that refusal amounts to fraud, a withholding what is owed. The pres. imperat. may mean that some of the Corinthians, in mistaken zeal, had been doing this; 'cease to defraud.' Three conditions are required for lawful abstention: it must be by mutual consent, for a good object, and temporary. It is analogous to fasting. Even so, the advice is given very tentatively, **εἰ μήτι ἄν.** Temporary abstention for a spiritual purpose is advised in O.T. ; Eccles. iii. 5 ; Joel ii. 16 ; Zech. xii. 12–14 :* but it is an exception for certain circumstances, not a rule for all circumstances : *illud sane sciendum quia mundae et sanctae sunt nuptiae, quoniam Dei jussu celebrantur* (Atto). For ἐπὶ τὸ αὐτό cf. xi. 20, xiv. 23 ; Luke xvii. 35 ; Acts i. 15, ii. 1, 44, 47, iv. 26 ; for ἀκρασία, Matt. xxiii. 25. Here διὰ τὴν ἀκρ. is probably to be taken as co-ordinate with the clause ἵνα μὴ πειρ., and as giving a second aspect of the reason for limiting the time of abstention. Aristotle made ἀκρασία a frequent term in Greek philosophy; in the Bible it is very rare. Calvin uses this verse as an argument against monasticism : *temere faciunt qui in perpetuum renuntiant*. To vow perpetual celibacy, without certainty of having received the necessary χάρισμα, is to court disaster. Forcing it on the clergy prevents good men from taking Orders and causes weak men to break their vow.

---

* σχολάζειν is very rare in LXX (Ps. xlv. 10), and is nowhere used in this sense ; but in class. Grk. it is frequent in the sense of being 'disengaged for,' or 'devoted to,' a pursuit or a person. We find a similar idea Exod. xix. 15 ; 1 Sam. xxi. 5 ; 2 Sam. xi. 4. Cf. Tibullus I. iii. 25. See also 1 Pet. iii. 7, iv. 7. Σύμφωνος occurs nowhere else in N.T.

The ἄν after ἔι μήτι (or εἰ μή τι) is omitted in B and bracketed by WH. Before τῇ προσευχῇ, KL, Syrr. Goth. Thdrt. insert τῇ νηστείᾳ καί: a manifest interpolation similar to καὶ νηστείᾳ in Mark ix. 29, and νηστεύων καί in Acts x. 30. In all three places ascetic ideas seem to have influenced copyists, but the evidence differs in the three cases. In Mark ix. 29 the words in question are omitted in ℵ B K, a very strong combination. In Acts x. 30 the words are wanting in ℵ A B C, Vulg. Copt. Arm. Aeth., a much stronger combination. Here the evidence against τῇ ν. καί is overwhelming; ℵ A B C* D* E F G 17, Latt. Copt. Aeth. The case of Matt. xvii. 21 is not parallel to these three. The whole verse is an interpolation from Mark ix. 29 after that passage had already been corrupted by the addition of καὶ νηστείᾳ. The practice of fasting has sufficient sanction in the N.T. (Matt. iv. 2, vi. 16–18, ix. 15 ; Mark ii. 20 ; Luke v. 35 ; Acts xiii. 2, 3, xiv. 23), without introducing it into places where it was not mentioned by the original writers, who, moreover, would not have placed it on the same level with prayer. Fasting is an occasional discipline, prayer an abiding necessity, in the spiritual life. Stanley attributes the readings σχολάζητε (KL) for σχολάσητε (ℵ A B C D, etc.), and συνέρχεσθε or συνέρχησθε (KLP) for ἦτε (ℵ A B C D, etc.) to ascetic influence : σχολάζητε would refer to general habit, ordinary and not extraordinary prayer, and ἦτε refers to what is usual, not exceptional. In commenting on these words, Origen makes a remark which is of no small liturgical interest. He quotes the case of Ahimelech, who was willing to let David have some of the shew-bread, εἰ πεφυλαγμένα τὰ παιδάριά ἐστιν ἀπὸ γυναικός (LXX of I Sam. xxi. 4). He assumes οὐκ οἷον δὲ ἀπὸ ἀλλοτρίας γυναικὸς ἀλλ᾽ ἀπὸ γαμετῆς, and continues, εἶτα ἵνα μέν ἄρτους προθέσεως λάβῃ τις, καθαρὸς εἶναι ὀφείλει ἀπὸ γυναικός· ἵνα δὲ τοὺς μείζονας τῆς προθέσεως λάβῃ ἄρτους, ἐφ᾽ ὧν ἐπικέκληται τὸ ὄνομα τοῦ Θεοῦ καὶ τοῦ Χριστοῦ καὶ τοῦ Ἁγίου Πνεύματος, οὐ πολλῷ πλέον ὀφείλει τις εἶναι καθαρώτερος, ἵνα ἀληθῶς εἰς σωτηρίαν λάβῃ τοὺς ἄρτους καὶ μὴ εἰς κρίμα. From this it is evident that "invocation of the name of God and of Christ and of the Holy Spirit" over the elements was regarded by Origen as the essential part of their consecration.

This passage is one of the few in N.T. which touch on the private devotions of Christians in the Apostolic age. See Bigg on 1 Pet. iii. 7, iv. 7.

6. τοῦτο δὲ λέγω. It is not clear how much the τοῦτο covers ; probably the whole of *vv.* 1–5. The least probable suggestion is that it refers solely to the resumption of married life, καὶ πάλιν κ.τ.λ.

συγγνώμην. 'Concession,' or 'indulgence,' or 'allowance.'* The word occurs nowhere else in N.T. and is very rare in LXX.

οὐ κατ' ἐπιταγήν. 'Not by way of command' (2 Cor. viii. 8).

---

* 'By permission' (AV.) is ambiguous ; it might mean, 'I am permitted by God to say as much as this.' It was translated *venia* in some Old Latin texts, and this rendering, understood (by Augustine) as meaning 'pardon,' led to far-reaching error. It means 'By way of concession' : he is telling people that they may marry, not that they must do so : *ex concessione non ex imperio* (Beza). There is similar uncertainty as to the scope of the τοῦτο in xi. 17, and the αὕτη in ix. 3. In 1 Tim. i. 1, κατ' ἐπιταγήν is used in a different sense : 'in obedience to the command.'

7. θέλω δὲ πάντας. This is in harmony with the καλὸν ἀνθρώπῳ from which he started. Surroundings so licentious as the Apostle had at Ephesus and Corinth might well inspire him with a longing for universal celibacy. For a similar wish about his own condition being that of others see Acts xxvi. 29 (ὁποῖος καὶ ἐγώ εἰμι): in both places we have the comparative use of καί, as again in *v.* 8 and x. 6.

ἀλλά. He admits that his own personal feeling is not decisive; indeed, is not in accordance with conditions of society which have their source in God. Here χάρισμα (see on i. 7) is used in the sense of a special gift of God, a special grace to an individual. Origen points out that if celibacy is a χάρισμα, so also is marriage, and those who forbid marriage forbid what has been given by God.

ὁ μὲν οὕτως. 'One in this direction and one in that.' The recognition that opposite courses may each of them be right for different individuals is more fully drawn out Rom. xiv. 1–12: and see Rom. xii. 6; 1 Pet. iv. 10. We have οὕτως . . . οὕτως, Judg. xviii. 4; 2 Sam. xi. 25, xvii. 15: it is not classical.

We perhaps understand the Apostle's wish better if we assume that it refers, not so much to the fact of remaining unmarried, as to the possession of the gift of continence, without which it was disastrous to remain unmarried. God had given him this gift, and he wishes that all men had it: but it does not follow that every man who has this gift is bound to a life of celibacy. In the Apostle's day (*v.* 26) the χάρισμα of continency was specially valuable. Cf. Matt. xix. 11.

We must read θέλω δέ (א* A C D* F G 17, Am. Copt., Orig.) rather than θέλω γάρ (B D² K L P, Syrr. Arm. Aeth.). The δέ marks a slight opposition to the concession just mentioned. That concession is not his own ideal; 'I rather wish that all men were as I myself also am.' Failure to see this has caused the substitution of γάρ for δέ.

K L, Arm. have χάρισμα before ἔχει: ἔχει χάρισμα is doubtless right: so also ὁ μὲν . . . ὁ δέ (א* A B C D F P) rather than ὃς μὲν . . . ὃς δέ (א³ K L).

VII. 8–40. Advice to Different Classes.

To the unmarried or widowed, to the married where both parties are Christians, to the married where one of the two is a heathen, I would advise, as a rule, that you should remain as you are, or as you were when you became Christians. The same principle would apply to circumcision, and also to slavery; but an opportunity for emancipation may be accepted.

[8] To the unmarried and to widows I affirm it to be an excellent thing for them, if they should continue to remain single, as I also remain. [9] If, however, they have not the special gift of self-control, let them marry; for it is better to marry than to be on fire. [10] But to those who have married as Christians I give a charge—and it is really not my charge, but Christ's—that a wife is not to seek divorce from her husband. [11] But if unhappily she does do this, she must remain single, or else be reconciled to her husband. In like manner a man is not to divorce his wife.

[12] To those whose cases are not covered by these directions I have this to say; and I say it as my own advice, not as Christ's command: if any member of the Church has a wife who is not a believer, and she consents to live with him, let him not divorce her; [13] and if a wife has a husband who is not a believer, and he consents to live with her, let her not divorce her husband. [14] And for this reason: the consecration of the believing partner is not cancelled by union with an unbeliever. On the contrary, the unbelieving partner is sanctified through union with a believer. If this were not so, the children would be left in heathen uncleanness; whereas in fact, as the offspring of a Christian parent, they are holy. [15] But if, on the other hand, the unbelieving partner insists on a separation, separation let there be. No servile bondage to a heathen yoke deprives a Christian man or woman of freedom in such cases. There need be no scruples, no prolonged conflict with the unbeliever who demands separation: it is in peace of mind that we have been placed by our calling as Christians. [16] For how can you tell, O wife, whether, by keeping your heathen husband against his wish, you will be able to convert him? Or how can you tell, O husband, whether you will be able to convert your reluctant wife?

[17] Still, the general principle is this: In each case let people be content with the lot which God assigned them, and with the condition in which God's call has come to them, and let them continue in that course so far as may be. This is the rule that I am laying down in all the Churches.

[18] This principle holds good with regard to circumcision. Were you already circumcised at the time of your call? Do not attempt to efface the circumcision. Or have you been

called in uncircumcision? Do not seek to be circumcised.
[19] Neither the one nor the other is of any consequence. What
really matters is keeping God's commandments, and that is
vital. [20] Each one of you, I say, should be content to remain
in the condition in which God called him. [21] And this applies
to slavery also. Were you a slave when you were called? Do
not be distressed at it; yet, if you can become free, make use
of the opportunity.

[22] I say that you need not be distressed at being a slave
when you became a Christian: every such slave is the Lord's
freed man. And the converse is true: he who was free when
he was called is Christ's slave. [23] You were bought with the
price of His blood, and to Him, whether you are bond or free,
you belong. Cease to regard yourselves as belonging to men
in the sense in which you belong to Him. [24] I repeat, Brothers,
the general rule. In that state in which each man was called,
let him be content to remain, remembering God's presence and
His protecting care.

8. τοῖς ἀγάμοις καὶ ταῖς χήραις. This includes bachelors,
widowers, and widows, but not unmarried girls, whose case is
discussed later (25–38), and who would not have much voice
in deciding the point in question. The conjecture of τοῖς χήροις
for ταῖς χήραις is worth considering. A word not found elsewhere in N.T. might be changed to one that is common. 'Even
as I' is more in place, if men only are addressed. Ἄγαμος
occurs vv. 11, 32, 34, and nowhere else in N.T.

καλόν. As in v. 1, this introduces the Apostle's own ideal,
as illustrated by his own life. As τοῖς ἀγάμοις covers both single
men and widowers, this passage does not tell us whether St Paul
had ever been married. The very early interpretation of γνήσιε
σύνζυγε (Phil. iv. 3) as meaning the Apostle's wife (Clem. Alex.
Strom. III. vi. p. 535, ed. Potter) may safely be set aside, for
this passage shows that, if he ever had been married, his wife
died before he wrote to the Philippians. And if he had been
married then, would he not have written γνησία in addressing
his wife. The argument that, as a member of the Sanhedrin
(Acts xxvi. 10), he must have been a married man and a father,
is not strong. This rule (*Sanh.* fo. 36 b), as a security for
clemency, may be of later date, and κατήνεγκα ψῆφον may be a
figurative expression for approving of the sentence. The probability is that St Paul was never married (Tertull. *De Monogam.*
8; *Ad Uxor.* ii. 1). In all his writings, as also in Acts, there

is no trace of wife or child.* The καί in ὡς κἀγώ, as in ὡς καὶ ἐμαυτόν (v. 7), is the comparative use of καί. He compares his own case with that of those whom he desires to keep unmarried, and emphasizes it. The aorist (μείνωσιν) suggests a life-long and final decision.

9. εἰ δὲ οὐκ ἐγκρατεύονται. 'But if they have not power over themselves' (midd.). It is doubtful whether the negative coalesces with the verb so as to express only one idea. In N.T. we more often have εἰ οὐ for 'if not' than εἰ μή, which means 'unless.' "Where a fact has sharply to be brought out and sharply to be negatived, there εἰ οὐ seems to be not only permissible, but logically correct" (Ellicott). See Burton, *Moods and Tenses*, §§ 242, 261, 469; and compare Rom. viii. 9; 2 Thess. iii. 10, 14, etc.

What is meant by this failure to have power over themselves is partly explained by πυροῦσθαι (present tense in both verbs). A prolonged and painful struggle seems to be intended, a condition quite fatal to spiritual peace and growth: cf. ix. 25; Gen. xliii. 30; 1 Sam. xiii. 12. Elsewhere we have πυροῦσθαι of burning with grief and indignation (2 Cor. xi. 29).† The advice given here is similar to that given in v. 5, διὰ τὴν ἀκρασίαν ὑμῶν, and to the younger widows in 1 Tim. v. 11–15.

κρεῖττον (א B D E) is here the better reading, κρεῖσσον in xi. 17, where see note. It is not easy to decide between γαμεῖν (א* A C* 17) and γαμῆσαι (א³ B C² D E F, etc.). Editors are divided. Perhaps γαμῆσαι was changed to γαμεῖν to conform to πυροῦσθαι. But the change of tense is intelligible ; 'better to marry once for all than to go on being on fire.' In this Epistle, as elsewhere in N.T., the later form of the aor. (ἐγάμησα) is more common (vv. 33, 34) than the earlier (ἔγημα) ; in v. 28 both forms occur.

10. τοῖς δὲ γεγαμηκόσιν παραγγέλλω. He passes from those to whom it is still open to marry or not to marry. 'But to those who have already married (since they became Christians) I give command.' To render, 'I *pass on* the order' from Christ to you, is giving too much force to the preposition. Christ does not 'pass on' the order. The meaning is, 'I give the order; no,

---

* See Max Krenkel, *Beiträge zur Aufhellung der Geschichte und der Briefe des Apostels Paulus*, pp. 26–46, a careful examination of the question, *War Paulus jemals verheiratet?* Baring Gould thinks that St Paul may have married Lydia (Acts xvi. 14, 40), and that it was she who supplied him with money (Acts xxiv. 26, xxviii. 30). This is not probable.

† Eph. vi. 16, it is used of the flaming darts of the evil one ; Rev. i. 15, iii. 18, of what has been refined by fire. It is frequent in the latter sense in LXX, and in 2 Macc., with τοῖς θυμοῖς added, of anger. Some understand it here as meaning 'unsatisfied affection' rather than ἀκρασία. In ix. 25 we have ἐγκρατεύεσθαι again, but nowhere else in N.T. See Hos. vii. 4 and Cheyne's note.

not I, Christ gives it.' In class. Grk. παραγγέλλω is used of the military word of command: see xi. 17; 1 Thess. iv. 11; often in 2 Thess., 1 Tim., Luke, and Acts. When the Apostle gives directions on his own authority (v. 12), he says 'speak,' not 'command.'

οὐκ ἐγὼ, ἀλλὰ ὁ Κύριος. Christ Himself had decided against divorce (Mark x. 9; Luke xvi. 18), and His Apostle repeats His teaching: see also Mal. ii. 16. St Paul is distinguishing between his own inspired utterances (v. 40) and the express commands of Christ, not between his own private views and his inspired utterances. And there is no need to assume (as perhaps in 1 Thess. iv. 15) that he had received a direct revelation on the subject. Christ's decision was well known. See Dobschütz, *Probleme des Ap. Zeitalters*, Leipzig, 1904, p. 109; Fletcher, *The Conversion of St Paul*, Bell, 1910, p. 57.

γυναῖκα ἀπὸ ἀνδρός. The fact that he begins with the unusual case of a wife divorcing her husband indicates that such a thing had actually occurred or was mentioned in their letter as likely to occur. Women may have raised the question.

χωρισθῆναι (אB C K L P) is certainly to be preferred to χωρίζεσθαι (A D E F G): patristic evidence is divided.

11. ἐὰν δὲ καὶ χωρισθῇ. 'But if (in spite of Christ's command) she even goes so far as to separate herself,' she is not to marry any other man. The divorce is her act, not her husband's. "Christianity had powerfully stirred the feminine mind at Corinth (xi. 5, xiv. 34). In some cases ascetic aversion caused the wish to separate" (Findlay). With the καί compare εἰ δὲ καί in iv. 7. Christ had forbidden marriage with a divorced wife (Luke xvi. 18), and His Apostle here takes the same ground. If the wife who has separated from her husband finds that, after all, she cannot live a single life, the only course open to her is to be reconciled to the husband whom she has injured. For the construction (καταλλ. c. dat.) see Rom. v. 10. Like εἰ δὲ ὁ ἄπιστος (v. 15) and ἀλλ' εἰ καὶ δύνασαι (v. 21), this ἐὰν δὲ καὶ κ.τ.λ. is a parenthesis to provide for an exceptional case. He then continues the Lord's command, that 'a husband is not to put away (ἀφιέναι = καταλύειν) his wife.'* St Paul, like our Lord, forbids divorce absolutely: πορνεία in the wife is not mentioned here as creating an exception; and it is possible that this exception

---

* The change from χωρισθῆναι of the wife to ἀφιέναι of the husband is intelligible. The home is his: she can leave it, but he sends her away from it. In LXX, χωρισθῆναι is frequent of separation in place. In papyri it is used of divorce; ἐὰν δὲ χωρίζωνται ἀπ' ἀλλήλων: so also χωρισμός. Polybius (XXXII. xii. 6) has κεχωρισμένη ἀπὸ τοῦ ἀνδρός. See Deissmann, *Bible Studies*, p. 247. In v. 13, ἀφιέναι is used of the wife, perhaps in order to make an exact parallel with v. 12.

(Matt. v. 32, xix. 9 ; see Allen and Plummer *ad loc.*) was unknown to the Apostle, because it had not been made by Christ.

12. τοῖς δὲ λοιποῖς. Having spoken of those converts who were still unmarried, and of those who had married since their conversion, he now treats of those who belonged to neither class. There were some who had married before their conversion and now had a heathen wife or a heathen husband. Were they to continue to live with their heathen partners? Yes, if the heathen partner consents to the arrangement. St Paul elsewhere uses οἱ λοιποί of a remainder which is wholly or largely heathen (Eph. ii. 3 ; 1 Thess. iv. 13, v. 6).

λέγω ἐγώ, οὐχ ὁ Κύριος. This is the right order (א A B C P 17), not ἐγὼ λέγω (D E F G). He means that he is not now repeating the teaching of Christ, who is not likely to have said anything on the subject. He does not mean that he is speaking now, not with Apostolic authority, but as a private individual. All his directions are given with the inspiration and power of an Apostle, and he speaks with confidence and sureness. He applies Christ's ruling as far as it will reach in the case of a mixed union. The Christian party must certainly not dissolve the marriage, if the heathen party does not desire to do so.

γυναῖκα ἔχει ἄπιστον. Here ἔχει must mean 'has,' not 'keeps,' 'retains,' and this shows the meaning of ἐχέτω in *v.* 2. It is the case of a Christian with a heathen wife whom he married when he himself was an unbeliever.

συνευδοκεῖ. 'Agrees in being content.' The compound verb (Rom. i. 32) indicates mutual consent, implying that more than one person is satisfied (Acts xxii. 20) ; often with a dative of the thing in which agreement is found (Luke xi. 48 ; Acts viii. 1 ; 2 Mac. xi. 24).

μὴ ἀφιέτω αὐτήν. AV. has 'let him not put her away' here, and 'let her not leave him' in *v.* 13 : RV. has 'leave' in both places. Perhaps 'put away' would be better in both, as St Paul is speaking of divorce. As in *v.* 11, ἀφιέναι = ἀπολύειν, which in class. Grk. would be ἀποπέμπειν. Vulg. has *dimittat* throughout.

13. καὶ οὗτος. The pronoun shows that αὕτη, and not αὐτή, is the right accentuation in *v.* 12. Here some inferior texts read αὐτός instead of οὗτος, and αὐτόν instead of τὸν ἄνδρα. The latter term has point, because it was a strong measure for a wife to try to divorce her husband. But the Apostle puts both sexes on a level by using ἀφιέτω, which is more commonly used of the husband, of both.

14. ἡγίασται. This refers to the baptismal consecration (i. 2, vi. 11), in which the unbelieving husband shares through union

with a Christian wife.. The purity of the believing partner over-
powers (νικᾷ) the impurity of the unbelieving one (Chrys.), so
that the union is pure and lawful; there is no profanation of
matrimony.   The principle εἰς σάρκα μίαν holds good in mixed
marriages (vi. 16), but not to the detriment of the believing
partner; as an unlawful union *desecrates*, so a lawful union *con-
secrates*: *pluris enim est pietas unius ad conjugium sanctificandum,
quam alterius ad inquinandum* (Calv.).   But he goes beyond
what is written when he adds, *interea nihil prodest haec sancti-
ficatio conjugi infideli.** Note the ἐν in both cases; the Christian
partner is the sphere in which the sanctification takes place, and
the heathen partner may be influenced by that sphere.   There
is no such intolerable difference of sphere as to necessitate dissolution of the marriage.

ἐπεὶ ἄρα.   'Since it would then follow,' *i.e.* if it was the impurity of the heathen partner which prevailed on the analogy of
Hag. ii. 11–13; there it is uncleanness that is communicated,
while consecration is not communicated.   The Apostle argues
back from the children to the parents.   The child of a parent
who is ἅγιος must *ipso facto* be ἅγιος: that he assumes as axiomatic.   He is not assuming that the child of a Christian parent
would be baptized; that would spoil rather than help his argument, for it would imply that the child was not ἅγιος till it was
baptized.   The verse throws no light on the question of infant
baptism.   He argues from the fact that the Corinthians must
admit that a Christian's child is 'holy.'   Consequently, it was
born in wedlock that is 'holy.'   Consequently, such wedlock
need not be dissolved.   But he is not approving such wedlock.
Marriages with heathen are wrong (2 Cor. vi. 14).   But, where
they have come into existence through the conversion of one
partner in a heathen marriage, the Christian partner is not to
seek divorce.

   D E F, Latt. add τῇ πιστῇ after γυναικί, ℵ A B C K L P omit. ἀδελφῷ
(ℵ* A B C D* E F G P 17, Copt. RV.) is to be preferred to ἀνδρί (ℵ³ D³
K L, Vulg. Syrr. Arm. Aeth. AV.), an unintelligent gloss by one who did
not see the point of ἀδελφῷ and wanted to make the usual balance to the
preceding γυναικί.   Vulg., Iren. Tert. add τῷ πιστῷ to ἀνδρί, making it
equivalent to ἀδελφῷ.   For νῦν δέ, D E F G have νυνί, which at the beginning of a clause is always in N.T. followed by δέ.
   With the argumentative use of ἐπεί, 'since, if that were so,' cf. xv. 29
and see note on Rom. iii. 6.   In v. 10, 11 we have a similar ἐπεί followed
by νῦν, as here.   See Burton, *Moods and Tenses*, §§ 229, 230.

* As Evans says, "He stands upon the sacred threshold of the Church:
his *surroundings* are hallowed.   United to a saintly consort, he is in daily
contact with saintly conduct: holy association may become holy assimilation,
and the sanctity which ever environs may at last penetrate.   But the man's
conversion is not a condition necessary to the sanctity of the subsisting conjugal union."   Origen compares such a union to a mixture of wine and water.

15. εἰ δὲ ὁ ἄπιστος χωρίζεται. 'But if it is the unbeliever that is for separating.' The emphasis is on ὁ ἄπιστος, and the present tense indicates the heathen partner's state of mind. What follows shows that ὁ ἄπιστος covers both sexes, and in such cases the Apostle has no injunction to give to the unbeliever. 'For what have I to do with judging them that are without'? (v. 12); so the responsibility rests with them, and they may do as they please, χωριζέσθω. If, therefore, the heathen partner seeks divorce, the Christian partner may consent. The Christian partner is under no slavish obligation to refuse to be set free. Just to this extent the law against divorce has its limits. Marriages between Jews ought not to be dissolved, and marriages between Christians ought not to be dissolved; but heathen marriages stand on a different basis. These ought to be respected as long as possible, even when one of the parties becomes a Christian. But if the one who remains a heathen demands divorce, the Christian is not bound to oppose divorce. In such matters the Christian οὐ δεδούλωται, has not lost all freedom of action; independence still survives.

We cannot safely argue with Luther that οὐ δεδούλωται implies that the Christian partner, when divorced by the heathen partner, may marry again. And Luther would have it that this implies that the Christian partner, when divorced by "a false Christian," may marry again. Who is to decide whether the Christian is "false" or not? And the principle, which is far older than Luther, that "reverence for the marriage-tie is not due to one who has no reverence for the Author of the marriage-tie" will carry one to disastrous conclusions. Basil (letter to Amphilochius, *Canonica Prima, Ep.* clxxxviii. 9) does not write with precision. All that οὐ δεδούλωται clearly means is that he or she need not feel so bound by Christ's prohibition of divorce as to be afraid to depart when the heathen partner insists on separation.

ἐν δὲ εἰρήνῃ κέκληκεν ὑμᾶς. 'It is in an atmosphere of peace that God has called you.' This is ambiguous. To what is the 'peace' opposed? If to *bondage*, which seems natural, then the meaning will be that to feel bound to remain with a heathen partner, who objects to your remaining, would violate the peace in which you were called to be a Christian. If 'peace' is opposed to *separation*, then the meaning will be that you ought to do your utmost to avoid divorce. The former is probably right: cf. Col. iii. 15. Heathen *animus* against Christianity would greatly increase the difficulty of insisting upon living with a heathen who was anxious for a divorce. In such a state of things Christian peace would be impossible. With ἐν εἰρήνῃ compare ἐν ἁγιασμῷ, 1 Thess. iv. 7. The δέ supplies the *positive* complement to the negative οὐ δεδούλωται.

Editors are much divided as to whether ὑμᾶς (ℵ* A C K, Copt.) or ἡμᾶς (ℵ³ B D E F, Latt. Syrr. AV. RV.) is the better reading.

16. τί γὰρ οἶδας, γύναι. As in *v.* 15, the case of the heathen husband desiring to divorce his Christian wife is uppermost, although the other case is also considered. And this verse is as ambiguous as the concluding part of *v.* 15. Either, 'Do not contend against divorce on the ground that, if you remain, you may convert your heathen partner; for how do you know that you will do that?' Or (going back to μὴ ἀφιέτω in 13, 14, and treating 15 as a rare exception to the almost universal rule), 'Avoid divorce, for it is possible—you never know—that you will convert your heathen partner.' This latter interpretation involves the rendering, 'How knowest thou whether thou wilt *not* save?' See the LXX of Esth. iv. 14; Joel ii. 14; Jon. iii. 9; 2 Sam. xii. 22. On the ground that these four passages express a hope rather than a doubt, Lightfoot prefers the interpretation that the chance of saving the unbelieving partner is "worth any temporal inconvenience." So also Findlay. But the other interpretation is probably right. The sequence of thought is then quite clear. 'If the unbeliever demands divorce, grant it: you are not bound to refuse. If you refuse, you will have no peace. The chance of converting your heathen spouse is too small a compensation for a strained and disturbed life, in which Christian serenity will be impossible.' To call the latter "temporal inconvenience" is a serious understatement. See Stanley. For σώζειν see Rom. xi. 14; 1 Tim. iv. 16; and for the history of the idea, Hastings, *DB.* iv. pp. 360 f.; *DCG.* ii. p. 556. The εἰ μή (*v.* 17) is almost decisive for this view.

17. This verse may be taken either as a summing up of what has just been stated, or as a fresh starting-point for what is to follow (18–24). It states the general principle which determines these questions about marriage, and this is afterwards illustrated by the cases of circumcision and slavery. Conversion to Christianity must make a radical change in the moral and spiritual life, but it need not make any radical change in our external life, and it is best to abide in the condition in which the call came to us. Therefore the Christian partner must not do anything to bring about a dissolution of marriage, any more than the Christian slave must claim emancipation. But if the heathen party insists on dissolution, or grants emancipation, then the Christian may accept freedom from such galling ties.*

* There is no good reason for suspecting with Baljon that *vv.* 17–22 are an interpolation, or with Clemen that they come from some other Pauline Epistle. Beza proposed to place them after *v.* 40. Equally needlessly, Holsten suspects that *v.* 14 is an interpolation.

Εἰ μὴ ἑκάστῳ ὡς μεμέρικεν ὁ Κύριος, ἕκαστον κ.τ.λ. 'Only as our Lord has appointed to each, as God has called each, so let him walk.' In both clauses 'each' is emphatic; and while the assignment of circumstances to each individual is attributed to Christ, the call to become a believer comes from the Father, as in Rom. viii. 28. The εἰ μή (introducing an exception or correction) defines and limits the somewhat vague 'is not under bondage in such cases.' There remains *some* obligation, viz. not to *seek* a rupture. One is not in all cases free to depart, simply because one cannot be compelled to stay. But nothing is here said against the improvement of one's circumstances after embracing Christianity. What is laid down is that, unless one's external condition of life is a sinful one, no violent change in it should be made, simply because one has become a Christian. One should continue in the same course (περιπατείτω), glorifying God by a good use of one's opportunities; *status, in quo vocatio quemque offendit, instar vocationis est* (Beng.). This general principle seems to the Apostle so important that he states that he has established it in all the Churches under his care, and then goes on to illustrate it by two frequent examples of its application. On περιπατεῖν and ἀναστρέφειν of daily conduct, see Hort on 1 Pet. i. 15 and Lukyn Williams on Gal. i. 13. See on iii. 3.

The verse reads better as a fresh starting-point (WH., Way, Weymouth, B. Weiss) than as a summary of what precedes (Alford, Ellicott). But even if the latter arrangement be adopted, there is no close connexion between *vv.* 16 and 17. Some join εἰ μή with εἰ τὴν γυναῖκα σώσεις, 'whether thou shalt save thy wife, whether not.' But that would require ἢ οὐ, as in Matt. xxii. 17. Others understand χωρίζεται after εἰ μή, 'If he does not depart'; others again understand σώσεις, 'If thou shalt not save her.' This makes very bad sense, and would almost certainly require εἰ δὲ μή. Theodoret runs the two verses into one sentence, 'How knowest thou . . . except in so far as our Lord has apportioned to each?' This is very awkward, and gives no good sense. 'Only' or 'Save only' is the best translation of εἰ μή. It introduces a caution with regard to what precedes, and this forms a preface to what follows. St Paul is opposing the restless spirit and desire for further change which the Gospel had excited in some converts.

καὶ οὕτως . . . διατάσσομαι. As in xi. 34; Tit. i. 5; Acts xxiv. 23, we have the middle; in ix. 14, xvi. 1 he uses the active. This is evidently spoken with Apostolic authority, and it indicates that the restlessness and craving for change, against which he here contends, was common among Christians. He lets the Corinthians know that they receive no exceptional treatment, either in the way of regulations or privileges. This checks rebelliousness on the one hand and conceit on the other. *Odiosum fuisset Corinthiis arctiore vinculo quam alios constringi* (Calv.). Cf. iv. 17.

Ought we to read μεμέρικεν (אּ* B) or ἐμέρισεν (אּ³ A C D, etc.)? Aor. might be changed to perf. to harmonize with κέκληκεν, and perf. (being less common) might be changed to aor. The perf. is preferable. Certainly ὁ Κύριος . . . ὁ Θεός (א A B C D E F) is to be preferred to ὁ Θεός . . . ὁ Κύριος (K L). Elsewhere it is God who calls (1 Thess. iv. 7; Rom. iv. 17, viii. 30; 2 Tim. i. 9), while the Lord distributes the gifts (xii. 5; Eph. iv. 11). D* F, Latt. substitute διδάσκω for διατάσσομαι.

18. Περιτετμημένος τις ἐκλήθη. The sentence is probably interrogative (AV., RV.), not hypothetical (Tyndale). The sense is much the same. A man who was circumcised before conversion is not to efface the signs of his Judaism. Jews did this sometimes to avoid being known as Jews in gymnastic exercises in the palaestra (1 Macc. i. 15; Joseph. *Ant.* XII. v. 1).* And an uncircumcised Gentile is not to seek circumcision; Gal. v. 2, 3; Acts xv. 1, 5, 19, 24, 28. St Paul, while proclaiming Gentile liberty, acts as a Jew to Jews (ix. 20). See Dobschütz, *Probleme*, p. 84.

κέκληταί τις (א A B P), τις κέκληται (D F G), τις ἐκλήθη (E K L). κέκληται τις is doubtless right; the perf. may indicate that these cases were generally earlier, Jews converted before Gentiles.

19. ἡ περιτομὴ οὐδέν ἐστιν, καὶ ἡ ἀκροβυστία οὐδέν ἐστιν. The Apostle repeats this in two somewhat different forms in Gal. v. 6 and vi. 15; ἐν γὰρ Χριστῷ Ἰησοῦ οὔτε περιτομή τι ἰσχύει οὔτε ἀκροβυστία, ἀλλὰ πίστις δι᾽ ἀγάπης ἐνεργουμένη, and οὔτε γὰρ περιτομή τι ἐστίν οὔτε ἀκροβυστία, ἀλλὰ καινὴ κτίσις. Having previously proclaimed the folly of *adopting* circumcision, when the freedom of the Gospel was open to them, as he has just done here in simpler terms (μὴ περιτεμνέσθω), he points out that the difference between circumcision and uncircumcision is a matter of small moment. Those who have it need not be ashamed of it, and those who have it not certainly need not seek it. "The peculiar excellence of the maxim is its declaration that those who maintain the absolute necessity of rejecting forms are as much opposed to the freedom of the Gospel as those who maintain the absolute necessity of retaining them" (Stanley).

Photius, **G.** Syncellus, and others say that the maxim is a quotation from an Apocalypse of Moses. It is extremely unlikely that such a principle would be contained in any Jewish book earlier than St Paul. Such a book, however, might after-

---

* St Paul's prohibition must be understood in a wider sense. A Jew, when he becomes a Christian, is not ostentatiously to drop all Jewish customs and modes of life. The verb occurs nowhere else in N.T.

wards be interpolated by a Christian with these words of the
Apostle. See Lightfoot on Gal. vi. 15; Weinel, *St Paul*, p. 56;
and consider the Apostle's action in circumcising Timothy and
not circumcising Titus.

ἀλλὰ τήρησις κ.τ.λ.   'But keeping of the commandments of
God *is everything*.' As in iii. 7 and x. 24, the strongly advers-
ative ἀλλά implies that the opposite of the previous negative is
understood. In Gal. v. 6 and vi. 15 the ἀλλά introduces two
different things (see above), both of them different from this.
Of all three of them we may say, *in his stat totus Christianismus*
(Beng).* Τήρησις ἐντολῶν occurs Ecclus. xxxii. 23, τηρ. νόμων,
Wisd. vi. 18: τηρεῖν τὰς ἐντολάς, Matt. xix. 17; 1 Tim. vi. 14;
1 John ii. 3, where see Westcott. On ἐντ. Θεοῦ see Deissmann,
Light, p. 381.

20. Repetition of the principle laid down; ' In the secular
surroundings of the calling in which he is called, in these let him
abide'; and ἐν ταύτῃ emphasizes the charge to make no change
of condition.† In N.T., κλῆσις is almost exclusively Pauline, and
it means either the act of calling (Phil. iii. 14) or the circumstances in which the calling took place (i. 26 and here): it does
not mean 'vocation.' Lightfoot quotes Epictetus (i. 29 § 46),
μάρτυς ὑπὸ τοῦ Θεοῦ κεκλημένος, and (§ 49) ταῦτα μέλλεις μαρτυ-
ρεῖν καὶ καταισχύνειν τὴν κλῆσιν ἣν κέκληκεν [ὁ Θεός].

21. δοῦλος ἐκλήθης; 'Wast thou a slave when thou wast
called? Do not mind that.' A slave can be a good Christian
(Eph. vi. 5; Col. iii. 22; Tit. ii. 9). Thackeray quotes the
iambic line in Philo, *Quod omn. prob. liber* 7, δοῦλος πέφυκας; οὐ
μέτεστί σοι λόγου. Here again, the clause might be either interrogative or hypothetical.

ἀλλ' εἰ καὶ . . . μᾶλλον χρῆσαι. 'But still, if thou canst also
become free, rather make use of it than not.' The καί affects
δύνασαι, not εἰ : 'if thou art also able to become free as well as
to remain a slave'; if the one course is as possible as the other;
then what? It is remarkable that the Apostle's advice is interpreted in opposite ways. He says, 'Rather make use of it.'
Make use of what? Surely, τῷ δύνασθαι ἐλεύθερος γενέσθαι, the
possibility of becoming free. This was the last thing mentioned;
and 'make use of' suits a new condition better than the old
condition of slavery. Still more decidedly does the aorist (χρῆσαι,

---

* Stanley has an interesting, but rather fanciful note, connecting this
passage with the Father, Gal. v. 6 with the Son, and Gal. vi. 15 with the
Holy Spirit.

† Manufacturers of idols who became Christians claimed this principle as
justifying their continuing to earn a living in this way. "Can't you starve?"
says Tertullian ; *fides famem non timet* (*De Idol.* 5, 12).

not χρῶ) imply a new condition. The advice, thus interpreted, is thoroughly in keeping with the Apostle's tenderness of heart and robustness of judgment. 'Do not be miserable because you are a slave; yet, if you can just as easily be set free, take advantage of it rather than not.' He regarded marriage as a hindrance to the perfection of the Christian life (vv. 32–35). Was not slavery, with its hideous temptations, a far greater hindrance? *

Nevertheless, various commentators, ancient and modern, insist on going back to δοῦλος for the dat. to be supplied with χρῆσαι and understand τῇ δουλείᾳ. *Utere servitute quasi re bona et utili: servitus enim valet ad humilitatem servandam et ad patientiam exercendam* (Herv.) It is urged that in this way the Apostle remains consistent with his rule, 'Abide in the calling in which thou wast called.' But ἀλλ' εἰ καὶ . . . χρῆσαι is a *parenthetic* mitigation given in passing; like ἐὰν δὲ καὶ . . . καταλλαγήτω in v. 11, it mentions a possible exception. The meaning will then be, 'Slavery is not intolerable for a Christian, but an opportunity for emancipation need not be refused.' The Christian slave is not to rebel against a heathen master, any more than a Christian wife against a heathen husband; but if the heathen is ready to grant freedom, the Christian slave, like the Christian wife, may take it without scruple. For this view, which is that of Luther, Erasmus, Calvin, and Beza, see Evans, Lightfoot, and Goudge; for the other, which is that of Bengel, Meyer, De Wette, and Edwards, see Alford, Ellicott and Schmiedel; but Schmiedel admits that χρῆσαι, if τῇ δουλείᾳ is to be understood, *hat allerdings etwas Seltsames*.

22. ὁ γὰρ ἐν κυρίῳ κληθεὶς δοῦλος. 'For he who, while in slavery, was called to be in the Lord is the Lord's freedman.' †
Or we may take ὁ with δοῦλος, 'For the slave who was called in the Lord'; but the next clause is against this. A slave 'called in the Lord' is in relation to Christ a freedman: ἀπελεύθερος, like *libertus*, is a relative term, used *c. gen.* of the emancipator. Although in his secular condition he remains a slave, in his spiritual condition he has been set free: he is κλητὸς ἅγιος (i. 1), and is free from the bondage of sin (Rom. vi. 6). There is no hint here that his master, if he were a Christian, would be sure to set him free; and even Philem. 21 does not imply that. See Harnack, *Mission and Expansion,* I. pp. 167 f.; Deissmann, *Light,* pp. 323, 326–333, 382, 392.

* Bachmann admits that the Apostle's recommending people to disregard an opportunity of being freed from slavery *zweifellos etwas Überraschendes hat.*
† In ordinary language, ἀπελεύθερος Κυρίου would mean that he had been the Lord's slave and that the Lord had manumitted him. He had been in slavery and the Lord had freed him from it, and this justifies the expression. The Lord was his προστάτης.

'In like manner, he that was called being free is Christ's slave'; or, 'the free man by being called is Christ's slave,' he can no longer do as he likes to his own hurt; he is bound to obey his new spiritual Master and Lord. Such a bondservant of Christ was the Apostle himself, and he gloried in the fact (Rom. i. 1; Phil. i. 1; Tit. i. 1). Nowhere else in the Bible is ἀπελεύθερος found.

K L, Copt. Aeth. Arm. add καὶ after ὁμοίως : D E F G add δὲ καὶ : ℵ A B P 17, Vulg. omit. καὶ or δὲ καὶ is usual after ὁμοίως, and hence the insertion ; but here neither is required.

23. τιμῆς ἠγοράσθητε. This recalls vi. 20 and applies it to both classes. The social slave, who has been set free by Christ, and the social freeman, who has become enslaved to Christ, have alike been bought by God, and are now His property. In one sense Christ's death was an act of emanicipation, it set free from the thraldom of sin; in another sense it was a change of ownership.* It is a mistake to suppose that the words are addressed only to those who are socially free, charging them not to lose their freedom. Such a charge would be superfluous. Moreover, the change from the singular to the plural intimates that both classes are now exhorted. See below.

In commenting on this verse, Origen lets us know that he was not the first to comment on this Epistle. He speaks of what οἱ λοιποὶ ἑρμηνευταί say on the subject. See on ix. 20.

μὴ γίνεσθε δοῦλοι ἀνθρώπων. ʼDo not become, do not show yourselves to be, bondservants of men.ʼ The words are obscure. It is very improbable that the prohibition is addressed to those who are free, and that it forbids them to sell themselves into slavery. Such a prohibition could not be needed. Moreover, the change from the 2nd pers. sing. to the 2nd pers. plur. shows that he is now addressing all his converts. Origen strangely interprets the slavery as meaning *marriage*, in which neither partner τοῦ ἰδίου σώματος ἐξουσιάζει, and from which both partners should seek freedom ἐκ συμφώνου. The bondage must mean ʼsome condition of life which is likely to violate God's rights of ownershipʼ (Lev. xxv. 42, 55). The interpretation, ʼDo not become enslaved to any *party-leader*,ʼ is remote from the context. More probably, ʼDo not let social relations or public opinion or evil advisers interfere with the absolute service which is due to Him who bought you with His Son's blood.ʼ

* " In the time of St Paul, ' Lord ' was throughout the whole Eastern world a universally understood religious conception. The Apostle's confession of his Master as ʼour Lord Jesus Christ,ʼ with the complementary idea that Christians were dearly bought 'slaves,' was at once intelligible in all the fulness of its meaning to every one in the Greek Orient " (Deissmann, *New Light on the N.T.*, p. 79). See Lietzmann, *Greek Papyri*, p. 4.

24. The general principle is stated once more with the addition of παρὰ Θεῷ. This may mean 'in the presence of God,' or 'in God's household,' or 'on God's side.' The last agrees well with μενέτω, and makes a good antithesis to ἀνθρώπων: 'let your attachments be heavenwards, not earthwards. With that proviso, all secular conditions, whether of family life, or caste, or service, are capable of being made the expression of a Christian character. Deissmann, *Light*, p. 330.

VII. 25–40. *Respecting unmarried women, the transitory and trying character of the present world is against a change of condition. The unmarried state leaves people more free for God's service.*

²⁵ With regard to unmarried daughters, I have no charge from the Lord to pass on to you; but I offer my opinion as that of a man who through the Lord's mercy is not unworthy of your confidence, and who perhaps knows Christ's mind, although he cannot quote any words of His. ²⁶ Well then, I think that owing to the distressful times that are upon us, it is an excellent thing for people to remain as they are. ²⁷ Are you united to a wife? Do not seek to be freed from the tie. Are you at present free from this tie? Do not seek to be bound by it. But if you do marry, you have committed no sin; ²⁸ and if a maiden marries, she has committed no sin. Yet people who make these ties are sure to have increased affliction in the affairs of this life. But I, as your adviser, would spare you this, if I could. ²⁹ This, however, I do affirm, Brothers. The time allowed before the Advent is now very narrow. This means that henceforth those who have wives should serve as strictly as those who have none, ³⁰ that those who weep should live as though no sorrow disturbed them, those who are enjoying life as not absorbed in their enjoyment, those who buy as not taking full possession, ³¹ and those who use this world as not eager to use it to the full: for transitory indeed is the outward fashion of this world. ³² Yet I want you to be free from the anxieties which the world produces. When a man is unmarried, he is anxious about our Lord's interests, studying how he may please our Lord; ³³ but when once he is married, he is anxious about worldly interests, studying how he may please his wife. ³⁴ Parted also by a similar division of interests are the married and the

unmarried woman (?). For the unmarried woman is anxious
about our Lord's interests, striving hard to be holy both in body
and in spirit ; but when once she is married, she is anxious about
worldly interests, studying how she may please her husband.
⁸⁵ Now I am saying all this simply for your own spiritual profit.
I have no wish to throw a halter over you and check Christian
liberty.   On the contrary, I want you to choose what is seemly,
and, like Mary, to wait upon our Lord without Martha's
distractions.

⁸⁶ That is my opinion ; but there are limitations.   If a father
think that the way in which he is acting towards his unmarried
daughter is not seemly, because she has long since reached a
marriageable age and ought now to marry without delay, seeing
that her nature seems to require it,—he must do as he thinks
best.   There is nothing sinful in it ; let the marriage take place.
⁸⁷ But when a father has settled convictions that a single life is
best for his daughter, and has no need to surrender these, but
has full right to carry out his own wishes, and has decided in his
own mind to do so,—he will act rightly if he keeps his daughter
free.   ⁸⁸ It comes to this, therefore, that both of them act rightly.
The father who gives his child in marriage does well, and he who
does not do so will be found to have done still better.

⁸⁹ A wife is bound as long as her husband lives ; but if he is
dead, she is free to marry any one she pleases, provided it be in
holy matrimony with a Christian.   ⁴⁰ But a widow is a happier
woman if she abides as she is to the end, according to my
judgment.   And I believe that I, no less than others, can claim
to have the guidance of God's Spirit.

25. Περὶ δὲ τῶν παρθένων. It is clear from the use of
παρθένος in *vv.* 28, 34, 36, 37, 38, that the word here applies to
women only; contrast Rev. xiv. 4.   On this subject no traditional teaching of Christ had reached the Apostle (*v.* 10); he
could not frame a judgment partly based upon His teaching
(*v.* 12) ; nor did he feel justified in giving an independent
Apostolic decision (*v.* 17), for the responsibility of deciding must
rest with the father.   He is willing, however, to state his own
opinion ; and he intimates that his wonderful conversion and
call are strong evidence that the opinion of one who has been so
divinely favoured is worthy of trust.   As in 1 Pet. ii. 10 (see
Hort), ἠλεημένος is used "in reference to the signal mercy of the
gift of the Gospel"; and this in his case included the call to be

an Apostle.   We have a similar use of ἠλεήθημεν in 2 Cor. iv. 1,
and of ἠλεήθην in 1 Tim. i. 13, 16.   Here πιστός, 'trustworthy,'
is used as in iv. 2 and 1 Tim. i. 12 ; cf. ἡ μαρτυρία Κυρίου πιστή
(Ps. xix. 8) ; not as in 2 Cor. vi. 15 and 1 Tim. iv. 10.

We have the same contrast between ἐπιταγή and γνώμη in
2 Cor. viii. 8, 10.   Here the Vulgate has *praeceptum* and *consilium* to distinguish the words, which led to the later distinction
between 'precepts' and 'counsels of perfection' (Stanley).

26. νομίζω οὖν.   'I think therefore.'   He does not mean that
he is not sure : what is stated in *v.* 25 shows that οὖν introduces
a decided conviction ; and perhaps the use of ὑπάρχειν rather
than εἶναι shows that the conviction is of long standing.   He holds
that this is a sound axiom to start from ; it is good in principle.

διὰ τὴν ἐνεστῶσαν ἀνάγκην.   These words are an important
qualification.   The Apostle's opinion is determined by 'the
present necessity,' 'the straitness now upon us' (Heb. ix. 9),
owing to the disturbances and dangers which he saw; and also
by the Advent which he believed to be very near (xvi. 22),
although not yet present (2 Thess. ii. 2).   We cannot assume
that his opinion would have been the same in a more peaceful
period, and after experience had proved that the Advent might
be long delayed.   For ἀνάγκη of external distress see Luke xxi. 23,
where the meaning is very similar to the meaning here ; 2 Cor.
vi. 4, xii. 10 ; 1 Thess. iii. 7 ; *Ps. Sol.* v. 8 ; *Testament of Joseph*
ii. 4.   Thackeray (*St Paul and Jewish Thought*, pp. 105 f.)
thinks that this passage may reflect Jewish beliefs in the "Woes
of the Messiah," the birth-pangs which were to precede His
Advent (2 Esdr. v. 1–12, vi. 18–24, ix. 1–9 ; *Jubilees* xxiii. 11–25 ;
Assump. of Moses x. 3–6 ; *Apoc. of Baruch* xxvii. 1 f., where see
Charles, xlviii. 31–39, lxx. 3–10).   Lightfoot (on Gal. i. 4)
contends that ἐνεστῶσαν means 'present' rather than 'imminent,'
but the difference is not great.   A trouble which is believed to
be near and certain is already a present distress.

ὅτι καλὸν ἀνθρώπῳ τὸ οὕτως εἶναι.   'That it is good, I say, for
a person so to be.'   The construction of the verse is not regular,
but quite intelligible : ὅτι is 'that,' not 'because,' and the
second καλόν picks up and continues the first.   But doubt
arises as to the meaning of τὸ οὕτως εἶναι.   'To be thus' is vague,
and 'thus' may have three meanings : (1) 'as he is,' *i.e.* he is to
remain without change of condition ; (2) ' as I am,' or as αἱ
παρθένοι are, *i.e.* unmarried ; (3) 'as I now tell you,' referring to
what follows.   The first is probably right ; it is a repetition of
the principle already given in *v.* 24, of which principle *v.* 27 is an
illustration.   The οὕτως in *v.* 40 and Rom. ix. 20 is similar.
There is not much difference in effect between (1) and (3)

Origen prefers (2), and points out that this is the fourth time
(*vv.* 1, 8, 26 *bis*) that the Apostle has used καλόν of celibacy,
whereas all that he says of marriage is that it is not sin.

27. δέδεσαι γυναικί ; Like *vv.* 18 and 21, this may be either
interrogative or hypothetical. The perfect indicates the settled
condition of the marriage-tie, and γυναικί means ' wife,' not
' woman ': betrothal to an unmarried woman is not included.
There could be no doubt about this case. The Lord had
prohibited divorce ; therefore μὴ ζήτει λύσιν, ' never at any time
(pres. imperat.) seek freedom.' The advice is permanent. Nowhere else in N.T. does λύσις occur. In LXX it is used only
of the solving of hard sayings (Eccles. viii. 1 ; Dan. xii. 8 ;
Wisd. viii. 8). See Milligan, *Greek Papyri*, p. 106.

λέλυσαι ἀπὸ γ. Here again the perfect means, ' Art thou in
a state of freedom from matrimonial ties ? ' It does not mean
' Hast thou been freed from a wife by death or divorce ? ' The
verb is chosen because of the preceding λύσιν, and bachelors as
well as widowers are addressed. Here it cannot be assumed
that such men are not to marry, because they were unmarried
when they were called to be Christians. The Lord had not
said this. But *in the existing circumstances* His Apostle advises
this. In neither clause need we translate μὴ ζήτει ' Cease to
seek.' We do not know that any Corinthian Christians had
been trying to be divorced from their wives, though probably
some were trying to be married.

28. ἐὰν δὲ καὶ γαμήσῃς. He at once hastens to assure those
who have already done what he now advises them not to do, that
they have done nothing wrong : ' But if it be that thou do
marry.' The καί, as in *v.* 11, intensifies the verb ; if it has
already gone as far as that. See Evans on this aorist.

> The ' and ' in ' but and if ' (AV., RV.) is not a translation of the καί,
> but an archaic reduplication of the ' if.' Perhaps ' and if ' is a corruption
> of ' an if,' for ' an '=' if,' as in the saying ' If *ifs* and *ans* were pots and
> pans.'
>
> In this verse we have both the later (γαμήσῃς) and the classical (γήμῃ)
> form of the aorist. But some texts (KL, Chrys.) have altered γαμήσῃς to
> γήμῃς, while D E F G have λάβῃς γυναῖκα, Vulg. *acceperis uxorem*. In
> ix. 21, 22 we have both κερδανῶ and κερδήσω.

οὐχ ἥμαρτες. The thought goes on to the marriage as a fact ;
' there was no sin in that.' This sounds incongruous in English,
and we must say ' thou hast not sinned.' Origen remarks that
Paul does not say ἐὰν γαμήσῃς, καλόν.

ἡ παρθένος. If the article is genuine, it is generic : a reference
to some particular case at Corinth is not likely.

θλίψιν δὲ τῇ σαρκὶ ἕξουσιν οἱ τ. ' But affliction for the flesh will be the lot of those who act thus.' *Quum diceret, habituros tribulationem carnis, vel in carne, significat, sollicitudines et angustias, quibus conjuges implicantur, ex negotiis terrenis provenire.* Caro *igitur hic pro homine externo capitur* (Calv.). This would be specially true in the persecutions which were to precede the Advent. As Bacon says, "He that hath wife and children hath given hostages to fortune "; and "children sweeten labours, but they make misfortunes more bitter." Origen makes θλίψις refer specially to the wife, quoting Gen. iii. 16. The dative may be locative; 'in the flesh' (AV., RV.); *tribulationem carnis* (Vulg.); *pressuram carnis* (Tert.); *afflictionem in carne* (Beza). Cf. σκόλοψ τῇ σαρκί, 'thorn for the flesh' (2 Cor. xii. 7).

ἐγὼ δὲ ὑμῶν φείδομαι. 'But I for my part spare you': this is his aim as their spiritual adviser. The emphatic ἐγώ makes 'I won't pain you by saying more' an improbable interpretation. In what way does he spare them? *Nolo vos illam tribulationem sentire* (Herv.). *Ideo quia, secundum indulgentiam conjugia non omnino prohibeo* (Primasius). Atto admits both reasons, but the former is probably right, and it almost excludes the latter. He aims at keeping them from affliction by persuading them not to marry. Cf. 2 Cor i. 23, xii. 6, xiii. 2.

γαμήσῃς (א B P [γαμήσῃ A] 17) rather than γήμῃς (K L, Orig. Chrys.) to agree with the following γήμῃ, or λάβῃς γυναῖκα (D F, Latt. *acceperis uxorem*), Tert. *duxeris uxorem*. It is less easy to decide whether ἡ before παρθένος should be inserted (א A D E K LP) or omitted (B F G). D* F insert ἐν before τῇ σαρκί.

29. Τοῦτο δέ φημι. 'But this I do declare.' The change from λέγω (*v.* 6, i. 12, vi. 5) to φημί should be marked in translation, whether the change has significance or not; but even the RV. fails to do this. The change probably gives special seriousness to the assertion. 'But, though I counsel none to change their state, I do counsel all to change their *attitude towards* all earthly things.' We have the same expression, introducing a solemn warning, xv. 50; cf. x. 15, 19 : nowhere else in N.T. or LXX does the 1st pers. sing. occur. The τοῦτο does not refer to what precedes ; he is not repeating what he has just said. He is reminding them of a grave fact, which has to be considered in connexion with marriage, and indeed with the whole of life. He has been insisting on the ἀνάγκη already present : he now insists on the (supposed) shortness of the interval before the Advent. Both facts confirm the advice which he gives.

ὁ καιρὸς συνεσταλμένος ἐστίν. 'The allotted time has become short,' lit. 'has been drawn together so as to be small in amount.' As in Rom. xiii. 11, ὁ καιρός is used almost as a technical term for the period before the Advent (Westcott on Heb. ix. 9). Hort (on 1 Pet. i. 11) thinks that it was owing probably to its use in Daniel (ix. 27, etc.) that in our Lord's time it was specially used with reference to national religious expectations.   But St Paul by no means always uses it in this special eschatological sense, although he commonly uses it of 'a fixed and limited time' or 'a fitting period,' while χρόνος is time generally, and is unlimited.   That he still believed that the Second Coming was near is evident from x. 11, xv. 51; but a little later his view seems to be changing (Sanday and Headlam, *Romans*, p. 379; Sanday, *Life of Christ in Recent Research*, p. 113). Calvin and others explain the words here of the shortness of human life; 'you are sure to die before long.'   This makes good sense, but probably not the right sense.

Some texts (D E F G) ins. ὅτι before ὁ καιρός : the best omit.   A more important point is the punctuation of what follows.   Should a stop, comma, or colon be placed after ἐστίν, and τὸ λοιπόν be taken with ἵνα κ.τ.λ. ?   Or should it be placed after τὸ λοιπόν, and τὸ λοιπόν be taken with what precedes ?   Editors are divided ; but the former is better for two reasons.   In the Pauline Epp. τὸ λοιπόν commonly leads (Phil. iii. 1, iv. 8 ; 2 Thess. iii. 1), as also does λοιπόν (2 Cor. xiii. 11 ; 1 Thess. iv. 1 ; 2 Tim. iv. 8).   And τὸ λοιπόν is weak after συνεστ. ἐστιν, 'is straitened as to its residue.'

τὸ λοιπὸν ἵνα καὶ οἱ ἐχ. γ.   'So that, henceforward those also who have wives may be as though they had none.'   St Paul rather frequently puts words in front of ἵνα for emphasis ; 2 Cor. ii. 4; Gal. ii. 10; Rom. vii. 13; Col. iv. 16.   It is quite clear that, if the conditions of the time are such that those who have wives ought to be as if they had none, then it is foolish to marry ; for as soon as one had taken a wife one would have to behave as if one had not got one, *i.e.* one would undertake a great responsibility, and then have the responsibility of trying to be free from it.   Far better, in such circumstances, never to undertake it.   In 2 Esdr. xvi. 40–48 there is a good deal that resembles this passage; but 2 Esdr. xv., xvi. are an addition made by a Christian about A.D. 265, and the writer very likely had this passage in his mind when he wrote.

The force of the καί is not quite certain.   He has been saying that in such times the unmarried state is best, and then goes on to say that not only the married, but also all bound in any earthly circumstances, should practise 'detachment'; then the καί would mean 'both' (AV., RV.).   Even when three or four things are strung together in Greek, the first may have καί as well as the rest.   In *Acta Pauli et Theclae* (p. 42, ed. Tisch.) we have μακάριοι οἱ ἔχοντες γυναῖκας ὡς μὴ ἔχοντες, ὅτι αὐτοὶ ἄγγελοι Θεοῦ γενήσονται.

The meaning of the illustrations is fairly clear.   Married men are apt to become absorbed in domestic cares, mourners in their sorrow, buyers in the preservation of what they have bought.   A

Christian, with dangers all round him and the Advent close at hand, ought not to be engrossed in any of his surroundings, knowing how temporary they are. He should learn how to sit loose to all earthly ties.

30. ὡς μὴ κατέχοντες. 'As not entering upon full ownership,' or 'keeping fast hold upon' (xi. 2, xv. 2; 2 Cor. vi. 10; 1 Thess. v. 21, where see Milligan, p. 155). Earthly goods are a trust, not a possession.

31. ὡς μὴ καταχρώμενοι. 'As not using it to the utmost'; lit. 'using it down to the ground,' and so, 'using it completely up.' We are not to try to get all we can out of externals. The rendering 'abusing' or 'misusing' is not the right idea.* Here and in ix. 18 only: in Ep. Jer. 28 of the idolatrous priests 'using up for their own profit' the sacrificial offerings. The man who remembers that he is only a sojourner in the world is likely to remember also that worldly possessions are not everything, and that worldly surroundings cannot be made permanent. Lightfoot quotes from Seneca (*Ep. Mor.* lxxiv. 18), "Let us use them, let us not boast of them: and let us use them sparingly, as a loan deposited with us, which will soon depart."

παράγει γὰρ τὸ σχῆμα τ. κ. τ. 'For transitory is the fashion of this world.' There is no need to take the γάρ back to ὁ καιρὸς συνεσταλμένος ἐστίν. Indeed, this does not make very good sense. The γάρ explains the reason for the preceding counsels, especially the last one. Τὸ σχῆμα τ. κ. is not a mere periphrasis for ὁ κόσμος: the phrase expresses 'the outward appearance,' all that can be apprehended by the senses. This may change, and does change, season by season, although the world itself abides. *Praeterit figura mundi, non natura, ut in aliam speciem mundus vertatur* (Herv.).† Cf. 2 Esdr. iv. 26; and see Deissmann, *Light*, p. 281; Resch, *Agrapha*, p. 274.

Because χρᾶσθαι commonly has the dative (2 Cor. i. 17, iii. 12) some texts have corrected τὸν κόσμον (the reading of אֿ* A B D* F G 17) to τῷ κόσμῳ. Even in class. Grk., καταχρᾶσθαι often has the accusative: in ix. 18 it has the dative.

32. ἀμερίμνους. 'Free from anxieties,' such as 'choke the word' (Mark iv. 19) and distract from the thought of 'that Day' (Luke xxi. 34). 'Without carefulness' (AV.) is not the meaning: cf. Matt. xxviii. 14; Wisd. vi. 15, vii. 23. 'Carefulness' formerly

---

* The Vulgate has *tanquam non utantur*, which seems to imply different Greek: Beza, *ut non abutentes*, which is right, for *abuti* often means 'to use up.' 'Misusing' would be παραχρώμενοι. In Philo (*De Josepho* xxiv.) we have χρῶ μὴ παραχρώμενος.

† Excepting Phil. ii. 8, σχῆμα occurs nowhere else in N.T., and, excepting Isa. iii. 17, nowhere in LXX. The destruction of the material universe is not a Pauline idea.

meant 'anxiety' (Ps. cxxvii. 3). Bacon couples it with 'trouble
of mind,' and Latimer calls it 'wicked' (Wright, *Bible Word-
Book*, p. 111). In papyri the wish that a person ἀμέριμνος γένῃ is
common. The Apostle goes on to give examples, and to show by
his wording that there is a right kind of μέριμνα as well as a wrong.

πῶς ἀρέσῃ τῷ Κυρίῳ. The thought of pleasing Christ and
God is frequent in the Pauline Epp. (Rom. viii. 8; 1 Thess. ii.
15, iv. 1; Col. i. 10; 2 Cor. v. 9). See on x. 33. Throughout *vv.* 32–34 ἀρέσῃ (אABDEFG) is certainly the right
reading, not ἀρέσει KLP). See Matt. vi. 24 and 2 Tim. ii. 4.

33. ὁ δὲ γαμήσας. The aorist points to the time when the
change of interest took place: 'once a man is married.'
Epictetus (*Enchir.* 18) holds that the care of external things (τὰ
ἐκτός) is fatal to devotion to one's higher nature: a man is sure
(πᾶσα ἀνάγκη) to neglect the one in caring for the other.

After τῇ γυναικί there is much doubt as to punctuation and reading.
Does καὶ μεμέρισται belong to *v.* 33 or *v.* 34? The Vulg. takes it with
v. 33, *et divisus est*, 'and he is a divided man,' 'he is no longer single-
hearted.' This spoils the balance of πῶς ἀρ. τ.κ. and πῶς ἀρ. τῇ γ. Moreover, it is a weak addition to the latter. The arrangement in AV. and
RV. seems better. Some texts (D³ E F G K L) omit the καὶ before μεμέρισται, and with that omission μεμέρισται must belong to what follows: but
this καὶ is probably genuine (א A B D* P 17, Vulg. Syrr. Arm. Aeth.). So
also the καὶ after μεμ. (א A B D³ F G K L P, Vulg. Aeth.). The position
of ἡ ἄγαμος is uncertain. Should it be inserted after ἡ γυνή only (B P
Vulg.), or after ἡ παρθένος only (D E F G K L Syrr. Arm.), or in both
places (א A F² 17, Aeth.)? This third reading cannot be right, and the
evidence for ἡ ἄγαμος after ἡ γυνή is thereby weakened. If, however, ἡ
ἄγαμος be read after ἡ γυνή only, then καὶ μεμέρισται must be taken with
v. 33. The alternative readings therefore are: τῇ γυναικὶ καὶ μεμέρισται,
καὶ ἡ γυνὴ ἡ ἄγαμος καὶ ἡ παρθένος μεριμνᾷ τ. τ. κ. (Lach. Treg. WH.) and:
τῇ γυναικί, καὶ μεμέρισται καὶ ἡ γυνὴ καὶ ἡ παρθένος, ἡ ἄγαμος μεριμνᾷ τ.τ.κ.
(Tisch. Alf. Rev. Ell.). Lightfoot (writing before the appearance of WH.)
says: "I venture to prefer this latter reading, though supported chiefly
by Western authorities, from internal evidence; for the sentences then
become exactly parallel. There is just the same distinction between the
married woman and the virgin as between the married and the unmarried
man. The other view throws sense and parallelism into confusion, for
καὶ μεμέρισται is not wanted with *v.* 33, which is complete in itself. It also
necessitates the awkward phrase ἡ γυνὴ καὶ ἡ παρθένος μεριμνᾷ. The
reading ἡ γυνὴ ἡ ἄγαμος καὶ ἡ παρθένος ἡ ἄγαμος illustrates the habitual
practice of scribes to insert as much as possible, and may be neglected."
Heinrici proposed a second μεμέρισται: τῇ γυναικὶ καὶ μεμέρισται, μεμέρισται καὶ ἡ γυνή. ἡ ἄγαμος καὶ ἡ παρθένος μεριμνᾷ, κ.τ.λ. This is pure conjecture; but it restores the balance of clauses and accounts for the double
καί. Findlay thinks it "tempting." Bachmann tabulates the confusing
evidence. See Resch, *Agrapha*, pp. 8, 183.

On the other hand, see Introd. § "Text." The question of reading
must precede and determine that of punctuation. The MS. evidence for
καὶ before μεμέρισται is overwhelming; that for ἡ ἄγαμος immediately after
γυνή scarcely less so. The sense given to μεμέρισται in AV. is "ill attested
and improbable" (WH.) and would require a plural verb.

34. ἵνα ᾖ ἁγία. Bengel remarks that ἁγία here means more than it does in *v.* 14: what is set apart from the world for God ought to conform to the purity of God and not to the defilements of the world: Trench, *Syn.* § 88 ; Cremer, pp. 598 f. See ɪ Tim. v. 5, and the art. *Heiligung* in Herzog (Hauck). Stanley quotes Queen Elizabeth, who said that England was her husband.

35. πρὸς τὸ ὑμῶν αὐτῶν σύμφορον. His aim is not to glorify his ministry as Apostle of the Gentiles (Rom. xi. 13), but to keep them free from cares (*v.* 32). Cf. **x.** 33, the only other place in N.T. in which σύμφορος occurs. The reading συμφέρον is probably wrong, as in **x.** 33.

βρόχον ὑμῖν ἐπιβάλω. 'Cast a snare upon you' (AV., RV.) gives a wrong idea : βρόχος is a halter or lasso, not a trap (here only, in N.T.). He has no wish to curtail their freedom, as one throws a rope over an animal that is loose, or a person that is to be arrested : *accesserat lictor injiciebatque laqueum* (Livy i. 26). Cf. Philem. 14; Prov. vi. 5. *Laqueo trahuntur inviti* (Beng.).

ἀλλὰ πρὸς τὸ κ.τ.λ. 'On the contrary, with a view to': what follows is an expansion of ἀμερίμνους : cf. Rom. xiii. 13.

εὐπάρεδρον. Cf. παρεδρεύοντες in ix. 13, and 'Give me wisdom, that sitteth by Thy throne,' τὴν τῶν σῶν θρόνων πάρεδρον (Wisd. ix. 4). The word occurs nowhere else in N.T. or LXX. Combined with ἀπερισπάστως it suggests the contrast between Mary sitting at the Lord's feet and Martha distracted by much serving, περιεσπᾶτο περὶ πολλὴν διακονίαν (Luke x. 40). Cf. ἵνα ἀπερίσπαστοι γένωνται τῆς σῆς εὐεργεσίας, 'that they might never be distracted from Thy goodness' (Wisd. xvi. 11); and see Ecclus. xl. 1, 2. The reading εὐπρόσεδρον has hardly any authority.*

36. The verse indicates that the Corinthians had asked him about the duty of a father with a daughter of age to marry. The question is what he ought to do, not what she ought to do : his wishes, not hers, are paramount. This is in accordance with the ideas of that age, and the Apostle does not condemn them.

There is no need to place a comma after νομίζει : her being of full age is what suggested to the father (who may have been warned also by friends) that he is not behaving becomingly towards his child in not furthering her marriage. Apparently νομίζει, like νομίζω in *v.* 26, is used, not of a hesitating opinion but of a settled conviction ; and verbally ἀσχημονεῖν looks back

---

* See the remarkable parallel in Epictetus (*Dis.* iii. 22 ; Long's translation, Bell, 1903, ɪɪ. p. 87) : " But in the present state of things, which is like that of an army placed in battle order, is it not fit that the philosopher should without any distraction (ἀπερίσπαστον) be employed only on the ministration (διακονίᾳ) of God, not tied down to the common duties of mankind, nor entangled in the ordinary relations of life ? "

to εὔσχημον in v. 35; but perhaps only verbally, because the spheres are so very different. 'Past the flower of her age' is perhaps too strong for ὑπέρακμος (Vulg. *superadulta*): Luther is right; *weil sie eben wohl mannbar ist*, and in Corinth there was danger that a girl, who was old enough to marry and anxious to marry, might go disastrously astray if marriage was refused. In Ecclus. xlii. 9 the father is anxious ἐν νεότητι αὐτῆς μή ποτε παρακμάσῃ. Plato (*Rep.* 460 E) speaks of μέτριος χρόνος ἀκμῆς as being 20 for a woman and 30 for a man. Ἀσχημονεῖν occurs here and xiii. 5 in N.T., and ὑπέρακμος nowhere else in the Bible.

οὕτως ὀφείλει γίνεσθαι. That he had better let her marry, not simply *propter voluntatem puellae* (Primasius), but because of the possible consequences of refusing. 'Let him do what he will' does not mean that it is a matter of indifference whether he allows the marriage or not, and that he can please himself; it means that he is free to do what his conviction (νομίζει) has led him to wish. It is wholly improbable that τις, αὐτοῦ and ὅς (v. 37) refer to the suitor, the prospective bridegroom. The Corinthians would not have asked about him. It is the father's or guardian's duty that is the question. Still more improbable is the conjecture that the Apostle is referring to a kind of spiritual betrothal between unmarried persons. It is supposed that Christian spinsters with ascetic tendencies, in order to avoid ordinary marriage, each placed themselves formally under the protection of a man, who was in some sense responsible for the woman. She might or might not share the same house, but she was pledged to share his spiritual life. And the meaning of v. 36 would then be that the man who has formed a connexion of this kind may, without sin, turn it into an ordinary marriage. In this way the plural γαμείτωσαν is free from all difficulty. But, quite independently of the improbability that St. Paul would sanction so perilous an arrangement, there is the obstacle of γαμίζων in v. 38, which everywhere in N.T. (Matt. xxii. 30, xxiv. 38; Mark xii. 25; Luke xvii. 27, xx. 35) means '*give* in marriage' (in LXX it does not occur). In spite of this, some make it mean 'marry'; while others accept the absurdity that the man who has formed a special union with a woman may give her in marriage to another man. The γαμίζων is decisive: the Apostle is speaking of a father or guardian disposing of an unmarried daughter or ward.

γαμείτωσαν. The plural is elliptic, but quite intelligible; 'Let the daughter and her suitor marry.' Cf. μείνωσιν, 1 Tim. ii. 15.

To avoid the awkwardness, D* F G, Arm., Aug. read γαμείτω, while d e f Vulg., Ambrst. have *non peccat si nubat*, 'he sinneth not if she marry.'

37. ὃς δὲ ἕστηκεν . . . ἑδραῖος. It is assumed that a father would originally be of the Apostle's opinion, that διὰ τὴν ἐνεστῶσαν ἀνάγκην, it is better for a daughter to remain single ; and the case is now stated of a father who is able to abide by that conviction, because his daughter's circumstances do not compel him to change it. There is in her condition no ὀφείλει γίνεσθαι, no ἀνάγκη to determine the father to act against his general principle. In N.T., ἑδραῖος is peculiar to Paul (xv. 58 ; Col. i. 23) ; in LXX it does not occur, but is frequent in Symm. Cf. 1 Tim. iii. 15.

ἐξουσίαν δὲ ἔχει περὶ τοῦ ἰδίου θ. 'He can do as he likes about his personal wishes' (ἔξεστιν, vi. 12, x. 23), *cum virgo non adversaretur sed assentiretur huic paternae voluntati* (Herv.). The repetition of ἴδιος respecting his will and heart, and the change to ἑαυτοῦ respecting his daughter, seem to mark the predominance of the father in the matter. Similarly, in *v.* 2 we have τὴν ἑαυτοῦ γυναῖκα, and in *v.* 4 τοῦ ἰδίου σώματος. With κέκρικεν compare κέκρικα in v. 3, and with the emphatic τοῦτο preparing for what is to follow, compare 1 Thess. iv. 3.

τηρεῖν. 'To keep her as she is,' 'guard her in a state of singleness,' not 'to keep her for himself.' On ποιήσει see *v.* 38.

ἑδραῖος comes last in its clause with emphasis (א A B D E P), not immediately after ἕστηκεν (K L) : F G, d e Aeth. Arm. omit ἑδραῖος. K L omit αὐτοῦ before ἑδραῖος. After κέκρικεν, ἐν τ. ἰδίᾳ κ. (א A B P) is to be preferred to ἐν τ. κ. αὐτοῦ (D E F G K L). τοῦ before τηρεῖν (D E F G K L) should be omitted (א A B P 17, e d).

38. καὶ ὁ γαμίζων . . . καὶ ὁ μή. This probably means ' *Both* he who does *and* he who does not ' : they both act well. Or, ' *It is equally true* that A. acts well, and that B. will act better.' By a dexterous turn, which perhaps is also humorous, the Apostle gives the preference to the one who does not give his daughter in marriage. The change from ποιεῖ to ποιήσει is also effective : the one 'does well,' the other 'will be *found* to do better,' for experience will confirm his decision. This καλῶς and κρεῖσσον may be said to sum up the results of the whole chapter.

γαμίζων (א A B D E 17) rather than ἐκγαμίζων (K L P). τὴν ἑαυτοῦ παρθένον (א A P) is perhaps preferable to τ. π. ἑαυτοῦ (B D E, Vulg. *virginem suam*) : K L, AV. omit the words. καλῶς ποιεῖ (א A D E K L P, Vulg.) rather than κ. ποιήσει (B) ; and κρεῖσσον ποιήσει (א A B 17, Copt.) rather than κρ. ποιεῖ (D E F G K L P, Vulg.). Copyists thought that both verbs must be in the same tense ; some changed ποιεῖ to ποιήσει, and others ποιήσει to ποιεῖ, as in AV.

39. A few words are added about the remarriage of widows. As their case is covered by *vv.* 8 and 34 we may suppose that the Corinthians had asked about the matter. In Rom. vii. 1–6 ᵔne principle stated here is used again metaphorically to illustrate transition from law to grace : ἐφ' ὅσον χρόνον appears in both passages. Romans was written soon after 1 Corinthians. There we have ἐὰν δὲ ἀποθάνῃ ὁ ἀνήρ : for κοιμηθῇ see on xi. 30.*

μόνον ἐν Κυρίῳ. 'Only as a member of Christ,' which implies that she marries a Christian.† To marry a heathen, especially in Corinth, would make loyalty to Christ very difficult : cf. *v.* 12, ix. 1, 2, xi. 11, xv. 58, xvi. 19. For the ellipse of the verb after μόνον see Lightfoot on Gal. ii. 10 and v. 13.

> Rom. vii. 2 has influenced the text here. ℵ³ D² E F G L P ins. νόμῳ after δέδεται, but ℵ* A B D* 17, Am. Copt. Aeth. Arm. omit. For κοιμηθῇ, A, Orig. Bas. have ἀποθάνῃ.

40. μακαριωτέρα. In the same sense as μακάριον μᾶλλον, Acts xx. 35. She will have more real happiness if she does not marry again. There is no inconsistency between this and 1 Tim. v. 14. The 'younger widows' come under the rule given in *v.* 9.

οὕτως. *In statu quo,* as in 2 Pet. iii. 4, πάντα οὕτως διαμένει. Here the word refers to the condition which she entered when her husband died. This confirms the interpretation of οὕτως in *v.* 26. In both cases the person had better make no change.

κατὰ τὴν ἐμὴν γνώμην. The ἐμήν is emphatic, and implies that there are other opinions.

δοκῶ δὲ κἀγώ. *Non dubietatem significat* (Primasius) any more than νομίζω (*v.* 26). 'And I also think,' not 'I think that I also' (RV.). Other people may believe that their views are inspired, but the Apostle ventures also to believe that he is guided in his judgment by God's Spirit. It seems to be clear from this that some of those who differed from him appealed to their spiritual illumination. See Goudge, p. 68 ; Stanley, pp. 117 f. ; Dobschütz, p. 64.

> On the authority of B 17, Aeth. and some other witnesses, WH. read γάρ in preference to δέ (ℵ A D E F G K L P, Latt. Copt.), placing δέ in the margin. A few texts have no conjunction.
>
> F G and some Latin texts (*habeo* or *habeam*) have ἔχω for ἔχειν.
>
> Alford remarks on ch. vii., "In hardly any portion of the Epistles has the hand of correctors and interpolators of the text been busier than here. The absence of all ascetic tendency from the Apostle's advice, on the point where asceticism was busiest and most mischievous, was too strong a testimony against it to be left in its original clearness."

Saepe apostoli in epistolis de conjugio agunt : unus Paulus, semel, nec sua sponte, sed interrogatus, coelibatum suadet, idque lenissime (Beng.). These words are an excellent summary of the

---

* Hermas seems to have *vv.* 39, 40, and 28 in his mind in *Mand.* IV. iv. 1.

† Harnack disputes this (*Mission and Expansion,* i. p. 81). Tertullian (*Ad Uxorem,* ii. 1, 2) implies that marriages between Christians and heathen did take place. See Cyprian (*Test.* iii. 62) ; *matrimonium cum gentilibus non jungendum.*

teaching in this chapter as to the comparative value of marriage and celibacy : the preference given to celibacy is tentative and exceptional, to meet exceptional conditions. " No condemnation of marriage, no exclusion of the married from the highest blessings of the Christian life, finds a place in the N.T." (Swete on Rev. xiv. 4, which he says " must be taken metaphorically, as the symbolical character of the Book suggests.") See also Goudge, pp. 63–65.

VIII. 1–XI. 1. FOOD OFFERED TO IDOLS.
VIII. 1–3. General Principles.

An idol represents nothing which really exists. Consequently, eating what is offered to such a nonentity is a matter of indifference : yet, in tenderness to the scruples of the weak, we ought to abstain from eating.

[1] Now, as to the subject of food that has been offered in sacrifice to idols, we are quite aware (as you say) that we all have knowledge ; we all are acquainted with the facts and understand them. But do not let us forget that knowledge may breed conceit, while it is love that builds up character. [2] If any one imagines that he has acquired knowledge, he may be sure that he has not yet attained to the knowledge to which he ought to have attained. [3] But if any one has acquired love of God, this is the man who is known by God, and God's recognition of him will not breed conceit. [4] Let us return then from these thoughts to the subject of eating the flesh of animals that have been sacrificed to idols. About that we are quite aware that there is no such thing in the world as the being that an idol stands for, and that there is no God but one. [5] For even if so-called gods do really exist,—if you like, in heaven, or, if you like, on earth ; and, in fact, there are many such gods and many such lords,— [6] nevertheless, for us there is but one God, who is the Source of all things and our Final End, and but one Lord, Jesus Christ, through whom the whole universe was made and through whom we were made anew. [7] Still, as I have intimated, we do not find in all men the knowledge to which you appeal. On the contrary, some of you, through being accustomed all their lives to look upon an idol as real, partake of sacrificed meat as if it were a real sacrifice to a god, and their conscience, being too weak to

guide them aright, is defiled with the consciousness of having
done something which they feel to be wrong. ⁸ But surely it is
not food that will affect our relation to God : if we do not eat,
we are none the worse in His sight, and if we do eat, we are
none the better. ⁹ Always take care, however, that this freedom
of yours to do as you like about eating or not eating does not
become an obstacle to the well-being of the weak. ¹⁰ For if any
such person sees you, who have the necessary knowledge, not
only eating this meat, but sitting and eating it in the court of the
idol, will not the very fact of his weakness cause his conscience
to be hardened—hardened into letting him eat what he still
believes to be a sacrifice to an idol? ¹¹ This must be wrong;
for it means bringing ruin to the weak man through your knowledge—ruin to the brother for whom Christ died. ¹² But in thus
sinning against your brethren, and in fact giving their conscience
a blow which it is too weak to stand, ye are sinning against
Christ. ¹³ Therefore, if what I eat puts a stumbling-block in my
brother's way, I will never eat meat again, so long as the world
lasts, rather than put a stumbling-block in my brother's way.

1. Περὶ δὲ τῶν εἰδωλοθύτων. St Paul is probably following the
order of the Corinthians' questions, but the connexion between
this subject and the advisability of marriage (vii. 2–5, 9, 36) is
close. Impurity and the worship of idols were closely allied
(Rev. ii. 14, 20), especially at Corinth, and either evil might lead
to the other (see Gray on Num. xxv. 1, 2). By τὰ εἰδωλόθυτα is
meant the flesh that was left over from heathen sacrifices. This
was either eaten sacrificially, or taken home for private meals,
or sold in the markets (4 Macc. v. 2 ; Acts xv. 29, xxi. 25 ; Rev.
ii. 14, 20). In x. 28 we have ἱερόθυτον, which, like θεόθυτον, gives
the heathen point of view.*

οἴδαμεν. See Rom. ii. 2, iii. 19, and Evans on 1 Cor. viii. 1,
additional note, p. 299. The expression is frequent in Paul.

πάντες γνῶσιν ἔχομεν. Perhaps a quotation, made with gentle
irony, from the Corinthians' letter. See Moffatt, *Lit. of N.T.*,
p. 112. They had claimed enlightenment—so dear to Greeks—
on this subject of the true nature of idol-worship. They knew
now that there were no gods ; the worship of them was a nullity.
The Apostle does not dispute that, but enlightenment is not
everything : and in the gift which is better than enlightenment
the Corinthians are lacking. Some commentators take πάντες
to mean all Christians, which has point. It can hardly mean

---

* In Aristoph. *Aves* 1265, mortals are forbidden to send ἱερόθυτον καπνὸν
to the gods through the air which belongs to the birds.

the Apostle and all who are similarly illuminated : he is urging that knowledge is not the prerogative of a privileged few.

ἡ γνῶσις φυσιοῖ. Enlightenment is not merely insufficient for solving these questions ; unless it is accompanied by love, it is likely to generate pride. While love builds up, mere knowledge puffs up. Thus in Col. ii. 18 (the only place outside 1 Cor. in which the verb occurs) we have, εἰκῇ φυσιούμενος ὑπὸ τοῦ νοός τῆς σαρκός. The Apostle once more glances at the inflated self-complacency which was so common at Corinth (iv. 6, 18, 19, v. 2). 'Puffed up' is just what ἀγάπη is not (xiii. 4). Cf. τυφόομαι, 1 Tim. iii. 6, vi. 4 ; 2 Tim. iii. 4. *Est genus scientiae, quo homines tumescunt ; quae quia charitate non est condita, ideo inflat. Ille qui putat se scire, propterea quia intelligit omnia licita, et non inquinare quod in nos intrat* (Matt. xv. 11, 20), *dum ad scandalum fratris licita sumit, nondum cognovit quemadmodum oporteat eum scire* (Atto). Loving consideration for the weakness of others buttresses them, and strengthens the whole edifice of the Church (Rom. xiv. 15). Ramsay, *Pictures of the Apostolic Church*, p. 257.

ἡ δὲ ἀγάπη οἰκοδομεῖ. For the first time in this letter St Paul uses this verb : but οἰκοδομή occurs iii. 9 and ἐποικοδομεῖν iii. 10. The earliest use of it in his writings is 1 Thess. v. 11, where he charges the Thessalonians to 'build up each the other,' and it becomes one of his favourite metaphors, especially in this Epistle (v. 10, x. 23, xiv. 4, 17), with οἰκοδομή still more frequent. It is possible that our Lord's use of the metaphor of building up His Church (Matt. xvi. 18) may have suggested it to the Apostle ; but it is a natural metaphor for any one to use. We find it in Acts ix. 31, xx. 32 ; 1 Pet. ii. 5 ; Jude 20 ; cf. Acts iv. 11. It is used of building up individuals, building up a society, and building up individuals to form a society (Hort on 1 Pet. ii. 5).* The metaphor is elaborately worked out Eph. ii. 20, 21 ; cf. 1 Cor. iii. 10–14. Jeremiah was set apart from his birth ἀνοικοδομεῖν καὶ καταφυτεύειν (Jer. i. 10 ; cf. xviii. 9, xxiv. 6 ; Ecclus. xlix. 7). In the hymn in praise of ἀγάπη (xiii.) this characteristic is not mentioned. Cf. Aristotle (*Eth. Nic.* I. iii. 6), τὸ τέλος ἐστὶν οὐ γνῶσις ἀλλὰ πρᾶξις : (II. ii. 1) ἡ παροῦσα πραγματεία οὐ θεωρίας ἕνεκά ἐστιν . . . ἀλλ᾽ ἵν᾽ ἀγαθοὶ γενώμεθα : also x. ix. 1. See Butler's "Thirdly" in the Sermon on the Ignorance of Man. On ἀγάπη see Deissmann, *Bible Studies*, pp. 198 f. ; *Light*, p. 18.

---

* In Spencer and other contemporary and earlier writers, 'edify' and 'edification' are used in their original sense of constructing buildings. See Kitchin on *Faery Queene*, I. i. 34, and Wright, *Bible Word-Book*, p. 219. It is found as late as 1670, "the re-edifying Layton Church " (Izaac Walton. *Life of G. Herbert*, sub fin.).

The punctuation of Griesbach, Bengel, etc., οἴδαμεν· ὅτι, 'Now about things offered we know ; because we all have knowledge,' is intolerably harsh. It would be almost impossible in *v.* 4, and οἴδαμεν ὅτι in the two places are evidently parallel. Lachmann conjectured that the original reading was οἴδαμεν ὅτι οὐ πάντες κ.τ.λ. See Alford.

St Bernard (*In Cantica*, xxxvi. 3) quotes Persius (i. 27), *Scire tuum nihil est, nisi te scire hoc sciat alter*, in commenting on this passage, and remarks : *Sunt qui scire volunt, ut sciantur ipsi ; et turpis vanitas est. Et sunt qui scire volunt, ut scientiam suam vendant ; et turpis quaestus est. Sed sunt quoque qui scire volunt ut aedificent ; et charitas est.*

2. εἴ τις δοκεῖ. 'If any one fancies (*existimat*, Vulg.; *sibi videtur*, Beza) that he knows anything.' The Corinthians fancied that they knew ; ἐγνωκέναι (perf.) that they had acquired knowledge, and that the knowledge was complete. If they had had more real knowledge they would have been less confident. It is the man of superficial knowledge that is ready to solve all questions ; and this readiness is evidence of want of real knowledge, for it shows that he does not know how ignorant he is. Cf. iii. 18, xi. 16 ; 1 Tim. i. 7. In οὔπω there is no reference to a future life.

3. εἰ δέ τις ἀγαπᾷ. This is the sure test, love ; and love of the highest of all objects, which is the highest form of love,— the love of Love Itself. This is a very different thing from thinking that one knows something.

οὗτος ἔγνωσται ὑπ' αὐτοῦ. The sentence is ambiguous in grammar, for either pronoun may refer to the man, and either to God ; but there is no reasonable doubt that οὗτος is the man, who is recognized and acknowledged by God as His. In a special sense, 'The Lord knoweth them that are His' (2 Tim. ii. 19 ; Ps. i. 6 ; Nahum i. 7 ; Jer. i. 5 ; Isa. xlix. 1). To Moses He said, 'I know thee by name,' Οἶδά σε παρὰ πάντας (Exod. xxxiii. 12, 17). It is in this sense that the man who loves God is known by God. We might have expected the Apostle to say, either, 'He who knows God is known by Him' (Gal. iv. 9), or 'He who loves God is loved by Him' (1 John iv. 19): but the combination of the two verbs is more telling, and more to his purpose. One who in this special sense is known by God may safely be assumed to possess what may rightly be called γνῶσις and not something which merely generates pride. He has the highest recognition of all in being known by God, and is not eager to show off in order to gain the recognition of men. *Ille veram habet scientiam qui Deum diligit ; et qui diligit Deum, fratris, ut suam, diligit salvationem* (Atto). Consequently, the man who loves God is the one who can rightly solve the question about food offered to idols. What effect will his partaking of it have on his fellow-Christian's progress in holiness ?

4. Περὶ τῆς βρώσεως οὖν. After these preliminary considerations (*vv.* 1–3), which indicate the direction in which a solution of the question is likely to be found, he returns with a resumptive οὖν (Gal. iii. 5) to the question mentioned in *v.* 1, and states it more definitely. We now learn that it was respecting the lawfulness of *eating* what had been offered to idols that the Corinthians wanted to have his decision. It was a question of very frequent occurrence. In private sacrifices certain portions of the animal were the perquisite of the priests, but nearly all the rest might be taken away by the offerer, to be eaten at home or sold. In public sacrifices made by the state the skins and carcases, which at Athens sometimes amounted to hundreds, were an important source of revenue and patronage, the skins being sold for the state (τὸ δερματικόν), and the flesh being distributed to magistrates and others, who would sell what they did not need for home consumption. Smith, *Dict. of Grk. and Rom. Ant.* II. p. 585. In the markets and in private houses εἰδωλόθυτα were constantly to be found.

οἴδαμεν. Here again he seems to be quoting from the Corinthian letter; 'What you say about the nullity of idols is quite true, but it does not settle the matter.' Cf. 1 Tim. i. 8.

ὅτι οὐδὲν εἴδωλον . . . ὅτι οὐδεὶς Θεός. These two clauses are parallel, and they should be translated in a similar way; and, as οὐδείς cannot be the predicate, οὐδέν is not the predicate, although most versions take it so (*quia nihil est idolum in mundo*, Vulg.; *dass ein Götze nichts in der Welt sei*, Luth.). Either, 'that there is no idol in the world, and that there is no God but one,' or 'that nothing in the world is an idol, and that no being is God except one,' is probably right, and the former is far better: cf. Mark x. 18; Luke xviii. 19. An idol professes to be an image of a god, not of the only God, and such a thing does not, and cannot, exist, for you cannot represent what has no existence. If there is no Zeus, an εἴδωλον of Zeus is an impossibility. It represents 'a no-god' (see Driver on Deut. xxxii. 17, 21), and the maker of it ἔπλασεν αὐτὸ χώνευμα, φαντασίαν ψευδῆ (Hab. ii. 18). This is what is meant by 'they ate the sacrifices of the dead' (Ps. cvi. 28; cf. cxv. 4–8, cxxxv. 15–18), deaf and dumb idols (xii. 2) in contrast to the living God. They are called νεκροί, Wisd. xiii. 10, xv. 17. Jews regarded them as 'nothing' (*aven*), mere 'lies' (*elilim*).

With ἐν κόσμῳ here compare Rom. v. 13. In the ordered universe there can be only one God, viz., the God who made it.

D³ E 17, Vulg. read περὶ δὲ τῆς βρώσεως without οὖν. D* has περὶ δὲ τῆς γνώσεως, and P 121, περὶ τῆς γνώσεως οὖν. After οὐδεὶς Θεός, א³ K L, Syrr. add ἕτερος, as in AV. None of these readings is likely to be right.

5. καὶ γὰρ εἴπερ κ.τ.λ.   'For even granted that there are so-called gods, whether in heaven or upon earth, just as there are gods many and lords many.'   Here εἴπερ εἰσίν and ὥσπερ εἰσίν are correlative, and εἰσίν must be taken in the same sense in both clauses.   If both refer to what really exists, the meaning will be, 'If you like to say that, because there are super-natural beings in abundance, as we all believe, therefore the so-called gods of the heathen really exist, nevertheless for us Christians there is only one God.'*   If both refer to heathen superstition, the meaning will be, 'Granted that there are so-called gods, as there are—plenty of them ; still for us,' etc.   He seems to mean that *to the worshippers* the idol *is* an object of adoration; so that, while actually they worship a nonentity, ethically they are worshippers of δαιμόνια (x. 20).   Jehovah is God of gods and Lord of lords (Deut. x. 17 ; Ps. cxxxvi. 2, 3), and therefore the second εἰσίν probably refers to actual existence. Moreover, St Paul, while denying that the heathen gods existed (see Lightfoot on Gal. iv. 8), yet held that heathen sacrifices were offered to beings that do exist (x. 19–21); there were supernatural powers behind the idols, although not the gods which the idols represented.   It is perhaps too much to say that εἴπερ, which in N.T. is peculiar to St Paul (2 Thess. i. 6 ; Rom. iii. 30, viii. 9, 17), is used of what the writer holds to be true or probable, yet it certainly does not imply that the hypothesis is improbable: 'granted that' is the meaning.   See Sanday and Headlam, p. 96 ; Thackeray, p. 144.   'Whether in heaven or on earth' gives the two main divisions of the κόσμος in *v.* 4.   *Dicuntur dii in caelo, ut sol, luna et varia sidera ; in terra, imago Jovis, Mercurii atque Herculis* (Atto).   More probably the latter are the heavenly, while the earthly are the nymphs, fauns, etc.   See Stanley's notes on this verse.

6. ἀλλ' ἡμῖν εἷς Θεὸς ὁ πατήρ.   'Nevertheless (whatever may be the truth about these), for us believers (emphatically) there is one God, the Father, from whom come all things, while we tend towards Him, and one Lord Jesus Christ, through whom are all things, we also through Him.†   There are two parallel triplets, θεοὶ πολλοί, εἷς Θεός, τὰ πάντα : κύριοι πολλοί, εἷς Κύριος, τὰ πάντα.   The one God is compared on the one side with many gods, on the other with the sum total of the universe: so also the one Lord.   The comparison results in opposition in the one case, in harmony in the other.   The πολλοί are intolerable rivals

---

* *Quocunque te flexeris, ibi illum videbis occurrentem tibi ; nihil ab illo vacat, opus suum ipse implet* (Seneca, *De Benef.* iv. 8 ; compare M. Aurelius, xii. 28 ; Xen. *Mem.* IV. iii. 13).   There is a close parallel in 1 Tim. ii. 5.

† With εἴπερ . . . ἀλλά here compare ἐάν . . . ἀλλά in iv. 15.   The context implies '*only* one God.'   See Deissmann, *New Light on the N.T.* p. 81.

to the εἰς Θεός and εἰς Κύριος : τὰ πάντα are welcome creatures. The ἡμεῖς, like the previous ἡμῖν, means 'we Christians.' *Bruta animalia et infideles homines in terram curvantur et terrena quaerunt;* * *nos vero per fidem et desiderium tendimus in eum a quo descendimus* (Herv.). God is the central Fount and the central Goal: all beings proceed from the former; only believers consciously work towards the latter. See Resch, *Agrapha*, p. 129.

In the case of Jesus Christ we have the same preposition (διά *c. gen.*) with both τὰ πάντα and ἡμεῖς.† But δι' οὗ does not refer to the same fact as δι' αὐτοῦ. The former points to the Son's work in creation, the latter to His work in the new creation of mankind. 'If any man is in Christ there is a new creation' (2 Cor. v. 17; see Lightfoot on Gal. vi. 15). "This verse contains the earliest statement in the N.T. as to the work of our Lord in creation. This is stated more fully in Col. i. 16–18. There, as here, the work of our Lord in creation and His work for the Church are spoken of together" (Goudge). *Per quem creati sumus ut essemus, per ipsum recreati sumus ut unum Deum intelligeremus, atque idolum nihil esse recognosceremus* (Atto). The statement is clear evidence of the Apostle's belief in the pre-existence of Christ; see on x. 4, where we have similar evidence. Schmiedel remarks that Paul nowhere else ascribes to Christ a share in the work of creation; but, as he frequently teaches the pre-existence, it is not going much further to ascribe to Him this work. Wace & Schaff, *Nicene Library*, IV. *Athanasius*, p. lxxi. n.; Sanday, *Life of Christ in Recent Research*, p. 131; J. Kaftan, *Jesus u. Paulus*, p. 64; Weinel, *St Paul*, p. 45.

B, Fay. omit ἀλλ' before ἡμῖν. אﬦ* omits Θεός. B, Aeth. have δι' ὅν for δι' οὗ.

7. Ἀλλ' οὐκ ἐν πᾶσιν ἡ γνῶσις. 'But not in all people is there the knowledge' which is necessary for eating idol-meats without harm. They do not know the principle on which the more enlightened do this. *Non omnes sciunt quod propter contemptum hoc faciatis, sed putant vos propter venerationem hoc facere* (Primasius); and they know that any veneration of an idol must be wrong. There is perhaps a difference intended

---

* But the unbelieving heathen must not be wholly excluded from the εἰς αὐτόν. While the Jew was being drawn by a special revelation through the Prophets towards God, the Gentile was groping his way in a general revelation through the order of Nature towards Him, till the course of both was completed by the revelation in Christ (Gwatkin, *Early Church History*, p. 15).

† The AV. is very inaccurate, translating εἰς 'in' instead of 'unto,' and διά 'by' instead of 'through.' B. W. Bacon regards *vv.* 6 and 8 as quotations from the Corinthians' letter.

between having knowledge (v. 1) and its being *in* them as an
effective and illuminating principle.

τινὲς δὲ τῇ συνηθείᾳ ἕως ἄρτι τοῦ εἰδώλου. To take ἕως ἄρτι
with ἐσθίουσιν, 'continue the practice of eating such food even
until now,' simplifies the translation, but it is not correct : τῇ σ.
ἕως ἄρτι τ. εἰδ. is all one expression, in which ἕως ἄρτι (iv. 13,
xv. 6) qualifies τῇ σ. It is the force of habit which lasts even
until now. They have been so accustomed to regard an idol
as a reality, as representing a god that exists, that even now,
in spite of their conversion, they cannot get rid of the feeling
that, by eating food which has been offered to an idol, they
are taking part in the worship of heathen gods ; they cannot
eat ἐκ πίστεως (Rom. xiv. 23). Consequently, when the example
of other Christians encourages them to eat meat of this kind,
they do what they feel to be wrong. 'But some, through the
force of habit which still clings to them respecting the idol, eat
the meat as being an idol sacrifice.' Missionaries at the present
day have similar experiences. A belief in witchcraft long continues to lurk in otherwise well-instructed Christians, and
(against their reason and their conscience) they allow themselves to be influenced by it. Note the emphasis on τῇ συνηθείᾳ
ἕως ἄρτι, and compare the datives in Gal. vi. 12 and Rom. xi. 31.

καὶ ἡ συνείδησις αὐτῶν ἀσθενὴς οὖσα μολύνεται. 'And so their
conscience, being weak, is defiled.' It is defiled, not by the
partaking of polluted food, for food cannot pollute (Mark vii.
18, 19; Luke xi. 41), but by the doing of something which the
unenlightened conscience does not allow. Cf. 2 Cor. vii. 1. An
uninstructed conscience may condemn what is not wrong, or allow
what is ; but even in such cases it ought to be obeyed. See notes
on Rom. xiv. 23. It is not quite clear what is meant by ἀσθενής.
It may mean 'too weak to resist the temptation of following
the example of others,' or 'weak through being unilluminated.'*
In either case it is defiled by a consciousness of guilt. The
man feels that he is doing what is wrong; and, until he knows
the real merits of the case, he is doing what is wrong. For
συνηθεία see xi. 16; John xviii. 39; 4 Mac. ii. 12 (ὁ γὰρ νόμος
καὶ τῆς φίλων συνηθείας δεσπόζει, διὰ πονηρίας αὐτοὺς ἐξελέγχων),
vi 13, xiii. 22, 27; and for συνείδησις see notes on Rom. ii. 15
and Westcott on Heb. ix. 9, p. 293: συνείδησις is rare in LXX,
frequent in the Pauline Epistles and Hebrews. See Hastings,

---

* Perhaps xi. 30 indicates that ἀσθενής here means 'unhealthy,' 'morbid,'
˙nd so 'incapable of healthy action': cf. Luke x. 9; Acts v. 15. Words
signifying weakness of body easily become used of mental and moral weakness. A healthy conscience would not be uneasy about eating such food,
and eating would then cause no defilement. In Ecclus. xxi. 28 the slanderer
μολύνει τὴν ἑαυτοῦ ψυχήν : in blackening his neighbour's character he violates
and blackens his own conscience.

DB. 1. pp. 468 f. The 'weakness' consists in giving moral value to things that are morally indifferent. That must lessen the power of conscience.

συνηθείᾳ (אּ* A B P 17, Copt. Aeth.) is to be preferred to συνειδήσει (אּ³ D E F G L, Vulg. Arm.), and ἕως ἄρτι should precede τοῦ εἰδώλου (אּ B D E F G, Latt.), not follow it (A L P). 'With conscience of the idol' (AV.) is hardly intelligible, and 'with consciousness of the idol' is not much better. If συνειδήσει be adopted, we must expand the meaning; 'with the scruple of conscience which they feel about the idol' (Evans).

8. βρῶμα δὲ ἡμᾶς οὐ παραστήσει τῷ Θεῷ. 'Commend' (AV., RV.) is perhaps a trifle too definite for παρίστημι: 'present' is accurate, meaning 'present for approbation or condemnation.' In this passage the Apostle probably had approbation chiefly in his mind, but in what follows both alternatives are given. Food will not bring us into any relation, good or bad, with God: it will have no effect on the estimate which He will form respecting us, or on the judgment which He will pronounce upon us. It is not one of the things which we shall have to answer for (Rom. xiv. 17). It is the clean heart, and not clean food, that will matter; and the weak brother confounds the two. The question of tense (see small print below) is important. The future can hardly refer to anything but the Day of Judgment. For the verb cf. Rom. vi. 13, xiv. 10; 2 Cor. iv. 14. The translation 'commend' obscures the reference to a judgment to come: 'will not affect our standing before God' is right.

οὔτε ἐὰν μὴ φάγωμεν, ὑστερούμεθα. 'If we abstain from eating we are not prejudiced (in God's sight), and if we eat we have no advantage.' We lose nothing by refraining from using our liberty in this matter, and we gain nothing by exercising it. Others explain ὑστερούμεθα of being inferior to the man who does not abstain, and περεσσεύομεν of being superior to the man who does abstain. This explanation is somewhat superficial and loses all connexion with the preceding sentence. Almost certainly τῷ Θεῷ is to be understood in both clauses. See Alexander, *The Ethics of St Paul,* p. 239.

For ἡμᾶς the evidence is overwhelming, but אּ* 17, 37 read ὑμᾶς. The two words are often confused in MSS. παραστήσει (אּ A B 17, Copt.) is to be preferred to παρίστησι (אּ³ D E L P, Latt.). The γάρ after the first οὔτε (D E F G L P, Vulg-Clem.) should be omitted (אּ A B 17, Am. Copt. Arm. Aeth.). And probably οὔτε ἐὰν μὴ φ., ὑστ. should precede οὔτε ἐὰν φ., περ. (A* B, Am. Copt. Arm.) rather than *vice versa* (אּ D F L P, Syrr.). The interchange of the verbs, ἐὰν μὴ φ., περ., οὔτε ἐὰν φ., ὑστ. (A² 17), is not likely to be right, although adopted by Lachm. The interchange of the clauses was a natural correction, in order to put the positive before the negative hypothesis. The Apostle puts the negative first, because that is the course which he recommends; 'If we do not eat, although we may, we are in no worse position before God.' The form περισσεύομεθα (B, Orig.), adopted by the Revisers, is probably a mechanical assimilation to ὑστερούμεθα.

9. βλέπετε δὲ μή πως ἡ ἐξουσία ὑμῶν. 'Take heed, however, lest this liberty of yours prove a stumbling-block to the weak.' It is lawful for those whose consciences are enlightened to do as they like about it (ἐξουσίαν as in vii. 37, ix. 4, and as ἔξεστιν in vi. 12); their eating will not do *them* any harm. But it may do harm to *others*, and thus may bring the eaters into a worse position before God. See notes on Rom. xiv. 13, 20 : excepting the quotation in 1 Pet. ii. 8, πρόσκομμα in N.T. is confined to this passage and Romans; in LXX it is not rare. It is that against which the man with weak sight stumbles; it is no obstacle to the man who sees his way; but the weak-sighted must be considered.*

ἀσθενέσιν (א A B D E F, etc.), as in *v.* 7 ; ἀσθενοῦσιν (L, Chrys. Thdrt.) perhaps from *v.* 11. P has ἡμῶν.

10. ἐν εἰδωλίῳ κατακείμενον. In order to show how the *offendiculum* (Vulg.) arises, he takes an extreme case. A Corinthian, in a spirit of bravado, to show his superior enlightenment and the wide scope of his Christian freedom, not only partakes of idol-meats, but does so at a sacrificial banquet within the precincts of the idol-temple. This was *per se* idolatrous; but St Paul holds the more severe condemnation in reserve : see on x. 14 f.† The τὸν ἔχοντα γνῶσιν may mean either that this is the man's own belief about himself, or that it is the weak brother's opinion of him. Εἰδώλιον, *vocabulum aptum ad deterrendum* (Beng.), is not classical : in LXX it occurs 1 Esdr. ii. 10 ; Bel 11 ; 1 Mac. i. 47 (*v.l.* εἴδωλα), x. 83 ; and in 1 Sam. xxxi. 10 we have the analogous Ἀσταρτεῖον, like Ἀπολλωνεῖον, Ποσειδωνεῖον, etc.‡ Such words are frequent in papyri.

ἀσθενοῦς ὄντος. 'Seeing that he is weak.' It is just because he is feeble in insight and character that this following of a questionable example 'builds up' his conscience in a disastrous

---

* "The stronger one can, for the sake of the weaker, refrain from using this liberty ; but the weaker cannot, on account of his conscience, follow the example of the stronger " (B. Weiss).

† Grenfell and Hunt (*Oxyrhynchus Papyri*, I. p. 177) give an invitation to sup at the κλίνη of the Lord Serapis in the Serapeium. There is another invitation to a meal in honour of Serapis in a private house. See Bachmann, p. 307 ; also Deissmann, *Light*, p. 355.

‡ It is possible that St Paul used the unusual word εἰδώλιον, because he was unwilling to put words with such sacred associations as ἱερόν or ναός to any such use (Edwards). But εἴδωλον (*v.* 4) suggests εἰδώλιον, and no other word would have expressed the meaning so clearly. It is also possible that οἰκοδομηθήσεται (a strange word in this connexion) is a sarcastic quotation of a Corinthian expression. Perhaps they talked of 'edifying' the weak brethren by showing them to what lengths they could go. This was "educating their consciences," but it was a *ruinosa aedificatio* (Calv.). The best MSS. have εἰδωλίῳ, not εἰδωλείῳ: compare δάνιον, Matt. xviii. 27. In Luke x. 34, πανδόχιον is well attested.

way. His conscience is not sufficiently instructed to tell him
that he may eat without scruple, and yet he eats. Doing
violence to scruples is no true edification: it is rather a pulling
down of bulwarks. Tertullian seems to have had this passage
in his mind when he says of those who are seduced into heresy;
Solent quidem isti infirmiores aedificari in ruinam (*De Praescr.
Haer.* 3). Atto paraphrases; *provocabitur manducare idolothyta,
non tamen ea fide qua tu.* It is *ruinosa aedificatio, quae in sana
doctrina fundata non est* (Calv.).

> The σέ before τὸν ἔχοντα is omitted by B F G, Vulg. Some editors
> bracket it, but it is well attested (אַ A D E L P, Syrr. Copt. Arm).
> ὁδοποιηθήσεται is an insipid conjecture for οἰκοδομηθήσεται, which is
> deliberately chosen with gentle irony, and needs no mending.

11. ἀπόλλυται γὰρ ὁ ἀσθενῶν ἐν τ. σ. γν. 'For it is destruction that he who is weak finds in thy knowledge.' Ruin, and
not building up, is what he is getting by following the example
of one who is better instructed than himself. There is the
tragedy of it; that the illumination of one Corinthian is precisely the field in which another Corinthian takes the road to
ruin. And the tragedy reaches a climax in the fact that the
one who is led astray is the brother in Christ of him who leads
him astray, and is one whom Christ died to save from ruin.
The last clause could hardly be more forcible in its appeal;
every word tells; 'the brother,' not a mere stranger; 'for the
sake of whom,' precisely to rescue him from destruction;
'Christ,' no less than He; 'died,' no less than that: cf. Rom.
xiv. 15. *Tu eris occasio mortis ejus propter quem Christus, ut
redimeret, mortuus est* (Herv.). See Matt. xviii. 6.

> ἀπολ. γάρ (אַ* B 17, Copt. Goth.) is to be preferred to καὶ ἀπολ.
> (אַ³ D*, d e) or ἀπολ. οὖν (A P 39). And καὶ ἀπολεῖται, though well sup-
> ported (D³ E F G L, Vulg. Syrr. Arm. Aeth.), looks like a correction to
> assimilate the tense with οἰκοδομηθήσεται and carry on the question through
> *v.* 11. The question ends at ἐσθίειν, and what follows is explanation.
> The emphatic position of ἀπόλλυται, and also the tense, have force; it
> is no less than destruction that results, and the destruction is already at
> work.

12. οὕτως δὲ ἁμαρτάνοντες εἰς τοὺς ἀδ. 'But by sinning
against your brothers in such a way as this': οὕτως is emphatic.
This verse confirms the view that εἰς τ. ἰδ. σῶμα ἁμαρτ. (vi. 18)
must mean 'sins *against* his own body.'

καὶ τύπτοντες. 'And by inflicting blows upon their conscience
in its weakness.' The καί makes the ἁμαρτάνοντες more definite,
by showing the kind of injury. The force of the present
participles should be noted: the wounding is a continued process, and so also is the weakliness; not ἀσθενῆ, but ἀσθενοῦσαν.
Nowhere else in N.T. is τύπτω used in a metaphorical sense:

elsewhere only in the Synoptists and Acts. But this sense occurs in LXX (1 Sam. i. 8 ; Prov. xxvi. 22 ; Dan. xi. 20). 'Wounding' and 'weakening' are in emphatic contrast : what requires the tenderest handling is brutally treated, so that its sensibility is numbed. The wounding is not the shock which the weak Christian receives at seeing a fellow-Christian eating idol-meats in an idoi-court, but the inducement to do the like, although he believes it to be wrong. His conscience is lamed by being crushed. This is the third metaphor used respecting the weak conscience ; it is soiled (*v.* 7), made to stumble (*v.* 9), wounded (*v.* 12). The order of the words is a climax ; ' inflicting blows, not on the back, but on the conscience, and on the conscience when it is in a weakly state.'

εἰς Χριστὸν ἁμ.   Like οὕτως and τύπτοντες, εἰς Χρ. is emphatic by position : ' it is against Christ that ye are sinning.'   St Paul may have known the parable of the Sheep and the Goats (Matt. xxv 40, 45), but Christ Himself had taught him that an injury to the brethren was an injury to Himself (Acts ix. 4, 5).

13. διόπερ.   'For this very reason,' *i.e.* to avoid sinning against Christ ; the πέρ strengthens the διό : here and x. 14 only, in N.T.   See 2 Mac. v. 20, vi. 27.

εἰ βρῶμα κ.τ.λ.   ' If food causes my brother to stumble, I will certainly never eat flesh again for evermore, that I may not make my brother to stumble.'   The declaration is conditional.   If the Apostle knows of definite cases in which his eating food will lead to others being encouraged to violate the dictates of conscience, then certainly he will never eat meat so long as there is real danger of this (x. 28, 29).   But if he knows of no such danger, he will use his Christian freedom and eat without scruple (x. 25–27).   He does not, of course, mean that the whole practice of Christians is to be regulated with a view to the possible scrupulousness of the narrow-minded.   That would be to sacrifice our divinely given liberty (2 Cor. iii. 17) to the ignorant prejudices of bigots.   The circumstances of this or that Christian may be such that it is his duty to abstain from intoxicants, although he is never tempted to drink to excess ; but Christians in general are bound by no such rule, and it would be tyranny to try to impose such a rule.

The change from βρῶμα to κρέα is natural enough.   If such a thing as food (which is always a matter of indifference) causes . . . I will never again eat flesh (which is in question here),' etc.   Note how he harps on ἀδελφός.

In dealing with both the question of fornication and that of eating idol-meats, the Apostle brings the solution ultimately from our relation to Christ.   Fornication is taking from Christ what is His property and giving it to a harlot.   Reckless eating of idol-

meats is an injury inflicted on Christ.   In neither case does he
appeal to the decree of the Apostles at the conference in Jerusalem
(Acts xv. 20, 29).   The principles to which he appeals were far
more cogent, especially for Greeks.*   Compare carefully Rom.
xiv. 14, 17, 21.

In his recent (1908) paper on the Apostolic Decree (Acts xv. 20–29),
Dr. Sanday says ; " The decree was only addressed in the first instance to a
limited area : and I can well believe that it soon fell into comparative disuse
even within that area.   It is true that, as we read it in the Acts, the decree
has the appearance of a very authoritative document.   Something of this
appearance may be due to a mistaken estimate on the part of St Luke himself.   But, even so, we are apt to read into it more than it really means.
For the moment the decree had a real significance : it meant a united
Christendom, instead of a disunited.   Many an official document has had
a temporary success of this kind, which the course of events has soon
caused to become a dead letter.   That was really the fate of the decree.
The tide of events ebbed away from it, and it was left on the beach
stranded and lifeless—lifeless at least for the larger half of the Church, for
that Gentile Church which soon began to advance by leaps and bounds."

" As to any further difficulty from St Paul's treatment of meats offered
in sacrifice to idols, I confess that I think little of it.   He could upon
occasion become a Jew to the Jews.   But the decree, we may be sure,
made no impression upon his mind.   It "contributed nothing" to his
Gospel.   It was no outcome of his religious principles.   It was just a
practical concordat, valid in certain specified regions and under certain
definite conditions.   But when he was altogether outside these, among his
own converts, he dealt with them by his own methods, and without any
thought of the authorities at Jerusalem."

The inference, from St Paul's silence, that Acts xv. belongs to a period
later than this Epistle, is quite untenable.

IX. 1-27. THE GREAT PRINCIPLE OF FORBEARANCE.

*I have not asked you to forego more rights than I forego
myself.   For the sake of others I surrender, not only what
any Christian may claim, but what I can claim as an
Apostle.*

¹ Can it be denied that I am a free agent, that I have the
authority and independence of an Apostle ?   I have seen our
Lord face to face and He made me His Apostle, and you who
were won over to Him through me are a standing proof of my
Apostleship.   ² It may be possible for other Christians to
question whether I am an Apostle or not, but you at least
cannot do so, for your very existence as a Christian Church is
the seal which authenticates my Apostleship.   ³ There you have
my answer to those who challenge my claim.

* See Gwatkin, *Early Church History*, i. 57, 63.

⁴ Surely we are free to do as we think best about eating and drinking at the cost of the Churches, ⁵ to do as we think best about taking with us on our journey a Christian sister as a wife, as also the rest of the Apostles do, and the brethren of the Lord, and Peter. ⁶ Or is it only I and Barnabas that are not free to do as we think best about working no longer for a living? ⁷ No soldier on service finds his own outfit and rations. If you plant a vineyard, you expect to partake of the produce, and if you tend cattle, you expect to get a share of the milk.

⁸ I am not saying all this merely from a worldly point of view. ⁹ The Divine Law assumes just the same principle. In the Law of Moses it stands written, Thou shalt not muzzle the ox while it is treading out the grain. Do you think that it was merely out of consideration for the oxen that God caused that to be written? ¹⁰ Surely He was looking beyond them, and it is really for us preachers that He says this. No doubt it was in our interest that this law was enacted; because thus the principle is laid down that the plougher ought not to plough, and the thresher ought not to thresh, without a good prospect of sharing in the profit. ¹¹ Well then, if it is we who in your hearts sowed the seeds of spiritual life, is it a very outrageous thing that we out of your purses shall reap some worldly benefit? ¹² If others get their share of this right of maintenance from you, have not we who taught you first a still better right? Nevertheless, we did not avail ourselves of this right. On the contrary, we put up with every kind of privation, rather than cause the spread of the Glad-tidings of Christ to be in any way hampered. ¹³ Of course you know that those who are engaged in the temple-services are maintained out of the temple-funds; those who serve at the altar share the sacrifices with the altar. ¹⁴ On the same principle the Lord directed that those who proclaim the Glad-tidings should out of this work get enough to live on. ¹⁵ But I have availed myself of none of these pleas.

Now do not think that I write all this in order that the maintenance due to preachers should henceforth be granted in my case. Indeed not; for it would be better for me by far to die than submit to that: no one shall make void my glorying in taking nothing for my work. ¹⁶ It is quite true that I do preach the Glad-tidings; but there is no glorying about that: it is a duty which I must perform,—must, because it will be the worse for me if I do not perform it. [17] If I did this spontaneously, I should have my pay : but seeing that I do it because I must, it is a stewardship which has been entrusted to me. [18] What pay then do I get? Why, the pleasure of being a preacher who gives the Glad-tidings free of charge, so as not to use to the full a preacher's right to maintenance.

[19] So far from claiming my full rights, I submit to great curtailments. For, free and independent though I am from all men, yet I made myself all men's slave, in order that I might win more of them. [20] Thus to the Jews I became as a Jew, that I might win Jews. That means that to those under the Mosaic Law I became like one of themselves (although, of course, I am nothing of the kind), that I might win those under the Law. [21] To the Gentiles who are free from the Law I became like one of them (although, of course, I am not free from God's law ; on the contrary, I am under Christ's law), that I might win those who are free from the Law. [22] To the men of tender scruples I became like one of them, that I might win such people as these. In short, to all kinds of men I have assumed all kinds of characters, in order at all costs to save some. [23] But all this variety I practise for one and the same reason, that I may not keep the Gospel to myself but share its blessings with others.

[24] You know that the competitors in a race all run, but only one gets the prize. [25] You must run like him, so as to secure it. Now, every one that competes in the games is in all directions temperate. They verily aim at winning a perishable crown, but we one that is imperishable. [26] I accordingly so run as being in no doubt about my aim ; I so fight as not wasting blows on the air. [27] Far from it ; I direct heavy blows against my body, and force it to be my slave, lest my preaching to others should end in my own rejection.

It is a mistake to regard this chapter as an independent section in defence of the writer's claim to be an Apostle. It is part of the discussion of the question as to eating food that has been offered to idols, in the midst of which it is inserted. Christians may eat such food, without fear of pollution ; but in doing so they may harm other Christians : therefore, where there is risk of harming others, they should forbear. To show that this forbearance ought not to seem hard, he points out that his habitual forbearance is greater than that which he would

occasionally claim from them. As in vi. 1, he begins with
animated questions. The conjecture that ix. 1–x. 22 is part of
the letter mentioned in v. 9 is not probable.

1. Οὐκ εἰμὶ ἐλεύθερος ; οὐκ εἰμὶ ἀπόστολος ; This is the order of
the questions in the best texts (see below). ' Have I not the
freedom of a Christian ? Have I not the rights of an Apostle ? '
Logically, this is the better order ; but even if it were not, the
evidence for it is too strong to be set aside on such grounds. It
is the thought that he forbears to claim, not only what any
Christian may claim, but also the exceptional claims of an
Apostle, that makes him digress on an explanation of what an
Apostle may claim. In *v.* 19 he glances back at his general
independence. Cf. Gal. ii. 4, 5.

οὐχὶ 'Ι. τ. Κ. ἡμῶν ἑώρακα ; This question and the next
vindicate the claim made in the second question. He is
certainly an Apostle, for he has the essential qualification of
having seen the Risen Lord (Acts i. 22, ii. 32, iii. 15, iv. 33, etc.),
and his preaching has had the power of an Apostle (2 Cor. iii. 1 f.,
xii. 12). The reference is to the Lord's appearance to him on
the way to Damascus,—ὤφθη κἀμοί (xv. 8) ; an appearance
which he regarded as similar in kind to the appearances to the
Eleven on the Easter Day and afterwards. Whether he is also
referring to the experiences mentioned in Acts xviii. 9, xxii. 17,
and 2 Cor. xii. 2–4 is uncertain. It is a mistake to say that we
are not told that he *saw* the Lord who spoke to him on the
way to Damascus. This is expressly stated, Acts ix. 17 (ὀφθείς),
27 (εἶδεν), xxii. 14 (ἰδεῖν).* Note that in this important question
we have the stronger form of the negative, which is specially
frequent in this argumentative Epistle (i. 20, iii. 3, v. 12, vi. 7,
viii. 10, x. 16, 18). In the N.T. Epistles it is almost confined
to this group of the Pauline Epistles.

Nowhere else does St Paul use the expression ' I have seen
Jesus the Lord,' and he seldom uses the name ' Jesus ' without
' Christ ' either before or after. See notes on Rom. i. 1, pp. 3 f.
When he does use the name ' Jesus ' he commonly refers to our
Lord's life on earth, especially in connexion with His Death or
Resurrection (1 Thess. i. 10, iv. 14 ; 2 Cor. iv. 10–14).   In
Rom. iv. 24 we have ' Jesus our Lord,' as here, and in both
cases the reference is to the risen Jesus. The use of ' Jesus '
without ' Christ ' is very rare in the later Epistles : once in
Philippians (ii. 10), once in Ephesians (iv. 21), and not at all
in Colossians or the Pastoral Epistles. See J. A. Robinson,
Ephesians, pp. 23, 107 ; Milligan, *Thessalonians*, p. 135 ; Selbie,

* See Weinel, *St Paul*, pp. 79 f. ; A. T. Robertson, *Epochs in the Life of
St Paul*, pp. 39 f., a valuable chapter.

Aspects of Christ, pp. 71 f., a careful discussion of the question whether it is possible to separate the Christ of St Paul from the Jesus of history. See also the lectures of Dr. Moffatt and Dr. Milligan in *Religion and the Modern World*, Hodder, 1909, pp. 205–253. The Christ who appeared to Saul on the road to Damascus declared Himself to be the historic Jesus whom Saul was persecuting, and he thus not merely saw Jesus our Lord, but received a 'voice from His mouth' (Acts xxii. 14). That rested on his own testimony; but the fact of his conversion and the work that he had done since that day was known to all (iv. 15; 2 Cor. xii. 12).

τὸ ἔργον μου. The founding of the Corinthian Church was a work worthy of an Apostle: *ab effectu jam secundo loco probat suum Apostolatum* (Calv.). Edwards quotes *meum opus es* (Seneca, *Ep.* 34). Lest he should seem to be claiming what he disclaims in iii. 5–7, he adds 'in the Lord': only in that power could such a work have been accomplished (iii. 9, iv. 15).

The order of the first two questions adopted above (ἐλεύθερος before ἀπόστολος) is that of ℵ A B P, Vulg. Copt. Arm. Aeth., Orig. Tert. The other is that of D E F G K L, Goth., which with P, Arm. insert Χριστόν either before or after Ἰησοῦν. ℵ A B, Am. and other versions omit Χριστόν.

2. εἰ ἄλλοις οὐκ εἰμὶ ἀπόστολος. The emphatic ὑμεῖς of the previous clause leads to an *argumentum ad hominem*. The Corinthians are the very last people who could reasonably question his claim to be an Apostle: at any rate to them he must be one.* 'For my certificate of Apostleship are *ye*' (2 Cor. iii. 2). They themselves are a certificate of the fact, a certificate the validity of which lies in the same sphere as the success of his work; it is 'in the Lord.' Authentication is the idea which is specially indicated by the figurative σφραγίς. No-where in N.T. does σφραγίς seem to be used, as often in later writings, with reference to baptism. See notes on Rom. iv. 11, p. 107; Lightfoot, *Epp. of Clem.* ii. p. 226; Hastings, *DB.* Art. 'Seal.' Preachers who were not Apostles might convert many, but the remarkable spiritual gifts which Corinthians possessed were a guarantee that one who was more than a mere preacher had been sent to them. *Paulus a fructu colligit se divinitus missum esse* (Calv.). The ἄλλοις may allude to the Galatians.

---

* ἀλλά γε occurs nowhere else in N.T., except Luke xxiv. 21, where see footnote, p. 553. He could not prove to any one that he had seen the Lord; but Corinthians at any rate had no need of such evidence to convince them that he was an Apostle. He seems to be glancing at the rival teachers who questioned his claim to the title. See Dobschütz, *Probleme des Ap. Zeitalters*, p. 105; Fletcher, *The Conversion of St Paul*, pp. 63 f. ; Ramsay, *Pictures of the Apostolic Age*, pp. 102 f.

μου τῆς ἀποστολῆς with ℵ B P 17, Orig., rather than τῆς ἐμῆς ἀπ. with D E F G K L.   A few inferior witnesses have ἐπιστολῆς.

3. ἡ ἐμὴ ἀπολογία . . . ἐστιν αὕτη.   WH. follow Chrysostom and Ambrose in making this verse refer to what follows; so also AV. and the Revisers.   RV. leaves it doubtful.   But it is more probable that it refers to what precedes.   'That I have seen the Risen Lord, and that you are such a Church as you are,—there you have my defence when people ask me for the evidence of my Apostleship.'   What follows tells us that he refrained from making his converts maintain him, and no one disputed his right to do that: but the Judaizers did dispute his right to be accounted an Apostle.   The ἐμή and ἐμέ look back to σφραγίς μου τῆς ἀποστολῆς.   'My reply to those who examine me is this': ἐμέ, not με.   Moreover vv. 4–11 are not so much a *defence* as a statement of *claims*.   Defence begins in the middle of v. 12; but a superfluous defence.   People blamed him for maintaining his independence, but they could not deny his right to do it.   See Alford, Findlay, Edwards, and B. Weiss: for the other view see Bachmann.

Both ἀπολογία and ἀνακρίνουσιν are forensic expressions, perhaps purposely chosen to indicate the high hand which the Judaizers assumed in challenging St Paul's claim.   But in its strictly forensic sense, of a judicial investigation, ἀνακρίνω is peculiar to Luke in N.T.   See on Luke xxiii. 14, and cf. Acts iv. 9, xii. 19, etc.   It does not much matter whether we take αὕτη as predicate (so better), or subject: in either case it means 'just what I have stated.'   Cf. τοῦτο in vii. 6 and xi. 17, and αὕτη in John i. 19, xvii. 3.   For the dative cf. Acts xix. 33; 2 Cor. xii. 19.

4. Μὴ οὐκ ἔχομεν ἐξουσιαν;   The μή is the interrogative *num*; the οὐκ belongs to the verb.   'Do you mean to say that we have no right?'   *Numquid non habemus potestatem* (Vulg.): cf. xi. 22; Rom. x. 19.   Here, as often in the Pauline Epistles, we are in doubt whether the plur. includes others with the Apostle: he may mean himself and Barnabas.   Where he means himself exclusively he commonly uses the singular: but it is more certain that the singular is always personal than that the plural commonly includes some one else.   See Lightfoot on 1 Thess. ii. 4.

φαγεῖν καὶ πεῖν.   'To eat and drink what those to whom we preach provide for us.'   He is not now thinking of eating idol-meats: that subject is for the moment quite in abeyance.   Still less is he contending that preachers are not bound to be ascetics.   He says that although he personally refuses entertainment at the cost of those to whom he ministers, yet he has a right to it.   He can do as he likes (ἔξεστί μοι) about it; he has the privilege of being maintained.   See *Clem. Hom.* iii. 71; Luke x. 7.

πεῖν (or πῖν) as 2nd aor. inf. of πίνω is well supported here and x. 7 (אֲ B* D* F G) against πιεῖν (A B³ D³ E K L P), and appears everywhere as a variant, except Matt. xx. 22. It is frequent in MSS. of LXX. See WH. II. *Notes*, p. 170.

5. ἀδελφὴν γυναῖκα περιάγειν. 'Do you mean to say that we have no right to take about (with us on our missionary journeys) a Christian person as a wife?' 'A sister (= Christian woman) as wife' is right. Even if γυναῖκα in this construction could mean 'woman,' it would be superfluous. The Vulgate encourages the mistranslation 'woman' with *mulierem sororem*. The Apostle is not contending that a missionary had a right to take about with him a woman who was not his wife. The fact that a group of women ministered to Christ could not be supposed to justify such indiscretion. But there is an early tradition that very few of the Apostles were married, and hence the temptation to make γυναῖκα mean 'woman' rather than 'wife.' Tertullian (*Exhort. Cast.* 8) translates rightly, *licebat et apostolis nubere et* uxores *circumducere*, and again (*Monogam.* 8), *potestatem* uxores *circumducendi*; but in the latter passage he suggests that only *mulieres*, such as ministered to the Lord, may be meant. This misinterpretation is followed by Augustine, Jerome, Ambrose, and others. It led to a great abuse, not confined to the clergy, in the early ages of the Church. Some Christians contracted a sort of spiritual union with unmarried persons, and the two lived together, without marriage, for mutual spiritual benefit. The women in such cases were known as ἀδελφαί, ἀγαπηταί, and συνείσακτοι. Under the last name they are strictly forbidden, in the case of any cleric, by the third Canon of the first Council of Nicaea (Hefele, *Councils*, p. 379; Suicer, *Thesaurus*, under all three words and under γυνή).

St Paul is not here claiming that Apostles had a right to marry; no one in that age would be likely to dispute that. He is claiming that they have a right to maintenance at the cost of the Church, and that, if they are married, the wife who travels with them shares this privilege. The whole of this passage (5–18) is concerned with the privilege (of which he refused to make use in his own case) of being maintained at the charges of the congregations. But here, as in Gal. i. 19 and elsewhere, we are left in doubt as to the exact meaning of ἀπόστολοι: see on xv. 5, 7.

The Sophists blamed Socrates and Plato for teaching gratuit-ously, thus confessing that their teaching was worth nothing (Xen. *Mem.* i. 6; Plat. *Gorg.* 520, *Apol.* 20; Arist. *Eth. Nic.* IX. i. 5). This kind of charge may have been made by the Judaizers at Corinth. Other Apostles accepted maintenance Why did Paul refuse it? Because he knew that he was no true

Apostle ; or, because he set up for being better than the Twelve ; or, because he was too proud to accept hospitality.*

For περιάγειν transitive see 2 Mac. vi. 10.

ὡς καὶ οἱ λοιποὶ ἀπόστολοι. It is probably on this that the interpolator of the Ignatian Epistles (*Philad.* 4) bases his statement that Peter and Paul and οἱ ἄλλοι ἀπόστολοι were married ; where the words *et Paulus* are omitted in some Latin texts. See on vii. 8. The only Apostles of whose marriage we have direct evidence on good authority are Peter and Philip (Papias in Eus. *H.E.* iii. 39): see Lightfoot, *Colossians*, p. 45. This passage would certainly lead us to suppose that most of the Apostles were married men ; it contends that all had the privilege of having themselves and their wives maintained by the Church, and it implies that some used the privilege, and therefore were married. The exact meaning of λοιποί is not clear : it may distinguish those who are included from 'the brethren of the Lord and Kephas,' or from Paul and Barnabas (*v.* 6). In the former case 'the brethren of the Lord' are Apostles, for the Apostolic body is divided into three parts ; 'Kephas,' 'the brethren of the Lord,' and 'the rest of the Apostles.'† But it is possible that, without any strictly logical arrangement, he is mentioning persons in high position in the Church who availed themselves of the privilege of having their wives maintained as well as themselves, when they were engaged in missionary work. See Lightfoot, *Galatians*, p. 95. In dictating, he mentions Peter, by himself, at the end, as a specially telling instance ; but we cannot safely infer from this that Peter had been in Corinth with his wife : i. 12 does not prove it. See Harnack, *Mission and Expansion*, I. p. 323, II. 99.

οἱ ἀδελφοὶ τοῦ Κυρίου. Here only does St Paul mention them, though he tells us (Gal. i. 19) that James was one. The question of their exact relation to Christ has produced endless discussion, and the question remains undecided. There is nothing in Scripture which forbids the natural interpretation, that they were the children of Joseph and Mary born after the birth of Christ. To some students of the problem, Matt. i. 25 seems to be decisive for this interpretation : see Plummer, *S. Matthew*, pp. 9, 10, and the literature there cited. There is wide agreement that Jerome's

---

* There was, of course, another reason. Owing to the influence of St Paul, a good deal of money that had previously supported Judaism now went elsewhere. The Jews said that he was making a fortune out of his new religion. Hence his protests that he never took maintenance.

† Here, as in 2 Cor. xii. 13 and Luke xxiv. 10, AV. ignores the article ; 'other apostles,' 'other churches,' 'other women.'

With ὡς καί compare καθὼς καί, 1 Thess. ii. 14 : it introduces an argument from induction ; *v.* 7 is an argument from analogy ; *v.* 8 is an appeal to authority.

theory, that they were our Lord's first cousins, children of a Mary who was sister to His Mother, cannot be maintained. But see Chapman, *JTS*. April 1906, pp. 412 f. The choice lies between the Helvidian and the Epiphanian theories. The decision does not affect the argument here. In any case they were persons whose close relationship to the Lord gave them distinction in the primitive Church : what they did constituted a precedent. Κηφᾶς, as almost always in Paul (i. 12, iii. 22, xv. 5).

6. ἢ μόνος ἐγὼ καὶ B. The ἤ, as in vi. 2, 9, puts the question from the other point of view ; that it adds "some degree of emotion" is not so clear. 'Or is it only I and Barnabas that have not a right to forbear working with our hands for a living?' The reason for including Barnabas is uncertain, and it seems to be an afterthought; hence the singular μόνος. It implies that Barnabas, like Paul, had refused maintenance ; and it is possible that there had been an agreement between them that on their missionary journey (Acts xiii. 3) they would not cost the Churches anything. It seems also to imply that the practice of Barnabas was well known.

ἐργάζεσθαι. Manual labour, to earn a livelihood, is commonly meant by the word, with (iv. 12 ; 1 Thess. iv. 11) or without (Matt. xxi. 28 ; Luke xiii. 14 ; Acts xviii. 3) ταῖς χερσίν added. Here again Greek sentiment would be against the Apostle's practice. That a teacher who claimed to lead and to rule should work with his hands for a living would be thought most unbecoming : nothing but the direst necessity excused labour in a free citizen (Arist. *Pol.* iii. 5). Contrast 2 Thess. iii. 6–12.

7. Three illustrations add force to the argument, and they are such as are analogous to the Christian minister, who wages war upon evil, plants churches, and is a shepherd to congregations.* It is perhaps accidental that in each case the *status* of the worker is different ; but this strengthens the argument. The soldier works for pay ; the vine-planter is a proprietor ; the shepherd is a slave. But to all alike the principle is applicable that labour may claim some kind of return. Cf. 2 Tim. ii. 6.

ὀψωνίοις. Though applying primarily to the soldier's food, it may cover his pay and his outfit generally. Cf. 2 Cor. xi. 8 ; Rom. vi. 23 ; Luke iii. 14, where see note. The word is late (1 Esdr. iv. 56 ; 1 Mac. iii. 28 ; xiv. 32), and is sometimes extended to mean the supplies of an army. See Lightfoot on Rom. vi. 23 ; Deissmann, *Bible Studies*, p. 266.

τὸν καρπόν . . . ἐκ τοῦ γάλακτος. The change of construction

---

* Origen points out that it is as a disciple of the Good Shepherd, who laid down His life for the sheep, that the Apostle uses this illustration.

is perhaps intentional. A proprietor disposes of the whole of the produce; a slave gets only a portion of it. Cf. Tobit i. 10. In some texts τὸν καρπόν has been corrected to ἐκ τοῦ καρποῦ (E K L, Latt. Syrr. Copt. Arm.). See Prov. xxvii. 18.

8. Μὴ κατὰ ἄνθρωπον. 'Do you think that I am speaking these things by man's rule?' It is not merely in accordance with human judgment of what is fitting that he lays down the principle that labour has a right to a living wage. There is higher authority than that. The expression κατὰ ἄνθρωπον occurs thrice in this Epistle (iii. 3, xv. 32) and thrice in the same group (Rom. iii. 5; Gal. i. 11, iii. 15), with slightly different shades of meaning: 'from a human point of view' is the leading idea.

ἢ καὶ ὁ νόμος. 'Or (v. 6) does the Law also not say these things?' Perhaps some one had urged that ὁ νόμος ταῦτα οὐ λέγει 'is silent on the subject': it is not laid down that congregations must maintain Apostles. The change from λαλῶ to λέγει is perhaps intentional, the one referring to mere human expression, the other to the substance of what is said. As in οὐκ ἔχομεν (v. 4), the negative belongs to the verb.

Neither Vulg. (*dico . . . dicit*) nor AV. distinguishes the verbs : they apparently follow D E F G in reading λέγω for λαλῶ. K L P have ἢ οὐχὶ καὶ ὁ νόμος ταῦτα λέγει : F G have ἢ εἰ καὶ ὁ ν.τ.λ. Doubtless ἢ καὶ ὁ ν.τ. οὐ λ. (א A B C D E, Vulg. Copt.) is right.

9. Philo (*De Humanitate*) quotes this prohibition as evidence of the benevolence of the Law; and Driver (on Deut. xxv. 4) says that it is "another example of the humanity which is characteristic of Dt." Cf. Exod. xx. 10, xxiii. 12; Prov. xii. 10. Oxen still, as a rule, thresh unmuzzled in the East. Conder says that exceptions are rare. Near Jericho, Robinson saw the oxen of Christians muzzled, while those belonging to Mahometans were not. Driver quotes these and other instances. Cf. 2 Sam. xxiv. 22; Isa. xxviii. 27 f.; Mic. iv. 12 f. Elsewhere (*De Spec. Leg.*) Philo says, οὐ γὰρ ὑπὲρ ἀλόγων ὁ νόμος, ἀλλὰ τῶν θυόντων.

It is not easy to decide between φιμώσεις (א A B³ C D³ E K L P) and κημώσεις (B* D* F G). There is the same difference of reading 1 Tim. v. 18, but there φιμώσεις is unquestionably right, as in LXX of Deut. xxv. 4. How could κημώσεις be so well attested, if it were not original? If it were original it would readily be corrected to the LXX, esp. as κημόω is rare : κημός is found in LXX (Ps. xxxi. 9; Ezek. xix. 4, 9), but not κημόω. Here Chrys. and Thdrt. support κημώσεις.

10. μὴ τῶν βοῶν μέλει τῷ Θεῷ; 'Do you suppose that it is for the oxen that God cares?' St Paul does not mean that God has no care for the brutes (Ps. civ. 14, 21, 27, cxlv. 9, 15; Matt. vi. 26, x. 30). Nor does he mean that in forbidding the muzzling, God was not thinking of the oxen at all. He means that the prohibition had a higher significance, in comparison with which the literal purport of it was of small moment. Jewish interpreters sometimes abandoned the literal meaning of Scripture, and turned it entirely into allegory. They not merely allegorized the words, but said that the literal meaning was untrue. In some cases they urged that the literal meaning was incredible, and that therefore the words were *intended* to be understood symbolically and in no other way. Thus Philo (*De Somn.* i. 16) says that Exod. xxii. 27 cannot be supposed to be meant literally, for the Creator would not be interested about such a trifle as a garment: and elsewhere (*De Sacrif.* 1) he says that the Law was not given for the sake of irrational animals, but for the sake of those who have mind and reason. Cf. *Ep. Barn.* x. 1, 2, xi. 1. St Paul elsewhere allegorizes the O.T., as Hagar and Sarah (Gal. iv. 24), and the fading of the light on Moses' face (2 Cor. iii. 13), but in neither case does he reject the literal meaning. It is not probable that he does so here ; even if πάντως be rendered 'entirely,' it need not be pressed to mean that the oxen were not cared for at all. Weinel, *St Paul*, p. 59.

ἢ δι' ἡμᾶς πάντως λέγει; 'Or is it for our sakes, as doubtless it is, that He saith it?' See RV. marg. For πάντως Vulg. has *utique* ; Beza, *omnino: utique* is probably right. It emphasizes the truth of this second suggestion 'assuredly'; cf. Luke iv. 23 , Acts xviii. 21, xxi. 22, xxviii. 4. In Rom. iii. 9, οὐ πάντως means 'entirely not,' 'not at all,' rather than 'not entirely,' 'not altogether.' See Thackeray, pp. 193 f. The ἡμᾶς probably means Christians;* but it may mean the Jewish nation, or mankind, to teach them to be just and humane. Origen prefers the former interpretation; οὐκοῦν δι' ἡμᾶς τοὺς τὴν καινὴν διαθήκην παρειληφότας εἴρηται ταῦτα, καὶ περὶ ἀνθρώπων γέγραπται, πνευμα-τικῶς τοῦ ῥητοῦ νοουμένου κατὰ τὸν θεῖον ἀπόστολον. Among Christians, Christian missionaries are specially meant. We might expect οὐ λέγει, as in *v.* 8. B. Weiss makes the sentence categorical; 'Rather for our sakes absolutely (v. 10) He says it.'

δι' ἡμᾶς γὰρ ἐγράφη. The γάρ, as in 1 Thess. ii. 20, implies an affirmative answer to the previous question. 'Yes indeed for our sakes it was written.' It was with an eye to men rather than to oxen that this prohibition was laid down. Weinel, *St Paul*, p. 53; Resch, *Agrapha*, pp. 30, 152, 336.

ὅτι ὀφείλει ἐπ' ἐλπίδι. The ὅτι is explanatory: '*to show that* it is in hope that the plougher ought to plough and the thresher (ought to thresh) in the hope of having a share (of the produce).' The sentence is condensed, but quite intelligible: ἐπ' ἐλπίδι is emphatic by position, and is then repeated for emphasis when

---

* The record of what was preparatory to the Gospel was made for the sake of those who received the Gospel.

the thing hoped for is stated.   RV. renders ὅτι 'because,' as if
the meaning were that the prohibition must have an eye to men,
because it is in accordance with common notions of what is fair:
which is unlikely.   The 'that' of AV. is too indefinite.   "Few
particles in the N.T. give greater difficulty to the interpreter
than ὅτι" (Ellicott).   Retaining 'Christian teachers' or 'Apostles'
as the meaning of ἡμᾶς, we must understand the ploughing and
threshing as metaphors for different stages of missionary work.
Such work, and indeed teaching of any kind, is often compared
to agriculture.   Some of the processes of agriculture represent
mission-work better than others, and St Paul would perhaps have
taken reaping rather than threshing, had not the quotation about
threshing preceded.   But threshing may represent the separation
of the true converts from the rest.*   To take ἐγράφη as referring
to what follows, and introducing another quotation, is a most
improbable construction : there is no such Scripture.

ὀφείλει ἐπ' ἐλπίδι ὁ ἀρ. ἀρ. (א* A B C P 17, Vulg., Orig. Eus.) is to
be preferred to ἐπ' ἐλπίδι ὀφ. ὁ ἀρ. ἀρ. (א³ D² K L, Chrys. Thdrt.), where
the desire to make ἐπ' ἐλπίδι still more emphatic has influenced the order.
Other texts are much confused.

καὶ ὁ ἀλοῶν ἐπ' ἐλπίδι τοῦ μετέχειν (א* A B C P 17, Syrr. Copt. Arm.
Aeth., Orig. Eus.) is to be preferred to κ. ὁ ἀλ. τῆς ἐλπίδος αὐτοῦ μετέχειν
ἐπ' ἐλπίδι (א³ D³ E K L, Chrys. Thdrt.) and to κ. ὁ ἀλ. τῆς ἐλπίδος αὐτοῦ
μετέχειν (D* F G, Ambst.).   Some scribe did not see that ἀλοᾶν must be
understood, and thus took μετέχειν to be the verb after ὀφείλει, making
alterations to suit this construction.

11. Εἰ ἡμεῖς ὑμῖν . . . εἰ ἡμεῖς ὑμῶν.   The ἡμεῖς in both places
is emphatic and by juxtaposition is brought into contrast with the
pronoun which follows.   Cf. σύ μου νίπτεις τοὺς πόδας (John xiii.
6).   There is possibly a slight vein of banter in the question.
'If it is we who in your hearts sowed spiritual blessings, is it an
exorbitant thing that we out of your possessions shall reap
material blessings?'   What the Apostle gave was incalculable in
its richness, what he might have claimed but never took, was a
trivial advantage : was it worth disputing about?   Was a little
bodily sustenance to be compared with the blessings of the
Gospel?   With μέγα εἰ cf. 2 Cor. xi. 15 : with τὰ σαρκικά cf. τὰ
βιωτικά (vi. 3) ; 'all that is necessary for our bodily sustenance.'

θερίσομεν (א A B K) seems preferable to θερίσωμεν (C D E F G L P).
The future indicative marks the reaping as more certain to follow, for
which reason Evans prefers the subjunctive.   The Apostle refused to reap.
See Lightfoot on Phil. iii. 11 : he thinks that there is only one decisive
instance of εἰ with subj. in N.T.

12. εἰ ἄλλοι τῆς ὑμῶν ἐξουσίας μετέχουσιν.   'If others (the
Judaizing teachers) have a share of the privilege which you

* Cf. the separation of the fruit of the Spirit from the works of the flesh,
Gal. v. 19-23.

bestow,' viz. the privilege of being maintained by the congregation.
It seems better to make ὑμῶν the subjective genitive. Yet most
commentators make it the objective genitive ; 'have a share of
the right exercised over you' (Mark vi. 7). But throughout the
passage the ἐξουσία is looked at from the Apostles' side, the
advantage which rightly belongs to them. This implies *power
over* the Corinthians to make them supply the maintenance ;
but that is not the side under consideration. And 'to have a
share in power over people' is a somewhat strange expression :
'to have a share of a privilege which people allow' is natural
enough. But the sense is the same, however the genitive is
interpreted. 'We have a better claim than others to the right
of maintenance.' Some conjecture ἡμῶν for ὑμῶν.

ἀλλ' οὐκ ἐχρησάμεθα τῇ ἐξουσίᾳ τ. 'Nevertheless,' he triumph-
antly exclaims, 'we never availed ourselves of this privilege';
after elaborately demonstrating his right to the privilege, as if he
were about to say, 'Therefore I hope that you will recognize the
right and give the necessary maintenance for us in future,' he
declares that he has never accepted it and never means to do
so ; * and he seems to include Silvanus and Timothy.

ἀλλὰ πάντα στέγομεν. 'On the contrary, we endure all
things'; 'we bear up under all kinds of privations and depriva-
tions, sooner than make use of this privilege.' The verb may mean
'we are proof against,' but it may be doubted whether πάντα
means "all pressure of temptation" to avail ourselves of maintenance. See on xiii. 7, and Milligan on 1 Thess. iii. 1. Beza
needlessly conjectures στέγομεν.

ἵνα μή τινα ἐνκοπὴν δῶμεν. 'In order that we may not furnish
any hindrance to the Gospel of Christ.' Neither in LXX nor
elsewhere in N.T. does ἐνκοπή occur, and the word is rare in
class. Grk. It is literally 'an incision,' and hence an 'inter-
ruption' or 'violent break,' as τῆς ἁρμονίας. It is perhaps a
metaphor from breaking bridges or roads to stop the march of
an enemy. The English 'hamper' had a similar origin, of
impeding by means of cutting. 'That we may not in any way
hamper the progress of the Gospel' is therefore the meaning.
Obviously, if he took maintenance, he might be suspected of
preaching merely for the sake of what he got by it. Moreover,
those who had to maintain him might resent the burden, and be
unwilling to listen to him. Chrysostom uses ἀναβολή, 'a mound
thrown up to stop progress,' as equivalent to ἐνκοπή. St Paul's
passionate determination to keep himself independent, especially

---

* *Dix fois il revient avec fierté sur ce détail, en apparence puéril, qu'il n'a
rien coûté à personne, quoique' il eût bien pu faire comme les autres et vivre
de l'autel. Le mobile de son zèle était un amour des ames en quelque sorte
infini* (Renan, *S. Paul,* 237).

at Corinth, appears in various places; 2 Cor. xi. 9, 10; 1 Thess. ii. 9; 2 Thess. iii. 8.   He must be free to rebuke, and his praise must be above the suspicion of being bought.   While labouring at Corinth, he could accept help from Macedonians, but not from Corinthians.   When Ignatius (*Philad.* 6) says that no one can accuse him of having been oppressive (ἐβάρησα), he probably refers to the suppression of opinion rather than the enforcing of maintenance.   Cf. ἐνέκοψεν, 1 Thess. ii. 18.

The MSS. vary between ὑμῶν ἐξουσίας (אABCDEFGP) and ἐξ. ὑμῶν: between τινα ἐγκ. (אABC) and ἐγκ. τινα: between ἐγκοπήν (ACD³FGKP), ἐνκοπήν (B* FG) and ἐκκοπήν (אD*L). There is no authority for ἡμῶν ἐξουσίας.

13. He has reminded them that he has never in the past taken maintenance.   Before stating what he means to do in the future, he strengthens the proof that he has a right to it. There is a higher and closer analogy than that of the soldier or of the different kinds of husbandmen.   The other analogies may have escaped their notice, but surely they must be aware of the usages of the Temple, which in this matter did not differ from heathen usage.   See Gray on Num. xviii. 8–20.

οὐκ οἴδατε; 'Do you not know that those who perform the temple-rites eat the food that comes out of the temple, those who constantly attend on the altar share with the altar' what is offered thereon?   The second half is not an additional fact; it repeats the first half in a more definite form.   See Num. xviii. 8–20 of the priest's portions, and 21–24 of the Levite's tithe, and contrast Deut. xiv. 23 (see Driver, p. 169).   Nowhere else in N.T. does συνμερίζομαι occur.

τὰ ἐκ τοῦ ἱεροῦ (אBD*FG, Copt.) is preferable to ἐκ τοῦ ἱεροῦ, without τά (ACD³EKLP, Syrr. Arm.): and παρεδρεύοντες (א*ABCDEFGP) to προσεδρεύοντες (א³KL).   Neither verb occurs elsewhere in N.T., and there is little difference of meaning between them.   See LXX of Prov. i. 21, viii. 3.

14. Just as God appointed that the priests and Levites should be supported out of what the people offered to Him, so did Christ also appoint that missionaries should be supported out of the proceeds of missions.   For the parallel between Christian preachers and Jewish priests see Rom. xv. 16.   It is clear that ὁ Κύριος means Christ; 'the Lord *also*,' just as Jehovah had done.   St Paul was familiar with what is recorded Matt. x. 10: Luke x. 7, 8.   See on vii. 10 and xi. 23.

15. οὐ κέχρημαι οὐδενὶ τούτων.   He repeats, in a stronger form, the statement of *v.* 12.   The change of tense brings it down to the present moment: 'I did not avail myself,' οὐκ ἐχρησάμην, and 'I have not availed myself,' οὐ κέχρημαι.   Moreover, the addition of the pronoun makes the statement more emphatic ; '*I*, however, have not availed myself of any of these advantages.' Others may have done so, but he has not. He now thinks no longer of Silvanus and Timothy, who were perhaps included in οὐκ ἐχρησάμεθα (v. 12), and speaks only of himself. Even the close analogy of the maintenance of the priests has not induced him to do that. He has now completely justified the plea that he is not asking them to forego more than he foregoes himself. *Si ego propter aliorum salutem a debitis sumptibus abstinui, saltem vos ab immolatis carnibus abstinete, ne multos fratrum praecipitetis in interitum* (Herv.). But *v.* 13 may possibly have been introduced for the sake of another parallel. 'Like the priests who partake of what has been sacrificed, I have a right to partake of offerings, but for the sake of others I forbear. Then may I not ask you, although you have a right to partake of what has been sacrificed, for the sake of others to forbear ? '

Having emphatically reminded them of his practice in the past, he now declares that he means to make no change. All this argument is not a prelude to requiring maintenance from them in future.

Οὐκ ἔγραψα δὲ ταῦτα. 'Now I did not write all this,' viz. all the pleas which he has been urging (*vv.* 4-14). Or δέ may be ' yet,' 'however,' and ἔγραψα may be the epistolary aorist, like ἡγησάμην and ἔπεμψα (Phil. ii. 25, 28), ἀνέπεμψα and ἔγραψα (Philem. 11, 19, 21); 'Yet I am not writing all this': Winer, p. 347. Deissmann gives examples from papyri, *Light*, pp. 157, 164.

ἵνα οὕτως γένηται ἐν ἐμοί . 'That it may be so done (for the future) in my case': not 'unto me,' as A.V. Vulg. has *in me* rightly, and *in eo*, Matt. xvii. 12, where both AV. and RV. have 'unto him.'

καλὸν γάρ μοι . . . οὐδεὶς κενώσει. Both reading and construction are doubtful. WH. make a rather violent aposiopesis after μᾶλλον ἀποθανεῖν ἤ : 'For a happy thing (it were) for me rather to die than—— No one shall make void my glorying,' *i.e.* his repeated declaration that he has never used his privilege of free maintenance. Lachmann's punctuation is still more violent ; ' For a happy thing it were for me rather to die than that my glorying should do so : no one shall make it void.'* The alternative is mentally to supply ἵνα, which with the fut. indic. is unusual, but not impossible (see *v.* 18). This difficulty led to the reading ἵνα τις κενώσῃ. It is impossible to get a satisfactory construction out of what seems to be the true text.

* Lachmann conjectures νὴ τὸ καύχημά μου : cf. xv. 31. Michelsen con jectures νὴ τὸ κ. μου ὃ οὐδεὶς κενώσει.

οὐ κέχρημαι οὐδενί (א* A B C D* E F G P 17) may safely be adopted : other texts vary the order, and some have ἐχρησάμην from v. 12. And οὐδεὶς κενώσει (א* B D* 17) is to be preferred to ἵνα τις κενώσῃ or κενώσει (א³ C D² K L P). But whatever text or construction we adopt the sense remains the same ; 'I would rather die than be deprived of my independence.' But 'rather die *of hunger* than accept food' is not the meaning. For καλὸν . . . ἤ see Swete on Mark ix. 43 ; Winer, p. 302 : the construction is not rare in LXX.

16. There must be no misunderstanding as to what he considers a matter for glorying. There can be no glory in doing what one is forced to do ; and he is forced to preach the Gospel, because if he refused to do so, God would punish him. But he is not forced to preach the Gospel *gratis* ; and he does preach *gratis*. In this there is room for glorying. See Chadwick, *Pastoral Teaching*, pp. 306 f.

ἀνάγκη γάρ μοι ἐπίκειται. He refers to the special commission which he had received on the way to Damascus (Acts ix. 6). He was 'a chosen vessel to bear Christ's name before the Gentiles and kings and the children of Israel' (Acts ix. 15) ; he was separated for the work to which the Holy Spirit had called him (Acts xiii. 2) ; and this commission had been repeated in the Temple (Acts xxii. 21). It was impossible for him to reject it : Rom. i. 14 ; Gal. i. 15 f. ; Ezek. iii. 17 f. 'Is laid' (AV., RV.) is not accurate for ἐπίκειται : 'lies' or 'presses upon me' is the meaning (Luke v. 1, xxiii. 23 ; Acts xxvii. 20) : ἐπίκειται ἡμῖν τὰ τῆς βασιλείας (1 Mac. vi. 57) ; κρατερὴ δ᾽ ἐπεκείσετ᾽ ἀνάγκη (Hom. *Il.* vi. 458). But St Paul's ἀνάγκη is the call of God, not the Greek's driving of blind fate.

17, 18. Various explanations have been given of these rather obscure verses, and it is not worth while to discuss them all. The following is close to the Greek and fits the context. 'For if by my own choice I make a business of this (as other teachers do), I get a reward (as they do).' As a matter of fact the Apostle does *not* do this ; he preaches because he must, and does not make a business of it or take any reward. But in order to make the argument complete, he states an alternative which *might* be a fact. He then states what *is* a fact. 'If, however, it is not of my own choice, then it is a stewardship that has been entrusted to me. What, then, is the reward that comes to me ? Why, that in preaching the Gospel I shall render the Gospel free of charge, so as not to use to the uttermost my privilege in the Gospel.' Or we may explain thus : (1) St Paul *had* a μισθός (v. 18) ; therefore εἰ γὰρ ἑκών . . . is not a *rejected* alternative ; (2) his μισθός is practically the same as his καύχημα (v. 15). Thus the alternatives of v. 17 are *both* true. He preached of obligation, but also in a way he was not obliged to adopt, *i.e.* without pay. The latter, not the former, secured him a reward. If he wished to exercise his privilege as an Apostle for all that it was worth (καταχρήσασθαι), he would insist upon full maintenance as his μισθός. But the μισθός which he prefers and gets is the delight of preaching without pay, of giving the Glad-tidings for nought, and taking no money for them. The idea of his μισθός being the commendation which he will receive at the Day of Judgment is quite foreign to the passage. Some editors carry the interrogation on to εὐαγγελίῳ. This makes a question of awkward length, and leaves the question to answer itself. To put the question at ὁ μισθός, and make what follows the answer to it, is more pointed. 'What is the pay that I get? Why, the pleasure of refusing pay.' An οἰκονόμος was often a slave (Luke xii. 42). With πεπίστευμαι compare Gal. ii. 7 and Lukyn Williams' note there; also 1 Tim. i. 11; Tit. i. 3; and see Deissmann, *Light*, p. 379. Nowhere else in the Bible does ἀδάπανον occur, and nowhere else in N.T. does ἄκων occur. See on vii. 31 for καταχρήσασθαι.

μοι ἐστίν (ℵ³ B L P) rather than ἐστίν μοι (D³ E), or μου ἐστίν (ℵ* A C K), or ἔσται μοι (D* F G). After τὸ εὐαγγέλιον, D² E F G K L P, Syrr. add τοῦ Χριστοῦ : ℵ A B C D*, Vulg. Copt. Arm. Aeth. omit.

19. Ἐλεύθερος γὰρ ὤν. 'For although I am free from all, yet I made myself a bondservant to all, in order that I might gain the more.'* He is about to show other ways in which he waives his rights, in order to serve others and help the spread of the Gospel. Others take these verses (19-23) as explaining the ways in which he gets his recompense by refusing recompense. But ἐλεύθερος ὤν seems to look back to *v.* 1 and to prepare the way for further instances of his forgoing his ἐλευθερία. Note the emphatic juxtaposition of πάντων πᾶσιν by chiasmus. Both πάντων and πᾶσιν are ambiguous as regards gender ; but πᾶσιν is almost certainly masculine, and that makes it almost certain that πάντων is masculine ; 'all *men*' (AV., RV.); *jedermann* (Luther); so also Calvin, though he regards the neuter as possible. Origen adopts the neuter as if it were certain. "To be free ἐκ πάντων," he says, "is the mark of a perfect Apostle. A man may be free from unchastity but be a slave to anger, free from avarice but a slave to vanity; he may be free from one sin but a slave to another sin. But to say, 'Although I am free from all,' is the mark of a perfect Apostle : and such was Paul." Strange that Origen should suppose that the Apostle would make any such claim. He rightly points

* The ἐκ expresses more strongly than ἀπό (Rom. vii. 3) that he is freed out of all dependence on others ; he is extricated from entangling ties.

out that there was no harm in Paul's going to Jewish synagogues
and observing Jewish customs, for he did not do this deceitfully,
ἀλλὰ θηρεύων τινὰς ἐξ αὐτῶν. In *interpreting*, Origen inserts the
article before νόμον, and each time writes οἱ ὑπὸ τὸν νόμον.
He says that people asked what was the difference between οἱ
Ἰουδαῖοι and οἱ ὑπὸ τὸν νόμον, and he thinks that the latter refers
to such people as the Samaritans. But, in *quoting*, he omits the
article. He points out that St Paul does not say μὴ ὢν Ἰουδαῖος,
for he was a Jew, although οὐκέτι ἐν τῷ φανερῷ: but he does say
μὴ ὢν ὑπὸ νόμον, for he was not a Samaritan. The meaning
of it all is, that he could find in all men something with which
he could sympathize, and he used this to win them. This was
hard work for one with so strong and pronounced an individu-
ality as he had.

τοὺς πλείονας. He could not expect to win *all*; but τούς
πλείονας does not mean 'the majority of mankind,' nor 'more
than any other Apostle,' but 'more than I should have gained if
I had not made myself a slave to all.' This is best expressed
by 'the more' (AV., RV.). With κερδήσω cf. Matt. xviii. 15;
1 Pet. iii. 1.*

20. He now gives examples of his becoming a slave to all.
He is the slave of Christ, and becomes a slave to others, in order,
like a faithful οἰκονόμος, to make gains for his Master. An
οἰκονόμος (see above) might be a slave. 'And (καί epexegetic)
I behaved to the Jews as a Jew,' *e.g.* in circumcising Timothy
at Lystra (Acts xvi. 3). Cf. Acts xxi. 26.

τοῖς ὑπὸ νόμον ὡς ὑπὸ νόμον. 'To them that are under Law
I behaved as one under Law.' The context shows clearly that
νόμος here means the Mosaic Law as a whole: but the sentence
is not a mere explication of the preceding one. The one
refers to nationality, the other to religion; and there were some
who were under the Mosaic Law who were not Jews by race.
The Apostle includes all who are not heathen.

μὴ ὢν αὐτὸς ὑπὸ νόμον. 'Though I knew that I was not
myself under Law.' He does not say οὐκ ὤν, which might refer
to a fact of which he was not aware: but οὐ with participles
is rare in N.T. The parenthesis is remarkable as showing how
completely St Paul had broken with Judaism. See Dobschütz,
Probleme, p. 82. In commenting on this verse Origen indicates
that he was not the first to do so; τινὲς ἐζήτησαν τίς ἡ διαφορὰ
τῶν ὑπὸ τὸν νόμον παρὰ τοὺς Ἰουδαίους. See on i. 24.

This parenthesis is omitted in D³ K, Copt. Aeth. AV., but is clearly to
be inserted with ℵ A B C D* E F G P, Vulg. Arm. RV. The omission
is probably due to homoeoteleuton, νόμον to νόμον.

* It is just possible that there is an allusion to the charge of making a gain
(2 Cor. xi. 12, xii. 17): his only gain was winning souls.

21. τοῖς ἀνόμοις. He goes a good deal further, and says that he was willing to behave as a heathen to heathen (cf. Gal. ii. 19). He did this, as Origen remarks, when he quoted heathen poets, and took as a text the inscription on a heathen altar, ἀγνώστῳ Θεῷ. See also Acts xiv. 15, xxiv. 25, where his arguments are such as a heathen would appreciate. Here ἄνομος does not mean 'lawless' in the sense of disregarding and transgressing law (Luke xxii. 37; Acts ii. 23; 1 Tim. i. 9), but = οἱ μὴ ὑπὸ νόμον, 'those who were outside Law'; Rom. ii. 14. Evans (following Estius, *exlex*, *inlex*) translates, 'To God's outlaws I behaved as an outlaw, not being (as I well knew) an outlaw of God, but an inlaw of Christ'; and Origen explains the latter as meaning τηρῶν τὴν πολιτείαν τὴν κατὰ τὸ εὐαγγέλιον. But even 'outlaw' has too much of the idea of lawlessness to be quite satisfactory. The genitives, Θεοῦ and Χριστοῦ mean 'in relation to.' *Qui est ἄνομος Θεῷ est etiam ἄνομος Χριστῷ: qui est ἔννομος Χριστῷ est ἔννομος Θεῷ:* and (on Gal. vi. 2) *lex Christi, lex amoris* (Beng.). It was the *lex amoris*, as followed by himself, that the Apostle would enforce on the Corinthians with regard to eating idol-meats; and this thought brings him to the last illustration of his forbearing conformity, τοῖς ἀσθενέσιν ἀσθενής. The Law of Christ, while freeing him from the Law of Moses, did not leave him free to do as he pleased: it restrained him, and kept him from wandering to other objects than the service of God and man (2 Cor. v. 14).

Θεοῦ and Χριστοῦ (א A B C D* F G P, Latt. Copt., Orig. Chrys.) rather than Θεῷ and Χριστῷ (D³ K L, Arm. Thdrt.): see Blass, § 36. 11. κερδάνω or κερδανῶ (א* A B C F G P 17) rather than κερδήσω (א³ D E K L, Orig. Chrys. Thdrt.), which is from *vv.* 19, 20. τοὺς ἀνόμους (א A B C D E P 17, Orig.) rather than ἀνόμους (א³ F G K L, Chrys. Thdrt.), perhaps to conform with Ἰουδαίους.

22. τοῖς ἀσθενέσιν ἀσθενής. 'To the weaklings I became a weakling' (no ὡς). When he had to deal with the over-scrupulous, he sympathized with their scruples, abstaining from things which seemed to them (though not to him) to be wrong. Cf. 2 Cor. xi. 29; Rom. xiv. 1, xv. 1. Certainly this is the meaning, not "those who had not strength to believe the Gospel." Origen says that he was weak to the weak when he allowed those who burn to marry. He points out that Paul does not say μὴ ὢν αὐτὸς ἀσθενής, which would have been ἀλαζονικόν and ὑπερήφανον: yet surely not so much so as Origen's own interpretation of ἐλεύθερος ἐκ πάντων (see on *v.* 19). See Resch, *Agrapha*, p. 132

τοῖς πᾶσιν γέγονα πάντα. 'To them all I am become all things.' The change from aorist to perfect is significant; this is the permanent result of his past action; he is always all-sided in all relations. His accommodation has no limit excepting the one just stated, that he is ἔννομος Χριστοῦ. See Lightfoot on Gal. ii. 5, where we see this limit operating; also *On Revision*, p. 92. Tarsus taught him to be many-sided. (Ramsay, *Pictures of the Apostolic Church*, pp. 346 f.)

ἵνα πάντως τινὰς σώσω. Another significant change; from κερδήσω to σώσω. When he sums up the various conciliations and accommodations he states the ultimate aim;—not merely to win this or that class to his side, but, by every method that was admissible, to save their souls. Peter sacrificed a Christian principle to save himself from Jewish criticism (Gal. ii. 12–14). Cf. for the πάντως Tobit xiv. 8; 2 Mac. iii. 13. See the remarkable comment on *vv.* 20- 22 in Cassian, *Conf.* xvi. 20.

Before ἀσθενής, **א**³ C D F G K L P, Syrr. Copt. Arm. Aeth. insert ὡς from *vv.* 20, 21 : **א*** A B, Latt. Orig. omit. Before πάντα, D² K L P, Orig. Thdrt. insert τά : **א** A B C D* F G omit. For πάντως τινάς some texts (D E F G, Latt.) have πάντας, or (17, Clem-Alex.) τοὺς πάντας. Clem-Alex. (*Strom.* v. 3) has three variations from the true text ; πάντα ἐγενόμην ἵνα τοὺς πάντας κερδήσω. Orig. varies between τοὺς πάντας, πάντας ἢ τινάς, and πάντα. Calv., rejecting *ut omnes facerem salvos* (Vulg.) for *ut omnino aliquos servem*, remarks ; *quia successu interdum caret indulgentia cujus Paulus meminit, optime convenit haec restrictio : quamvis non proficeret apud omnes, non tamen destitisse, quin paucorum saltem utilitati consuleret.*

23. πάντα δὲ ποιῶ διὰ τὸ εὐαγγέλιον. 'Yet all that I do, I do because of the Gospel.' * Not, 'for the Gospel's sake,' in order to help its progress, but because the Gospel is so precious to himself. He has just been stating how much he does for the salvation of others ; he now adds that he is also careful of his own salvation, and thus anticipates the conclusion of *v.* 27. What follows shows that this is the meaning ; he must secure his share in that eternal life which the Gospel offers.

ἵνα συνκοινωνὸς αὐτοῦ γένωμαι. 'In order that I may prove to be a fellow-partaker thereof,' *i.e.* not lose his share in the salvation which he tries to bring to others.† Even in speaking of his own salvation he does not regard it as the main thing, or as something apart by itself. Salvation is offered by the Gospel to all ; and he must strive to be one of those who receive it. The prize is not yet won : *σύν et γίγνομαι magnam habent modestiam* (Beng.).

24. The thought of possible failure, where failure would be so disastrous, suggests an exhortation to great exertion, which is

* '*This* I do' (AV.) comes from a wrong reading ; τοῦτο (K L, Syrr.), instead of πάντα.

† This gives some support to the view that, in iii. 9, Θεοῦ συνεργοί meant 'sharers in work for God,' but it does not make that view probable.

illustrated by the practice of runners and boxers in the Isthmian games. These were held once in three years close to Corinth. See Hastings, *DB.* art. 'Games'; Smith, *D. of Grk. and Rom. Ant.* art. 'Isthmia.' The reference to the games is certain; such contests were common everywhere. The reference to the *Isthmian* games is much less certain. See Ramsay, *Pauline Studies*, p. 332, *Pictures of the Apostolic Church*, p. 363.

οἱ ἐν σταδίῳ τρέχοντες . . . βραβεῖον. 'The runners in a race-course all of them run, but one taketh the prize.'* Does that mean, asks Origen, that only one Christian is saved, while the rest of us are lost? Not so, for all who are in the way of salvation are one, 'one body.' It is the Christian Church that runs, and there is a prize for each of its members. But the prize is not in all cases the same: God gives to each according to his merit. The derivation of βραβεῖον (*brabeum, brabium, bravium*) is unknown. It occurs Phil. iii. 14; Clem. Rom. *Cor.* 5; Tatian, *Ad Graec.* 33.

25. οὕτως τρέχετε, ἵνα καταλάβητε. 'So run, that ye may secure it.' The οὕτως may look back to the successful competitor; 'run as he does': or it may simply anticipate the ἵνα.† The change from λαμβάνει to καταλάβητε marks the difference between mere receiving and securing as one's own possession, and this play on words cannot be reproduced in English. Evans suggests 'take' and 'overtake.' This would be excellent, if we had οὕτως διώκετε, ἵνα καταλάβητε, for διώκειν and καταλαμβάνειν are common correlatives for 'pursue' and 'overtake.' But here the idea of one Christian overtaking another is alien to the context, and 'to overtake a prize' is not a natural expression. In Phil. iii. 12 we have the same play on words, but there we have διώκω, as also in Rom. ix. 30.

πᾶς δὲ ὁ ἀγωνιζόμενος. It is easy to talk about securing the prize, '*but* every one who enters for a contest, in everything practises self-control'; he goes into strict training, which for a Greek athlete lasted ten months. Ἐγκρατ. occurs vii. 9, and nowhere else in N.T. Cf. Hor. *Ars Poet.* 412 f. AV. puts a colon, RV. a full stop, here, so that what follows is an inde-pendent sentence. More probably, ἐκεῖνοι μέν and ἡμεῖς δέ are two classes which make up the whole company of athletes, πᾶς ὁ ἀγωνιζόμενος. With WH. put only a comma after ἐγκρατεύεται. Emphasis on πᾶς and πάντα.

φθαρτὸν στέφανον. In the Isthmian games a pine-wreath: cf. 1 Pet. v. 4; Wisd. iv. 2. Philo (*De Migr. Abr.* 6), "Thou

---

* Compare the contrast between πάντες and οὐκ ἐν τοῖς πλείοσιν (x. 1. 5).

† In any case it means *perseveranter nec respicientes retro.—Recte dictum est, Deum adverbia, non verba remunerare ; nempe eos qui fortiter et juste, non autem qui fortia et justa operatur* (Salmeron in Denton).

hast proved thyself to me a perfect athlete, and hast been deemed
worthy of prizes and wreaths (βραβείων καὶ στεφάνων), while
Virtue presides over the games and holds forth to thee rewards
of victory." Even Pindar has not succeeded in making the
wreath of glory ἄφθαρτος: the victors in the games are not those
who are remembered in history. *Non solum corona, sed etiam
memoria ejus perit* (Beng.). The οὖν is independent of the μέν,
which anticipates the following δέ (contrast vi. 4, 7); 'they
verily,' or 'they of course, in order to receive a perishable
crown.'

ἡμεῖς δὲ ἄφθαρτον. The exact expression is not found elsewhere in N.T., but we have ἀμαράντινον τῆς δόξης στέφανον
(1 Pet. v. 4), where 'made of immortelles' is perhaps the meaning rather than 'which fadeth not away': see Bigg *ad loc.* But
'amaranth' and 'immortelles' are flowers that do not fade, so
that the meaning is much the same. Elsewhere we have τὸν
στέφανον τῆς ζωῆς (Jas. i. 12; Rev. ii. 10), ὁ τῆς δικαιοσύνης
στέφανος (2 Tim. iv. 8). In all these places, as here, it is a
crown of victory that is meant, rather than a royal crown,
διάδημα (Rev. xii. 3, xix. 12; Isa. lxii. 3; 1 Esdr. iv. 30; 1 Mac.
xi. 13, xiii. 32). The contrast between φθαρτός and ἄφθαρτος
occurs in 1 Pet. i. 23. In LXX of Zech. vi. 14 we have ὁ δὲ
στέφανος ἔσται τοῖς ὑπομένουσιν: but more to the point is the
description of Virtue in Wisd. iv. 2, ἐν τῷ αἰῶνι στεφανηφοροῦσα
πομπεύει, τὸν τῶν ἀμιάντων ἄθλων ἀγῶνα νικήσασα. The figure is
frequent in 4 Mac.

Lightfoot (*St Paul and Seneca*) quotes from Seneca (*Ep. Mor.*
lxxviii. 16) a remarkable parallel; "What blows do athletes
receive in their face, what blows all over their body. Yet they
bear all the torture from thirst of glory. Let us also overcome
all things, for our reward is not a crown or a palm branch or
the trumpeter proclaiming silence for the announcement of our
name, but virtue and strength of mind and peace acquired
ever after."

Epictetus also (*Dis.* iii. 21) has a fine passage on the
qualifications and responsibilities of teachers; "The thing is
great, it is mystical, not a common thing, nor is it given to every
man. But not even wisdom perhaps is enough to enable a man
to take care of youths: a man must have a certain readiness and
fitness for this purpose; and above all things he must have God
to advise him to occupy this office (*vv.* 16, 17; vii. 40), as God
advised Socrates to occupy the place of one who confutes error.
Why then do you act at hazard in things of the greatest importance? Leave it to those who are able to do it, and to do it
well." And again (iii. 22), "He who without God attempts so
great a matter, is hateful to God."

26. ἐγὼ τοίνυν. Instead of going on with his exhortation to others, he looks to himself. *He* cannot dispense with painful effort. 'I for my part, therefore, am so running, as one with no uncertain course.' He knew the goal quite well, and he knew the road which led to it (Gal. ii. 2). Here οὕτως anticipates ὡς (iv. 1), which adds weight to the view that in *v.* 24 οὕτως anticipates ἵνα. But οὕτως τρέχω does not make it probable that οὕτως τρέχετε is indicative. To render οὐκ ἀδήλως 'not without certainty of reaching the goal' makes it almost contradict the fear expressed in μή πως ἀδόκιμος γένωμαι. *Scio quod petam et quomodo* (Beng.) is better. In N.T., τοίνυν generally begins a sentence (see on Luke xx. 25 and cf. Heb. xiii. 13): St Paul has the usual classical order (cf. Wisd. i. 11, viii. 9). Nowhere else in the Bible is ἀδήλως found: but see 2 Mac. vii. 34; Phil. iii. 14.

οὕτως πυκτεύω. 'I so box as smiting not the air.' It is unlikely that he means 'I do not smite the *air*, but I beat my *body*,' in which case μου τὸ σῶμα would have preceded ὑπωπιάζω, and it is rash to say that οὐκ negatives ἀέρα, because the negative of δέρων would have been μή. We may regard οὐκ ἀέρα δέρων as one term, 'no air-smiter': he uses his fists as one in deadly earnest, and does not miss: he plants his blow. And οὐ with participles still survives in N.T., where the writer feels "that the proper negative for a statement of downright fact is οὐ."

There are eleven other instances in Paul : four in 2 Cor. iv. 8, 9 ; two in a quotation in Gal. iv. 27 ; one each in Rom. ix. 25 ; Gal. iv. 8 ; Phil. iii. 3 ; Col. ii. 19 ; 1 Thess. ii. 4. See also Matt. xxii. 11 ; Luke vi. 42 ; John x. 12 ; Acts vii. 5, xxvi. 22, xxviii. 17, 19 ; Heb. xi. 1, 35 ; 1 Pet. i. 8 (see Hort), and a quotation in ii. 10. J. H. Moulton (*Gr.* i. p. 231) gives numerous illustrations from papyri, and concludes with a remark which applies to this passage. "The closeness of the participle to the indicative in the kinds of sentence found in this list makes the survival of οὐ natural." See Blass, § 75. 5.

'Beating the air,' whether literally or metaphorically, is common in literature. Virgil's Dares (*Aen.* v. 377), *verberat ictibus auras*, and *Entelius vires in ventum effudit* (446) may occur to any one ; also *ventosque lacessit ictibus* (xii. 105 ; *Geor.* iii. 233). Ovid, *Met.* vii. 786, *vacuos exercet in aera morsus.* Valerius Flaccus, *Arg.* iv. 302, *vacuas agit inconsulta per auras brachia.* Hom. *Il.* xx. 446, τρὶς δ'ἠέρα τύψε βαθεῖαν. Cf. also εἰς ἀέρα λαλεῖν (xiv. 9). But we are not to understand the Apostle as speaking of *practising* boxing : both τρέχω and πυκτεύω refer to the actual contest. We see the close of it in 2 Tim. iv. 7, 8.

27. ἀλλ' ὑπωπιάζω . . . δουλαγωγῶ. 'But I bruise my body black and blue and lead it along as a bond-servant.' The renderings of ὑπωπιάζω (lit. give a black eye by hitting τὸ ὑπώπιον) are various ; *castigo* (Vulg.), *lividum facio* (d), *contundo* (Beza), *subigo* (Calv.). See on Luke xviii. 5, where Vulg. has *sugillo.** It is perhaps too much to say that St Paul regards his body as an antagonist. Rather, it is something which becomes a bad master, if it is not made to be a good servant. It is like the horses in a chariot race, which must be kept well in hand by whip and rein if the prize is to be secured. The Apostle was no Gnostic, regarding the body as incurably evil, and here he says σῶμα and not σάρξ. But the body must be made the δοῦλος of the spirit. Nowhere else in the Bible does δουλαγωγῶ occur: cf. δουλόω in Rom. vi. 18, 22. The purpose of δουλαγωγῶ is τοῦ μηκέτι δουλεύειν τῇ ἁμαρτίᾳ (Rom. vi. 6). Ignatius recalls what follows (*Trall.* 12). See Lietzmann, *Greek Papyri*, p. 6.

μή πως ἄλλοις κηρύξας αὐτὸς ἀδόκιμος γένωμαι. The thought of possible failure, which is just discernible in *v.* 23, is here expressed with full distinctness, and the metaphor of contests in the games perhaps still continues. There was a κῆρυξ at the games who announced the coming contest and called out the competitors: "Then our herald, in accordance with the prevailing practice, will first summon the runner" (Plat. *Laws*, viii. p. 833). This the Apostle had done in preaching the Gospel; he had proclaimed, οὕτως τρέχετε, ἵνα καταλάβητε. But he was not only the herald to summon competitors and teach them the conditions of the contest; he was a competitor himself. How tragic, therefore, if one who had instructed others as to the rules to be observed for winning the prize, should himself be rejected for having transgressed them!† Excepting Heb. vi. 8, ἀδόκιμος is found only in Paul: 2 Cor. xiii. 5–7; Rom. i. 28; Tit. i. 16; 2 Tim. iii. 8: δόκιμος also (xi. 19) is mainly Pauline. Manifestly exclusion from the contest, as not being qualified, is not the meaning; he represents himself as running and fighting: it is exclusion from the prize that is meant.‡ He might prove to be disqualified. His effective preaching and his miracles (x. 9–11, xiv. 18, 19; 2 Cor. xii. 12; Rom. xv. 18, 19; Gal. iii. 5) will avail nothing if he has broken the rules of the course (see on Matt. vii. 22, 23). *In quo monentur omnes, ut timendo sperent et sperando timeant, quatenus spes foveat laborantes et timor incitet negligentes* (Atto). *Ita certus est de praemio, ut timeat illud amittere; et ita metuit amittere, ut certus sit de eo* (Herv.). *Potest*

---

* Cf. Cic. *Tusc.* ii. 17, *Inde pugiles caestibus contusi ne ingemiscunt quidem, gladiatores quas plagas perferunt, accipere plagam malunt quam turpiter vitare.*

† 'There is one that is wise and teacheth many, and yet is unprofitable to his own soul' (Ecclus. xxxvii. 19), μισῶ σοφιστὴν ὅστις οὐχ αὑτῷ σοφός (Menander).

‡ There was a herald who proclaimed the victors, and was himself crowned for his services. Nero proclaimed his own success at the games, and thus competed with the heralds. *Victorem se ipse pronunciabat: qua de causa et praeconio ubique contendit* (Suet. *Nero*, 24).

*etiam conjungi cum superiore dicto, in hunc modum ; Ne Evangelio
defrauder, cujus alii mea opera fiunt participes* (Calv.).

ὑπωπιάζω (אA B C D* 17) is to be preferred to ὑποπιάζω (F G K L P),
ὑπωπιέζω (D³), or ὑποπιέζω (22). 'Keep under' (AV.) is from ὑποπιάζω.
For σῶμα F has στόμα.   For ἀδόκιμος, *reprobus* (Vulg.), *rejectaneus* (Beza).
Schmiedel suspects *vv.* 24–27 as an interpolation.

X. 1–XI. 1. THESE PRINCIPLES APPLIED.

The fear expressed in ix. 27 suggests the case of the
Israelites, who, through want of self-control, lost the promised
prize.   They presumed on their privileges, and fell into idolatry,
which they might have resisted (1–13).   This shows the danger
of idolatry : and idol-feasts are really idolatry, as the parallels of
the Christian Eucharist and of the Jewish sacrifices show.   Idol-
feasts must always be avoided (14–22).   Idol-meats need not
always be avoided, but only when the fact that they have been
sacrificed to idols is pointed out by the scrupulous (23–xi. 1).

X. 1–13. *Take warning from the fall of our fathers in
the wilderness.   Distrust yourselves.   Trust in God.*

¹ The risk of being rejected is real.   Our ancestors had
extraordinary advantages, such as might seem to ensure success.
They were all of them protected by the cloud, and they all
passed safely through the sea, ² and all pledged themselves to
trust in Moses by virtue of their trustful following of the cloud
and their trustful march in the sea ; ³ all ate the same supernatural
food, ⁴ and all drank the same supernatural drink ; for they used
to drink from a supernatural Rock which attended them, and the
Rock was really a manifestation of the Messiah.   ⁵ Yet, in spite
of these amazing advantages, the vast majority of them frustrated
the good purpose of God who granted these mercies.   This is
manifest ; for they were overthrown by Him in the wilderness.

⁶ Now all these experiences of theirs happened as examples
which we possess for our guidance, to warn us against lusting
after evil things, just as those ancestors of ours actually did.
⁷ And so you must not fall into idolatry, as some of them fell ;
even as it stands written, The people sat down to eat and to
drink, and rose up to sport.   ⁸ And let us not be led on to
commit fornication, as some of them committed, and died in a
single day, 23,000 of them.   ⁹ And let us not strain beyond all

bounds the Lord's forbearance, as some of them strained it, and
were destroyed, one after another, by serpents. ¹⁰ Nor yet
murmur ye, which is just what some of them did, and were
destroyed forthwith by the destroying angel. ¹¹ Now all these
experiences by way of example occurred one after another to
them, and they were recorded with a view to admonishing us,
unto whom the ends of the ages, with their weight of authority,
have come down. ¹² Therefore if, like our forefathers, you think
that you are standing securely, beware lest self-confidence cause
you, in like manner, to fall. ¹³ And you can avoid falling. No
temptation has taken you other than a man can withstand. Yes,
you may trust God : He will not let you be tempted beyond your
strength. While He arranges the temptation to brace your
character, He will also arrange the necessary way of escape, and
the certainty that He wlll do this will give you strength to
endure.

1. Οὐ θελω . . . ἀδελφοί. See on xii. 1. The γάρ shows the
connexion with what precedes : ' Failure through lack of self-
discipline is not an imaginary peril : if you lack it, your great
spiritual gifts will not save you from disaster.' *

οἱ πατέρες ἡμῶν. Just as Christ spoke of the ancestors of the
Jews as ' your fathers' (Matt. xxiii. 32 ; Luke xi. 47 ; John vi.
49), so the Apostle calls them ' our fathers': some members of
the Church of Corinth were Jews, and the expression, was literally
true of them, as of St Paul. But he may mean that the Israelites
were the spiritual ancestors of all Christians. In Gal. vi. 16
' the Israel of God ' means the whole body of believers. Clem.
Rom. (*Cor.* 60) uses τοῖς πατράσιν ἡμῶν in the same sense, and
speaks to the Corinthians of Jacob (4), and Abraham (31) as
ὁ πατὴρ ἡμῶν. See on Rom. iv. 1.

πάντες. The emphatic repetition in each clause marks the
contrast with οὐκ ἐν τοῖς πλείοσιν (*v.* 5). All, without exception,
shared these great privileges, but not even a majority (in fact
only two) secured the blessing which God offered them. No
privilege justifies a sense of security : privilege must be used
with fear and trembling.

ὑπὸ τὴν νεφέλην. 'Under the cloud' which every one
remembers (Exod. xiii. 21, 22, xiv. 19, 24, xl. 38 ; etc.). The

---

* The ' Moreover' of AV. is from a false reading δέ (א³ K L, Syrr.) : the
evidence for γάρ is overwhelming. It introduces further justification of his
demand that they should imitate him in his forbearance and *Entsagung.*
The οὐ θ. ὑμᾶς ἀγν. (xii. 1 ; 2 Cor. i. 8 ; Rom. i. 13 ; 1 Thess. iv. 13)
implies no reproach : contrast οὐκ οἴδατε (iii. 16, v. 6. vi. 2, etc.).

acc. perhaps indicates movement. They marched with the cloud above them.* The pillar of fire is not mentioned, as less suitable for the figurative ἐβαπτίσαντο which follows: Wisd. xix. 7.

2. εἰς τὸν Μωϋσῆν ἐβ. 'They received baptism unto Moses,' as a sign of allegiance to him and trust in him ; or 'into Moses,' as a pledge of union with him. Comparison with baptism 'into Christ' (Rom. vi. 3 ; Gal. iii. 27) is suggested, and it is implied that the union with Moses which was the saving of the Israelites was in some way analogous to the union with Christ which was the salvation of the Corinthians. Throughout the paragraph, the incidents are chosen from the Pentateuch with a view to parallels with the condition of the Corinthian Christians. The Israelites had had a baptism into Moses, just as the Corinthians had had a baptism into Christ. For a contrast between Christ and Moses, see Heb. iii. 1-6. With the aor. mid. compare ἀπελούσασθε, vi. 11 ; with the εἰς, Acts xix. 3.

ἐν τῇ νεφέλῃ καὶ ἐν τῇ θαλάσσῃ. Both cloud and sea represent "the element in which their typical baptism took place." To make the cloud the Holy Spirit and the sea the water is forced and illogical; both are material and watery elements, and both refer to the water in baptism. In what follows it is the material elements in the Eucharist which are indicated.

Editors are divided between ἐβαπτίσαντο (B K L P) and ἐβαπτίσθησαν (‎א A C D E F G). But the latter looks like a correction to the expression which was generally used of Christian baptism (i. 13, 15, xii. 13 ; etc.). Cf. vi. 11.

3. τὸ αὐτὸ βρῶμα πνευματικόν. The manna which typified the bread in the Eucharist (Jn. vi. 31, 32) was 'spiritual' as being of supernatural origin, ἄρτος ἀγγέλων (Ps. lxxviii. 25), ἀγγέλων τροφή (Wisd. xvi. 20). In all three passages, as here and Neh. ix. 15, 20, the aorist is used throughout ;—quite naturally, of an act which is past, and the repetition of which is not under consideration. It is possible that πνευματικόν also means that "the immediate relief and continuous supply of their bodily needs tended to have an effect upon their spirit ; that is, to strengthen their faith" (Massie). *Israelitis, una cum cibo corporis, alimentum animarum datum est* (Beng.). Others take it as meaning that the manna and the water had a spiritual or allegorical meaning. It is remarkable that St Paul chooses the manna and the rock, and not any of the Jewish sacrifices, as

---

* Onkelos paraphrases Deut. xxxiii. 3 ; "With power He brought them out of Egypt, they were led under Thy cloud ; they journeyed according to Thy word." Onkelos is said to have been, like St Paul, a disciple of Gamaliel. Cf. Ps. cv. 39.

parallels to the Eucharist. In class. Grk. πῶμα is more common than πομα.

WH. bracket the first τὸ αὐτό, which ℵ*, Aeth. omit, while A C* omit αὐτό: but τὸ αὐτό is very strongly attested (ℵ³ B C² D E F G K L P, Latt.). MSS. vary between πν. βρ. ἐφ. (ℵ* B C² P), βρ. πν. ἐφ. (ℵ³ D E F G K L), and πν. ἐφ. βρ. (A 17). A omits the second αὐτό, and again there is difference as to the order; πν. ἐπ. πόμα (ℵ A B C P), πόμα πν. ἐπ. (D E F G K L).

4. ἔπινον γὰρ ἐκ πν. ἀκολουθούσης πέτρας. 'For they used to drink from a spiritual rock accompanying them,' or 'from a spiritual accompanying rock.' The change to the imperfect is here quite intelligible: they habitually made use of a source which was always at hand. It is not so easy to determine the thought which lies at the back of this statement. That the wording of the passage has been influenced by the Jewish legend about a rock following the Israelites in their wanderings and supplying them with water, is hardly doubtful; but that the Apostle believed the legend is very doubtful. In its oldest form, the legend made the well of Beer (Num. xxi. 16 f.) follow the Israelites; afterwards it was the rock of Kadesh (Num. xx. 1 f.) which did so, or a stream flowing from the rock. St Paul seems to take up this Rabbinic fancy and give it a spiritual meaning. The origin of the allusion is interesting, but not of great importance: further discussion by Driver (*Expositor*, 3rd series, ix. pp. 15 f.); Thackeray, pp. 195, 204 f.; Selbie (Hastings, *DB*. art. 'Rock'); Abbott (*The Son of Man*, pp. 648 f., 762).

Of much more importance is the unquestionable evidence of the Apostle's belief in the pre-existence of Christ. He does not say, 'And the rock *is* Christ,' which might mean no more than, 'And the rock is a type of Christ,' but, 'And the rock *was* Christ.' In Gal. iv. 24, 25 he uses the present tense, Hagar and Sarah '*are* two covenants,' *i.e.* represent them, are typical of them. Similarly, in the interpretation of parables (Matt. xiii. 19–23, 37–38) we have 'is' throughout. The ἦν implies that Christ was the source of the water which saved the Israelites from perishing of thirst; there was a real Presence of Christ in the element which revived their bodies and strengthened their faith. The comment of Herveius, *Sic solet loqui Scriptura, res significantes tanqam illas quae significantur appellans*, is true, but inadequate; it overlooks the difference between ἐστι and ἦν. We have an approach to this in Wisd. xi. 4, where the Israelites are represented as calling on the Divine Wisdom in their thirst, and it is Wisdom which grants the water. Philo (*Quod deterius potiori*, p. 176) speaks of the Divine Wisdom as a solid rock which gives imperishable sustenance to those who desired it; and he then goes on to identify the rock with the manna. The pre-existence of Christ is implied in ἐπτώχευσεν (2 Cor. viii. 9), in ἐξαπέστειλεν ὁ Θεὸς τὸν υἱὸν αὐτοῦ (Gal. iv. 4), and in ὁ Θεὸς τὸν ἑαυτοῦ υἱὸν πέμψας (Rom. viii. 3). Cf. Phil. ii. 5, 6, and see Jülicher, *Paulus u. Jesus*, p. 31 ; J. Kaftan, *Jesus u. Paulus*, p. 64 ; Walther, *Pauli Christentum Jesu Evangelium*, p. 24. Justin (*Try.* 114) probably had this passage in his mind when he wrote of dying for the name τῆς καλῆς πέτρας, καὶ ζῶν ὕδωρ ταῖς καρδίαις βρυούσης, καὶ ποτιζούσης τοὺς βουλομένους τὸ τῆς ζωῆς ὕδωρ πιεῖν. By the statement that the life-saving rock was a manifestation of the power of Christ, present with the Israelites, the Apostle indicates that the legend, at which he ' seems to glance in ἀκολουθούσης, is not to be believed literally. What clearly emerges is that, as the Israelites had something analogous to Baptism, so also they had something analogous to the Eucharist ; and this is the only passage in N.T. in which the two sacraments are mentioned together.

MSS. vary between ἡ πέτρα δε (א B D*³), ἡ δὲ πέτρα (A C D² K L P), and πέτρα δέ (F G).

5. ἀλλ᾽ οὐκ ἐν τοῖς πλείοσιν αὐτῶν ηὐδόκησεν ὁ Θεός. 'Howbeit, not with most of them was God well pleased.' Although *all* of them had great blessings (and, in particular, those which resembled the two sacraments which the Corinthian Church enjoyed), there were very few in whom God's gracious purpose respecting them could be fulfilled. In οὐκ ἐν τοῖς πλείοσιν we have a mournful understatement: only two, Caleb and Joshua, entered the Promised Land (Num. xiv. 30–32). *All* the rest, thousands in number, though they entered the lists, were disqualified, ἀδόκιμοι ἐγένοντο (ix. 27), by their misconduct.

In the Epistles, the evidence as to the augment of εὐδοκέω varies greatly ; in i. 21, εὐδόκησεν is undisputed ; here the balance favours ηὐδ. (A B* C): see WH. II. *Notes* p. 162.

The construction εὐδ. ἔν τινι is characteristic of LXX and N.T., while Polybius and others write εὐδ. τινι: but exceptions both ways are found (2 Thess. ii. 12; 1 Mac. i. 43). In Matt. xii. 18 and Heb. x. 6 we have the accusative.

κατεστρώθησαν γὰρ ἐν τῇ ἐρήμῳ. The γάρ introduces a justification of the previous statement. God cannot have been well pleased with them, *for* κατέστρωσεν αὐτοὺς ἐν τῇ ἐρήμῳ (Num. xiv. 16). They did not die a natural death ; their death was a judicial overthrow. The verb is frequent in Judges and 2 Maccabees; cf. Eur. *Her. Fur.* 1000 : nowhere else in N.T. It gives a graphic picture, the desert strewn with dead (Heb. iii. 17).

6. Ταῦτα δὲ τύποι ἡμῶν ἐγενήθησαν. 'Now these things came to pass as examples for us to possess.' The examples were of two kinds ; *beneficia quae populus accepit et peccata quae idem*

admisit (Beng.).   The one kind was being followed; the Corinthians had sacraments and spiritual gifts: they must take care
that the other kind was avoided.   This is better than understanding τύποι in the sense of types, the Israelites being types
and the Corinthians antitypes; in which case ἡμῶν would be the
subjective genitive.*   Origen understands it in the sense of
examples to warn us.   The transition from τύπος (τύπτω) as 'the
mark of a blow' (John xx. 25) to 'the stamp of a die,' and
thence to any 'copy,' is easy.   But a 'copy' may be a thing to
be copied, and hence τύπος comes to mean 'pattern' or 'example.'
See Milligan on 1 Thess. i. 7.   *Deus, inquit, illos puniendo
tanquam in tabula nobis severitatem suam repraesentavit, ut inde
edocti timere discamus* (Calv.).   *Ea potissimum delicta memorantur,
quae ad Corinthios admonendos pertinent* (Beng.).   See Weinel,
St Paul, pp. 58, 59.

εἰς τὸ μὴ εἶναι.   This confirms the view that τύπος does not
mean 'types,' but examples for guidance, 'to the intent that we
should not be.'   In saying εἶναι ἐπιθυμητάς rather than ἐπιθυμεῖν
he is probably thinking of ἐκεῖ ἔθαψαν τὸν λαὸν τὸν ἐπιθυμητήν
(Num. xi. 34).   The substantive occurs nowhere else in N.T.

καθὼς κἀκεῖνοι ἐπεθύμησαν.   'Even as they also lusted.'   The
καί is not logical, and perhaps ought to be omitted in translation;
it means 'they as well as you,' which assumes that the Corinthians
have done what they are here charged not to do: cf. 1 Thess. iv.
13.   Longing for past heathen pleasures may be meant.

7. μηδὲ εἰδωλολάτραι γίνεσθε.   'Neither become ye idolaters.'
The μηδέ is not logical; it puts a *species* on a level with its *genus*.
'Lusting after evil things' is the class, of which idolatry and
fornication are instances; and the μηδέ, 'nor yet,' implies that
idolatry is a new class.   It was, however, the most important of
the special instances, because of its close connexion with the
Corinthian question.   But this is another point in which Greek
idiom is sometimes rather illogical.   We should say '*Therefore
do not become.*'   The τινες is another understatement, like οὐκ
ἐν τοῖς πλείοσιν: the passage quoted shows that the whole people
took part in the idolatry.   St Paul seems to be glancing at the
extreme case in viii. 10, of a Christian showing his superior
γνῶσις by sitting at an idol-banquet in an idol-temple.   Such
conduct does amount to taking part in idolatrous rites.   The
Apostle intimates, more plainly than before, that the danger
of actual idolatry is not so imaginary as the Corinthians in their
enlightened emancipation supposed.

παίζειν.   The quotation is the LXX of Exod. xxxii. 6, and

* This would imply that the Corinthians were predestined to fall as the
Israelites did.

we know that the 'play' or 'sport' included χοροί, which Moses saw as he drew near.* These dances would be in honour of the golden calf, like those of David in honour of the Ark of God, as he brought it back (2 Sam. vi. 14). The quotation, therefore, indicates an idolatrous banquet followed by idolatrous sport.

Calvin asks why the Apostle mentions the banquet and the sport, which were mere accessories, and says nothing about the adoration of the image, which was the essence of the idolatry. He replies that it was in these accessories that some Corinthians thought that they might indulge. None of them thought that they might go so far as to join in idolatrous worship.

No doubt ὥσπερ (א A B D³ L) before γέγραπται is to be preferred to ὡς (C D* K P), and perhaps πεῖν (B* D* F G) to πιεῖν (A B³ C D³ E K L P): πῖν (א) supports πεῖν. See on ix. 4.

8. The relationship of idol-worship and fornication is often very close, and was specially so at Corinth (Jowett, 'On the Connexion of Immorality and Idolatry,' *Epp. of St Paul*, II. p. 70). Hence fornication is taken as the second instance of lusting after evil things. In the matter of Baal-Peor (Num. xxv. 1–9), to which allusion is made here, it was the intimacy with the strange women which led to participation in the idolatrous feasts, not *vice versa* as the RV. suggests; 'the people began to commit whoredom with the daughters of Moab: *for* they called the people unto the sacrifices of their gods.' It is remarkable that precisely at this point the Apostle changes the form of this exhortation and passes from the 2nd pers. (γίνεσθε) to the 1st (πορνεύωμεν), thus once more putting himself on a level with his readers. But there is nothing in the brief reference to the sins of the Israelites to show that, when the Moabite women invited the Israelites to the sacrifices of their gods, immoral intercourse had preceded the invitation.† In Wisd. xiv. 12 the connexion between idolatry and fornication and the consequent destruction are pointed out; Ἀρχὴ γὰρ πορνείας ἐπίνοια εἰδώλων, εὑρέσεις δὲ αὐτῶν φθορὰ ζωῆς, where the rendering '*spiritual* fornication' (AV.) is unnecessary, and probably incorrect.

ἔπεσαν μιᾷ ἡμέρᾳ εἴκοσι τρεῖς χιλιάδες. Here we have, in the most literal sense, φθορὰ ζωῆς. In Num. xxv. 9 the number is

---

* Aristoph. *Ran.* 450, τὸν ἡμέτερον τρόπον τὸν καλλιχορώτατον παίζοντες. The verb is found nowhere else in N.T. In LXX it is frequent.

† But in Num. xxv. we have two different stories combined and somewhat confused: *vv.* 1–5 come from one source, *vv.* 6–18 from another. The locality in one case is Shittim, in the other Peor; the god in one case is presumably Kemosh the God of Moab, but he is called in both cases the Baal of Peor; the punishment in one case is execution by the judges, in the other plagues sent by God; the cause of the evil in one case is Moabite, in the other Midianite. See Gray, *Numbers*, pp. 380 f., and cf. the interchange of Ishmaelite with Midianite, Gen. xxxvii. 25–36.

24,000. St Paul quotes from memory, without verifying, the exact number being unimportant. But harmonizers suggest that 1000 were slain by the judges; or that 23,000 and 24,000 are round numbers for a figure which lay between the two; or that, of the 24,000 who died of the plague, 23,000 died on one day.* All these suggestions are the result of a 'weak' (viii. 9 f., ix. 22) theory of inspiration; and the first does not avoid the charge of error, for we are told that 'those that died by the *plague* were 24,000.' For ἔπεσαν see 1 Chron. xxi. 14.

For πορνεύωμεν (א A B D³ E) and ἐπόρνευσαν (*ibid.*) D* F G have ἐκπορνεύωμεν and εξεπόρνευσαν from LXX of Num. xxv. 1. Excepting Jude 7, the compound is not found in N.T. ἔπεσαν (א A B C D* F G P 17) is to be preferred to ἔπεσον (D³ K L): see W H. II. *Notes* p. 164. א³ A C D² K L P insert ἐν before μιᾷ: א* B D* F G, Latt. omit. 'In one day' augments the terror of the punishment.

9. μηδὲ ἐκπειράζωμεν τὸν Κύριον. 'Neither let us sorely tempt the Lord,' try Him out and out, provoke Him to the uttermost, till His longsuffering ceases. This the Israelites did by their frequent rebellion. It is rather fanciful to connect this with *v.* 8, as *v.* 8 is connected with *v.* 7. It is true that "fornication leads to tempting God"; but is that the Apostle's reason for passing from πορνεύωμεν to ἐκπειράζωμεν? The compound occurs (in quotations from LXX of Deut. vi. 16) Matt. iv. 7; Luke iv. 12; also Luke x. 25; in LXX, both of man trying God (Ps. lxxviii. 18), and of God trying man (Deut. viii. 2, 16). It implies prolonged and severe testing. See on iii. 18. Here the meaning is that God was put to the proof, as to whether He had the will and the power to punish. In class. Grk. ἐκπειρᾶσθαι is used. It is doubtful whether the Apostle is thinking of anything more definite than the general frailty and faultiness of the Corinthian Christians. Misuse of the gift of tongues (Theodoret) and a craving for miracles (Chrysostom) are not good conjectures.

ὑπὸ τῶν ὄφεων ἀπώλλυντο. 'Perished day by day by the serpents.' The imperfect marks the continual process, and the article points to the well-known story. 'Perished' = 'were destroyed,' and hence ὑπό is admissible. In class. Grk. ὑπό is used of the agent after an intrans. verb, but it is not very frequent in N.T. We have πάσχειν ὑπό, Matt. xvii. 12 and 1 Thess. ii. 14, where Milligan quotes from papyri, βίαν πάσχων ἑκάστοτε ὑπὸ Ἑκύσεως. See Winer, p. 462.

We may safely prefer τὸν Κύριον (א B C P 17, Aeth. Arm.) to τὸν Χριστόν (D E F G K L, Latt.) or τὸν Θεόν (A). No doubt Χριστόν, if original, might have been changed to Κύριον or Θεόν because of the diffi-

* The μιᾷ ἡμέρᾳ increases the horror: *omnia ademit Una dies infesta tibi tot praemia vitae* (Lucr. iii. 911): cf. Rev. xviii. 8.

culty of supposing that the Israelites in the wilderness tempted Christ. On the other hand, either Χριστόν or. Θεόν might be a gloss to explain the meaning of Κύριον. Epiphanius says that Marcion substituted Χριστόν for Κύριον, that the Apostle might not appear to assert the lordship of Christ. Whatever may be the truth about this, it is rash to say that "Marcion was right in thinking that the reading Κύριον identifies the Lord Jehovah of the narrative with the historical Jesus Christ." It is safer to say with Hort on 1 Pet. ii. 3, "No such identification can be clearly made out in the N.T." But see on Rom. x. 12, 13. In the N.T. ὁ Κύριος commonly means 'our Lord'; but this is by no means always the case, and here it almost certainly means Jehovah, as Num. xxi. 4–9 and Ps. lxxviii. 18 imply. There seems to be no difference in LXX between Κύριος and ὁ Κύριος, and in N.T. we can lay down no rule that Κύριος means God and ὁ Κύριος Christ. See Bigg on 1 Pet. i. 3, 25, ii. 3, iii. 15; Nestle, *Text. Crit. of N.T.* p. 307.

καθώς τινες (א A B C D* F G P 17) rather than καθώς καί τινες (D³ E K L). ἐπείρασαν (A B D³ K L) rather than ἐξεπείρασαν (א C D* F G P 17), the latter being an assimilation to ἐκπειράζωμεν. It is more difficult to decide between ἀπώλλυντο (א A B) and ἀπώλοντο (C D E F G K L P): but ἀπώλλυντο would be more likely to be changed to ἀπώλοντο (*v.* 10) than *vice versa.*

10. μηδὲ γογγύζετε. Rebellious discontent of any kind is forbidden; and there is nothing said as to the persons against whom, or the things about which, murmuring is likely to take place. But the warning instance (καθάπερ τινες) can hardly refer to anything but that of the people against Moses and Aaron for the punishment of Korah and his company (Num. xvi. 41 f.), for we know of no other case in which the murmurers were punished with death.* From this, and the return to the 2nd pers. (γογγύζετε), we may conjecture that the Apostle is warning those who might be disposed to murmur against him for his punishment of the incestuous person, and for his severe rebukes in this letter.†

ὑπὸ τοῦ ὀλοθρευτοῦ. Not Satan, but the destroying angel sent by God to smite the people with pestilence. The Apostle assumes that there was such an agent, as in the slaying of the firstborn (τὸν ὀλεθρεύοντα, Exod. xii. 23), and in the plague that punished David (2 Sam. xxiv. 16; ἄγγελος Κυρίου ἐξολεθρεύων, 1 Chron. xxi. 12), and in the destruction of the Assyrians (2 Chron. xxxii. 21; Ecclus. xlviii. 21). Cf. Acts xii. 23: Heb. xi. 28. Vulg. nas *ab exterminatore,* Calv. *a vastatore*; in Heb. xi. 28 Vulg. has *qui vastabat,* in Exod. xii. 23 *percussor.* The angelology and demonology of the Jews was confused and unstable. Satan is sometimes the destroyer (Wisd. ii. 24). By introducing sin he brought men under the power of death;

---

* The murmuring against the report of the spies can hardly be meant, for that was punished by the murmurers dying off in the wilderness, not by any special destruction (Num. xiv. 1, 2, 29).

† It is perhaps for this reason that he changes from καθώς to καθάπερ. which implies the very closest resemblance, 'exactly as.'

Rom. v. 12; Heb. ii. 14; John viii. 44. Nowhere else in the
Bible does ὀλοθρευτής occur.

Assimilation has produced four corruptions of the text in this verse:
γογγύζετε (A B C K L P, Vulg. Syrr. Aeth.) has been corrected to γογγύ-
ζωμεν (א D E F G): καθάπερ (א B P) has been corrected to καθώς (A C D
E F G K L): K L inserts καί before τινες: and A corrects ἀπώλοντο to
ἀπώλλυντο.

11. ταῦτα δὲ τυπικῶς συνέβαινεν ἐκείνοις. 'Now these things
by way of lesson happened one after another to *them*': emphasis on ἐκείνοις. The imperfect sets forth the enumerated
events as in process of happening; the singular sums them up
as one series. In *v.* 6 we had the plural, ἐγενήθησαν, attention
being directed to the separate τύποι in *vv.* 1–5; moreover, there
may be attraction to τύποι, Winer, p. 645.

ἐγράφη δὲ π. ν. ἡμ. 'And were written for our admonition,'
ne similiter peccantes similia patiamur. The written record was
of no service to those who had been punished; *quid enim
mortuis prodesset historia? vivis autem quo modo prodesset, nisi
aliorum exemplis admoniti resipiscerent?* (Calv.). Note the
change from imperfect to aorist.

εἰς οὓς τὰ τέλη τῶν αἰώνων κατήντηκεν. 'Unto whom the ends
of the ages have reached.' The common meaning of καταντάω
in N.T. is 'reach one's destination': see on xiv. 36. The point
of the statement here is obscure. 'The ages' are "the successive
periods in the history of humanity, and perhaps also the parallel
periods for different nations and parts of the world" (Hort on ἐπ'
ἐσχάτου τῶν χρόνων, 1 Pet. i. 20).* In what sense have the ends
of these ages reached us as their destination? 'The ends' of
them implies that each one of them is completed and summed
up; and the sum-total has come down to us for whom it was
intended. That would seem to mean that we reap the benefit
of the experience of all these completed ages. Such an interpretation comes as a fit conclusion to a passage in which the
Corinthians are exhorted to take the experiences of the Israelites
as lessons for themselves. *Pluralis habet vim magnam: omnia
concurrunt et ad summam veniunt; beneficia et pericula, poenae
et praemia* (Beng.).

Or it may mean that the ends of the ages have reached us,
and therefore we are already in a new age, which is the final

---

* The education of the Gentiles went on side by side with the education
of the Jews, and both streams met in the Christian Church. "The Church
is the heir of the spiritual training of mankind" (Findlay). The temptation
to make τὰ τ. τῶν *al.* singular produced corruptions; *in quos finis sacculorum
devenit* (Iren. IV. xiv. 3), *in quos finis seculorum obvenit* (Aug. *De cat. rud.*
3). Tert. preserves the plural; *ad nos commonendos, in quos fines aevorum
decucurrerunt* (*Marc.* v. 7); also Vulg.; *ad correptionem nostram, in quos
fines seculorum devenerunt.*

one and will be short (vii. 29 : see Westcott on Heb. ix. 26 and
1 John ii. 18). The interpretation will then be that "the last
act in the drama of time is begun" (Rutherford), and therefore
the warnings contained in these examples ought at once to be
laid to heart. The Day of Judgment is near and may come at
any moment (xvi. 22); it is madness not to be watchful.

AV. has 'Now all these things,' and 'all' is well supported; ταῦτα δὲ
πάντα (C K L P, Vulg. Syrr. Copt. Arm.); πάντα δὲ ταῦτα (א D E F G,
Aeth.); A B 17, Theb. omit πάντα: Orig. and Tert. sometimes omit.
The fact that πάντα is inserted in different positions, and that insertion is
more intelligible than omission, justifies exclusion. τυπικῶς (א A B C K P,
Vulg. *in figura*) is to be preferred to τύποι (D E F G L), and συνέβαινεν
(א B C K L) to συνέβαινον (A D E F G L), which looks like assimilation to
v. 6; also κατήντηκεν (א B D* F G) to κατήντησεν (A C D³ K L).

12, 13. The Apostle adds two admonitions : to those who
are so self-confident that they think that they have no need
to be watchful; and to those that are so despondent that they
think that it is useless to struggle with temptation.

12. Ὥστε. See on iii. 21. 'So then, let him that thinketh
that he is standing securely beware lest he fall'; *i.e.* fall from
his secure position and become ἀδόκιμος. The Apostle does
not question the man's opinion of his condition; he takes
the security for granted : but there is danger in feeling secure,
for this leads to carelessness. Perhaps there is special reference
to feeling secure against contamination from idol-feasts. It is
less likely that there is a reference to one who "thinks that
through the sacrament he *ipso facto* possesses eternal life with
God." See Rom. xi. 20, xiv. 4. Μὴ τοίνυν ἐπὶ τῇ στάσει φρόνει
μέγα, ἀλλὰ φυλάττου τὴν πτῶσιν (Chrys.).

Both AV. and RV. disregard the difference between ὥστε
here and διόπερ in v. 14, translating both 'wherefore.' In
Phil. ii. 12, AV. has 'wherefore,' and RV. 'so then,' for ὥστε.
Vulg. rightly distinguishes, with *itaque* here and *propter quod* in
v. 14. Διόπερ indicates more strongly than ὥστε that what
follows is a reasoned result of what precedes.

13. πειρασμὸς ὑμᾶς οὐκ εἴληφεν. An appeal to their past
experience. Hitherto they have had no highly exceptional,
superhuman temptations, but only such as commonly assail
men, and therefore such as a man can endure. The τύποι just
mentioned show that others have had similar temptations.
This ought to encourage them with regard to the future, which
he goes on to consider. It is reading too much into the verse
to suppose that Corinthians had been pleading that they must
go to idol-feasts; otherwise they might be persecuted and
tempted to apostatize. In three of his letters, however (to the

Alexandrians, to the clergy of Samosata, and to Acacius and others), Basil applies this text to persecution (*Epp.* 139, 219, 256). With εἴληφεν compare Wisd. xi. 12 ; Luke v. 26, vii. 16, ix. 39.

πιστὸς δὲ ὁ Θεός. 'On the contrary, God is faithful,' *id est verax in hac promissione, ut sit semper nobiscum* (Herv.). Both AV. and RV. have 'but' for δέ. But the opposition is to what is negatived in what precedes ; this clause continues the encouragement already given. The perfect tense (οὐκ εἴληφεν) brings us down to the present moment ; there never has been πειρασμὸς μὴ ἀνθρώπινος. In addition to this there is the certainty that God will never prove faithless : *est certus custos suorum* (Calv.).

ὃς οὐκ ἐάσει ὑμᾶς. 'And therefore He will not suffer you to be tempted beyond what ye are able to endure.' This follows from His faithfulness, 'as being one who will not allow,' etc. For a similar use of ὅς see 1 Tim. ii. 4.

ἀλλὰ ποιήσει κ.τ.λ. 'But will provide, with the temptation, the way of escape also.' '*A* way to escape' (AV.) ignores the article before ἔκβασιν, 'the necessary way of escape,' the one suitable for such a difficulty. The σύν and the articles imply that temptations and possibilities of escape always go in pairs : there is no πειρασμός without its proper ἔκβασις, for these pairs are arranged by God, who permits no unfairness. He knows the powers with which He has endowed us, and how much pressure they can withstand. He will not leave us to become the victims of circumstances which He has Himself ordered for us, and *impossibilia non jubet*. For ἔκβασις Vulg. has *proventus* ; Beza and Calv. (better) *exitus*, which Vulg. has Heb. xiii. 7 ; *egressus* might be better still. On the history of πειράζειν see Kennedy, *Sources*, p. 106. As to God's part in temptation, see Matt. vi. 13 ; 1 Chron. xxi. 1 ; Job i. 12, ii. 6 ; Exod. xvi. 4 ; Deut. viii. 2 ; and, on the other side, Jas. i. 13.

τοῦ δύνασθαι ὑπενεγκεῖν. This τοῦ with the infinitive to express purpose or result * is very frequent in Luke (i. 77, 79, ii. 24, where see note) and not rare in Paul (Gal. iii. 10 ; Phil. iii. 10 ; Rom. i. 24, vi. 6, vii. 3, viii. 12, xi. 8, 10). Ὑποφέρειν means 'to bear up under,' 'to endure patiently' (2 Tim. iii. 11 ; 1 Pet. ii. 19 ; Prov. vi. 33 ; Ps. lxix. 7 ; Job ii. 10). Temptation is probation, and God orders the probation in such a way 'that ye may be able to endure it.' The *power* to endure is given σὺν τῷ πειρασμῷ, the endurance is not given ; that depends on

---

* J. H. Moulton (*Gr.* I. p. 217) prefers to call this use of τοῦ *c. infin.* 'epexegetic,' and thinks that "when Paul wishes to express purpose he uses other means." Bachmann makes τοῦ δύνασθαι the genitive of the substantival infinitive, dependent on ἔκβασιν, 'the escape of being able to bear it' ; *i.e.* the ἔκβασις consists in the power to endure.

ourselves. On the liturgical addition to the Prayer, 'Lead us not into temptation *which we are not able to bear*,' see Resch, *Agrapha*, pp. 85, 355 ; Hastings, *DB*. III. p. 144.

Cassian (*Inst*. v. 16) says that "some not understanding this testimony of the Apostle have read the subjunctive instead of the indicative mood : *tentatio vos non apprehendat nisi humana*" (so Vulg.). The verse is a favourite one with Cassian.

A few texts insert οὐ before δύνασθε and ὑπενεγκεῖν after it : a few insert ὑμᾶς before or after ὑπενεγκεῖν : ℵ* A B C D* F L P 17 omit ὑμᾶς.

14-22. *The Lord's Supper and the Jewish sacrifices may convince you of the fact that to participate in a sacrificial feast is to participate in worship. Therefore, avoid all idol-feasts, which are a worship of demons.*

¹⁴ Yes, God provides escapes from temptations, and so my affection for you moves me to urge you to escape from temptation to idolatry ; avoid all contact with it. ¹⁵ I appeal to your good sense ; you are capable of judging for yourselves whether my arguments are sound.

¹⁶ The cup of the blessing, on which we invoke the benediction of God in the Lord's Supper, is it not a means of communion in the Blood-shedding of Christ? The bread which we break there, is it not a means of communion in the Body of Christ ? ¹⁷ Because the many broken pieces are all one bread, we, the assembled many, are all one body ; for we, the whole congregation, have with one another what comes from the one bread. ¹⁸ Here is another parallel. Consider the Israelites, as we have them in history with their national ritual. Is it not a fact that those Israelites who eat the prescribed sacrifices enter into fellowship with the altar of sacrifice, and therefore with Him whose altar it is ? The altar unites them to one another and to Him. ¹⁹ You ask me what I imply by that. Not, of course, that there is any real sacrifice to an idol, or that there is any real idol, such as the heathen believe in. ²⁰ But I do imply that the sacrifices which the heathen offer they offer to demons and to a no-god : and I do not wish you to enter into fellowship with the company of demons. ²¹ Is my meaning still not plain ? It is simply impossible that you should drink of a cup that brings you into communion with the Lord and of a cup that brings you into communion with demons ; that you should eat in common with others at the table of the Lord

and at the table of demons. ^{22} Or do we think so lightly of this, that we persist in doing just what the Israelites did in the wilderness,—provoking the Lord to jealousy by putting Him on a level with demons? Are we able, any more than they were, to defy Him with impunity?

14. Διόπερ. Here and viii. 13 only. 'Wherefore, my beloved ones (the affectionate address turns the command into an entreaty), flee right away from idolatry.' Flight is the sure ἔκβασις in all such temptations, and they have it in their own power: all occasions must be shunned. They must not deliberately go into temptation and then expect deliverance. They must not try how near they can go, but how far they can fly. *Fugite idolatriam: omnem utique et totam* (Tert. *De Cor.* 10). This might seem a hard saying to some of them, especially after expecting a wide measure of liberty, and he softens it with ἀγαπητοί μου. It is his love for them that makes him seem to be severe and compels him to lay down this rule. Cf. xv. 58; 2 Cor. vii. 1; Phil. ii. 12, etc. St Paul more commonly has the simple accusative after φεύγειν (vi. 18; 1 Tim. vi. 11; 2 Tim. ii. 22), and it is not clear that φεύγειν ἀπό, which is more common in Gospels and Rev., is a stronger expression. The accusative would not have implied that the Corinthians were already involved in idolatry: that would require ἐκ.

15. ὡς φρονίμοις. Cf. iii. 1; Eph. v. 28. There is no sarcasm, as in 2 Cor. xi. 19. They have plenty of intelligence, and can see whether an argument is sound or not, so that *pauca verba sufficiunt ad judicandum* (Beng.). Yet there is perhaps a gentle rebuke in the compliment. They ought not to need any argument in a matter, *de quo judicium ferre non erat difficile* (Calv.). Resch, *Agrapha*, p. 127.

κρίνατε ὑμεῖς ὃ φημι. The ὑμεῖς is emphatic, and the change from λέγω to φημί should be marked in translation, although it may be made merely for variety; 'Judge for *yourselves* what I declare.' Vulg. has *loquor* and *dico*; in Rom. iii. 8 *aiunt* (φασί) and *dicere* (λέγειν).

16. Τὸ ποτήριον τῆς εὐλογίας. 'The cup of the blessing,' *i.e.* over which a benediction is pronounced by Christian ministers, as by Christ at the Last Supper. It does not mean 'the cup which brings a blessing,' as is clear from what follows. We know too little about the ritual of the Passover at the time of Christ to be certain which of the Paschal cups was the cup of the Institution. There was probably a Paschal 'cup of the thanksgiving' or 'blessing,' and the expression here used may come from that, but the addition of 'which we bless' in our Christian assemblies shows that the phrase is used with a fuller meaning. Cf. ποτήριον σωτηρίου (Ps. cxv. 4). Εὐλογεῖν and εὐχαριστεῖν express two aspects of the same action : see on xi. 24. The plurals, εὐλογοῦμεν and κλῶμεν, do not necessarily mean that the whole congregation took part in saying the benediction or thanksgiving and in breaking the bread, except so far as the minister represented the whole body. The Apostle is speaking of Christian practice generally, without going into details. See notes on xi. 23–25, where he does give some details, and cf. Acts ii. 42, 46. Evans enlarges on the εὖ in εὐλογοῦμεν, 'over which we speak the word *for good*,' and concludes, "the bread and wine, after their benediction or consecration, are not indeed changed in their nature, but become in their use and their effects the very body and blood of Christ to the worthy receiver."

οὐχὶ κοινωνία ἐστὶν τ. αἷμ. τ. Χριστοῦ; 'Is it not communion in the Blood of Christ?' The RV. margin has 'participation in.' But 'partake' is μετέχειν : κοινωνεῖν is 'to have a share in'; therefore κοινωνία is 'fellowship' rather than 'participation.' This is clear from what follows respecting the bread. It is better not to put any article before 'communion' or 'fellowship.' AV. has 'the,' which is justifiable, for κοινωνία, being the predicate, does not need the article. RV. has 'a,' which is admissible, but is not needed. Strangely enough, Vulg. varies the translation of this important word; *communicatio sanguinis*, but *participatio corporis: communio* (Beza) is better than either. As κοινωνεῖν is 'to give a share to' as well as 'to have a share in,' *communicatio* is a possible rendering of κοινωνία. The difference between 'participation' and 'fellowship' or 'communion' is the difference between having a share and having the whole. In Holy Communion each recipient has a share of the bread and of the wine, but he has the whole of Christ : οὐ γὰρ τῷ μετέχειν μόνον καὶ μεταλαμβάνειν ἀλλὰ τῷ ἑνοῦσθαι κοινοῦμεν (Chrys.).*

Here, as in Luke xxii. 17, and in the *Didache* 9, the cup is mentioned first, and this order is repeated *v.* 21 ; but in the account of the Institution (xi. 23) the usual order is observed. This may be in order to give prominence to the Blood-shedding, the characteristic act of Christ's sacrifice, and also to bring the

---

* Ellicott says that this distinction between μετέχειν and κοινωνεῖν "cannot be substantiated. All that can properly be said is that κοινωνεῖν implies more distinctly the idea of a community with others" : and that is sufficient. See Cremer, p. 363. Lightfoot points out the caprice of AV. in translating κοινωνοί first 'partakers' and then 'have fellowship,' while κοινωνία is 'communion,' and μετέχειν is 'to be partakers' (*On Revision*, p. 39).

eating of the bread into immediate juxtaposition with the eating at heathen sacrifices. As regards construction, τὸ ποτήριον and τὸν ἄρτον are attracted to the case of the relatives which follow.

ὃν κλῶμεν. It is clear from εὐχαριστήσας (xi. 24) that St Paul does not mean to limit εὐλογοῦμεν to the cup: there was a benediction or thanksgiving over this also. There is no action with regard to the cup which would be parallel to breaking the bread, and therefore we cannot say that κλῶμεν is equivalent to, or a substitute for, εὐλογοῦμεν. Nor would "πίνομεν correspond to κλῶμεν": eating would correspond to drinking, and both are assumed. The transition from the Body of Christ to the Church, which in another sense is His Body, is easily made, but it is not made here: that comes in the next verse.

It is evident from xi. 18 f. that the mention of the cup before the bread here does not imply that in celebrating the rite the cup ever came first. Here he is not describing the rite, but pointing out a certain similarity between the Christian rite and pagan rites. Ramsay (*Exp. Times*, March 1910, p. 252) thinks that he names the cup first "partly because the more important part of the pagan ceremony lay in the drinking of the wine, and partly because the common food in the pagan ceremony was not bread, but something eaten out of a dish," which was one and the same for all. To this we may add that in the heathen rite it seems to have been usual for each worshipper to bring his own loaf. The worshippers drank out of the same cup and took sacrificial meat out of the same dish, but they did not partake of the same bread: εἷς ἄρτος was not true of them (Hastings, *DB*. v. p. 132 b). This is said to be "the usual practice of simple Oriental meals, in which each guest has his own loaf, though all eat from a common dish." There was therefore less analogy between the heathen bread and the Christian bread than between the heathen cup and the Christian cup, and for this reason also the cup may have been mentioned first. For this reason again he goes on (*v.* 17) to point out the unity implied in the bread of the Christian rite. The single loaf is a symbol and an instrument of unity, a unity which obliterates the distinction between Jew and Gentile and all social distinctions. There is only one Body, the Body of Christ, the Body of His Church, of which each Christian is a member. That is the meaning of 'This is My Body.'

The main point to which the Apostle is leading his readers, is that to partake ceremonially of the Thing Sacrificed is to become a sharer in the Sacrificial Act, and all that that involves.

It is not easy to decide whether the first ἐστιν should follow κοινωνία (A B P, Copt. Arm.) or Χριστοῦ (ℵ C D E F G K L, Latt.). Probably the latter order arose through assimilation to the position of the second

FIRST EPISTLE TO THE CORINTHIANS

ἐστίν. A and a few other authorities put the second ἐστιν after the second κοινωνία, probably for assimilation. אֵ B C D F K L P have the second ἐστιν after Χριστοῦ. For the second Χριστοῦ, D* F, Latt. have Κυρίου.

17. ὅτι εἷς ἄρτος, ἓν σῶμα οἱ πολλοί ἐσμεν. It is not difficult to get good sense out of these ambiguous words, but it is not easy to decide how they should be translated. Fortunately the meaning is much the same, whichever translation is adopted. The ὅτι may = 'because' and introduce the protasis, of which ἓν σῶμα . . . ἐσμεν is the apodosis; 'Because there is one bread, one body are we the many,' *i.e.* Because the bread, although broken into many pieces, is yet one bread, we, although we are many, are one body. Vulg. seems to take it in this way; *quoniam unus panis, unum corpus multi sumus.** The awkwardness of this is that there is no particle to connect the statement with what precedes. The Syriac inserts a 'therefore'; 'as, therefore, that bread is one, so are we one body.' Or (better) ὅτι may = 'for' (AV.), or 'seeing that' (RV.), and be the connecting particle that is required; 'Seeing that we, who are many, are one bread, one body' (RV.). But, however we unravel the construction, we have the parallel between many fragments, yet one bread, and many members, yet one body. See Lightfoot on Ign. *Eph.* 20, where we have πάντες συνέρχεσθε ἐν μιᾷ πίστει καὶ ἑνὶ Ἰησοῦ Χριστῷ followed by ἕνα ἄρτον κλῶντες. See also *Philad.* 4. The Apostle's aim is to show that all who partake of the one bread have fellowship with Christ. This is plain from what follows. See Abbott, *The Son of Man*, p. 496.

οἱ γὰρ πάντες ἐκ τοῦ ἑνὸς ἄρτου μετέχομεν. 'For we all have our share from the one bread,' *i.e.* the bread which is the means of fellowship with Christ. Nowhere else have we μετέχειν with ἐκ: the usual construction is the simple genitive (21, ix. 12), which may be understood (30, ix. 10); but compare ἐκ in xi. 28. The meaning seems to be that we all have a share which is taken from the one bread, and there is possibly a suggestion that the one bread remains after all have received their shares. . All have communion with the Body, but the Body is not divided. The idea of Augustine, that the one loaf composed of many grains of corn is analogous to the one body composed of many members, however true in itself, is foreign to this passage. We have the same idea in the *Didache* 9; "As this broken bread was scattered (as grain) upon the mountains and gathered together became one, etc." "*How* the sacramental bread becomes in its use and effects the body of Christ, is a thing that passes all understanding:

* *Quoniam unus est panis, unum corpus nos, qui multi sumus* (Beza). *Weil Ein Brod es ist das wir brechen, sind Ein Leib wir, die Vielen* (Schmiedel).

the *manner* is a mystery" (Evans). He adds that οἱ πάντες = 'all as one,' 'all the whole congregation.' It is remarkable how St Paul insists upon the *social* aspect of both the sacraments; 'For in one Spirit were we all baptized *into one body*' (xii. 13).

18. The sacrifices of the Jews furnish a similar argument to show that participation in sacrificial feasts is communion with the unseen.

βλέπετε τὸν Ἰσραὴλ κατὰ σάρκα. 'Look at Israel after the flesh,' the actual Israel of history. Christians are a new Israel, Israel after the Spirit, τὸν Ἰσραὴλ τοῦ Θεοῦ (Gal. vi. 16, iii. 29; Phil. iii. 3), whether Jews or Gentiles by birth.

οὐχ οἱ ἐσθίοντες κ.τ.λ. 'Are not they who eat the sacrifices in fellowship with the altar?' They are in fellowship with the altar, and therefore with the unseen God, whose altar it is. To swear by the Temple is to swear by Him that dwelleth therein (Matt. xxiii. 21), and to have fellowship with the altar is to have fellowship with Him whose sacrifices are offered thereon. As in the Holy Communion, therefore, so also in the Temple services, participating in sacrificial feasts is sacrificial fellowship with an unseen power, a power that is Divine. There is something analogous to this in the sacrificial feasts of the heathen; but in that case the unseen power is not Divine. See Lev. vii. 6, 14, vi. 26, and Westcott on Heb. xiii. 10.

19. τί οὖν φημι; 'What then do I declare?' This refers back to the φημί in *v.* 15 and guards against apparent inconsistency with viii. 4. 'Do I declare that a thing sacrificed to an idol is something, or that an idol is something?' In neither case was there reality. The εἰδωλόθυτον professed to be an offering made to a god, and the εἴδωλον professed to represent a god. Both were shams. The εἰδωλόθυτον was just a piece of flesh and nothing more, and its being sacrificed to a being that had no existence did not alter its quality; the meat was neither the better nor the worse for that. The εἴδωλον was just so much metal, or wood, or stone, and its being supposed to represent a being that had no existence did not alter its value; it was neither more nor less useful than before. As a sacrifice to a god, and as the image of a god, the εἰδωλόθυτον and the εἴδωλον had no reality, for there was no such being as Aphrodite or Serapis. Nevertheless, there was something behind both, although not what was believed to be there.

AV., following KL, Syrr., has 'idol' first; and, without authority, inserts the article, 'the idol.' ℵ B C D E P, Vulg. Copt. Arm. Aeth. have ὅτι εἰδωλόθυτον . . . ὅτι εἴδωλον. The accentuation of Tisch., ὅτι εἰδωλόθυτον τι ἔστιν, ἢ ὅτι εἴδωλόν τι ἔστιν, is probably wrong: better, τί ἐστιν in each case ; 'that it is *something*' (*aliquid*) is the meaning, not 'that any such thing exists.' The omission of ἢ ὅτι εἴδωλόν τί ἐστιν (א* A C*) is no doubt owing to homoeoteleuton, τί ἐστιν to τί ἐστιν.

20. ἀλλ᾽ ὅτι ἃ θύουσιν τὰ ἔθνη. 'But (what I do declare is) that the things which the Gentiles sacrifice.' Here (according to the best texts), as in Rom. ii. 14, xv. 27, ἔθνη has a plural verb: in Rom. ix. 30 it has the singular. As τὰ ἔθνη are animate and numerous, the plural is natural. On the history of the term ἔθνος see Kennedy, *Sources*, p. 98.

δαιμονίοις καὶ οὐ θεῷ θύουσιν. The Apostle seems to have LXX of Deut. xxxii. 17, ἔθυσαν δαιμονίοις καὶ οὐ θεῷ, θεοῖς οἷς οὐκ ᾔδεισαν, 'They sacrificed to demons (*Shêdim*) and to a no-god, to gods whom they knew not,' in his mind. That καὶ οὐ θεῷ means 'and to a no-god' rather than 'and not to God' is confirmed by Deut. xxxii. 21 ; αὐτοὶ παρεζήλωσάν με ἐπ᾽ οὐ θεῷ . . . κἀγὼ παραζηλώσω αὐτοὺς ἐπ᾽ οὐκ ἔθνει, 'They have made me jealous with a no-god . . . and I will make them jealous with a no-people'; see Driver's notes. In Bar. iv. 7 we have the same expression, probably based on Deut. xxxii. 17 ; θύσαντες δαιμονίοις καὶ οὐ θεῷ 'by sacrificing to demons and no-god.' The *Shêdim* are mentioned nowhere else, excepting Ps. cvi. 37, a late Psalm, possibly of the Greek period : according to it human sacrifices were offered to the *Shêdim* ; see Briggs *ad loc*. In Ps. xcvi. 5, 'All the gods of the nations are idols,' LXX πάντες οἱ θεοὶ τῶν ἐθνῶν δαιμόνια, the word rendered 'idols' and δαιμόνια means 'things of nought' (Lev. xix. 4, xxvi. 1 ; Ps. xcvii. 7 ; cf. Is. xl. 18 f., xliv. 9 f.). Asmodaeus, the evil spirit of Tob. iii. 8, vi. 14, is called in the Aram. and Heb. versions 'king of the Shêdim'; and it is possible that St Paul has the *Shêdim* in his mind here. See Edersheim, *Life and Times*, II. pp. 759–763. Here, the translation, 'and not to God,' introduces a thought which is quite superfluous : there was no need to declare that sacrifices to idols are not offered to God. But 'to a no-god' has point, and is probably a reminiscence of O.T The Apostle is showing that taking part in the sacrificial feasts of the heathen involves two evils,—sharing in the worship of a thing-of-nought, and (what is still worse) having fellowship with demons. This latter point is the main thing, and it is expressly stated in what follows. See Hastings, *DB*. art. 'Demon'; Thackeray, p. 144. The primitive and wider-spread idea that there is, in sacrifice, communion between deity and worshippers, and between the different worshippers, greatly aided St Paul in his teaching.

The idea that evil spirits are worshipped, when idols which represent non-existent pagan deities are worshipped, was common among the Jews, and passed over from them into the Christian Church, with the support ot various passages in both O.T. and N.T.   In addition to those quoted above may be mentioned Is. xiii. 21, xxxiv. 14, where both AV. and RV. have 'satyrs' and LXX δαιμόνια.   In Lev. xvii. 7 and 2 Chron. xi. 15, AV. has 'devils,' RV. 'he goats,' RV. marg. 'satyrs,' and LXX μάταια: see Curtis on 2 Chron. xi. 15.   In Enoch xcix. 7, "Others will make graven images of gold and silver and wood and clay, and others will worship impure spirits and demons and all kinds of superstitions not according to knowledge," quoted by Tertullian (De Idol. 4).   Book of Jubilees i. 11, "They will worship each his own (image), so as to go astray, and they will sacrifice their children to demons"; and again, xxii. 17, "They offer their sacrifices to the dead and they worship evil spirits."   In Rev. ix. 20, ἵνα μὴ προσκυνήσουσιν τὰ δαιμόνια καὶ τὰ εἴδωλα. In the Gospels, and probably in the Apocalypse, δαιμόνια seem to be the same as πνεύματα ἀκάθαρτα, and that is likely to have been St Paul's view. The close connexion between idolatry and impurity would point to this (see Weinel, St Paul, pp. 31–34).   By entering into fellowship with demons or unclean spirits, they were exposing themselves to hideous temptations of terrific violence.

οὐ θέλω δὲ κ.τ.λ.   'And I do not wish that you should become fellows of the demons': 'have fellowship with' (AV.) or 'have communion with' (RV.) does not give the force of γίνεσθαι. The article shows that 'the demons' are regarded here as a *society*, into which the worshipper of idols is admitted.

The text of *v.* 20 has been much varied by copyists, and some points remain doubtful.   θύουσιν (א A B C D E F G P) is to be preferred to θύει (K L), which is a grammatical correction in both places.   After the first θύουσιν, א A C K L P, Vulg. Syrr. Copt. have τὰ ἔθνη: B D E F omit. WH. bracket.   The second θύουσιν follows καὶ οὐ θεῷ (א A B C P, Arm.), not precedes (D E F G, Vulg. Syrr. Copt.).   For κοινωνοὺς τῶν δαιμονίων, D* E F G have δαιμονίων κοινωνούς.   For γίνεσθαι, F, Syrr. Copt. have εἶναι.

21. οὐ δύνασθε.   Of course it is not meant that there is any impossibility in going to the Lord's Supper, and then going to an idol-feast: but it is morally impossible for one who has real fellowship with Christ to consent to have fellowship with demons. For one who does so consent οὐκ ἔστιν κυριακὸν δεῖπνον φαγεῖν. Only those who do not realize what the Supper is, or do not realize what an idol-feast is, could think of taking part in both: cf. 2 Cor. vi. 15; Matt. vi. 24.   The genitives may be possessive genitives, but the context indicates that they mean 'the cup which brings you into fellowship with,' genitives of relation.

τραπέζης Κυρίου.   In Mal. i. 7, 12, 'My table,' *i.e.* the Lord's table, means the altar; see also Ezek. xli. 22, xliv. 16.   Here it can only mean the Lord's Supper, 'table' (as often) including what was on it, especially food; hence the expression, τραπέζης μετέχειν.   Wetstein quotes Diod. iv. 74, μετασχὼν κοινῆς τραπέζης. Deissmann (New Light on the N.T., p. 83; see also Light, p. 355) quotes the invitation to "dine at the κλίνη of the Lord Serapis in the house of Cl. Serapion."   Probably from this

passage, and perhaps also from Luke xxii. 30, 'the Lord's Table'
came to mean the Lord's Supper. Augustine calls it 'the table
of Christ' and 'that great table'; Ambrose and Gregory
Nazianzen, 'the mystical table'; etc.

22. ἢ παραζηλοῦμεν τὸν Κύριον; A reminiscence of Deut.
xxxii. 21 quoted above; see on Rom. x. 19, xi. 11 : 'Or are we
provoking the Lord to jealousy?' 'Is that what we are engaged
in—trying whether the Lord will suffer Himself to be placed on
a level with demons?' In Deut. 'the Lord' of course means
Jehovah, and some understand it so here; but *v.* 21 almost
necessitates a reference to Christ. The ἢ introduces the alternative, 'Or (if you think that you *can* eat of Christ's table and of
the table of demons) are we going to provoke His jealousy?'

μὴ ἰσχυρότεροι αὐτοῦ ἐσμεν; 'Surely we are not stronger than
He?' His anger cannot be braved with impunity; Job ix. 32,
xxxvii. 23; Eccles. vi. 10; Isa. xlv. 9; Ezek. xxii. 14; some of
which passages may have been in the Apostle's mind when he
thus reduced such an argument εἰς ἄτοπον. It is as when
Jehovah answers Job out of the whirlwind. Cf. i. 13.

x. 23–xi. 1. *Idol-meats need not always be avoided, but
brotherly love limits Christian freedom. Abstain from idol-
meats when an over-scrupulous brother tells you that they
have been sacrificed to idols. In this and in all things seek
God's glory. That is my rule, and it keeps one from injuring
others. And it is my rule because it is Christ's.*

[23] As was agreed before, In all things one may do as one
likes, but not all things that one may do do good. In all things
one may do as one likes, but not all things build up the life of
the Church. [24] In all open questions, it is the well-being of the
persons concerned, and not one's own rights, that should determine one's action.

[25] See how this works in practice. Anything that is on sale
in the meat-market buy and eat, asking for no information that
might perplex your conscience; [26] for the meat in the market,
like everything else in the world, is the Lord's, and His children
may eat what is His without scruple. [27] Take another case. If
one of the heathen invites some of you to a meal, and you care
to go, anything that may be set before you eat, asking for no
information, as before. [28] But if one of your fellow-guests should
think it his duty to warn you and say, This piece of meat has
been offered in sacrifice, then refrain from eating it, so as to

avoid shocking your informant and wounding conscience. [29] Of course I do not mean your own conscience, but the conscience of the over-scrupulous brother who warned you. For to what purpose should I, by using my liberty, place myself in a false position, judged by the conscience of another? [30] Fancy 'saying grace' for food which causes offence and involves me in blame!

[31] In short, that aim solves all these questions. Whether you are eating or drinking or doing anything else, let your motive always be the promotion of God's glory. [32] Beware of putting difficulties in the way of Jews by ill-considered liberty, or of Greeks by narrow-minded scruples, or of the Church of God by unchristian self-seeking. [33] That is just my own principle. I try to win the approval of everybody in everything, not aiming at my own advantage, but at that of the many, that they may be saved from perdition. [1] In this I am only following in the footsteps of Christ. Will not you follow in mine?

The whole discussion of εἰδωλόθυτος, accordingly, issues in three distinct classes of cases, for each of which St Paul has a definite solution:

(1) Eating at sacrificial feasts. This is idolatry, and absolutely forbidden.

(2) Eating food bought in the shops, which may or may not have an idolatrous history. This is unreservedly allowed.

There remains (3) the intermediate case of food at non-ceremonial feasts in private houses. If no attention is drawn to the "history" of the food, this class falls into class (2). But if attention is pointedly called to the history of the food, its eating is prohibited, not as *per se* idolatrous, but because it places the eater in a false position, and confuses the conscience of others.

23. Πάντα ἔξεστιν. A return, without special personal reference, to the principle stated (or perhaps quoted) in vi. 12; where see notes. Of course he means all things *indifferent*, with regard to which a Christian has freedom. He repeats this principle, with its limitation, before dealing finally with the question of idol-meats. See Moffatt, *Lit. of N.T.*, p. 112.

οὐ πάντα οἰκοδομεῖ. This explains οὐ πάντα συμφέρει. There are some things which do not build up either the character of the individual, or the faith which he professes, or the society to which he belongs. A liberty which harms others is not likely to benefit oneself, and a liberty which harms oneself is not likely to benefit others. Cf. xiv. 26; Rom. xiv. 19.

Before ἔξεστιν, in both clauses, ℵ³ H K L, Syrr. AV. insert μοι from vi. 12: ℵ* A B C* D E, Am. Copt. omit.   Through homoeoteleuton, πάντα to πάντα, F G omit the first clause and 17 omits the second.

24. μηδεὶς τὸ ἑαυτοῦ ζητείτω. This is the practice which really συμφέρει and οἰκοδομεῖ: 'Let no one seek his own good.' The prohibition is, of course, relative: seeking one's own good is not always wrong, but it is less important than seeking the good of others; and when the two conflict it is one's own good that must give way: cf. *v.* 33, vi. 18; Luke x. 20, xiv. 12, 13, xxiii. 28.

ἀλλὰ τὸ τοῦ ἑτέρου. The μηδείς of course is not the subject, but ἕκαστος, understood from the μηδείς. Such ellipses are as common in English as in Greek. Here, as in iii. 7 and vii. 19, the ἀλλά implies the opposite of the previous negative. Here, D² E K L add ἕκαστος after ἑτέρου. The Apostle now returns to viii. 1-13 to finish the subject.

25. ἐν μακέλλῳ. The word occurs nowhere else in Biblical, and is rare in classical, Greek; = *macellum*, which may be derived from *macto* = 'slaughter' or *maceria* = 'enclosure.' It means 'provision-market,' and especially 'meat-market.' Probably a great deal of the meat offered for sale (πωλούμενον) came from the sacrifices, especially what was sold to the poor. See Deissmann, *Light*, p. 274.

μηδὲν ἀνακρίνοντες. 'Making no inquiry' as to whether the meat had been offered in sacrifice. It is not likely that the meaning is, 'not examining any piece of meat,' because of *v.* 27 In the market, it might be possible to distinguish sacrificial meat, but not after it had been served at table.

διὰ τὴν συνείδησιν. 'Out of regard to conscience.' Is this clause to be taken with μηδὲν ἀνακρίνοντες, or with ἀνακρίνοντες only? If the latter, the meaning is 'making no conscientious inquiries,' asking no questions prompted by a scrupulous conscience. Had the order been μηδὲν διὰ τ. συν. ἀνακρ., this would no doubt be the meaning. As the words stand, the former construction is better; 'For the sake of your conscience making no inquiry,' asking no questions which might trouble conscience. It is not wise to seek difficulties. The connexion with ἐσθίετε, 'eat, because your conscience is an enlightened one,' may safely be rejected.

26. τοῦ Κυρίου γάρ. Quotation from Ps. xxiv. 1 to justify the advice just given. The emphasis is on τοῦ Κυρίου, 'To the *Lord* belongs the earth.' Meat does not cease to be God's creature and possession because it has been offered in sacrifice: what is His will not pollute any one. This agrees with Mark vii. 19, καθαρίζων πάντα τὰ βρώματα, and with Acts x. 15, ἃ ὁ

Θεὸς ἐκαθάρισεν. It is stated that the words here quoted are used by Jews as grace at meals. Whether or no they were so used in St Paul's day, the principle laid down in 1 Tim. iv. 4 was recognized; 'Every creature of God is good, and nothing to be rejected, if it be received with thanksgiving.'

τὸ πλήρωμα αὐτῆς. 'That which fills it,' 'its contents.' See J. A. Robinson, *Ephesians*, p. 259. Cf. Ps. xcvi. 11, 'The sea and all that therein is,' ἡ θάλασσα καὶ τὸ πλήρωμα αὐτῆς.

27. καλεῖ ὑμᾶς. The pronoun here has a slight change of meaning. He has been addressing all the Corinthian Christians, but this ὑμᾶς can only mean 'some of you.' All of them had heathen acquaintances, one of whom might invite several of them. And the emphasis is on καλεῖ : he suggests that without an express invitation they surely would not go.

καὶ θέλετε πορεύεσθαι. 'And you care to go': an intimation that he does not advise their going, though he does not forbid it ; *satius fore si recusarent* (Calv.).

πᾶν τὸ παρατιθέμενον. Placed first with emphasis, like πᾶν τὸ ἐν μ. πωλ. : 'Anything that is put before you'; 'Anything that is for sale,' etc. Cf. Luke x. 8.

εἴ τις (א A B D* F G P, Latt.) is to be preferred to εἰ δέ τις (C D² E H K L, Syrr.).

28. ἐὰν δέ τις ὑμῖν εἴπῃ. The change from εἰ to ἐάν is perhaps intentional, although the difference between the two is less in late Greek than in earlier. 'If any one invites you,' a thing which is very possible and may have happened. 'If any one should say to you,' a pure hypothesis, and not so very probable. In Gal. i. 8, 9 we have a change from ἐάν to εἰ. See J. H. Moulton, *Gr.* p. 187. This shows clearly that the meal is a private one, and not such as is mentioned in viii. 10. The Apostle has already ruled that banquets ἐν εἰδωλίῳ must be avoided, and at such a banquet there would be no need to say Τοῦτο ἱερόθυτόν ἐστιν. It is less easy to decide who the speaker is. Certainly not the host, whose conscience would not be mentioned, but a fellow-guest. And we are almost certainly to understand a fellow-Christian, one of the 'weak' brethren, who, being scrupulous himself about such things, thinks that he ought to warn others of what he chances to know. That a heathen would do it out of malice, or amusement, or good-nature ("I dare say, you would rather not eat that"), is possible, but *his* conscience would hardly come into consideration. And his using ἱερόθυτον rather than εἰδωλόθυτον would seem to indicate that he was a Gentile Christian : when he was a heathen and regarded sacrifices to the gods as sacred, he would use ἱερόθυτον

and not εἰδωλόθυτον : and he uses the old word still.* It shows
how St Paul has realized the situation. The word occurs
nowhere else in Bibl. Grk. See Deissmann, *Light*, p. 355 n.

μὴ ἐσθίετε. This cannot mean 'Cease from eating.' As
ἐσθίετε (*v.* 25) means 'make a practice of eating,' μὴ ἐσθίετε
means 'make a practice of abstaining from eating.'

δι' ἐκεῖνον . . . καὶ τὴν συνείδησιν. We expect αὐτοῦ after
συνείδησιν, but the Apostle purposely omits to say whose conscience is considered, in order to leave an opening for the
emphatic statement which follows : 'out of regard to your
informant and to conscience.' He would be shocked, and the
shock would be a shock to conscience.

ἱερόθυτον (‭‭N‬ A B H, Sah.) is to be preferred to εἰδωλόθυτον (C D E F
G K L P, Copt. Arm.), which is a correction to a more usual and apparently
more correct term. There would be little temptation to change εἰδωλόθυτον
into ἱερόθυτον, which occurs nowhere else in N.T. or LXX. The AV.,
following H² K L, Goth., Chrys. Thdrt., adds from *v.* 26 'The earth is the
Lords,' etc. ‭N‬ A B C D E F G H* P, Latt. Copt. Aeth. Arm. omit.

29. συνείδησιν δὲ λέγω. 'Now by conscience I mean, not
one's own, but the other's,' not the guest's who received the
information, but the fellow-guest's who gave it. There is no
need to regard ἑαυτοῦ as second person ('thine own,' AV., RV.)
for σεαυτοῦ : it may be indefinite, 'one's own.' In the plural,
ἑαυτῶν, etc. is regularly used in N.T. for ἡμῶν αὐτῶν and ὑμῶν
αὐτῶν, etc. (xi. 31 ; Phil ii. 12, etc.) ; but, in the singular, there
is not one decisive example of this use. In Rom. xiii. 9 ; Gal.
v. 14 ; Matt. xxii. 39, σεαυτόν is the better reading ; in John
xviii. 34, σεαυτοῦ. Here, ἑαυτοῦ is the right reading.

ἵνα τί γὰρ ἡ ἐλευθερία μου ; The Apostle graphically puts
himself in the place of the Christian guest who has been placed
in a difficulty by the officiousness of his scrupulous informant ;
ex sua persona docet. ἵνα τί γάρ : the force of the ἵνα is lost
in most explanations of this clause (except Godet). ἵνα τί (see
small print) never means 'by what right,' but rather 'for what
object'? St Paul's main point in the context is μὴ ἐσθίετε, for
which γάρ introduces a reason : 'Eat not, . . . for what good
will you gain?' (cf. viii. 8). What follows is really a characteriza-
tion of the act of eating. The clue to the tense is in Rom. xiv. 16,
where the same verb, βλασφημεῖσθω, is used in a very similar
connexion, 'What good shall I gain by (eating, *i.e.*) by suffering
my liberty to incur judgment (as xi. 31 ; Rom. ii. 12 ; Acts xiii.

---

* See Origen (*Cels.* viii. 21 *sub init.*), where he says that Celsus would
call ἱερόθυτα what are properly called εἰδωλόθυτα, or, still better, δαιμονιόθυτα.
There is no improbability in a 'weak' Christian accepting the invitation of a
heathen. There would be plenty of food that had never been sacrificed : and
he might avoid the word εἰδωλόθυτον out of consideration for his entertainer.

27) at the hands of another's conscience? Why incur blame
for food for which I give thanks, if I "say grace" for it?' In the
last clause, the point is in the incongruity of 'saying grace' for
what places me in a false position; the structure exhibits a slight
logical inversion closely similar to that in Rom. vii. 16 (see
Introd. § on Style).

For ἑαυτοῦ (ℵ A B C D² E, etc.), D*, Latt. (*tuam*) have σεαυτοῦ, and H
has ἐμαυτοῦ, which are manifest corrections. For ἄλλης, F, d g Goth.,
Ambr. have ἀπίστου, which is wrong both as reading and as interpretation.

The interrogative ἵνα τί (with γένηται or γένοιτο understood) is found
in several places, both in N.T. (Matt. ix. 4, xxvii. 46; Luke xiii. 7; Acts
iv. 25, vii. 25) and in LXX (Ruth i. 11, 21; Ecclus. xiv. 3; 1 Mac. ii. 7);
also in Plato and Aristophanes. Cf. *ut quid?* and *in quid?* and *ad quid?*

30. εἰ ἐγὼ χάριτι μετέχω. 'If I with thanksgiving partake,
why do I receive reviling about that for which I give thanks?'
This suggests, if it does not imply, that one's being able to
thank God for it is evidence that the enjoyment is innocent.
One cannot thank God for a pleasure which one knows to be
wrong. The connexion between χάριτι and εὐχαριστῶ should be
preserved in translation. Apparently both refer to grace at
meals, and the meaning is that all food, whether sacrificial or
not, is sanctified, 'if it be received with thanksgiving,' μετὰ εὐχα-
ριστίας, ἁγιάζεται γὰρ διὰ λόγου Θεοῦ καὶ ἐντεύξεως (1 Tim. iv. 4).
Evans translates, 'If I with grace *said* have *meat* with others,
why am I evil spoken of *for having meat* for which I have said
grace?' AV. and RV. render χάριτι 'by grace,' which means
'by God's grace' (xv. 10), either His grace in providing food, or
His grace in enlightening the conscience (Chrys.). So also
Calvin; *quum Dei beneficium sit, quod omnia mihi licent.* But
this is less likely than 'thanksgiving.' See Ellicott.

The δέ between εἰ and ἐγώ (C D³ E H K L, Syrr.) may be safely
omitted (ℵ B D* F G P, Latt.). AV. has 'For,' which has no authority.
No connecting particle is required, and δέ interrupts the sense. In any
case ἐγώ is emphatic, 'If I for my part.' For χάριτι without the article cf.
Eph. ii. 5; Heb. ii. 9, xiii. 9.

31. Εἴτε οὖν ἐσθίετε. The οὖν gathers up the results of the long
discussion, and introduces a comprehensive principle which
covers this question and a great many other things. All is to
be done to God's glory; and this aim will be a good guide in
doubtful cases.* It has been suggested before, vi. 20.

εἴτε τι ποιεῖτε. 'Or do anything'; the active side of life as
distinct from enjoyment and refreshment. Cf. ὅ τι ἐὰν ποιῆτε,
πάντα ἐν ὀνόματι Κυρίου Ἰησοῦ, and ὃ ἐὰν ποιῆτε, ἐργάζεσθε ὡς τῷ

---

* Epictetus (Arr. *Dis.* ii. 19) says; "I have this purpose, to make you
free from constraint, compulsion, hindrance, to make you free, prosperous,
happy, looking to God in everything small and great," εἰς Θεὸν ἀφορῶντας ἐν
παντὶ μικρῷ καὶ μεγάλῳ.

Κυρίῳ (Col. iii. 17, 23). Foregoing our rights out of Christian charity would illustrate this. *Abstaining* from action, for a good motive, is included in τι ποιεῖτε as well as deeds, whether simple or heroic. Ignatius repeatedly has the phrase, εἰς τιμὴν Θεοῦ (Eph. 21 *bis*, *Smyrn.* 11, *Polyc.* 5; cf. *Magn.* 3, *Trall.* 12). Here again, as in *v.* 28, we have the refrain interpolated; 'For the earth is the Lord's,' etc. (C³). See Deissmann, *Light*, p. 459.

32. ἀπρόσκοποι γίνεσθε. 'Behave without giving offence,' 'prove yourselves to be averse to causing others to stumble'; *sine offensione estote* (Vulg.). The term here, as in Ecclus. xxxii. 21, is certainly transitive, 'not making to stumble': in Acts xxiv. 16 it is certainly intransitive, 'without stumbling': in Phil. i. 10 it may be either, but is probably intransitive. The use of the term here, in continuation of the great principle set forth in *v.* 31, shows that *refraining* from doing is much in his mind when he says εἴτε τι ποιεῖτε.

καὶ Ἰουδαίοις γ. καὶ Ἕλλησιν καὶ τῇ ἐκκλησίᾳ τοῦ Θεοῦ. These are three separate bodies; the third does not include the other two. Therefore unconverted Jews and unconverted Greeks are meant; they are οἱ ἔξω (v. 12), and it is an Apostolic principle that Christian conduct must be regulated with reference to those outside the Church as well as those within : ἵνα περιπατῆτε εὐσχη-μόνως πρὸς τοὺς ἔξω (1 Thess. iv. 12; cf. Col. iv. 5). An ill-advised exhibition of Christian freedom might shock Jews and an ill-advised rigour about matters indifferent might excite the derision of Greeks, and thus those who might have been won over would be alienated. In καὶ τῇ ἐκ. τοῦ Θ. (i. 2, xi. 16, 22, xv. 9) he is again thinking of the weak brethren who have needless scruples.* See on xii. 12.

καὶ Ἰουδαίοις γίνεσθε is the order in ℵ* A B C 17, Orig. There would be obvious temptation to correct to γίνεσθε τοῖς Ἰ., as in ℵ³ D E F G K L P; and versions follow suit.

33. καθὼς κἀγὼ . . . ἀρέσκω. 'Just as I also am ready to render service to all men in all things.' The rendering 'please' for ἀρέσκω is somewhat misleading, for it seems to mean that the Apostle habitually curried favour with every one and tried to be liked by all. Cf. Gal. i. 10. 'Please' is used from his own point of view of what ought to please.† Ἀρέσκειν is sometimes almost 'to be a benefactor to.' "In monumental inscriptions the words ἀρέσαντες τῇ πόλει, τῇ πατρίδι, etc. are used to describe those who have proved themselves of use to the commonwealth,

---

* There is no "harsh note of ecclesiasticism" here. It is the glory of God that is put in the first place, and, after that, the good of others.

† Ignatius recalls these words and iv. 1, when he writes (*Trall.* 2), δεῖ δὲ καὶ τοὺς διακόνους ὄντας μυστηρίων Ἰ. Χριστοῦ κατὰ πάντα τρόπον πᾶσιν ἀρέσκειν.

as in O. G. I. S. 646, 12, ἀρέσαντα τῇ τε αὐτῇ βουλῇ καὶ τῷ δήμῳ"
(Milligan on 1 Thess. ii. 4). What follows shows that his aim
was not popularity.

μὴ ζητῶν τὸ ἐμαυτοῦ σύμφορον. The conclusion shows what
kind of σύμφορον is meant, viz. spiritual profit. The saving of
his own soul is not his main object in life ; that would be a
refined kind of selfishness. He seeks his own salvation through
the salvation of others. The unity of the Church as the Body of
Christ is such that the spiritual gain of one member is to be
sought in the spiritual gain of the whole (*v.* 17, xii. 12, 25, 26).
It is for this reason that he prefers inspired preaching to speaking
in a Tongue (xiv. 4, 19). It is a commonplace among philosophers that the man who seeks his own happiness does not
find it : it is in seeking the happiness of others that each man
finds his own. See Phil. ii. 4 ; Rom. xv. 1. Josephus (*B.J.* iv.
v. 2) praises Ananus as πρὸ τῶν ἰδίων λυσιτελῶν τὸ κοινῇ συμφέρον
τιθέμενος.

ἵνα σωθῶσιν. As in ix. 22. This effort must be to the glory
of God, for it is carrying on His work (Col. i. 13, 14). Cf. i. 21 ;
1 Thess. ii. 16 ; 1 Tim. ii. 4. This shows what πᾶσιν ἀρέσκω means.

As in vii. 35, σύμφορον (א* A B C) is to be preferred to συμφέρον
(א³ D E F G K L P). Nowhere else in N.T. does σύμφορος occur ; in LXX
only 2 Mac. iv. 5. Hence the change to a more familiar word. In xii. 7,
συμφέρον is right : συμφέρειν is frequent.

XI. 1. The division of the chapters is unfortunate. This verse
clearly belongs to what precedes. He has just stated his own
principle of action, and he begs them to follow it, because it is
Christ's : *Hinc apparet, quam ineptae sint capitum sectiones* (Calv.).
There is no connexion with what follows.

μιμηταί μου γίνεσθε. 'Become imitators of me.' Excepting
Heb. vi. 12, μιμητής is in N.T. peculiar to Paul (iv. 16 ; Eph. v.
1 ; 1 Thess. i. 6, ii. 14): not found in LXX. Everywhere it is
joined with γίνεσθαι, which indicates moral effort; 'Strive to
behave as I do.' Everywhere the more definite 'imitator' (RV.)
is to be preferred to 'follower' (AV.) : '*Be* ye *followers* of me'
is doubly defective. Cf. ὥσπερ καὶ τῶν ἄλλων ἔργων οἱ διδάσκαλοι
τοὺς μαθητὰς μιμητὰς ἑαυτῶν ἀποδεικνύουσιν (Xen. *Mem.* 1. vi. 3).

καθὼς κἀγὼ Χριστοῦ. This addition dispels the idea that it is
in any spirit of arrogance that he asks them to imitate him ;
once more he is only asking them to do what he does himself,
to follow the example of one whom they recognized as their
teacher : *nihil praescribit aliis quoâ non prior observaverit ;
deinde se et alios ad Christum, tanquam unicum recte agendi
exemplar revocat* (Calv.). It is as an example of self-sacrifice
that he takes Christ as his model ; the whole context shows this.

And it is commonly this aspect of Christ's life that is regarded,
when He is put before us in N.T. as an example : Rom. xv. 2, 3 ;
2 Cor. viii. 9 ; Eph. v. 2 ; Phil. ii. 4, 5. "The details of His
life are not generally imitable, our calling and circumstances
being so different from His. Indeed, the question, 'What
would Jesus do?' may be actually misleading" (Goudge). The
wiser question is, ' Lord, what wilt Thou have me to do?' It is
seldom that St Paul mentions any of the details of our Lord's
life on earth, and it is therefore unlikely that he is thinking of
anything but the subject in hand—sacrificing one's own rights
and pleasures for the good of others. Nevertheless, the knowledge which St Paul displays of details is sufficient to show that
he knew a great deal more than he mentions, and exaggerated
statements have been made respecting his supposed ignorance.
See Knowling, *The Testimony of St Paul to Christ*, Lect. x. ;
Jacquier, *Histoire des Livres du N.T.*, II. 22–24 ; *The Fifth
Gospel*, pp. 75, 195 f. On the supposed difference between the
teaching of Christ and that of St Paul see Kaftan, *Jesus und
Paulus*, Tübingen 1906, esp. pp. 24, 32, 58 ; Walther, *Pauli
Christentum Jesu Evangelium*, Leipzig, 1908, esp. pp. 25–30 ;
Jülicher, *Paulus und Jesus*, Tübingen, 1907, esp. pp. 35 f.

XI. 2–XIV. 40. DISORDERS IN CONNEXION WITH PUBLIC WORSHIP AND THE MANIFESTATION OF SPIRITUAL GIFTS.

This constitutes the third * main division of the Epistle, and
it contains three clearly marked sections ; respecting (1) the
Veiling of Women, xi. 2–16 ; (2) Disorders connected with the
Lord's Supper, xi. 17–34 ; (3) Spiritual Gifts, especially Prophesying and Tongues, xii. 1–xiv. 40. At the outset there is a
possible reference to the Corinthians' letter to the Apostle ; but
the sections deal with evils which had come to his knowledge in
other ways.

XI. 2–16. The Veiling of Women in Public Worship.

*Although in respect of religion men and women are on
an equality, yet the Gospel does not overthrow the natural
ordinance, which is really of Divine appointment, that woman
is subject to man. To disavow this subjection before the congregation must cause grave scandal ; and such shamelessness
is condemned by nature, by authority, and by general custom.*

* The fourth, if the Introduction (i. 1–9) be counted.

[2] Now, as to another question, I do commend you for remembering me, as you assure me you do, in all things, and for loyally holding to the traditions just as I transmitted them to you. [3] But I should like you to grasp, what has not previously been mentioned, that of every man, whether married or unmarried, Christ is the head, while a woman's head is her husband, and Christ's head is God. [4] Every man, whether married or unmarried, who has any covering on his head when he publicly prays to God or expounds the will of God, thereby dishonours his head: [5] whereas every woman, whether married or unmarried, who has her head uncovered when she publicly prays to God or expounds the will of God, thereby dishonours her head; for she is then not one whit the better than the wanton whose head is shaven. [6] A woman who persists in being unveiled like a man should go the whole length of cutting her hair short like a man. But seeing that it is a mark of infamy for a woman to have her hair cut off or shorn, let her wear a veil. [7] A man has no right to cover his head; he is by constitution the image of God and reflects God's glory: whereas the woman reflects man's glory.

[8] Man was created first; he does not owe his origin to woman, but woman owes hers to him; [9] and, what is more, she was made for his sake, and not he for hers. [10] For this reason she ought, by covering her head, publicly to acknowledge her subjection. Even if she does not shrink from scandalizing men, she might surely fear to be an offence to angels.

[11] Nevertheless, this dependence of the woman has its limits: in the Lord neither sex has any exclusive privileges, but each has an equal share. [12] For as, at the first, the woman came into being from the man, so, ever since then, the man has come into being by means of the woman; and, like everything else, both are from God.

[13] Use your own powers of discernment. Is it decent that a woman should have her head uncovered when she publicly offers prayer to God? [14] Surely even nature itself teaches you that for a man to wear his hair long is degrading to him; [15] whereas this is a glory to a woman, because her long hair is God's gift to her, to serve her as a covering. [16] Yet, if any one is so contentious as to dispute this conclusion, it will suffice to say that both Christian authority and Christian usage are against him.

2. Ἐπαινῶ δὲ ὑμᾶς. 'Now I do praise you that in all things ye remember me and hold fast the delivered instructions exactly as I delivered them to you.' The verse is introductory to the whole of this division of the letter which treats of public worship. With his usual tact and generosity, the Apostle, before finding fault, mentions things which he can heartily and honestly praise.* The δέ marks the transition to a new topic, and perhaps from topics which the Corinthians had mentioned in their letter to others which he selects for himself. Ἐπαινῶ looks forward to οὐκ ἐπαινῶ which is coming (v. 17): here he can praise, in some other matters he cannot. He may be referring to his own letter (v. 9); 'Now, it is quite true that I praise you.' Or he may be referring to their letter, 'Now, I do praise you that, as you tell me, in all things you remember me'; comp. viii. 1. Primasius, in any case, gives the right key; *Quid erat, quod subito laudat quos ante vituperavit? Ubi legis auctoritatem non habet, blandimentis provocat ad rationem.* The translation, 'that ye remember everything of mine,' is possible but not probable: μέμνημαι : acc. is fairly common in classical Greek, but is not found in N.T. Both πάντα and καθὼς παρέδωκα ὑμῖν are emphatic: their remembrance of him was unfailing, and they observed with loyal precision what he had told them—by word of mouth or in the lost letter. Neither παραδίδωμι (in this sense) nor παράδοσις (Gal. i. 14; Col. ii. 8; 2 Thess. ii. 15, iii. 6) are common in the Pauline Epp. It is possible that in some of these passages, as in v. 23 and xv. 3, we have an allusion to some rudimentary creed which was given to missionaries and catechists †: comp. 2 Thess. ii. 5. There had been a Jewish παράδοσις of monstrous growth, and it had done much harm (Matt. xv. 6; Mark vii. 8; Gal. i. 14). There is now a Christian παράδοσις to supersede it, and it was from the first regarded as precious (1 Tim. vi. 20; 2 Tim. i. 14). See Mayor, *St Jude and 2 Peter*, pp. 23, 61; A. E. Burn, *Intr. to the Creeds*, ch. ii. This παράδοσις contained the leading facts of the Gospel and the teaching of Christ and the Apostles. As yet there were no written Gospels for St Paul to appeal to, although there may have been written collections of the Sayings of our Lord. For κατέχετε cf. xv. 2; 1 Thess. v. 21; Heb. x. 23; Luke viii. 15; and see Milligan, *Thessalonians*, p. 155. There may be a reference to v. 1; in this they are imitating him; or a reference to their own letter.

---

* Atto of Vercelli seems to be mistaken in saying, *Haec nempe verba per ironiam dicta sunt.* So also Herveius; *Per ironiam incipit loqui. His verbis plus illos tangit, quam si manifeste increparet eos. Quasi diceret; Vos obliti estis mei, et traditiones meas non tenetis, sed volo ut ista quae subjungo, sciatis.* There is no sarcasm. Cf. i. 4–9.

† See Basil *De Spir.* xxix. 71. The μέμνησθε rather implies a considerable time since he had been at Corinth. It may have been over two years.

The 'brethren' in AV., following D E F G K L, Latt., is an interpolation : א A B C P Copt. Arm. Aeth. omit.

3. θέλω δὲ ὑμᾶς εἰδέναι. 'But I would have you know'
something not previously mentioned, but of more importance
than they supposed, because of the principles involved. In Col.
ii. 1 we have the same formula, but more often οὐ θέλω ὑμᾶς
ἀγνοεῖν (x. 1, xii. 1; 2 Cor. i. 8; Rom. i. 13, xi. 25), which is
always accompanied by the affectionate address, ἀδελφοί. He
feels bound to insist upon the point in question, and perhaps
would hint that the Corinthians do not know everything.

παντὸς ἀνδρός. 'Of *every* man Christ is the head': παντός is
emphatic, every male of the human family. He says ἀνδρός rather
than ἀνθρώπου (xv. 45) to mark the contrast with γυνή, and he
takes the middle relationship first; 'man to Christ' comes
between 'woman to man' and 'Christ to God.' By κεφαλή is
meant supremacy, and in each clause it is the predicate ; ' Christ
is the head of man, man is the head of woman, and God is the
head of Christ': iii. 23; Eph. i. 22, iv. 15, v. 23, comp. Judg.
xi. 11; 2 Sam. xxii. 44. God is supreme in reference to the
Messiah as having sent Him. This was a favourite Arian text ;
it is in harmony with xv. 24–28, and, like that passage, it
implies more than the inferiority of Christ's human nature ;
John vi. 57. See Ellicott, 1 *Corinthians*, pp. 64, 65 ; H. St
J. Thackeray, *St Paul and Contemporary Jewish Thought*, p. 49 ;
Godet, *ad loc.*

4. προσευχόμενος ἢ προφητεύων κατὰ κεφαλῆς ἔχων. 'When he
prays or prophesies having (a veil) down over his head.' The
participles are temporal and give the circumstances of the case.
With κατὰ κεφ. ἔχων comp. λυπούμενος κατὰ κεφ. of Haman
(Esth. vi. 12), Vulg. *operto capite* ; here *velato capite*. The
'prophesying' means public teaching, admonishing or comfort-
ing ; delivering God's message to the congregation (xiii. 9, xiv. 1,
3, 24, 31, 39). Such conduct 'dishonours his head' because
covering it is a usage which symbolizes subjection to some
visible superior, and in common worship the man has none :
those who are visibly present are either his equals or his inferiors.
There is no reason for supposing that men at Corinth had been
making this mistake in the congregation. The conduct which
would be improper for men is mentioned in order to give point
to the censure on women, who in this matter had been acting as
men. It is doubtful whether the Jews used the *tallith* or veil
in prayer as early as this. We need not suppose that the
Apostle is advocating the Greek practice of praying bare-headed
in opposition to Jewish custom : he is arguing on independent
Christian principles. Tertullian's protest to the heathen (*Apol.*

30), that the Christians pray with head uncovered, because they have nothing to be ashamed of, is not quite in point here.

If in 'dishonoureth his head' (not 'Head') there is any allusion to Christ (*v.* 3), it is only indirect. The head, as the symbol of Christ, must be treated with reverence; so also the body (vi. 19), as the temple of the Spirit. And there may be a hint that, in covering his head in public worship, the man would be acknowledging some head other than Christ. See Edwards and Ellicott; also Art. 'Schleier' in Kraus, *Real-Ency. d. christ. Alt.* ii. p. 735.

5. 'Praying or prophesying' must be understood in the same way in both verses: it is arbitrary to say that the man is supposed to be taking the lead in full public worship, but the woman in mission services or family prayers. Was a woman to be veiled at family prayers? Yet in public worship women were not to speak at all (xiv. 34; 1 Tim. ii. 12). Very possibly the women had urged that, if the Spirit moved them to speak, they must speak; and how could they speak if their faces were veiled? In that extreme case, which perhaps would never occur, the Apostle says that they must speak veiled. They must not outrage propriety by coming to public worship unveiled because of the bare possibility that the Spirit may compel them to speak.* Comp. Philip's daughters (Acts xxi. 9), and the quotation from Joel (Acts ii. 18). In neither men nor women must prophesying be interpreted as speaking with Tongues. The latter was addressed to God and was unintelligible to most hearers; prophesying was addressed to the congregation. The women perhaps argued that distinctions of sex were done away in Christ (Gal. iii. 28), and that it was not seemly that a mark of servitude should be worn in Christian worship; or they may have asked why considerations about the head should lead to women being veiled and men not. And perhaps they expected that the Apostle who preached against the bondage of the Law would be in favour of the emancipation of women. See De Wette, *ad loc.*

The unveiled woman dishonours her head, because that is the part in which the indecency is manifested. Also by claiming equality with the other sex she disgraces the head of her own sex; she is a bare-faced woman, 'for she is one and the same thing (neut. Blass, *Gr.* § 31. 2) with the woman that is shaven,' either as a disgrace for some scandalous offence, or out of bravado. Aristoph. *Thesm.* 838; Tac. *Germ.* 19; and other illustrations in Wetst. The Apostle has married women chiefly

* See Harnack, *The Mission and Expansion of Christianity,* ii. pp. 65, 395-6, ed. 1902. See also Tert. *De Virgin vel.* 13; *De Orat.* 21.

in view. In Corinth anything questionable in Christian wives was specially dangerous, and the Gospel had difficulties enough to contend against without shocking people by breaches of usage Christianity does not cancel the natural ordinances of life; and it is by the original ordinance of God that the husband has control of the wife. Only here and *v.* 13 does ἀκατακάλυπτος occur in N.T. Having decided the matter in question (*vv.* 4, 5), St Paul now proceeds (*vv.* 6-16) to justify his decision.

6. If a woman refuses to be veiled, let her be consistently masculine and cut her hair close; no veil, short hair : the verbs are middle, not passive, and express her own action (Blass, *Gr.* § 55. 2). If she flings away the covering provided by Divine ordinance, let her also fling away the covering provided by nature (Chrys.). The combination of the aor. mid. with the pres. mid. (κείρασθαι ἢ ξυρᾶσθαι) is so unusual that some editors prefer ξύρασθαι, aor. mid. from ξύρω, a late form found in Plutarch (Veitch, *s.v.*; Blass, *Gr.* § 24).

7. The connexion between ὀφείλει (*v.* 10) and οὐκ ὀφείλει here must be marked : the woman is morally bound, the man is not morally bound, to veil his head. But 'not bound to' may be an understatement for 'bound not to'; comp. Acts xvii. 29 : St Paul can hardly mean that the man may please himself, while the woman may not—*magis liber est viro habitus capitis quam mulieri* (Beng.); for he has just said that the man puts his head to shame by covering it, as a woman puts her head to shame by not doing so. *Sicut vir professione libertatis caput suum honorat, ita mulier, subjectionis* (Calvin). The man *ought* not to wear a covering, 'since he is by original constitution (ὑπάρχων) God's image and glory,' reflecting the Creator's will and power, 'while the wife is her husband's glory.' This she is as a matter of fact (ἐστίν, not ὑπάρχει). See Abbott, *The Son of Man*, p. 674. She also was made κατ' εἰκόνα Θεοῦ, for in Gen. i. 26 ἄνθρωπον includes both sexes, but this fact is omitted here, because it is the relation of woman to man, not of woman to God, that is under consideration; and, as she has a superior, she does not so well represent Him who has no superior. Moreover, it is the son, rather than the wife, who is the εἰκών of the *man*. Comp. 1 Tim. ii. 13.

8, 9. Parenthetical, to confirm the statement that the woman is man's glory by an appeal to both initial (ἐκ) and final (διά *c. acc.*) causes. Woman was created *out of* man, and moreover (καὶ γάρ) *for* man, not *vice versa*. The articles in *v.* 9, τὴν γυναῖκα . . . τὸν ἄνδρα, may mean the woman and the man in Gen. ii. 18-22, Eve and Adam. For καὶ γάρ see Blass, § 78. 6.

10. διὰ τοῦτο. Because * man is a reflexion of the divine glory, while woman is only a reflexion of that reflexion, "there-fore the woman (generic) is morally bound to have [the mark of *his*] authority upon her head." The passage is unique, no satisfactory parallel having been found. There is no real doubt as to the meaning, which is clear from the context. The diffi-culty is to see why the Apostle has expressed himself in this extraordinary manner. That 'authority' (ἐξουσία) is put for 'sign of authority' is not difficult; but why does St Paul say 'authority' when he means 'subjection'? The man has the symbol of *authority*, no veil on his head; the woman has the symbol of *subjection*, a veil on her head. For ἐξουσία we should expect ὑποταγή (1 Tim. ii. 11, iii. 4, of the subjection of women), or ὑπειξις (Plut. 2. 751D of the subjection of women; comp. ὑπείκειν, Heb. xiii. 17), or ὑπακοή (Rom. v. 19, vi. 16, xvi. 19). Is it likely that St Paul would say the exact opposite of what he means? The words put in square brackets can scarcely be the true explanation. For conjectural emendations of ἐξουσίαν (all worthless) see Stanley, *ad loc.* p. 184.

In Rev. xi. 6, ἐξουσίαν ἔχουσιν ἐπὶ τῶν ὑδάτων means 'have control over the waters'; xiv. 18, ἔχων ἐξουσίαν ἐπὶ τοῦ πυρός, 'having control over fire'; xx. 6, ἐπὶ τούτων ὁ δεύτερος θάνατος οὐκ ἔχει ἐξουσίαν, 'over these the second death has no control.' Comp. Rom. ix. 21; 1 Cor. vii. 37; the LXX of Dan. iii. 30 (97). Can the meaning here be, 'ought to have control over her head,' so as not to expose it to indignity? If she unveils it, every one has control over it and can gaze at her so as to put her out of countenance. Her face is no longer under her own control.

Ramsay (*The Cities of St Paul,* pp. 202 ff.) scouts the common explanation that the 'authority' which the woman wears on her head is the authority to which she is subject, "a preposterous idea which a Greek scholar would laugh at any where except in the N.T." Following Thomson (*The Land and the Book,* p. 31) he explains thus. "In Oriental lands the veil is the power and the honour and dignity of the woman. With the veil on her head she can go anywhere in security and profound respect. She is not seen; it is a mark of thoroughly bad manners to observe a veiled woman in the street. She is alone. The rest of the people around are non-existent to her, as she is to them. She is supreme in the crowd. . . . But without the veil the woman is a thing of nought, whom any one may insult. . . . A

* One might say, 'Precisely for this reason,' διὰ τοῦτο being stronger than οὖν, and introducing a special, if an exclusive reason. This helps to decide the explanation of διὰ τοὺς ἀγγέλους, which must mean something that is at least a very important reason for women being veiled in public worship, if not the only reason.

woman's authority and dignity vanish along with the all-covering
veil that she discards. That is the Oriental view, which Paul
learned at Tarsus." In his Preface (vi.) Ramsay adds; "In the
Hebrew marriage ceremony, as it is celebrated in modern
Palestine, I am informed that the husband snatches off the
bride's veil and throws it on his own shoulder, as a sign that he
has assumed authority over her." Was Rebekah's veiling
herself a sign of subjection? Gen. xxiv. 65. See Glover, *The
Conflict of Religions in the Roman World*, p. 154.

διὰ τοὺς ἀγγέλους. These words have produced much
discussion, but there is not serious doubt as to their meaning.
They are not a gloss (Baur), still less is the whole verse an
interpolation (Holsten, Baljon). Marcion had the words, and
the evidence for them is overwhelming.* An interpolator would
have made his meaning clearer. Accepting them, we may
safely reject the explanation that 'angels' here mean the bishops
(Ambrose) or presbyters (Ephraem) or all the clergy (Primasius).
Nor can evil angels be meant (Tert. *De Virg. vel.* vii., xvii.); the
article is against it: οἱ ἄγγελοι always means good angels
(xiii. 1; Matt. xiii. 49, xxv. 31; Luke xvi. 22; Heb. i. 4, 5, etc.).
And the suggestion that the Apostle is hinting that unveiled
women might be a temptation to angels (Gen. vi. 1, 2) is somewhat childish. Is it to be supposed that a veil hides a human
face from angels, or that public worship would be the only
occasion when an unveiled woman might lead angels into
temptation? It is a mistake to quote the Testament of the
XII. Patriarchs (*Reuben* v. 6), or the Book of Jubilees (iv. 15,
22), or Theodotus (Frag. 44; C. R. Gregory, *Enleit. in d. N.T.*,
p. 151), in illustration of this passage. The meaning is plain. If
a woman thinks lightly of shocking men, she must remember
that she will also be shocking the angels, who of course are
present at public worship. Compare iv. 9, and ἐναντίον ἀγγέλων
ψαλῶ σοι (Ps. cxxxviii. 1), and 'O ye angels of the Lord, bless ye
the Lord' (Song of the Three Children, 37). Ancient liturgies
often bear witness to this belief, as does our own; "Therefore with
Angels and Archangels," etc., Chrysostom says, "Knowest thou
not that thou standest in the midst of the angels? with them
thou singest, with them thou chantest, and dost thou stand
laughing?" See Luke xv. 7, 10, xii. 8, 9.

One other suggestion is worth considering, viz. that διὰ τ.
ἀγγέλους might mean 'because the angels do so.' Angels, in
the presence of their direct and visible Superior, veil their faces

* St Paul assumes, as obvious to his readers, a connexion no longer
obvious to us. We can hardly regard the reason intended as falling outside
the scope of the διὰ τοῦτο (see above). The question is, what point of
contact for διὰ τ. ἀγγ. is furnished in *vv.* 3–9?

(Isa. vi. 2); a woman, when worshipping in the presence of her
direct and visible superior (man), should do the same.

Conjectural emendations (all worthless) are quoted by Stanley: see
also *Expositor*, 1st series, xi. p. 20. "None of the known emendations
can possibly be right; and the intrinsic and obvious difficulty is itself
enough to set aside the suggestion that the whole verse is an interpolation"
(WH. *App.* p. 116).

11. πλήν. Limitation. Although by original constitution
woman is dependent on man, yet he has no right to look down
on her. In the Christian sphere each is dependent on the other,
and both are dependent on God (viii. 6; Rom. xi. 36); and it
is only in the Christian sphere that woman's rights are duly
respected. Each sex is incomplete without the other.

ἐν Κυρίῳ. There can be no separation between man and
woman when both are members of Christ. Cf. for ἐν Κυρίῳ
1 Thess. iv. 1; 2 Thess. iii. 4; Gal. v. 10; Eph. iv. 17.

ℵ A B C D* D³ E F G H P, RV. have οὔτε γυνὴ χ. ἀ. before οὔτε ἀνὴρ
χ. γ. D³ K L, Vulg. AV. transpose the clauses.

12. This mutual dependence of the sexes is shown by the
fact that, although originally woman sprang from man, yet ever
since then it is through woman that man comes into existence:
if he is her initial cause (ἐκ), she is his instrumental cause
(διά c. gen.). But (another reason why man must not be contemptuous) the whole universe—man and woman and their
whole environment—owes its origin to God. Cf. xv. 27; Eph.
v. 23; and see Basil, *De Spiritu*, v. 12, xviii. 46.

13. In conclusion he asks two questions, the second of
which clinches the first. He appeals to their general sense of
propriety, a sense which is in harmony with the teaching of φύσις
and is doubtless inspired by φύσις. Their ideas of what is
πρέπον are in the best sense *natural*. It should be noted that
both in AV. and RV. the second question is brought to a close
too soon. The note of interrogation should be placed after
'it is a glory to her,' as in the Vulgate, Luther, Tyndale, and
Coverdale. Beza and others make three questions, breaking up
the second into two.

ἐν ὑμῖν αὐτοῖς κρίνατε. In their own inner judgment (vi. 2),
cannot they decide (x. 15)? 'Is it becoming that a woman
should pray to God unveiled?' Usually προσεύχομαι has no
case after it, but here τῷ Θεῷ is added to emphasize the principle that when she is addressing God she ought not to be
asserting her equality with men or trying to draw the attention
of men: comp. Matt. vi. 6. For πρέπον see Westcott on Heb
ii. 10.

14. A further argument, supporting the previous one. Instinctively they must feel the impropriety; and then external nature confirms the instinctive feeling. Even if the internal feeling should not arise, does not even nature by itself show that, while doubtless man, being short-haired, is by Divine order unveiled, woman, being long-haired, is by Divine order veiled? *Naturae debet respondere voluntas* (Beng.).* While fanaticism defies nature, Christianity respects and refines it; and whatever shocks the common feelings of mankind is not likely to be right. At this period, civilized men, whether Jews, Greeks, or Romans, wore their hair short. 'Long hair is a permanent endowment (δέδοται) of woman, to serve as an enveloping mantle' (Heb. i. 12 from Ps. ci. 27; Judg. viii. 26; Ezek. xvi. 13, xxvii. 7; Isa. lix. 17). Note the emphasis on ἀνήρ and γυνή, also on the clause introduced by δέ. Nowhere else in Biblical Greek does κομάω occur. Milligan, *Grk. Papyri*, p. 84.

16. This is best taken as concluding the subject of the veil; it makes a clumsy opening to the next subject. 'But if any one seemeth to be (or is minded to be)† contentious, *we* have no such custom, nor yet the Churches of God.' There are people who are so fond of disputing that they will contest the clearest conclusions, and the Corinthians were fond of disputation. But the Apostle will not encourage them. If such should question the dictates of decorum and of nature in this matter, they may be told that the teachers have no such usage as permitting women to be unveiled,—a thing unheard of in Christian congregations. It is possible that ἡμεῖς means only himself, but he probably means that he knows of no Apostle who allows this.‡

Throughout the section he appeals to *principles*. The wearing or not wearing a veil may seem to be a small matter. Everything depends upon what the wearing or not wearing implies, and what kind of sanction the one practice or the other can claim. He does not use δεῖ about the matter;

---

* Was the obscure metaphor of 'the veil,' which Dante (*Purg.* xxix. 27) uses of Eve, *Non sofferse di star sotto alcun velo*, suggested by the revolt of the women of Corinth against "standing under any veil" in public worship?

† Comp. iii. 18, viii. 2, and especially xiv. 37, where we have a summary conclusion similar to this.

‡ Herveius interprets ἡμεῖς as 'we Jews.' *Post rationes ponit auctoritatem, ut contentiosos vincat, quia neque Judaismus hoc habuit, nec Ecclesia Dei, ostendens quia neque Moyses neque Salvator sic tradidit.* Atto has the same idea. '*Nos' propter Judaeos, 'Ecclesia' dicit propter gentes. Quapropter, si hanc consuetudinem habetis, non solum non Christi, sed nec Moysi discipulos fore monstratis.* Nowhere else in N.T. or LXX is φιλόνεικος found, excepting Ezek. iii. 7, where all Israel are said to be such.

there is no intrinsic necessity (*v.* 19): but he does use both ὀφείλει (7, 10) and πρέπον ἐστί (13); for there is both moral obligation and natural fitness. His final appeal—to the practice of all congregations—would be of special weight in democratic Corinth. For αἱ ἐκκλησίαι τοῦ Θεοῦ comp. 2 Thess. i. 4. See Hort, *The Christian Ecclesia*, pp. 108, 117, 120. There is no need to conjecture that *v.* 16 is an interpolation, or that συνήθεια refers to contentiousness. Would St Paul think it necessary to say that Apostles have no habit of contentiousness?

For Greek and Roman customs respecting the hair and veils, see Smith, *Dict. of Ant.* Artt. 'Coma,' 'Flammeum,' 'Vestales.' The cases in which males, both Greek and Roman, wore long hair do not interfere with the argument.* Such cases were either exceptional or temporary; and they were temporary because nature taught men otherwise. For men to wear their hair long, and for women to wear it short, for men to veil their heads in public assemblies, and for women not to do so, were alike attempts to obliterate natural distinctions of sex. In the Catacombs the men are represented with short hair.

XI. 17–34. Disorders connected with the Lord's Supper.

There are abuses of a grave kind in your public worship; a chronic state of dissension, and gross selfishness and excess in your love-feasts and celebrations of the Lord's Supper. This profanation brings grievous judgments on you. Avert the judgments by putting a stop to the profanation.

¹⁷ Now, in giving you this charge about the veiling of women, I do *not* commend you that your religious gatherings do you more harm than good. ¹⁸ First of all, when you meet as a Christian congregation, you are split into sets :—so I am told, and to some extent I am afraid that it is true. ¹⁹ Indeed, party-divisions among you can hardly be avoided if men of proved worth are not to be lost in the crowd.

²⁰ Well then, as to your religious gatherings : it cannot be said that it is the *Lord's* Supper that you eat. ²¹ For everybody's first thought is to be beforehand in getting his *own* supper; and so, while the poor man who brings nothing cannot get enough even

---

* Hom. *Il.* ii. 472, 542 ; Hdt. i. 82, v. 72 ; Aristoph. *Eq.* 580. Cf. our Cavaliers.

to eat, the rich man who brings abundance takes a great deal too
much even to drink. [22] Surely you do not mean that you have no
homes in which you can satisfy hunger and thirst? Or do you
think that you need have no reverence for God's congregation;
or that because a man is poor you may treat him with contempt?
What am I to say to you? Do you expect me to commend
you? In this matter that is impossible.

[23] Quite impossible; for I know that you know better. I
myself received from the Lord that which in turn I transmitted
to you, namely, that the Lord Jesus, in the night in which He
was being delivered up, took bread: [24] and when He had given
thanks, He brake it, and said, 'This is My Body, which is for
you. This do ye, in remembrance of Me.' [25] In like manner
also the cup, after supper was over, saying, 'This cup is the new
covenant in virtue of My Blood. This do ye, as often as ye
drink it, in remembrance of Me.'

[26] Yes, He gave this command; for as often as you eat this
bread and drink this cup, it is the death of the Lord that you
are proclaiming,—nothing less than that,—until His return.
[27] It follows, therefore, that whoever eats the bread or drinks the
cup of the Lord in a way that dishonours Him, shall be held
responsible for profaning the Body and Blood of the Lord.
[28] But, in order to avoid this profanation, let a man scrutinize
his own spiritual condition and his motives; then, and not till
then, let him eat of the bread and drink of the cup. [29] For he
who eats and drinks is thereby eating and drinking a sentence
on himself, if he fails to recognize the sanctity of the Body.
[30] The proof of this is within your own experience; for it is
because people fail to recognize this sanctity that so many of
you are sick and ill, while not a few have died. [31] But if we
recognized our own condition and motives, we should escape this
sentence. [32] Yet, when we are thus sentenced, we are being
chastened by the Lord, to save us from being involved in the
final condemnation of the world.

[33] So then, my brothers, at your religious gatherings for a
common meal, wait until all are ready. [34] If any one is too
hungry to wait, let him stay at home and eat; so that your
gatherings may not have these fatal results. All the other
matters in which you need instruction I will regulate whenever
I come.

The shocking desecration of the Lord's Supper by the disorders which St Paul here censures was, no doubt, the primary
reason why he is so severe in his condemnation of the conduct
of those Corinthians who profaned it by their selfish misbehaviour, but it was not the only reason for distress and
indignation. "In the whole range of history there is no more
striking contrast than that of the Apostolic Churches with the
heathenism round them. They had shortcomings enough, it is
true, and divisions and scandals not a few, for even apostolic
times were no golden age of purity and primitive simplicity
Yet we can see that their fulness of life, and hope, and promise
for the future was a new power in the world. Within their own
limits they had solved almost by the way the social problem
which baffled Rome, and baffles Europe still. They had lifted
woman to her rightful place, restored the dignity of labour,
abolished beggary, and drawn the sting of slavery. The secret
of the revolution is that the selfishness of race and class was
forgotten in the Supper of the Lord, and a new basis for society
found in love of the visible image of God in men for whom
Christ died" (Gwatkin, *Early Church History*, p. 73). The
Corinthian offenders were reviving the selfishness of class, were
treating with contumely the image of God visible in their fellow-
men, and were thus bringing into serious peril the best results
of this blessed revolution. The Apostle does not hesitate to
declare (*vv.* 30–32) that this evil work of theirs is bringing upon
them the manifest judgments of God.

It is worth noting that he appeals to what '*the Lord* Jesus'
did at the Supper, not to what 'Jesus' did. There is no basis
for the hypothesis that St Paul did not regard Jesus as the Son
of God until after His Resurrection, comp. v. 4, 5. See Introduction, § 'Doctrine.'

17. Τοῦτο δὲ παραγγέλλων οὐκ ἐπαινῶ. The reading is somewhat doubtful (see below), as also is the meaning of τοῦτο. If
τοῦτο refers to the charge which he gives respecting the Love-
feasts (28–34), then the interval between this preface and the
words which it anticipates is awkwardly prolonged. It is not
impossible that τοῦτο refers to the charge about women wearing
veils.* The connexion between the two subjects is close, both
being concerned with proper behaviour at public worship. 'Now
in giving you this charge I do not praise [you], that your
religious gatherings do you harm instead of good.' It is an

---

* There is similar doubt as to the scope of the τοῦτο in vii. 6, and the
αὕτη in ix. 3. Here the doubt is considerable. The παραγγ. about veiling
was prefaced by praise (*v.* 2): and τοῦτο δέ may introduce another παραγγ.
where praise is impossible ; 'In giving *this* charge I have no praise to give.'

understatement, purposely made in contrast to *v.* 2, that he does not praise them. He censures them severely. What was intended for their wealth they had made an occasion of falling. These gatherings, instead of quickening their spiritual life, had led to grievous misconduct and consequent suffering. For εἰς, of result, comp. Col. iii. 10.

The evidence for παραγγέλλων οὐκ ἐπαινῶ is somewhat stronger than for παραγγέλλω οὐκ ἐπαινῶν. B is neutral with παραγγέλλων οὐκ ἐπαινῶν, and D with παραγγέλλω οὐκ ἐπαινῶ: Vulg. *praecipio non laudans*. There is no ὑμᾶς in the Greek ; but neither AV. nor RV. put 'you' in italics.

Both the Attic κρεῖττον (vii. 9) and the un-Attic κρεῖσσον (here and vii. 38) are well attested : τὸ ἧσσον here only ; comp. 2 Cor. xii. 15. It is possible that both κρεῖσσον and ἧσσον were pronounced in a similar way (*kreesson heesson*) ; if so, we have a play upon sound.

18. 'For, to begin with.' The Apostle hastens to justify his refusal to give praise. The πρῶτον μέν has no δεύτερον δέ or ἔπειτα δέ afterwards, and possibly there is no antithesis ; but some find it in the section about spiritual gifts (xii. 1 f.) : cf. Rom. i. 8, iii. 2, x. 1, xi. 13 ; 2 Cor. xii. 12 : Blass, *Gr* § 77. 12.

ἐν ἐκκλησίᾳ. 'In assembly,' *i.e.* in a gathering of the members of the Corinthian Church. "This use is at once classical and a return to the original force of *qāhāl*" (Hort, *The Chr. Eccles.* p. 118) : xiv. 19, 28, 35 ; comp. 3 John 6 and ἐν συναγωγῇ, John vi. 59, xviii. 20. 'Church' in the sense of a building for public worship cannot be meant ; there were no such buildings.

ἀκούω σχίσματα ἐν ὑμῖν ὑπάρχειν. 'I continually hear (pres.) that dissensions among you prevail' (not simply εἶναι) : these splits are the rule. In the Love-feasts they seem to have been chiefly social, between rich and poor. Possibly what St James condemns (ii. 1–4) took place ; the wealthy got the best places at the tables. Yet neither σχίσματα (see on i. 10) nor αἱρέσεις are separations from the Church, but dissensions within it. Wherever people deliberately choose (αἱρεῖν) their own line independently of authority, there is αἵρεσις : Gal. v. 20.

μέρος τι πιστεύω. The Apostle has the love which 'hopeth all things' (xiii. 7), and he will not believe that all that he hears to their discredit is true ; *miti sermone utitur* (Beng.).

The reading ἐν τῇ ἐκκλ. (TR., 'in the Church' AV.) is found only in a few cursives. There is no reason for suspecting that ἐν ἐκκλ. (all uncials) is an interpolation.

μέρος τι is the accusative of the extent to which the action applies : comp. πάντα πᾶσιν ἀρέσκω (x. 33). We might have had ἐκ μέρους (xiii. 9, 12).

19. δεῖ γὰρ καὶ αἱρέσεις. Comp. Matt. xviii. 7. In the nature of things, if there are splits of any kind, these are sure

to settle down into parties,—factions with self-chosen views.
Human nature being what it is, and Corinthian love of faction
being so great, if a division once became chronic, it was certain
to be intensified. But here perhaps there is not much difference
between σχίσματα and αἱρέσεις. Justin M. (*Try.* 35) mixes the
words ἔσονται σχίσματα καὶ αἱρ. with Matt. xxiv. 5, 11, 24, vii. 15,
and attributes them to our Lord. Comp. *Clem. Hom.* xvi. 21,
and see Resch, p. 100. For αἵρεσις comp. Acts v. 17, xv. 5,
xxvi. 5, etc.

ἵνα [καὶ] οἱ δόκιμοι φανεροὶ γένωνται. Divine Providence turns
this evil tendency to good account: it is the means of causing
the trusty and true to become recognizable. Either by coming
to the front in the interests of unity, or by keeping aloof from
all divisions, the more stable characters will become manifest:
2 Thess. ii. 11, 12. To have religious zeal, without becoming a
religious partizan, is a great proof of true devotion. Contrast
ἀδόκιμος (ix. 27).

D F G, Latt. omit ἐν ὑμῖν before εἶναι. B D, Latt. insert καί before οἱ
δόκιμοι: ℵ A C E F G K L P, Syrr. omit. The δόκιμοι are those who have
been 'accepted' after being tested like metals or stones (Gen. xxiii. 16);
hence 'proved' and 'approved' (Rom. xvi. 10; 2 Cor. x. 18, xiii. 7).
See Origen, *Con. Cels.* iii. 13, *Philocalia* xvi. 2. Quite needlessly, some
suspect that ἵνα . . . ἐν ὑμῖν is an interpolation.

20. Συνερχομένων οὖν ὑμῶν ἐπὶ τὸ αὐτό. 'When therefore you
come together to one place' (Acts i. 15, ii. 1, 44, iii. 1), 'when
you are assembled ἐν ἐκκλησίᾳ, *i.e.* for a religious purpose.' Or
ἐπὶ τὸ αὐτό might (less probably) mean 'for the same object.'
The place is not yet a building set apart. In any case, ἐπὶ τὸ
αὐτό emphasizes the contrast between the external union and the
internal dissension. Compare vii. 5, xiv. 23.

οὐκ ἔστιν κυριακὸν δεῖπνον φαγεῖν. The adjective is emphatic
by position: 'there is no eating a *Lord's* supper.' A supper they
may eat, but it is not the Lord's: οὐκ ἔστιν, 'there is no such
thing,' for such conduct as theirs excludes it. Hence οὐκ ἔστιν
may be rendered 'it is not possible,' *non licet* (Ecclus. xiv. 16);
but this is not necessary. At first, the Eucharist proper seems to
have followed the Agape or Love-feast, being a continuation of
it. Later the Eucharist preceded and was transferred from
evening to morning. Here, κυριακὸν δεῖπνον probably includes
both, the whole re-enactment of the Last Supper including the
Eucharist. *Placuit Spiritui Sancto ut in honorem tanti sacramenti
in os Christiani prius Dominicum corpus intraret quam exteri cibi*
(Aug. *Ep.* cxviii. 6, 7, *ad Januar.*). See Hastings, *DB.* III.
p. 157; Smith, *D. Chr. Ant.* I. p. 40; *Ency. Bibl.* II. 1424. We
cannot be sure from the use of κυριακόν instead of τοῦ κυρίου that
the name κυριακὸν δεῖπνον was already in use. The expression

must have had a beginning, and this may be the first use of it. Inscriptions and papyri show that, as early as A.D. 68, κυριακός was in use in the sense of 'pertaining to the Emperor,' 'imperial' (Deissmann, *New Light on the N.T.* p. 82, *Bible Studies*, p. 217, *Light*, p. 361). The word δεῖπνον occurs only here and Rev. xix. 9, 17, outside the Gospels; in LXX, only in Daniel and 4 Macc.

21. ἕκαστος γὰρ τὸ ἴδιον δεῖπνον προλαμβάνει. 'For each one takes before the rest (instead of with them) his *own* supper': he anticipates the partaking in common, and thus destroys the whole meaning and beauty of the ordinance. It was thus not even a κοινὸν δεῖπνον, much less κυριακόν. The ἐν τῷ φαγεῖν is not an otiose addition: it is a mere eating, which he might just as well or better have done elsewhere and elsewhen.*

καὶ ὃς μὲν πεινᾷ. 'The consequence is that one man cannot even satisfy his hunger, while another even drinks to excess.' These are probably respectively the rich and the poor. The poor brought little or nothing to the common meal, and got little or nothing from the rich, who brought plenty; while some of the rich, out of their abundant supplies, became drunk. There is a sharp antithesis between deficiency in necessary food and excess in superfluous drink. There is no need to water down the usual meaning of μεθύειν (Matt. xxiv. 49; John ii. 10; Acts ii. 15; 1 Thess. v. 7). Even in a heathen ἔρανος such selfish and disgusting behaviour would have been considered shameful, as the directions given by Socrates show; they are very similar to those of St Paul (Xen. *Mem.* III. iv. 1). Certainly such meetings must have been 'for the worse'; hungry poor meeting intoxicated rich, at what was supposed to be a supper of the Lord! In these gatherings the religious element was far more important than the social; but the Corinthians had destroyed both. For this late use of the relative, ὃς μὲν . . . ὃς δὲ . . . comp. Rom. ix. 21; 2 Tim. ii. 20; Matt. xxi. 35, xxii. 5, xxv. 15. Coincidence is implied.

For προλαμβάνει (אBCDEFGKLP) A and some cursives have προσλαμβάνει, the active of which does not occur in the N.T., except as a variant here and Acts xxvii. 34.

22. μὴ γὰρ οἰκίας οὐκ ἔχετε. 'For surely you do not mean that you have not got houses to eat and to drink in!' Comp. μὴ οὐκ ἔχομεν (ix. 4, 5, 6), and εἰς τὸ . . . ἐσθίειν (viii. 10); and

---

* Comp. "And no prophet that orders a table in the spirit eats of it himself: but if he does, he is a false prophet" (*Didache* xi. 9). This calling for a Love-feast in a state of ecstasy (ἐν πνεύματι) is a curious possibility, which had probably been experienced. Only a false prophet would do this in order to get food for himself.

see Abbott, *Johannine Grammar*, 2702 *b*. 'Well, then, if that is
not true (and of course it is not), there is only one alternative,'
which is introduced by $\mathring{\eta}$. 'Ye despise the congregation that is
assembled for the worship of God, and ye put the poor to shame.'
They treated a religious meal as if it were a licentious entertainment, and therein exposed the poverty of those who were in need.
There can be little doubt that, as οἱ ἔχοντες = 'the rich,' οἱ μὴ
ἔχοντες = 'the poor.'   Here it might mean 'those who have not
houses for meals' (Alford); so also Wiclif, 'han noon'; but this
is very improbable.   The τοῦ Θεοῦ is added with solemnity (*v.* 16,
x. 32) to give emphasis to the profanity.   The addition is frequent
in the two earliest groups of the Pauline Epistles (Hort, *The Chr.
Eccles.* pp. 103, 108, 117): καταφρονεῖτε, as Rom. ii. 4; Matt.
xviii. 10; καταισχύνετε, as Rom. v. 5.   The majority of the
Corinthian Christians would be poor.*

τί εἴπω ὑμῖν; ἐπαινέσω ὑμᾶς; Deliberative subjunctives:
'What am I to say to you?   Am I to praise you?'   The ἐν
τούτῳ may be taken with what precedes (AV., RV.), or with
what follows (Tisch., WH., Ell.).   The latter seems to be better,
as limiting the censure to this particular, and also as preparing
for what follows.

23. ἐγὼ γὰρ παρέλαβον ἀπὸ τοῦ Κυρίου.   'I cannot praise you,
for what *I* received from the Lord, and also delivered to *you*,
was this.'   We cannot tell *how* St Paul received this.   Neither
does the ἐγώ imply that the communication was direct, nor does
the ἀπό that it was not direct, although, if it was direct, we
should probably have had παρά (Gal. i. 12; 1 Thess. ii. 13, iv. 1;
etc.).   The ἐγώ balances ὑμῖν: the Apostle received and transmitted to them this very thing, so that both know exactly what
took place.   He was a sure link in a chain which reached from
the Lord Himself to them.   They did not receive it from the
Lord, but they received it from one who had so received it, and
therefore they have no excuse.   This is one of the παραδόσεις
which they professed to be holding fast (*v.* 2).   See Ramsay,
Exp. Times, April 1910; Jülicher, *Paulus u. Jesus*, p. 30.

It is urged that in a matter of such moment a direct revelation to the Apostle is not incredible.   On the other hand, why
assume a supernatural communication when a natural one was
ready at hand?   It would be easy for St Paul to learn everything from some of the Twelve.   But what is important is,
not the *mode* of the communication, but the *source*.   In some
way or other St Paul received this from Christ, and its authen-

* Rutherford translates; 'Or do you think that you need stand on no
ceremony with the Church of God; that because men are poor you may
affront them?'

ticity cannot be gainsaid; but his adding ἀπὸ τοῦ Κυρίου is no guide as to the way in which he received it. More important also than the mode are the *contents* of the communication, and it is to them that παραλαμβάνειν frequently points (1 Thess. ii. 13; 2 Thess. iii. 6; 1 Cor. xv. 1, 3): see Lightfoot on Gal. i. 1, 13. It certainly does not point to anything *written*: St Paul does not say that he had *read* what he delivered to them. See Knowling, *The Testimony of St Paul to Christ*, pp. 275 f. Zahn and Schmiedel are here agreed that St Paul is appealing to historical tradition. See also *Camb. Bibl. Ess.* pp. 336 f.; *Mansfield College Essays*, pp. 48 f.

ὃ καὶ παρέδωκα ὑμῖν. 'Which I also delivered to you.' He transmitted to them the very thing which he had received from the Lord, so that they were well aware of what ought to have made these disorders impossible. This would be St Paul's own reply to the assertion that he, and not Jesus, is the founder of Christianity.

ἐν τῇ νυκτὶ ᾗ παρεδίδετο. 'In the night in which He was being delivered up.' St Paul mentions the sad solemnity of the occasion in contrast to the irreverent revelry of the Corinthians. Neither AV. nor RV. keeps the same translations for παραδίδωμι in this verse, nor marks the imperfect. The delivery to His enemies had already begun and was going on at the very time when the Lord instituted the Eucharist. Moreover, to translate 'was betrayed' confines the meaning to the action of Judas; whereas the Father's surrender of the Son is included, and perhaps is chiefly meant, and the Son's self-sacrifice may also be included (E. A. Abbott, *Paradosis*, §§ 1155, 1202, 1417). It is plain that St Paul assumes that his readers are acquainted with the details of the Passion; and the precision with which he writes here and xv. 3–8 is evidence that "he is drawing from a well-furnished store" (Sanday, *DCG.* II. p. 888). He himself is well acquainted with the chief facts in the life of Christ (A. T. Robertson, *Epochs in the Life of St Paul*, p. 89; Fletcher, *The Conversion of St Paul*, pp. 55 f.).

ἔλαβεν ἄρτον. 'Took a loaf,' one of the thin cakes of bread used for the Paschal meal. It was perhaps more like our biscuit or oatcake than ordinary loaves. Hastings, *DCG.* I. pp. 230 f.

24. εὐχαριστήσας ἔκλασεν. All four accounts of the Institution have ἔκλασεν here, a detail of Divinely-appointed ritual. Luke also has εὐχαριστήσας, for which Mark and Matthew substitute εὐλογήσας. The two words doubtless refer to the same utterance of Christ, in which He gave thanks and blessed God, and both contain the significant εὖ: comp. εὐαγγέλιον, εὐδοκία, and see T. S. Evans *ad loc.* Mark has these features, which are omitted here; 'as they were eating,' 'Take ye,' 'they all drank of it,' 'which is shed for many.' For the third of these Matthew substitutes 'Drink ye all of it'; he has the other three. Luke has none of them. Mark, Matthew, and Luke have εὐχαριστήσας, of the cup also, and here ὡσαύτως covers it. The three, moreover, give, what is omitted here, 'I say to you I will in no wise drink of the fruit of the vine until' . . . 'the Kingdom.' The details which are common to all four accounts are (1) the taking bread, (2) the giving thanks, (3) the breaking, (4) the words, 'This is My Body,' (5) the cup; and, if the disputed passage in Luke be retained, (6) the words 'blood' and 'covenant.' The disputed passage is almost *verbatim* as *vv.* 24, 25 here, from τὸ ὑπὲρ ὑμῶν . . . αἵματι.

Of the four accounts of the Institution this is the earliest that has come down to us, and the words of our Lord which are contained in it are the earliest record of any of His utterances; for this Epistle was written before any of the Gospels. It is, however, possible that Mark used a document in giving his account, and this document might be earlier than this Epistle.

Τοῦτό μου ἐστὶν τὸ σῶμα τὸ ὑπὲρ ὑμῶν. All carnal ideas respecting these much-discussed words are excluded by the fact that the Institution took place before the Passion. Our Lord's human Body was present, and His Blood was not yet shed. What is certain is that those who rightly receive the consecrated bread and wine in the Eucharist receive spiritually the Body and the Blood of Christ. How this takes place is beyond our comprehension, and it is vain to claim knowledge which cannot be possessed, or to attempt to explain what cannot be explained. "If there is a point on which the witness of Scripture, of the purest ecclesiastical tradition, and of our own Church, is more express and uniform than another, it is the peculiar and transcendent quality of the blessing which this Sacrament both represents and exhibits, and consequently of the Presence by which that blessing is conferred. How this Presence differs from that of which we are assured by our Lord's promise, where two or three are gathered together in His name—whether only in degree or in kind—it is beyond the power of human language to define and of human thought to conceive. It is a subject fit, not for curious speculation, but for the exercise of pious meditation and devotional feeling; and it is one in which there is a certainty that the highest flight of contemplation will always fall short of the Divine reality" (Bishop Thirlwall, *Charges*, vol. i. p. 278; see also pp. 245, 246). "I could not consent to make our Church answerable for a dogma committing those who hold it to the belief that, in the institution of the Supper, that which our Lord held in His hand, and gave to His disciples, was nothing less than His own Person, Body, Soul, and Godhead" (*Ibid.* vol. ii. p. 251; see also the appendix on Transubstantiation, pp. 281 f.). The notes of Ellicott and Evans *ad loc.*, with Gould on Mark xiv. 22; Westcott on John vi. and xiii.; Gore, *Dissertations*, pp. 230 f.; Hastings, *DB.* iii. pp. 148 f., with the bibliography there given, may be consulted. Excellent remarks and summaries of doctrine will be found in Beet, *A Manual of Theology*, pp. 380-96. Happily, no theory of the manner of Christ's Presence in the Eucharist is necessary for the fruitful reception of it, and to have this demonstrated would not make us better Christians, any more than a knowledge of the chemical properties of bread makes us better able to digest it. Stanley, *Christian Institutions*, ch. vi.

τοῦτο ποιεῖτε εἰς τὴν ἐμὴν ἀνάμνησιν. 'Perform this action (continue to take bread, give thanks, and break it) in remembrance of Me' (Num. x. 10; Ps. xxxviii. 1, lxx. 1). This implies that hereafter He is to be absent from sight. The words are not in Mark or Matthew, nor in Luke, except in the disputed verses. Therefore the command to continue the celebration of the Lord's Supper rests upon the testimony of St Paul. This, however, does not for a moment imply that he was the first to repeat the celebration, or the first to teach Christians to do so. This passage plainly implies that repeated celebrations were already a firmly established practice. The authority of St Paul was quite inadequate to this immense result. Nothing less than the authority of Christ would have sufficed to produce it. See Knowling, pp. 279 f.

The proposal to give to τοῦτο ποιεῖτε the meaning 'sacrifice this' must be abandoned. As the Romanist commentator Estius says, it is *plane praeter mentem Scripturae.** So also Westcott; "I have not the least doubt that τοῦτο ποιεῖτε can mean only *do this act* (including the whole action of hands and lips), and not *sacrifice this*; and that the Latin also can have only the same rendering" (in a letter quoted in his *Life*, II. p. 353): and Bachmann, τοῦτο *geht auf die ganze Handlung, wie sie durch das Tun Jesu und seiner Jünger dargestellt ist:* and Herveius; '*Hoc facite,*' *id est, corpus meum accipite et manducate per successionem temporis usque in finem saeculi, in memoriam passionis meae.* See Ellicott and Goudge *ad loc.*; *Expositor*, 3rd series, vii. 441; T. K. Abbott, *Essays on the*

---

* *Hoc facite, id est accipite et date* (Card. Hugo de Sto. Caro, d. 1263); *Mandat fieri quod ipse fecit, scilicet accipere panem, gratias agere, frangere, consecrare, sumere, ac dare* (Card. Thomas de Vio, Caietanus, d. 1534).

Original Texts of O. and N.T. p. 110; *A Reply to Mr. Supple's and other Criticisms*; and notes on Luke xxii. 19 in the *Int. Crit. Com.* p. 497.

Edwards translates τὴν ἐμὴν ἀνάμνησιν, 'My commemoration,' in contrast to that of Moses (x. 2), thus making τὴν ἐμήν parallel to καινή (*v.* 25). See Blass, *Gr.* § 48. 7. The Eucharist perpetually calls to mind the redemption by Christ from the bondage of sin, as the Passover recalled the redemption from the bondage of Egypt. Christ did not say, 'in remembrance of My death.' The recorded words, 'as My memorial,' are of wider import; they imply 'in remembrance of all that I have done for you and all that I am to you.' The early Christians seem to have regarded the Eucharist as a commemoration of the Resurrection as well as the Death, for they selected the first day of the week for this memorial. Wetstein compares the address of T. Manlius to the troops after his colleague Decius had devoted himself to secure their success; *Consurgite nunc, memores consulis pro vestra victoria morte occumbentis* (Livy, viii. 10).

Λάβετε, φάγετε (C³ K L P, Syrr. Aeth.) are an interpolation from Matt. xxvi. 26; ℵ A B C* D E F G, Lat-Vet. Aegyptt. Arm. omit. After τὸ ὑπὲρ ὑμῶν, ℵ³ C³ E F G K L P insert κλώμενον, D* inserts θρυπτόμενον, Vulg. (*quod . . . tradetur*) and some other versions have a rendering which implies διδόμενον. ℵ* A B C* 17 and other witnesses omit. The interpolation of any of these words weakens the *nervosa sententia* (Beng.), τὸ ὑπὲρ ὑμῶν, which means 'for your salvation' (Mark x. 45). AV. inserts 'Take, eat,' and 'broken'; RV. gives the latter a place in the margin.

25. ὡσαύτως τὸ ποτήριον. He acted with the cup as with the bread: He took it, gave thanks, and administered it to the disciples. '*The* cup' means 'the usual cup,' the well-known one (x. 16). The addition of μετὰ τὸ δειπνῆσαι shows that the bread was distributed during the meal, ἐσθιόντων αὐτῶν (Mark xiv. 22): but it was after supper was over, *postquam caenatum est* (Aug.), not *postquam coenavit* (Vulg.), that the cup was administered. Perhaps the Apostle is pointing out that the cup, against which they had so grievously offended by intoxication, was no part of the meal, but a solemn addition to it. But we must not translate, 'the after-supper cup,' which would require τὸ μετὰ τὸ δ. ποτήριον. Thomas Aquinas would give a meaning to the fact that the bread was distributed during the meal, while the cup was not administered till the meal was over. The one represents the Incarnation, which took place while the observances of the Law still had force; but the other represents the Passion, which put an end to the observances of the Law. And Cornelius à Lapide regards Christ's taking the cup into His hands as a token of His voluntarily taking death for us. Such thoughts are admissible, if it is not maintained that they are the meaning which is intended in Scripture.*

Τοῦτο τὸ ποτήριον ἡ καινὴ διαθήκη ἐστὶν ἐν τῷ ἐμῷ αἵματι. *Hic calix novum testamentum est in meo sanguine.* The position of ἐστίν is against combining ἐν τῷ ἐμῷ αἵματι with ἡ καινὴ διαθήκη. Rather, 'This cup is the new covenant, and it is so in virtue of My Blood.' 'In My Blood' is an expansion or explanation of the 'is,' and is equivalent to an adverb such as 'mystically.' The cup represents that which it contains, and the wine which it contains represents the Blood which seals the covenant. The Atonement is implied, without which doctrine the Lord's Supper is scarcely intelligible. Only St Paul (and Luke?) has the καινή. The covenant is 'fresh' as distinct from the former covenant which is now obsolete. It is καινή in its contents, in the blessings which it secures, viz. forgiveness and grace: and τῷ ἐμῷ αἵμ. is in contrast to the blood with which the old covenant was confirmed (Exod. xxiv. 8). See Jer. xxxi. 31, the only place in O.T. in which διαθήκη καινή occurs. The choice of διαθήκη, rather than συνθήκη, which is the common word for covenant, is no doubt deliberate, for συνθήκη might imply that the parties to the covenant contracted on equal terms. Between God and man that is impossible. When He enters into a contract He disposes everything, as a man disposes of his property by will: hence διαθήκη often means a testament or will. In the LXX συνθήκη is freq.; in the N.T. it does not occur. Westcott, *Hebrews*, p. 299. On the meaning of 'blood,' 'which is the life,' in connexion with Christ's Sacrifice, see Westcott, *Hebrews*, pp. 293 f.; *Epp. of St John*, pp. 34 f.; Sanday and Headlam, *Romans*, pp. 89, 91.

τοῦτο ποιεῖτε κ.τ.λ. St Paul alone has these words of the cup. In the disputed passage in Luke they are wanting.

ὁσάκις ἐὰν πίνητε. This makes the command very comprehensive; *quotiescunque*: comp. ὁσάκις ἐὰν θελήσωσιν (Rev. xi. 6). Every time that they partake of the sacramental cup (τοῦτο τὸ ποτήριον), they are to do as He has done in remembrance of Him. He does not merely give permission; He commands. It is perverse to interpret this as a general command, referring to all meals at which anything is drunk. What precedes and

* On the other hand, "the crude suggestion of Professor P. Gardner (*The Origin of the Lord's Supper*, 1893), that St Paul borrowed the idea of the Eucharist from the Eleusinian Mysteries, which he may have learned about at Corinth," is not admissible. The theory ignores the evidence of the Mark-tradition, and involves misapprehension of the Eleusinian Mysteries. See E. L. Hicks, *Studia Biblica*, iv. 12. Ramsay thinks that the interval between the bread and the cup "was occupied with instruction in the meaning of the symbolism" (*Exp. Times*, March 1910).

follows limits the meaning to 'the cup of blessing.' The Lord commands that the Supper be often repeated, and His Apostle charges those who repeat it to keep in view Him who instituted it, and who died to give life to them. In liturgies these words are transferred to Christ; 'ye proclaim *My* death till *I* come.'

With regard to the Lord's presence in Holy Communion, Bishop Westcott wrote to the Archbishop of York, 8th Oct. 1900; "The circumstances of the Institution are, we may say, spiritually reproduced. The Lord Himself offers His Body given and His Blood shed. But these gifts are not either separately (as the Council of Trent) or in combination Himself . . . I shrink with my whole nature from speaking of such a mystery, but it seems to me to be vital to guard against the thought of the Presence of the Lord ' in or under the forms of bread and wine.' From this the greatest practical errors follow " (*Life and Letters of B. F. Westcott*, II. p. 351).

It is very remarkable that "the words of institution" differ widely in the four accounts. There is substantial agreement in meaning; but the only clause in which all four agree is 'This is My Body'; and even here there is a difference of order between Τοῦτό μου ἐστὶν τὸ σῶμα (1 Cor.) and Τοῦτό ἐστιν τὸ σῶμά μου (Mark, Matt., Luke). It is quite clear that in all four accounts these words are words of administration, not of consecration. This is specially manifest in Mark, where they are preceded by 'Take ye' (Λάβετε), and in Matt., where they are preceded by 'Take, eat' (Λάβετε, φάγετε). The same may be said of 'This is My Blood' (Mark, Matt.): they are words of administration, not of consecration. The consecration has preceded, and would seem to be included in εὐχαριστήσας or εὐλογήσας. "All liturgies of every type agree in bearing witness to the fact that the original form of consecration was a thanksgiving"; and the form of words in which our Lord gave thanks has not been preserved. In the Eastern liturgies "the words of institution were not recited as of themselves effecting the consecration, but rather *as the authority in obedience to which the rite is performed*" (W. C. Bishop, *Ch. Quart. Rev.*, July 1908, pp. 387–92). In the main lines of Eucharistic teaching in the fourth, fifth, and sixth centuries, "The moment of consecration is associated with the invocation of God the Word (Serapion, 1), or with the invocation of God the Holy Ghost (St. Cyril of Jerusalem, *Cat.* xxi. 3), or with the Invocation of the Holy Trinity (*Ibid.* xix. 7),* or with the recital of the words recorded to have been used by our Lord at the institution (Pseudo-Ambrose, *De Sacr.* iv. 21–23)" (Darwell Stone, *Ch. Quart. Rev.*

---

* To this may be added the still earlier testimony of Origen ; see on vii. 5.

Oct. 1908, p. 36). Cyril of Jerusalem quotes St Paul as saying
(*v.* 25), "And having taken the cup and given thanks, He said,
Take, drink, this is My Blood," which is wide of St Paul's words,
and agrees exactly with none of the other accounts (*Cat.* xxi. 1).
It would thus appear that we know the exact words of institution only very imperfectly, and the exact words of consecration
not at all. Again, just as we do not know the manner of our
Lord's Presence in the rite as a whole, so we do not know
"the supreme moment of consecration." It is lawful to believe
that we should *not* be in a better position for making a good use
of this mystery if all these things *were* known.*

26. ὁσάκις γὰρ ἐὰν ἐσθίητε. In *Apost. Const.* viii. **12, 16**
these words are put into Christ's mouth, with the change, "*My*
death, till *I* come." The γάρ introduces the Apostle's explanation of the Lord's command to continue making this commemor-
ative act. Or possibly γάρ refers to the whole passage (23–25);
"Such being the original Institution, it follows that as often as
ye eat," etc. To make the γάρ co-ordinate with the γάρ of
v. 23, as giving an additional reason for οὐκ ἐπαινῶ, is very
forced. St Paul gives no directions as to *how* frequently the
Lord's Supper is to be celebrated, but he implies that it is to be
done frequently, in order to keep the remembrance of the Lord
fresh. We may conjecture that at Corinth celebrations had been
frequent, and that it was familiarity with them that had led to
their being so dishonoured. By 'this bread' (τὸν ἄρτον τοῦτον)
would seem to be meant bread used in the manner prescribed
by Christ (*vv.* 23, 24).

The τοῦτο with τὸ ποτήριον ('*this* cup,' AV.) is a manifest interpolation :
א* A B C* D* F G, Latt. Arm. omit. Note the chiasmus between ἐσθίητε
and πίνητε, but the change of order seems to have no significance. What
is significant is the addition of καὶ τὸ ποτήριον πίνητε, which can hardly be
reconciled with the practice of denying the cup to the laity.

τὸν θάνατον τοῦ Κυρίου καταγγέλλετε. 'Ye proclaim ('shew'
is inadequate) continually (pres. indic.) the death of the Lord.'
The Eucharist is an *acted* sermon, an *acted* proclamation of the
death which it commemorates ; † but it is possible that there
is reference to some *expression of belief* in the atoning death of
Christ as being a usual element in the service. The verb is
indicative, not imperative.

ἄχρι οὗ ἔλθῃ. The Eucharist looks backwards to the Cruci-

---

* See art. *Abendmahl* in Schiele, *Die Religion in Geschichte und Gegenwart*, in which the doubtful points in the history of the institution are clearly
stated ; also Plummer, *S. Matthew*, pp. 361 f. ; Dobschütz, *Probleme d. Ap.
Zeitalters*, p. 73 ; Hastings, *DB.* iii. p. 146, *DCG.* ii. p. 66.

† Comp. Cyprian (*De zelo et livore*, 17) ; *De sacramento crucis et cibum
sumis et potum.*

fixion and forwards to the Return: *hoc mysterium duo tempora extrema conjungit* (Beng.). But at the Second Advent Eucharists will come to an end, for the commemoration of the absent ceases when the absent returns. "No further need of symbols of the Body, when the Body itself appears" (Theodoret). Then instead of their drinking in memory of Him, He will drink with them in His Kingdom (Matt. xxvi. 29).

The ἄν between ἄχρι or ἄχρις οὗ and ἔλθῃ is not likely to be genuine אּ* A B C D* F and Fathers omit. If it were genuine, it would indicate that the Coming is uncertain, and this can hardly be the Apostle's meaning. How near the Coming may be is not here in question; but Eucharists must continue till then.

27. ὥστε . . . ἔνοχος ἔσται. 'Consequently . . . he will be guilty.' Seeing that partaking of the bread and of the cup is a proclaiming of the Lord's death, partaking unworthily must be a grievous sin. No definition of 'unworthily' is given; but the expression covers all that is incompatible with the intention of Christ in instituting the rite. It is quite certain that selfish and greedy irreverence is incompatible. But what follows shows that not only external behaviour but an inward attitude of soul is included. There must be brotherly love towards all and sure faith in Christ. Weinel fails to notice this (p. 259).

ἢ πίνῃ. As the cup followed the bread at a considerable interval, it was possible to receive one unworthily without receiving the other at all. In either case the whole sacrament was profaned. It is on the use of ἢ here, and not καί, that an argument is based for communion in one kind only; and it is the only one that can be found in Scripture. But the argument is baseless. Because profaning one element involves profaning both, it does not follow that receiving one element worthily is the same as worthily receiving both.* It is eating this bread *and* drinking the cup that proclaims the death of the Lord (*v.* 26): we have no right to assume that eating without drinking, or *vice versa*, will suffice. The whole passage, especially *vv.* 22, 26, 28, 29, may be called *proof* that we are to eat *and* drink. And see Blass, § 77. 11 on the quasi-copulative sense which ἢ has in such sentences : *vel* (Vulg.), *aut* (Calvin).

τὸ ποτήριον τοῦ Κυρίου. The cup which has reference to the Lord and brings us into communion with Him, as the 'cup of demons' (ποτήριον δαιμονίων) brings the partakers into communion with them (x. 21): comp. κυριακὸν δεῖπνον (*v.* 20). Nowhere else in N.T. does ἀναξίως occur: in vi. 2 we have ἀνάξιος.

ἔνοχος ἔσται τοῦ σώματος κ.τ.λ. 'Shall be under guilt of

---

* To break one commandment is to break the whole Law, but to keep one command is not to keep the whole Law. See Abbott, *Johannine Grammar*, 2759 f., and comp. ἢ in Rom. i. 21.

violating, be guilty of a sin against, the Body and the Blood of
the Lord.' The dignity of that of which they partake (x. 16) is
the measure of the dignity which their irreverence profanes
He does not say ἔνοχος ἔσται τοῦ θανάτου τ. Κ., *par facit, quasi
Christum trucidaret* (Grotius).   The guilt is rather that of
deliberate injury or insult to the king's effigy or seal, or profane
treatment of a crucifix.   Dishonour to the symbols is dishonour
to that which they represent; and to use the bread and the
wine as the Corinthians used them was to treat the memorials
of Christ's death, and therefore that which they commemorated,
with insult.

The use of ἔνοχος is varied: *c. gen.* of the offence (Mark iii. 29), of
that which is violated (here and Jas. ii. 10), and of the penalty (Mark
xiv. 64; Heb. ii. 15); *c. dat.* of that which is violated (Deut. xix. 10)
and of the tribunal (Matt. v. 21, 22).

After τὸν ἄρτον, K L P, Vulg. AV. add τοῦτον : ℵ A B C D E F G
Lat.-Vet. RV. omit.   For ἤ before πίνῃ A, Aegypt. Aeth. AV. read καί,
a manifest correction.   After ἀναξίως, D L, Pesh. Goth. add τοῦ Κυρίου.
A few unimportant witnesses support the TR. in omitting τοῦ before
αἵματος.   The AV. inserts 'this' before 'cup of the Lord,' without
authority.

28. δοκιμαζέτω δὲ ἄνθρωπος ἑαυτόν. 'But (in order to avoid
all this profanity) let a man (iv. 1; Gal. vi. 1) prove himself'
(1 Thess. v. 21; Gal. vi. 4).   Let him see whether he is in a
proper state of mind for commemorating and proclaiming the
death of the Lord.   The emphasis is on δοκιμαζέτω.   It is
assumed that the result of the testing will either directly or
indirectly be satisfactory.   This is sometimes implied in δοκιμάζειν as distinct from πειράζειν : Lightfoot on 1 Thess.
v. 21 ;
Trench, *Syn.* § lxxiv.   The man will either find that he is already in
a right condition to receive, or he will take the necessary means
to become so.   Nothing is said here either for or against employing the help of a minister, as in private confession : but δοκιμαζέτω
ἑαυτόν shows that the individual Christian can do it for himself,
and perhaps implies that this is the normal condition of things.*
Those who are unskilful in testing themselves may reasonably
seek help; and confession, whether public or private, is help
supplied by the Church to those who need it.   But when the
right condition has been reached, by whatever means, then and
not till then (οὕτως) let him come and partake.

ἐκ τοῦ ἄρτου . . . ἐκ τοῦ ποτηρίου.   The prepositions seem to
imply that there are other communicants (x. 17); but the change
of construction in ix. 7 renders this doubtful.   Evans interprets
the ἐκ of "the mystical *effects* of the bread eaten."

* Chrysostom insists on this ; " He does not order one man to test
another, but each man himself ; thus making the court a private one and the
verdict without witnesses."   *Unicuique committitur suimet judicium* (Cajetan).

29. It is impossible to reproduce in English the play upon words which is manifest in these verses (29–34), in which changes are rung upon κρίμα and κρίνω with its compounds : Blass, *Gr* § 82. 4. Such things are very common in 2 Cor. (i. 13, iii. 2, iv. 8, vi. 10, x. 6, 12, xii. 4). The exact meaning of this verse is uncertain. Either (1) 'For the (mere) eater and drinker,' who turns the Supper into an ordinary meal ; or, (2) 'For he who eats and drinks (unworthily, or without testing himself).' There is not much difference between these two, and in either case μὴ διακρίνων must mean '*because* he does not rightly judge,' or '*without* rightly judging.' Or else, (3) 'He who eats and drinks, eats and drinks judgment to himself, *if* he does not rightly judge.' In any case κρίμα is a neutral word, 'judgment' or 'sentence,' not 'condemnation,' still less 'damnation.' The context implies that the judgment is adverse and penal (*v.* 30) ; but it also implies that the punishments are temporal, not eternal. These temporal chastisements are sent to save offenders from eternal condemnation. For κρίμα, not κρίσις, comp. Rom. iii. 8, v. 16 ; Gal. v. 10 ; and see Thayer's Grimm.

It seems to be safe to assume that διακρίνω has the same meaning in *vv.* 29 and 31. In that case 'discern' or 'dis-criminate' (RV. and marg.) can hardly be right, for this meaning makes poor sense in *v.* 31. 'Judge rightly' makes good sense in both places. Of course one who forms a right judgment will discern and discriminate (in this case, will distinguish the Body from ordinary food), but 'distinguish' is not the primary idea. Chrysostom paraphrases, μὴ ἐννοῶν, ὡς χρή, τὸ μέγεθος τῶν προκει- μένων, μὴ λογιζόμενος. It is not likely that, because the bread symbolizes the many grains of Christian souls united in one Church, τὸ σῶμα here means the body of Christians ; * still less that it means 'the substance' which is veiled in the bread, as some Lutherans interpret.

The addition of ἀναξίως after πίνων, and of τοῦ Κυρίου after τὸ σῶμα in a number of texts, are obvious interpolations. Why should א* A B C* and other authorities omit in both cases, if the additions were genuine?

Editors differ as to the accent of κρίμα. In classical Greek κρῖμα is right, but in this later Greek the earlier witnesses for accents give κρίμα. Much the same difference is found with regard to στῦλος, which Tisch. accents στύλος. See Lightfoot on Gal. ii. 9, v. 10.

On the insoluble problem as to *what* it is that the wicked receive in the Lord's Supper, see E. H. Browne and E. C. S. Gibson on article xxix '

---

* Stanley strongly contends for this meaning ; it was "the community and fellowship one with another which the Corinthian Christians were so slow to discern" ; and he appeals to xii. 12, 13, 20, 27 ; Rom. xii. 4, 5 ; Eph. ii. 16, iii. 6, iv. 12, 16 ; Col. i. 18, ii. 19, iii. 15 (*Christian Institutions*, p. 111). In any case we may compare the striking saying of Ignatius (*Rom.* vii., *Trall.* viii.), that "the Blood of Jesus Christ is *love.*"

the correspondence between Keble and Pusey at the end of vol. iii. of *The Life of Pusey*; and J. B. Mozley, *Lectures and other Theological Papers*, p. 205. "If he receive unworthily, he verily rejects the Body and Blood of Christ" (Khomiakoff, *Essay on the Church*, in Birkbeck, *Russia and the English Church*, p. 207). Some problems respecting the Eucharist are the result of theories (which may be erroneous) respecting the *manner* of Christ's Presence in the Eucharist : if the theory is relinquished, the difficulty disappears. It is clear from *vv.* 28, 29, which have καί and not ἤ between ἐσθ. and πιν., that communion in both kinds was usual, and there is no mention of special ministers who distributed the bread and the wine. But these abuses might suggest the employment of ministers.

30. διὰ τοῦτο. He proceeds to prove the truth of κρίμα ἑαυτῷ ἐσθίει καὶ πίνει from the Corinthians' own experiences. It is because of their irreverence at the Lord's Supper that many among them have been chastised with sickness, and some even with death. To interpret this of spiritual weakness and deadness is inadequate ; and no ancient commentator thus explains the words. Their spiritual deadness produced the irreverence, and for this irreverence God chastised them with bodily suffering. Had spiritual maladies been meant, we should probably have had ἐν πνεύματι, or ἐν ταῖς καρδίαις ὑμῶν. Perhaps at this time there was much sickness in the Church of Corinth, and St Paul points out the cause of it. We need not assume that he had received a special revelation on the subject. It is possible that the excess in drinking may have led in some cases to illness. Both ἀσθενεῖς and ἄρρωστοι imply the weakness of ill-health (Mark vi. 5, 13 ; Matt. xiv. 14), and it is not clear which is the stronger word of the two : *infirmi et imbecilles* (Vulg.) ; but ἀρρωστεῖν (2 Chron. xxxii. 24) is perhaps more than ἀσθενεῖν. By ἱκανοί is meant 'enough to be considerable' : in this sense the word is frequent in Luke and Acts, and in 1 and 2 Mac., but is rare elsewhere : in Rom. xv. 23 the reading is somewhat doubtful. See Swete on Mark x. 46.

κοιμῶνται. 'Are sleeping' (in death), *dormiunt*, rather than 'are falling asleep,' *obdormiunt* : here and elsewhere the Vulg. has *dormio*. The word was welcomed by Christians as harmonizing with the belief in a resurrection, but it was previously used by Jews and heathen without any such belief. Test. of XII. Patr. *Joseph* xx. 4, ἐκοιμήθη ὕπνῳ καλῷ, where some texts read ἐκ. ὕπνον αἰώνιον: comp. ὅπως καρωθῶσιν καὶ ὑπνώσωσιν ὕπνον αἰώνιον, and ὑπνώσουσιν ὕπνον αἰώνιον καὶ μὴ ἐξεγερθῶσιν (Jer. li. 39, 57) ;* Book of Jubilees xxiii. 1 ; *Tum consanguineus Leti Sopor* (Virg. *Aen.* vi. 278. See Milligan on 1 Thess. iv. 13). Calvin points out that these consequences of profanation must

---

* With αἰώνιος here comp. κοιμήσατο χάλκεον ὕπνον (Hom. *Il.* xi. 241) ; *ferreus urget somnus* (Virg. *Aen.* x. 745), *perpetuus sopor urget* (Hor. *Od.* I. xxiv. 5). These illnesses and deaths would be all the more remarkable in a Church which had a χάρισμα ἰαμάτων (xii. 9).

254 FIRST EPISTLE TO THE CORINTHIANS [XI. 30-33

be regarded as admonitions : *neque enim frustra nos affligit Deus,
quia malis nostris non delectatur ; argumentum copiosum et amplum.*
He also seems to regard solitary masses as a repetition of the
offence in *v.* 21 ; *ut unus seorsum epulam suam habeat, abolita
communicatione.*

31. εἰ δὲ ἑαυτοὺς διεκρίνομεν. 'But if we made a practice
(imperf.) of rightly judging *ourselves*': ἑαυτούς is emphatic, and
ἑαυτοὺς διεκρ. is stronger than the middle. The reference is to
v. 28. 'If we habitually tested ourselves, and reached a right
estimate, we should not receive judgment' (such as these sicknesses and deaths). For the construction comp. John v. 46,
viii. 19, 42, xv. 19, xviii. 36 ; and for ἑαυτούς with the 1st pers.
Acts xxiii. 14 ; 1 John i. 8. In using the 1st pers. the Apostle
softens the admonition by including himself. What follows is
much less stern than what precedes. He is anxious to close
gently.

εἰ δέ (אٌ* A B D E F G, Vulg, Aeth. Goth. RV.) is certainly to be preferred to εἰ γάρ (א³ C K L P, Syrr. Aegyptt. AV.).

32. κρινόμενοι δέ. 'But when we do receive judgment (as is
actually the case by these sicknesses), we are being chastened by the
Lord, in order that we may not receive judgment of condemnation
(be judged to death) with the world.' These temporal sufferings
are indeed punishments for sin, but their purpose is disciplinary
and educational (1 Tim. i. 20), to induce us to amend our ways
and escape the sentence which will be pronounced on rebels at
the last day. The κόσμος here is, not God's well-ordered
creature, but His enemy, as commonly in St John. 'I beseech
therefore those who read this book, that they be not discouraged because of the calamities, but account that these
punishments were not for the destruction, but for the chastening
of our race' (2 Mac. vi. 12). For παιδευόμεθα (as implying
moral training as distinct from mere teaching), see Westcott on
Heb. xii. 7 ; Trench, *Syn.* § 32 ; Milligan, *Grk. Papyri,* p. 94.*

33. ὥστε, ἀδελφοί μου. In *vv.* 31, 32 he has been regarding
offences generally. He now returns to the disorders in connexion with the Lord's Supper in order to close the subject, and
in so doing he repeats the affectionate address (i. 11) which
still further mitigates the recent severity. This conclusion
indicates where the great fault has been : in the common meal
of Christian love and fellowship there has been no love or fellowship. Having charged them to secure the necessary internal

* "The Apostle did not say κολαζόμεθα, nor τιμωρούμεθα, but παιδευόμεθα.
For his purpose is to admonish, not to condemn ; to heal, not to requite ;
to correct, not to punish " (Chrys.).

feeling by means of self-examination, he now insists upon the necessity for the external expression of it. To the last he harps upon συνέρχεσθαι. These are *meetings*, Christian *gatherings*, the object of which is to manifest mutual love. Moreover, the purpose of the congregational meal is spiritual, not physical ; not to satisfy hunger, but to commemorate and to hold communion with Christ. Let them cease to come together εἰς ἧσσον, εἰς κρίμα. As in *v.* 21, τὸ φαγεῖν is a general expression for a common meal.

ἀλλήλους ἐκδέχεσθε. 'Wait for one another,' *invicem expectate* (Vulg.). This is the usual meaning of the verb in the N.T. (xvi. 11; Heb. x. 13, xi. 10; Acts xvii. 16; Jas. v. 7). The meaning 'receive ye one another' (common in the LXX and in class. Grk.) is less suitable : for this he would perhaps have used προσλαμβάνεσθαι (Rom. xiv. 1, xv. 7). The waiting would prevent the greedy προλαμβάμειν (21): and Chrysostom points out the delicacy of the expression. It is the rich who are to wait for the poor ; but neither rich nor poor are mentioned.

34. The mere satisfying of hunger should be done ἐν οἴκῳ (xiv. 35), not ἐν ἐκκλησίᾳ (*v.* 18). Comp. κατ᾽ οἶκον (Acts ii. 46, v. 42). The abrupt conclusion is similar to the conclusion of the discussion about women wearing veils (*v.* 16). He is not going to argue the matter any further; the difference between the Supper and ordinary meals must be clearly marked: that is final.

The δέ after εἰ,—εἰ δέ τις (א³ D³ EK L P, Syrr. AV.) is a manifest interpolation (א* A B C D* F G, Latt. RV. omit). The asyndeton makes an abrupt conclusion.

τὰ δὲ λοιπά. One may guess for ever, and without result, as to what things the Apostle was going to set in order, just as one may guess for ever as to what directions our Lord gave to the Apostles respecting Church order during the forty days. Here 'all the other matters' possibly refers to matters about which the Corinthians had asked, and probably to matters connected with the Love-feasts and the Eucharist. The use of διατάξομαι (vii. 17, ix. 14, xvi. 1 ; Tit. i. 5) suggests that these had reference to externals, εὐταξία, rather than to the inner meaning of the rite. But the evidence is slight, and does not carry us far.

ὡς ἂν ἔλθω. 'Whensoever I shall have come,' or 'according as I come.' The ἂν makes both event and time uncertain. Comp. ὡς ἂν πορεύωμαι εἰς τὴν Σπανίαν (Rom. xv. 24); ὡς ἂν ἀπίδω τὰ περὶ ἐμέ (Phil. ii. 23). J. H. Moulton, i. p. 167. Meanwhile there seems to be no overseer or body of elders to act for him.

ADDITIONAL NOTE ON XI. 17–34.

This passage throws considerable light upon the manner of celebrating the Lord's Supper in St Paul's day.   On the negative side we have important evidence.   As J. A. Beet *in loc.* points out very incisively, the Apostle says nothing about ' consecration ' by a 'priest'; and, had there been anything of the kind, would he not have said, 'Wait for the consecration,' rather than 'Wait for one another' (*v.* 33)?   Beet points out further (*Manual of Theology*, p. 388) that private members were able to appropriate beforehand the food designed for the communion, which implies that they were not in the habit of receiving the bread and wine from the *church officers*.   And St Paul does not tell them that they must not help themselves to the bread and wine, although this would have effectually put a stop to the abuses in question ; which shows that he did not look upon reception of the elements as essential to the validity of the rite.   From this we infer with certainty that, when Christ ordained the Supper, He did not direct, and that, when 1 Corinthians was written, the Apostles had not directed, that the sacred rite should be administered by the church officers and them alone.   Nor have we in the N.T. any evidence that the Apostles afterwards gave this direction. What we *have* is evidence that a body of church officers was being developed : and it is reasonable to suppose that, when a distinction had been made between laity and clergy, the duty of celebrating the Lord's Supper would very soon be reserved for the clergy.

On the positive side we may assume from τοῦτο ποιεῖτε that the Christian Supper was closely modelled, in all essentials, on what Christ did at the Paschal Supper.   This carries with it—

(α) The Blessing and Breaking of Bread and the Blessing of a Cup, as then by Christ, so later by a presiding person.

(β) The Meal itself, originally meant, like the Passover, to be a genuine meal, for satisfying hunger and thirst.

But (*v.* 22) St Paul began a change which tended to make the meal connected with the Lord's Supper a mere ceremony. The genuine meal, for satisfying hunger, is to be taken at home, and the Lord's Supper is not to be used for that purpose by all communicants as a matter of course, although the poor are to have an opportunity of satisfying their appetites.   This change naturally tended to the goal which was ultimately reached, viz., the complete separation of the Eucharist from the Supper, which became a mere 'Agape.'   The contributions of food brought by the worshippers survived in later times as the First Oblation, the Εὐλογίαι.   See *Dict. of Chr. Ant.* Artt. 'Agape,' 'Eulogia,' 'Eucharist'; Kraus, *Real-Enc. d. christ. Alt* I. Artt.

'Eucharistie,' 'Eulogien'; Hastings, *DB.* and *DCG.* Artt. 'Lord's Supper,' 'Communion.'

XII. 1–XIV. 40. SPIRITUAL GIFTS, ESPECIALLY PROPHESYING AND TONGUES.

This is the third and longest section of the fourth main division of the Epistle; and, as at the beginning of this division (xi. 2), there is a possible reference to the letter of the Corinthians to the Apostle; but he would no doubt have treated of a number of the topics which are handled, even if they had not mentioned them.

In all three of the sections we are reminded that he is dealing with a young Church in which some of the faults of their former state of life are reappearing. This is specially the case with the Corinthian love of faction. There were rivalries, cliques, and splits, hardening sometimes into parties with party-leaders. About the veils, there was the rivalry between men and women. At the love feasts, there was the rivalry between rich and poor. And here we have evidence of rivalries as to the possession of spiritual gifts, and especially as to those which were most demonstrative, and therefore seemed to confer most distinction.

The difficulty of this section lies in our ignorance of the condition of things to which it refers. The phenomena which are described, or sometimes only alluded to, were to a large extent abnormal and transitory. They were not part of the regular development of the Christian Church. Even in Chrysostom's time there was so much ignorance about them as to cause perplexity. He remarks that the whole of the passage is very obscure, because of our defective information respecting facts, which took place then, but take place no longer. Some members of the Corinthian Church, in the first glow of early enthusiasm, found themselves in possession of exceptional spiritual endowments. These appear to have been either wholly supernatural endowments or natural gifts raised to an extra-ordinarily high power. It seems to be clear that these endowments, although spiritual, did not of themselves make the possessors of them morally better. In some instances the reverse was the case; for the gifted person was puffed up and looked down on the ungifted. Moreover, the gifts which were most desired and valued were not those which were most useful, but those which made most show.

The chapter falls into two clearly marked parts: (1) The **Variety, Unity, and true Purpose of Spiritual Gifts**, 1–11; (2)

Illustration from Man's Body of the truth that, though the Gifts
may be various, those who possess them are one organic Whole,
12–31. The first three verses are introductory, to supply a test
which a Church consisting chiefly of converts from heathenism
would be likely to require. Converts from Judaism might know
from their own history and previous experience what manifestations of power were divinely inspired, and what not. But
converts from idolatry would not be able to distinguish:
incantations and spells were all alike to them. Then follows
(4–11) the paragraph on the oneness of the origin of all gifts
that are beneficial.

*A sure test of the origin of any spiritual gift is, Does it
promote the glory of Jesus Christ? What dishonours Him
cannot be from above. The good gifts are very various in
their manifestations, but they have only one Source—God's
Holy Spirit.*

¹ Now concerning spiritual manifestations, Brethren, I am
anxious that you should be under no delusions. ² You remember
that, when you were heathens, you were led away, just as the
impulse might take you, to the dumb idols that could tell you
nothing. ³ Those experiences do not help you now; and therefore
I would impress upon you this as a sure test. No one who is
speaking under the influence of God's Spirit ever says, Jesus is
anathema; and no one can say, Jesus is Lord, except under the
influence of the Holy Spirit.

⁴ Now there are various distributions of gifts; but it is one
and the same Spirit who bestows them. ⁵ And there are various
distributions of ministrations; and it is to one and the same
Lord that they are rendered. ⁶ And there are various distributions of effects; yet it is the same God who causes every one of
them in every Christian that manifests them. ⁷ But to each
Christian the manifestation of the Spirit is granted with a view
to some beneficent end. ⁸ For to one man is granted through
the Spirit the utterance of wisdom; to another, the utterance of
knowledge according to the leading of the same Spirit; ⁹ to a
third, potent faith by means of the same Spirit; and to another,
manifold gifts of healings by means of the one Spirit; ¹⁰ and to
another, various miraculous effects; to another, inspired utterance; to another, powers of discriminating between inspirations;
to yet another, different kinds of Tongues; and to another,

the interpretation of Tongues. ¹¹ But every one of these manifestations of power is caused by one and the same Spirit, who
distributes them to each individual singly, exactly as He wills.

1. Περὶ δὲ τῶν πνευματικῶν. 'Now concerning spiritual
powers' or 'gifts.' The περί, as in vii. 1 and viii. 1, probably
refers to topics mentioned by them; and the δέ, as in xi. 2,
marks the transition from one topic to another, and probably
from one topic about which they had asked to another about
which they had asked. With less probability some make the δέ
antithetical, as distinguishing what he deals with at once from
what he has decided to postpone; 'But, while I postpone τὰ
λοιπά, I must not delay to instruct you about τὰ πνευματικά.'
Some again would make τῶν πνευματικῶν masculine, as in ii. 15
and xiv. 37; but it is certainly neuter, as in xiv. 1. What
follows treats of the spiritual gifts, rather than those who are
endowed with them; but the difference is not very important.
*Spiritualia dona vocat, quia solius Spiritus Sancti opera sunt,
industria humana nihil ad hoc conferente* (Natalis Alexander):
see Denton on the Ep. for 10th Sunday after Trinity.

οὐ θέλω ὑμᾶς ἀγνοεῖν. As in x. 1; comp. Rom. i. 13, xi. 25;
2 Cor. i. 8; 1 Thess. iv. 13. The formula marks the introduction
of an important subject which must not be overlooked, and is
always softened by the addition of the affectionate ἀδελφοί: he
will not leave his brethren in ignorance. Moreover, this addition
reminds them that there ought to be no jealousies between
brethren as to the possession of spiritual gifts.

2. οἴδατε ὅτι ὅτε . . . ἀπαγόμενοι. The sentence is not
grammatical, and the simplest remedy is to understand ἦτε with
ἀπαγόμενοι, which is not a violent supplement. The main
sentence in that case is οἴδατε ὅτι πρὸς τὰ εἴδωλα ἀπαγόμενοι
(ἦτε). 'Ye know that, when ye were heathen, ye were led away,
as from time to time ye might be led,* to worship the idols, the
speechless things.' They were hurried along, like dumb brutes,
to pay reverence to the dumb idols,—objects of worship which,
so far from inspiring others to speak, could not speak themselves.
They had no revelation to give, and could not have communicated it, if they had. 'They have mouths and speak not'
(Ps. cxv. 5, Hab. ii. 18; Wisd. xiii. 17–19; Baruch vi. 8), and
can neither answer questions nor make known their own will:
coeci ad mutos ibatis, muti ad coecos (Beng.). The insertion of 'as
at any time ye might be led,' added to ἀπαγόμενοι, emphasizes
the idea of senseless, and almost unconscious following. They

---

* This is one of the places in which the old *iterative* force of ἄν seems to
survive in the N.T. Comp. Acts ii. 45, iv. 35. J. H. Moulton, p. 167.

were led, not by any revelation of Divine will, but by local custom, or by the command of priests or rulers.* But ἀπαγό-μενοι does not mean 'led *astray*' : the heathen were not seduced from a better religion to idolatry. Here only is ἀπάγειν found in the N.T., except in the Synoptics and Acts ; and there the common meaning is to lead away by *force*, rather than by seductive guile, to trial, prison, or punishment (Matt. xxvi. 57, xxvii. 2, 31 ; etc. ; Acts xii. 19, xxiv. 7). The agent who led them on to the worship of idols is not mentioned ; but we are probably to understand the evil one as at the back of custom or command, Satan, "the wily wire-puller of moral mischief" (Evans). Contrast πνεύματι ἄγεσθαι (Gal. v. 18 ; Rom. viii. 14), and with ὅτε ἔθνη ἦτε comp. ὅτε ἦμεν νήπιοι (Gal. iv. 3). On the verse as a whole Calvin rightly remarks, *perturbata est constructio, sed tamen clarus est sensus.*

We may safely adopt ὡς ἂν ἤγεσθε rather than ὡς ἀνήγεσθε. Other doubts are not so easily settled.

Some regard ὡς ἂν ἤγεσθε as a resumption of the clause introduced by ὅτι : ' Ye know that, when ye were heathen,—how ye were led to those voiceless idols, being carried away.' This makes the ἀπαγόμενοι come in very awkwardly. Both ὅτι and ὅτε are found in ℵ A B C D E L P, Vulg. Arm., but some texts omit ὅτε and some omit ὅτι. WH. suspect a primitive error, and for ὅτι ὅτε conjecture ὅτι πότε. The error might easily arise in dictation. This is very attractive ; it gets rid of all grammatical difficulty and is in accordance with Pauline usage ; ' Ye know that *once* ye were heathen, carried away to those voiceless idols, as on occasions ye might be led.' St Paul often contrasts his readers' previous unhappy paganism (πότε) with their happy condition as believers (νῦν) : Rom. xi. 30 ; Col. i. 21, iii. 8 ; Eph. ii. 11-13, v. 8. But whichever reading or con-struction we adopt, the import of the verse is clear : it is because they once were idolaters that he is so anxious that they should be properly instructed about τὰ πνευματικά.

3. διὸ γνωρίζω ὑμῖν. 'On which account I make known to you' (xv. 1 ; Gal. i. 11). Excepting the Pastoral Epistles, διό is frequent in the Pauline Epp. Seeing that in their heathen state they could know nothing about spiritual gifts, nor how to discern whether a person was speaking by the Spirit or not, he must tell them by what kind of spiritual power God makes revelations to man.† No utterance inspired by Him can be *against* Christ. Every word *for* Christ is inspired by Him.

* "Much of the immorality which St Paul so graphically describes was associated with religious worship. So that the Apostle assigns as the cause of the universal condition of moral corruption in the world the universal prevalence not so much of no religion as of false religion " (Du Bose, *The Gospel according to St Paul*, p. 63). On the idea of Christians ceasing to belong to the ἔθνη, see Harnack, *The Mission and Expansion of Christianity*, i. pp. 60, 89.

† Chrysostom thinks that he is contrasting Christian inspiration with the frenzy of the Dionysiac and other mysteries ; this may be true *in part*.

ἐν Πνεύματι Θεοῦ. The ἐν may express either sphere or instrumentality : comp. Rom. ix. 1, xiv. 17, xv. 16; Luke iii. 16. Although it is perhaps more common to have the article where direct agency is meant (vi. 11), yet active influence rather than surrounding element seems to be implied here. See J. A. Robinson on Eph. v. 18. The difference between λαλεῖν and λέγειν may be noted, the one of uttering sounds, the other of articulately saying something : comp. ch. xiv. *passim*; Acts ii. 4, 6, 7, 11. The blasphemous ᾿Ανάθεμα ᾿Ιησοῦς would be more likely to be uttered by a Jew than a Gentile; *faciebant gentes, sed magis Judaei* (Beng.). It is possible that it was uttered against Jesus by His bitter enemies even during His life on earth. It is not improbable that Saul himself used it in his persecuting days, and strove to make others do so (Acts xxvi. 11). When the Gospel was preached in the synagogues the fanatical Jews would be likely to use these very words when Jesus was proclaimed as the Messiah (Acts xiii. 45, xviii. 6). Unbelievers, whether Jews or Gentiles, were admitted to Christian gatherings (xiv. 24), and therefore one of these might suddenly exclaim in the middle of public worship, ᾿Ανάθεμα ᾿Ιησοῦς. To the inexperienced Corinthians a mad shout of this kind, reminding them of the shrieks of frenzied worshippers of Dionysus and the Corybantes, might seem to be inspired : see Findlay *ad loc.* St Paul assures them that this anti-Christian utterance is absolutely decisive : it cannot come from the Spirit.* For ἀνάθεμα comp. xvi. 22; Gal. i. 8, 9; Trench, *Syn.* § v.; Cremer, p. 547; Suicer, 268. It is one of the 103 words which in N.T. are found only in Paul and Luke (Hawkins, *Hor. Syn.* p. 190). It is less likely that St Paul is thinking of cases of *apostasy*. Fifty years later, those who denied that they were Christians were required to blaspheme Christ : this was the crucial test. *Qui negabant esse se Christianos aut fuisse, cum praeeunte me deos appellarent et imagini tuae ture ac vino supplicarent*, praeterea male dicerent Christo, *quorum nihil posse cogi dicuntur qui sunt re vera Christiani, dimittendos esse putavi* (Pliny to Trajan, *Ep.* x. 96).

Κύριος ᾿Ιησοῦς. This comprehensive utterance is as wide as Christendom : every loyal Christian is inspired. Those who have received special gifts, such as those which are mentioned below (4–11), must not regard those who have not received them as devoid of the Spirit. This is one of the ways in which the

---

* Origen says that the Ophites required this utterance from those who joined them : ἔστι τις αἵρεσις ἥτις οὐ προσίεται τὸν προσιόντα εἰ μὴ ἀναθεματίσῃ τὸν ᾿Ιησοῦν. See *JTS.* x. 37, p. 30.

Here the RV. is right in making ' Jesus is anathema ' and ' Jesus is Lord ' the *oratio recta* : ℵ A B C have ἀνάθεμα ᾿Ιησοῦς, not ᾿Ιησοῦν, and Κύριος ᾿Ιησοῦς, not Κύριον ᾿Ιησοῦν.

Spirit glorifies Jesus (John xvi. 14), by enabling many to confess Him as Lord. Comp. the similar double test, negative and positive, given in 1 John iv. 2–4; but while St John has in view those who denied the humanity of Christ, St Paul has in view those who denied His Divinity. In Gal. iv. 6 we have the parallel cry, 'Abba, Father,' as a mark of Christian adoption; and in Acts viii. 16, xix. 5 we have the formula, baptized 'into the name of the *Lord* Jesus.'*

4–6. These verses give the keynote of the passage. Having given the negative and positive criterion of genuine spiritual endowments as manifested in speech, the Apostle goes on to point out the essential oneness of these very varied gifts. In doing so he shows clearly, and perhaps of set purpose, that Trinitarian doctrine is the basis of his thought. We have the three Persons in inverse order, the Fount of Deity being reached last,—Πνεῦμα, Κύριος, Θεός. We have the same order, and similar thought in Eph. iv. 4–6; one body, quickened by one Spirit, dependent upon one Lord, and having the origin of its being in one God and Father of all. And there, as here, the Trinitarian Unity is at once followed by a statement of the distribution of grace to each separate individual; ἑνὶ δὲ ἑκάστῳ ἡμῶν ἐδόθη ἡ χάρις. Still more clear is the benediction at the end of 2 Cor. (xiii. 14); see notes in the Camb. Grk. Test. Comp. Clem. Rom. *Cor.* xlvi. 3; "one God and one Christ and one Spirit of grace"; and lviii. 2; "as God liveth, and the Lord Jesus Christ liveth, and the Holy Spirit." See also Sanday in Hastings, *DB.* II. p. 213; Goudge, 1 *Corinthians*, pp. xxix ff. This language of St Paul, in which the Trinitarian point of view is not paraded, but comes out quite naturally and incidentally, gives confirmation to the authenticity of Matt. xxviii. 19. This Epistle was written a dozen years or more before the First Gospel; but St Paul's language is all the more intelligible if it was well known that our Lord had spoken as Matt. reports.

4. Διαιρέσεις δὲ χαρισμάτων εἰσίν. Although every one who knows the significance of 'Jesus is Lord,' and can heartily affirm it, is inspired, 'yet there are distributions of special gifts'— *divisiones gratiarum* (Vulg.). Διαίρεσις occurs nowhere else in the N.T., and it may mean either 'differences,' 'distinctions,' or 'distributions,' 'apportionings,' 'dealings out.'† The use of

---

* Our Lord uses a similar argument (Mark ix. 39; Luke ix. 50). It is quite possible that, at baptism, the convert made some short confession of faith, such as Κύριος Ἰησοῦς. He confessed the Name, when he was baptized in the Name.

† It is frequent in LXX, especially in Chronicles, of the 'courses of priests, Levites, and troops.'

διαιροῦν in v. 11 seems to decide for the latter. In all three
cases here the word refers to the gifts being distributed among
different individuals rather than to the distinctions between the
gifts themselves. Both meanings are true; but it is the dealing
out of the gifts, rather than the variety of them, that is insisted
upon here.* Χάρισμα is almost exclusively a N.T. word, and
(excepting 1 Pet. iv. 10) is peculiar to Paul. It is found as a
doubtful reading twice in Ecclus.; in vii. 33 χάρις is probably
right, and in xxxviii. 34 (30) χρῖσμα may be right. The word is
frequent in 1 Cor. and Rom., and is found once each in 2 Cor.
and 1 and 2 Tim. See especially Rom. xii. 3–8, which was
perhaps written when the Apostle had this chapter in his mind.
From neither passage can we gather that there were definite
ministers, differing in function, and each endowed with special
and appropriate χαρίσματα. The impression conveyed is that
these gifts were widely diffused, and that perhaps there were not
many Christians at Corinth who were not endowed with at least
one of them. See P. W. Schmiedel, *Ency. Bibl.* iv. 4755 f.; Hort,
The Chr. Eccles., pp. 153 f.; W. E. Chadwick, *The Pastoral
Teaching of St Paul*, ch. iii. ; J. Wilhelm in *The Catholic Cyclo-
paedia*, iii. Art. 'Charismata'; Sanday and Headlam, *Romans*,
pp. 358 f.; Cremer, p. 577; Suicer, 1500. The word is sometimes used in a wider sense of any gift of grace, *e.g.* continence
(vii. 7), or faith (Rom. i. 11).

τὸ δὲ αὐτὸ Πνεῦμα. The δέ marks the antithesis between the
one Fount and the many streams. The Spirit which bestows all
these special gifts is the same as that which enables Gentile or
Jew to confess Christ; consequently the test given in *v.* 3 is
available in each case. See Dale, *Ephesians*, pp. 133 ff.

5. διακονιῶν. Like χάρισμα, the word has both a general
and a special meaning: (1) any Christian ministration or service
(here; Rom. xi. 13; Eph. iv. 12), whether of an Apostle or of
the humblest believer; (2) some special administration, as of
alms, or attendance to bodily needs (xvi. 15; 2 Cor. viii. 4).
"Spiritual service of an official kind" is not included in the
meaning, but may be implied in the context. See Hort,
Christian Ecclesia, pp. 202 f.

καὶ ὁ αὐτὸς Κύριος. Here there is no antithesis (καί, not δέ)
between the many and the one: the two facts are stated as
parallel. On the one side are the apportionments of ministrations; on the other is He who 'came not to be ministered
to, but to minister' (Mark x. 45), but who counts all service
to others as service done to Himself (Matt. xxv. 40). 'Ye serve

---

* Comp. Maharbal's words to Hannibal; *Non omnia nimirum eidem dii
dedere* (Livy, xxii. 51).

the Lord Christ' (Col. iii. 24): it is He who is glorified by the
diverse distribution of ministries.

6. ἐνεργημάτων. These are the results or effects of the ἐνέργεια given by God (Eph. iii. 7; Col. i. 29, ii. 12), the outward
manifestations of His power. Among these ἐνεργ. are certainly
χαρίσματα ἰαμάτων. The word occurs again v. 10, but nowhere
else in Biblical Greek: it is almost co-extensive with χαρίσματα,
but it gives prominence to the idea of power rather than that of
endowment. Cremer, pp. 262, 713; he quotes Polyb. iv. 8. 7,
αἱ τῶν ἀνθρώπων φύσεις ἔχουσί τι πολυειδές, ὥστε τὸν αὐτὸν ἄνδρα
μὴ μόνον ἐν τοῖς διαφέρουσιν τῶν ἐνεργημάτων: and Diodor. iv. 51,
τῶν δὲ ἐνεργημάτων ὑπὲρ τὴν ἀνθρωπίνην φύσιν φανέντων.

ὁ δὲ αὐτὸς Θεός. If this is the right reading, we again have
a contrast between the oneness of the Operator and the multi-
plicity of the operations, as before in v. 4. The Operator
(ὁ ἐνεργῶν) is always God: every one of the gifts in every person
that manifests them (τὰ πάντα ἐν πᾶσιν) is bestowed and set in
motion by Him. See J. A. Robinson, *Eph.* p. 241; Westcott,
Eph. p. 155.

ὁ δὲ αὐτός is the reading of ℵ A K L P, Latt. Syrr. Arm., and the δέ is
supported by the ὁ αὐτὸς δέ of D E F G. But καὶ ὁ αὐτός is found in B C,
some cursives, and Origen. If καὶ ὁ αὐτός may be due to assimilation to
v. 5, ὁ δὲ αὐτός may be due to assimilation to v. 4. St Paul would be as
likely to repeat the καί as to go back to the δέ.

7. The emphasis is on the first word and on the last. One
and the same Divine Unity works throughout, as Spirit, Lord,
and God : 'but to *each* one is being given the manifestation of the
Spirit with a view to *profiting*.' The purpose of all these various
gifts, like their origin, is one and the same—the good of the
congregation ; they are bestowed to be exercised for the benefit
of all: Eph. iv. 7–16. The AV. is unfortunate ; 'to *every* man'
is wrong and wrongly placed. In ἡ φανέρωσις (2 Cor. iv. 2 only)
τοῦ Πνεύματος, the genitive is probably objective, 'the operation
which manifests the Spirit, rather than subjective, 'the manifestation which the Spirit produces.' There are many such
doubtful genitives ; Moul.-Win. p. 232.

πρὸς τὸ συμφέρον. 'With a view to advantage,' *i.e.* 'the profit
of all.' We are probably to understand that it is common weal
that is meant, not the advantage of the gifted individual. These
charismata are not for self-glorification, nor merely for the
spiritual benefit of the recipient, but for that of the whole Church.
Here συμφέρον is certainly right ; comp. Acts xx. 20 ; Heb. xii.
10: in vii. 35 and x. 33 σύμφορον is to be preferred, but in x. 33
the Revisers have συμφέρον, as here.

The import of *vv.* 6 and 7 is, that the very various gifts, bestowed not for merit but of free bounty—*gratiae gratis datae*, are being distributed to each individual according to his capacity ; and he must use the new powers, opportunities, and activities for the well-being of the whole. They are talents out of one and the same treasury of love, and must be used for the profit of the one body. What follows is the explanation of ἑκάστῳ δίδοται (8–11), and then we have an amplification of πρὸς τὸ συμφέρον (12 ff.).

8–11. The details of the continual giving are now stated. It is by no means certain that St Paul is consciously classifying the nine gifts which he mentions ; still less is it certain that the ἑτέρῳ in *vv.* 9 and 10 marks the beginning of a new class. The change to ἑτέρῳ may be made merely to break the intolerable monotony of ἄλλῳ eight times in succession ; and we might render the first ἑτέρῳ 'to a third,' and the second ʻto an eighth.' Comp. ἄλλῳ . . . ἄλλῳ . . . ἑτέρῳ . . . ἄλλῳ in Hom. *Il.* xiii. 730–2. Nevertheless, if we take each ἑτέρῳ as marking a new division, we get an intelligible result. Of the three classes thus made, the first is connected with the intellect, the second with faith, and the third with the Tongues. Note that the Tongues come last. For Origen's comment, see *JTS.* x. 37, p. 31.

8. ᾧ μὲν . . . λόγος σοφίας, ἄλλῳ δὲ λόγος γνώσεως. In each case it is the λόγος which is divinely imparted, the power of communicating to others : the σοφία and the γνῶσις may come from above, or from human study or instruction. The λόγος σοφίας is discourse which expounds the mysteries of God's counsels and makes known the means of salvation. It is a higher gift than λόγος γνώσεως, and hence is placed first, and is given by the instrumentality (διὰ τοῦ) of the Spirit, whereas the latter is given in accordance with (κατὰ τό) the Spirit. Commentators differ as to the exact differences between σοφία and γνῶσις ; but σ. is the more comprehensive term. By it we know the true value of things through seeing what they really are ; it is spiritual insight and comprehension (Eph. i. 17 ; 2 Esdras xiv. 22, 25). By γν. we have an intelligent grasp of the principles of the Gospel ; by σ. a comprehensive survey of their relations to one another and to other things. Contrast the shallow σοφία λόγου, so valued at Corinth (i. 17). In itself, γν. may be the result of instruction guided by reason, and it requires no special illumination ; but the use of this knowledge, in accordance with the Spirit, for the edification of others, is a special gift. But our ignorance of the situation makes our distinctions between the two words precarious : to the Corinthians, among whom these two gifts were of common occurrence, the difference between σ. and γν. would be clear enough.

9. ἑτέρῳ πίστις. 'To a third, faith.' This cannot mean the
first faith of a convert's self-surrender to the truth, nor the saving
faith which is permanently possessed by every sincere Christian,
but the wonder-working faith (xiii. 2; Matt. xvii. 20) which mani
fests itself in ἔργα rather than in λόγος; potent faith; *ardentissima
et praesentissima apprehensio Dei in ipsius potissimum voluntate*
(Beng.); πίστιν οὐ τὴν τῶν δογμάτων, ἀλλὰ τὴν τῶν σημείων
(Chrys.); the faith which produces, not only miracles, but
martyrs. We are perhaps to understand the next four gifts, or
at any rate the next two, as grouped under πίστις. If πίστις is
thus regarded as generic, and as including some of the gifts
which follow, then the six gifts which follow πίστις, like the two
which precede it, fall into pairs: λόγος σ. and λόγος γν., χαρίσματα ἰαμάτων and ἐνεργήματα δυνάμεων, προφητεία and διακρίσεις
πνευμάτων, γένη γλωσσῶν and ἑρμηνεία γλωσσῶν.

χαρίσματα ἰαμάτων. 'Gifts of healings,' 'gifts which result in
healings': ἴαμα in this chap. only, in the N.T., and always in
this phrase (*vv.* 28, 30), but frequent in the LXX. Cf. Acts
iv. 30. The plur. seems to imply that different persons each had
a disease or group of diseases that they could cure: that any one
could cure πᾶσαν νόσον καὶ πᾶσαν μαλακίαν (Theophyl.) is not
stated. The means may have been supernatural, or an excep-
tionally successful use of natural powers, such as 'suggestion':
see Jas. v. 14.*

ἐνεργήματα δυνάμεων. This may be added to cover wonderful
works which are not healings, such as the exorcizing of demons;
and such chastisements as were inflicted on Elymas the sorcerer,
or on Hymenaeus and Philetus may be included. Cf. Gal. iii. 5;
Heb. ii. 4.

10. προφητεία. Not necessarily predicting the future, but
preaching the word with power (xiv. 3, 24, 30): comp. *Didache*
xi. This gift implies special insight into revealed truths and a
great faculty for making them and their consequences known to
others. It was about the two pairs of gifts mentioned in this
verse that the Corinthians were specially excited. See *Ency. Bibl.*
III. 3886, IV. 4760.

---

* Harnack holds that St Luke was "a physician endowed with peculiar
'spiritual' gifts of healing, and this fact profoundly affects his conception of
Christianity" (*The Acts of the Apostles*, p. 133). Again, "whose own we-
account shows him to have been a physician endowed with miraculous gifts of
healing" (p. 143; comp. p. 146).

It is remarkable that although there are allusions to signs and wonders in
the Apostolic age (2 Cor. xii. 12; Gal. iii. 5; Rom. xv. 19; Heb. ii. 4), there
is no allusion to miracles wrought by Christ. It cannot be said that in the
age in which the Gospels were being framed there was a tendency to glorify
Christ by attributing miracles to Him. See L. Ragg, *The Book of Books,*
p. 221.

διακρίσεις πνευμάτων. 'The gift of discerning in various cases (hence the plur.) whether extraordinary spiritual manifestations were from above or not'; they might be purely natural, though strange, or they might be diabolical. An intuitive discernment is implied, without the application of tests. Perhaps the expression chiefly refers to the prophetic gift, which might easily be claimed by vainglorious persons or by those who made a trade of religion. The *Didache* (xi. 8) says that "not every one that speaks in the spirit is a prophet, but only if he has the ways of the Lord. By their ways therefore the false prophet and the true shall be known." The whole chapter should be read in this connexion: but the *Didache* gives certain external tests, about which St Paul says nothing either here or 1 Thess. v. 19–21. He implies that the discrimination between true and false manifestations of power is a purely spiritual act (ii. 15). Döllinger (*First Age of the Chruch*, p. 312) remarks; "How St Paul distinguished the gift of wisdom, which he claimed for himself also, from the gift of knowledge, must remain doubtful. The special gift of faith which he mentions can only have consisted in the energetic power and heroic confidence of unlimited trust in God. The gift of discerning spirits enabled its possessor to discriminate true prophets from false, and judge whether what was announced came from God or was an illusion. Such a gift was indispensable to the Church at a time when false prophets abounded, forced their way into congregations, and increased every year in numbers and audacity. There were false teachers, as St John intimates (1 John iv. 1 f.), who preached their own doctrine as a revelation imparted to them from above."

γένη γλωσσῶν. St Paul places last the gifts on which the Corinthians specially prided themselves, and which they were most eager to possess, because they made most display. Their enthusiasm for the gift of Tongues was exaggerated. The undisciplined spirit which had turned even the name of Christ into a party-cry (i. 12), and the Lord's Supper into a drunken revel, turned spiritual gifts into food for selfish vanity, instead of means for the good of all. And here again they would not 'wait for one another,' but each was eager to take his turn first, and numbers were speaking all at once (xiv. 27). The γένη indicates that the manifestations of this gift varied much ; comp. γένη φωνῶν (xiv. 10): but it seems to be clear that in all cases persons who possessed this gift spoke in ecstasy a language which was intelligible to themselves, but not to their hearers, unless some one was present who had the gift of interpretation. The soul was undergoing experiences which ordinary language could not express, but the Spirit which caused the experiences supplied also a language in which to express them. This

ecstatic language was a blissful outlet of blissful emotions, but
was of no service to any one but the speaker and those who
had the gift of interpretation.   The gift of interpreting these
ecstatic utterances might be possessed by the person who
uttered them (xiv. 5, 13); but this seems to have been exceptional: comp. Acts x. 46, xix. 6; [Mark] xvi. 17.   From
xiv. 27, 28 it seems to be clear that this ecstatic utterance was
not uncontrollable: it was very different from the frenzy of
some heathen rites, in which the worshipper parted with both
reason and power of will.   And whatever may be the relation
of this gift to the Tongues at Pentecost, the two are alike in
being exceptional and transitory (see below on xiv.).

The conjunctions in these two verses (9, 10) are somewhat uncertain.
In v. 9 there should probably be no δέ after ἑτέρῳ: ℵ* B D* E F G, Latt.
Arm. omit.   In v. 10 there should perhaps be no δέ until the last clause,
ἄλλῳ δὲ ἑρμ. γλ.   But there is considerable authority for a δέ after the
first and the second ἄλλῳ: yet B D E F G, Latt. omit.

In v. 9, ἐν τῷ ἑνί (A B, cursives, Latt.) is to be preferred to ἐν τῷ
αὐτῷ, which comes from the previous clause.   The temptation to alter
ἑνί to αὐτῷ would be great; and v. 11 confirms the ἑνί.   In v. 10 διακρίσεις
(A B K L) is to be preferred to διάκρισις (ℵ C D* F G P).   The plur. would
be changed to the sing. to harmonize with προφητεία and ἑρμηνία.   Ἑρμηνία
occurs again xiv. 26, and nowhere else in N.T.

11. πάντα δὲ ταῦτα.   The πάντα is very emphatic, and the
δέ marks the contrast of transition from the manifold gifts and
powers to the one Source of them all.   This Source is the Spirit
of God; so that there is no contradiction between v. 6 and v. 10.
What God works, the Spirit works.   Nor is there any contradiction between v. 10 and v. 31.   Our earnest desire for the
best gifts is one of the things which fits us to receive them,
and each man receives in proportion to this desire, a desire
which may be cultivated.   The Spirit knows the capacity of
each; iii. 8, vii. 7, xv. 23.

τὸ ἓν καὶ τὸ αὐτὸ Πνεῦμα.   This is a combination of τῷ ἑνί
Πν. with τῷ αὐτῷ Πν. in v. 9, and is so far a confirmation of
the reading, τῷ ἑνί.   This one and the same Spirit has already
been defined as 'God's Spirit' (v. 3), who is here said to do
what God does (v. 6).   But here there is something added;
the Spirit 'distinguishes and distributes severally to each, exactly
as He willeth.'   Throughout the verse, but especially in the
last words (καθὼς βούλεται), the personality of the Spirit is
implied.*   It is in the will that personality chiefly consists.

* St Paul commonly uses ἐνεργεῖν with a personal subject (v. 6; Gal. ii. 8,
iii. 5; Eph. i. 11, 20, ii. 2, as here; Phil. ii. 13), but ἐνεργεῖσθαι with an
impersonal subject (Rom. vii. 5; 2 Cor. i. 6, iv. 12; Gal. v. 6; Eph. iii. 20;
Col. i. 29; 1 Thess. ii. 13; 2 Thess. ii. 7).   See J. A. Robinson, *Ephesians*,
p. 246.   See also Basil, *De Spir.* xvi. 37, xxvi. 61, and *Ep.* xxxviii. 4.

The Apostle here teaches the Corinthians that they ought not
to plume themselves upon the possession of one or more of
these gifts. They may be evidence of capacity, but they are
no proof of merit. It is the will of the Spirit that decides, a
will which discriminates, but which cannot be compelled by
anything which man can do: *singulis dat singula, vel aliqua,
varia mensura* (Beng.). The Church consists of many persons
very variously endowed, and the gifts bestowed upon individuals
benefit the whole. Διαιρέω in NT. is found only here and Luke
xv. 12.

The addition of ἰδίᾳ (sc. ὁδῷ) emphasizes the fact that the Spirit deals
with men, not *en masse*, but one by one, 'to each according to his several
ability'(Matt. xxv. 15; Rom. xii. 6; Eph. iv. 11). In N.T. we commonly
have κατ' ἰδίαν in this sense: here only ἰδίᾳ, and 2 Mac. iv. 34 only in
LXX. But ἰδίᾳ is not rare in class. Grk.

12-31. We pass on to an illustration (taken from the human
body) of the truth that, though the gifts of God's Spirit may
be many and various, yet those who are endowed with them
constitute one organic whole. The illustration is a common
one, and is used several times by the Apostle: Rom. xii. 4, 5;
Eph. iv. 16, v. 30; Col. ii. 19. See J. A. Robinson on
Eph. iv. 16. The difference between the famous parable of
Menenius Agrippa (Livy ii. 32) and this simile of St Paul is
that the Apostle does not say anything about a centre of
nourishment: it is not the feeding of the body, but its unity,
and the dependence of the members on one another, that is
the lesson to be instilled.* In the brute creation, as Buckland
taught his Oxford pupils, and among brutalized men, it is the
stomach that rules the world. The ultimate aim of the violence
and cunning of each animal is to feed itself, and often at the
cost of the lives of other animals: this determines its activities.
The ultimate aim of the Christian is the well-being of the whole
body, of which the controlling power is Christ, who is at once
the Head and the Body, for every Christian is a member of
Him (vi. 15; Eph. v. 30), and represents Him (Matt. xxv.
40, 45). Hence, *inter Christianos longe alia est ratio* (Calvin).
The Church is neither a dead mass of similar particles, like
a heap of sand, nor a living swarm of antagonistic individuals,
like a cage of wild beasts: it has the unity of a living organism,
in which no two parts are exactly alike, but all discharge different

* The Emperor Marcus Aurelius frequently insists on this; Γεγόναμεν
γὰρ πρὸς συνεργίαν, ὡς πόδες, ὡς χεῖρες, ὡς βλέφαρα, ὡς οἱ στοῖχοι τῶν ἄνω καὶ
τῶν κάτω ὀδόντων· τὸ οὖν ἀντιπράσσειν ἀλλήλοις, παρὰ φύσιν (ii. 1). Τὰ λογικὰ
ζῶα ἀλλήλων ἕνεκεν γέγονε (iv. 3). Οἷόν ἐστι ἐν ἡνωμένοις τὰ μέλη τοῦ
σώματος, τοῦτον ἔχει τὸν λόγον ἐν διεστῶσι τὰ λογικά, πρὸς μίαν τινὰ συνεργίαν
κατεσκευασμένα (vii. 13).

functions for the good of the whole. All men are not equal,
and no individual can be independent of the rest: everywhere
there is subordination and dependence. Some have special
gifts, some have none; some have several gifts, some only
one; some have higher gifts, some have lower: but every
individual has some function to discharge, and all must work
together for the common good. This is the all-important point
—unity in loving service. The Church is an organic body, an
organized society, of which all the parts are moved by a spirit
of common interest and mutual affection. Weinel, *St Paul*,
pp. 130—133.

*In considering these various gifts, remember that there
is in the Christian body, just as there is in the frame of
the living man, a divinely ordained diversity of members,
combined with a oneness in mutual help and in devotion to
the whole: so that no member can be despised as useless,
either by himself or by other members; for each has his
proper function, and all are alike necessary. This unity
involves mutual dependence, and therefore it excludes discontent and jealousy on the one hand, arrogance and contempt
on the other.*

[12] Just as the human body is one whole and has many
organs, while all the organs, although many, form only one
body, so is it with the Christ, in whom all Christians are one.
[13] For it was by means of one Spirit, and in order to form one
body, that we all of us were baptized—Jews and Greeks, slaves
and freemen, without distinction,—and were all made to drink
deeply of that one Spirit. [14] For, I repeat, the human body
consists, not of one organ, but of many. [15] Suppose the foot
were to grumble and say, 'As I am not as high up as the hand,
I do not count as part of the body,' not for all it can say does
it cease to belong to the body. [16] And suppose the ear were
to grumble and say, 'As I am not as well placed as the eye,
I do not count as part of the body,' not for all it can say does
it cease to belong to the body. [17] If the whole body were one
monstrous eye, where would the hearing be? If the whole
were hearing, where would the smelling be? [18] But, as a
matter of fact, God gave every one of the organs its proper
place in the body, exactly as He willed. [19] Now, if all made
only one organ, where would the body be? [20] But, as it is,

although there be many organs, there is only one body. ²¹ And
the eye has no right to look down on the hand and say, 'Thou
art of no use to me'; nor the head to look down on the feet
and say, 'Ye are of no use to me.' ²² On the contrary, it is
much truer to say that those organs of the body which seem
to be somewhat feeble are really as indispensable as any, ²³ and
the parts of the body which we regard as less honourable are
just those which we clothe with more especial care, and in
this way our uncomely parts have a special comeliness;
²⁴ whereas our comely parts have all that they need, without
special attention. Why, yes; God framed the body on principles of compensation, by giving additional dignity to whatever
part showed any deficiency, ²⁵ so as to prevent anything like
disunion in the body, and to secure in all organs alike the
same anxious care for one another's welfare. ²⁶ And, accordingly, if one of them is in pain, all the rest are in pain with it;
and honour done to one is a joy to all. ²⁷ Now you are a body
—the Body of Christ, and individually you are His members.
²⁸ And God gave each his proper place within the Church,—
Apostles first, inspired preachers next, teachers third; besides
these, He gave miraculous powers and gifts of healing, powers
of succouring, powers of governing, ecstatic utterance. ²⁹ Surely
you do not all of you expect to be Apostles, or inspired preachers,
or teachers: surely you do not all of you expect to have all
these wonderful gifts, and even more than these! ³¹ What
you ought to do is persistently to long for yet greater gifts.
And accordingly I go on to show you a still more excellent
way by which you may attain to them.

12. πάντα δὲ τὰ μέλη. 'While *all* the members of the body,
though they be many, are one body, so also is the Christ,' in
whose Nature they share, in whom they all form one body
(*v.* 27), and whom they all serve (*v.* 5). From one point of
view Christ is the Head, but that is not the thought here.
Here He is the whole Body, as being that which unites the
members and makes them an organic whole. We might have
had οὕτως καὶ ἡ ἐκκλησία, for Christ or the Church is only one
Body with many members. The superfluous τοῦ σώματος after
τὰ μέλη emphasizes the idea of unity; and some texts make
this still more emphatic by interpolating τοῦ ἑνός after τοῦ
σώματος. The human body is a unique illustration of unity
in diversity. Comp. Justin M. *Try.* **42**. In Eph. and Col.

τὸ σῶμα has become a common designation of the Church. The congregation, having to serve one and the same Lord, must be united.

13. καὶ γὰρ ἐν ἑνὶ Πνεύματι. The 'one body' suggests the 'one Spirit,' for it is in a body that spirit has a field for its operations. 'For in *one* Spirit also we *all* were baptized so as to form *one* body.' An additional reason (καὶ γάρ, v. 7, xi. 9) for the oneness of the many. The Spirit is the element in (ἐν) which the baptism takes place, and the one body is the end to (εἰς) which the act is directed: *ut simus unum corpus uno Spiritu animatum* (Beng.); ἐπὶ τούτῳ ὥστε εἰς ἓν σῶμα τελεῖν (Theod.). St Paul insists here on the social aspect of Baptism, as in x. 17 on the social aspect of the Eucharist.

εἴτε Ἰουδαῖοι εἴτε Ἕλληνες, εἴτε δοῦλοι εἴτε ἐλεύθεροι. The insertion of this parenthetical explanation shows in the clearest way how diverse were to be the members and how close the oneness of the body. The racial difference between Jew and Greek was a fundamental distinction made by nature; the social difference between slave and freeman was a fundamental distinction made by custom and law: and yet both differences were to be done away, when those who were thus separated became members of Christ. In Gal. iii. 28 this momentous truth is stated still more broadly, and with more detail in Col. iii. 11. In each case the wording is probably determined by the thought of those to whom the Apostle is writing. See Lightfoot on Col. iii. 11, and cf. vii. 22; Rom. x. 12; Eph. ii. 14, with J. A. Robinson's note.

πάντες ἓν πνεῦμα ἐποτίσθημεν. 'Were *all* watered, saturated, imbued, with *one* Spirit.' The πάντες and the ἓν are placed together in emphatic antithesis. The Christ is the ἓν σῶμα, and this suggests ἓν Πνεῦμα, for in man σῶμα and πνεῦμα are correlatives. Comp. Ἀπολλὼς ἐπότισεν.

The verse is taken in three different ways. (1) The whole refers to Baptism under two different figures,—being immersed in the Spirit, and being made to drink the Spirit as a new elixir of life. But, as ποτίζειν is used of irrigating lands, there is perhaps not much change of metaphor. (2) The first part refers to Baptism, the second to the outpouring of spiritual gifts after Baptism. (3) The first refers to Baptism, the second to the Eucharist (Aug. Luth. Calv.). This is certainly wrong; the aorists refer to some definite occasion, and 'drinking the Spirit' is not used of the Eucharist. Both parts refer to Baptism. Compare the thought in Gal. iii. 26 f., and see *JTS.*, Jan. 1906, p. 198.

Before ἐν πν. ἐποτ., K L, Vulg. AV. insert εἰς, to agree with the first clause : א B C D* F P, Syrr. Aeth. Arm. RV. omit. For ἐν πν. ἐποτ., A has ἐν σῶμά ἐσμεν. For ἐποτίσθημεν, L and some cursives have ἐφωτίσθημεν, a verb which in ecclesiastical Greek is often used of baptism.

In the active ποτίζω has two accusatives, γάλα ὑμᾶς ἐπότισα, and therefore retains one acc. in the passive : comp. 2 Thess. ii. 15 , Luke xii. 47, xvi. 19.

14. καὶ γὰρ τὸ σ. Additional confirmation ; 'For the body also is not one member, but many.' *

15. 'If the foot should say, Because I am not hand, I am not of the body, it is not on account of this (discontented grumbling) not of the body.' The παρὰ τοῦτο ('all along of this,' 4 Mac. x. 19) refers to the pettish argument of the foot, rather than to the fact of its not being a hand. In each case it is the inferior limb which grumbles, the hand being of more value than the foot, and the eye than the ear. And Chrysostom remarks that the foot contrasts itself with the hand rather than with the ear, because we do not envy those who are very much higher than ourselves so much as those who have got a little above us ; οὐ τοῖς σφόδρα ὑπερέχουσιν, ἀλλὰ τοῖς ὀλίγον ἀναβεβηκόσι. For εἰμὶ ἐκ, 'belong to,' and so 'dependent on,' see John iv. 22 ; and for the double negative, 2 Thess. iii. 9. Bengel compares Theoph. Ant. (ad Autol. 3) ; οὐ παρὰ τὸ μὴ βλέπειν τοὺς τυφλοὺς ἤδη καὶ οὐκ ἔστι τὸ φῶς τοῦ ἡλίου φαῖνον : and Origen (con. Cels. vii. 63) ; οὐ διὰ τοῦτο οὐ μοιχεύουσιν. Some would take οὐ παρὰ τοῦτο in vv. 15, 16 interrogatively, as in the AV. But this would require μή.

17. εἰ ὅλον τὸ σῶμα. 'If the whole body (Luke xi. 34) were eye (Num. x. 31), where were the hearing?' Each member has a function which it alone can discharge, and no organ ought to think little of its own function, or covet that of another organ.† In class. Grk. ὄσφρησις is common, but it occurs nowhere else in the Bible.

---

* M. Aurelius, as we have seen, says that we are made to co-operate with one another, as feet, and hands, and eyelids, and upper and lower jaws. To act in opposition to one another is unnatural (ii. 1). Socrates points out how monstrous it would be if hands and feet, which God made to work in harmony, were to thwart and impede one another (Xen. Mem. ii. iii. 18).

† Wetstein quotes Quintilian, viii. 5 ; Neque oculos esse toto corpore velim, ne caetera membra suum officium perdant. Cic. De Off. i. 35 ; Principio corporis nostri magnam natura ipsa videtur habuisse rationem, quae formam nostram, reliquamque figuram, in qua esset species honesta, eam posuit in promptu ; quae partes autem corporis ad naturae necessitatem datae adspectum essent deformen habiturae atque turpem, eas contexit atque abdidit. De Off. iii. 5 ; Si unumquodque membrum sensum hunc haberet, ut posse putaret se valere, si proximi membri valetudinem ad se traduxisset, debilitari et interire totum corpus necesse est.

Primasius turns v. 17 thus ; Si toti docentes, ubi auditores? Si toti auditores, quis sciret discernere bonum vel malum?

18. νῦν δὲ ὁ Θεὸς ἔθετο. 'But, as it is, God placed the members, each one of them, in the body, even as He willed.' As we see from manifest facts, God made unity, but not uniformity; He did not level all down to monotonous similarity. The aorists refer to the act of creation, and there is no need to turn either into a perfect ('hath set,' AV., RV.). From the very first it was ordered so, as part of a *plan*; therefore 'placed' rather than 'set.' Every member cannot have the same function, and therefore there must be higher and lower gifts. But pride and discontent are quite out of place, for they are not only the outcome of selfishness, but also rebellion against God's will. This has two points ; it was not our fellow-men who placed us in an inferior position, but God; and He did it, not to please us or our fellows, but in accordance with His will, which must be right. Who is so disloyal as to gainsay what God willed to arrange? Rom. ix. 20. Compare καθὼς βούλεται (v. 11), but the change of verb and of tense should be noted : it is not mere repetition. Deissmann (*Bible Studies*, p. 252) quotes ὡς ὁ Θεὸς ἤθελεν from a private letter of about 200 A.D.

19. 'Now, if they all (τὰ πάντα) were one member, where were the body?' This is the second absurdity : the first was 'where were the other members?' The very idea of body implies many members, and if all the members tried to have the honour of the highest member, the body would be lost. *Quanta ergo insania erit, si membrum unum, potius quam alteri cedat, in suum et corporis interitum conspiret* (Calv.). See Pope, *Essay on Man*, i. 259 f., "What if the foot," etc.

20. 'But, as it is (But now you see), there are many members, yet one body.' Perhaps there was already a proverb—πολλὰ μέλη, ἐν σῶμα. St Paul reiterates this truth, for on it everything which he desires to inculcate turns. From the oneness of the whole the mutual dependence of the parts follows of necessity. See M. Aurelius, ii. 3 ; in the universe, part and whole must co-operate.

νῦν δέ is specially frequent in 1 Cor. (v. 11, vii. 14, xii. 20, xiv. 6) ; but both here and elsewhere authorities are divided between νῦν and νυνί : in xiii. 13 and xv. 20 νυνί is probably right. In v. 19, B F G omit the τά before πάντα, and in v. 20 the μέν after πόλλα is omitted by B D*, Arm. Goth. If we retain μέν, 'yet one body' or 'but one body' may be strengthened to 'yet but one body' (AV.), *unum vero corpus* (Beza).

21. Hitherto he has been regarding the inferior organs, who grumbled because they were not superior. Now he takes the superior, who looked down on the inferior. All, of course, with reference to evils at Corinth. 'But the eye cannot say to the hand'—cannot, without stultifying itself: it is manifestly untrue. What would become of the desire of the eyes if there were no hand to grasp it? There is no such thing as independence either in an organism or in society. All parts are not equal, and no one part can isolate itself. From the first there is dependence and subordination.

The article before ὀφθαλμός is certainly genuine (א A B C D E F G L P), and the δε before ὁ ὀφθαλμός is probably genuine (א B D E K L, Latt.). Arm. omits both.

22. 'Nay, on the contrary (ἀλλά), much rather those members of the body which seem to be naturally (ὑπάρχειν) somewhat feeble, are necessary.' The humbler parts not only are indispensable, but are as indispensable as the rest. So also in society. It is the humblest workers, the day-labourers in each trade, that are not only *as* necessary as the higher ones, but are more necessary. We can spare this artizan better than this poet; but we can spare all the poets better than all the artizans. With this use of the comparative to soften the meaning, comp. 2 Tim. i. 8; Acts xvii. 22. St Paul does not specify the 'somewhat feeble' members, and we need not do so.

23. καὶ ἃ δοκοῦμεν ἀτιμότερα . . . περιτίθεμεν. 'And the parts of the body which we deem to be less honourable, these we clothe with more abundant honour.' Elsewhere in the N.T. περιτίθημι occurs only in the Gospels and there only in the literal sense, and generally of clothing (Matt. xxvii. 28), or the crown of thorns (Mark xv. 17), or a fence (Matt. xxi. 33; Mark xii. 1), etc.; but in the LXX we have this same metaphor; καὶ οὕτως πᾶσαι αἱ γυναῖκες περιθήσουσιν τιμὴν τοῖς ἀνδράσιν ἑαυτῶν (Esth. i. 20): τιμὴν ἑαυτῷ περιτιθείς (Prov. xii. 9).

The division of the verses is unfortunate, and the punctuation of the AV. is wrong, while that of the RV. might be improved. Put a comma at the end of *v.* 23, and a full stop at the end of the first clause of *v.* 24. 'And so our uncomely parts have a comeliness more exceeding, whereas our comely parts have no need.' This is the result of giving more abundant honour to the less honourable; acting on that principle, we give *most* honour to the *least* honourable. The 'more exceeding comeliness' refers to the abundance of clothing, which, even when other parts are unclothed, τὰ ἀσχήμονα receive. For these the Vulg. has *inhonesta*, Beza *indecora*, Calv. *minus honesta*. There are three classes; τὰ εὐσχήμονα, which have no need of clothing or adornment, and are commonly exposed to view; τὰ ἀτιμότερα, which are usually clothed and often adorned; and τὰ ασχήμονα, which are always carefully clothed, *ut membra quae turpiter paterent, lateant honeste* (Calv.). The least honourable are not only not despised, they are treated with exceptional care.* There is no doubt that here, as elsewhere, εὐσχημοσύνη refers to *external* grace, elegance, or decorum. It does not refer to dignity of function. It is true that fatherhood has high responsibility, and that the womb and the breast are sacred, but εὐσχημοσύνη is not the word to express that. Throughout the passage the Apostle is thinking of the members of the Church, and therefore more or less personifies the organs of the body. We might render οὗ χρείαν ἔχει '*feels* no need,' no need of anything additional, *nullius egent* (Vulg.), which is better than the more definite *iis decore non est opus* (Beza). We do not adorn the eye, or protect the face as we protect the feet. Ἀσχήμων occurs several times in LXX, but nowhere else in N.T. ; εὐσχημοσύνη in 4 Mac. vi. 2, but nowhere else in N.T. or LXX. See Abbott, *Son of Man*, p. 178.

24. ἀλλὰ ὁ Θεὸς συνεκέρασεν τὸ σῶμα. The nominative is emphatic. 'But the fact is, it was God who compounded (blended) the body together, by giving to that which feeleth lack more abundant honour.' The two aorists are contemporaneous, δούς with συνεκέρασεν: in giving, or by giving, He tempered ; and in tempering, or by tempering, He gave. In the LXX and N.T. συγκεραννύναι is rare (Dan. ii. 43 ; 2 Mac. xv. 39 ; Heb. iv. 2), but it is common in class. Grk. Comp. the speech of Alcibiades (Thuc. VI. xviii. 6) ; νομίσατε νεότητα μὲν καὶ γῆρας ἄνευ ἀλλήλων μηδὲν δύνασθαι, ὁμοῦ δὲ τό τε φαῦλον καὶ τὸ μέσον καὶ τὸ πάνυ ἀκριβὲς ἂν ξυγκραθὲν μάλιστ' ἂν ἰσχύειν: also σύγκρασίς τίς ἐστιν ἐν πᾶσιν (Clem. Rom. *Cor.* 37). In *v.* 23 the Apostle shows how men, led by a natural instinct, equalize the dignity of their members. Here he shows that it is in reality God who blends and balances the whole by endowing men with this instinctive sense of propriety. What is in accordance with the common feelings of mankind is evidence of what is right (xi. 14).

We should read τῷ ὑστερουμένῳ (א A B C) rather than τῷ ὑστεροῦντι (D E F G K L). The former expresses the member's *sense* of inferiority.

25. ἵνα μὴ ᾖ σχίσμα ἐν τ. σ. 'That there should be no disunion in the body, but that (on the contrary) the members should have the *same* care one for another': τὸ αὐτό is emphatic, and μεριμνῶσιν is plural because the argument requires that the members be thought of as many and separate : 1 Tim. v. 25 ; Rev. v. 14 ; Luke xxiv. 11. The verb implies anxious care, thoughtful trouble.

* Atto of Vercelli illustrates this principle by the honour which is paid to those who, out of humility, go bare-footed and wear shabby clothing.

26. καί. 'And so (as a consequence of the perfect blending), whether one member suffereth, all the members rejoice with it.' Not only are the members united to one another and careful for one another, but what is felt by one is felt by all. See St Paul's own sympathy, 2 Cor. xi. 28, 29. Plato (*Repub.* v. 462) points out that when one's finger is hurt, one does not say, "My finger is in pain," but "*I* have a pain in my finger"; and Chrysostom (*ad loc.*) graphically describes how the various organs are affected when a thorn runs into the foot, and also when the head is crowned. 'Is glorified' may mean either by adornment, or by healthy action, or by special cultivation. In συγχαίρει the personification of the organs is complete: *congaudent* (Vulg.), *congratulantur* (Beza). But Beza, by substituting *simul dolent* for *compatiuntur* (Vulg.), makes συμπάσχει imply as much personification as συγχαίρει. The Christian principle is the law of sympathy. The interests of all individuals, of all classes, and of all nations are really identical, although we are seldom able to take a view sufficiently extended to see that this is so: but we must try to believe it. The benefit of one is the benefit of every one; and a wrong done to one is a wrong done to every one. *Salva esse societas, nisi amore et custodia partium, non potest* (Seneca).* The verb in N.T. is found only in Paul and Luke.

> God, in the nature of its being, founds
> Its proper bliss, and sets its proper bounds:
> But as He framed a whole the whole to bless,
> On mutual wants built mutual happiness.
> Thus God and nature linked the general frame,
> And bade self-love and social be the same.
>
> Pope, *Essay on Man*, iii. **109, 217.**

27. ὑμεῖς δέ ἐστε σῶμα Χριστοῦ. 'Now *ye* are *Body* of Christ': no article. 'Body of Christ' is the quality of the whole which each of them individually helps to constitute. Comp. ὁ Θεὸς φῶς ἐστι (1 John i. 5), ὁ Θεὸς ἀγάπη ἐστίν (1 John iv. 8), πνεῦμα ὁ Θεός (John iv. 24), Θεός ἦν ὁ λόγος (John i. 1); 1 Cor. iii. 9, 16. It does not mean, 'Ye are *the* Body of Christ,' although that translation is admissible, and indicates the truth that each Christian community is the Universal Church in miniature; nor, 'Ye are Christ's Body,' which makes 'Christ's ' emphatic, whereas the emphasis is on σῶμα as the antithesis of μέλη. Least of all

---

* "One of the most remarkable sides of the history of Rome is the growth of ideas which found their realization and completion in the Christian Empire. Universal citizenship, universal equality, universal religion, a universal Church, all were ideas which the Empire was slowly working out, but which it could not realize till it merged itself in Christianity" (Ramsay, *The Church in the Roman Empire*, p. 192).

does it mean, 'Ye are *a* Body of Christ,' as if St Paul were insisting that the Corinthians were only *a* Church and not *the* Church,
a meaning which is quite remote from the passage.   Nowhere in
the Pauline Epistles is there the idea that the one Ecclesia is
made of many Ecclesiae.   "The members which make up the
One Ecclesia are not communities but individual men.   The
One Ecclesia includes all members of partial Ecclesiae ; but its
relations to them all are direct, not mediate. . . . There is no
indication that St Paul regarded the conditions of membership
in the universal Ecclesia as differing from the conditions of
membership in the partial local Ecclesiae" (Hort, *The Chr. Eccl.*
pp. 168–9).   He means here that the nature of the whole of
which the Corinthians are parts is that it is Body of Christ,
not any other kind of whole.   Consequently, whatever gift each
one of them receives is not to be hidden away, or selfishly
enjoyed, or exhibited for show, but to be used for the good of
the whole community.   The δέ marks a return to what was laid
down in *v.* 12.

μέλη ἐκ μέρους.   *membra de membro* (Vulg.) ; *membra ex parte*
(Calv.) ; *membra particulatim* (Beza).   The meaning is uncertain,
but probably, 'members each in his assigned part,' 'apportioned
members of it.'   Chrysostom and Bengel explain that the
Corinthians were not the whole Church, but 'members of a
part' of the *Universalis Ecclesia.*   This seems to Calvin to be
sensus coactior, and he prefers the other interpretation.   Still
less satisfactory is the explanation 'partial members of it,'
i.e. imperfect members, which does not suit the context at
all.   Cf. Eph. iv. 16.

The Vulgate, with d e f Arm., supports D* in reading μέλη ἐκ μέλους.
Origen and Eusebius commonly have μέρους, but once each has μέλους :
Theodoret the same.   Chrysostom always μέρους.

28. Καὶ οὓς μὲν ἔθετο ὁ Θεὸς ἐν τῇ ἐκκλησίᾳ.   The correspondence with *v.* 18 is manifest, and it must be marked in translation.
'And some God placed in the Church,' or 'in His Church'
(i. 2, x. 32, xi. 16, 22, xv. 9).   Just as God in the original constitution of the body placed differently endowed members in it,
so in the original constitution of the Church He placed (Acts
xx. 28) differently endowed members in it.   The mid. implies
that He placed them for His own purpose, καθὼς ἠθέλησεν.   The
Church is the Church Universal, not the Corinthian Church ;
and this is perhaps the first Epistle in which we find this use :
comp. x. 32, xi. 22, xv. 9 ; Hort, p. 117.   The sentence should
have run, οὓς μὲν ἀποστόλους, οὓς δὲ προφήτας, but the original
construction is abandoned, perhaps intentionally, because
an arrangement in order of dignity seemed better than a

mere enumeration, the last place being again reserved for the
Tongues. Later he drops into a mere enumeration. Moul.
Win. p. 710.

πρῶτον ἀποστόλους. Not to be restricted to the Twelve.
The term included Paul and Barnabas, James the Lord's brother
(xv. 7; Gal. i. 19; comp. ix. 5), apparently Andronicus and
Junias (Rom. xvi. 7), and probably others (xv. 5, 7). There
could not have been false apostles (2 Cor. xi. 13) unless the
number of Apostles had been indefinite. From this passage,
and from Eph. iv. 11 (comp. ii. 20), we learn that Apostles were
the first order in the Church; also that St Peter is not an order
by himself. Apparently it was essential that an Apostle should
have seen the Lord, and especially the risen Lord (ix. 1, 2;
Luke xxiv. 48; Acts i. 8, 21–23): he must be a 'witness of
His resurrection.' This was true of Matthias, James, and Paul;
and may easily have been true of Barnabas, Andronicus, and
Junias; but not of Apollos or Timothy. The Apostles were
analogous to the Prophets of the O.T., being sent to the
new Israel, as the Prophets to the old. They had administrative functions, but no local jurisdiction: they belonged to
the whole Church. Nevertheless various ties made local
Churches to be more under the control of one Apostle than of
others. See Lightfoot, *Galatians*, pp. 92 f. The 'evangelists'
and 'pastors' of Eph. iv. 11 are perhaps included here under
'prophets and teachers.' But evangelists are not *ad rem* here,
because the subject is the spiritual life of members of the
Church, and their relations to one another *in* the Church, rather
than their external activity among the heathen. The enumeration here is more concrete than that in *vv.* 8–10, but less
concrete than in Eph. iv. 11. The first three are explicitly in
order of eminence; but the ἔπειτα with the next two probably
means no more than that these come after the first three. The
gifts that follow the first three are not connected with particular
persons, but are distributed 'at will' for the profit of the whole
congregation; and it is remarkable that δυνάμεις and χαρίσματα
ἰαμάτων are placed after διδασκάλους. See Dobschütz, *Probleme*,
p. 105.

προφήτας. See on *v.* 10 and xiv. 3, 24, 25. They were
inspired to utter the deep things of God, for the conviction of
sin, for edification, and for comfort; sometimes also for predicting the future, as in the case of Agabus.

διδασκάλους. Men whose natural powers and acquired knowledge were augmented by a special gift. It is evident from 'Are
all teachers?' (*v.* 29) that there was a class of teachers to which
only some Christians belonged, and the questions which follow
show that 'teachers,' like 'workers of miracles,' were distinguished

by the possession of some gift.* In Eph. iv. 11 we are not
sure whether ' pastors and teachers ' means one class or two, but
at any rate it is probable that whereas ' Apostles,' ' prophets,'
and ' evangelists ' instructed both the converted and the unconverted, ' pastors and teachers ' ministered to settled congregations.
In Acts xiii. 1 we are equally in doubt whether ' prophets and
teachers ' means one class or two. St Luke may mean that of
the five people mentioned some were prophets and some were
teachers, or he may mean that all were both. ' Teacher ' might
be applied to Apostles, prophets, and evangelists, as well as to
the special class of teachers. In 1 Tim. ii. 7 St Paul calls
himself a ' preacher ' (κῆρυξ), an ' Apostle,' and a ' teacher.' In
the *Didache* the ' teacher ' seems to be itinerant like the
' prophet ' (xiii. 2). When the ministry became more settled
the ' bishops ' and ' elders ' seem to have become the official
teachers ; but perhaps not all elders taught (1 Tim. v. 17). In
the *Shepherd of Hermas* the teachers are still distinct from the
bishops ; " The stones that are squared and white, and that fit
together in their joints, these are the Apostles and bishops and
teachers and deacons " (*Vis.* iii. 5). See Hastings, *DB.* iv.
p. 691 ; *Ency. Bibl.* iv. 4917.

ἔπειτα δυνάμεις, ἔπειτα χαρίσματα ἰαμάτων. Change from the
concrete to the abstract, perhaps for the sake of variety ; in
Rom. xii. 7 the converse change is made. We must not
count ἔπειτα, ἔπειτα as equivalent to ' fourthly, fifthly ' : the
classification according to rank ends with ' teachers,' but γένη
γλωσσῶν are purposely placed last. ' Gifts of healing ' are
a special kind of ' miraculous powers' : see on *v.* 9, where the
less comprehensive gift is placed first, while here we descend
from the general to the particular. It would be a lesson to the
Corinthians to hear these brilliant gifts expressly declared to be
inferior to teaching ; the ἔπειτα clearly means that.

ἀντιλήμψεις. This and the next gift form a pair, referring to
general management of an external character. This term occurs
nowhere else in the N.T., but it comes from ἀντιλαμβάνεσθαι
(Luke i. 54 ; Acts xx. 35 ; 1 Tim. vi. 2 ; comp. Rom. viii. 26),

---

* " It is impossible to determine exactly how people were recognized as
teachers. One clue, however, seems visible in Jas. iii. 1. From this it
follows that to become a teacher was a matter of personal choice—based, of
course, upon the individual's consciousness of possessing a charisma "
(Harnack, *The Mission and Expansion of Christianity*, I. p. 336 ; p. 243,
ed. 1902). The whole chapter (1st of the 3rd Book) should be read. It
shows that the order ' Apostles, prophets, and teachers ' is very early.
" St Paul is thinking without doubt of some arrangement in the Church
which held good among Jewish Christian communities founded apart from
his co-operation, no less than among the communities of Greece and Asia
Minor."

which means to take firm hold of some one, in order to help.
These 'helpings' therefore probably refer to the succouring of
those in need, whether poor, sick, widows, orphans, strangers,
travellers, or what not; the work of the diaconate, both male
and female. We have those who need ἀντίλημψις (Ecclus. xi. 12,
li. 7). The word is fairly common in the Psalms and 2 and
3 Mac. See also Psalms of Solomon vii. 9, xvi. title.

κυβερνήσεις. 'Governings' or 'administrations.' This probably refers to those who superintended the externals of organization, οἱ προϊστάμενοι (Rom. xii. 8; 1 Thess. v. 12), or οἱ ἡγού-
μενοι (Heb. xiii. 7, 17, 24; Acts xv. 22; Clem. Rom. *Cor.* 1).
See Hort, *The Chr. Eccl.* p. 126. The word is derived from the
idea of piloting a ship (Acts xxvii. 11; Rev. xviii. 17), and hence
easily acquires the sense of directing with skill and wisdom : οἷς μὴ
ὑπάρχει κυβέρνησις, πίπτουσιν ὡς φύλλα, *ubi non est gubernator,
populus corruet* (Prov. xi. 14). The term, which is found nowhere
else in N.T., may be equivalent to ἐπίσκοποι and πρεσβύτεροι.
We must, however, remember that we are here dealing with
gifts rather than with the offices which grew out of the gifts.

These two classes, ἀντιλήμψεις and κυβερνήσεις, are not
mentioned in *vv.* 5–10; nor are they repeated in *vv.* 29, 30.
But Stanley would identify the former with the *help* rendered in
the 'intepretation of tongues,' and the latter with the *guidance*
given in the 'discerning of spirits.' This is not at all probable.
See Deissmann, *Bible Studies*, p. 92.

With regard to the subordinate position which these two
gifts have in the one list which contains them, Renan (*Saint
Paul*, pp. 409, 410) has a fine passage. "Malheur à celui qui
s'arrêterait à la surface, et qui, pour deux ou trois dons chimér-
iques, oublierait que dans cette étrange énumération, parmi les
diaconies et les *charismata* de l'Église primitive, se trouve le soin
de ceux qui souffrent, l'administration des deniers du pauvre,
l'assistance réciproque ! Paule énumère ces fonctions en dernier
lieu et comme d'humbles choses. Mais son regard perçant sait
encore ici voir le vrai. ' Prenez garde,' dit-il ; ' nos membres
les moins nobles sont justement les plus honorés.' Prophètes,
docteurs, vous passerez. Diacres, veuves dévouées, vous
resterez ; vous fondez pour l'éternité." *

ἔπειτα ... ἔπειτα is right (א A B C), not ἔπειτα ... εἶτα (K L, f Vulg.
deinde ... exinde), nor ἔπειτα, without either to follow (D E F G).
Vulg. after *genera linguarum* adds *interpretationes sermonum* from *v.* 10.
But whence comes the change to *sermonum*? Tertullian (*Adv. Marcion.
v. 8) has *genera linguarum ... interpretatio ... linguarum.*

* The shortness of the list of charismata in Eph. iv. 11 as compared with
the list here is perhaps an indication that the regular exercise of extraordinary
gifts in public worship was already dying out. Hastings, *DB.* III. p. 141.

29. μὴ πάντες ἀπόστολοι; 'Surely all are not Apostles?' These rhetorical questions explain μέλη ἐκ μέρους (*v.* 27) and look back to τὸ σῶμα οὐκ ἔν μέλος ἀλλὰ πολλά (*v.* 14). God did not give all these spiritual gifts to all. That would have been to make each member a kind of complete body, independent of the other members; and this would have been fatal to the whole. He has made no one member self-sufficient; each needs much from others and supplies something to them. See Godet. Here all the illustrations are concrete, with the possible exception of δυνάμεις. But seeing that δυνάμεις and χαρ. ἰαμάτων form a pair, we may put the two questions together and take ἔχουσιν with both terms; 'Have all (the power of working) miracles, all gifts of healing?' The Vulgate may be taken in a similar manner; *Numquid omnes virtutes, numquid omnes gratiam habent curationum?* but again, why the change from *gratias* (*v.* 28) to *gratiam?* For the third time the gift of Tongues is placed last.

30. The compound verb διερμηνεύω here has led to the reading διερμηνεία (or -ια) in *v.* 10 (A D*). The compound (xiv. 5, 13, 27; Luke xxiv. 27; Acts ix. 36) is more common in the N.T. than the more classical ἑρμηνεύω (John i. 43, ix. 7; Heb. vii. 2). As language weakens, the tendency to strengthen by means of compounds increases. With the general sense of the two verses compare Hom. *Il.* xiii. 729; Ἀλλ' οὐ πως ἅμα πάντα δυνήσεαι αὐτὸς ἐλέσθαι, and the familiar *non omnia possumus omnes.*

31. ζηλοῦτε δὲ τὰ χαρίσματα τὰ μείζονα. 'Continue to desire earnestly (pres. imperat.) the greater gifts.' The Corinthians coveted the greater gifts, but they had formed a wrong estimate as to which were the greater. The Hymn of Love, which follows, is to guide them to a better decision: not those which make most show, but those which do most good, are the better. As members of one and the same body they must exhibit self-sacrificing love, and they must use their gifts for the benefit of the whole body. This is the lesson of ch. xiv. We cannot all of us have all the best gifts; but (δέ) by prayer and habitual preparation we can strive to obtain them: and a continual desire is in itself a preparation. Μένετε ἐπιθυμοῦντες χαρισμάτων, as Chrysostom says. For ζηλοῦτε comp. xiv. 1, 39; and ἐζήλωσα τὸ ἀγαθόν (Ecclus. li. 18). The verb is also used in a bad sense, 'be moved with envy or hatred' (xiii. 4; Acts vii. 9, xvii. 5). See Hort and also Mayor on Jas. iv. 2. It is perhaps with a *double entendre* that it is used here, as an indirect rebuke to the jealousy with which some of them regarded the gifts bestowed on others. Chrysostom (*Hom.* xxxi. 4) has some strong remarks on jealousy, as the chief cause of dissension, and as even more deadly in its effects than avarice. *Hucusque revocavit illos a schismate ad concordiam et unionem, ut nullus*

glorietur de charismate superiori, nullusque doleat de inferiori
Hinc eos in charitatem innuit, ostendens sine ea nihil caetera
valere (Herveius). *Sicut publica via excelsior est reliquis viis at*
semitis, ita et charitas via est directa, per quam ad coelestem
metropolim tenditur (Primasius).

καὶ ἔτι καθ᾽ ὑπερβολὴν ὁδὸν ὑμῖν δείκνυμι. There is no contrast with what precedes ('And yet,' AV.): on the contrary, καί
means 'And in accordance with this charge to desire what is
best,' while ἔτι belongs to what follows; 'And a still more
excellent way show I to you,' καθ᾽ ὑπερβολήν being equivalent
to a comparative, *excellentiorem viam* (Vulg.). If ἔτι be taken
with καί, it means 'moreover,' *et porro* (Beza); 'And besides, I
show you a supremely excellent way.' What is this way κατ᾽
ἐξοχήν? Is it the way by which the greater gifts are to be
reached? Or is it the way by which something better than
these gifts may be reached? The latter seems to be right.
'Yearn for the best gifts; that is good, as far as it goes. But
the gifts do not make you better Christians; and I am going to
point out the way to something better, which will show you the
best gifts, and how to use them.'* xiv. 1 confirms this view.

There is considerable evidence (D E F G K L, Vulg. Arm.) for κρείττονα
or κρείσσονα, and Chrys. expressly prefers the reading; but μείζονα (ℵ A B C,
Am. Aeth., Orig.) is probably right.

In the N.T. ὑπερβολή is confined to this group of the Pauline Epp.
(1 and 2 Cor. Gal. Rom.), and generally in this phrase, καθ᾽ ὑπερβολήν.
Comp. Rom. vii. 13.

Klostermann adopts the reading of D*; καὶ εἴ τι καθ᾽ ὑπερβολήν, ὁδὸν
ὑμῖν δείκνυμι, 'And if (ye desire earnestly) something superlatively good,
I show you a way.' But the earliest versions confirm the other MSS. in
reading ἔτι.

The Spiritual Gifts.

In this chapter we have had three enumerations of these gifts (*vv.* 8–10,
28, 29–30); and in Romans (xii. 6–8) and Ephesians (iv. 11) we have other
lists. It will be useful to compare the five statements.

1 Cor. xii. 8–10	xii. 28	xii. 29, 30
1. λόγος σοφίας	1. ἀπόστολοι	1. ἀπόστολοι
3. λόγος γνώσεως	2. προφῆται	2. προφῆται
πίστις	3. διδάσκαλοι	3. διδάσκαλοι
5. χαρ. ἰαμάτων	4. δυνάμεις	4. δυνάμεις
4. ἐνεργ. δυνάμεων	5. χαρ. ἰαμάτων	5. χαρ. ἰαμάτων
2. προφητεία	6. ἀντιλήμψεις	
διακρ. πνευμάτων	7. κυβερνήσεις	
8. γένη γλωσσῶν	8. γένη γλωσσῶν	8. γλώσσαις λαλεῖν
9. ἑρμ. γλωσσῶν	9.	9. διερμηνεύειν

---

* Comp. the use of ἡ ὁδός, 'the Way' *par excellence*, for Christianity
(Acts ix. 2, xix. 9, 23, xxii. 4, xxiv. 14, 22). Bengel has *via maxime vialis*;
it has the true characteristic of a way in perfection.

Rom. xii. 6–8.	Eph. iv. 11.
2. προφητεία	1. ἀπόστολοι
διακονία	2. προφῆται
3. διδασκαλία	εὐαγγελισταί
παράκλησις	ποιμένες καὶ
μεταδιδόναι	3. διδάσκαλοι
προΐστασθαι	

It will be observed that in four of the lists there are at least two gifts which are not mentioned in the other lists: in 1 Cor. xii. 8–10, πίστις and διάκρισις πνευμάτων ; in xii. 28, ἀντιλήμψεις and κυβερνήσεις : in Rom. xii. 6–8, διακονία, παράκλησις, μεταδιδόναι, and προΐστασθαι; and in Eph. iv. 11, εὐαγγελισταί and ποιμένες, if ποιμένες is a separate class from διδάσκαλοι. We must not assume that in all cases the difference of name means a difference of gift or of function. We may tentatively identify διακονία with ἀντίλημψις, and οἱ προιστάμενοι with κυβερνήσεις, and perhaps with ποιμένες. We have St Paul's own authority for placing ἀπόστολοι, προφῆται, and διδάσκαλοι above all the rest, and in that order ; and for placing γένη γλωσσῶν with ἑρμηνεία γλωσσῶν last. Taking xii. 28 as our guide, we notice that, of the nine gifts enumerated, three are those in which teaching is the common element, two are wonder-working, two are administrative, and two are ecstatic. The three pairs are valuable, especially the first two, yet they are not indispensable ; but powers of teaching are indispensable. If there is no one to teach with sureness and authority, the Christian Church cannot be built up and cannot grow. But it must be remembered once more that we are treating of various gifts bestowed upon various persons, some of whom had more than one gift, and that some Christians had no special endowment. We are not dealing with classes of officials, each with definite functions ; *munus* in the sense of *donum* has not yet passed into *munus* in the sense of *officium*, and the process of transition has scarcely begun. In correcting the errors into which the Corinthians had fallen, the Apostle does not tell any officials to take action, but addresses the congregation as a whole. The inference is that *there were no officials in the ecclesiastical sense*, although, as in every society, there were leading men. See *Ency. Bibl.* I. 1038, III. 3108, IV. 4759 ; Hastings, *DB.* III. 377 ; Hort, *Chr. Eccles.* pp. 203 f.

Novatian (*De Trinitate* xxix.) paraphrases this passage thus ; *Hic est enim qui prophetas in ecclesia constituit, magistros erudit, linguas dirigit, virtutes et sanitates facit, opera mirabilia gerit, discretiones spirituum porrigit, gubernationes contribuit, consilia suggerit, quaeque alia sunt charismatum dona componit et digerit ; et ideo ecclesiam domini undique et in omnibus perfectam et consummatam facit ;* where (as in ix. and xii.) Novatian evidently uses *sanitates* in the sense of ' cures.'

On our scanty knowledge of the organization of the Apostolic Churches see Gwatkin, *Early Church History*, i. pp. 64–72.

ADDITIONAL NOTE ON XII. 3.

If the theory is correct that the Christ party were docetists, who used the name of Christ in opposition, not merely to the names of Paul, Apollos, and Kephas, but also to the name of Jesus, then the cry ' Jesus be anathema' might express their contempt for ' knowing Christ after the flesh.' They would have nothing to do with any external or material reality, and in this spirit perhaps denied that there could be any resurrection of the *body*, either in the case of Christ or of any one else. See B. W. Bacon, *Introd. to N. T.* p. 92. There may have been docetists at Corinth, whether they belonged to the Christ party or not.

XIII. 1–13. A PSALM IN PRAISE OF LOVE.

The thirteenth chapter stands to the whole discussion on Spiritual Gifts in a relation closely similar to that of the digression on self-limitation (ch. ix.) to the discussion of εἰδωλόθυτα. Either chapter raises the whole subject of its main section to the level of a central principle. The principle is in each case the same *in kind*, namely, that of subordinating (the lower) self to the good of others; but in this chapter the principle itself is raised to its highest power: from forbearance, or mere self-limitation, we ascend to love.

The chapter, although a digression, is yet a step in the treatment of the subject of Spiritual Gifts (xii. 1–xiv. 40), and forms in itself a complete and beautiful whole. After the promise that he will point out a still more surpassing way, there is, as it were, a moment of suspense; and then *jam ardet Paulus et fertur in amorem* (Beng.). Stanley imagines "how the Apostle's amanuensis must have paused to look up in his master's face at the sudden change in the style of his dictation, and seen his countenance lit up as it had been the face of an angel, as this vision of Divine perfection passed before him" (p. 238). Writer after writer has expatiated upon its literary and rhythmical beauty, which places it among the finest passages in the sacred, or, indeed, in any writings.* We may compare ch. xv., Rom. viii. 31–39, and—on a much lower plane—the torrent of invective in 2 Cor. xi. 19–29. This chapter is a divine προφητεία, which might have for its title that which distinguishes Ps. xlv.,—'A Song of Love' or 'of Loves.' And it is noteworthy that these praises of Love come, not from the Apostle of Love, but from the Apostle of Faith. It is not a fact that the Apostles are one-sided and prejudiced, each seeing only the gift which he specially esteems. Just as it is St John who says, 'This is the victory which overcometh the world, even our faith,' so it is St Paul who declares that greater than all gifts is Love.

No distinction is drawn between love to God and love to man. Throughout the chapter it is the root-principle that is meant; ἀγάπη in its most perfect and complete sense. But it is specially in reference to its manifestations to men that it is praised, and most of the features selected as characteristic of it are just those in which the Corinthians had proved defective.

---

* "The greatest, strongest, deepest thing Paul ever wrote" (Harnack).

"I never read 1 Cor. xiii. without thinking of the description of the virtues in the *Nicomachean Ethics*. St Paul's ethical teaching has quite an Hellenic ring. It is philosophical, as resting on a definite principle, viz. our new life in Christ; and it is logical, as classifying virtues and duties according to some intelligible principle" (E. L. Hicks, *Studia Biblica*, iv. p. 9).

And this deficiency is fatal. Christian Love is that something without which everything else is nothing, and which would be all-sufficient, even were it alone. It is not merely an attribute of God, it is His very nature, and no other moral term is thus used of Him (1 John iv. 8, 16). See W. E. Chadwick, *The Pastoral Teaching of St Paul*, ch. vi.; Moffatt, *Lit. of N.T.*, pp. 57, 58).

This hymn in praise of love is of importance with regard to the question of St Paul's personal knowledge of Jesus Christ. It is too often forgotten that Saul of Tarsus was a contemporary of our Lord, and the tendency of historical criticism at the present time is to place the date of Saul's conversion not very long after the Ascension. Furrer and Clemen would argue for this. Saul may not have been in Jerusalem at the time of the Crucifixion and Resurrection; but he would have abundant means of getting evidence at first hand about both, after the Appearance on the road to Damascus had made it imperative that he should do so; and some have seen evidence of exact knowledge of the life and character of Jesus of Nazareth in this marvellous analysis of the nature and attributes of Love. We have only, it is said, to substitute Jesus for Love throughout the chapter, and St Paul's panegyric "becomes a simple and perfect description of the historic Jesus" (*The Fifth Gospel*, p. 153). Intellect was worshipped in Greece, and power in Rome; but where did St Paul learn the surpassing beauty of love? "It was the life of love which Jesus lived which made the psalm of love which Paul wrote possible" (*ibid.*). In this chapter, as in Rom. xii., "we note that very significant transference of the centre of gravity in morals from *justice* to the sphere of the affections." See Inge, in *Cambridge Biblical Essays*, p. 271.

> Most commentators and translators are agreed that here, as in the writings of St John, ἀγάπη should be rendered 'love' rather than 'charity'; for the contrary view see Evans, p. 376. In the Vulgate, ἀγάπη is usually translated *caritas*, but *dilectio* is fairly common, and to this variation the inconsistencies in the AV. are due. The RV. has abolished them, and the gain is great. 'Charity' has become greatly narrowed in meaning, and now is understood as signifying either 'giving to the poor' or 'toleration of differences of opinion.' In the former and commonest sense it makes *v.* 3 self-contradictory,—almsgiving without 'charity.' See Sanday and Headlam, *Romans*, p. 374; Stanley, *Corinthians*, p. 240.

The chapter falls into three clearly marked parts. (1) The Necessity of possessing Love, 1–3; (2) Its glorious Characteristics, 4–7; Its eternal Durability, 8–13.

The one indispensable gift is Love. If one were to have all the special gifts in the highest perfection, without having Love, one would produce nothing, be nothing, and gain nothing. Love includes all the most beautiful features of moral character, and excludes all the offensive ones. Moreover, it is far more durable than even the best of the special gifts. They are of use in this world only; Love, with Faith and Hope, endures both in this world and in the next.

[1] I may talk with the tongues of men, yea of angels; yet, if I have no Love, so far from doing any good to a Christian assembly, I am become like the senseless din in heathen worships. [2] And I may have the gift of inspired preaching, and see my way through all the mysteries of the Kingdom of God and all the knowledge that man can attain; and I may have all the fulness of faith, so as to move mountains; yet, if I have no Love, so far from being a Christian of great account, I am nothing. [3] I may even dole out with my own hands everything that I possess,—may even, like the Three Children, surrender my body to the flames; yet, if I have no Love, so far from becoming a saint or a hero, or from winning a rich recompense from Heaven, I am not one whit the better. Love is the one thing that counts.

[4] For Love is patient and kind; Love knows no hatred or envy.
It is never a braggart in mien, or swells with self-adulation;
[5] It never offends good feeling, or insists on all it has claim to;
It never blazes with rage, and it stores up no resentment.

> [6] It delights not over the wrong that men do,
> But responds with delight to true dealing.
> [7] Unfailingly tolerant, unfailingly trustful,
> Unfailingly hopeful, unfailingly strong.

[8] The time will never come for Love to die.
There will be a time when our prophesyings will be useless;
There will be a time when these Tongues will cease;
There will be a time when our knowledge will be useless.

> [9] For our knowledge is but of fragments,
> And our prophesyings but of fragments.

[10] But when absolute completeness shall have come,
Then that which is of fragments will have no use.
The difference is far greater than that which distinguishes childhood from manhood; and yet, even there, how marked the

change! ¹¹ When I was a child, I used to talk as a child, to think as a child, to reason as a child. Since I am become a man, I have done away with childhood's ways. ¹² In a similar way, what we now see are but reflexions from a mirror which clouds and confuses things, so that we can only guess at the realities; but in the next world we shall have them face to face. The knowledge that I now have is only of fragments; but then I shall know as completely as God from the first knew me.

¹³ So then, Faith, Hope, and Love last on—just these three : but chiefest and best is Love.

1–3. All four classes of gifts (xii. 28) are included here : the ecstatic in *v.* 1 ; the teaching (προφητεία) and the wonder-working (πίστις) gifts in *v.* 2 ; and the administrative in *v.* 3. The Apostle takes the lowest of these special gifts first, because the Corinthians specially needed to be set right about them, and also because the least valuable of the special gifts made the strongest contrast to the excellence of Love. Speaking with Tongues and having no Love was only too common at Corinth. There is a climax in the succession, γλῶσσαι, προφητεία, πίστις, ψωμίσω καὶ παραδῶ. To mark this one may perhaps translate καὶ ἐάν in *v.* 3 'even if' ; but in strict grammar καὶ ἐάν is throughout simply 'and if.'

Ἐὰν ταῖς γλώσσαις . . . λαλῶ. A mere objective possibility connected with the future; 'If I should speak with the tongues of men and of angels,' not ' *Though* I speak' (AV.). The addition of καὶ τῶν ἀγγέλων gives the supposition about rapturous utterances the widest possible sweep ; 'Supposing that I had all the powers of earthly and heavenly utterance.' The reference to the Tongues need not be questioned. For the combination, 'angels and men,' comp. iv. 9. The language of angels was a subject which the Jews discussed, some Rabbis maintaining that it was Hebrew. Origen suggests that it is as superior to that of men as that of men is to the inarticulate cries of infants ; but χωρὶς ἀγάπης, γλῶσσα κἂν ἀγγέλων ἐν ἀνθρώποις καθ᾿ ὑπόθεσιν ᾖ, ἀτράνωτός ἐστιν (*JTS.* x. 37, p. 33), Ambrose (*De off. ministr.* ii. 27), *Si volumus commendare nos Deo, caritatem habeamus.* See Chadwick, *Pastoral Teaching,* p. 245. With the supposition here comp.

Οὐδ᾿ εἴ μοι δέκα μὲν γλῶσσαι δέκα δὲ στόματ᾿ εἶεν,
φωνὴ δ᾿ ἄρρηκτος, χάλκεον δέ μοι ἦτορ ἐνείη.

Hom. *Il.* ii. 489.

Non, mihi si linguae centum sint, oraque centum,
Ferrea vox.   Virg. *Georg.* ii. 44 ; *Aen.* vi. 625.

Godet has useful warnings against the " religious sybaritism "
which, especially during the excitement of religious " revivals," is
apt to turn Christianity into sentiment and fine speaking.   The
gift of Tongues might lead to this.   The Apostle sets an example
of love and of humility in taking himself as the illustration of
failure.   He might have said, ' If *you* should speak,' or ' Although
you speak.'   But he remembers his own gift of Tongues (xiv. 18),
and gives the warning to himself all through these three verses.

ἀγάπην δὲ μὴ ἔχω, γέγονα κ.τ.λ.   ' And should not have love '
(viii. 1), or, ' while I have not love,' on that assumption 'I am
become (Gal. iv. 16) sounding brass or a clanging cymbal.'   The
χαλκός probably means something of the nature of a gong rather
than a trumpet ; and ἀλαλάζον imitates loud and prolonged noise,
often of the shout of victory (Josh. vi. 20 ; 1 Sam. xvii. 52), but
sometimes of grief (Jer. iv. 8 ; Mark v. 38).   Cymbals are often
mentioned in the O.T., but nowhere else in the N.T. ; and in
St Paul's day they were much used in the worship of Dionysus,
Cybele, and the Corybantes.   Seeing that he insists so strongly
on the unedifying character of the Tongues (xiv.), as being of no
service to the congregation without a special interpreter, it is
quite possible that he is here comparing unintelligible Tongues
in Christian worship with the din of gongs and cymbals in pagan
worship.   Or he may be pointing out the worthlessness of
extravagant manifestations of emotion, which proceed, not from
the heart, but from hollowness.   Cymbals were hollow, to
increase the noise.   Or he may be merely saying that Tongues
without Christian love are as senseless as the unmusical and
distracting noise of a soulless instrument.   Δωδωναῖον χαλκεῖον is
said to have been a proverbial expression for an empty talker ;
and it was probably on account of his vainglorious loquacity that
Apion the grammarian, against whom Josephus wrote, was called
by Tiberius *cymbalum mundi*: φορτικός τις καὶ ἐπαχθὴς τοῖς
πολλοῖς, as Chrysostom paraphrases here.

On ἀγάπη see above ; Trench, *Syn.* § xii. ; Cremer, pp. 13 f. ;
Suicer, i. pp. 18 f. ; Hastings, *DB*. iii. p. 156 ; Deissmann, *Bible
Studies*, p. 199, *Light*, pp. 18, 70, and see 150, 399.   Ἠχεῖν is
frequent in LXX, but is found nowhere else in N.T.

2. κἂν ἔχω προφητείαν κ.τ.λ.   ' And if I should have the gift
of prophesying (preaching with special inspiration), and should
know *all* the mysteries (of God's counsels and will), and *all*
possible knowledge about them (xii. 8), and if I should have *all*
possible faith (xii. 9), so as to remove mountains, while I have
no love, I am nothing '—spiritually a cipher.   Having said that
the ecstatic gifts are worthless without love, he now says that the
teaching gifts are equally worthless : and perhaps he is here

indicating the three kinds of spiritual instructors (xii. 8, 10, 28), for τὰ μυστήρια πάντα may refer to the σοφία of the ἀπόστολοι, and πᾶσαν τὴν γνῶσιν to the γνῶσις of the διδάσκαλοι. Comp. Rom. xi. 33, xv. 14. By πίστις is meant wonder-working faith, not saving faith ; ' enough to displace mountains ' : comp. τὰ ὄρη μεταστήσεσθαι (Isa. liv. 10). It is possible that St Paul is alluding to our Lord's saying (Mark xi. 22 ; Matt. xvii. 20, xxi. 21), although of course not to Gospels which were not yet written. But it is quite as probable that both He and the Apostle used a proverbial expression, moving mountains being a common metaphor for a great difficulty. See Abbott, *The Son of Man*, p. 387. In N.T. the verb is found only in Paul and Luke. Balaam and Samson were instances of persons who had supernatural gifts and yet were morally degraded. For the combination of faith and knowledge, comp. 2 Cor. viii. 7, and for the emphatic repetition of πᾶς, 2 Cor. ix. 8. The abruptness of οὐθέν εἰμι, after the prolonged hypothesis of three clauses, is impressive.

In *vv.* 2 and 3 the MSS. differ considerably between κἂν and καὶ ἐάν and καὶ ἄν. But it is probable that κἂν is right throughout, the evidence for it being stronger in *v.* 3 than in *v.* 2, but not decisive. For μεθιστάναι (אBDEFG) the external evidence is stronger than for μεθιστάνειν (ACKL, Orig. Chrys.) ; but, on the other hand, the unusual μεθιστάνειν would be likely to be altered to the common form. And οὐθέν (אABCL) is to be preferred to οὐδέν (D* FGK).

3. We now pass on to the administrative gifts, ἀντιλήμψεις (xii. 28), ministering to the bodily needs of the brethren, and that in what *seems* to be a specially self-denying form.

κἂν ψωμίσω πάντα τὰ ὑπάρχοντά μου. 'And if I should give away in doles of food all my possessions.' There is no need to say anything about the recipients of the bounty, τοὺς πένητας (Chrys.), *pauperum* (Vulg.), 'the poor' (AV., RV.) : it is the giver, not the recipients, that is in question. The verb implies *personal* distribution to *many*, and that the act is done once for all : he could not habitually give away *all* his goods. The 'all' continues the emphatic repetition of πᾶς : throughout he makes the supposition as strong as possible. We have ψωμίζω in Rom. xii. 20 and in the LXX (Num. xi. 4, 18 ; Deut. viii. 3, 16 of the manna ; and often). In class. Grk. it is used of feeding children and young animals with ψωμοί, 'morsels' (freq. in LXX) : ψωμίον, 'sop,' John xiii. 26. *Si distribuero in cibos pauperum* (Vulg.), *insumam in alimoniam* (Calv.), *insumam alendis egenis* (Beza).

κἂν παραδῶ . . . ἵνα καυθήσομαι. 'And (even) if I deliver up myself to be burned.' Literally, ' deliver up my body, so that I shall be burned.' In the N.T. ἵνα is often used where result is

prominent and purpose in the background. It expresses a
"purposive result," the subjective intention shading off into the
objective effect ; and hence the use of the future : ix. 18 ; Gal.
ii. 4 ; John vii. 3, xvii. 2, etc.   True love, as he proceeds to
show, does not need the supreme crises which call for the
sacrifice of all that one possesses or of one's life,—a sacrifice
which might be made without true love : it manifests itself at all
times and in all circumstances.   Sacrifices made without love may
profit other people, but they do not profit the man himself.
Non charitas de martyrio, sed martyrium nascitur ex charitate
(Primasius).   St Paul is not thinking of burning as a punishment,
which it was not, nor of the branding of slaves, but of the most
painful death which any one can voluntarily suffer.   It was from
this text that Dr. Richard Smith, Regius Professor of Divinity,
preached at Oxford before the burning of Ridley and Latimer,
16th October 1555.   Comp. παρέδωκαν τὰ σώματα αὐτῶν εἰς πῦρ
(Dan. iii. 28, Theod. 95), which may be in the Apostle's mind, and
πυρὶ τὸ σῶμα παραδόντες, of the Indians (Joseph. *B.J.* vii. viii. 7).

In each of the three suppositions we have a different result :
'I produce nothing of value' (*v.* 1) ; 'I am of no value' (*v.* 2) ;
'I gain nothing of value' (*v.* 3).   The man who possessed all the
gifts mentioned might be useful to the Church, but in character
he would be worthless, if the one indispensable thing were
lacking.   The gifts are not valueless, but he is.

It is by no means certain that καυθήσομαι (D E F G L, Latt. Syrr. Arm.
Aeth. Goth., Method. Bas. Tert.), to which καυθήσωμαι (C K, Chrys.) give
additional support, is the right reading.   The evidence for καυχήσωμαι
(ℵ A B 17, Aegyptt., Orig. Lat. MSS. known to Jer.) is very strong, and
WH. (*App.* p. 117) argue strongly in favour of it.   Clement of Rome (*Cor.*
lv.) may be referring to the passage with this reading when he says,
"Many gave themselves up (ἑαυτοὺς παρέδωκαν) to slavery, and receiving
the price paid for themselves fed (ἐψώμισαν) others."   If καυχήσωμαι be
adopted, it belongs to both clauses, not to the second only ; 'If I should
dole away my goods in alms, and if I should give up my very body, all
for the sake of glory, while I have no love, I am not a whit the better.'

But, as in the case of μεθιστάνειν (*v.* 2), we must consider more than the
external evidence.   Which would the Apostle be more likely to write, and
which would be more likely to be changed by a copyist?   'Surrender my
body,' without saying how or to whom, is an unlikely expression.   In the
two preceding verses nothing is said about the presence of an unworthy
motive, but only the absence of the one indispensable motive.   And the
introduction of the unworthy motive spoils the all-important 'and have no
love.'   No need to say that, if the motive is self-glorification.   If the
thought of Dan. iii. might have led a copyist to change καυχήσωμαι into
καυθήσωμαι, it might equally well have led the Apostle to write καυθήσωμαι
or καυθήσομαι : comp. ἔσβεσαν δύναμιν πυρός (Heb. xi. 34).   And if the
original reading had been καυχήσωμαι, would not καυθήσομαι have been a
more common reading than καυθήσομαι?   Cyprian twice quotes, *si tradidero
corpus meum ut ardeam, caritatem autem non habeam* (*Test.* iii. 3 ; *De
cath. eccl. unit.* 14), and the author of the tract on Re-baptism (13) has

etsi corpus meum tradidero, ita ut exurar igni, dilectionem autem non habeam.

The attractive suggestion of Stanley (p. 231) and of Lightfoot *Colossians*, p. 156, ed. 1875; p. 394, ed. 1892) that St Paul is thinking of "the Indian's tomb," with its boastful inscription, which he may have seen at Athens, confirms the reading καυθ. rather than καυχ., but it suits either. The tomb was still to be seen in Plutarch's time (*Alexander* 69), and the inscription ran thus ; "Zarmano-chegas, an Indian from Bargosa, according to the traditional customs of Indians, made himself immortal, and lies here" (ἑαυτὸν ἀπαθανατίοας κεῖται). He had burnt himself alive on the funeral pyre. But it is more likely that St Paul would think of Jewish examples (1 Macc. ii. 59).

ψωμίζω (K) for ψωμίσω (א A B C D, etc.) is the correction of a copyist who did not see the significance of the aorist.

With οὐδὲν (B C D F K L, not οὐθέν, א A) ὠφελοῦμαι, comp. Matt. vi. 1, vii. 22, 23, xvi. 26.

4-7. The Apostle, having shown the moral worthlessness and unproductiveness of the man who has many supernatural gifts and performs seemingly heroic acts without love, now depicts in rapturous praise the character that consists of just this one indispensable virtue. Every one of the moral excellences which he enumerates tells, for they are no mere abstractions, but are based on experience, and are aimed at the special faults exhibited by the Corinthians. And just as he personifies Sin, Death, and the Law in Romans, so here he personifies Love. The rhythm becomes lyrical.

We have fourteen descriptive statements in pairs. The first pair of characteristics has both members positive. Four pairs of negative characteristics follow, the last member being stated both negatively and positively (*v.* 6); and then we have two more pairs of positive characteristics (*v.* 7).

> Ἡ ἀγάπη μακροθυμεῖ, χρηστεύεται·
> Ἡ ἀγάπη οὐ ζηλοῖ, οὐ περπερεύεται,
> οὐ φυσιοῦται, οὐκ ἀσχημονεῖ,
> οὐ ζητεῖ τὰ ἑαυτῆς, οὐ παροξύνεται,
> οὐ λογίζεται τὸ κακόν, οὐ χαίρει ἐπὶ τῇ ἀδικίᾳ,
>   συνχαίρει δὲ τῇ ἀληθείᾳ·
> πάντα στέγει, πάντα πιστεύει,
> πάντα ἐλπίζει, πάντα ὑπομένει.

4. μακροθυμεῖ. 'Is long-suffering, long-tempered,' *longanimis* (Erasm.): it is slow to anger, slow to take offence or to inflict punishment.* While ὑπομονή (2 Cor. i. 6, vi. 4, xii. 12 ; Luke only in the Gospels, etc.) is endurance of suffering without giving way, μακροθυμία (2 Cor. vi. 6; Rom. ii. 4, ix. 22, etc.; not in the Gospels) is patience of injuries without paying back.

---

* Quod si te illud movet, quod solemus eam quam Graeci μακροθυμίαν vocant, *longanimitatem* interpretari, animadvertere licet a corpore ad animum multa verba transferri, sicut ab animo ad corpus (Aug. *De quantitate animae* xvii. 30).

It is the opposite of ὀξυθυμία, 'quick' or 'short temper':
comp. Jas. i. 19, and the adaptation of these verses in Clem.
Rom. *Cor.* 49.

χρηστεύεται. 'Is kind in demeanour,' 'plays the gentle
part.' While μακροθ. gives the passive side in reference to
injuries received, χρηστ. gives the active side in reference
to benefits bestowed. Nowhere else in the Bible is χρηστεύεσθαι
found, but χρηστότης and χρηστός are frequent in both the LXX
and N.T. See Clem. Rom. *Cor.* 18.

ἡ ἀγάπη οὐ ζηλοῖ. Ἡ ἀγάπη is repeated at the beginning
of the negative characteristics; it is to be taken with οὐ ζηλοῖ,
not with χρηστεύεται. 'Love knows neither jealousy nor envy.'
The verb covers both vices, and perhaps others; 'boil (ζέω)
with hatred or jealousy' is apparently the original meaning
(Acts vii. 9, xvii. 5; Jas. iv. 2). Contrast xii. 31, xiv. 1, 39;
2 Cor. xi. 2. To covet good gifts is right, to envy gifted
persons is wrong; for envy and jealousy lead to division and
strife (iii. 1).

οὐ περπερεύεται. 'Does not play the braggart' (πέρπερος);
late Greek, and not elsewhere in the Bible. Marcus Aurelius
couples it with γλισχρεύεσθαι, καὶ κολακεύειν, καὶ ἀρεσκεύεσθαι
(*v.* 5). Ostentation is the chief idea. Clem. Alex. (*Paed.* III.
i. p. 251) says; Περπερεία γὰρ ὁ καλλωπισμός, περιττότητος
καὶ ἀχρειότητος ἔχων ἔμφασιν. Origen applies it especially to
intellectual pride; Cicero (*Epp. ad Attic.* I. xiv. 4) uses it of
rhetorical display. Tert. (*De Pat.* 12) translates; *non protervum
sapit*, which is not so very different from Chrys. (*ad loc.*) οὐ
προπετεύεται. Hesychius says that the πέρπερος is μετὰ βλακείας
ἐπαιρόμενος. Evidently the word had various shades of meaning:
see Wetstein and Suicer. But the idea of ostentatious boasting
leads easily to the next point.

οὐ φυσιοῦται. 'Does not puff itself out' (iv. 6, 18, 19, v. 2,
viii. 1; Col. ii. 18; and not elsewhere in the N.T.). "He
who subjects himself to his neighbour in love can never be
humiliated" (Basil to Atarbius, *Ep.* 65).

A third ἡ ἀγάπη between οὐ ζηλοῖ and οὐ περπερ. (א A C D E F G K L,
Syrr. Goth.) is probably not genuine (om. B 17 and other cursives, Vulg.
Copt. Arm. Grk. and Lat. Fathers). Ἡ ἀγάπη at the beginning of the
positive and of the negative characteristics is in place; a third is superfluous. If it be inserted, it belongs, like the other two, to what follows.
The punctuation, ἡ ἀγάπη μακροθυμεῖ, χρηστεύεται ἡ ἀγάπη, οὐ ζηλοῖ ἡ
ἀγάπη, is clumsy.

5. οὐκ ἀσχημονεῖ. Comp. vii. 36. In both places 'behave
unmannerly,' rather than 'suffer shame' or 'seem vile' (Deut.
xxv. 3), is the meaning. Love is tactful, and does nothing
that would raise a blush: *non agit indecenter* (Calv.), *indecore*

(Beza), rather than *non est ambitiosa* (Vulg.), *fastidiosa* (Erasm.). The verb occurs in LXX, but nowhere else in N.T., excepting vi. 36. M. Aurelius (xi. 1) assigns properties to the rational soul (λογικὴ ψυχή) which remind us of those which the Apostle assigns to ἀγάπη, *e.g.* τὸ φιλεῖν τοὺς πλησίον, καὶ ἀλήθεια, καὶ αἰδώς.

τὰ ἑαυτῆς. 'Its own interests': x. 24, 33. This makes nobler sense than the reading τὸ μὴ ἑαυτῆς (B, Clem-Alex.). That Love does not try to defraud would be bathos here. This statement perhaps looks back to the law-suits in ch. vi.

οὐ παροξύνεται. Not merely 'does not fly into a rage,' but 'does not yield to provocation': it is not embittered by injuries, whether real or supposed. Elsewhere in N.T. only of St Paul's spirit being provoked at the numerous idols in Athens (Acts xvii. 16): in LXX frequent of great anger. The 'contention' between Paul and Barnabas (Acts xv. 39) was a παροξυσμός: see Westcott on Heb. x. 24.

οὐ λογίζεται τὸ κακόν. When there is no question that it has received an injury, Love 'doth not register the evil'; it stores up no resentment, and bears no malice. Comp. τὴν κακίαν τοῦ πλησίου μὴ λογίζεσθε ἐν ταῖς καρδίαις ὑμῶν (Zech viii. 17). For this sense of 'reckoning' see 2 Cor. v. 19; Rom. iv. 8; cf. Philem. 18. Neither *non cogitat malum* (Vulg.) nor *non suspicatur malum* (Grot.) does justice to either the verb or the article: τὸ κακόν is '*the* evil done to it.'

6. οὐ χαίρει ἐπὶ ἀδικίᾳ. 'Rejoiceth not over unrighteous-ness,' the wrongdoing committed by others (Rom. i. 32). It cannot sympathize with what is evil. Chrys. misses the point in saying that Love does not rejoice over those who *suffer* wrong, τοῖς κακῶς πάσχουσι. It is quite true that there is no *Schadenfreude* in Love, no gloating over the misfortunes of others; but that is not the meaning here. Love cannot share the glee of the successful transgressor.

συνχαίρει δὲ τῇ ἀληθείᾳ. So far from feeling satisfaction at the misdeeds of others, Love 'rejoices with the Truth.' Here Truth is personified, and Love and Truth rejoice together: comp. 2 Cor. xiii. 8; Jas. iii. 14; 1 John v. 6. The truth of the Gospel is not meant, but Truth in its widest sense, as opposed to ἀδικία (2 Thess. ii. 12; Rom. ii. 8), and therefore equivalent to Goodness. The change of preposition, from ἐπί to συν-, is ignored in the AV. *Non gaudet super iniquitatem, congaudet autem veritati* (Vulg.). Love sympathizes with all that is really good in others.

The seven negatives would become monotonous if they were continued. By giving an affirmative antithesis to the last of them St Paul prepares the way for a return to positive characteristics.

7. πάντα στέγει. The meaning of the verb is somewhat uncertain. It occurs only Ecclus. viii. 17 in LXX, of the fool who will not be able to *conceal* the matter, λόγον στέξαι: and only here, ix. 12, and 1 Thess. iii. 1, 5 in N.T. 'Covereth,' and so 'excuseth' would make sense here, but not such good sense as the other meaning of the verb, 'is proof against,' and so 'forbeareth, endureth,' which seems to be the meaning in all four places in the N.T. The second meaning springs from the first. 'To cover' is 'to protect,' and 'to protect' is 'to keep off' rain, foes, troubles, etc., and therefore to be proof against them or endure them. See Lightfoot on 1 Thess. iii. 1, where the Vulg. has *non sustinentes, v. 5, non sustinens,* and in ix. 12, *omnia sustinemus,* while here it has *omnia suffert.* The root is connected with *tegere,* 'deck,' 'thatch.'

πάντα πιστεύει. This does not mean, as Calvin points out, that a Christian is to allow himself to be fooled by every rogue, or to pretend that he believes that white is black. But in doubtful cases he will prefer being too generous in his conclusions to suspecting another unjustly. While he is patient with (στέγει) the mischief which his neighbour undoubtedly does, he credits him with good intentions, which he perhaps does not possess.

This characteristic, with the next pair, forms a climax. When Love has no evidence, it believes the best. When the evidence is adverse, it hopes for the best. And when hopes are repeatedly disappointed, it still courageously waits. The four form a chiasmus, the second being related to the third as the first to the last. While στέγει refers to present trials, ὑπομένει covers the future also. It is that cheerful and loyal fortitude which, having done all without apparent success, still stands and endures, whether the ingratitude of friends or the persecution of foes. Throughout the Pauline Epistles it is assumed that the Christian is likely to be persecuted; 1 Thess. i. 6, iii. 3, 7; 2 Thess. i. 4, 6; Rom. v. 3, viii. 35, xii. 12, etc.

One result of all this is closely connected with the subject of the preceding and of the following chapter—the well-being of the Christian body, as a whole consisting of many unequally gifted members: *praecipuus scopus est quam sit necessaria caritas ad conservandam ecclesiae unitatem* (Calvin).

8–13. Having shown the worthlessness of supernatural gifts, if love is absent, and the supreme excellence of a character in which love is dominant, St Paul now shows that love is superior to all the gifts, because they are for this world only,

whereas love is for both time and eternity. "This is the
crowning glory of love, that it is imperishable" (Stanley); it
abides until and beyond the supreme crisis of the Last Day.

8. Ἡ ἀγάπη οὐδέποτε πίπτει.   In making this new point
the nominative is again repeated, and with good effect. And
the new point is reached without difficulty. From ὑπομένει to
οὐδ. πίπτει is an easy transition.   That which withstands all
assaults and is not crushed by either the shortcomings of
comrades or the violence of opponents, will stand firm and
unshaken.   In the N.T., πίπτειν is nearly always literal; but
comp. τοῦ νόμου μίαν κεραίαν πεσεῖν (Luke xvi. 17).   In class.
Grk., οὐδέποτε is stronger than οὔποτε; but in late Grk. strong
forms lose their strength and become the common forms:
οὐδέποτε occurs fifteen or sixteen times in the N.T., οὐ . . .
πότε only 2 Pet. i. 21; comp. Eph. v. 29; 1 Thess. ii. 5;
2 Pet. i. 10.

From the statement that 'Love never faileth' but 'abideth'
after death, has been inferred the doctrine that the saints at
rest pray for those on earth.   Calvin vigorously attacks this
inference, as if it were harmful to believe in such a result
of love.   The inference is, no doubt, somewhat remote from the
context.

The reading πίπτει (ℵ* A B C* 17, 47, Nyss. Ambrst. Aug.) is to be
preferred to ἐκπίπτει (D E F G K L P, Vulg., Tert. Cypr.), which perhaps
comes from Rom. ix. 6.   Chrys. reads ἐκπίπτει, and explains that
Christians must never hate their persecutors.   They hate the evil deeds,
which are the devil's work, but not the doers, for they are the work of
God.   But οὐδέποτε πίπτει means more than this, as what follows shows.

εἴτε δὲ προφητεῖαι, καταργηθήσονται.   St Paul now takes up
again the comparison between Love and the special gifts.
Tested by the attribute of durability, Love exceeds all these
χαρίσματα.   And here the AV. improves on the Greek.   The
varied rendering of καταργεῖσθαι, 'fail,' 'vanish away,' 'be done
away,' is more pleasing than the repetition of the same word;
and the making the first καταργ. a *verbal* contradiction of
οὐδέποτε πίπτει is effective.

The repeated εἴτε is depreciatory; it suggests indifference
as to the existence of gifts of which the use was at best
temporary.   'But as to prophesyings, if there be any, they
shall be done away.'   Excepting Luke xiii. 7 and Heb. ii. 14,
καταργεῖν, 'to put out of action,' is wholly Pauline in the N.T.
It is found in all four groups, but is specially common in this
group of the Pauline Epp.   In the LXX, only in Ezra.   Three
prominent χαρίσματα are taken in illustration of the transitory
character of the gifts: to have gone through all would have

been tedious. And the γλῶσσαι are dropped in *v.* 9. Obviously, they will be 'rendered idle.' Tongues were a rapturous mode of addressing God; and no such rapture would be needed when the spirit was in His immediate presence. But Tongues seem to have ceased first of all the gifts. The plur. προφητεῖαι indicates different kinds of inspired preaching; but γνώσεις (א A, etc.) is a corruption to harmonize with the preceding plurals.

9. Again we have a chiasmus: prophesyings, knowledge (*v.* 8), know, prophesy (9). Both will be done away, for it is from a part only, and not from the whole, that we get to know anything of the truth, and from a part only that we prophesy. We cannot know, and therefore cannot preach, the whole truth, but only fragments. Knowledge and prophecy are useful as lamps in the darkness, but they will be useless when the eternal Day has dawned; ὁ γὰρ μέλλων βίος τούτων ἀνενδεής. In both clauses ἐκ μέρους is emphatic. Bishop Butler has shown that here complete knowledge even of a part is impossible, for we cannot have this until we know its full relation to the whole; and, in order to do that, we must have full knowledge of the whole, which is impossible.*

10. 'But when there shall have come that which is complete, that which is from a part will be done away'; chiasmus again. *Ubi perventum ad metam fuerit, tunc cessabunt adjumenta cursus* (Calv.). We might have expected St Paul to put it in this way, yet he does not. He does not say, 'But when we shall have come to the perfection of the other world,' etc. He is so full of the thought of the Second Advent, that he represents the perfection as coming to us. '*When* it shall have come'; then, but not till then. The Apostle is saying nothing about the cessation of χαρίσματα in this life: prophesyings and knowledge might always be useful. All that he asserts is, that these things will have no use when completeness is revealed; and therefore they are inferior to Love. Luther renders τὸ ἐκ μέρους, *das Stückwerk*.

In order to make the 'then and not till then' clearer, K L, Syrr. Chrys. and some other witnesses insert τότε before τὸ ἐκ μέρους: om. א A B D* F G P, Latt. Arm. Aeth. Goth., etc. Chrys. points out that it is only the partial, fragmentary knowledge that will be done away.

11. Illustration suggested by τὸ τέλειον: it is very inadequate, but it will serve. The difference between a νήπιος and a τέλειος

---

* Ἐκ μέρους is fairly common in both LXX and N.T. Other adverbial expressions are ἀπὸ μέρους, which marks a contrast with the whole less clearly than ἐκ μ. (2 Cor. i. 14, ii. 5), ἀνὰ μέρος (xiv. 27), and κατὰ μέρος (Heb. ix. 5).

is as nothing compared with the difference between the twilight of this world and the brightness of the perfect Day, but it will help us to understand this. In order to confirm *vv.* 8–10, the Apostle appeals to personal experience. 'When I was a child, I used to talk, think, and reason as a child: now that I am become a man, I have done away with the child's ways.' RV, has 'felt' for ἐφρόνουν, which is no improvement on the 'understood' of AV. A mental process is meant (Rom. xii. 3, etc.), of which ἐλογιζόμην, 'calculated' (2 Cor. v. 19, xi. 5 etc.), is a development. *Loquebar, sapiebam, cogitabam* (Vulg.); but *ratiocinabar* (Beza, Beng.) is better than *cogitabam.* Comp. *Numera annos tuos, et pudebit eadem velle quae volueras puer* (Seneca, *Ep.* 27).

The antithesis between τέλειος (ii. 6) and νήπιος (iii. 1) is freq. (xiv. 20; Eph. iv. 13, 14). The mid. imperf. ἤμην is not found, except as a doubtful reading, in class. Grk., but it is not rare in later writers: Gal. i. 10; Matt. xxiii. 30, xxv. 35, 36, 43 ; Acts xxvii. 37, and perhaps xi. 11. See Veitch, p. 200. The perf. κατήργηκα indicates a change of state which still continues; the emancipation from childish things took place as a matter of course, *ultro, libenter, sine labore* (Beng.), and it continues.
In each case ὡς νήπιος follows the verb (א A B 17, Vulg. Aeth.), and the δέ after ὅτε is an interpolation (om. א* A B D*); the contrast is more emphatic without it.

12. βλέπομεν γὰρ ἄρτι δι' ἐσόπτρου ἐν αἰνίγματι. 'For we see at present by means of a mirror in a riddle.' The γάρ confirms the preceding illustration ; *for* as childhood to manhood, so this life to the life to come. The argument is *a fortiori.* If adults have long since abandoned their playthings and primers, how much more will the reflected glimpses of truth be abandoned, when the whole truth is directly seen. Almost certainly, δι' ἐσόπτρου means '*by means of* a mirror,' not '*through* a mirror.' Ancient mirrors were of polished metal, and Corinthian mirrors were famous; but the best of them would give an imperfect and somewhat distorted reflexion, and Corinthian Christians would not possess the best (i. 26). To see a friend's face in a cheap mirror would be very different from looking at the friend. This world reflects God so imperfectly as to perplex us ; all that we see is ἐν αἰνίγματι. The word occurs nowhere else in the N.T., but is freq. in the LXX. Probably Num. xii. 8 is in St Paul's mind : στόμα κατὰ στόμα λαλήσω αὐτῷ, ἐν εἴδει καὶ οὐ δι' αἰνιγμάτων.* Other words for 'mirror' are ἔνοπτρον and κάτοπτρον. Comp.

---

* This passage led to the Rabbinical tradition that Moses had seen God through a clean window, but the Prophets through a dirty one (Bachmann, *ad loc.* p. 409 n.). There are two metaphors in Num. xii. 8, which St Paul mixes : βλέπειν ἐν αἰνίγματι is somewhat incongruous. But to condemn ἐι αἰν. as a gloss is a violent expedient. A gloss would have been more harmonious with the text.

2 Cor. iii. 18. Tertullian wrongly thinks of a window-pane made of horn, which is only semi-transparent; *per corneum specular*. But a window with horn or *lapis specularis* would be διόπτρον, not ἔσοπτρον. See Smith, *D. Ant.* i. p. 686. Others explain the διά as meaning that in a mirror one seems to see *through* the surface to the reflected objects.

τότε δὲ πρόσωπον πρὸς πρόσωπον. 'But then (when τὸ τέλειον shall have come) face to face'; πρόσωπον π. πρ being an adverb after βλέπομεν. The expression is Hebraistic; Gen. xxxii. 30: comp. πρ. κατὰ πρ. Deut. xxxiv. 10.

Our knowledge of divine things in this life cannot be direct: all comes through the distorting medium of human thought and human language, figures, types, symbols, etc. Even those who are illumined by the Spirit can give only a few rays of the truth, and those not direct, but reflected. Even the Gospel is a riddle, compared with the full light of the life to come. Here our knowledge is mediate, the result of inference and instruction; it is partial and confused; a piecemeal succession of broken lights. There it will be immediate, complete, and clear; a connected and simultaneous illumination. The imperfection of our knowledge, even of revealed truth, is not sufficiently recognized; and hence the rejection of Christianity by so many thoughtful people. Christians often claim to know more than it is possible to know. They forget how much of the Bible is symbolical. See Goudge, p. 122.

ἄρτι γινώσκω ἐκ μέρους. In realizing what is true of all of us, St Paul returns to his own personal experience; 'At present I get to know from a part only, but then I shall know in full even as I was known also in full, once for all,' by God from all eternity. Or the aorist may refer to Christ's knowledge of him at his conversion. For ἐπιγινώσκειν, which is very frequent in Luke (i. 4, v. 22, etc.) and in St. Paul (Rom. i. 32; 2 Cor. vi. 9, etc.), see Lightfoot on Col. i. 9, and J. A. Robinson on Eph. i. 17, p. 248. It is difficult to believe that here the compound is not meant to indicate more complete knowledge than the simple verb: but it does not follow from this that the compound always does so. In any case, καθὼς καὶ ἐπεγνώσθην is a bold way of expressing the completeness of future illumination; human knowledge is to equal (καθώς, 'exactly as') divine. Comp. Philo (*De Cherub.* § 32, p. 159;) νῦν ὅτε ζῶμεν γνωριζόμεθα μᾶλλον ἢ γνωρίζομεν. In this verse we have γίνωσκω in all three voices.

D* F G, Vulg. Arm. Goth., Tert. Cypr. omit. γάρ, but it is well attested (א A B K L P, Copt.).

13. νυνὶ δὲ μένει. 'So then, when all the other gifts have been reduced to nothing by the glories of the Return, there

remain just these three.' The νυνί is not temporal, but logical,
and the δέ expresses the contrast between the transitory gifts just
mentioned and those here; 'But, as you see, there abideth':
comp. xii. 18, 20; Heb. ix. 26. The singular μένει is not a slip
in grammar: the three virtues are a triplet distinguished by a
durability which the brilliant χαρίσματα, so coveted by the
Corinthians, do not possess; for the triplet will survive the
Second Advent.* In the progress which is possible in the other
world there will be room for Faith and Hope, but there will be
no room for Tongues, prophesyings, healings, or miracles. The
character which is built upon those three survives death and
abides in eternity. Goodness is far more enduring, because far
more akin to God, than the greatest capacities for usefulness.
Even in this world these gifts are not indispensable. One can
be a good Christian without Tongues or prophesying; but one
cannot be a good Christian without Faith, Hope, and Love.

μείζων δὲ τούτων ἡ ἀγάπη. 'And out of these (partitive
genitive) Love is greater.' Mentally, perhaps, the Apostle puts Love,
about which he has said so much, into one class, and the other
two virtues into another. But, however we explain the comparative (cf. Mt. xxiii. 11), and the simplest explanation is that
μέγιστος had become almost obsolete (J. H. Moulton, Gr. i.
p. 78), there is no doubt about the meaning; Love is superior to
the other two. Why is it superior, seeing that all three are
eternal? Not perhaps because Faith and Hope concern the
individual, while Love embraces the whole Christian society: sua
enim cuique fides ac spes prodest; caritas ad alios diffunditur
(Calv.). Rather, Love is the root of the other two; 'Love
believeth all things, hopeth all things.' We trust those whom
we love, and we hope for what we love. Again, Faith and Hope
are purely human; or, at most, angelic; the virtues of creatures.
Love is Divine. Deus non dicitur fides aut spes absolute, amor
dicitur (Beng.).

For the triplet comp. 1 Thess. i. 3, v. 8; Gal. v. 5, 6; Col.
i. 4, 5; Heb. vi. 10–12; Resch, Agrapha, pp. 155 f. Comp.
also St John's triplet, Light, Life, and Love.

* But "when a verb occurs in the 3rd person in an introductory manner
it is often used in the singular number, though the subject may be in the
plural." Thus "what cares these roarers for the name of king?" Yet, even
without this inversion, two or more kindred subjects may have a singular verb
(Mark iv. 41; Matt. v. 18, vi. 19). J. H. Moulton, Gr. i. p. 58; Blass,
§ 11. 3, § 44. 3.

XIV. 1-40. THE SUBJECT OF SPIRITUAL GIFTS CONCLUDED.

In ch. xii. the human body was given as an instructive illustration of a Christian Church. In xiii. it was shown that the principle which ought to quicken and regulate every member of the Church is love. In xiv. the influence of this principle is traced in the selection of the gifts that are most useful to the whole body, and also in the manner of employing them. Following after love does not impede the desire for special gifts, but it regulates it. The love which seeks not its own advantage must prefer a gift which benefits all to one which is a delight and a help to no one but its possessor. Not that the latter is to be despised; God does not bestow worthless gifts: but it is possible to mar any gift by misusing it.

The chapter has four divisions: (1) Prophesying or inspired preaching is superior to Tongues, both in reference to believers and to unbelievers, 1–25. (2) Regulations for the orderly exercise of these two gifts in Christian assemblies, 26–33. (3) Regulations respecting women, 34–36. (4) Conclusion of the subject, 37–40.

In the first and main portion of the chapter the superiority of inspired preaching to Tongues is stated at once (2–5); and this is supported by two series of arguments (6–11 and 14–19) connected with two exhortations (12, 13). The whole chapter shows that 'prophesying' is not the gift of prediction, but that of preaching; and that 'Tongues' are not foreign languages, but a mode of utterance different from all human language.

The main result of the chapter is that, just as it is love which gives value to character and conduct (xiii.), so it is love which teaches the true value and proper use of the charismata. See Zahn, *Introd. to N.T.* i. p. 280.

You are right in desiring these supernatural gifts, but take care that you do so from the right motive; and the right motive is love. Those gifts which benefit others are to be preferred to those which glorify ourselves; hence inspired preaching is more to be desired than Tongues. In the congregation, Tongues (unless interpreted at once) are a hindrance to worship. Even the experienced cannot join in

devotions which they do not understand, while the inex-
perienced or the unbelievers, if any be present, are lost in
contemptuous amazement. But inspired preaching is a great
help to all who hear it, whether believing or unbelieving.

Unless an interpreter is present, Tongues should be
exercised in private. In public worship, all who are inspired
to preach may do so in turn, and the whole Church, including
themselves, will be the gainer.

This does not apply to women. So far from preaching,
they ought not even to ask questions.

In all matters of public worship decorum and order must
be studied.

[1] What you have to do, therefore, is persistently to strive to make this love your own, while you continue to long to have the gifts of the Spirit, and especially to be inspired to preach. [2] For he who speaks in a Tongue is speaking, not to men, but to God, for no man can understand one who in a state of rapture is speaking mystic secrets. [3] It is otherwise with one who is inspired to preach : he does speak to men, and to good purpose, —words of faith to build them up, words of hope to quicken them, words of love to hearten and console. [4] Not that Tongues are useless ; one who exercises this gift may build up his own spiritual life by it : but the inspired preacher builds up the spiritual life of the Church. [5] Now I could wish that you should all have the gift of Tongues ; but I would greatly prefer that you should be inspired to preach, this being far more important, unless, of course, the Tongues should at once be interpreted, so that the Church may thereby receive spiritual advantage. [6] But, Brethren, seeing that Tongues without explanation are useless, suppose that, when next I visit you, I speak with Tongues, what good shall I do you, if I shall fail to explain to you some glimpse of the unseen or some knowledge of truth, the one to inspire you, the other to instruct you ? [7] Why, there are instruments which, although lifeless, make a sound,—a pipe, for instance, or a harp ; yet if they make no distinction in the notes, how is one to know the tune which the pipe or the harp is playing? [8] A trumpet-blast is a still stronger instance : if that gives an uncertain sound, who will get ready for battle? [9] It is just the same with you : if with your tongue you do not make

intelligible speech, how is one to know what you are saying? For you might as well be saying it to the winds. [11] Well, then, if I show that I do not understand the meaning of the language used, the person who speaks to me will conclude that I talk gibberish, just as from my point of view he is talking gibberish to me; and we both wish that we could talk to some advantage. [12] It is just the same with you: seeing that you are so enthusiastic for inspirations, let it be for the spiritual advantage of the Church that you seek to abound in them. [13] Therefore he that speaks in a Tongue should pray that he may be able to interpret what he utters. [14] For if I am praying in a Tongue, it is quite true that my spirit is praying, but my understanding is doing no good. [15] What does that imply? I must go on praying with the spirit, that, of course, for my own sake: but for the sake of others I must pray with the understanding also. I must sing with the spirit, but I must sing with the understanding also. [16] Else, suppose that you are blessing God in ecstasy, how is he who has no experience of such things to say the Amen at your giving of thanks, seeing that he does not know what you are saying? [17] For although you are giving thanks beautifully, yet the other is getting no spiritual advantage. [18] I thank God I have the gift of Tongues in a higher degree than all of you. [19] Nevertheless, in public worship I would rather speak five words with my understanding, and thereby give others also some solid instruction, than thousands and thousands of words in an ecstatic Tongue.

[20] My brethren, do not behave as if you were still children in mind: and it is childish to prefer what glitters to what does good. Of course, in jealousy and ill-will be children, nay, be very babes; but in mind behave as full-grown men. [21] In the great Prophet of the old Covenant it stands written that, because Israel would not obey God's word spoken in language which they could understand, thay would be punished in being conquered by Assyrians whose language they could not understand, and that even this sign would fail to teach them obedience. [22] This shows us that unintelligible Tongues are a sign, not of course to those who believe, but to those who fail to do so; while inspired preaching is for the benefit, not of those who do not believe, but of those who do. [23] Consequently, if, when you all meet together in one place for public worship, you one after another do nothing but speak with Tongues, and there come in

those who have no experience of such things,—and still more so if unbelievers come in,—will they not say that you must be mad? [24] Whereas, if one after another you utter inspired teaching, and there comes in an unbeliever,—and still more so if an inexperienced brother comes in,—by preacher after preacher he is convinced of his sinfulness, his heart is searched, [25] its secret evils are revealed to him, and the blessed result will be that he humbles himself before God and man, and from that moment proclaims that, little as he thought so till then, it is God who is with you.

[26] How then does the matter stand, Brethren? Whenever you meet together for worship, each of you is ready to manifest some gift,—to sing a song of praise, to give instruction, to reveal a truth, to utter a Tongue, or to interpret one. By all means exercise the gifts with which you have been endowed, always provided that they are exercised to build up the spiritual life of others and not to glorify yourselves. [27] If those who speak with Tongues are preferred, let only two, or at most three, speak in any one meeting, and one at a time, and let one interpreter serve for each. [28] But if no interpreter be present, let whoever has this gift be silent in public worship, and exercise it in private between himself and God. [29] And of those who are inspired to preach, let two or three speak in each meeting, and let the rest of them exercise the gift of discernment as to what is being spoken. [30] But if a revelation be made to one of those who thus sit listening, let the preacher give place to him. [31] For he *can* stop and be silent, and in this way it will be in the power of all of the inspired to preach one by one, so that all, whether inspired or not, may learn something and be quickened. [32] Yes, he can stop: an inspired man's spirit is under the inspired man's control, for the God who inspires him is a God, not of turbulence, but of peace. This holds good of all the assemblies of His people.

[34] When I say that all in turn may preach, I do not include your wives. They must keep silence in the assemblies. Utterance, whether in a Tongue or in preaching, is not allowed to them, for this would violate the rule of subjection which has been imposed upon them since the Fall. [35] Even their asking questions, which might seem to be compatible with subjection, cannot be allowed in the assemblies. Let them ask their own husbands at home, and the husbands can ask in the assembly. It is shameful

for a woman to speak there. ⁸⁶Perhaps you think that you have the right to do as you please in such matters. What? are you the Mother-Church, or the only Church, that you make such claims?

⁸⁷If any one claims to be inspired as a preacher or in any other way, let him give evidence of his inspiration by recognizing that what I am writing to you is inspired; it is the Lord's command. ⁸⁸But if any one fails to recognize this, I have no more to say. God deals with such. ⁸⁸So then, my Brethren, the sum of the whole discussion is this. Long earnestly to be inspired to preach, and if any one has the gift of Tongues, do not forbid him to use it. But let everything be done in accordance with natural feelings of propriety as well as established rule.

1. Διώκετε τὴν ἀγάπην, ζηλοῦτε δὲ τὰ πνευματικά. This verse looks back to xii. 31, and sums up the two preceding chapters. The Corinthians are to follow with persistence (Rom. ix. 30, 31, xiv. 19; 1 Thess. v. 15, etc.) 'the more excellent way,' and to desire with intensity (xii. 31, xiv. 39; 2 Cor. xi. 2; Gal. iv. 17) supernatural gifts; but (more than all the rest) that they may be inspired to preach. The ἵνα is definitive, not telic. For the other meaning of ζηλοῦν, 'boil with envy and hatred,' comp. xiii. 4. Love is a *grace*, which all Christians by earnest endeavour can attain. Prophesying, Tongues, etc. are *gifts*, which may be eagerly desired, but which no amount of effort can secure. Those alone receive them to whom they are given (xii. 11). The Apostle assures them that his praise of love does not mean that the gifts are to be despised. But no man is made morally the better by a gift, for character depends upon personal effort. Yet the gifts may be instruments of personal improvement, as well as of service to others, although the latter is of higher importance: hence μᾶλλον δὲ ἵνα προφητεύητε. For ζηλοῦτε see Mayor on Jas. iv. 2, p. 128.*

2. 'For he who speaketh in a Tongue, not to men doth he speak, but to God, for no man heareth him (to any purpose). This meaning of ἀκούειν comes out clearly in comparing Acts ix. 7 and xxii. 9. In the one place the men hear the voice; in the other they did not hear the voice of Him who was speaking to Saul, *i.e.* they heard a sound but did not hear it as words

---

* *Magna distantia est inter res temporales et spiritales: temporales enim, cum non habentur, multum desiderantur; si vero habeantur, fastidiunt atque vilescunt: spiritales autem, cum non habentur, minus desiderantur; cum vero habentur, magis magisque desiderium in nobis accendunt* (Atto of Vercelli).

addressed to any one. Also in the story of Babel; Συγχέωμεν ἐκεῖ αὐτῶν τὴν γλῶσσαν, ἵνα μὴ ἀκούσωσιν ἕκαστος τὴν φωνὴν τοῦ πλησίον (Gen. xi. 7; comp. xlii. 23). Verse after verse shows that speaking in foreign languages cannot be meant. Tongues were used in communing with God, and of course this was good for those who did so (v. 4). Tongues were a sort of spiritual soliloquy addressed partly to self, partly to Heaven. Compare the proverb, *Sibi canit et Musis*. It is equally clear that οὐδεὶς ἀκούει does not mean that Tongues were inaudible, or that no one listened to them, but that no one found them intelligible. One might as well have heard nothing.

πνεύματι δὲ λαλεῖ μυστήρια. 'As it is in the spirit that he speaketh what are in effect mysteries.' Explanatory use of δέ; not uncommon after a negative, but in *v.* 4 without a negative. 'In the spirit,' but not 'with the understanding' (*v.* 14), and therefore unintelligible to others. Μυστήριον in the N.T. commonly means 'truth about God, once hidden, but now revealed.' In this sense it is very common in St Paul: see Lightfoot on Col. i. 26 and Swete on Mark iv. 11; Beet on 1 Cor. iii. 4, p. 40. Mysteries must be revealed to be profitable; but in the case of Tongues without an interpreter there was no revelation, and therefore no advantage to the hearers. See Hatch, *Essays in Bibl. Grk.* pp. 57 f.

3. ὁ δὲ προφητεύων. 'Whereas he who exerciseth the gift of prophesying does speak to men, what is in effect edification and exhortation and consolation.' With λαλεῖ οἰκοδομήν comp. κρίμα ἐσθίει and τοῦτό μου ἐστὶ τὸ σῶμα (xi. 24, 29): in each case 'what is *in effect*' is the meaning. The metaphorical sense of οἰκοδομή, 'building up the spiritual life,' is peculiar to St Paul in the N.T., in Rom., 1 and 2 Cor., and Eph.: elsewhere (Matt. xxiv. 1; Mark xiii. 1, 2) of actual buildings or edifices. Παράκλησις, 'a calling near,' is sometimes 'supplication' (2 Cor. viii. 4), 'exhortation' (Phil. ii. 1), 'consolation' (2 Cor. i. 4–7) or a combination of the last two, 'encouragement' (Heb. vi. 18, xii. 5). 'Exhortation' or 'encouragement' is right here. 'Consolation' or 'comfort' must be reserved for παραμυθία, which occurs nowhere else in the N.T.; in the LXX, Wisd. xix. 12. But in Phil. ii. 1 we have παραμύθιον coupled with παράκλησις, and in 1 Thess. ii. 11 we have παρακαλοῦντες καὶ παραμυθούμενοι. Prophesying was the power of seeing and making known the nature and will of God, a gift of insight into truth and of power in imparting it, and hence a capacity for building up men's characters, quickening their wills, and encouraging their spirits. The three are co-ordinate: not build up by quickening and encouraging, nor build up and quicken in order to encourage.

Compare Barnabas = 'son of prophecy' = υἱὸς παρακλήσεως (Act⁻ iv. 36). *Exhortatio tollit tarditatem, adhortatio timiditatem.* See W. E. Chadwick, *The Pastoral Teaching of St Paul,* ch. ix.; Weinel, *St Paul,* 113 f.

4. ὁ λαλῶν γλώσσῃ ἑαυτὸν οἰκοδομεῖ. By communing with God in supernatural language the man who spoke in a Tongue built up himself. But, as Chrysostom says, What a difference between one person and the Church! Although there is no τήν before ἐκκλησίαν, 'the Church' is nearer the meaning than 'a Church' or 'a congregation'; yet either of the latter is admissible. See Alford and Ellicott, *ad loc.* But there is no sarcasm; *se ipsum aedificat, ut ipse quidem putat; sibi placet. Revera autem neminem aedificat.*

In both *v.* 2 and *v.* 4, D E with Arm. and other authorities have γλώσσαις for γλώσσῃ. Some (A E K L) insert τῷ before Θεῷ in *v.* 2, but here none insert τήν before ἐκκλησίαν.

5. θέλω δὲ πάντας ὑμᾶς λαλεῖν γλώσσαις, μᾶλλον δὲ ἵνα προφητεύητε. The change from the infinitive to ἵνα is perhaps meant to make the wish more intense; but this is sufficiently expressed by the μᾶλλον. See J. H. Moulton, *Gr.* p. 208. Nowhere else does St Paul use θέλω ἵνα, but it is not rare (Matt. vii. 12; Mark vi. 25, ix. 30; Luke vi. 31; John xvii. 24): in such cases the telic force is lost, and the ἵνα gives the object of the wish. 'Now I wish that all of you might speak with Tongues, yet I wish still more that ye should prophesy; as (δέ as in *v.* 2) greater is he,' etc. The 'for' of AV. is a little too pronounced, but is defensible, even without γάρ for δέ: see below. The Corinthians are exhorted *ne, praepostero zelo, quod praecipuum est minoribus postponant* (Calv.). As M. Aurelius (viii. 59) says, "Men are made for one another." As for the unsatisfactory ones, "either teach them better or put up with them."

The apodosis (τί ὑμᾶς ὠφελήσω;) is placed between two protases, which are co-ordinate, the second, on the negative side, being complementary to the first, on the positive side; 'If I come speaking with Tongues, instead of speaking either in the way of revelation,' etc.

ἐκτὸς εἰ μὴ διερμηνεύῃ. Pleonastic combination of ἐκτὸς εἰ and εἰ μή: 'with this exception, unless he interpret'; comp. xv. 2; 1 Tim. v. 19. The man who spoke in a Tongue might also have the gift of interpreting Tongues, and *si accedat interpretatio, jam erit prophetia* (Calv.). The δια- in διερμηνεύειν may indicate either 'being a go-between' or 'thoroughness.' One who interprets his own words intervenes between unintelligible utterance and the hearers: comp. 13, 27, xii. 30.

μείζων δέ (℘ A B P, Copt.) is to be preferred to μείζων γάρ (D F K L, Latt. Syrr. Arm. Aeth.). *Nisi forte interpretetur* (Vulg.), 'unless possibly he should interpret,' is not exact : this would require ἐάν. Omit *forte* : the εἰ intimates that his interpreting decides the point. It would be known that he possessed the gift of interpretation. On ἐκτὸς εἰ μή see Deissmann, *Bible Studies*, p. 118, and on εἰ with the subjunctive see J. H. Moulton, *Gr.* i. p. 187, and Ellicott on 1 Cor. ix. 11, where some good texts have θερίσωμεν. This is the only sure instance in the N.T., and it means that his subsequent interpretation is regarded as quite possible.

6. The first of a series of three arguments, drawn from their experience of him as a teacher. They are hoping to see him again. What good would he do them, if all that they got from him was ecstatic language, in which he excelled, but which they would not understand. To do them good he must speak intelligible language, of which he gives four examples in pairs that correspond : revelation is imparted by inspired preaching, and knowledge by doctrine; *i.e.* ἀποκάλυψις and γνῶσις are the internal gifts of which προφητεία and διδαχή are the external manifestation.* The ἐν expresses the form in which the λαλεῖν takes place. Dionysius of Alexandria seems to have had this passage in his mind in famous criticism of the Johannine writiags (Eus. *H.E.* vii. xxv. 26).

'But, as it is (seeing that without interpretation there can be no general edification), if I should come unto you (xvi. 3) speaking in Tongues, what shall I profit you (Gal. v. 2)? What shall I profit you, unless I should speak to you either in the way of revelation?' etc. See the paraphrase above.

νῦν (℘ A B D* F G P) rather than νυνί (E K L). The νῦν is logical, as in v. 11, vii. 14, xii. 18, 20, and as νυνί in xiii. 13, not temporal ; and in the construction of the verse τί ὑμᾶς ὠφ. is virtually repeated. 'Teaching,' the act of giving instruction,' is better than 'doctrine' (AV.) for διδαχή : 'doctrine' would be διδασκαλία (Eph. iv. 14 ; Col. ii. 22 ; 1 Tim. i. 10, etc.). But the distinction is not always observed.

7. Second argument, from the sounds of inanimate instruments. What use would they be, if the notes were indistinguishable? The αὐλός (here only in N.T.) and κιθάρα (Rev. xiv. 2) are given as representatives of all wind and stringed instruments. They were the commonest in use at banquets, funerals, and religious ceremonies. The music must be different, if it is to guide people to be joyous, or sorrowful, or devout. Soulless instruments can be made to speak a language, but not if all the notes are alike.

'Yet things without life giving a voice, whether pipe or harp, if they should give no distinction to the sounds, how shall be

---

* Thus Origen says, προφητεία ἐστὶν ἡ διὰ λόγου τῶν ἀφανῶν σημαντικὴ γνῶσις. διδαχὴ ἐστὶν ὁ εἰς τοὺς πολλοὺς διανεμόμενος διδασκαλικὸς λόγος (*JTS.* x. 37, p. 36). See Abbott, *The Son of Man*, pp. 200 f.

known what is piped and what is harped?' AV. has 'sound' for both φωνή and φθόγγος, and both AV. and RV. ignore the repetition of the τό. Except for Rom. x. 18, φθόγγοις might be translated 'notes.' Perhaps, as in Gal. iii. 15, the ὅμως is attracted out of its place, and the sentence is meant to run—'Inanimate things, although giving a voice, yet, unless,' etc. Ἄψυχος occurs Wisd. xiii. 17, xiv. 29, but nowhere else in N.T.

> In Judith xiv. 9 we have ἔδωκεν φωνήν, and in Wisd. xix. 18, ὥσπερ ἐν ψαλτηρίῳ φθόγγοι τοῦ ῥυθμοῦ τὸ ὄνομα διαλλάσσουσιν. For τοῖς φθόγγοις (א A D E K L P, Vulg.), B, d e Arm., Ambrst. have φθόγγον, and for δῷ (א A B D*), E F L P have διδῷ. See Matt. xxiv. 31; Rev. xiv. 2, xviii. 22 for φωνή, of musical sound; and Rom. iii. 22, x. 12 for διαστολή as meaning 'distinction' and not 'interval' (διάστημα). But in music the difference of meaning is not great.

8. Another and stronger illustration. Of all musical sounds the military trumpet is the most potent, and far clearer than pipe or lyre. If sound is to be a signal, it must differ from other sounds.

'For if a trumpet also should give an uncertain voice, who will make ready for battle?'* The context makes 'battle' more probable than 'war.' In Homer and Hesiod the meaning of 'battle' is commonest (*Il.* vii. 174 of a duel), in class. Grk. that of 'war.' Cf. Num. x. 9; Jer. l. 42; Ezek. vii. 14. In the Synoptists, 'war' is the better translation. In Jas. iv. 1 πόλεμοι καὶ μάχαι means bitter quarrels between individuals. Compare Clem. Rom. *Cor.* 46. On military signals with trumpets see Smith, *Dict. Ant.* 'Exercitus,' i. p. 801; 'Tuba,' ii. p. 901. For ἄδηλος see the unmarked graves, τὰ μνημεῖα τὰ ἄδηλα (Luke xi. 44): the word is found nowhere else in N.T. and is rare in LXX. Here, ἄδηλον σάλπ. φων. is the right order, and also the most effective.

9. If the military trumpet is more potent than pipe or lyre, still more expressive is the human tongue; but that also can produce sounds which convey no meaning.

'So also ye, unless by means of the tongue ye give speech that is distinct, how shall it be known what is spoken?' The tongue here means the organ of speech, not the ecstatic Tongue, which never gave εὔσημον λόγον, but rather what was ἄσημον, excepting to one who had the gift of interpretation. Εὔσημος (here only, but classical) means 'well-marked,' 'definite,' 'significant.' Origen suggests that this text intimates that the obscure

---

* Here 'make ready' or 'make preparations' is better than 'prepare himself.' The intransitive use of the middle is older and more common than the reflexive. Undoubted instances of the reflexive are rare in the N.T. J. H. Moulton, *Gr.* p. 156. The καί may be 'even'; 'For if even a trumpet.'

portions of Scripture, such as the account of the sacrifices in Leviticus and of the Tabernacle in Exodus, ought not to be read in public worship, unless some one explains their meaning.

ἔσεσθε γὰρ εἰς ἀέρα λαλοῦντες. 'For ye will be speaking into the air'—to the winds. The periphrastic tense indicates the lasting condition to which the unintelligible speaker is reduced. Compare ἀέρα δέρων, ix. 26; also Wisd. v. 11, 12: except in Wisd., ἀήρ is rare in the LXX.* *Tu fac ne ventis verba profundam* (Lucr. iv. 932).

10. Third argument, from the sounds of human language. Speech is useless to the hearer, unless he understands it.

τοσαῦτα, εἰ τύχοι, γένη φωνῶν . . . καὶ οὐδὲν ἄφωνον. 'There are, it may be, so many kinds of voices (Gen. xi. 1, 7) in the world, and no kind (of course) is voiceless' (xii. 2; Acts viii. 32). But here ἄφωνος does not mean 'dumb' but, what may be worse, 'unintelligible.' Voiceless voice, *i.e.* meaningless sound, had better be inaudible; it is mere distracting noise. This was just the case with Tongues in a congregation without an interpreter. Wetstein gives many examples of εἰ τύχοι, 'if it so happens,' or 'I dare say.' It implies that the number is large, but that the exact number does not matter: 'There are, I dare say, ever so many kinds.' For ἐν κόσμῳ without the article, 'in existence,' comp. viii. 4; 2 Cor. v. 19.† Probably γένος is to be understood with οὐδέν: to say that nothing is without a voice of some kind would hardly be true. But the Vulg. takes it so; *nihil sine voce est; nihil horum mutum* (Calv.); *nihil est mutum* (Beza); which moreover destroys the oxymoron in φωνὴ ἄφωνος: comp. χάρις ἄχαρις, βίος ἄβιος or ἀβίωτος, γάμος ἄγαμος, πλοῦτος ἄπλουτος. *Nullum genus vocum vocis expers* is better. Speech without meaning is a contradiction in terms.

No doubt ἐστίν (K L, Chrys. Thdrt.) is a grammatical correction of εἰσίν (א A B D E F G P); but the plural is deliberate, to emphasize the number of different kinds. A few authorities insert τῷ before κόσμῳ, αὐτῶν after οὐδέν, and ἐστίν after ἄφωνον: in all cases א* A B P with other witnesses omit.

11. All kinds of languages met at commercial Corinth with its harbours on two seas, and difference of language was a frequent barrier to common action. Moreover, it was well known how exasperating it could be for two intelligent persons to be unintelligible to one another. Yet the Corinthians were

---

* The rare compounds, ἀεροβατεῖν and ἀερομετρεῖν do not illustrate this expression: they suggest vagueness rather than futility.

† ἐν οὐρανῷ, ἐν οἴκῳ, ἐν πόλει, ἐν ἐκκλησίᾳ, ἐπὶ γῆς are similar phrases: in such cases the idea is definite enough without the article. There was a tendency, apparent in the papyri, to drop the article after a preposition. J. H. Moulton, *Gr.* p. 82, and on εἰ τύχοι, p. 196.

introducing these barriers and provocations into Christian worship, and all for the sake of display!

ἐὰν οὖν μὴ εἰδῶ . . . ἐν ἐμοὶ βάρβαρος. 'Unless, therefore, I
know the meaning of the voice, I shall be to him who speaks to
me a barbarian, and he who speaks will in *my* estimation be a
barbarian.' The second result is more obvious than the first;
but the Apostle assumes that the foreigner sees quite plainly that
his words are not understood. Comp. Rom. i. 14; Col. iii. 11;
Acts xxviii. 2, 4. Βάρβαρος, like 'gibberish,' is probably meant
to imitate unintelligible sounds. AV., with D E F G, Latt. Syrr.
Copt. Arm., Chrys., omits the ἐν before ἐμοί: 'unto me.' Compare Hdt. ii. 158; Ovid, *Trist.* v. 10, 11; and see J. H. Moulton,
p. 103.

12. οὕτως καὶ ὑμεῖς . . . ἵνα περισσεύητε. 'So also ye (*v.* 9),
seeing that ye are earnestly desirous of spiritual manifestations
(enthusiastic after spirits), let it be for the edifying of the Church
that ye seek to abound.' The Corinthians were eager for these
brilliant charismata. St Paul does not blame them, but charges
them to have a right motive for desiring them, viz. the building
up of others rather than their own gratification. Origen says
that the way to increase one's charismata is to use them for the
good of others: otherwise the gifts may wane. Cf. Philo, *De
Decalogo*, 105. For οὕτως see vi. 5, viii. 12; for ζηλωταί, Gal.
i. 14; Acts xxii. 3; for πνευμάτων in this sense, xii. 10; for the
inversion of order for the sake of emphasis, iii. 5, vii. 17; Rom.
xii. 3. Some would translate; 'For the edifying of the Church
seek (them), that ye may abound (in them).' This is not so
probable as the other. There is perhaps a touch of irony or of
rebuke in 'seeing that ye are so eager for.' This exhortation
closes the first series of arguments. The next verse (13) is a
corollary from πρὸς τὴν οἰκοδομὴν . . ., and leads to the second
series.

13. Διὸ ὁ λαλῶν γλώσσῃ προσευχέσθω ἵνα διερμηνεύῃ. 'It
follows from this (xii. 3; Gal. iv. 31, etc.) that he who speaks
in a Tongue should pray that he may interpret,' *i.e.* have the
gift of interpretation also. This prayer might precede or follow
the ecstatic speech. The verse does not necessarily mean 'Let
him in his ecstasy pray that he may be allowed to interpret';
still less, 'Let him in his ecstasy pray in such a way as to make
his utterance intelligible.' It was characteristic of glossolalia
that the speaker could not make his speech intelligible; and
apparently he had no control over the sounds that he uttered,
although he could abstain from uttering them. It does not
follow that, because we have προσεύχωμαι γλώσσῃ in *v.* 14, therefore γλώσσῃ is to be understood with προσευχέσθω in *v.* 13:

γλώσσῃ is indispensable in *v.* 14. Διό is found in all groups of the Pauline Epp., except the Pastorals, and is specially frequent in this group.

14. First argument of the second series. The gift of Tongues is inferior to other gifts, because in it the reason has no control; and the Apostle has misgivings about devotions in which the reason has no part (*v.* 19). Strange that Corinthians should need to be told that intellect is not to be ignored, but ought to be brought to full development (*v.* 20). " Feeling is a precious gift; but when men parade it and give way to it, it is weakness instead of strength" (F. W. Robertson, *Corinthians*, p. 228).

ἐὰν γὰρ προσεύχωμαι γλώσσῃ. 'For if ever I pray in a Tongue, my spirit prayeth, but my understanding is unfruitful,' because it does no good to others. There is no οἰκοδομή for the congregation, because what he utters is not framed by his intellect to convey any meaning to them. Hilary says that Latins sometimes sang Greek songs for the mere pleasure of the sound, without understanding what they sang. Note that it is the πνεῦμα, not the ψυχή, that prays; and prayer here includes praise and thanksgiving. The preacher's fruit is to be sought in the hearer's progress, not in his own delight or in their admiration of his gift. Aristotle (*Eth. Nic.* IV. iii. 33) speaks of τὰ καλὰ καὶ ἄκαρπα, objects of beauty which do not pay, though they delight all and dignify the possessor. For νοῦς see Luke xxiv. 45; Rev. xiii. 18, xvii. 9.

15. τί οὖν ἐστίν; 'What then is the outcome?' How do we stand after this discussion (*v.* 26; Rom. iii. 9, vi. 15; Acts xxi. 22) as to the conditions of being of use to others in one's devotions? Unreasoning emotionalism will not do. 'I will pray with the spirit (that of course); but I will pray with the understanding also,' so as to be able to edify others: 'I will sing praise with the spirit, but,' etc. There is no thought here of liturgical music; it is the individual spontaneously using a special gift in the congregation; "impromptu utterance of sacred song" (Beet). Comp. Eph. v. 19; Col. iii. 16: ψάλλω originally meant playing on a stringed instrument; then singing to the harp or lyre; finally, singing without accompaniment, especially singing praise—τῷ κυρίῳ, τῷ ὀνόματι αὐτοῦ κ.τ.λ. It is possible that the ecstatic utterances sometimes took the form of an inarticulate chant, songs without intelligible words or definite melody. Compare ψάλατε συνετῶς (Ps. xlvii. 8).

16. Second argument. Tongues are a stumbling-block to the ungifted, for ineffable emotion is a hindrance rather than a help to those who witness it.

'For else, if ever thou art blessing God in spirit,' *i.e.* thanking Him in ecstasy, 'how shall he who occupies the place of the ungifted say the (usual) Amen after thy giving of thanks, seeing that he knows not what thou art saying?' You may be engaged in the highest kind of devotion, *nobilissima species orandi* (Beng.), but it conveys no meaning to those who cannot interpret the language used. It is obvious that εὐχαριστία here cannot mean the Eucharist. The minister at that service would not speak in a Tongue. Nor is it probable that in 'the Amen' there is indirect reference to the Eucharist. The use of the responsive Amen at the end of the prayers, and especially of the reader's doxology, had long been common in the synagogues (Neh. v. 13, viii. 6; 1 Chron. xvi. 36; Ps. cvi. 48), and had thence passed into the Christian Church, where it at once became a prominent feature (Justin M. *Apol.* i. 65; Tertul. *De Spectac.* 25; Cornelius Bishop of Rome in Eus. *H.E.* vi. xliii. 19; Chrys. *ad loc.*), especially at the end of the consecration prayer in the Eucharist. So common did it become at the end of every prayer in Christian worship that the Jews, it is said, began to abandon it; Jerome says that it was like thunder. The Rabbis gave similar instructions about the ἰδιώτης: the language should be such as he can understand. Hastings, *DCG.* i. p. 51, *DB.* i. p. 80; Dalman, *The Words of Jesus*, p. 226. In the LXX the Hebrew word is retained in the responsive passages (Neh. v. 13, viii. 6; 1 Chron. xvi. 36; 1 Esdr. ix. 47; Tobit viii. 8), but in the Psalms and elsewhere it is translated γένοιτο. The Vulgate has *fiat* in the Psalms, elsewhere 'Amen.' It is evident from this passage that a great deal of the service was extempore, and both the *Didache* and Justin show that this continued for some time. Apparently the prophets had more freedom in this respect than others. For ἐπί see Phil. i. 3; 1 Thess. iii. 7.

The precise meaning of both τόπος and ἰδιώτης is uncertain. But it is unlikely that at this early period, when the Christians in each town met for common worship in private houses, there was a portion of the room set apart for the ἰδιῶται, or that these were laymen as distinct from officials. No clearly marked distinctions had as yet been drawn between ministers and laity. In Acts iv. 13 (see Knowling's note), 'without special training,' 'uneducated,' seems to be the meaning, and in 2 Cor. xi. 6 the Apostle probably means that he was not a trained orator or professional speaker. Here 'unlearned' or 'inexperienced' may be the meaning; but RV. margin is probably right; 'without gifts,' *i.e.* having no gift of Tongues, or of interpretation, or of prophesying. It would therefore be somewhat like ἀμύητος, 'uninitiated.' Tyndale and Coverdale have 'laye people' in Acts and 'unlearned' here. In any case the Apostle's argument is clear. It would be ἄτοπον that one who has a place in public worship should be prevented from joining in it, owing to the language used being unintelligible. Tongues were not given to encourage vanity, or to hinder the devotions of others. Wetstein gives abundant illustrations of the different meanings of ἰδιώτης: see also Suicer on both ἰδιώτης and Ἀμήν. Conybeare and Howson explain ἰδιώτης as one "who takes no part in the particular matter in hand"—an outsider, *unbetheiligt*.

εὐλογῇς (א A B D E P) rather than εὐλογήσῃς (F G K L, Latt. *benedixeris*), and πνεύματι (א* A F G 17, Vulg. Syrr. Arm.) rather than ἐν πνεύματι (B D) or τῷ πν. (K L, Chrys.), or ἐν τῷ πν. (P).

17. σὺ μὲν γὰρ καλῶς εὐχαριστεῖς. The σύ is emphatic, εὐχαριστεῖς is synonymous with the preceding εὐλογῇς, and there is perhaps a touch of irony in the καλῶς: 'Thy beautiful thanksgiving is quite lost on the poor ἰδιώτης.' Or the καλῶς may mean, 'Do not think that I consider Tongues to be worthless; God's gifts, if rightly used, are always valuable to the receiver; *but* Tongues are no good to the ungifted hearer.' Note ἀλλά instead of δέ after μέν, intensifying the contrast; 'but none the less.'

18. Third argument, from his own case; comp. *v.* 6, iv. 6, ix. 1 f., xiii. 1-3. He, if any one, has a right to speak with Tongues in the congregation, yet he will not. He knows what he is talking about; he is not depreciating a gift of which he has no experience. In xiii. 1 he spoke hypothetically of possessing this gift. Here he says plainly that he possesses it with greater intensity than all of them, which perhaps implies that the fact was not generally known, because he exercised the gift in private. Here we have strong evidence that Tongues are not foreign languages. He does not say that he speaks 'in *more* tongues'; and he could use his understanding in speaking Latin or Syriac just as much as in speaking Greek. In saying that the man who was most richly endowed with this gift was one who abstained from using it in public, he perhaps hints that those who were not greatly endowed were the people who gave themselves most airs about it.

εὐχαριστῶ τῷ Θεῷ. This cannot refer to the Eucharist, and to some extent confirms the view that *vv.* 16, 17 do not.

πάντων ὑμῶν μᾶλλον. The emphatic position of πάντων perhaps means 'more than all of you put together': but 'more than any of you' is sufficient for the argument. The omission of ὅτι before πάντων raises the second sentence in importance, making it co-ordinate instead of dependent. How "perfectly sane and sober" the Apostle is in all this is well pointed out by Weinel, *St Paul*, pp. 142 f.

The AV. inserts 'my' before 'God,' with K L, Vulg. But nearly all other authorities omit. It is more difficult to decide between γλώσσῃ (א A D E F G 17, Latt. Arm.) and γλώσσαις (B K L P, Syrr. Copt. Aeth. Chrys. Thdrt.). But λαλῶ (א B D E P 17, Latt. Syrr. Copt. Arm.) is to be preferred to λαλῶν (KL, Chrys. Thdrt.), which is a correction arising from the absence of ὅτι. The omission of μᾶλλον is curious ; *omnium vestrum lingua loquor* (Vulg. d f). A omits λαλῶ ; 'I give thanks in a Tongue.'

19. ἀλλὰ ἐν ἐκκλησίᾳ. 'But (whatever I may do in private) in an *assembly* I had rather speak five words with my understanding.' For θέλω . . . ἤ, 'I prefer,' comp. 2 Mac. xiv. 42 ; the use is classical (Hom. *Il.* i. 117), and is found in papyri (Deissmann, *Light*, p. 179): and λαλῆσαι rather than λαλεῖν, because of the definite number of words spoken on the contemplated occasion. Κατηχήσω (Rom. ii. 18 ; Gal. vi. 6 ; Luke i. 4) implies thorough instruction by word of mouth ; of what is sounded down into the ear. The verb in N.T. is found in Paul and Luke only. La Rochefoucauld (*Max.* 142) contrasts the *grands esprits* who convey much meaning in few words with those who have *le don de beaucoup parler et de rien dire.**

20. This verse is better taken as the beginning of a new portion of the subject rather than as the conclusion of what precedes. It opens affectionately. Comp. x. 14 ; Rom. x. 1 ; Gal. iii. 15, vi. 1 ; 1 Thess. v. 25 : in each case the opening Ἀδελφοί makes a fresh start.

'Brethren, do not prove children in your minds, but in jealousy of one another show yourselves (not merely children but) babes : in your minds (Prov. vii. 7, ix. 4) prove full-grown men' ; *i.e.* 'Play the part of babies, if you like, in freedom from malice : but in common sense try to act like grown-up people.' A severe rebuke to those who prided themselves on their intelligence. Children prefer what glitters and makes a show to what is much more valuable ; and it was childish to prefer ecstatic utterance to other and far more useful gifts.† Nowhere else in N.T. does φρένες occur, but in LXX it is frequent in Proverbs in the phrase ἐνδεὴς φρενῶν, which St Paul may have in his mind. AV. and RV. are probably right in translating κακία 'malice' or 'maliciousness,' rather than 'wickedness' or 'vice,' in all the places in which it occurs in St Paul (v. 8 ; Rom. i. 29 ; Eph. iv. 31 ; Col. iii. 8 ; Tit. iii. 3, where it is joined with φθόνος). In

* On this verse Erasmus remarks ; "They chant nowadays in our churches what is an unknown tongue and nothing else, while you will not hear a sermon once in six months telling people to amend their lives. Modern church music is so constructed that the congregation cannot hear one distinct word. The choristers themselves do not understand what they are singing" (Froude, *Life and Letters of Erasmus*, p. 117).

† *Repuerascere nos et apostolus jubet secundum deum, ut malitia infantes per simplicitatem, ita demum sapientes sensibus* (Tert. *Adv. Valent.* 2).

1 Pet. ii. 1 (see Hort) it is joined with δόλος, φθόνοι, and καταλαλιαί. In class. Grk. κακία in the moral sense is opposed to ἀρετή, and is vice of any kind, but especially cowardice. Later it comes to mean maliciousness and ill-will; often in the Testaments of the XII. Patriarchs; *Symeon* iv. 6; *Zabulon* viii. 5; *Gad* vi. 7; and especially *Benjamin* viii. 1; ἀπόδρατε τὴν κακίαν, τὸν φθόνον καὶ τὴν μισαδελφίαν. See 2 Mac. iv. 4. Everywhere in St Paul the Vulgate has *malitia*, and even in Matt. vi. 34; but in Acts viii. 22 *nequitia*. Νηπιάζειν occurs nowhere else in the Bible: comp. xiii. 11; Rom. xvi. 19.

21. ἐν τῷ νόμῳ γέγραπται.   'In the Law it stands written.' The reference is to Isa. xxviii. 11, 12, and ὁ νόμος here means Scripture generally; Rom. iii. 19; John x. 34, xii. 34, xv. 25. See Orig. *Philocalia* ix. 2; Suicer, ii. p. 416: πᾶσαν τὴν παλαιάν, οὐ μόνον τὰ Μωσαϊκά (Theoph.). But the connexion of the quotation with the argument here is not easy: perhaps something of this sort; 'I have pointed out that Tongues are a blessed experience to the individual believer, and that, if interpreted, they may benefit the believing congregation. Tongues have a further use, as a sign to *un*believers; not a convincing, saving sign, but a judicial sign. Just as the disobedient Jews, who refused to listen to the clear and intelligible message which God frequently sent to them through His Prophets, were chastised by being made to listen to the unintelligible language of foreign invaders, so those who now fail to believe the Gospel are chastised by hearing wonderful sounds which they cannot understand.' If this is correct, we may compare Christ's use of parables to veil His meaning from those who could not or would not receive it. The quotation is very free, and is not from the LXX.*

1 Cor. xiv. 21.	LXX of Isa. xxviii. 11, 12.
Ὅτι ἐν ἑτερογλώσσοις καὶ ἐν χείλεσιν ἑτέρων λαλήσω τῷ λαῷ τούτῳ, καὶ οὐδ᾽ οὕτως εἰσακούσονταί μου, λέγει Κύριος.	διὰ φαυλισμὸν χειλέων, διὰ γλώσσης ἑτέρας· ὅτι λαλήσουσιν τῷ λαῷ τούτῳ λέγοντες αὐτοῖς, Τοῦτο τὸ ἀνάπαυμα τῷ πεινῶντι καὶ τοῦτο τὸ σύντριμμα, καὶ οὐκ ἠθέλησαν ἀκούειν.

'For with alien-tongued men and with lips of aliens will I speak to this people, and not even thus will they hearken

---

* Origen says, ταῦτα τὰ ῥήματα εὕρομεν παρὰ Ἀκύλᾳ καὶ ταῖς λοιπαῖς ἐκδόσεσιν, οὐ μὴν παρὰ τοῖς ἑβδομήκοντα: and again, εὗρον τὰ ἰσοδυναμοῦντα τῇ λέξει ταύτῃ ἐν τῇ τοῦ Ἀκύλου ἑρμηνείᾳ κείμενα (*Philocalia* ix. 2). On γέγραπται of Scripture, see Deissmann, *Bible Studies*, pp. 112 f. The connexion with the argument may be; 'Tongues do not *engender* faith, while prophecy does' (*v.* 24); or, 'Tongues *appeal* to no faith, as prophecy does, in the hearers. Tongues, then, are a sign to *un*believers.'

unto Me, saith the Lord.' The ὅτι is not recitative, but is part of the quotation, representing what might be rendered 'Yea' or 'Truly for.' In Isaiah the men with alien tongue are the Assyrians. Isaiah's opponents are supposed to have jeered at him for repeating the same simple message; "We are not children, requiring to be told the same thing over and over again." Then he threatens them with the terrible gibberish (like stammering) of foreign invaders. See W. E. Barnes, *ad loc.* The main part of the application here is the conclusion, οὐδ' οὕτως εἰσακούσονταί μου, where the compound is stronger than the simple ἀκούειν, and perhaps represents '*willing* to listen': Luke i. 13; Acts x. 31; Heb. v. 7—of God's listening to prayer.

ἐτέραις γλώσσαις (F G, Vulg. *in aliis linguis*, Tert.) for ἐτερογλώσσοις, and ἐτέροις (D E F G K L P, Latt.) for ἐτέρων (א A B 17 and other cursives) are probably corrections of scribes. Ἑτερόγλωσσος is found in Aquila, but not in LXX.

22. ὥστε. 'So then (*i.e.* in harmony with this passage of Scripture), the Tongues are for a sign to men who do not believe.' He does not say that they *are* a sign, but that they are intended to *serve* as such—εἰς σημεῖον : Gen. ix. 13 ; Num. xvi. 38, xvii. 10 ; Deut. vi. 8, xi. 18, etc. Nor does he say what kind of a sign, but the context shows that it is for judgment rather than for salvation : comp. εἰς μαρτύριον (Mark i. 44, vi. 11, etc.), which is equally indefinite. No εἰς ση. after προφητεία.

23. But it is obvious that, even for unbelievers, prophesying is more valuable than Tongues. ' If, therefore, the whole Church be come together to one place, and all are speaking with Tongues, and there come in ungifted people or unbelievers, will they not say that ye are raving?' It was strange that what the Corinthians specially prided themselves on was a gift which, if exercised in public, would excite the derision of unbelievers. The Corinthians *were* crazy, although not exactly as heathen might suppose. Compare the charge of drunkenness at Pentecost; Acts ii. 13.

If ἐπὶ τὸ αὐτό means ' for the same object,' the object might be the Tongues : the Corinthians came together to enjoy this spiritual luxury and exhibit it to others : but both here and xi. 20 it probably means ' to the same place ' (Luke xvii. 35 ; Acts i. 15, ii. 1, iii. 1). In any case, πάντες does not mean that they all spoke at once : πάντες cannot mean that in *v.* 24, and therefore does not mean it here. It means that one after another they uttered unintelligible language, and no one said anything that ordinary persons could understand ; the service consisted of glossolalia. Note the changes of tense ; συνέλθῃ and εἰσέλθωσιν of what took place once for all, λαλῶσιν of what continued for some time.   Perhaps in both verses (23, 24) he is assuming an extreme case for the sake of argument, that all present have the gift of Tongues, and that all present have the gift of prophesying. The latter would be very much better.

Evidently, the heathen sometimes obtained admission to Christian assemblies as to the synagogues. This may have depended upon local custom, or upon the character of the intruders, who might be friends of the family in whose house the assembly was held.   See Swete on Rev. iii. 8.

24. ἐὰν δὲ πάντες προφητεύωσιν.   'Whereas, if all should be prophesying, and there should come in some unbeliever or ungifted person.'   The change to the singular and the change of order have point.   A good effect would be more probable in the case of an individual than of a group ; and if the ἄπιστος was deeply moved by what he heard, *a fortiori* the ἰδιώτης would be.   In the former case the argument is the other way : if ἰδιῶται said that they were demented, still more would ἄπιστοι do so.   Speaking with Tongues *infidelem sibi relinquit*; inspired preaching *ex infidelibus credentes facit, et fideles pascit* (Beng.).

ἐλέγχεται ὑπὸ πάντων.   'He is convicted by all'; by all the inspired speakers, whose preaching arouses his conscience (Heb. iv. 12). 'He is convinced of all' (AV.) is ambiguous and misleading. 'Convince' formerly = 'convict' or 'refute' (John viii. 46 ; Job xxxii. 12).   For 'of' = 'by' see xi. 32 ; Phil. iii. 12 ; Matt. vi. 1 ; Luke xiv. 8 ; and "may of Thee be plenteously rewarded."

ἀνακρίνεται ὑπὸ πάντων.   'He is searched into by all'; ix. 3, x. 25, 27 ; Luke xxiii. 14, etc.   There are three stages in the process of conversion : (1) he is convinced of his sinful condition ; (2) he is put upon his trial, and the details of his condition are investigated ; (3) the details are made plain to him.   On the unsatisfactory renderings of κρίνω and its compounds in the AV. see Lightfoot, *On Revision*, pp. 69 f.

25. The scrutiny in the court of conscience (ἀνάκρισις) produces self-revelation, self-condemnation, and submission. 'The secrets of his heart become manifest, and thus, falling upon his face, he will worship God.'   A spontaneous expression of submission and thankfulness ; but the homage is to God, not to the inspired speaker. The gift of prophesying, however successful, is no glory to the possessor of it. It is the Spirit of God, not the preacher's own power, that works the wonderful effect.   This verse seems to be at variance with *v.* 22 ; 'prophesying is not for the unbelieving': but the discrepancy

is only apparent. The comparison with the disobedient Israelites shows that the ἄπιστοι in *v.* 22 have heard the word and
rejected it. Here the context shows that the ἄπιστος has not
previously heard. Comp. Saul and his messengers (1 Sam. xix.
20–24). With 'fall down on his face' comp. the Samaritan
leper (Luke xvii. 16). In the Gospels προσκυνεῖν is frequent,
but here only in St Paul. The ἰδιώτης is almost forgotten in
this stronger instance: if an unbeliever is thus τετραχηλισμένος
(Heb. iv. 13), how much more the ungifted or inexperienced
Christian.

ἀπαγγέλλων ὅτι ὄντως ὁ Θεὸς ἐν ὑμῖν ἐστίν. 'Proclaiming that
(so far from your being mad, and little as he had hitherto
supposed that you were thus blessed) verily God is among you.'
In ἀπαγγέλλων the sender rather than the destination (ἀναγγ.) of
the message is thought of: he spreads it abroad *from* (*abkündigen*).
This declaration begins there and then, and is continued afterwards: *ultro, plane, diserte pronuncians Deum vere esse in vobis et
verum Deum esse qui in vobis est* (Beng.); ὄντως, in spite of his
previous scoffs and denials, there is the Real Presence of the
true God. The article before Θεός is doubtless genuine
(א³ B D² D³ E K L); it has special point in the unbeliever's
confession. Both 'among you' as a congregation and 'in your
hearts' as individuals would be included in ἐν ὑμῖν, but the
former most strongly. Compare the confession of Alcibiades as
to the effect of Socrates upon him; "I have heard Pericles and
other great orators, but I never had any similar feeling; my soul
was not stirred by them, nor was I angry at the thought of my
slavish state. But Socrates makes me confess that I ought not
to live as I do, neglecting the wants of my soul. And he is the
only person who ever made me ashamed: for I know that I
cannot answer him or say that I ought not to do as he bids," etc.
(Plato, *Symposium*, 215, 216). For ὄντως, see Gal. iii. 21; Mark
xi. 32.

The AV., with some inferior MSS., has 'and thus' (καὶ οὕτω or καὶ
οὕτως) at the beginning of the verse (א A B D* F G, Vulg. omit), and
repeats 'and so' in the proper place.

26–33. Regulations for the Orderly Exercise of Tongues and Prophesying in the Congregation.

St Paul has here completed his treatment (xii.–xiv.) of
πνευματικά. He now gives detailed directions as to their use.

26. Τί οὖν ἐστίν, ἀδελφοί; 'What then is the result, brethren,'
of this discussion? Comp. *v.* 15. In answering his own
question he first gives the facts of the case, then states the

indispensable principle that all things are to be done unto edifying, and finally gives practical directions for applying this principle.

ὅταν συνέρχησθε. 'Whenever ye are coming together (v. 23, xi. 17, 18, 20), each has ready (comp. πάντες, vv. 23, 24) a psalm to improvise, a lesson to give, a revelation to make known, a Tongue to utter, an interpretation to explain the Tongue.' All these gifts are there in the several individuals ready to be manifested. By all means let them be manifested. But never lose sight of the more excellent way of love: let the edification of others be the end ever in view.*

The spontaneous character of the manifestations is graphically indicated. There was no lack of persons eager to manifest some gift. But perhaps the Apostle intimates that they do not come to public worship quite in the right spirit. This readiness to come to the front would be sure to lead to abuse unless carefully controlled. What they ought to be eager to do is to use their gifts for the good of all. This is the *optima norma*. But we cannot safely infer that we have here the *order* in which the manifestations commonly took place at Corinth,—first a psalm, then instruction, and so on. Compare the account of Christian assemblies in Tertullian (*Apol.* 39). The account of the Therapeutae ought not to be quoted in illustration, still less as Philo's : the περὶ βίου θεωρητικοῦ is possibly a Christian fiction, and perhaps wholly imaginative. With ἕκαστος ἔχει compare ἕκαστος λέγει (i. 12), and for improvised psalms see Moses and Miriam (Exod. xv.), Balaam (Num. xxiii., xxiv.), Deborah (Judg. v.), and the Canticles (Luke i., ii.). It is remarkable that there is no προφητείαν ἔχει. Was that gift so despised at Corinth that those who possessed it did not often come forward? Ψαλμός occurs in N.T. in Paul and Luke only. Ἑρμηνία occurs nowhere else in N.T., excepting xii. 10.

The ὑμῶν after ἕκαστος (D E F G K L, Vulg. AV.) is probably spurious : א A B 17, Copt. RV. omit. And ἀποκάλυψιν ἔχει should precede γλῶσσαν ἔχει (א A B D E F G 17, Latt. Syrr. Copt. Aeth. RV.), not follow it (L, Chrys. Thdrt., AV.). The Tongue and the interpretation would be mentioned together.

27. εἴτε γλώσσῃ τις λαλεῖ. As in xii. 28 (οὓς μέν), a construction is begun and left unfinished. This is the first member of a distributive sentence, which ought to have gone on εἴτε . . ., εἴτε. But there is no second member : at *v.* 29, where it might

* Abbott, *Johannine Grammar*, 2534[b], expands the passage thus ; 'Just when ye are assembling for sacred worship, and ought to be thinking of Christ and of Christ's Body, the congregation, each one is perhaps thinking of himself, 'I have a Psalm,' 'I have a Doctrine,' 'I have a Revelation.' Have done with this ! Let all be done to edification.'

have come, a new construction is started, perhaps because the εἴτε is forgotten, or perhaps deliberately, because the presence of prophets in the assembly is assumed as certain. Moreover, there is no verb with κατὰ δύο κ.τ.λ., but λαλείτωσαν is readily understood (1 Pet. iv. 11). There might be many ready to speak with Tongues, but the number was to be limited down to (distributive use of κατά) two, or at most three, who were to speak in turn. The insertion of ἀνὰ μέρος perhaps implies that sometimes two tried to speak at once.* One, and one only (εἷς not τις), was to interpret; there was to be no interpreting in turn, which might lead to profitless discussion. Moreover, this would be a security against two speaking with Tongues at the same time, for one interpreter could not attend to both. Possibly the gift of interpretation was more rare, for the possibility of there being no interpreter present is contemplated.

28. σιγάτω ἐν ἐκκλησίᾳ. In strict grammar, this should mean that the interpreter must keep silence, but the change of subject is quite intelligible, and indeed necessary. The verb is one of many which in N.T. are found only in Paul and Luke (Hawkins, *Hor. Syn.* p. 191).

ἑαυτῷ δὲ λαλείτω. The pronoun is emphatic : ' to *himself* let him speak,' that is, in private, not in the congregation. It cannot mean that he is to 'commune with his own heart,' in *public,* 'and be still.'† The whole point of λαλεῖν throughout the chapter is that of making audible utterance. If he cannot interpret his Tongue, and there is no interpreter present, he must not exercise his gift until he is alone. The difference between διερμηνευτής (A E K L) and ἑρμηνευτής (B D* F G) is unimportant. The latter occurs Gen. xlii. 23, the former nowhere else in Biblical Greek.

29. The directions with regard to prophesying are much the same as those with regard to Tongues, but are less explicit. Not more than three are to prophesy on any one occasion, and of course only one at a time ; but ἢ τὸ πλεῖστον is here omitted. Of those who speak with Tongues, three in one assembly, with one interpreter, is an absolute maximum ; of those who prophesy, three would generally be a convenient limit.

οἱ ἄλλοι διακρινέτωσαν. 'Let the others discern,' *caeteri dijudicent*; let them discriminate whether what is being said is really inspired. This 'discerning of spirits,' διάκρισις πνευμάτων

---

* In St Paul ἀνά occurs only here and vi. 5. In the N.T. it is generally distributive, as here, or in the phrase ἀνὰ μέσον, as vi. 5. Nowhere else in N.T. does τὸ πλεῖστον, 'at the most,' occur : δύο ἢ τό γε πλεῖστον τρεῖς is found in papyri.

† ἀψοφητὶ καὶ ἠρέμαι καθ᾽ ἑαυτόν (Theoph.).

(xii. 10), was a gift, and it is assumed that an inspired preacher would possess it. There was the possibility that ἑαυτῷ τις λαμβάνει τὴν τιμήν of prophesying, without being καλούμενος ὑπὸ τοῦ Θεοῦ (Heb. v. 4). The listening prophets are therefore to use this gift : they are *etiam tacendo utiles Ecclesiae* (Calv.) by preserving the congregation from being misled by one who is not really guided by the Spirit, but "by some evil spirit fashioning himself into an angel of light," as Origen puts it. It is a mistake to say that in the *Didache* a contrary instruction to this is given. There the command is : πάντα προφήτην λαλοῦντα ἐν πνεύματι οὐ πειράσετε οὐδὲ διακρινεῖτε· πᾶσα γὰρ ἁμαρτία ἀφεθήσεται, αὕτη δὲ ἡ ἁμαρτία οὐκ ἀφεθήσεται (xi. 7). The prophet has been tested, and found to be a true prophet, and it is expressly stated that he is speaking ἐν πνεύματι : therefore to question his utterances would be ἡ τοῦ Πνεύματος βλασφημία (Matt. xii. 31).

As in Phil. ii. 3 (ἀλλήλους) and iv. 3 (τῶν λοιπῶν), 'the other' (AV.) is here plural : comp. Josh. viii. 22 ; 2 Chron. xxxii. 32 ; Job xxiv. 24. But 'let the other judge' now seems to apply to only one of the listening prophets : comp. *v.* 17.

οἱ ἄλλοι (א A B E K, Vulg.) is to be preferred to ἄλλοι (D* F G L), and διακρινέτωσαν (א A B E K L) to ἀνακρινέτωσαν (D* F G), 'examine' (Arm.).

30. ἐὰν δὲ ἄλλῳ ἀποκαλυφθῇ καθημένῳ. 'But if a revelation be made to another sitting by.' As in the synagogue, the congregation sat to listen to reading or preaching, and perhaps we may infer that the reader or preacher stood (Luke iv. 16 ; Acts xiii. 16). The ἄλλος would no doubt give some sign that he had received a call to speak, and in that case the one who was then speaking was to draw to a close. The Apostle does not say σιγησάτω, 'let him *at once* be silent,' but σιγάτω, which need not mean that. Those who often addressed the congregation would be open to the temptation of continuing to speak after their message was delivered, and they would certainly need the exhortations and warnings of other inspired preachers. No one was to occupy the whole time to the exclusion of others, and each ought to rejoice that others possessed this gift as well as himself (Num. xi. 28).

31. δύνασθε γὰρ καθ' ἕνα πάντες προφητεύειν. 'For ye have the *power*, one by one, *all* of you, to prophesy.' If each preacher stops when another receives a message, all the prophets, however many there may be, will be able to speak in successive assemblies, three at each meeting. They are capable of making room for one another, and (like the rest of the congregation) they are capable of receiving instruction and encouragement. The congregation would learn more through a change of preachers, and the preachers also would learn more through listening to one another.*

32. καὶ πνεύματα προφητῶν προφήταις ὑποτάσσεται. 'And prophets' spirits are subject to prophets.' The present tense states an established fact or principle. The spirits of sibyls and pythonesses were not under their control; utterance continued till the impulse ceased. But this is not the case with one who is inspired by God; a preacher without self-control is no true prophet: and uncontrolled religious feeling is sure to lead to evil. This therefore is a second justification of ὁ πρῶτος σιγάτω: he *can* hold his peace, for prophets always have their own spirits under the control of their understanding and their will.

Some would make προφητῶν refer to those who speak, and προφήταις to those for whom the speakers have to make room. But the juxtaposition of the two words is against this. Moreover, he does not say '*ought* to be subject to,' as a matter of order, but, '*are* subject to,' as a matter of fact. Again, why say 'spirits of prophets' instead of 'prophets'? It would have been much simpler to say 'Prophets *must* be in subjection to *one another*' if this had been his meaning. It is probable that πνεύματα means the prophetic charismata rather than the spirits of the persons who possess them, although the interpretation of the sentence is much the same in either case: comp. xii. 10 and see Swete on Rev. xxii. 6. The omission of the article in all three places makes the saying more like a maxim or proverb; comp. 'Jews have no dealings with Samaritans' (John iv. 9).

πνεύματα (‭א‬ A B K L, Vulg. Copt.) may safely be preferred to πνεῦμα (D F, Aeth.), which probably was substituted under the influence of xii. 4–13. Novatian has *spiritus prophetarum prophetis subjectus est* (*De Trin.* xxix.).

33. οὐ γάρ ἐστιν ἀκαταστασίας ὁ Θεός. Proof that the prophetic gift is under control, and that therefore an inspired speaker can stop and give place to another. The God who gives the inspiration is not on the side of disorder and turbulence, but on that of peace. He cannot be a promoter of tumult, and therefore cannot inspire two people to speak simultaneously to the same audience. The fact of His inspiring a second speaker is proof that the first can stop and ought to do so. Inspiration is no

---

* Perhaps, as Origen takes it, St Paul contemplated the possibility of all the congregation being prophets. There must, he says, have been something of a prophetic spirit in Israel, sufficient for the discerning of prophets; for the utterances of the false prophets, who were such favourites at court, have all perished, while the utterances of the Prophets of God, who were so persecuted, have been preserved (*JTS.* x. 37, p. 41).

excuse for conflict and confusion, and jealousies and dissensions are not signs of the presence of God (*v.* 25); ἡ ἀγάπη οὐκ ἀσχημονεῖ. The principle here stated justifies us in maintaining that miracles are not violations of law; God is not on the side of violations of law, but is on the side of peace, which results from preserving law: comp. ὁ Θεὸς τῆς εἰρήνης (Rom. xvi. 20). For ἀκαταστασία, which is a strong word—*dissensio* (Vulg.), *seditio* (Calv.)—compare 2 Cor. xii. 20; Jas. iii. 16; Luke xxi. 9.*

ὡς ἐν πάσαις ταῖς ἐκκλησίαις τῶν ἁγίων. Added, as in xi. 16, as conclusive, and the addition of τῶν ἁγίων is made with some severity. Orderly reverence is a characteristic of *all* the Churches of the saints, a fact which raises doubts as to whether the Church at Corinth is a Church of saints: comp. iv. 17, vii. 17. Some editors place these words at the beginning of the next paragraph, where ἐν ταῖς ἐκκλησίαις makes them seem somewhat superfluous. Moreover, it is more probable that St Paul would begin the paragraph with the subject of it, αἱ γυναῖκες, as in Eph. v. 22, 25, vi. 1, 5; Col. iii. 18–22; 1 Pet. iii. 1, 7. Chrysostom mixes this clause with iv. 17 and vii. 17 and quotes οὕτω γὰρ ἐν πάσαις ταῖς ἐκκλησίαις τῶν ἁγίων διδάσκω.† If St Paul had written this, it would of necessity belong to what precedes, and not to *v.* 34. Assuming that it is best taken with what precedes, to which of the preceding clauses does it belong? Possibly to οὐ γάρ ἐστιν κ.τ.λ. Reverent submission to order is everywhere a note of the Church. Others take it with καὶ πνεύματα προφητῶν κ.τ.λ., making οὐ γάρ ἐστιν parenthetical. WH. make from καὶ πνεύματα to εἰρήνης parenthetical, and take this clause with ἵνα πάντες μανθάνωσιν κ.τ.λ. This makes a very awkward parenthesis, and ὡς ἐν πάσαις τ. ἐκ comes in too late to add much force to ἵνα πάντες μανθάνωσιν. Perhaps the worst punctuation is to take ὡς ἐν πάσαις τ. ἐκ. with what precedes, and τῶν ἁγίων with αἱ γυναῖκες ἐν ταῖς ἐκ. See Hort, *The Chr. Eccl.* pp. 117, 120.

34-40. Directions as to Women; Concluding Exhortations.

34. The women are to keep silence in the public services. They would join in the Amen (*v.* 16), but otherwise not be heard. They had been claiming equality with men in the matter of the veil, by discarding this mark of subjection in Church, and apparently they had also been attempting to preach, or at any rate had been asking questions during service. We are not sure whether St Paul contemplated the *possibility* of women prophesy-

---

* St James (iii. 8) calls the tongue ἀκατάστατον κακόν, as promoting the disorder which is directly opposed to God's will: see Hort *ad loc.*

† *Sicut et in omnibus ecclesiis sanctorum doceo* (Vulg.).

ing in exceptional cases.* What is said in xi. 5 may be hypothetical. Teaching he forbids them to attempt; διδάσκειν δὲ
γυναικὶ οὐκ ἐπιτρέπω, a rule taken over from the synagogue and
maintained in the primitive Church (1 Tim. ii. 12). Discarding
the veil was claiming equality with man; teaching in public was
αὐθεντεῖν ἀνδρός. Hence the command here.

ὑποτασσέσθωσαν, καθὼς καὶ ὁ νόμος λέγει. So far from their
having dominion over men, 'let them be in subjection, even as
also the Law saith.' The reference is to the primeval command,
Gen. iii. 16: comp. Eph. v. 22. Had the Apostle heard of
Gaia Afrania, wife of Licinius Buccio, a contentious lady who
insisted on pleading her own causes in court, and was such a
nuisance to the praetors that an edict was made prohibiting
women from pleading? She died B.C. 48. For Greek sentiment
on the subject see Thuc. II. xlv. 2.

There should probably be no ὑμῶν after αἱ γυναῖκες (א A B 17, Vulg.
Copt. Arm. Aeth. omit): but if it be accepted (D E F G K L, Syrr.), it is
in contrast to τῶν ἀγίων. 'Let *your* women (or your wives) not act
differently from those among the saints.'

If ὑποτάσσεσθαι (D F G K L, Vulg. Arm.) be read instead of ὑποτασσέσθωσαν (א A B 17, Copt. Aeth.) there is a touch of irony: 'women are not
permitted to speak; they *are* permitted to keep their proper place': *non
enim permittitur eis loqui, sed subditas esse.* So also Chrys., who with K
has ἐπιτέτραπται, for ἐπιτρέπεται, perhaps on the analogy of γέγραπται.

35. εἰ δέ τι μαθεῖν θέλουσιν, ἐν οἴκῳ κ.τ.λ. 'And moreover, if
they wish to learn anything, let them ask their own husbands *at
home.*' The women might urge that they did not always understand
the prophesying: might they not ask for an explanation. Asking
to be taught was not self-assertion but submissiveness. But the
Apostle will not allow this: questions may be objections to what
is preached, or even contradictions of it : ἐν οἴκῳ (in emphatic
contrast to ἐν ταῖς ἐκκλησίαις) they can ask their own husbands,
and if these do not know, *they* can ask in the assemblies. It is
assumed that only married women would think of asking questions
in public; unmarried women could get a question asked through
the married. Origen quotes, πρὸς τὸν ἄνδρα σου ἡ ἀποστροφή σου
(Gen. iii. 16). Perhaps husbands, by analogy, would cover
brothers and sons. Compare Soph. *Ajax* 293, γύναι, γυναιξὶ
κόσμον ἡ σιγὴ φέρει. Eur. *Phoeniss.* 200; *Tro.* 649. But *ne*

---

* Tertullian takes it so; *caeterum prophetandi jus et illas habere jam
ostendit, cum mulieri etiam prophetanti velamen imponit* (*Adv. Marcion.*
v. 8). So also does Harnack, *The Mission and Expansion of Christianity*,
ii. pp. 65, 71 ; pp. 395, 400, ed. 1902. Weinel suspects that this verse is an
interpolation by a later hand, and that 1 Tim. ii. 12 also is late. Hilgenfeld,
Holsten, Schmiedel, and others regard *vv.* 34, 35 as an interpolation : see
Moffatt, *Historical N.T.*, pp. 727 f. In some MSS of Ambrosiaster, *vv.* 34
and 35, with the notes, are transferred to the end of the chapter, after *v.* 40
(A. Souter, *A Study of Ambrosiaster*, p. 189).

videretur eas etiam discere prohibuisse, ostendit eas domi debere discere (Primasius).

αἰσχρόν. A strong word, used of women being clipped or shorn (xi. 6): comp. Eph. v. 12; Tit. i. 11—the only other instances in the N.T. It is really a scandalous thing for a woman to address the congregation or disturb it by speaking. What follows is still more severe, but it is put sarcastically.

γυναικὶ λαλεῖν ἐν ἐκκλησίᾳ (א A B 17, Vulg. Copt. Aeth.) rather than γυναιξὶν ἐν ἐκκ. λαλεῖν (D E F G K L, Syrr.). A few authorities have γυναικὶ ἐν ἐκκ. λαλ. or γυναιξὶν λαλ. ἐν ἐκκ. The plural is an obvious correction to agree with the preceding plurals.

36. Ἢ ἀφ᾽ ὑμῶν ὁ λόγος τοῦ Θεοῦ ἐξῆλθεν, ἢ εἰς ὑμᾶς μόνους κατήντησεν; 'What? was it from you that the word of God came forth? or was it to you alone that it reached?' The AV. has three inaccuracies: (1) a false accent is thrown on to the prepositions 'from' and 'unto,' as if the two questions gave two alternatives; (2) ἐξῆλθεν and κατήντησεν are both rendered 'came'; (3) μόνους is rendered 'only,' which is ambiguous. The meaning is, 'Were you the starting-point of the Gospel? or were you its only destination? Do you mean to contend that you have the right to maintain these irregularities? women discarding veils in public worship, people getting drunk at the Supper, people speaking in Tongues and no one interpreting, prophets refusing to give place to one another, women claiming to prophesy and ask questions in public worship? If you defend such scandals as these, one can only suppose that you claim to be the A and Ω of the Gospel, the fount and reservoir of all Church teaching, the starting-point and the goal of all Church discipline.'* Compare ἡ ἔξοδος αὐτοῦ καὶ τὸ κατάντημα αὐτοῦ (Ps. xix. 6); and see J. A. Robinson on Eph. iv. 13. For Corinthian assumption of independence see iv. 6, v. 2.

We cannot infer from εἰς ὑμᾶς being used rather than πρὸς ὑμᾶς that the idea of "entering as it were into them" is included; for εἰς is the regular construction after καταντάω (x. 11; Eph. iv. 13; Phil. iii. 11); also in the literal sense of arriving at a place (Acts xvi. 1, xviii. 19, 24, etc.). In the N.T. the verb is peculiar to Acts and St Paul. Nor must we infer that, if Corinth had been the Mother-Church, the Apostle would have allowed that it had the right to sanction such things. His sarcastic argument is that they seem to be claiming a monstrous amount of authority and independence. The verse sums up his indignation.

* *Haec quae vobis trado, tenere debetis, non vestra instituta meis traditionibus praeferre, et caeteris fidelibus quasi fontem religionis velle tradere. Quoniam a nobis qui de circumcisione sumus coepit evangelica praedicatio, non a vobis; nec beneficium vos dedistis, sed accepistis. Nec quasi singulariter electi debetis gloriari, aut de singulari scientia extolli* (Herveius).

37, 38. He here sums up his own authority in a mannei very similar to xi. 16: both passages begin with εἴ τις δοκεῖ. Comp. also iii. 18, viii. 2. The meaning of δοκεῖ must in each case be determined by the context. 'If any man thinketh him-self to be a prophet or endowed with any spiritual gift'; not 'seemeth to be,' *videtur* (Vulg.) but *'sibi videtur'* (Beza). It is what the man is in his own eyes that is the point here.

ἐπιγινωσκέτω ἃ γράφω ὑμῖν, ὅτι Κυρίου ἐστὶν ἐντολή. 'Let him continually take knowledge of what I am writing to you, that it is the *Lord's* commandment.' Κυρίου is very emphatic. 'Let him prove his own inspiration by fully recognizing my absolute authority.' The sureness of a divinely appointed Apostle is in the verse: *non patitur Paulus demum quaeri an recte scribat* (Beng.). He is conscious that what he says does not come from himself; he is the mouthpiece of Christ: ii. 10–16, vii. 40; 2 Cor. xiii. 3; comp. 1 John iv. 6.* But he is not claiming authority to regulate these details for the whole Church through-out all time: no such vast extension is in his mind. What he is claiming is authority to regulate them for the Corinthian Chris-tians at that time (ix. 2). And the ἃ γράφω covers all that he has been saying about disorders in public worship (xi.–xiv.). His indignation in *v.* 36 is provoked by all these irregularities, and ἃ γράφω has the same extension. It is a mistake to limit either to the question of women speaking in Church.

εἰ δέ τις ἀγνοεῖ ἀγνοείτω. 'But if any one is ignorant (that Christ is the Source of my rulings in these matters), let him be ignorant.' His ignorance does not alter facts, and he must be left in his unedifying condition. *Si quis ignorat, ignoret* (Calv.). *Qui vero ignarus est, ignarus esto* (Beza). "Why does he add this?" asks Chrysostom: "To show that he does not use compulsion and is not contentious; which is a mark of those who do not wish to establish their own advantage but seek what is beneficial to others."

But it is possible that the true reading is ἀγνοεῖται, 'he is ignored' by God; he fails to recognize God's Apostle, and God refuses to recognize him. But St Paul does not say 'if he refuses to admit my authority,' but 'if he is not aware of it'; and being ignored by God seems to be an excessive requital for mere ignorance. 'I do not care to dispute with him' is more reasonable. The evidence is rather evenly balanced: ἀγνοεῖται (א* A* D* F G 17, *ignorabitur* Vulg.: ἀγνοείτω (B E K L and the cor-rectors of א A D, Syrr. Copt. Aeth. Arm., Orig. Chrys. Thdrt.), see viii. 3; Gal. iv. 9. But in one passage Origen has expressly ἀγνοεῖται ὑπὸ τοῦ Θεοῦ (*JTS.* x. 37, p. 30.

---

* It is possible that with D* F G, Orig. we ought to omit ἐντολή: the brief ὅτι Κυρίου ἐστίν is impressive. The AV. follows E K L, Vulg. Syrr. in reading εἰσὶν ἐντολαί. Resch assumes an unrecorded saying of Christ *'Agrapha*, p. 211.

39. ὥστε, ἀδελφοί μου. As in xi. 33, these words introduce an affectionate summing up after severe censure: *Post multas correptiones, fratres eos appellat, ut subleventur* (Atto). For ὥστε see vii. 38, x. 12, xv. 58. 'So then, my brethren, continue to desire earnestly the gift of prophesying, and that of speaking with Tongues hinder ye not.' * A vast difference ; the one gift to be greatly longed for, the other only not forbidden ; for, as Chrys. points out, τὸ τῶν γλωσσῶν οὔτε πάντη ἄχρηστον, οὔτε σφόδρα ὠφέλιμον καθ᾽ ἑαυτό. See 1 Thess· v. 19, 20.

40. πάντα δὲ εὐσχημόνως καὶ κατὰ τάξιν γινέσθω. 'Only (δέ) let all things be carried on (pres. imperat.) with seemliness and in order.' For εὐσχημόνως comp. Rom. xiii. 13 ; 1 Thess. iv. 12, where see Milligan's note and quotations from papyri. Ecclesiastical decorum is meant; beauty and harmony prevail in God's universe, where each part discharges its proper function without slackness or encroachment; and beauty and harmony ought to prevail in the worship of God. In κατὰ τάξιν we probably have a military metaphor. The exact phrase occurs nowhere else in either N.T. or LXX, but is used of the Greeks' manner of fighting at Salamis as opposed to the disorderly efforts of the barbarians (Hdt. viii. 86). Possibly εὐσχημόνως refers to the celebration of the Supper and the behaviour of the women, κατὰ τάξιν to the exercise of the gifts.

In these three chapters (xii.–xiv.) the Apostle has been contending with the danger of *spiritual anarchy*, which would be the result if every Christian who believed that he had a charisma were allowed to exercise it without consideration for others. He passes on to the danger of one form of *philosophic scepticism,—* doubt as to the possibility of resurrection.

XV. THE DOCTRINE OF THE RESURRECTION OF THE DEAD.

Having treated of various social, moral, ecclesiastical, and liturgical questions, the Apostle now takes up a doctrinal one, which he has kept to the last because of its vital importance.†

---

* μὴ κωλύετε cannot mean '*cease* to hinder,' for they had been too eager to encourage speaking with Tongues. Perhaps the previous ζηλοῦτε has caused the pres. imperat. to be used. Or, St Paul may be alluding to his own apparent discouragement of the exercise of this gift. 'Do not, in consequence of what I have said, attempt to hinder.' Comp. μὴ ἀμέλει, μηδενὶ ἐπιτίθει, μηδὲ κοινώνει (1 Tim. iv. 14, v. 22), where 'cease to' seems to be quite out of place. J. H. Moulton, *Gr.* p. 125.

† Calvin suggests that St Paul did not wish to treat of so momentous a subject until, by the rebukes and exhortations of the previous chapters, he had brought the Corinthians to a proper state of mind.

The Epistle begins with the subject of Christ Crucified (i. 13-ii. 5); it ends with that of Christ Risen (xv.). This chapter has been called "the earliest Christian doctrinal essay," and it is the only part of the letter which deals directly with doctrine.

There is here no trace of a question asked by the Corinthians: this subject St Paul starts himself, in consequence of information which has reached him. Thus the letter begins and ends in a similar way. At the outset he treated of a subject which had been reported to him (i. 11), and he closes with one which again was suggested by what he had heard (v. 12),—that there were certain people at Corinth who denied the doctrine of the Resurrection. Who these persons were we do not know; but it is very improbable that they were converts who had originally been Sadducees, and who still retained some of their Sadducean leanings. The Corinthian Church was mainly a Gentile Church; and the errors with which the Apostle has been dealing were of Greek rather than Jewish origin. The Book of Daniel and Isaiah xxiv.-xxvii., with other passages in the O.T., had made the Jew familiar with the doctrine of the bodily resurrection of individuals, at any rate of individual Jews; but to the Greeks, even to those who accepted the immortality of the soul, the idea of a bodily resurrection was foolishness.* We shall be safe in concluding that the sceptics alluded to in v. 12 were Greeks and not Jews.

The gentleness of tone with which the preceding section closed is continued. The Apostle is anxious not to give offence. With gentle words he goes back to teaching of which they have already experienced the value, and disclaims all originality respecting it. He has merely passed on to them what he himself, on the highest authority, received. "There is no historical fact more certain," says Harnack, "than that the Apostle Paul was not the first to emphasize so prominently the significance of Christ's Death and Resurrection, but that in recognizing their meaning he stood exactly on the same ground as the primitive community" (*What is Christianity?* p. 153).

The chapter contains three sections, each of which is capable of subdivision, and perhaps some of these subdivisions are almost as important as the three sections, which are these; (1) The Resurrection of Christ is an Essential Article of the Gospel, 1–11. (2) If Christ is risen, the Dead in Christ will

---

* See Acts xvii. 18, 32, and St Paul's speech in the Areopagus (22–31), "the most wonderful passage in the Book of Acts: in a higher sense (and probably in a strictly historical sense at some vital points) it is full of truth" (Harnack, *The Mission and Expansion of Christianity*, i. p. 383; comp. p. 88).

rise, 12–34. (3) Answers to Objections; the Nature of the Body of the Risen, 35–58. The conclusion reached in *vv.* 1–34 is that Christianity stands or falls with the fact of the Resurrection. The conclusion of the whole is that Victory over Death has been won, and that Christians must live in accordance with this certainty. See Swete, *The Ascended Christ*, pp. 163 f.

XV. 1–11. The Resurrection of Christ is an Essential Article of the Gospel.

Here we have three subdivisions; (*a*) The Creed delivered to the Corinthians by St Paul, 1–4; (*b*) The Official Witnesses of the Resurrection of Christ, 5–8; (*c*) The Agreement between St Paul and the other Apostles respecting this Creed, 9–11.

The substance of my preaching has been and is the historical fact of the Resurrection of Christ, which was predicted in Scripture, and is vouched for by competent witnesses, most of whom are still living. Among these are the other Apostles and myself; and, greatly as they differ from me in calling and work, we are absolutely agreed about this.

¹ Now I have to remind you, Brothers, of the purport of the Glad-tidings with which I once gladdened you, which also you then received, in which also you now stand firm, ² by means of which also you are in the way of salvation, if you are holding fast the Gospel with which I gladdened you,— unless, of course, you became Christians without thinking of the faith which you professed. ³ You remember the purport of my preaching; for I handed on to you in the forefront of everything what was no invention of my own, but what I also received, that Christ died for our sins, as the Scriptures have predicted, ⁴ and that He was buried, and that He has been raised from the dead—on the third day, as the Scriptures have predicted; ⁵ and that He appeared to Kephas, then to the Twelve. ⁶ Afterwards He appeared to upwards of five hundred brethren at once, the majority of whom survive to the present day, but some have gone to their rest. ⁷ Next He appeared to James; then to the Apostles in a body: ⁸ and last of all, just as if to the untimely-born Apostle, He appeared also to me. ⁹ For I am the very least of the Apostles, and I am not

fit to have the name of an Apostle, because I persecuted the Church, the Church of God. ¹⁰ But by the grace of God I have been made equal to being an Apostle; and His grace, which reached even to me, did not prove ineffectual. Quite the contrary; I toiled more effectually than all of them: yet not I, of course; it was the grace of God working with me. ¹¹ Well, it is of no importance whether I or the other Apostles laboured more effectually: what does matter is this, that we all continue to preach the Death and Resurrection of Christ, and it was the Death and Resurrection of Christ that, at your conversion, you accepted and believed.

1, 2. Γνωρίζω δὲ ὑμῖν. 'Now I proceed to make known to you the Good-tidings (Isa. lii. 7) which I once brought to you, the Good-tidings which ye received, the Good-tidings in which ye stand firm, the Good-tidings by which ye are being saved.' The καὶ . . . καὶ . . . καὶ . . . is a climax, and in English a repetition of the substantive gives the effect better than a repetition of the conjunction. Stanley follows Theodoret in making γνωρίζω = ἀναμιμνήσκω, 'I remind you,' with which Chrysostom seems to agree. They had forgotten their own belief, so he has to call their attention to it. But γνωρίζω is simply 'I make known,' *notum facio* (Vulg.), and is often used in the N.T. of preaching the Gospel. There is a gentle reproach in the word. He has to begin again and teach them an elementary fact, which they had already accepted. He can claim themselves as witnesses to its truth and efficacy. In the Pauline Epp. both γν. ὑμῖν (xii. 3; Gal. i. 11; 2 Cor. viii. 1) and εὐαγγέλιον εὐαγγελίζομαι (ix. 18; Gal. i. 11; 2 Cor. xi. 7) are peculiar to this group. The latter is an attractive expression, emphasizing the goodness and gladness of the message; but the repetition cannot well be reproduced in English: see above. The verses here are badly divided.

ὃ καὶ παρελάβετε κ.τ.λ. He adduces three proofs that their own experience has shown to them the value of his doctrine: παρελάβετε looks to the past, ἑστήκατε to the present, σώζεσθε to what is being done for the future. They accepted his teaching; in it they stand with a firm foothold; and they are thus among οἱ σωζόμενοι (i. 18; Acts ii. 47; 2 Cor. ii. 15), those who are in the way of salvation. Compare Eph. i. 13. Quite incidentally (vi. 14), the Apostle has previously assumed that the doctrine of Christ's Resurrection and our consequent resurrection is admitted. See C. H. Robinson, *Studies in the Resurrection of Christ*, pp. 38 f. and 50 f.; F. H. Chase, *Cambridge Theological Essays*, pp. 391 ff.

Τίνι λόγῳ εὐηγγελισάμην ὑμῖν εἰ κατέχετε. 'If ye are holding fast with what word I preached it to you.' Not ᾧ λόγῳ, 'the word with which,' but τίνι λ., 'with what word,' the λόγος covering both the form and the substance of his teaching. Their standing erect in the way of salvation depends upon their keeping a firm hold (xi. 2) on what he taught and the very expressions which he used: *quo sermone* (Beza), rather than *qua ratione* (Vulg.), or *quo pacto* (Calv.). In xi. 2 he affirms that they are holding fast the traditions of doctrine and discipline; here he puts it hypothetically, and εἰ κατέχετε is displaced in order to give an emphatic position to τίνι λ. εὐηγγ. Such inversions of order are common. Blass, however, § 80. 6, thinks this very awkward.

The RV. takes τίνι λόγῳ differently; '*I make known, I say, in what words I preached* it unto you, if ye hold it fast.' But this is scarcely tenable. St Paul's making known could not depend on their holding fast: he writes what he pleases, whatever their condition may be.*

ἐκτὸς εἰ μὴ εἰκῇ ἐπιστεύσατε. 'With this proviso—unless ye believed haphazard': see on xiv. 5. There are two defects possible; they may not be holding fast what he taught, or they may have received it so hastily that they do not comprehend it. Belief adopted in a hurry is not likely to be very sure. He begins the discussion with this fear respecting them, and he ends it with a charge to be steadfast and unshifted (*v.* 58). Εἰκῇ is not 'in vain' (AV., RV.), nor 'without cause' (RV. marg.), but 'without consideration,' 'heedlessly,' 'rashly'; *temere* rather than *frustra.*† This ἐκτὸς εἰ μὴ εἰκῇ states a misgiving which lies at the back of the whole chapter. Has the conversion of the Corinthians been superficial and unreal? Was it a shallow enthusiasm, or a passing fancy for some new thing? See Evans and Edwards on εἰκῇ. Ellicott and others prefer 'in vain.'

3. παρέδωκα γὰρ ὑμῖν ἐν πρώτοις. 'For I delivered to you (xi. 2) in the foremost place (Gen. xxxiii. 2) what I also received.' Foremost in importance, not in time; the doctrine of the Resurrection is primary and cardinal, central and indispensable. The γὰρ may look back either to γνωρίζω ὑμῖν, or (better) to τίνι λόγῳ, 'You remember *how* I preached, *for*.' St Paul lingers over this preface, *qua eos quasi suspensos tenet* (Beng.).

---

* The reading ὀφείλετε κατέχειν (D* F, g, Ambrst.) for εἰ κατέχετε is an attempt to simplify the construction: so also is the conjecture of ὅ for εἰ.

† οἱ πρὸς καιρὸν πιστεύοντες καὶ ἐν καιρῷ πειρασμοῦ ἀφιστάμενοι, εἰκῇ πιστεύουσι (Origen).

Many scholars prefer εἰκῆ to εἰκῇ. The orthography is not important.

What follows is almost a creed; but we need not suppose that it had already been formulated. Rather, this passage supplied material for the formulating of creeds.

ὃ καὶ παρέλαβον. 'Which also I received.' Nothing is said as to the source from which he received it, or the way in which the communication was made. It is *possible* that he received it from Christ by special revelation; but this is even less probable than in xi. 23 (see notes there). Here there is neither ἐγώ nor ἀπὸ τοῦ Κυρίου to emphasize the authority either of the person who made the communication or of the Source from which he derived it. Neither of these is the question here. The point is that St Paul did not invent what he communicated to them; he received just what they received. The καί indicates the exact agreement of what he received with what he passed on to them. He appeals (*vv.* 5–7) to human testimony prior to his own experience, and it is reasonable to suppose that this is what is implied in παρέλαβον. In any case, it is clear that he does not appeal to documents either here or in xi. 23. St Paul knows nothing of written Gospels; and ὃ καὶ παρέλαβον seems to refer to something quite different from ὤφθη κἀμοί (*v.* 8). And he knows nothing of a formulated Creed, neither in Rom. vi. 17, 'the standard of teaching to which ye were committed,' nor in 2 Tim. i. 13, 'the pattern of sound words which thou hast heard from me.' See Dobschütz, *Probleme*, pp. 11, 106. He received the facts from the Apostles and others; the import of the facts was made known to him by Christ (Gal. i. 12).

ἀπέθανεν ὑπὲρ τῶν ἁμαρτιῶν ἡμῶν. 'He died for our sins,' *i.e.* 'on account of our sins,' not 'on behalf of them,' which is hardly sense. One may die on behalf of sinners, but hardly on behalf of sins (2 Cor. v. 14, 15; Gal. iii. 13). On the whole, περί is used of things, τοῦ δόντος ἑαυτὸν περὶ τῶν ἁμαρτιῶν ἡμῶν (Gal. i. 4, where see Lightfoot), and ὑπέρ of persons, Χριστὸς ἅπαξ περὶ ἁμαρτιῶν ἀπέθανεν, δίκαιος ὑπὲρ ἀδίκων (1 Pet. iii. 18), but exceptions abound. Neither preposition implies vicarious action, which would require ἀντί, but vicarious action may be implied in the context. *Pro peccatis nostris abolendis* (Beng.) gives the right meaning. There is a real connexion, beyond our comprehension, between Christ's death and the forgiveness of men's sins. This is in agreement with the O.T. (Isa. liii. 4–12), and this agreement is part of the εὐαγγέλιον which St Paul proclaimed to them. Nowhere else does he use the expression ὑπὲρ τ. ἁμαρτιῶν: comp. Gal. ii. 20; Eph. v. 2, 25; Tit. ii. 14. See Knowling, *Messianic Interpretation*, pp. 90 f.

κατὰ τὰς γραφάς. The double appeal to Scripture in so brief a statement is deliberate and important; and the divine

prediction of what would take place is appropriately placed
before the Apostolic testimony as to what did take place. The
agreement of what did take place with what was foretold in
Scripture is pointed out with special frequency in the writings
of St Luke (xxii. 37, xxiv. 25–27, 44–46; Acts ii. 25–27, iii. 35,
xiii. 34, 35, xvii. 3, xviii. 28). See Cyril, *Cat. Lect.* xiv., which
is a commentary on these verses.

καὶ ὅτι ἐτάφη. The inclusion of this detail in so brief a statement of facts is remarkable. But the burial is carefully recorded
in all four Gospels, and was evidently regarded as of importance.
The importance there and here is that the burial was evidence
of a bodily resurrection. The body was laid in the tomb, and
the tomb was afterwards found to be empty.*

καὶ ὅτι ἐγήγερται. 'And that He hath been raised—on the
third day.' Change from aorists of what took place once for
all to the perfect of a result which abides; He remains alive as
the Risen One. By death and burial He came down to our
level, by Resurrection He raised us to His: *mortuus est iste
nobiscum, ut nos cum ipso resurgamus* (Calv.). 'On the third
day' does not harmonize well with a perfect, but it is added as
of importance (1) as evidence of a bodily resurrection (comp.
Acts ii. 24 f.), and (2) to show the exact coincidence with
prophecy (Hos. vi. 2; comp. Ps. xvi. 10, 11; xvii. 15–24).
Christ is said to have included 'on the third day' in what was
predicted in Scripture (Luke xxiv. 46).† Matt. xii. 40 cannot
safely be quoted here, for there are strong reasons for believing
that there we have the Evangelist's misunderstanding of Christ's
words rather than the words themselves. Christ was not three
days and three nights in the grave. See Allen *ad loc.* "In any
case we have here irresistible evidence that this difficult clause,
'raised on the third day in accordance with the Scriptures'
formed part of the earliest Christian creed; and its difficulty,

---

* The connexion between the Body which disappeared from the tomb and
the Body which the disciples afterwards saw and were told to handle is beyond
our comprehension. See Latham, *The Risen Master*, p. 73.

† There τῇ τρίτῃ ἡμέρᾳ is the right reading; but here the more emphatic
τῇ ἡμέρᾳ τῇ τρίτῃ (ℵABDE 17, Cyr.) is right. "The 'third day' is
hardly less firmly rooted in the tradition of the Church than the Resurrection
itself. We have it not only in the speech ascribed to St Peter (Acts x. 40),
but in the central testimony of St Paul, and then in the oldest form of the
Apostles' Creed. It is strange that so slight a detail should have been preserved at all, and still stranger that it should hold the place it does in the
standard of the Church's faith" (Sanday, *Outlines of the Life of Christ*,
p. 183). Matt. xii. 40 is evidence of the Evangelist's belief in it and estimate
of its importance. See J. H. Moulton, *Gr.* pp. 137, 141; Knowling, *Test.
of St Paul to Christ*, p. 307. Max Krenkel (*Beiträge z. Aufhellung d. Geschichte u. d. Briefe d. Ap. Paulus*, pp. 385 f.) thinks that 2 Kings xx. 5 was
regarded as a prophecy of resurrection on the third day.

and its antiquity, justify the conviction that the words proceeded
from Christ Himself" (Abbott, *The Son of Man*, p. 188; see also
pp. 186, 200).

5-8. We now have a list of the official Witnesses to the
Resurrection of Christ, beginning with the first of the Apostles
and ending with 'the least' of them. The form of the sentence
shows that at least the first two on the list, St Peter and the
Twelve, had been quoted by St Paul to the Corinthians. Very
likely the others had been quoted also, although the cessation
of the ὅτι after *v.* 5 (perhaps simply to end a prolix sentence)
leaves this doubtful. Of course St Paul had told them of his
own experiences respecting the Risen Christ; and he probably
knew of other witnesses not mentioned here. See Thorburn,
The Resurrection Narratives and Modern Criticism, pp. 86 f.

5. καὶ ὅτι ὤφθη Κηφᾷ. 'And that He appeared to Kephas.'
The coincidence with the incidental remark Luke xxiv. 34
(comp. Mark. xvi. 7) is noteworthy. Peter is first in all the
four lists of the Apostles, and is expressly designated as πρῶτος
in Matt. x. 2 For this reason a special appearance to him
would be natural. But we may venture to say that his denial
of his Lord and consequent dejection made an appearance to
him necessary. He needed to be absolved and restored.
When he and John ran to the sepulchre after the tidings
brought by Mary Magdalen, John believed, but apparently
Peter did not, that the Lord had risen. And then the Lord
appeared to him, and the completeness of his restoration was
brought home to him by the fact that he was allowed to be
the means of convincing the other Apostles (Luke xxii. 32) that
the Lord had risen indeed, because He had appeared to Simon
(Luke xxiv. 34). "The Apostle who had risen from his fall
through the words of absolution that came from the Risen
Christ was the first to bring the Gospel of the Resurrection
home to the hearts of his fellows" (Swete, *The Appearances of
our Lord after the Passion*, p. 16).* St Paul no doubt received
this testimony from St Peter himself, when some eight years
after the Resurrection he 'went up to Jerusalem to make the

---

* Chrysostom says that Kephas is placed first here as being τὸν πάντων
ἀξιοπιστότερον, and that it was likely that Christ would appear to him first
among males, because he had been the first to confess Him as the Messiah,
and because he desired so much to see Him again. Although St Paul
ignores the non-official testimony of the women who visited the sepulchre, he
does not say that the Lord appeared *first* to Peter. *Nota quia non dicit
primo visus est Cephae* (Atto). But the way in which he speaks of Peter
shows that he does not consider Peter as one of the Kephas party, who are condemned in i. 12 (Zahn, *Introd. to N. T.* i. p. 283). See also A. T. Robertson,
Epochs in the Life of St Paul, pp. 81, 82; Burkitt, *Earliest Sources for the
Life of Jesus*, p. 71.

acquaintance of Kephas' (ἱστορῆσαι Κηφᾶν, Gal. i. 18), and spent a fortnight with him. Henceforward, 'He appeared to Kephas' was part of St Paul's own testimony respecting the Resurrection. It was during the same fortnight that St Paul had also seen 'James, the Lord's brother,' and therefore was able to give the testimony which he had received at first hand from him also (v. 7). Both Peter and James had great weight with the party at Corinth which was opposed to St Paul. The Kephas party of course appealed to Kephas (i. 12), and it is probable that the Christ party appealed to the Lord's brother.

Excepting St John (i. 43), St Paul is the only N.T. writer who uses the Aramaic name 'Kephas' of the first Apostle, always in this letter (i. 12, iii. 22, ix. 5, xv. 5), and usually in Gal. (i. 18, ii. 9, 11, 14), the only letters in which he mentions Peter, whom he calls 'Peter' twice (Gal. ii. 7, 8).

The meaning of ὤφθη is determined by the context; either 'was seen by,' or 'appeared in a vision to.' Here ἐγήγερται decides for the former. Moreover, a mere vision would not make our being raised more probable; it was Christ's having been raised and having been seen by competent witnesses that did that. The appearances to Mary Magdalen and to the two on the way to Emmaus are not mentioned, as not being official. St John does not count either of them when he counts three manifestations (ἐφανερώθη) of Jesus to His disciples (xxi. 14), although he himself narrates the manifestation to Mary in much detail (xx. 11–18). Besides ὤφθη and ἐφανερώθη, we have also ἐφανέρωσεν ἑαυτόν (John xxi. 1) and ἐφάνη ([Mark] xvi. 9) used of these appearances of Christ.

εἶτα τοῖς δώδεκα. 'The Twelve' is here an official name for the Apostolic body: only ten were present, for both Judas and Thomas were away. Similarly, the *decemviri* and *centumviri* were so called, whatever the exact number may have been. The name *centumviri* was retained after the number was increased beyond the hundred. Origen and Chrysostom needlessly conjecture that, after the Ascension, our Lord appeared to Matthias; and even that would not affect this statement.

In *vv.* 5, 6 there is frequent confusion in the MSS. between εἶτα and ἔπειτα. Here, εἶτα (B K L P) is to be preferred to ἔπειτα (א A 17, Eus. Chrys.) or καὶ μετὰ ταῦτα (D* F G). ἔνδεκα (D* F G, Latt. Goth.) for δώδεκα (א A B K L P, Syrr. Copt. Aeth.) is a manifest correction. St Paul nowhere else speaks of 'the Twelve,' and here he is repeating a traditional formula : Rev. xxi. 14 ; Matt. xix. 28 ; Acts vi. 2.

6. ἔπειτα ὤφθη ἐπάνω πεντακοσίοις ἀδελφοῖς ἐφάπαξ. *Illustris apparitio* (Beng.). The ὅτι is now dropped, probably to simplify the construction. It is likely that St Paul had previously cited this instance to the Corinthians; it was one which they could easily verify, as so many of the witnesses survived. The occasion of the appearance to the 500 is unknown; but it is probably to be identified with Matt. xxviii. 16, where only the Eleven are mentioned, because only to them was the great commission (18–20) given, although the presence of others seems to be implied in 'some doubted.' St Paul naturally mentions the large number of witnesses. See Swete, *Appearances of our Lord*, pp. 82, 83; Ellicott, *Life of our Lord*, Lect. viii. p. 410; Andrews, *Life of our Lord*, p. 628.*

When ἐπάνω qualifies a cardinal number, the cardinal retains its own case : it is not governed by ἐπάνω. In Mark xiv. 5, τριακοσίων δηναρίων is the genitive of price. Moul.-Win. p. 313. Chrysostom interprets ἐπάνω as ἄνω ἐκ τῶν οὐρανῶν· οὐ γὰρ ἐπὶ γῆς βαδίζων, ἀλλ' ἄνω, καὶ ὑπὲρ κεφαλῆς αὐτοῖς ὤφθη, which cannot be right. *Plus quam* (Vulg.) is certainly the meaning. And ἐφάπαξ clearly does not mean 'once for all' (Rom. vi. 10; Heb. vii. 27, ix. 12), but 'at once,' *simul* (Vulg.).

οἱ πλείονες μένουσιν ἕως ἄρτι. 'The majority survive until now,' abide upon earth (Phil. i. 25; John xxi. 22). Those who had seen Christ after the Resurrection would soon become marked men. He had doubtless found most of His disciples among the younger generation; hence the large number who were still living more than twenty-five years after the Ascension, and could be questioned : *eo significat, non allegoricam sed veram et naturalem fuisse resurrectionem; nam spiritualis resurrectionis oculi testes esse non possunt* (Calv.).

τινὲς δὲ ἐκοιμήθησαν. While he speaks of his own life as a daily dying (*v.* 31), he speaks of actual death as a sleep. The expression is common both in Jewish and heathen literature, and does not of itself imply any belief in a future life. The resemblance between "Death and his brother Sleep" (Virg. *Aen.* vi. 278) is too obvious to escape notice. Nevertheless, it was because the word suggested a future awakening that Christians adopted it, and it has special point here : see on xi. 30, and Ellicott and Milligan on 1 Thess. iv. 13. A poetic euphemism contains a blessed truth. These τινες had seen the Risen One and believed in Him, and had died in this faith. If there was no resurrection in store for them, how strange was their lot !

For πλείονες (אABDEFG) KLP read πλείους. KLP also add καὶ after τινὲς δέ, and K adds ἐξ αὐτῶν. Correctors of א A D ins. the καί, with Orig. Eus. Chrys. and others ; but it is not likely to be genuine. On the use of the aorist here, 'fell asleep (at various times),' and therefore 'have fallen asleep,' see J. H. Moulton, p. 136.

7. ἔπειτα ὤφθη Ἰακώβῳ. Nothing is known of this appearance, or as to which James is meant. But there is little doubt

* Dobschütz (*Ostern und Pfingsten*) would identify 1 Cor. xv. 6 and John xx. 21–23 with Acts ii. 1–4. The same event is the basis of all three passages. Could traditions have become so different in so short a time ?

that the James is the Lord's brother, who became president of
the Church in Jerusalem, and that he is placed here among the
chief witnesses because of his high position at Jerusalem.   There
may also be another reason, viz. the resemblance between his
case and that of St. Paul.   Our Lord's brethren had refused to
believe on Him during His ministry (John vii. 5), but are found
among believers after the Ascension (Acts i. 14).   What converted them?   The appearance of the Risen Lord to the eldest
of them may have done so, and the appearance may have been
granted for this very purpose.   In that case St James was converted in the same way as St Paul.   Three years after his own
conversion St Paul met the Lord's brother at Jerusalem, and
probably heard of this appearance from St James himself.   Each
told the other his experiences.   But it may be doubted whether
either James or Peter (v. 5) told St Paul what the Lord had *said*
to him.   In any case, such details are not needed here.   What
is of importance here is the fact that within ten years of the
Resurrection St Paul had the opportunity of talking with St
Peter and St James and comparing their experiences of the
Risen Lord with his own, and that within thirty years of the
Resurrection he records their testimony.   For James and Peter
see ix. 5; Gal. i. 18, 19, ii. 9–12.

For the narrative about an appearance to James recorded in
the Gospel according to the Hebrews (Jerome, *De Viris illustr.*
2), see Nicholson, pp. 62 f.; Lightfoot, *Galatians*, pp. 265, 274;
Swete, *Appearances of our Lord*, p. 89; Resch, *Agrapha*, pp.
248 f.   The narrative may be mere legend; but if it is historical,
it is not likely that St Paul is alluding here to what is there
recorded.

εἶτα τοῖς ἀποστόλοις πᾶσιν.   'Then to the whole body of the
Apostles.'   There is no emphasis on πᾶσιν, which does not look
back to Ἰακώβῳ.   The antithesis, 'to *one*, then to *all*,' is false,
for the πᾶσιν does not imply that James was an Apostle.   He
was not one of the Twelve, and it is unlikely that St Paul here
thinks of him as an Apostle in the wider sense, an idea quite
foreign to the context.   The meaning here is, 'then to the
Apostolic body as a whole,' Thomas being now present.   The
addition of πᾶσιν here confirms the view that τοῖς δώδεκα (v. 5)
is official and not numerical.*   As St Paul at once passes on

---

* "That the Twelve henceforth rank in history as the Twelve Apostles,
and in fact as *the* Apostles, was a result brought about by St Paul; and, para-
doxically enough, this was brought about by him in the very effort to fix the
value of his own Apostleship.   He certainly did not work out this conception,
for he neither could nor would give up the more general conception of the
Apostleship. . . . St Paul holds fast to the wider conception of the Apostolate,
but the twelve disciples form in his view the original nucleus" (Harnack,
The Mission and Expansion of Christianity, i. p. 323; p. 232, ed. 1902).

to the appearance to himself, he evidently means this manifestation to the whole body of the Apostles as the final one to others,
viz. at the time of the Ascension. The conjecture of πάλιν for
πᾶσιν is unnecessary.

Respecting St Paul's testimony, Professor Percy Gardner
remarks; "As regards his own life, and the phenomena of
Christianity which came under his direct observation, he is as
good an authority as we can have in regard to any events in
ancient history. . . . However confused and inconsistent may
be the accounts in the Gospels of the appearances of the risen
Lord, there can be no doubt that the society believed such
appearances to have taken place. No other cause can be
suggested for the sudden change in the minds of the disciples
from consternation and terror to confidence and boldness. And
the well-known Pauline passage as to the witnesses of the
Resurrection is as historic evidence of the belief of the first
disciples unimpeachable. Paul himself claims with perfect
confidence that he has seen the risen Lord" (*Hibbert Journal
Supplement*, 1909, pp. 49, 51).

8. ἔσχατον δὲ πάντων ὡσπερεὶ τῷ ἐκτρώματι ὤφθη κἀμοί. 'But
last of all, as if to the abortion (of the Apostolic family), He
appeared also to me.' As in Mark xii. 22, there is a doubt
whether πάντων is masc. or neut. After a series of persons (5–7)
the masc. is more probable; and ἔσχατον is used adverbially,
like ὕστερον. Nowhere else in N.T. or LXX does ὡσπερεί occur:
in a few texts it is a *v.l.* in iv. 13. In calling himself the ἔκτρωμα
among the Apostles, he refers to the suddenness and violence of
the transition (ἐκτιτρώσκω), while he was still in a state of im-
maturity.* The Twelve were disciples of Jesus before He called
them to be Apostles, and He trained them for promotion: Saul
was suddenly torn from opposition to Jesus to become His
Apostle. Theirs was a gradual and normal progress; his was
a swift and abnormal change. Possibly his Jewish adversaries
had called him an abortion, an insult to which his small stature
may have given a handle; but no such hypothesis is needed to
account for the use of the expression here. It indicates his
intense feeling respecting the errors of his career previous to
his conversion. For the word, comp. Num. xii. 12; Job iii. 16;

* The proposal to read τῳ (=τινι) instead of τῷ need not be seriously
considered : context and usage are against it.

*Sicut abortivus quadam naturae violentia ante tempus compellitur nasci,
ita ego par terribilem Domini visionem et luminis oculorum amissionem co-
actus sum, antequam vellem, exire de caeco synagogae utero, et ad lucem fidei
atque libertatem prodire* (Herveius). Primasius adds a stronger point of
similarity ; *mortua matre vivus educitur.* The Judaism from which he was
so violently taken was a defunct religion.

Eccles. vi. 3; and see Suicer, i. p. 1073; Lightfoot on Ign *Rom.* 9.

St Paul uses the same word, ὤφθη, of the appearances to himself as he uses of the appearances to the others. He regards it as the same in kind. He saw the Risen Lord as really as they did. The Lord appeared to him at other times (Acts xxii. 18; comp. xviii. 9, xxvii. 23; 2 Cor. xii. 2–4), but doubtless it is the appearance on the way to Damascus that is meant here. "There is no greater life in history than that which S. Paul spent in the service of Christ, and it was what it was because S. Paul believed from the bottom of his heart that Jesus had appeared to him from heaven and sent Him to do His work" (Swete, *Appearances*, p. 126). On this unique occasion God chose him 'to see the Righteous one, and to hear a voice from His mouth' (Acts xxii. 14), and his whole work as an Apostle was built upon that.* See Thorburn, pp. 83, 85.

The καμοί comes at the end with deep humility: 'to me also.' This appearance to the Apostle of the Gentiles completed the official evidence. He evidently knew of no later manifestation, and that to St John in Patmos was after St Paul's death. The fact that the manifestations had ended with the one to St Paul is against the theory of hallucinations. If all the appearances had been hallucinations, they would probably have continued, for such things are infectious, because people see what they expect to see. But neither the Twelve nor St Paul expected to see the Risen Lord, and some of them for a time doubted, not only the statements of others, but the evidence of their own eyes, for it seemed to be far too good to be true.

It is important to notice that two of the witnesses cited in this list, St James and St Paul himself, had previously been unbelievers. Indeed, St Paul had not only refused to believe that Jesus was the Messiah, but had strenuously persecuted those who accepted Him as such. Afterwards, the intensity of his conviction that he 'had seen the Lord' became "the determining factor in St Paul's theology." See Inge, in *Cambridge Biblical Essays*, p. 267. It is also remarkable that he does not mention the appearance to St Stephen (Acts vii. 55, 56). It was not "official."

9–11. The status of St Paul as one of the Apostles, and their absolute agreement with him with regard to the fundamental doctrine of the Resurrection. Different as they were from him in other things,—they before him in Apostleship, he before them

---

* *Il n'est pas un seul critique, aujourd'hui, qui ne reconnaisse que Paul a gardé toute sa vie, la ferme conviction d'avoir été le temoin d'une apparition extérieure du Christ ressuscité* (A. Sabatier, *L'Apôtre Paul*, p. 46).

in labours,—they and he were wholly agreed in preaching this, *uno ore, omnes Apostoli* (Beng.).

9. Ἐγὼ γάρ εἰμι ὁ ἐλάχιστος τ. ἀπ. Explanation of the strong word ἔκτρωμα, given with much emphasis. In ἐλάχιστος there is no reference to 'Paulus' = 'little.' See Eph. iii. 8; 1 Tim. i. 15. Both names, Saul and Paul, were probably given him by his parents, in accordance with Jewish custom, which still prevails, of giving a child two names, one religious and one secular. Like his namesake he was a Benjamite. Saul the son of Kish was τῆς φυλῆς τῆς ἐλαχίστης (1 Sam. ix. 21).

ὃς οὐκ εἰμὶ ἱκανός. As distinguished from ἄξιος, ἱκανός = 'reaching up to,' 'competent,' 'adequate' (2 Cor. ii. 16) rather than 'meriting,' but when moral sufficiency is meant the difference is not great. Comp. Matt. iii. 11 (= Mark i. 7) with John i. 27. This is the argumentative use of the relative; 'seeing that I am not fit to be called an Apostle.' Comp. Rom. ix. 25; Heb. ii. 11. The violent ἔκτρωσις was rendered necessary by his having been a persecutor. This blot in his past life he never forgot: Gal. i. 13; 1 Tim. i. 12–14; Acts xxvi. 9.* For τὴν ἐκκλησίαν τοῦ Θεοῦ see on xi. 22. The addition of τοῦ Θεοῦ prepares for what follows.

10. χάριτι δὲ Θεοῦ εἰμι ὃ εἰμι. 'But by God's grace I am what I am'—an Apostle who has seen the Lord and laboured fruitfully for Him. In spite of his unfitness to bear the name, the grace of God has made him equal to it. The persecutor has been forgiven and the abortion adopted. On the eleventh Sunday after Trinity this humble boast of Paul the Pharisee is placed side by side with the arrogant boast of the typical Pharisee.

ἡ εἰς ἐμὲ οὐ κενὴ ἐγενήθη. 'Which was manifested towards *me*' (or, was extended to *me*), 'did not prove empty,' *i.e.* fruitless, without result; or perhaps, 'did not turn out to be worthless.' Comp. *vv.* 14, 58; εἰς κενόν, Phil. ii. 16; 1 Thess. iii. 5; ματαία, *v.* 17.†

ἀλλά. 'So far from that being the case, I laboured more abundantly than they all.' This may mean either (1) 'than all of them together,' or (2) 'than any one of them (xiv. 18).' Though (1) seems extravagant, it may be the meaning, seeing that God's

---

* *Le souvenir d'avoir persécuté cette Église de Dieu est resté pour Paul, durant toute sa vie, le sujet d'une douloureuse humiliation. Il s'en afflige comme s'il avait persécuté le Seigneur lui-même* (Sabatier, *L'Apôtre Paul*, p. 8). Both Luke (Acts ix. 21) and Paul (Gal. i. 13, 23) use πορθεῖν as well as διώκειν of Saul's destructive work. No other N.T. writer uses πορθεῖν.

† The Vulg. is capricious in its translation of κενός. Nearly always it has *inanis* (vv. 14, 58; Eph. v. 6; Col. ii. 8, etc.), but here and Mark xii. 3 it has *vacuus*, although in Luke xx. 10 it has *inanis*: μάταιος is always *vanus* (iii. 20; Tit. iii. 9; Acts xiv. 15, etc.).

grace is the chief cause of it. Apart from that, his energy and
toil would have been without fruit (Rom. xv. 19). In himself
he is greatly inferior to the Twelve ; in his work, which is God's,
greatly superior. His labour (κόπος) means his work as a whole,
including his success ; and his great success was evidence that he
was an Apostle. See on xvi. 16. Thus his great work was
evidence of the Resurrection, for it would never have been
undertaken if the Risen Lord had not appeared to him, nor
would it have had such results without His help.

ἀλλὰ ἡ χάρις τοῦ Θεοῦ σὺν ἐμοί. 'So far from its being I (alone)
who did all this, it was the grace of God with me.' There were
two who laboured, two co-operators, grace with himself (Acts xiv.
27) ; but it was grace which made the labour effective (Gal. ii. 20).
The Apostle's satisfaction with his own labours "from a human
point of view is as the joy of a child who gives his father a birth-
day present out of his father's own money" (Weinel, p. 178).
Dobschütz (*Probleme*, p. 58) shows how true this estimate of his
labours is. The reading ἡ σὺν ἐμοί (see below), which Calvin
characteristically adopts, makes grace the sole worker ; 'not I,
but the grace of God which was with me, did the abundant and
fruitful work.' Atto more reasonably says ; *quibus verbis, 'gratia
Dei mecum,' ostendit quia nec gratia sine libero arbitrio, nec liberum
arbitrium sine gratia, hominis salutem operatur.* So also Augustine ; *nec gratia Dei sola, nec ipse solus, sed gratia cum illo.*

For οὐ κενὴ ἐγενήθη, D* has πτωχὴ οὐκ ἐγενήθη, while F G have πτωχὴ
οὐ γέγονεν. A E K L P have ἡ σὺν ἐμοί, but ℵ* B D* F G, Latt. Goth.
omit ἡ.

11. εἴτε οὖν ἐγὼ εἴτε ἐκεῖνοι, οὕτως κ.τ.λ. 'Whether then it
were I or they (who laboured most abundantly after seeing the
Risen Christ), so we continually preach (i. 23), and so ye once
for all believed,' when ye accepted the preaching. He does not
mean that they had ceased to believe, but that there was a
definite time when they accepted this belief as the result of
Apostolic preaching. The οὖν resumes the main argument
(*vv.* 3–8) after the digression (*vv.* 9, 10), and οὕτως looks back
to τίνι λόγῳ. Evans, somewhat hesitatingly, questions this, and
prefers to render οὖν 'however.'

Harnack points out that "legends concerning the appearances of the Risen Christ and the Ascension are difficult to
explain, on the assumption that they arose before the destruction
of Jerusalem" (*The Acts of the Apostles*, p. 291). It is quite
clear from these verses that appearances of the Risen Christ
were firmly believed in long before A.D. 70. Harnack himself
places 1 Corinthians in A.D. 52 or 53. The inference is that the
reports about the appearances were not "legends."

There is nothing to show that St Paul meant this list of the appearances to be exhaustive, and that he mentions no others because he knew of no others. He omits five of the appearances which are mentioned in the Gospels: to the women, to Mary Magdalen, to the two on the way to Emmaus, to Thomas with the other Apostles on the second Lord's Day, and to certain disciples at the Sea of Tiberias. He probably knew of some of these, if not of all. His reason for confining himself to those which he mentions can be easily conjectured. The witnesses whom he cites were persons well known to the Corinthians as leaders of the Church; Kephas, the Apostolic body, James, and himself; to which he adds a large company, some of whom could be easily found and questioned. The evidence would not have been strengthened by mentioning appearances to persons of whom the Corinthians had never heard. See F. H. Chase and A. J. Mason in *Cambridge Theological Essays*, pp. 396–401, 424–429; also J. O. F. Murray, pp. 329–332.

"It is curious that, in Paul's time, it was the principle of the resurrection which was denied by the Corinthians to whom he is writing, while the actual fact of the resurrection of Jesus was admitted. Now, it is the principle which is admitted, while the actual resurrection of Jesus is denied." But the life and teaching of St Paul, and the evolution and continued existence of the Christian Church cannot be explained, if the belief in the resurrection of Jesus Christ was based on hallucination. Can any Christian believe that Christianity is built upon this fundamental error?

"The reality of the resurrection is maintained, so long as the cause of the appearances of Jesus is attributed to Jesus, and not to the imaginations of the disciples. To the twentieth-century mind a spiritual manifestation seems open to less objection than the reanimation of the physical body which had been laid in the grave. We do not know, however, sufficient either of matter or spirit to justify any dogmatism either in the one direction or the other. The narratives will support either theory. The story of the empty tomb, however, certainly implies that the physical body of Jesus disappeared, though what finally became of it is not expressly explained. It must be admitted that the reanimation of the physical body of Jesus presents difficulties to the modern mind in the way of its final disposal which cannot lightly be ignored. The old conception of its literal ascension into heaven is in these days inconceivable. Our ignorance on this matter, however, ought not to invalidate the knowledge we undoubtedly possess of the empty tomb, nor ought we to allow the difficulty of accounting for the final disposal of the body to lead us to reject the plain story of its disappearance. Certainly, on the hypothesis of pure hallucinations, the speedy cessation of the appearances is a difficulty more easily ignored than explained" (*The Fifth Gospel*, pp. 169, 191–194).

XV. 12–34. If Christ is risen, the Dead in Christ will rise.

Here again we have three subdivisions: (*a*) The Consequences of denying the Doctrine of the Resurrection, 12–19; (*b*) The Consequences of accepting the Resurrection of Christ 20–28; (*c*) Arguments from Experience, 29–34.

How is it that, in the face of this Apostolic proclamation, some people go about and declare that a resurrection of dead people is impossible; thus making Apostolic preaching to be a lie, and your faith to be a delusion, and the condition of

*dead Christians to be quite hopeless, and the condition of
living Christians to be pitiable in the extreme?*

*But they are quite wrong; for Christ has risen, and
therefore resurrection is for us certain. For in this matter
Christ is the first sheaf of a vast harvest; and when He
has conquered all that opposes Him, including death itself,
then, as the Son of God, He will yield up everything to His
Father, and God will be supreme.*

*Baptism for the sake of the dead would lose all its
meaning, and Christian self-sacrifice would lose most of its
inspiration and comfort, if there were no resurrection and
no future life.*

[12] Now, if Apostles are continually proclaiming Christ as
having been raised from the dead, how is it that some are
declaring among you that there is no such thing as a resurrection
of dead people?   [13] If there is no such thing, then Christ Himself cannot have been raised.   [14] And if Christ has not been
raised, then our proclamation of the Gospel is empty verbiage,
and your faith in it is empty credulity.   [15] And, what is more, we
are found guilty of misrepresenting God, because we have represented Him as having raised the Christ, whereas He did nothing
of the kind, if as a matter of fact dead people are never raised.
[16] For it is quite clear that, if dead people are never raised, Christ
Himself has not been raised.   [17] And in that case your faith is
futile; you are still living in your sins.   [18] Yes, and it follows
that all those who went to their rest trusting in Christ, forthwith
perished utterly and are now lost to Christ!   [19] If our case is no
better than this, that just in the present life we have had hope in
Christ, there are no human beings more truly to be pitied than
we are.

[20] But this dismal doctrine is not true. Christ has been
raised from the dead; and He is no solitary exception, but the
first and foremost example of many that are to be awakened.
[21] For since it is through a man that we have death, it is through
a Man also that we have resurrection from the dead.   [22] For as
in virtue of our union with Adam we all die, so also in virtue of
our union with Christ we shall all be made alive.   [23] But each in
his proper order; Christ the first sheaf; afterwards Christ's own
harvest in the Day of His Coming.   [24] After that will come the

End, when He is to give up His Kingship into the hands of His
God and Father; and that will be when He has brought to
nought all other rule and all other authority and power. 25 For
He must retain His Kingship until God has put all His enemies
under His feet. 26 The last foe to be brought to nought is
death. 27 For God has put all things, death included, in subjection under Christ's feet. (Now, when it is said that all things
have been put in subjection to Christ, it is obvious that God,
who put them thus in subjection, is not included.) 28 But when
every power has been made subject to the Son, then, but not till
then, even the Son Himself will become subject to the Father
who put all things under Him, in order that God may be everything in every creature, and the Divine immanence be perfect
and complete.

29 Otherwise, what will be the position of those who from
time to time are being baptized out of consideration for the
dead? If dead men never rise at all, why in the world are
people baptized out of consideration for them? 30 And why do
so many of us stand in peril every hour? 31 I protest to you, my
Brothers, as surely as I glory over you—and you know that I do
that in Christ Jesus our Lord, there is not a day that I do not
stand face to face with death. 32 If, looking at it from a purely
human point of view, I was near being torn in pieces at
Ephesus, what did I gain by it? If dead men do not rise, the
human point of view gives as a practical inference, ' Let us eat
and drink, for to-morrow we die.' 33 Do not make the serious
mistake of supposing that there is no risk in being friendly to
these views and to those who advocate them. ' Fair characters
are marred by foul companionships.' 34 You must rouse yourselves from this paralysing delusion in a right spirit, and cease
to persist in culpable error. You pride yourselves upon your
religious enlightenment: crass ignorance as to the very meaning of
God is what some of you have. It is to make you ashamed of
yourselves that I speak like this.

12. Εἰ δὲ Χριστὸς κηρύσσεται ὅτι ἐκ νεκρῶν ἐγήγερται κ.τ.λ.
' Now if Christ is continually preached that He hath been raised
from the dead, how comes it that it is said among you by some
persons that resurrection of dead men does not take place? ' * St

---

* The reading ἐκ ν. ὅτι ἐγ. (D E F G) puts an unintelligible emphasis on
ἐκ νεκρῶν.

Paul has just shown how full and unanimous is the testimony to the fact of the Resurrection of Christ, and from that solid basis he now passes on (δέ) to the main question, using a current sceptical assertion as a text. It is one statement against another. On the one hand the declaration of all the Apostles, from the first to the last of them, and of many other eye-witnesses, that Christ has been raised and abides for ever as the Risen Lord (this is the force of the perfect ἐγήγερται throughout the argument) ; on the other the *a priori* dictum of certain cavillers, unsupported by any evidence, that there is no such thing as a resurrection of dead people. The latter position is analogous to the modern one ; " Miracles *don't* happen." Which will the Corinthians, who long ago accepted Apostolic preaching, hold to now ? And a decision is necessary, for the conflict of statement continues. The Apostles continue to preach the Resurrection of Christ (κηρύσσομεν, κηρύσσεται), and the sceptics continue to assert (λέγουσιν) that resurrection is impossible. And this is the situation which has to be explained. If resurrection is impossible, how do you account for the large volume of testimony from official and unofficial witnesses, who are still alive to be questioned, that one resurrection has taken place ? * It is possible that these teachers did not deny that Christ had risen ; and if so, this indicates how strong they felt the evidence for it to be. They may have declared that His case was unique, and proved nothing as to the rest of mankind. But this the Apostle cannot allow. If it is certain that any one man has risen, then the position that resurrection is impossible is untenable. If Christ is risen, others can rise. Indeed, when His relation to mankind is considered, we may say that others *will* rise. Deny this consequent in either form, " Others will not rise," or " Others cannot rise," and you thereby deny the antecedent, " Christ is not risen." There is no escape from this logic ; but some Corinthians did not see it.

It has been pointed out already that the τινες were almost certainly Gentiles, brought up under the influence of Greek philosophy, not Jews with Sadducean prejudices. Possibly they held that matter was evil, and that it was incredible that a soul, once set free by death, would return to its unclean prison. Or they may have been influenced by a popular form of Epicurean materialism. They had been brought up in the belief that at death existence either ceases entirely, or becomes so shadowy as

---

* This problem still remains. We do not free ourselves from difficulty by rejecting the Resurrection of Christ as unhistorical. How can we explain the origin of the evidence that He said that He would rise and of the evidence that He did rise ? And how can we explain the existence of the Christian Church ?

to be worthless: in any case the body perishes utterly. The idea of a glorified body, in which the highest part of man's nature would be supreme, without opposition or hindrance from any other part, was beyond even Plato's vision, and they could not attain to it. Aeschylus (*Eum.* 647) makes Apollo say,

> ἀνδρὸς δ'ἐπειδὰν αἷμ' ἀνασπάσῃ κόνις
> ἅπαξ θανόντος, οὔτις ἔστ' ἀνάστασις.

And that is just what these Corinthians declared. See also the view of Cebes (Plato, *Phædo*, 70 A). There is no evidence of such theories as those of Hymenaeus and Philetus (2 Tim. ii. 17, 18).

St Paul's treatment of these dangerous doubters is to be noticed. He does not suggest that they should be excommunicated; he argues with them through those who are in danger of being perverted by them. And in his arguments he is less severe than he is with some other victims of false teaching. The πῶς λέγουσιν here is more gentle than the indignant astonishment of Θαυμάζω ὅτι οὕτως ταχέως μετατίθεσθε κ.τ.λ. and Ὦ ἀνόητοι Γαλάται, τίς ὑμᾶς ἐβάσκανεν κ.τ.λ. (Gal. i. 6, iii. 1). The πῶς reminds us rather of Gal. ii. 14, iv. 9; 1 John iii. 17: it expresses surprise at something incongruous. Moreover, he does not name these teachers of error; there is no need to brand them: compare iv. 18; 2 Cor. x. 2; Gal. i. 7, ii. 12; Acts xv. 24; and it is not likely that they are to be identified with any of the four parties in i. 12.

Χριστός is attracted from the dependent clause into the main sentence in order to make the word more prominent. Christ is the sum and substance of the Gospel, the central fact of which is His Resurrection. Throughout the passage νεκροί has no article: it is not 'the dead' as a class that are under consideration, but individuals who are in this condition, 'dead persons,' 'dead men.'

ἐν ὑμῖν τινές (ℵ A B P 17, Syrr., Orig. Chrys.) is to be preferred to τινὲς ἐν ὑμῖν (D E F G K L, Arm.), and ἐν ὑμῖν belongs to λέγουσιν. It is in Christian society (i. 11) that this statement is made.

13. These sceptics are supposed to hold to their doctrine: they deny the consequent in the Apostle's conditional proposition. If Christ is risen, dead people can rise. Dead people cannot rise. Therefore, Christ is not risen. 'But if resurrection of dead men does not take place, Christ *also* hath not been raised,' and οὐδέ may be kept in the front place by rendering, 'neither hath Christ been raised' (RV.). But οὐδέ must not be rendered 'not even,' which would rather obscure the line of argument. The fact of the Incarnation involves a difference in *kind* between the Resurrection of the Son of God and that of His *adopted* children. The connexion between antecedent and consequent is therefore not logical merely, but *causal*: the

Resurrection of Christ is not viewed by the Apostle as *one particular case* of a general law, but as the source of Divine Power which *effects* the Resurrection in store for His members (*v.* 23). Deny the effect, and you overthrow the cause; accept the cause as a fact, and the effect will certainly follow.

14. The sceptics still persist, and accept the denial of the antecedent: Christ is not risen. St Paul goes on to show what this denial involves, viz. (1) the falsification of Apostolic teaching and of Christian faith (14–17), and (2) the destruction of all Christian hope (18, 19). Thus by a *reductio ad impossibile* the denial is disproved. In short, the Resurrection of Christ is not an isolated fact or doctrine which can be accepted or rejected independently of other truths: it is the very centre of the Gospel.

εἰ δὲ Χρ. οὐκ ἐγήγερται. 'But if Christ hath *not* been raised (οὐκ emphatic), void certainly (ἄρα) is our preaching, void also is your faith.'* Τὸ κήρυγμα looks back to κηρύσσομεν (*v.* 11), and means, 'what we preach,' the substance of it (i. 21, ii. 4); and πίστις looks back to ἐπιστεύσατε (*v.* 11): ἄρα, 'in that case,' 'then,' as an inevitable result; κενός, *inanis* (see above on *v.* 10), 'empty,' 'hollow,' 'devoid of reality': comp. κενὴ ἡ ἐλπὶς αὐτῶν (Wisd. iii. 11); κεναὶ ἐλπίδες καὶ ψευδεῖς (Ecclus. xxxi. 1). Here κενόν and κενή are emphatic by position. But, as Origen points out, 'Seeing that our preaching is *not* void, and your faith is *not* void, then Christ has been raised.' Cf. Eph. v. 6; Col. ii. 8.

15. εὑρισκόμεθα δὲ καὶ ψευδομάρτυρες τοῦ Θεοῦ. 'And (as a further consequence) we are found to be also false witnesses of God (obj. gen.), because (in preaching) we bore witness respecting God that He raised the Christ, whom He did not raise, if indeed after all dead men are not raised'; *si videlicet mortui non suscitantur* (Beza). AV. has 'rise not'; but ἐγείρονται is passive, not middle. Εὑρίσκω is often used of moral judgments respecting character, and conveys the idea of discovering or detecting: iv. 2; 2 Cor. xi. 12, xii. 20; Gal. ii. 17; Phil. iii. 9. We may take τοῦ Θεοῦ as the subjective genitive, 'false witnesses in the service of God,' 'Divine witnesses telling lies,' but this is less suitable; and 'falsely claiming to be God's witnesses' is certainly not the meaning. There is a similar doubt respecting κατὰ τοῦ Θεοῦ, which would usually mean 'against God,' *adversus Deum* (Vulg. Luth.), but may mean 'about God,' 'of God,' *de Deo* (Erasm. Beza), although not *a Deo* (Calv.). The meaning

---

* The καί after ἄρα should probably be omitted (BL, Latt. Syrr. Copt. Arm. Aeth.); also δέ after κενή (אABD* FP, Latt. Copt.). And ὑμῶν (אAFGKP, Latt. Syrr. Copt. Arm.) is to be preferred to ἡμῶν (BD*, Basm. Goth.).

'respecting' or 'about' is fairly common in class. Grk., although
not in the N.T., and is perhaps to be preferred here (Tyn.
Genev. Rhem. AV. RV.). For, although every lie dishonou₁s
God, yet there is no special dishonour in saying that He raised
Christ, if He did not do so; and if St Paul had meant 'against
God,' he would probably have put κατὰ τ. Θ. after ψευδομάρτυρες
rather than after ἐμαρτυρήσαμεν. Nevertheless, 'against God'
(Wic. Cov.) may be justified on the ground that to attribute to
a person a good or glorious act, which it is well known that he
never performed, is to cause him to be suspected of having
prompted the false assertion. The Apostles, if they falsely
declared that God had raised Christ, would lead people to think
that God had inspired them to tell lies about Him. This,
however, is rather far-fetched. St Paul's evident horror of being
convicted at the bar of Divine justice of bearing false witness
in this matter shows his estimate of the importance of the
matter. And it is to be noted that the alternative possibility,—
that he and the other Apostles were honest, but deluded
witnesses, does not occur to him at all. The modern theory,
that those who believed that they had seen the Risen Lord were
victims of an hallucination, is wholly absent from his thought,
even as a possibility. The force of the article before Χριστόν
perhaps is 'the Christ of whom we have all along been speaking.'
For εἴπερ see on viii. 5: here the addition of ἄρα indicates that
the hypothesis is not St Paul's own.

16. A solemn repetition of the argument in *v.* 13; *sublato
effectu, tollitur et causa.* Here the form is slightly changed, and
additional inferences (17, 18) are drawn from it.

17. A solemn repetition and enlargement of *v.* 14, showing
more clearly what the loss to the Corinthians would be if this
theory were true. Both AV. and RV. render κενή in *v.* 14
and ματαία here 'vain,' and sometimes there is little difference
between the two words: but here there is; κενή is 'wanting in
reality,' ματαία 'wanting in result,' 'fruitless,' 'futile' (Tit. iii. 9;
4 Macc. xvi. 7). In class. Grk. μάταιος is of two terminations
(Jas. i. 26); but here and 1 Pet. i. 18 the fem. occurs, as often
in LXX.

ἔτι ἐστὲ ἐν ταῖς ἁμαρτίαις ὑμῶν. This may mean one of two
things. If Christ has not been raised for our justification
(Rom. iv. 25), His death is made a nullity, for there is no
redemptive power in it. It does not save us from the guilt and
penalty of sin; for how can a dead Christ save others from death,
which is the penalty of sin? And how can He secure for others
a life beyond the grave which He Himself does not possess?
Comp. Rom. vi. 1–11; Phil. iii. 10; Col. iii. 1. Or, the words

may be an appeal to their personal experience. If Christ had
not risen, they would still be living in their original heathen
wickedness, for baseless credulity could never have delivered
them. It was faith in a living Christ that had done that.
Therefore Christ has been raised. This is a more telling argument than the other, because it is based on what the Corinthians
could not help knowing. They were as sure that they were not
continuing their old heathen life as the Apostles were that they
were not lying witnesses. But the former is closer to the
context, and to St Paul's doctrinal purpose.

18. ἄρα καὶ οἱ κοιμηθέντες ἐν Χριστῷ ἀπώλοντο. 'So then, they
also who were laid to sleep in Christ have perished'; an
amazing result! By ἐν Χρ. is meant 'believing in Christ,
and in communion with Him.' It is those who are *not* ἐν
Χριστῷ when they die that perish. This denial of the resurrection of the dead throws everything into confusion. The ἀπώλεια
is the utter loss consequent upon dying in sin. This meaning
is frequent in St Paul (i. 18, viii. 11 ; 2 Cor. ii. 15, iv. 3 ; 2 Thess.
ii. 10). See Cremer, p. 452 ; also Beet, *The Last Things*, pp.
122 f., a valuable discussion. They have surrendered everything
in order to have eternal life with Christ at His Coming, and they
have died. If they are dead beyond possibility of restoration,
then death separates us for ever from Christ. Is that credible?
This is not an appeal to mere sentiment : it is an appeal to our
sense of what is morally fitting, and this is a good supplement to
the appeal to fact (*v.* 17).

In class. Grk. ἄρα rarely, if ever, stands first, as here ; 2 Cor. v. 15 ;
Gal. ii. 21, v. 11 ; etc. It is a little doubtful whether οἱ κοιμηθέντες is not
a true passive, 'those who were put to sleep,' rather than middle, 'those
who fell asleep,' both here and 1 Thess. iv. 14. See J. H. Moulton, *Gr.*
p. 162, and on the other side Milligan on 1 Thess. iv. 14, a passage
which throws much light on this verse. The expression does not imply
that the departed are unconscious, but that they are at rest, and may be
raised again to full activity. See above on xi. 30.

19. εἰ ἐν τῇ ζωῇ ταύτῃ ἐν Χριστῷ ἠλπικότες ἐσμὲν μόνον. The
first and last words, 'in this life' and 'only,' are emphatic ;
nevertheless, they should not be taken together ; 'in this life
only.' The μόνον qualifies either ἠλπικότες or the whole
clause, and ἐσμέν is the copula, not the auxiliary to the participle
to form an analytical tense. 'If we are having only hope in
Christ in this life' ; or, 'If in this life we are hopers in Christ
and have nothing beyond'; *i.e.* If all that Christians have got
is hope in Christ, without possibility of life with Him hereafter,
what can be more pathetic ? See RV. marg.

ἐλεεινότεροι πάντων ἀνθρώπων ἐσμέν. 'We are more to be

pitied than all men'; not 'more miserable,' 'more wretched,' but 'more deserving of compassion.'* In that case, Christians would be toiling and suffering here under a great delusion, a hope that has no foundation and will never be fulfilled—and such a glorious hope! For ἐλεεινός see Rev. iii. 17 and LXX of Dan. ix. 23, x. 11, 19.

The right order is ἐν Χριστῷ ἠλπ. ἐσμὲν (א A B D* E F G), not ἠλπ. ἐσμὲν ἐν Χρ. (K L P); and πάντων ἀνθρ. ἐσμέν (א A B E F G K L P), not ἐσμέν π. ἀνθρ. (D, Latt., Orig.).

20-28. The sum of the arguments in *vv.* 13–19 is that the doctrine maintained by the τινές (*v.* 12) cannot be true, because it involves such monstrous consequences. And it is *not* true, so that the consequences are of a wholly different character, and we can rejoice abundantly. Christ has been raised, and His Resurrection carries with it that of all those who are Christ's, for the Risen One is the first fruit of a vast harvest (vi. 14). Apostolic preaching is not void; their faith is neither void nor futile; they are not in their sins; those that are asleep have not perished; Christian hope is not limited to this life; and Christians are not the most pitiable of men (*die bedauernswürdigsten* or *bejammernswerthesten unter allen Menschen*).

In these verses the Apostle ceases to argue, and authoritatively declares the truth. Human logic is for the moment dropped, and the inspiration of the Prophet takes its place. Confident in the possession of knowledge which transcends experience and reason, he authoritatively declares what has been revealed to him respecting the relations between mankind and Christ, and between Christ and the Father. See Evans, pp. 354, 361; Schiele, *Die Religion in Geschichte und Gegenwart,* 1719–1731.

20. Νυνὶ δέ. These words begin a joyous outburst in contrast to the dreary pictures which he has been drawing. The denial which produced those pictures is not true; 'But, as it is, Christ has been raised from the dead, first of those that are asleep.' The addition of ἐκ νεκρῶν implies a bodily resurrection, for Christ could not be thought of as among the spiritually dead. And 'firstfruit' implies community of nature. The first sheaf offered in the Temple on the morrow of the Passover was the same in kind as the rest of the harvest, and was a sort of

---

* In the Apocalypse of Baruch (xxi. 13) we have a similar thought; "For if there were this life only, which here belongs to all men, nothing could be more bitter than this"; because happiness is so short-lived (14, 15) and life itself must end (22). The writer may have known 1 Corinthians. See on *v.* 35. Novatian may have had this passage in his mind when he argued (*De Trin.* xiv.) thus; *Si homo tantummodo Christus, cur spes in illum ponitur, cum* spes in homine maledicta *referatur* (Jer xvii. 5)?

consecration of the whole (Lev. xxiii. 10, 11).* For ἀπαρχή comp. xvi. 15 ; Rom. viii. 23, xi. 16, xvi. 5 ; Jas. i. 18, where see Mayor ; Rev. xiv. 4, where see Swete ; Clem. Rom. *Cor.* 24, 42. Christ is the first instalment, an earnest that many more are to follow. Comp. πρωτότοκος ἐκ τῶν νεκρῶν (Col. i. 18), πρ. τ. ν (Rev. i. 5).

The AV. has, ' *and* become the firstfruits of them that slept.' There is neither ' and ' nor ' become ' in the true text : ἐγένετο (K L, Syrr. Goth.) is a manifest correction ; ℵ A B D* F P 17, Latt. Copt. Arm., Orig. omit. 'Απαρχή is in apposition with Χριστός, *Christus resurrexit, primitiae dormientium* (Vulg.).

21. Christ leads the way in resurrection, as Adam did in death. In each case a man was the instrument of a great change in the condition of mankind, the one of a great disaster, the other of a great deliverance. 'For since through man (by Adam's sin) is death, through man also is resurrection of the dead' : Rom. v. 12, where see Sanday and Headlam. He says διὰ ἀνθρώπου, not ἐξ ἀνθρ. The deadly wound came ἐκ τοῦ πονηροῦ : similarly the cure comes διὰ Χριστοῦ ἐκ τοῦ Πατρός.

How can Adam be said to have led the way in death,— to have been the means of introducing death, where death was previously unknown ? Death, as geology teaches us, was in the world long before man existed on the earth. Granted ; but death *as the penalty of sin* could not be in the world, until there was sin. Possibly St Paul believed Genesis ii. and iii. to be literally true ; † at any rate he regards the narrative as sufficiently true to be made the basis of a lesson. Genesis does not tell us that man was created immortal ; it implies the contrary. But man was created with the opportunity of becoming immortal, for he was placed within reach of the tree of life. Because of his sin he was deprived of this opportunity, was driven from the tree of life, and consequently died. In this sense death came to the human race through his instrumentality. The fact that the brutes had been dying for ages before man existed does not affect the question. See Goudge, p. 149.

And how can Christ be said to have led the way in resur

---

* εἰ ἀνέστη Χριστὸς ἐκ νεκρῶν, πρωτότοκος δὲ ἐκεῖνός ἐστιν ἐκ νεκρῶν, οὐδεὶς δὲ πρωτότοκός ἐστιν ἑτερογενῶς, ἀνάγκη ὁμογενῆ εἶναι τὴν ἀνάστασιν αὐτοῦ τῇ ἀναστάσει τῶν ἀνισταμένων (Origen). *Si caput resurrexit, necesse est ut caetera quoque membra sequantur* (Primasius). On St Paul's know- 'edge of the details of Christ's life, see *Camb. Bibl. Ess.* pp. 336 f. On his ase of the contrast between Christ and Adam, see Abbott, *The Son of Man*, pp. 80 f.

† The article before 'Αδάμ and before Χριστῷ points to both as historical persons, each producing an effect.

rection, and to be ἀπαρχὴ τῶν κεκοιμημένων? Others had been raised from the dead before He was; He had raised some Himself. But only to die again. None of those who had been restored to life remained for ever alive, for death had not yet been conquered. Christ was the first, and thus far is the only human being, who *non moriturus surrexit*—rose never to die again.

22. Transition from abstract to concrete. 'For as in Adam all die, so also in Christ shall all be made alive.'* By 'in Adam' and 'in Christ' is meant 'in the person of,' as having a community of nature with. In different ways, Adam and Christ were each of them Head of the human race and could represent it. But the simple 'in' is as intelligible as any paraphrase. It is more important to determine the meaning of πάντες in each clause. The argument, that πάντες must have the same meaning in both clauses; πάντες in the first clause must mean the whole human race; therefore πάντες in the second clause must mean the whole human race, is somewhat precarious. The meaning may be, 'As it is in Adam that all who die die, so it is in Christ that all who are made alive are made alive.' It is still more precarious to argue that 'in Christ shall all be made alive' implies that all mankind will at last be saved.† The meaning may be that all will be raised, will be quickened, which is not the same as saying that all will be saved. See Dan. xii. 2, where a resurrection of the wicked is taught for the first time in the O.T., together with a belief in future rewards and punishments; but of Israelites only, and perhaps not all of them, for the 'many' (not 'all') possibly refers to great saints and great sinners, and to no others. 'Many of them that sleep (Jer. li. 39, 57) in the ground of dust (Job xx. 11, xxi. 26) shall awake (Isa. xxvi. 19), some to eternal life (Ps. of Sol. iii. 16; 4 Macc. xv. 3; Enoch xxxvii. 4, xl. 9, lviii. 3, lxii. 14), and some to reproaches and eternal abhorrence' (Isa. lxvi. 24). See Driver, *ad loc.*; Dalman, *The Words of Jesus*, pp. 156 f.; and the parallel passage John v. 28, 29. In *v.* 36, as in Rom. iv. 17, ζωοποιεῖν is used in a natural sense, in John v. 21, vi. 63 in a spiritual sense: in each case the context must decide. See Hatch, *Ess. in Bibl Grk.*, p. 5, for the Hellenistic use of the word.

* Nothing is said about the saints being "caught up in the clouds to meet the Lord in the air" (1 Thess. iv. 17) either here or in later Epistles. Perhaps St Paul has recognized that such language is symbolical and may mislead. And nothing is said about the wicked: their fate is not much in the Apostle's mind. He gives no hint of either further probation or annihilation: but that does not allow us to say that he denied either.

† See iii. 17, vi. 9, 10, xi. 32.

23. ἕκαστος δὲ ἐν τῷ ἰδίῳ τάγματι. 'But each in his own division.' There is little doubt that τάγμα is a military metaphor; 'company,' 'troop,' 'band,' or 'rank.' We are to think of each 'corps' or body of troops coming on in its proper position and order: 2 Sam. xxiii. 13; 1 Sam. iv. 10; Josephus *B.J.* i. ix. 1, iii. iv. 2. In *B.J.* ii. viii. 14, after mentioning the Pharisees, he goes on, Σαδδουκαῖοι δέ, τὸ δεύτερον τάγμα, . . . ψυχῆς τε τὴν διαμονὴν καὶ τὰς καθ᾽ ᾅδου τιμωρίας καὶ τιμὰς ἀναιροῦσι. Of these τάγματα there are two, clearly marked, in the present passage; Christ, who has already reached the goal of Resurrection; and Christ's Own, who will reach it when He comes again. Perhaps St Paul is thinking of a third τάγμα, those who are not Christ's Own, to be raised from the dead some time before the End. But throughout the passage, the unbelievers and the wicked are quite in the background, if they are thought of at all. The whole context is governed by ἐν Χρ. ζωοποι. (*v.* 22). It is perhaps because only the good are under consideration that St Paul used παρουσία rather than κρίσις or ἡμέρα κρίσεως. With the beautiful expression, οἱ τοῦ Χριστοῦ, comp. iii. 23; Gal. v. 24; John x. 3, 14: it means all the saved, whether Christians, Jews, or heathen. Deissmann (*Light*, pp. 372, 382) has shown that παρουσία was a technical term for the arrival of a potentate or his representative, and that Καίσαρος "belonging to the Emperor," was used in much the same sense as Χριστοῦ is used here.

24. εἶτα τὸ τέλος. 'After this will come the End' is perhaps to be preferred to 'Then cometh the End'; but the latter has the advantage of being as indefinite in meaning as the Greek seems to be. It is evident that there is an interval (ἔπειτα), which still continues, between the first and the second τάγμα. Christ's Own are still waiting. Is there also to be an interval between His Coming and the End? Or does St Paul mean that the Coming is the End—that the two are simultaneous? It is impossible to say, for εἶτα, like 'then,' may introduce either what is subsequent or what is immediately consequent. In *vv.* 5 and 7 there is an interval: comp. 1 Tim. ii. 13, iii. 10, the only other passages in which St Paul uses εἶτα: and what follows seems to imply an interval. See Thackeray, *The Relation of St Paul to Contemporary Jewish Thought*, pp. 120 f., and comp. 1 Pet. iv. 7. 'The End' may be compared with ἡ συντέλεια τοῦ αἰῶνος (Matt. xiii. 40, 49, xxiv. 3, xxviii. 20); it balances ἀπαρχή.

ὅταν παραδιδῷ τὴν βασιλείαν τῷ Θεῷ καὶ πατρί. 'Whenever He delivereth the Kingdom to the God and Father.' The ὅταν indicates that the time for this is quite uncertain. As no

ἡμῶν is expressed, the meaning probably is 'His God and Father.'
It is to God that the Kingdom belongs, and it is to Him both
as God and as Father that the Son delivers it. Comp. 2 Cor.
i. 3, xi. 31; Rom. xv. 6; Eph. i. 3, 17; Mark xv. 34; John
xx. 17; Rev. i. 6, iii. 2, 12; 1 Pet. i. 3, where see Hort's note.
Our Lord Himself spoke of the Father as His God, and His
Apostles are not afraid of asserting the same truth. Usually
ὁ Θεὸς κ. πατήρ is followed by a genitive to show whose God
and Father is meant, but in Eph. v. 20 and Jas. i. 27 there is
no genitive, as here, and 'of us' may be included with 'of
Him.' What exactly is meant by παραδῷ τὴν βασιλείαν, is beyond
our comprehension. Sovereignty has been committed to the
Son for a definite purpose: when that purpose has been fulfilled,
the sovereignty returns to the original Source. We need not
think of Christ as losing anything or as ceasing to rule, but
as bringing to a triumphant conclusion a special dispensation.
It is His work to put an end to all that opposes the sovereignty
of God. When all opposition is brought to nought, the Divine
sovereignty, in which the Son shares (John xvii. 10; Eph. v. 5;
Rev. xi. 15, xxii. 1, 3), will be complete, and the reign of God,
which is the reign of love, will no more have let or hindrance.
We lose ourselves, when we try to define the details of this consummation: it is wiser to adopt a reverent reticence and reserve.

ὅταν καταργήσῃ πᾶσαν ἀρχὴν καὶ πᾶσαν ἐξουσίαν καὶ δύναμιν.
'Whenever He shall have done away with every principality,
and every authority and power.' Although this clause is placed
after ὅταν παραδῷ, it precedes it in time, as is shown by the
change from present subjunctive to aorist. The 'doing away'
is prior to the 'delivering up.' The order of events is (1) the
abolition of all that opposes, (2) the handing over of the
sovereignty, which is the End. This is not argument, but a
revelation of mysteries. Nevertheless, the revelation has a
place in the argument, for it shows how death, which at present
has dominion over the human race, will at last be done away
in the removal of every power that opposes the will of God.
The terms, ἀρχή, ἐξουσία, and δύναμις, do not necessarily imply
evil powers (Rom. viii. 38; Eph. i. 21, iii. 10, vi. 12; Col. i. 16):
the context must decide.* Here they are evil—τοὺς ἐχθρούς,
and all evil influences, human (2 Thess. ii. 8) and superhuman,
are included. The verb is frequent in this Epistle, and has
various shades of meaning; 'reduce to inactivity,' 'supersede,'
'subdue,' 'abolish,' 'destroy.' See Cremer.

---

* "Originally terms of Jewish speculation, they came in after times to
play a large part in Christian thought. The Apostle's purpose in mentioning
them is to emphasise the exaltation of Christ above them all" (J. A. Robinson
on Eph. i. 21, p. 41). See Westcott on Heb. ii. 5–8.

It is not easy to decide between παραδιδῷ (א A D E P) and παραδιδοῖ (B F G), and it is not important to do so, for παραδιδοῖ may be a sub-junctive: comp. Mark iv. 29, v. 43, ix. 30. Both forms are found in papyri; see Milligan on 1 Thess. v. 15. παραδῷ (K L) is a correction, to make agreement in tense with καταργήσῃ.

25. δεῖ γάρ. This explains why the Son continues to hold the βασιλεία. It has been so decreed by God, and the decree has been made known in prophecy (Ps. cx. 1; Mark xii. 36): βασιλεύειν, 'to be King, remain King' (imperf. infin.). See Luke i. 33, and Pearson, *On the Creed*, Art. vi. p. 282. The nominative to θῇ is Christ, not God, as is clear both from the syntax of the sentence, and the context generally. For the constr. comp. xi. 26; Gal. iii. 19; Rom. xi. 25. In the Pauline Epp., as in the N.T. generally, ἄχρι is more common than μέχρι, but ἄχρι occurs only in this group, excepting Phil. i. 5, 6.

The MSS. vary much between ἄχρι and ἄχρις, and K L add ἄν after ἄχρις οὖ. A F G 17 and several versions add αὐτοῦ after τοὺς ἐχθρούς.

26. ἔσχατος ἐχθρὸς καταργεῖται ὁ θάνατος. No article; there can be only one last: comp. ἐσχάτη ὥρα (1 John ii. 18). 'As the last enemy, Death is brought to nought—is done away': present tense of what is certain. Death is brought to nought when all his victims are restored to life. This same truth is expressed by St John in symbolical language when he says that Death and Hades were cast into the Lake of Fire (Rev. xx. 14, where see Swete).* As *vv.* 54, 55 show, St Paul probably has in his mind Isa. xxv. 8 and Hos. xiii. 14. Here καταργεῖται seems to imply total destruction; but, whatever may be said on other grounds for the theory of the ultimate annihilation of the wicked, it can hardly be said that the destruction of Death lends support to it. See Beet, *Last Things*, pp. 236 f.; Langton Clarke, *The Eternal Saviour Judge*, pp. 91, 181, 306, 336; Briggs, *The Messiah of the Apostles*, pp. 114 f. B. Weiss contends that the depriving Death of all power does not exclude the possibility that those who have definitely rejected salvation will, *in accordance with God's will*, remain in death because they remain in sin. But it is only because God wills it that Death ever has any power. Does He will that in certain cases that power should continue for ever?

27. πάντα γὰρ ὑπέταξεν. The first word is emphatic. 'For *all* things (and therefore Death among them) did God put under Christ's feet.' The aorist points to some remote past,

---

* It is possible that some of the objectors urged that, if dead people were to be raised, they ought, like Christ, to be raised soon after death. St Paul intimates that a great deal must happen before the victory over Death is complete. See Swete, *The Ascended Christ*, pp. xii. f., 16 f., 32 f.

and should not be made a perfect, as 'hath put' (AV.). The meaning cannot be that God put all things under *Death's* feet; for this is not true, and is not the meaning of Ps. viii. 4–7, which tells of man's marvellous dignity as God's vice-gerent in the universe (Gen. i. 26, 28). This dignity the first Adam and his descendants lost through disobedience, but the Second Adam, through His obedience, has it in untold fulness, and at the Second Advent it will be complete.*

ὅταν δὲ εἴπῃ ὅτι πάντα ὑποτέτακται. Strict grammar requires that the nominative to ὑπέταξεν be the nominative to εἴπῃ, and this on other grounds is probable. It also requires that εἴπῃ be treated as the *futurum exactum*: 'when God shall have said' at some time in the future. *Quando autem dixerit, omnia subjecta sunt* (Iren. v. xxxvi. 2); when the End shall have come and God shall have proclaimed, 'All things have been brought into subjection.' Others refer the εἴπῃ to God's declaration by the mouth of the Psalmist; *cum autem dicat* (Vulg.), 'But when He hath thus said' (Ellicott), which is much the same as 'But when He saith' (AV., RV.), *quum autem dicit* (Beza). Those who make 'Christ' the nominative to εἴπῃ, *must* make the verb refer to His final triumph; 'When Christ shall have said,' as He will say at some time in the unknown future. The change from ὑπέταξεν to ὑποτέτακται is in favour of the reference to a future declaration rather than to what is said in the Psalm: 'have been subjected and remain in subjection.' In that case, after δῆλον ὅτι we must supply πάντα ὑποτετάξεται, 'it is manifest that (all will be subjected) with the exception of Him (God) who subjected the all to Him (Christ)'; or, more simply, 'of course with the exception,' etc.

The ὅτι before πάντα ὑποτέτακται is of doubtful authority: B, Vulg. and other Latin texts omit. The αὐτῷ, 'under Him' (AV.), after ὑποτέτακται has very little authority.

28. ὅταν δὲ ὑποταγῇ αὐτῷ τὰ πάντα, τότε κ.τ.λ. 'When, however, the all shall have been subjected to Him (the Son), then (and not till then) shall the Son Himself also be subjected to Him (the Father) who subjected the all to Him (the Son), that God may be all in all.' The passage is a summary of mysteries which our present knowledge does not enable us to explain, and which our present faculties, perhaps, do not enable us to understand. See Cyril of Jerusalem, *Cat. Lect.* x. 9,

---

* Schmiedel urges that the use of Ps. viii. here (comp. Heb. ii. 5) shows that the title 'Son of Man' was known to St Paul and other Apostles. They may have avoided the expression as likely to lead Gentiles to believe that Jesus was the son of some particular man (Knowling, *The Testimony of St Paul to Christ*, p. 272).

xv. 29–31; Hooker, *Eccl. Pol.* v. lv. 8. Perhaps τότε καὶ αὐτὸς ὁ υἱός should be rendered, 'then shall *even* the Son Himself,' or 'then shall the Son *of His own free will.*' But the καί is of doubtful authority; B D* E F G 17 and other witnesses omit.

ἵνα ᾖ ὁ Θεὸς πάντα ἐν πᾶσιν. The ἵνα depends on ὑποταγήσεται, not on τῷ ὑποτάξαντι. This is the purpose of the ultimate subjection of the Son to the Father, 'that God, and God alone, may be everything in everything,' *i.e.* may fulfil all relations in all creatures. The πᾶσιν is probably neuter, but the comprehensive neuter, including both persons and things: see J. A. Robinson on Eph. i. 23, p. 44, and comp. iii. 22, viii. 6, xi. 12; xii. 6; Col. iii. 11. Wetstein gives examples of πάντα and τὰ πάντα being used as predicates of persons; *e.g.* πάντ᾽ ἐκεῖνος ἦν αὐτοῖς (Dem. *De Cor.* p. 240). The meaning seems to be that there will no longer be need of a Mediator: all relations between Creator and creatures, between Father and offspring, will be direct. *Nunc adhuc non est omnia in omnibus, quia singuli sancti diversas virtutes ejus in se habent. Tunc autem universa unus habebit, et erit ipse omnia in omnibus* (Primasius). *Tunc remoto velo palam cernemus Deum in sua majestate regnantem, neque amplius media erit Christi humanitas, quae nos ab interiore Dei conspectu conhibeat* (Calvin). *Deus immediate se ostendens, vivificans et effundens in beatos suam mirandam lucem, sapientiam, justitiam, et laetitiam* (Melanchthon). See also Origen *De Prin.* III. v. 7; Gregory of Nyssa on 1 Cor. xv. 28, on the Soul and the Resurrection, and the Great Catechetical Oration; Weinel, *St Paul,* p. 50; Knowling, *Messianic Interpretation,* pp. 45, 110 f. See on πάντες in *v.* 22.

It is uncertain whether we should read τὰ πάντα (א E F K L P, Ath. Chrys.) or πάντα (A B D* 17, Arm., Hipp.). Origen has both readings.

29–34. Once more there is an abrupt change of tone;— "one of the most abrupt in St Paul's Epistles. He leaves the new topic just when he has pursued it to the remotest point, and goes back to the general argument as suddenly as if nothing had intervened" (Stanley). He ceases to prophesy and reveal mysteries, and again begins to reason, as in the paragraph before *v.* 20. Two subsidiary arguments are here added, one based on baptism for the dead (*v.* 29), the other on the motive of the Christian life (30–34); and each has given rise to so much perplexity that some have proposed to omit ὑπὲρ τῶν νεκρῶν and ὑπὲρ αὐτῶν, or the whole of *v.* 29, or even the whole paragraph, as an interpolation.* But, apart from the violence of such emendations, what induced an interpolator to insert enigmas?

---

* Others propose δαπανώμενοι and δαπανῶνται for βαπτιζόμενοι and βαπτίζονται, or ἀπ᾽ ἔργων νεκρῶν (Heb. vi. 1) for ὑπὲρ τῶν νεκρῶν.

29. Ἐπεὶ τί ποιήσουσιν οἱ βαπτιζόμενοι ὑπὲρ τῶν νεκρῶν; 'Otherwise, what will they do who receive baptism for the dead?' 'Otherwise' or 'Else' (v. 10, vii. 14) means, εἰ ἀναστασις νεκρῶν οὐκ ἔστιν (v. 13): and τί ποιήσουσιν may mean either, 'what will they have recourse to?' or, 'what will they gain?' The second question, εἰ ὅλως κ.τ.λ., is in favour of 'what will they gain?' Neither Mark xi. 5 nor Acts xxi. 13 is quite parallel, for there the verb is present, not future. Jer. iv. 30 and Hos. ix. 5 have the future, with the meaning, 'what will you resort to?' The question here implies that they will be in an absurd and piteous state. We might render, 'what will be the position of those who receive baptism for the dead?'

The meaning of οἱ βαπτιζόμενοι ὑπὲρ τῶν νεκρῶν will remain doubtful. J. W. Horsley (*Newbery House Magazine*, June 1890) has collected thirty-six explanations; see also Meyer. Only three need be noticed.

1. The Greek expositors (ably supported by Evans) explain the expression as referring to ordinary Christian baptism, ὑπὲρ τῶν νεκρῶν being taken as meaning 'with an interest in the resurrection of the dead,' *i.e.* in expectation of the resurrection. But is there any authority for this use of ὑπέρ? And is not the supposed ellipse of τῆς ἀναστάσεως very violent? If St Paul had wanted to abbreviate ὑπὲρ τῆς ἀναστάσεως τῶν νεκρῶν, he would have left out τῶν νεκρῶν, not τῆς ἀναστάσεως. Lastly, the article with the present participle, οἱ βαπτιζόμενοι, seems to imply a class of people who practise something exceptional.

2. The reference is to some abnormal baptismal rite known to the Corinthians, which would be meaningless without a belief in the resurrection. This hypothesis, when left quite indefinite, is admissible. But when it is defined as vicarious baptism, *i.e.* of baptizing living proxies in place of those who had died unbaptized, it becomes highly improbable. This practice existed in some quarters in Tertullian's day (*De Resur.* 48; *Adv. Marcion.* v. 10), but perhaps only among heretics. There is no evidence that this vicarious baptism was practised anywhere in St Paul's time; and if it had been, would he have used such a superstitious rite as an argument? Granted that such an argument does not necessarily imply approval of the rite, yet it would have laid him open to the retort, "But *we* do not practise anything of the kind; what is that to us?"

3. The reference is to something exceptional, but which may often have occurred at Corinth and elsewhere, and which the Apostle would approve. Persons, previously inclined to Christianity, sometimes ended in being baptized out of affection or respect for the dead, *i.e.* because some Christian relation or friend had died, earnestly desiring and praying for their con-

version. Such might reasonably be designated as 'those who
receive baptism on behalf of the dead.' See Findlay, *ad loc.*; also
Hastings, *BD.* i. p. 245. Stanley gives thirteen interpretations,
but not this last, which is one of the best. With regard to the
arguments as a whole he says; "They may fail of themselves in persuading us of a future state, but they cannot fail in persuading us
of his intense conviction of the reality of Christ's resurrection;
and not of its reality only, but of its supreme importance as a
turning-point in the destinies of the human race" (p. 313).

εἰ ὅλως νεκροὶ οὐκ ἐγείρονται. To be taken with what follows
(RV.), rather than with what precedes (AV.). "If dead people
are not raised at all (if this is quite certain), why in the world
(καί intensive) are they baptized for them?" Comp. εἰ μὴ γὰρ
τοὺς προπεπτωκότας ἀναστῆναι προσεδόκα, περισσὸν καὶ ληρῶδες ὑπὲρ
νεκρῶν εὔχεσθαι (2 Macc. xii. 44), an instructive passage in connexion with this verse. With ὅλως here comp. μὴ ὀμόσαι ὅλως
(Matt. v. 34), and see on v. 1, vi. 7. In all four places the Vulg.
has *omnino*, a word which has as many shades of meaning as
ὅλως. 'Actually' or 'absolutely' might serve here, as in v. 1
With the intensive καί comp. the readings Rom. viii. 24, τί καὶ
ἐλπίζει and τίς καὶ ὑπομένει. If resurrection is absolutely a fiction,
then baptism for the dead is an absurdity.

Both 2. and 3. have the decisive merit of satisfying the ὑπὲρ
αὐτῶν at the end of the verse. These words would be superfluous, or even inexplicable, if St Paul were speaking simply of
ordinary Christian baptism.

30. Another practical result of denying the possibility of
resurrection is that it makes a great deal of the Christian life
seem absurd, and that it destroys a very powerful motive for
good behaviour. The hope of rewards is not the highest motive
for virtue, but, if the reward hoped for is not an ignoble one,
such as sensual pleasure or financial gain, to be influenced by
the hope of rewards is not immoral. Righteousness simply for
righteousness' sake is not a sufficient motive for all of us at all
times; and even to those who find it sufficient, the thought of
reward may be a help, especially such reward as the joy of a
good conscience in this life and the inconceivable bliss of the
beatific vision in the next. Destroy the belief in a future life,
and, although the joy of a good conscience would still remain,
yet a powerful motive for good conduct, and therefore a powerful
defence against temptation, would be lost.

After βαπτίζονται we must read ὑπὲρ αὐτῶν (א A B D* E F G K P,
Vulg. Copt. Arm. RV.) rather than ὑπὲρ τῶν νεκρῶν (D³ L, AV.).

τί καὶ ἡμεῖς κινδυνεύομεν πᾶσαν ὥραν; 'Why do we also stand
in jeopardy every hour?' The καί is not intensive as in the

previous question; not, 'Why in the world do we stand in jeopardy?' The καί means that 'we also, as well as those who receive baptism for the dead, are affected by the denial of this doctrine.' The καὶ ἡμεῖς therefore implies that the Apostle and others like him are not among those who receive baptism for the dead. And ἡμεῖς must not be made more definite, as 'we Apostles' or 'we preachers.' It includes all those who, like St Paul, incur great risks for the Gospel. 'Every hour' is a vivid after-thought; danger is never absent from such lives; Rom. viii. 36; 2 Cor. iv. 10–12.

31. And the danger is neither rare nor trifling. Every day he goes about with his life in his hands: *obsideor assiduis mortibus quotidie* (Calv.). Possiby he refers also to the moribund condition of his body, but the chief reference is to external perils which might any day be fatal; 2 Cor. i. 8, 9; xi. 23, ἐν θανάτοις πολλάκις. What assurance is he to give them for the truth of this strong statement? The estimation in which (as they know) he holds them. 'As surely as I am proud of you,' or, 'I affirm it by the glorying in you which I have in Christ Jesus our Lord.' It is, however, not in any earthly sphere that he has this feeling, but ἐν Χριστῷ Ἰησοῦ τῷ Κυρίῳ ἡμῶν. The full titles show how great the security is, and the ἔχω perhaps implies that he regards his exultation over them as a valuable possession. We have similar asseverations 2 Cor. i. 23, ii. 17, xi. 10, xii. 19. Origen asks whether the Apostle does not here violate the evangelical command, Swear not at all, and leaves the question unanswered. Atto remarks that the fact that the Apostle here uses an oath proves that an oath is not always wrong; *quod ipse Dominus manifestat, dum non dicit quod amplius malum est, sed a malo* (Matt. v. 37). Νή occurs here only in the N.T., and in the LXX only Gen. xlii. 15, 16, νὴ τὴν ὑγίειαν Φαραώ: but comp. 1 Sam. i. 26, iii. 17; 2 Sam. iii. 35. Outside the Pauline Epistles, καύχησις, καύχημα, καυχᾶσθαι are rare in the N.T.; comp. 1 Thess. ii. 19; Phil. ii. 16; and for the feeling without this word, Col. i. 4. The affectionate ἀδελφοί (which D E F G L, Orig. Chrys. omit) comes very naturally in the middle of the affectionate asseveration; 'I assure you by the brotherly pride in your faith with which I am possessed in Christ Jesus our Lord'(Rutherford).

32. εἰ κατὰ ἄνθρωπον ἐθηριομάχησα ἐν Ἐφέσῳ. 'If from merely human motives I fought with wild beasts at Ephesus.' The exact meaning of κατὰ ἄνθρωπον (iii. 3, ix. 8; Rom. iii. 5; Gal. i. 11, iii. 15) depends on the context. Here it is placed first with emphasis, to show that the Apostle is speaking hypothetically from the ordinary secular point of view. It is beside the mark to say that he ought to have had a much higher view.

Taking common human estimates as his standard, he would have asked, Is it worth the risk? Will it *pay*? And he would have said, No. *Humanae vitae respectu, ita ut nobis constet praemium in hoc mundo* (Calv.); *humano auctoramento, spe vitae praesentis* (Beng.). No doubt, ἐθηριομάχησα, 'I was a θηριομάχος, a wild-beast fighter,' is metaphorical.* St Paul was a Roman citizen, and could not be compelled to fight as a *bestiarius* or *venator* in the arena, nor could he be flung as a criminal *ad leonem*. If, in spite of his citizenship, this had taken place, he would have mentioned the outrage and miraculous escape in 2 Cor. xi. 23 f., and St Luke would hardly have omitted it in Acts. He means that he was near being torn to pieces by infuriated men. *Per allegoriam bestiae intelliguntur adversariae potestates. Sicut in Psalmo; Ne tradas bestiis confitentem tibi* (Primasius). Heraclitus is said to have called the Ephesians θηρία, and to have given this as a reason for not being one of their rulers. Pompey at Pharsalus said, οἷοις θηρίοις μαχόμεθα (Appian *B.C.* ii. 11). Origen characteristically remarks, ἔστι καὶ θηρία νοητά. Comp. Ps. xxii. 13, 14; Tit. i. 12; 2 Tim. iv. 17; and Ignat. *Rom.* 5, *Smyrn.* 4, with Lightfoot's notes. The uproar caused by Demetrius (Acts xix.) was probably later than this. The climax, peril (κινδυνεύομεν), peril of death (ἀποθνήσκω), peril of a horrible death (ἐθηριομάχησα), is perhaps intentional. We have θεομάχος (Acts v. 39), θεομαχεῖν (Acts xxiii. 9, TR.).†

τί μοι τὸ ὄφελος; 'What is *the* profit to me?' Where is the gain to compensate a man for such dreadful dangers? Τί ὄφελος, without the article (Jas. ii. 14, 16), is more colloquial; so also in Plato and Philo. In LXX, ὄφελος occurs Job xv. 3 only. Here the sentence ends: it has its conditional clause in front of it. The next conditional clause belongs to the next sentence.

εἰ νεκροὶ οὐκ ἐγείρονται. For the sixth time we have the foolish dogma of the τινες quoted, 'Dead people are not raised.' If that disastrous dictum were true, they might be advising one another to adopt the impious conduct of the people in Jerusalem, Let us eat and drink, etc. (LXX of Isa. xxii. 13). *St Paul is not stating his own view*, but the common view, the inevitable moral result of denying a future life (Isa. lvi. 12; Eccles. ii. 24, iii. 12,

---

* Ramsay (*St Paul*, p. 230) regards it as "an interesting mixture of Greek and Roman ideas," the Greek idea that the mob is a dangerous beast, and the Roman idea of fighting with beasts in the circus. The verb occurs nowhere else in N.T. or LXX.

† Marcus Aurelius (x. 8) says that to desire to live on under debasing conditions is like the half-devoured beast-fighters (τοῖς ἡμιβρώτοις θηριομάχοις), who, in spite of their ghastly wounds, beg to be respited till the morrow, only to be exposed to the same teeth and claws. The question is thoroughly discussed by Max Krenkel, *Beiträge zur Aufhellung der Geschichte und der Briefe des Ap. Paulus*, pp. 126-152.

v. 18, viii. 15, ix. 7; Luke xii. 19; and esp. Wisd. ii. 6–9). Similar passages abound in classical writers; Hdt. ii. 78; Thuc. ii. 53; Eur. *Alc.* 788 f.; Hor. *Od.* II. iii. 13. At Trimalchio's banquet (Petron. *Satyr.* 34), the thought of the dead makes the guests exclaim,

> Heu! heu! nos miseros! quam totus homuncio nil est!
> Sic erimus cuncti postquam nos auferet Orcus.
> Ergo vivamus dum licet esse bene.

The advice is despondent rather than defiant; but in any case the Apostle suggests that it is shocking, and therefore the doctrine of annihilation, on which it is based, must be untrue. No Christian can accept it, but those who deny that there is a life after death are only too likely to accept it. Belief in a resurrection is a moral safeguard. See Lightfoot, *Cambridge Sermons*, pp. 123–125. St Paul has no sympathy with moral ideals which provide no forgiveness of sins; and without Christ's Death and Resurrection there is no forgiveness.

33. Having quoted the natural but fatal advice which might be given to them, he passes on to give advice which is wholesome and necessary. Here we get his own view.

μὴ πλανᾶσθε. 'Do not *begin* to be led astray' (vi. 9), *nolite seduci* (Vulg.); or (better), '*Cease* to be led astray' by such Epicurean principles: vi. 9; Gal. vi. 7; Jas. i. 16, where see Hort's note. He perhaps wishes to intimate that some of them have been captivated by this specious, but immoral doctrine. The quotation that follows confirms this.

φθείρουσιν ἤθη χρηστὰ ὁμιλίαι κακαί. 'Evil companionships mar good morals,' or 'Bad company spoils noble characters.' It is uncertain whether Menander adopted a popular proverb, or the saying passed from the *Thais* into popular use. St Paul may have got the saying from either source; but the form χρηστά (for the reading χρησθ' has hardly any authority) points to the proverb rather than the play. The saying is specially true of the Christian life, and the friends and acquaintances of the Corinthian Christians were mostly heathen; vii. 12, viii. 10, x. 27; 2 Cor. vi. 14–16. Neither ὁμιλίαι nor ἤθη is found elsewhere in the N.T. The former combines the meanings of 'conversations' and 'societies' or 'companies,' *colloquia* (Vulg.), *commercia* (Beza), LXX of Prov. vii. 21; Wisd. viii. 18. We cannot infer from this passage, combined with Acts xvii. 28 and Tit. i. 12, that St Paul was well acquainted with classical writers; his quotations may have been common-places. Origen (*Hom.* xxxi. *in Luc.*) says that St Paul borrows words even from heathen in order to hallow them.

34. ἐκνήψατε δικαίως καὶ μὴ ἁμαρτάνετε. Aor. imperat., between two presents with the negative: μὴ πλανᾶσθε . . . ἐκνήψατε . . . μὴ ἁμαρτάνετε. 'Once for all shake off your drowsiness in a right spirit, and do not *begin* to sin,' *i.e.* do not let yourselves drift into evil courses by dallying with false opinions; or, 'Get rid of your stupor with a righteous resolve, and *cease* to go wrong' in bad company. The strong metaphor, ἐκνήψατε, implies that they were already in a grievous case. He addresses them, says Chrysostom, as if they were drunk or mad. Hence, *evigilate* (Vulg.) is hardly strong enough. The verb is used in a literal sense Gen. ix. 24; 1 Sam. xxv. 37; Joel i. 5: cf. ἀνανήψωσιν ἐκ τῆς διαβόλου παγίδος (2 Tim. ii. 26). Of its use here Beng. says; *exclamatio plena majestatis apostolicae*: nowhere else in N.T.

It is possible that these sceptics claimed to be sober thinkers, and condemned the belief in a resurrection as a wild enthusiasm. If so, we have an explanation of the rather strange combination of δικαίως with ἐκνήψατε.

ἀγνωσίαν γὰρ Θεοῦ τινες ἔχουσιν. 'For utter ignorance of God is what some (*v.* 12) have got.' This is their disease, and they must get rid of it: for ἔχειν in this sense see Mark iii. 10, ix. 17, Acts xxviii. 9. He says ἀγνωσίαν ἔχειν rather than ἀγνοεῖν or οὐκ εἰδέναι or οὐ γινώσκειν (i. 21) as being much stronger; and rather than γνῶσιν οὐκ ἔχειν as intimating that they not merely fail to possess what is good and necessary, but possess what is evil. Agnosticism is not so much privation and poverty, as positive peril. Is St Paul thinking of Wisd. xiii. 1? Μάταιοι μὲν γὰρ πάντες ἄνθρωποι φύσει, οἷς παρῆν Θεοῦ ἀγνωσία. On "the unquestionable acquaintance of St. Paul with the Book" of Wisdom see Hastings, *DB.* iv. pp. 930 f. Ἀγνωσία is not ἄγνοια, *ignorantia*, the absence of knowledge, but *ignoratio*, the failure or inability to take knowledge. These Corinthians had no power of appreciating God's existence or presence, His nature or will. See Hort on 1 Pet. ii. 15; also on Jas. ii. 18.

πρὸς ἐντροπὴν ὑμῖν λαλῶ. 'It is to move you to shame (vi. 5; Ps. xxxiv. 26) that I am speaking to you in this manner.' It was indeed a bitter thing for Corinthians, who prided themselves on their intelligence, to be told that as regards the knowledge of God they were more purblind than the heathen. *Paulus ignorantiam Dei illis exprobans, omni prorsus honore eos spoliat* (Calv.). Their inability to recognize the power and goodness of God was shown in their dogmatic assertion that He does not raise the dead. See on iv. 14 and vi. 5; also Milligan, *Greek Papyri*, p. 22.

λαλῶ (א B D E P 17) is certainly to be preferred to λέγω (A F G K L); *loquor* (Vulg.), *dico* (f g).

XV. 35-58. ANSWERS TO OBJECTIONS; THE NATURE OF THE BODY OF THE RISEN.

Again we have three subdivisions; (*a*) The Answers of Nature and of Scripture, 35–49; (*b*) Victory over Death, 50–57; (*c*) Practical Result, 58.

Plato in the *Phaedo*, and Cicero in the *Tusculan Disputations*, argue for a future life; but resurrection is beyond their view. Does St Paul confuse the resurrection of the body with the immortality of the soul? Only so far as those with whom he is arguing confused the two. According to current ideas, to deny the possibility of resurrection was coming very near to denying any real life beyond the grave. The body was commonly regarded as the security for the preservation of personality. If the body was never to be preserved, the survival of the soul would be precarious or worthless. Either the finite spirit would be absorbed in the Infinite Spirit, or its separate existence would be shadowy, insipid, and joyless. St Paul shapes his argument to meet both classes,—those who denied the resurrection of the body, but allowed the survival of the soul, and those who denied both. Christ, in refuting the Sadducees, treated the two doctrines as so closely connected that to admit immortality and deny resurrection was illogical.* Christ argues from the Living God, as St Paul from the Risen Christ. The continued relation of the Living God to each one of the patriarchs implied the permanence of their personal life. The continued relation of believers to the Christ who has been raised in the body implies the permanence of their bodily life. See Swete, *The Ascended Christ*, p. 138.

In working onwards to the triumphant conclusion, St Paul frequently falls into the rhythmical parallelism which distinguishes Hebrew poetry: see especially *vv.* 42 f. and 51 f.

People ask how the body that dies and the body that is raised can be the same. Nature itself shows that there is no necessity for their being the same. The seed and the plant that rises from it are so far from being the same, that the one must die in order that the other may live. Even between bodies that are material there are endless possibilities of difference; and not all bodies are material. There may

---

* *Possibly* Christ meant no more than "that Abraham, Isaac, and Jacob were already enjoying a life fuller and more complete than that which the Jews were accustomed to associate with Sheol"; but such an answer seems to be hardly adequate. In 4 Maccabees, which is a philosophical Jewish homily, it is stated that the godly do not die, but live to God (ζῶσιν τῷ Θεῷ), like the Patriarchs; vii. 19, xvi. 25.

be immense differences, yet real relationship, between the body that dies and the body that is raised. Scripture confirms this.

The transformation of the material body that dies into a glorified body that will not die is not only possible, but necessary and certain ; and hence the completeness of the victory over Death.

With this certainty before you, be steadfast, working in sure hope of eternal life.

35 But some one is sure to object, Is it possible for the dead to be raised? Why, with what kind of a body will they come back? 36 The question may seem to be clever, but it is really very foolish, and daily experience answers it. The seed which you yourself sow can have no new life given to it, unless it dies: 37 and what you sow is not the body that is to be, but just a leafless grain; say a grain of wheat, or of any other plant. 38 But it is God who gives it a body just as He ordained it from the first, and to every one of the seeds the kind of body that is appropriate to it. 39 Even now, without taking account of resurrection, flesh is not all of it the same in kind: there is flesh of men, and of beasts, and of birds, and of fishes,—all different. 40 Moreover, there are bodies fitted for existence in heaven, and bodies fitted for existence on earth; but the beauty of the heavenly bodies is quite different from the beauty of the earthly. 41 The sun has a splendour of its own ; so has the moon; and so have all the stars, for no two stars are the same in splendour. 42 These differences are very great, yet we think them natural. There is just as much difference between the body that dies and the body that is raised, and the change need not seem incredible. Think of the body as a seed committed to the ground.

It is sown a thing perishable, it is raised imperishable.

43 It is sown in disability, it is raised in full glory.

It is sown in powerlessness, it is raised in full vigour.

44 It is sown an animal body, it is raised a spiritual body.

As surely as there exists an animal body,
So surely there exists a spiritual one.

45 Yes, this is the meaning of that which stands written,
The first man Adam became a life-having soul ;
The last Adam became a life-giving spirit.

⁴⁶ Yet not first in time is the life-giving spirit ;
But the animate comes first, and then the spiritual.
⁴⁷ The first man is from the dust of the earth ;
The Second Man is from heaven.
⁴⁸ And each gives his nature to those of his race.
As the earthy one is, such also are those who are earthy,
And as the Heavenly One is, such also are those who are
heavenly.
⁴⁹ So, just as we have borne the likeness of the earthy,
We shall also bear the likeness of the Heavenly.
⁵⁰ Now this I assure you, Brothers, that flesh and blood can
have no share in the Kingdom of God, nor yet what is perishable
in what is not perishable. ⁵¹ And here I reveal to you a truth
that has hitherto been kept secret respecting our future estate.
We shall all of us—not sleep in death,
⁵² But we shall all be transformed ;
In a moment, in the twinkling of an eye,
At the last trumpet-call.
For the trumpet will sound,
And the dead will be raised, never again to perish,
And we who are then alive shall be transformed.
⁵³ For this perishable nature of ours
must put on what is imperishable ;
And this mortal nature of ours
must put on what is immortal.
⁵⁴ Now when this perishable nature
shall have put on imperishability,
And this mortal nature
shall have put on immortality,
Then indeed shall come true the word that has been written,
Death hath been swallowed up into victory.
⁵⁵ Where, O death, is thy victory ?
Where, O death, is thy sting ?
⁵⁶ Its sting is given to death by sin ;
Its power is given to sin by the Law.
⁵⁷ But thanks be to God who is giving us the victory
Through our Lord Jesus Christ.

⁵⁸ So then, my dear Brothers, prove yourselves firm and unmoveable, abounding unceasingly in the work which the Lord

appoints for you, for you know that your toil cannot be in vain, with the Lord as your security for a blessed immortality.

35. Ἀλλὰ ἐρεῖ τις, Πῶς ἐγείρονται οἱ νεκροί ; As in Jas. ii. 18, the ἀλλά is the writer's word, not the objector's. ' But (some one will say) how are the dead raised?' is probably wrong. Compare Ἐρεῖς μοι οὖν and ἐρεῖς οὖν (Rom. ix. 19, xi. 19). Where St Paul has some sympathy with an objection he says, τί οὖν ἐροῦμεν (Rom. iv. 1, vi. 1, vii. 7, viii. 31, ix. 14, 30) : here he has none. The objection is still urged. Granted that historical testimony and natural fitness are in favour of believing that Christ rose again as an earnest that we shall be raised, is our bodily resurrection possible ? Can we conceive such a thing? We cannot be expected to believe what is impossible and inconceivable.

ποίῳ δὲ σώματι ἔρχονται ; 'And with what kind of a body do they come?' This second question is made in support of the first. Will it be the same body as that which died? But that body has perished. Or will it be quite a different body? Then how is that a resurrection ? The ἔρχονται *seems* to imply a rather crude idea of the resurrection, as if they were seen coming out of their graves. Yet such a conception is almost inevitable, if resurrection is to be pictured to the imagination (John v. 29). The Talmud shows that the Rabbis believed that the particles of the body which died would reunite at the resurrection and form the same body again.* So gross a conception could easily be held up to ridicule then, and is less credible than ever now that we know that the particles form several bodies in succession and may pass in time from one human body to another. See C. H. Robinson, *Studies in the Resurrection*, p. 14. For scientific answers to various objections, see Stewart and Tait, *The Unseen Universe*, ch. vii.

The τις is one of the τινες of *vv.* 12 and 34. The πῶς implies, What is the force that will raise the dead, and in what way does it act? The ποίῳ σώματι implies, What is the result of its action ? What are the nature and properties of the raised body? Chrysostom asks, Why does not the Apostle appeal to the omnipotence of God? and replies, Because he is dealing with people who do not believe, ὅτι ἀπίστοις διαλέγεται. These objectors ἀγνωσίαν Θεοῦ ἔχουσιν and are incapable of appreciating such an appeal.

---

* " In what shape will those live who live in Thy day ? Will they then resume this form of the present, and put on these entrammeling members? And He answered and said to me ; The earth will assuredly restore the dead, which it now receives in order to preserve them, making no change in their form, but as it has received, so will it restore them " (Apocalypse of Baruch xlix. 2, 3, l. 1, 2 ; see Charles *ad loc.*).

They do not apprehend even their own operations, and how can they understand His? *

It is possible that ἔρχονται is equivalent to 'come *back*,' as often respecting Christ's Return: comp. Matt. xxv. 19, 27; Luke xii. 45 : but this is not necessary. How do they *come on the scene*? In what form is one to picture them? The question may imply that the coming cannot be a return.

36. ἄφρων, σὺ ὃ σπείρεις κ.τ.λ. This is the answer to the first question, and it is given with a severity which implies that the objector plumes himself on his acuteness. But he is not at all acute. There is strong emphasis on the σύ. '*Your own* experience might teach you, if you had the sense to comprehend its significance. Every time you sow, you supply the answer to your own objection.' The σύ is in marked antithesis to ὁ Θεός in *v.* 38. *Ex tui operis consuetudine considerare debuisti quod dicimus* (Primasius). Only by dissolution of the material particles in the seed is the germ of life, which no microscope can detect, made to operate. The new living organism is not the old one reconstructed, although it has a necessary and close connexion with it; it is neither identical with the former, nor is it a new creation (John xii. 24).† Dissolution and continuity are not incompatible; *how* they are combined is a mystery beyond our ken, but the fact that they can be combined is evident, and death setting free a mysterious power of new life is part of the *how*. *Nihil in resurrectione futurum doceo quod non subjectum sit omnium oculis* (Calv.). Yet this ἄφρων (Ps. xciii. 8 ; Luke xi. 40 ; five times in 2 Cor.) thinks his objection unanswerable. St Paul speaks thus πρὸς ἐντροπήν.

On the anarthrous nominative for the vocative see J. H. Moulton, *Gr* p. 71. K L here read ἄφρον : so also T R. Comp. Luke xii. 20; Acts xiii. 10. See Abbott, *The Son of Man*, p. 624.

37. καὶ ὃ σπείρεις κ.τ.λ. This is the answer to the second question, introduced by καί. The grain, before being sown, is stripped of all the sheaths which protected it on the plant, as the human body, before burial, is stripped of its usual clothing. The γυμνόν has no reference to the soul stripped of the body,

* *Tu, inquit, qui te sapientem putas, dum per mundi sapientiam asseris, mortuos non posse resurgere, audi ex rebus mundi, unde tua sapientia probetur insapientia* (Herveius).

† It seems clear from *vv.* 36, 37 combined with *v.* 50 that St Paul did not believe that at the Resurrection we shall be raised with a body consisting of material particles. There is a connexion between the body that dies and the body that is raised, but it is not a material connexion, not identity of 'flesh and blood.' See Burton, *Lectures*, pp. 429-431, quoted by Conybeare and Howson *ad loc.* See also Lightfoot, *Cambridge Sermons*, pp. 74-79.

an idea which is quite alien to the passage. The epithet, which is emphatic, looks forward rather than backward: τὸ σῶμα τὸ γενησόμενον, *quod futurum sit* (Vulg.), *quod nascetur* (Calv. Beng.), *oriturum* (Beza), will be clothed with green coverings, as the resurrection-body (2 Cor. v. 2) with glory.* As in xiv. 10, εἰ τύχοι indicates an indefiniteness which is unimportant. For the argument there, the exact number of γένη φωνῶν was of no consequence: here the particular kind of grain is of no moment, —'wheat, if you like, or anything else.'

38. ὁ δὲ Θεός. This is the important point. Neither the seed itself, nor the sower, provides the new body; 'but it is God that giveth it a body exactly as He willed, and to each of the seeds a body of its own,' *i.e.* the right body, the one that is proper to its kind. Therefore to every buried human being He will give a proper resurrection-body. The use of σῶμα of vegetation reminds us that the illustration has reference to the human body: and καθὼς ἠθέλησεν, as in xii. 18 (not καθὼς θέλει, or καθὼς βούλεται, as in xii. 11), shows that God does not deal with each case separately, just as He *pleases* at the moment, but according to fixed laws, just as it *pleased* Him when the world was created and regulated.† From the first, vegetation has had its laws κατὰ γένος καὶ καθ' ὁμοιότητα (Gen. i. 11, 12), and great as is the variety of plants, the seed of each has a body of its own, in which the vital principle, to be brought into action by death and decay, resides. See Orr, *Expositor*, Nov. 1908, p. 436; Milligan, *Greek Papyri*, pp. 91, 101.

39. οὐ πᾶσα σὰρξ ἡ αὐτὴ σάρξ. 'Not all flesh is the same flesh.' The difference between our present body and our risen body may be greater than that between a seed and the plant which springs from it. It may be greater than that between men and fishes. In Gen. i. 20—27 fishes are mentioned before fowls, and we have an ascending scale, fishes, birds, beasts, man; here we have a descending one. The use of κτηνῶν rather than τετραπόδων (Rom. i. 23; Acts x. 12, xi. 6), and of πτηνῶν (here only) rather than πετεινῶν (*ibid. et saepe*), is for the sake of alliteration, of which St Paul is fond (2 Cor. vii. 4, viii. 22, ix. 5, x. 6, xiii. 2).

* The future participle is rare in N.T. Nowhere else does γενησόμενος occur; ἐσόμενος in Luke xxii. 49 only.

† Deissmann, *Bible Studies*, p. 252, quotes similar expressions from private letters of the 2nd cent. A.D.

Even a heathen could teach that it is our wisdom to accept God's will as expressed in the ruling of the universe; "Dare to look up to God and say, Deal with me for the future as Thou wilt; I am of the same mind as Thou art; I am Thine; I refuse nothing that pleases Thee; lead me whither Thou wilt" (Epictetus, *Dis.* ii. 16).

T R inserts σάρξ after ἄλλη μέν with many cursives and some versions, and AV. follows: ℵ A B D E F etc. omit. A K L P omit σάρξ before πτηνῶν: ℵ B D E F G insert. D* F G correct πτηνῶν to the more usual πετεινῶν. F K L transpose πτηνῶν and ἰχθύων, perhaps influenced by the order in Gen. i. 20, and AV. follows. Already in Gen. i. 25, ii. 20 κτῆνος is used of beasts generally, and not merely such as are acquired and possessed (κτᾶσθαι) by men; it need not be restricted to cattle, *pecorum* (Vulg.), still less to beasts of burden, *jumentorum* (d).

40.   καὶ σώματα ἐπουράνια, καὶ σώματα ἐπίγεια. 'Bodies also celestial there are, and bodies terrestrial,' *i.e.* some suitable for existence in heaven, and some for existence on earth. We cannot be certain what St Paul means by σώματα ἐπουράνια. He can hardly be thinking of *the inhabitants of other planets*; nor is it likely that the Fathers are right in making the distinction between ἐπουρ. and ἐπιγ. to be that between *saints* and *sinners*. Throughout the passage the differences between the various σώματα are physical, not ethical. Is he thinking of *angels*, which may be supposed to have σώματα, and are always represented as appearing to men in the form of men? * This is possible, but it does not seem to fit the argument. St Paul is appealing to the Corinthians' experience of nature, to the things which they see day by day: and they had no experience of angels. '*Heavenly bodies*' in the modern sense is more likely (*v.* 41) to be right. As there are differences on the earth, so also in the sky. There is a wide difference (ἑτέρα) between terrestrial and celestial bodies; and there is a further difference (ἄλλη) between one celestial body and another. The God who made these myriads of differences in one and the same universe can be credited with inexhaustible power. It is monstrous to suppose that He cannot fit a body to spirit. Therefore we must not place any limit to God's power with regard either to the difference between our present and our future body, or to the relations between them. He has found a fit body for fish, fowl, cattle, and mortal man: why not for immortal man? Experience teaches that God finds a suitable body for every type of earthly life and every type of heavenly life. Experience cannot teach that there is a type of life for which no suitable body can be found. Phil. iii. 21.

41.   ἀστὴρ γὰρ ἀστέρος κ.τ.λ. 'I say "stars" and not "a star," *for* star differs from star in glory'; the differences in light and lustre are endless. It is legitimate to apply these

---

* It is not likely that he is thinking of sun, moon, and stars as the bodies of angels: comp. Enoch xviii. 13, 14; Jubilees ii. 2, 3. 'Body' here does not mean an organism, but what is perceptible, "a permanent possibility of sensation." Müller (*Orientalische Literaturzeitung*, June 1900, Art. 'Zum Sirachproblem') suggests that St Paul is here quoting from the Hebrew Sirach.

differences in the heavenly bodies to possible differences in the
glories of the risen saints, and it is not impossible that the
Apostle had this thought in his mind. See Tert. *De Res.*
49, 52. But his main argument is that God, who made all
these *known* differences and connexions, may have made
differences and connexions between our present and future
bodies which are quite beyond our comprehension. Immense
differences there are certain to be. See some excellent remarks
of Origen in Jerome, *Letter to Pammachius against John of
Jerusalem,* 26.

42. Hitherto the answer to the second question (ποίῳ δὲ
σώματι ἔρχονται;) has been indirect: it now becomes direct.
The risen body is incorruptible, glorious, powerful, spiritual. It
is quite obvious that the corpse which is 'sown' is none of these
things. It is in corruption before it reaches the grave; it has
lost all rights of citizenship (ἀτιμία), and, excepting decent
burial, all rights of humanity; it is absolutely powerless, unable
to move a limb. The last epithet, ψυχικόν, is less appropriate
to a corpse, but it comes in naturally enough to distinguish the
body which is being dissolved from the body which will be
raised. The former was by nature subject to the laws and
conditions of physical life (ψυχή), the latter will be controlled
only by the spirit (πνεῦμα), and this spirit will be in harmony
with the spirit of God. In the material body the spirit has
been limited and hampered in its action; in the future body
it will have perfect freedom of action and consequently complete
control, and man will at last be, what God created him to be,
a being in which the higher self is supreme. The connexion
between 'spirit' and 'power' is frequent in Paul (ii. 4, v. 4;
Rom. i. 4, xv. 13, 19): cf. Luke i. 35; Acts i. 8. Evidently,
ψυχικόν does not mean that the body is made of ψυχή, consists
entirely of ψυχή: and πνευματικόν does not mean is made and
consists entirely of πνεῦμα. The adjectives mean 'congenital
with,' 'formed to be the organ of.' The ψυχή, in combination
with the physical germ, enables the latter to develop according
to the law of the γένος. The πνεῦμα, in combination with an
immaterial germ, enables the latter to develop according to a
higher law which is quite beyond our comprehension. The
πνεῦμα is the power by which the ψυχή in our present body has
communion with God; it is also the future body's principle of
life. Only in this Epistle does St Paul use ψυχικός (*vv.* 44, 46,
ii. 14; elsewhere Jas. iii. 15 and Jude 19; see Mayor on both
passages, and Hort on Jas. iii. 15): ψυχή is found in all groups,
except the Pastoral Epp. In the liturgies we frequently have
the order, ψυχή, σῶμα, πνεῦμα, perhaps suggesting that σῶμα is

the link between the other two (*JTS.* Jan. 1901, p. 273). See Additional Note, pp. 380 f.

44. εἰ ἔστιν . . . ἔστιν καί. The emphasis is on ἔστιν in both clauses ; ' If there *is* a natural body (and of course you cannot deny that), there *is* also a spiritual.' Is it likely that the highest development of all is left blank ? * This *a priori* argument may be confirmed by Scripture.

45. ' Thus also it stands written ; The first man Adam became a life-having soul; the last Adam a life-giving spirit.' The second clause is not in Gen. ii. 7, but is St Paul's comment on it (Thackeray, *St Paul and Contemporary Jewish Thought*, p. 201). Comp. John iii. 31, v. 21, where the Evangelist may be combining his own reflexions with quotation. The ψυχή results from the union of the breath of life with a lifeless body. God's breathing the vital principle into a lifeless human body shows that He gave man a soul-governed body, a body that was to be the organ of the ψυχή. Must not the last Adam be something much higher than that? St Paul says 'the last Adam' (Rom. v. 12–19) rather than 'the second Adam,' because here the point is that He is the supreme result in the ascending development. There will be no other Head of the human race. Our first parent was in one sense Head of the race ; its ideal representative was head in a different sense ; and there can be no third Head.† To those who believed that the world would soon come to an end it was specially obvious that Christ was the last Adam. Even in Jesus Himself there was development until He *became* ζωοποιοῦν, 'able to communicate a higher form of life' to the race of which He was Head : comp. John xx. 22. He became such at the Resurrection, and perhaps still more so at the Ascension. Before His death, His σῶμα, like ours, was ψυχικόν. See Thackeray, pp. 40–49 ; Dalman, *Words of Jesus*, p. 247 ; Abbott, *The Son of Man*, p. 79 ; Evans *ad loc.*

46. ἀλλ' οὐ πρῶτον τὸ πνευματικόν. This states a general law, not merely what took place in a particular instance : understand ἐστι, not ἐγένετο. 'The spiritual' is more comprehensive than 'spiritual body.' Adam could not be created morally perfect, but only capable of attaining to perfection ; indeed, even his physical and mental powers needed development. Therefore the lower moral stage must precede the higher.

* The AV. omits the 'if' with K L, and on the same weak authority adds 'body' to spiritual. There is no σῶμα before πνευματικόν in the true text.

† Primasius points out that the first Adam and the last were alike in being produced without human father and without sin. Dr. E. A. Abbott thinks that the idea of the Messiah as 'the Last Adam' and 'the Second Man comes from Ezekiel (*The Message of the Son of Man*, p. 5).

Holiness cannot be given ready made. It is the result of the
habitual free offering of self, the constant choice of good and
refusal of evil, and it is capable of indefinite increase. There is
nothing final in the universe, except God. All came from Him,
and it may be that all is tending (with whatever interruptions)
towards Him. Man's appointed task and privilege is to be
ever drawing nearer to Him.

47. ὁ πρῶτος ἄνθρωπος ἐκ γῆς χοϊκός. 'The first man is
of the earth, made of dust': ἔπλασεν ὁ Θεὸς τὸν ἄνθρωπον χοῦν
ἀπὸ τῆς γῆς (Gen. ii. 7). Otherwise we might have had γήϊνος
or γηγενής : comp. γηγενοῦς ἀπόγονος πρωτοπλάστου (Wisd. vii. 1).
In Mark vi. 11, χοῦς is used for κονιορτός (Matt. x. 14; Luke
ix. 5; Acts xiii. 51): comp. Rev. xviii. 19. But χοῦς (χέω) is
'soil' loosened and heaped up rather than 'dust': χοϊκός occurs
nowhere else in ·Biblical Greek. *De terra terrenus* (Vulg.);
better, *e terra pulvereus* (Beza). What is ἐκ γῆς is liable to
decay, death, and dissolution ; what is ἐξ οὐρανοῦ is imperishable.

ἐξ οὐρανοῦ. This refers to the Second Advent rather than
to the Incarnation. The Apostle is answering the question,
'With what kind of a body do they come ? ' It was ἐξ οὐρανοῦ,
e caelo, that the Risen Lord appeared to St Paul. From the
Ascension to the Return, Christ is ἐξ οὐρανοῦ in His relation to
mankind. They are still 'of earth,' He is now 'of heaven.'
See Briggs, *Church Unity*, pp. 282 f., for some valuable remarks
on this passage in its bearing on eucharistic doctrine.

The AV., with A K L P, Syrr. Arm. Goth., Chrys., inserts 'the Lord,'
ὁ κύριος, before ἐξ οὐρανοῦ : ℵ* B C D* E F G 17, Latt. Copt. Aeth., Tert.
Cypr. Hil. omit. Tertullian attributes the insertion, or rather the substitution of κύριος for ἄνθρωπος, to Marcion : Primus *inquit* (*stultissimus
haereticus*), homo de humo terrenus, secundus dominus de caelo. *Quare
secundus, si non homo, quod et primus ? Aut numquid et primus dominus,
si et secundus* (*Adv. Marcion.* v. 10). Tertullian himself gives two renderings ;
Primus homo de terrae limo, secundus homo de caelo (*De Carne Chr.* 8) ;
*Primus homo de terra choicus, id est limaceus, id est Adam, secundus homo
de caelo* (*De Res.* 49). Cyprian has *de terrae limo* repeatedly, and once
e terrae limo.

48, 49. Each race has the attributes of its Head. As a consequence of this law (καί), we who once wore the likeness of
the earthly Adam shall hereafter wear that of the glorified
Christ. What Adam was, made of dust to be dissolved into
dust again, such are all who share his life ; and what Christ is,
risen and eternally glorified, such will be all those who share
His life. A body, conditioned by ψυχή, derived from Adam, will
be transformed into a body conditioned by πνεῦμα, derived from
Christ. See 1 Thess. iv. 16 ; 2 Thess. i. 7 ; Phil. iii. 20, 21 ;
Eph. ii. 6, 20 ; also Swete, *The Ascended Christ*, p. 138.

If, with the best editors, we follow the greatly preponderating external evidence and read φορέσωμεν rather than φορέσομεν, 'let us wear' or 'let us put on for wear' rather than 'we shall wear,' the meaning will be that the attaining to the glorified body depends upon our own effort: see Goudge, p. 155. "But not only the context and the whole tenor of the argument are in favour of the future, but the hortative subjunctive is here singularly out of place and unlooked for" (Ellicott). Perhaps we have here "a very early instance of itacism." Compare Jas. iv. 15, where the balance of evidence is very different and the future is undoubtedly right. Alford thinks that here "a desire to turn a physical assertion into an ethical assertion" has corrupted the reading.

φορέσομεν, B 17 46 Arm. Aeth., Theodoret expressly (τὸ γὰρ φορέσομεν προρρητικῶς, οὐ παραινετικῶς εἴρηκεν): φορέσωμεν, אACDEFGKLP, Latt. Copt. Goth., Chrysostom expressly (τοῦτ' ἐστιν, ἄριστα πράξωμεν).

50–57. The two objections are now answered. How is resurrection possible after the body has been dissolved in the grave? Answer; The difficulty is the other way: resurrection would be impossible without such dissolution, for it is dissolution that frees the principle of new life. Then what kind of a body do the risen have, if the present body is not restored? Answer; A body similar to that of the Risen Lord, *i.e.* a body as suitable to the spiritual condition of the new life as a material body is to the present psychical condition.

But a further question may be raised. What will happen to those believers who are alive when the Lord comes? The radical translation from ψυχικόν to πνευματικόν must take place, whether through death or not. Mortal must become immortal. God will make the victory over death in all cases complete.

50. Τοῦτο δέ φημι. 'Now this I assert' (vii. 29). The assertion confirms *v.* 49 and prepares for *v.* 51: it introduces a fundamental principle which covers and decides the case. A perishable nature cannot really have possession of an imperishable Kingdom. For the Kingdom an incorruptible body wholly controlled by spirit is necessary, and this 'flesh and blood' cannot be. By σὰρξ καὶ αἷμα * is meant our present mortal nature, not our evil

---

* This is the usual order (Gal. i. 16 ; Matt. xvi. 17), but αἷμα καὶ σάρξ is also found (Eph. vi. 12 ; Heb. ii. 14). Perhaps the transitory and perishable character of man is specially meant ; οὕτως γενεὰ σαρκὸς καὶ αἵματος, ἡ μὲν τελειτᾷ, ἑτέρα δὲ γεννᾶται (Ecclus. xiv. 18; comp. xvii. 31). In Enoch xv. 4–6 an offspring that is flesh and blood is contrasted with spiritual beings who have immortal life.

The two meanings of 'inherit' are illustrated by the two renderings *obtinere* (Novatian) and *possidere* (Vulg.). See Dalman, *Words*, p. 125 ; Abbott, *The Son of Man*, p. 576. On St Paul's idea of the Kingdom of God see Sanday in *JTS.*, July 1900, pp. 481 f. ; Robertson, Bampt. Lect. ch. ii.

propensities, which would be σάρξ without αἷμα (Rom. viii. 12, 13).
The expression here refers to those who are still living, whereas
ἡ φθορά refers to those who have died.　If living flesh cannot
inherit, how much less dead and corrupted flesh.　Our present
bodies, whether living or dead, are absolutely unfitted for the
Kingdom: there must be a transformation.　See Briggs, *The
Messiah of the Apostles,* pp. 116–9; and for ἀφθαρσία, J. A.
Robinson on Eph. vi. 24.　'Flesh and blood' is treated as one
idea and has a singular verb: comp. ἕως ἂν παρέλθῃ ὁ οὐρανὸς καὶ
ἡ γῆ (Matt. v. 18): ὅπου σὴς καὶ βρῶσις ἀφανίζει (vi. 19).　Here
many witnesses have δύνανται, but δύναται (א B P) is no doubt
correct.　See J. H. Moulton, *Gr.* p. 58, and comp. Exod.
xix. 13.　The construction is found in papyri.

51.　ἰδοὺ μυστήριον ὑμῖν λέγω.　Emphatic introduction of information of great moment.　This mystery of the sudden transformation of the living has been revealed to him: comp. Rom.
xi. 25.　For μυστήριον comp. ii. 1, 7, iv. 1, xiii. 2, xiv. 2: see
Beet on ii. i. 7, pp. 60 f.　'Behold, it is a mystery that I am
telling you: all of us will not sleep, but all of us will be changed.'
The desired antithesis requires that both clauses should begin
with πάντες: hence πάντες οὐ in the first clause, not οὐ πάντες.
Two things have to be stated regarding 'all of us.'　That all of
us will undergo death is not true; that all will undergo the great
transformation is true.　Of course St Paul does not mean that
all will escape death, any more than πάντας δὲ οὐ μὴ ἴδῃς (Num.
xxiii. 13) means 'Thou shalt not see any of them.'　The first
person plural does not necessarily imply that St Paul felt confident of living till the Second Advent; but it does imply
expectation of doing so in company with most of those whom he
is addressing.　Those who die before the Advent are regarded
as exceptions.　This expectation is more strongly expressed in
the earlier letter to the Thessalonians (iv. 15); ἡμεῖς οἱ ζῶντες οἱ
περιλειπόμενοι εἰς τὴν παρουσίαν.　In the later letter (2 Cor. v. 4 f.)
the expectation seems to be less strong.　But the belief that the
Advent is near would seem to have been constant (xvi. 22; Phil.
iv. 5; comp. 1 Pet. iv. 7; Jas. v. 8; *Barnabas* 21).　Evidently
the Apostle had no idea of centuries of interval before the
Advent.　Perhaps the fact that he and all his readers did fall
asleep before the Advent had something to do with the confusion
of the text of this verse.　Knowling, p. 309.

　　The οἱ before πάντες (A) may safely be rejected.　The μέν after the first
πάντες (א A E F G K L P, Vulg. Copt.) is probably not genuine: B C* D*,
e Arm. Aeth. omit.　The other variations are more important.　οὐ κοιμηθη-
σόμεθα, πάντες δὲ ἀλλαγησόμεθα (B E K L P and MSS. known to Jerome,
Syrr. Copt. Aeth. Goth., Chrys.) is to be preferred to κοιμησόμεθα, οἱ

πάντες δὲ ἀλλαγησόμεθα (א C F G 17 and MSS. known to Jerome, Arm.), and to ἀναστησόμεθα, οὐ πάντες δὲ ἀλλαγησόμεθα (D, Latt., Hil.). See WH. ii. p. 118.

52. ἐν ἀτόμῳ, ἐν ῥιπῇ ὀφθαλμοῦ. Neither expression occurs elsewhere in N.T. or LXX : compare the classical ἐν ἀκαρεῖ χρόνου. The marvellous change from death to life and from mortal to immortal will not be a long process, but instantaneous ; and it will be final.

ἐν τῇ ἐσχάτῃ σάλπιγγι. For this idea see 1 Thess. iv. 16 ; Matt. xxiv. 31 ; Rev. viii. 2, where see Swete ; 2 Esdr. vi. 23. We need not suppose that St Paul believed that an actual trumpet would awaken and summon the dead. The language is symbolical in accordance with the apocalyptic ideas of the time. The point is that the resurrection of the dead and the transformation of the living will be simultaneous, as of two companies obeying the same signal. Here the Apostle classes himself and most of his hearers very distinctly among the living at the time of the Advent. "We, who shall not have put off the body, shall be changed, not by putting it off, but by putting on over it the immortal that shall absorb the mortal" (Evans).[*]

D* E F G have ῥοπῇ for ῥιπῇ, and A D E F G P have ἀναστήσονται for ἐγερθήσονται. σαλπίσει is a late form for σαλπίγξει, and the nom. is not the trumpet, but the trumpeter, ὁ σαλπιγκτής. Later Jewish speculation makes *God* sound a trumpet seven times at the end of the world to raise the dead. See Charles, Apocalypse of Baruch, p. 82.

53. δεῖ γὰρ τὸ φθαρτὸν τοῦτο ἐνδύσασθαι. The δεῖ looks back to the principle stated in *v.* 50 : τὸ φθαρτόν is more comprehensive than τὸ θνητόν, but the two terms are meant to be synonymous and to refer to the living rather than the dead. By τοῦτο the Apostle's own body is specially indicated (Acts xx. 34) ; and ἐνδύσασθαι (aor. of sudden change) is a metaphor which implies that there is a permanent element continuing under the new conditions. In a very real sense it is the same being which is first corruptible and then incorruptible. Compare 2 Cor. v. 4 ; Cicero (*Tusc. Disp.* i. 49), *supremus ille dies non nostri extinctionem sed commutationem affert loci* ; Seneca (*Ep. ad Lucil.* 102), *dies iste, quem tamquam extremum reformidas, aeterni natalis est.*

54. The Apostle dwells on the glorious change and repeats the details in full. As soon as it takes place, then, at that solemn moment and in this mysterious way, the prophetic utterance which stands written (Deissmann, *Bible Studies*, p. 112) will have its realization, and "the farthest-reaching of all O.T. prophecies" (Dillmann) will become an accomplished fact (γενήσεται).

[*] At the time when Philippians was written, the Apostle still believed ὁ Κύριος ἐγγύς (iv. 5), and perhaps he always did believe this.

In Isa. xxv. 8 it is said that God will swallow up death—the death which came by the hand of the Assyrian.* In the Prophet's vision the deliverance from death is limited by the necessities of his own age. The Apostle's view is much wider. He knows that all death will be swallowed up now that Christ has conquered death by rising again. The doom pronounced upon Adam (Gen. iii. 19) is removed; and the result (εἰς) is victory, absolute and everlasting triumph. Death is annihilated, and God is all in all. This thought makes the Apostle burst out into a song of triumph of death which is a free adaptation of another prophetic utterance. With the constr. compare v. 28.

It is not certain that τὸ φθαρτὸν τ. ἐνδ. ἀφθ. καὶ is part of the true text. A B D E K L P, Syrr., Chrys. support the reading; א* C* I M, Vulg. Copt. Aeth. Goth. Arm. omit. Accidental omission is possible. Deliberate insertion in conformity with the preceding v. is also possible. The balance seems to be in favour of retaining the words ; and the rhythmical solemnity of the passage seems to require them.
In LXX, εἰς νῖκος = 'for ever' (2 Sam. ii. 26 ; Job xxxvi. 7 ; Amos i. 11, viii. 7 ; etc.). Tertullian read νεῖκος : he renders *in contentionem* or *in contentione* (*De res. carn.* 51, 54). So also Cyprian (*Test.* iii. 58).

55. ποῦ σου, θάνατε, τὸ νῖκος; 'Where is that victory of yours,' hitherto so universal and so feared? It is annihilated (i. 20 ; Rom. iii. 27). The fear that hath punishment (1 John iv. 18) has vanished, and the transition out of death into life (John v. 24 ; 1 John iii. 14) has taken place. By κέντρον death is represented as a venomous creature, a scorpion or a hornet, which is rendered harmless, when it is deprived of its sting. The serpent has lost its poison-fang. The word is used of a 'goad' (Acts xxvi. 14 ; Prov. xxvi. 3) ; of the 'sting' of a bee (4 Macc. xiv. 19) ; of the 'sting' of the infernal locusts (Rev. ix. 10).

In Hos. xiii. 14, the Heb. and the LXX differ, and the differences have affected the text here, scribes having been influenced by one or the other. The νῖκος clause should precede the κέντρον clause (א B C I M 17, Vulg. Copt.), and θάνατε is right in both clauses (א B C D E F G I, Latt. Copt.) rather than ᾅδη (K L M P, Syrr. Arm. Goth. Aeth.). St Paul never uses ᾅδης, perhaps because the word might have erroneous associations for Greek readers. The AV. has 'sting' before 'victory,' and 'grave' for 'death' in the 'victory' clause.

56. The thought of death deprived of its sting suggests the thoughts of sin and of the law ; for it was by sin that death acquired power over man, and it is because there is a law to be transgressed that sin is possible (Rom. v. 13 ; vii. 7). Where there is no law, there may be faults, but there can be no rebellion,

* Theodotion has the same wording as St Paul, κατεπόθη ὁ θάν. εἰς ν. Aquila, καταποντίσει τὸν θάν. εἰς ν. LXX, the unintelligible κατέπιεν ὁ θάνατος ἰσχύσας.

no conscious defiance of what authority has prescribed. But against law there may be rebellion, and rebellion merits death. Christ by His obedience had law on His side and conquered death, because death was not His due. When the Christian is clothed with immortality, and all that is mortal is dissolved or absorbed, then sin will be abolished and the restrictions of law will be meaningless. The verse harmonizes with the context, and there is no need to suspect that it is a gloss. On the relation of sin to death see Hort on Jas. i. 15.

57. τῷ δὲ Θεῷ χάρις. Sudden transition to thanksgiving, as in 2 Cor. ii. 14; Rom. vii. 25; 1 Tim. i. 17.

τῷ διδόντι ἡμῖν τὸ νῖκος. Pres. partic.; 'Who is giving us the victory': it is a process which is continually going on, as Christians appropriate what has been won for them by Christ, and in His strength conquer sin; 2 Cor. xii. 9; 1 Thess. iv. 8; comp. Rom. viii. 37.* Quite naturally, St Paul retains the rarer form νῖκος, which has already been used (vv. 54, 55). In LXX, νῖκος is nearly as common as νίκη (1 John v. 4).

58. Practical result of this great assurance. They must get rid of the unsettled and unfruitful state of mind caused by habitual scepticism, and must learn to be firmly seated, so as to be able to resist the false teaching and other hostile forces that would carry them away (Col. i. 23). Let there be less speculation and more work. See Thorburn, *The Resurrection Narratives*, pp. 183 f., on modern speculations.

Ὥστε. See on xiv. 39. Compare especially Phil. iv. 1, where, as here, the Apostle adds ἀγαπητοί to ἀδελφοί: he rarely uses both words, but either ἀγαπητοί (x. 14) or ἀδελφοί (iii. 1; iv. 6, etc.). Here he desires to assure them that, in spite of the severe language which he has sometimes employed, there is no diminution in his affection: comp. iv. 14. *Post multas correctiones, non solum fratres, sed et dilectos appellat, ut saltem hoc remedio sublevati ad pristinam fidem reverterentur* (Atto).

ἑδραῖοι γίνεσθε. Not, 'continue to be,' but, 'become, prove yourselves to be' (x. 32, xi. 1). They have still much to learn; they are not yet stable either in belief or behaviour (vv. 2, 33). They need to be τῇ πίστει τεθεμελιωμένοι in order to become ἑδραῖοι τῇ πίστει (Ign. *Ephes.* 10): comp. Polycarp *Phil.* 10, where this is quoted. He is speaking ὡς σαλευομένοις. He says ἀμετακίνητοι, 'unmoveable' (here only), not ἀκίνητοι, 'unmoved': they must not allow themselves to be loosed from their moorings; comp. Arist. *Eth. Nic.* II. iv. 3.

περισσεύοντες ἐν τῷ ἔργῳ τοῦ Κυρίου πάντοτε. Every word tells. In the abundance of results they may be equal to Apostles

* D and Chrys. have δόντι, Vulg. *qui dedit*, which spoils the sense.

(*v.* 10); but it must be in work, not in disputation; and in the Lord's work, which He always has ready for each one of His servants to do; and there must be no relaxing of effort, no shirking. This involves κόπος, wearisome toil. But what of that, with the full knowledge which they possess of what the conditions are? Τί λέγεις; πάλιν κόπος; Ἀλλὰ στεφάνους ἔχων, καὶ ὑπὲρ τῶν οὐρανῶν (Chrys.).

ὁ κόπος ὑμῶν οὐκ ἔστιν κενὸς ἐν Κυρίῳ. This may mean either that the effort of doing the work of the Lord abundantly is no idle pastime, or that it is not fruitless, but is sure to have blessed results here and hereafter; *vv.* 10 and 14 favour the latter. If there were no Resurrection, their labour would be fruitless; but in such conditions as have been established, in such an atmosphere as that in which they work, viz. ἐν Κυρίῳ, that is impossible. We need not confine ἐν Κυρίῳ to κενός, still less to κόπος, from which it is too far removed; it probably belongs to the whole sentence. The Apostle goes on to give them an illustration of doing God's work.

ADDITIONAL NOTE ON XV. 42–44.

A considerable number of scholars, and among them J. H. Bernard, R. H. Charles, G. G. Findlay, and W. Milligan, contend that σπείρεται in *vv.* 42–44 cannot refer to the 'sowing' of the corpse in the ground. No such use of σπείρειν, it is said, has been produced. Moreover, the analogy about the difference between the seed sown and the plant that rises from it shows that St Paul cannot mean burial when he speaks of 'sowing.' His argument is that the seed is *not* dead when it is sown, but that it must die before it is quickened. In the animal world, death precedes burial; but, in vegetation, the burial of the seed precedes death, the death that is necessary for the new life. The same holds good of John xii. 24, where πεσὼν εἰς τὴν γῆν is used for being sown, and the 'falling into the earth' precedes the dying. In human existence, what precedes the death that prepares the way for resurrection is life in this world, and this is what is meant by σπείρεται.* The vital germ is placed in

---

* Calvin points out this interpretation as a possible alternative; *aut si mavis, illam similitudinem retinens praesentis vitae tempus metaphorice sationi comparat.* The original meaning of *serere* is 'to bring forth'; *non temere nec fortuito sati et creati sumus* (Cic. *Tusc.* I. xlix. 118). He speaks of a *maturitatem serendi generis humani; quod sparsum in terras atque satum, divino auctum sit animorum munere* (*De Leg.* I. ix. 24).

material surroundings, like seed in soil, and continues in them until death sets the vitality free to begin a new career under far more glorious conditions. With this interpretation the contra-diction involved in calling a corpse a σῶμα ψυχικόν is avoided; and the sudden intrusion of the thought of burial, which occurs nowhere in the argument from *v.* 12 onwards, is avoided also.

It is possible that this is correct; nevertheless, the marked inclusion of Christ's burial (καὶ ὅτι ἐτάφη) in the very brief Creed given in *vv.* 3, 4, gives considerable support to the common interpretation. Moreover, sowing is a very natural figure to use respecting the dead body of one who is to rise again.

XVI. PRACTICAL AND PERSONAL: THE CONCLUSION.

The Epistle now rapidly draws to an end with a number of brief directions, communications, salutations, exhortations, and good wishes. It will suffice to make six subdivisions; (*a*) The Collection for the Poor at Jerusalem, 1-4; (*b*) St Paul's intended Visit to Corinth, 5-9; (*c*) Timothy and Apollos commended, 10-12; (*d*) Exhortation interjected, 13, 14; (*e*) Directions respecting Stephanas and others, 15-18; (*f*) Concluding Salutations, Warning, and Benediction, 19-24.

1-4. Here, as at xv. 49, the Apostle suddenly descends from very lofty heights to matters of ordinary experience. It is as if he had suddenly checked himself in his triumphant rhapsody with the thought that 'the work of the Lord' in this life must be attended to. There is still much labour to be undertaken by those who still remain alive waiting for the final victory, and he must return to business.

St Paul had the collection of money for the poorer members of the Church in Jerusalem very much at heart, as is seen from this passage and 2 Cor. viii., ix., with which should be compared Rom. xv. 26, Gal ii. 10, and Acts xxiv. 17. In "the ablest and most convincing section of Paley's *Horae Paulinae*" (ii. 1) it is shown how these four passages, while having each their distinctive features, "fit and dovetail into one another and thus imply that all are historical." We thus have "singular evidence of the genuineness" of the documents which contain these different but thoroughly consistent accounts. See Sanday and Headlam

(p. 413), and Jowett (p. 419), on Rom. xv. 29; also the *Camb. Grk. Test.* on 2 Cor. viii. and ix. The directions given here are so brief that we may suppose that the Corinthians already knew a good deal about the matter, possibly from Titus, who may have been in Corinth before this. Moreover, Titus may have been the bearer of this letter, and in that case would be able to tell them in detail what the Apostle desired them to do. We know that Titus did organize the collection at Corinth. In 2 Cor. ix. 1, St Paul says that 'it is superfluous for him to write' on the subject. Nevertheless, in his intense anxiety about the fund, he says a great deal more than he says here, supporting the appeal with strong arguments.

His anxiety about the collection is very intelligible. The distress at Jerusalem was great and constant. Jews often made collections for impoverished Jews; Christians must do at least as much. It was specially to be wished that Gentile Christians should help Jewish Christians, and thus promote better feeling between the two bodies. Still more was it to be wished that Christians at Corinth, where the Apostle's work was regarded with suspicion and dislike by the Jewish party, should send liberal help to Christians at Jerusalem, where the suspicion and dislike originated. This would prove two things; (1) that his Apostolic authority was effectual in a Gentile Church, and (2) that he had loyal affection for the Church at Jerusalem.

Augustine suggests that the poverty at Jerusalem was the result of the community of goods (Acts iv. 32), a view that is still held, and is probably part of the explanation: communism without careful organization of labour is sure to end in disaster. But there were other causes. Jerusalem had a pauperized population, dependent on the periodical influx of visitors. The Jewish world, from Cicero's time at least, supported the poor of Jerusalem by occasional subventions. As the Christian Jews came to be regarded as a distinct body, they would lose their share in these doles; and the 'communism' of Acts iv. 32 was but a temporary remedy. Most of the converts were, therefore, poor at the outset. They were probably 'boycotted' and otherwise persecuted by the unconverted Jews (1 Thess. ii. 14; Jas. ii. 6, v. 1-6), and their position would be similar to that of Hindoo Christians excluded from their caste, or Protestants in the West of Ireland. And the belief that 'the Lord was at hand' (*v.* 22)

may have checked industry at Jerusalem, as it did at Thessalonica
(2 Thess. iii. 10; *Didache* xii.). See Knowling on Acts xx. 4,
p. 422; Beet on 2 Cor. viii. 15, pp. 426 f.; Hort, *Romans and
Ephesians*, pp. 39 f., 173; Ramsay, *St Paul the Traveller*,
pp. 287 f.; Rendall, *Expositor*, Nov. 1893, p. 321.

1. Περὶ δὲ τῆς λογίας. The abrupt transition leads us to
suppose that the Corinthians had asked about the matter: comp
vii. 1, viii. 1, xii. 1. At any rate the sudden introduction of this
topic implies that they were already acquainted with it; comp.
the sudden transition to Apollos in *v.* 12. St Paul uses seven
words in speaking of this collection; λογία (*v.* 1); χάρις (*v.* 3;
2 Cor. viii. 4); κοινωνία (2 Cor. viii. 4, ix. 13; Rom. xv. 26);
διακονία (2 Cor. viii. 4, ix. 1, 12, 13); ἁδρότης (2 Cor. viii. 20);
εὐλογία (2 Cor. ix. 5); λειτουργία (2 Cor. ix. 12); to which may
be added ἐλεημοσύναι (Acts xxiv. 17, in the report of his speech
before Felix) and προσφοραί (*ibid.*). The classical word συλλογή
is not found in N.T.; in LXX, only of David's scrip (1 Sam.
xvii. 40). It used to be supposed that λογία or λογεία was found
only here and in ecclesiastical writers (Ellicott *ad loc.*, Suicer, ii.
p. 247); and Edwards thought that St Paul had coined the
word. Deissmann (*Bible Studies*, pp. 142 f.) shows that it was
"used in Egypt from the 2nd cent. B.C. at the latest," and gives
various examples from papyri: in one, λογεία is associated with
λειτουργία. He thinks that in 2 Cor. ix. 5 the first εὐλογίαν may
be a corruption of λογείαν. See also *Light*, pp. 104, 366.

εἰς τοὺς ἁγίους. He does not mean that the Christians at
Jerusalem were in a special sense 'holy'; he indicates *why* the
Corinthians ought to give. Those in need are their fellow-
Christians (i. 2; 2 Cor. i. 1): *sic mavult dicere quam 'pauperes';
id facit ad impetrandum* (Beng.). He perhaps also indicates
that those in need were the source and original headquarters of
the Corinthians' Christianity (Rom. xv. 27). Although he does
not say so, we might suppose from this passage that all the
Jerusalem Christians were poverty-stricken. Rom. xv. 26 shows
that this was not so: it was εἰς τοὺς πτωχοὺς τῶν ἁγίων τῶν ἐν Ἱερ.
that the κοινωνία was to be made. With this use of εἰς *c. acc.* for
the *dat. commodi* comp. 2 Cor. viii. 4, ix. 1, 13: it is found in
LXX, and is probably not a Hebraism but an Alexandrian idiom.
It is found in papyri; Deissmann, pp. 117 f.

ὥσπερ διέταξα ταῖς ἐκκλ. τ. Γ. 'Just as I made arrangements
for the Churches of Galatia.' There is a tone of authority in the
verb; as Chrysostom remarks, "He did not say, 'I exhorted
and advised,' but, 'I made arrangements,' as being more absolute;
and he does not cite the case of one city, but of a whole nation."
And the compound verb indicates that *detailed* directions had

been given to the Galatians,—possibly by St Paul in person.
What follows is no doubt a summary of these directions, to be
enlarged by Titus. 'The Churches of Galatia' are mentioned
to show the Corinthians that they are not the only Gentiles who
are asked to contribute to the support of Jewish Christians,
and also to move them to imitate such good examples. *Galat-
arum exemplum Corinthiis, Corinthiorum exemplum Macedonibus*
(2 Cor. ix. 2), *Corinthiorum et Macedonum Romanis* (Rom. xv.
26) *proponit* (Beng.).

οὕτως καὶ ὑμεῖς ποιήσατε. 'So also do *you* act.' He writes
with confidence: he has only to give directions, and they are
sure to be followed. There is none of the anxious pleading of
2 Cor. viii., ix. And it was perhaps this apparent peremptoriness
which his opponents used as an argument against him. See
G. H. Rendall, p. 107. We may infer from this that the plan
adopted in Galatia had not proved unsuccessful. The ὥσπερ . . .
οὕτως implies that the details of that plan are to be exactly
followed, and ὑμεῖς is emphatic (Gal. ii. 10). We need not
infer from Gal. vi. 6, 7, that the appeal to the Galatians had
failed; the Apostle is writing there respecting the support of
teachers in Galatia, not of the poor at Jerusalem.

2. κατὰ μίαν σαββάτου. 'On every first day of the week.'
The expression is Hebraistic; Mark xvi. 2; Luke xxiv. 1; John
xx. 1, 19; Acts xx. 7. For the sing. σάββατον = 'week,' Luke
xviii. 12; [Mark xvi. 9]. This is our earliest evidence respecting
the early consecration of the first day of the week by the
Apostolic Church. Apparently, the name 'Lord's Day' was not
yet in use, and the first day of the week is never called 'the
sabbath' in Scripture. If it was right to do good on the Jewish
sabbath (Matt. xii. 12; Mark iii. 4), how much more on the
Lord's Day? καὶ γὰρ ἡ ἡμέρα ἱκανὴ ἦν ἀγαγεῖν εἰς ἐλεημοσύνην,
for it reminded them of the untold blessings which they had
received (Chrys.). Hastings, *DB*. iii. p. 140; *D. Chr. Ant.* ii.
p. 2031; Knowling, *Test. of St Paul to Christ*, pp. 281 f.

ἕκαστος ὑμῶν. It is assumed that every one, however poor,
will give something; but the giving is to be neither compulsory
nor oppressive. Some of them would be slaves.

παρ' ἑαυτῷ τιθέτω θησαυρίζων. This cannot mean, 'Let
him assign a certain sum as he is disposed, and put it into the
Church treasury.' It is improbable that at that time there was
any Church treasury, and not until much later was money
collected during public worship. Each is to lay by something
weekly 'in his own house, forming a little hoard, which will
become a heavenly treasure' (Matt. vi. 19–21; Luke xii. 21).
Chrysostom says that the accumulation was to be made in private,

because the additions might be so small that the donor would be ashamed to make them in the congregation. The Apostle virtually says, 'Become a guardian of holy possessions, a self-elected steward of the poor'—γενοῦ φύλαξ χρημάτων ἱερῶν, αὐτοχειροτόνητος οἰκονόμος πενήτων.*

ὅ τι ἂν εὐοδῶται. 'Whatsoever he may prosper in,' 'whatever success he may have,' 'whereinsoever he is prospered by God'; *quod pro Dei benignitate licuerit* (Beza). The idea of a prosperous journey (ὁδός)has dropped out of the word. The verb is frequent in this more general sense in LXX, especially in Chronicles, Daniel, and Tobit: comp. the Testaments, *Judah* i. 6; *Gad.* vii. 1. It is not certain what tense εὐοδῶται is. WH. (ii. *App.* p. 172) decide for the perfect; either εὐόδωται, perf. indic., or εὐοδῶται, a very rare perf. mid. subjunctive. J. H. Moulton (*Gr.* i. p. 54) follows Blass and Findlay in deciding for the pres. subj., which seems to be more probable. In any case, the meaning is that the amount is to be fixed by the giver in proportion to his weekly gains; and there is no dictation as to the right proportion, whether a tenth, or more, or less. A tenth is little for some, impossible for others; but week by week each would see how much or how little he had got, and would act accordingly.

ἵνα μὴ ὅταν ἔλθω τότε λογίαι γίνωνται. 'So that, whenever I come, collections may not be going on then.'† Each will have his contribution ready, instead of having to decide at the last moment how much he ought to give, and how the money is to be found. St Paul does not wish to go round begging, when he comes; he will have other things to do. Moreover, he does not wish to put pressure upon them by asking in person (2 Cor. ix. 7): he desires to leave them quite free. The τότε is emphatic; 'then' would be the worst possible time.

σαββάτων (K L M) is an obvious correction of the less usual σαββάτου (A B C D E F G I P): א* has σαββατω. For ἂν, B I M have ἐάν. εὐοδῶται (א*B D E F G L P) is to be preferred to εὐοδωθῇ (A C I K M). Vulg. has *quod ei bene placuerit*, which seems to imply a reading ὅ τι ἐὰν εὐδοκῇ, and Latin translations of Chrys. have *quod sibi videatur* or *videbitur*. ὅταν εὐοδῶται is pure conjecture.

* Calvin remarks that Christians, who know that they have God for their debtor, ought to feel the blessedness of giving, when even a heathen poet (Mart. v. 42) could write, *Quas dederis solas semper habebis opes*: and Primasius says that by giving a little at a time they will not feel oppressed, and so can be the cheerful givers who are beloved by God. Compare καὶ συνήγανον ἀργύριον καθὰ ἑκάστου ἠδύνατο ἡ χείρ (Bar. i. 6).

† It illustrates the caprice of the AV. that in *v.* 1 λογία is rendered 'collection,' and in *v.* 2 'gathering.' Tyndale and the Genevan have 'gathering' in both places, while the Rhemish has 'collection' in both. Contrast the ὅταν in 2, 3, 5 with the ἐάν in 10.

3. ὅταν δὲ παραγένωμαι κ.τ.λ. 'But whenever I arrive,
whomsoever ye may approve, these with letters (commendatory)
will I send to take your bounty to Jerusalem.' He is represented
as using the same verb respecting this subject in his speech
before Felix (Acts xxiv. 17); ἐλεημοσύνας ποιήσων εἰς τὸ ἔθνος μου
παρεγενόμην. AV., RV., and various modern scholars take δι'
ἐπιστολῶν with δοκιμάσητε, in which case the letters are written by
the Corinthians as credentials for the delegates to be sent to
Jerusalem with the money: so also Arm., Calv., Beza. But it is
more natural to take the words with πέμψω, in front of which
they are placed in emphatic contrast to σὺν ἐμοί which is similarly
placed before πορεύσονται. He will either write letters with
which to send the delegates (2 Cor. iii. 1; Acts ix. 2), or he will
take the delegates with himself. The delegates were not to be
sent off until the Apostle arrived at Corinth. What need, therefore, for the Corinthians to write letters? Syr., Copt., Aeth.,
Chrys., Tisch., Treg., and others take δι' ἐπ. with πέμψω. 'Letters'
is probably a true plural, not the "plural of category." The
Apostle would write to more than one person at Jerusalem.*

In N.T., δοκιμάζειν often implies that what has been tested
(iii. 13) has stood the test and been approved (xi. 28; Rom. i.
28, ii. 18; 1 Thess. ii. 4, where see Milligan), as here. Just as
St Paul does not dictate what proportion of their gains they
ought to give, so he does not select the bearers of the fund, still
less claim to have charge of it himself. In no case will he do that,
to avoid all suspicion of enriching himself out of it. Those who
find the money are to entrust it to persons tested and approved
by themselves, and these persons are to have letters from the
Apostle as credentials, unless he goes himself. The two aorists,
παραγένωμαι and δοκιμάσητε, indicate that his arrival and the
selection of the delegates are regarded as contemporaneous.†

Very often ἀποφέρειν does not mean 'carry *away*' so much
as 'take *home*,' 'bring *to its destination*,' and in some cases
'bring *back*.' It was not the removal of the money from Corinth,
but its being conveyed to Jerusalem, that was the important
point: comp. Luke xvi. 22. And he speaks of it as their
'gracious gift,' τὴν χάριν ὑμῶν (2 Cor. viii. 4–7, 19), *beneficentiam
vestram* (Beza), because he would regard it as free bounty, like
the graciousness of God.

* In Galatians, St Paul uses the later Graecized political form Ἱεροσόλυμα
of the actual city (i. 17, 18, ii. 1), and the ancient theocratic Hebrew form
Ἱερουσαλήμ of the typical city (iv. 25, 26; comp. Heb. xii. 22; Rev. iii. 12;
xxi. 2, 10). But here and Rom. xv. 19, 25, 26, 31 he uses Ἱερουσαλήμ of
the actual city, "lovingly and reverently," as of the mother Church and the
home of suffering saints. See Deissmann, *Bible Studies*, p. 316.

‡ Papyri seem to show that οὓς ἐὰν δοκιμάσητε was a phrase in common
use. On commendatory letters see Deissmann, *Light*, p. 158.

4. ἐὰν δὲ ἄξιον ᾖ τοῦ κἀμὲ πορεύεσθαι. 'But if it be fit that I also should go.' The ἄξιον is purposely put without a substantive, and πορεύεσθαι is used in its common sense of going on a mission, going with a purpose, with a work to be done : see Westcott on John vii. 33. 'If the amount collected makes it worth while for *me* also to go on this business' is another possible meaning. He could not abandon other work in order to present a paltry sum ; and an Apostle could not take the lead in so unworthy a mission. It would look like approving niggardliness. There is no pride of office here, but proper respect for himself and them. It is with consciousness of his authority that he says, 'they shall go with me,' not 'I will go with them.'

Were the Corinthians niggardly, or at least somewhat backward in giving? One is inclined to think so by the doubt expressed here : see also ix. 11, 12 ; 2 Cor. xi. 8, 9, xii. 13. No Corinthian delegates are mentioned Acts xx. 4. That might mean that the Corinthians sent their contribution independently. But it might mean that they were not represented because their contribution was so small. St Paul twice went to Jerusalem with money for the poor (Acts xi. 29, 30, xxiv. 17). It was perhaps because he was known to have charge of such funds that he was expected by Felix to pay for his release (xxiv. 26).

5-9. He gives further information about the proposed (*v.* 3) visit to Corinth. He will come, but he must postpone his visit for the present. This postponement will be compensated by the increased length of his visit, when he does come ; and they will be able to help him for his next journey. He cannot, however, leave Ephesus just yet, for there is great opportunity for good work, and his presence there is necessary. This will give them all the more time for laying money by for the Jerusalem poor.

5. ὅταν Μ. διέλθω, Μ. γὰρ διέρχομαι. 'Whenever I shall have journeyed through Macedonia, for I intend journeying through M.' In Acts (xiii. 6, xiv. 24, xv. 3, 41, xviii. 23, xix. 1, 21, xx. 2), διέρχομαι seems to be almost a technical term for a missionary tour or evangelistic journey, the district traversed being in the accusative without a preposition : Ramsay, *St Paul*, pp. 72, 384 ; Knowling on Acts xiii. 6. In contrast to this tour through Macedonia he intends making a long stay (παραμενῶ) at Corinth.

The erroneous note at the end of this Epistle, " written from Philippi," is based on a misunderstanding of διέρχομαι : as if it meant 'I am at the present moment passing through M.,' instead of 'M. I pass through,' *i.e.* 'such is my intention ; I make no long stay anywhere.' It is clear from *v.* 8 that he writes from Ephesus.

6. πρὸς ὑμᾶς δὲ τυχὸν παραμενῶ. 'But with *you* (first, in emphatic contrast to Macedonia) perchance I shall stay or even winter.' With πρὸς ὑμᾶς comp. Gal. i. 18 ; Matt. xiii. 56 ; and see Westcott on John i. 1 and 1 John i. 2. The πρός implies more than μετά or σύν, and means 'in active intercourse with you.' The acc. abs. τυχόν is not found elsewhere in Biblical Greek, but it occurs in Plato and Xenophon : * comp. the colloquial "happen I shall come." In xiv. 10, εἰ τύχοι. His remaining at Corinth through the winter might be necessary, because navigation then would be perilous or impossible. After 14th Sept. navigation was considered dangerous; after 11th Nov. it ceased till 5th March : see Blass on Acts xxvii. 9 ; Ramsay, *St Paul*, p. 322 ; and Zahn, *Introduction to N.T.*, i. p. 319. Orelli on Hor. *Od.* i. iv. 2 quotes Vegetius, *De re mil.* v. 9, *ex die iii. Id. Novembr. usque in diem vi. Id. Mart. maria claudi.*

ἵνα ὑμεῖς με προπέμψητε κ.τ.λ. 'In order that *you* may be the people to set me forward on my journey, whithersoever I may go.' He would rather have his 'send-off' from them. For this, προπέμπειν is the usual verb (2 Cor. i. 16 ; Rom. xv. 24 ; Acts xv. 3, etc.). He is not asking for money or provisions ; the verb does not necessarily mean more than good wishes and prayers. The last clause is purposely indefinite (οὗ ἐὰν π.). He may go to Jerusalem, but that depends upon various circumstances. With οὗ for οἷ comp. Luke x. 1, xxiv. 28 ; it is freq. in late Greek (Gen. xx. 13, xxviii. 15 ; etc.).

WH., following B M 67, prefer καταμενῶ to παραμενῶ (אACDE FGIP). There would be temptation to make the verb similar to παρα-χειμάσω, all the more so as παραμένειν is more common (Phil. i. 25 ; Heb. vii. 23 ; Jas. i. 25) than καταμένειν (Acts i. 13). Nevertheless the balance for παραμενῶ is considerable.

7. οὐ θέλω γὰρ ὑμᾶς ἄρτι ἐν παρόδῳ ἰδεῖν. 'For I do not care in your case to get a sight (aor.) just in passing.' † For the third time in two verses πρὸς ὑμᾶς, ὑμεῖς, ὑμᾶς), he lays an affectionate emphasis on the pronoun. In the case of such friends as they are, a mere passing visit would be very unsatisfying ; all the more so, because there is much to be arranged at Corinth (xi. 34). There is no emphasis on ἄρτι, as if he meant, 'I paid a passing visit to you once, and it was so painful that I do not mean to repeat the experiment now.' The ἄρτι fits in well with the hypothesis of a previous short visit (2 Cor. xii. 14, xiii. 1),

---

* It has been found in a letter written on a leaden tablet from Athens about B.C. 400 (Deissmann, *New Light on the N.T.*, p. 56).

† With this use of πάροδος compare 2 Sam. xii. 4, ἦλθε πάροδος τῷ ἀνδρὶ τῷ πλουσίῳ, 'there came a *visit* to the rich man' ; and Wisd. ii. 5, where life is called σκιᾶς πάροδος, the 'passing of a shadow.' In Gen. xxxviii. 14, ἐν παρόδῳ seems to mean 'on a by-way' or 'by the wayside' (see Skinner *ad loc.*). The word occurs nowhere else in N.T.

but it does not imply it : it need not be much stronger than
'just.' But he is thinking less of their need of him to keep them
in order (*nam et medicus ibi moram habet ubi plures aegrotant*),
than of his need of them to satisfy his yearning. Lightfoot,
who contends for the previous short visit, says that this passage
cannot be used as evidence for it (*Biblical Essays*, p. 275, note).

χρόνον τινα. Emphatic : 'For I am hoping to stay on in
intercourse with you for some little time.' He is looking forward
to living among them. He does not say ' to stay on *at Corinth*' :
it is the people, not the place, that he cares about. Excepting
i. 2, he never mentions Corinth, and then only as their home.

ἐὰν ὁ Κύριος ἐπιτρέψῃ. It is of no importance whether
this means God or Christ. But there may be point in the
change from θελήσῃ (iv. 19), 'If the Lord *wills* me to do this
painful thing,' to ἐπιτρέψῃ, 'If He *allows* me this pleasure'
(Heb. vi. 3). This, however, cannot be pressed : Jas. iv. 15 ;
Acts xviii. 21. St Paul's own practice shows that it is not
necessary always to express this condition when announcing
one's plans (*v.* 5; Rom. xv. 28 ; Acts xix. 21). Ben Sira is
said to have ruled that no one ought to say that he will do
anything without first saying, "If the Lord will"; and both
St Paul and St James may be influenced by a form of Jewish
piety which was sure to commend itself to Christians. Mayor
on James iv. 15 has collected various examples from Greek
and Roman writers, but the O.T. does not supply any. Deissmann (*Bible Studies*, p. 252) gives several illustrations from
papyri ; and see Eur. *Alc.* 780–5. Hort (*Romans and Ephesians*,
pp. 42 f.) points out how uncertain St Paul's future must have
seemed to him (Rom. i. 10).

'For I hope' (RV.) is to be preferred to 'But I trust' (AV.) : ἐλπίζω
γάρ (‭א‬ A B C D E F G I M P), ἐλπίζω δέ (K L) : ἐπιτρέψῃ (‭א‬ A B C I M),
ἐπιτρέπῃ (D E F G K).

8. 'But I propose to stay on at Ephesus until Pentecost.'
Evidently he is writing in or near Ephesus, and probably about
Easter (v. 7, xv. 20). At that time navigation would have
begun again, and therefore it would be possible for him to
come. It does not much matter whether we read ἐπιμενῶ
(= παραμενῶ, παραχειμάσω) or ἐπιμένω (= διέρχομαι) : in either
case he is expressing his intention. WH. prefer ἐπιμένω, 'I am
staying on.' Pentecost is probably mentioned as a rough
indication of time, a few weeks later. He does not mean
that he must keep the Feast of Pentecost at Ephesus. His
reasons for staying on are quite different. There is a grand
opening for effectual work, and there is a powerful opposition :
he must utilize the one and check the other.

9. θύρα γάρ μοι ἀνέῳγεν μεγάλη καὶ ἐνεργής. 'For a door is standing open for me, great and effective.' The metaphor of a door for an opportunity is simple enough (2 Cor. ii. 12; Col. iv. 3, where see Lightfoot). In all three places an *opening* for preaching the Gospel seems to be meant, although in 2 Cor. ii. 12 the meaning might be that Troas was a good avenue for reaching the country beyond (Ramsay in Hastings, *DB*. iv. p. 814). It is possible that εἴσοδος is used in a similar sense 1 Thess. i. 9, ii. 1. In Acts xiv. 27 the 'door' is opened to the hearers, not to the preachers. But it is not quite clear what ἐνεργής means, or in what sense a door can be called ἐνεργής. Probably St Paul is thinking more of the opportunity than of the 'door.' The 'door' means an opportunity, and he applies to it an epithet which suits the fact better than the symbol. It may mean either 'effective, influential, productive of good results,' or 'calling for much activity, full of employment'; Philem. 6; Heb. iv. 12. In Heb. iv. 12, the Vulg. has *efficax*; in Philem. 6 and here, *evidens* (other Latin texts, *manifesta*), which is a translation of ἐναργής, a word which is not found in Biblical Greek; nor is ἐνεργής found in LXX. On the 'opened door' given to the Church in Philadelphia (Rev. iii. 8), see Swete *ad loc.* and Ramsay, *Letters to the Seven Churches*, p. 404. See also Deissmann, *Light*, p. 302.

ἀντικείμενοι πολλοί. 'There are many opposing my entrance,' hindering him from making use of the great opportunity (Phil. i. 20). Among these are the wild beasts of xv. 32, and they would include both Jews and heathen. Acts xix. shows how true this estimate of the situation proved. "The superstition of all Asia was concentrated at Ephesus. Throughout the early centuries the city mob, superstitious, frivolous, swayed by the most common-place motives, was everywhere the most dangerous and unfailing enemy of Christianity, and often carried the imperial officials further than they wished in the way of persecution" (Ramsay, *St Paul*, p. 277). But this determines St Paul, not to fly, but to stay on: *quod alios terruisset, Paulum invitat* (Grotius).

The intransitive ἀνέῳγεν is late Greek for ἀνέῳκται.

10–12. His intended stay at Corinth reminds him of the visit which Timothy is to pay in preparation for his (iv. 17); and the thought of the helper who has already started reminds him of another helper, Apollos, who refuses to start at present.

10. Ἐὰν δὲ ἔλθῃ Τ. Timothy had been sent with Erastus from Ephesus to Corinth; but as he had to go through Macedonia (Acts xix. 22), and as his time was limited (*v.* 11), St Paul did not feel sure that he would reach Corinth; and he possibly did not do so. In 2 Cor. we read a good deal about the visit of Titus to Corinth, but nothing is said about Timothy's visit. On the other hand, while the Apostle explains and defends his own changes of plan about visiting Corinth, he says nothing about Timothy's having failed to visit them. If Timothy is the ἀδικηθείς of 2 Cor. vii. 12, he must have reached Corinth and have been grossly insulted by some one; but more probably the ἀδικηθείς is St Paul himself. Timothy was in Macedonia when 2 Cor. was written (i. 1), and perhaps had never been further.*

βλέπετε ἵνα ἀφόβως γένηται πρὸς ὑμᾶς. 'See that he comes to feel at home with you without fear': comp. Col. iv. 17; 2 John 8; but βλέπετε μή (viii. 9, x. 12; Gal. v. 15; Col. ii. 8, etc.) is more common than βλέπετε ἵνα. They are to take care that there is no painful awkwardness in Timothy's intercourse with them. Was Timothy timid? There are passages which agree with such a supposition, although they do not necessarily imply it (1 Tim. v. 21–23; 2 Tim. i. 6–8, ii. 1, 3, 15, iv. 1, 2). See Hastings, *DB*. iv. p. 768). He was certainly young, for some eight years later St Paul still speaks of his νεότης (1 Tim. iv. 12); and the Corinthians could certainly be rude, even to the Apostle himself (2 Cor. x. 10).

'For he is working the work of the Lord (xv. 58), as I also am.' Therefore, if they put difficulties in Timothy's way, they will be hindering the work which God has given to the Apostle to do: iv. 17; Phil. ii. 19–21.

κἀγώ (‭א‬ A C K L P), καὶ ἐγώ (D E F G), ἐγώ (B M 67). WH. adopt the last, on the same evidence as καταμενῶ (*v.* 6). In Luke ii. 48, xvi. 9, and Acts x. 26, καὶ ἐγώ seems to be right; almost everywhere else κἀγώ is the better reading, but the evidence is frequently divided. In the three exceptions the ἐγώ is rather pointedly co-ordinated with some one else. See Gregory, *Prolegomena*, p. 96.

11. μή τις οὖν αὐτὸν ἐξουθενήσῃ. 'Let no one therefore set him at nought—treat him as of no account' (i. 28, vi. 4; 2 Cor. x. 10; Gal. iv. 14; 1 Thess. v. 20). Except Mark ix. 12, the verb is found only in Paul and Luke. It is stronger than καταφρονείτω (1 Tim. iv. 12; comp. xi. 22). Beng. quotes, νεώτερος ἐγώ εἰμι καὶ ἐξουδενωμένος (Ps. cxix. 141 : *adolescentulus sum ego et contemptus*; but here the Vulg. has *spernat*, with *contemnere* for καταφρονεῖν.

ἐν εἰρήνῃ. To be taken with προπέμψατε, not with ἵνα ἔλθῃ, which would have little point. 'When he departs, let him see that he has your good will, and that he leaves no bad feeling in any of you.' 'In peace' at the conclusion of his intercourse with them will be a fitting result of 'without fear' at the beginning of it. The last clause shows *why* they ought

* Lightfoot, *Biblical Essays*, p. 276; Zahn, *Introd. to N.T.*, i. p. 344.

to set Timothy forward on his journey with peace and good will; he will be on his way to the Apostle, who is expecting him.

μετὰ τῶν ἀδελφῶν. Erastus is the only one mentioned in Acts xix. 22; but there may have been others, or St Paul may have expected others. The words need not mean more than that Timothy is not likely to come alone. This, however, is so unimportant a meaning that some prefer taking μετὰ τ. ἀδ. with ἐκδέχομαι: 'I am expecting him and so are the brethren.' This is an awkward construction, but it has more point. 'The brethren' in this case will be the same as 'the brethren' in v. 12, viz. those who brought the letter from Corinth and are waiting to take back the Apostle's reply. The meaning would then be, 'Send him back to me in peace, and then the brethren who are waiting for him will be able to start with my answer to you.'

12. Περὶ δε Ἀπολλώ. This looks as if the Corinthians had asked that Apollos should visit them again (v. 1, vii. 1, 25, viii. 1, xii. 1). At any rate St Paul knew that they would be glad to have Apollos among them once more, and he is anxious to assure them that he is quite willing that Apollos should come. He is not jealous of the able and attractive Alexandrian, and is not at all afraid that he may join the Apollos party (i. 12, iii. 4–6, iv. 6; Tit. iii. 13). He has urged him strongly to go with the brethren who are to take 1 Cor. to Corinth, and it is not his fault that Apollos does not do so.

καὶ πάντως οὐκ ἦν θέλημα ἵνα ἔλθῃ κ.τ.λ. 'And, in spite of all I could say, he had no wish to come *now*; but he will come whenever the right time arrives.' The παρεκάλεσα αὐτόν shows whose 'will' is meant; 'I exhorted and entreated him, and there was absolutely no wish to come at present.' Chrysostom assumes that it is the will of Apollos that is the impediment, and points out how St Paul excuses himself without blaming Apollos. To suppose that the will of God is meant (Theoph., Beng., Evans) is at variance with the context. When St Paul means the will of God, which is very frequently, he says so (i. 1; 2 Cor. i. 1, viii. 5, etc.).* In the N.T., πάντως

---

* But see Lightfoot, *On Revision*, p. 118, who quotes Ign. *Ephes.* 20, *Rom.* 1, *Smyr.* 1; where, however, the context shows that the Divine will is meant, and where some texts have τοῦ Θεοῦ expressed.

It is quite clear that St Paul did not regard Apollos as the leader of the Apollos party, any more than he regarded Peter as leader of the Cephas party, or himself as leader of the Paul party. But it is possible that Apollos had some reason, which the Apostle does not care to mention, for not wishing to return to Corinth then. Origen speaks of him as being ἐπίσκοπος at Corinth.

is found only in Paul and Luke (ix. 10; Luke iv. 23; Acts
xxviii. 4): it expresses strong affirmation, *utique* (Vulg.). The
νῦν softens the refusal: Apollos has not made up his mind
never to visit Corinth again, but he cannot be induced to
come now. Although St Paul was not afraid that Apollos
would join the Apollos party, Apollos may have been afraid
that this party would try to capture him. If this is correct,
ὅταν εὐκαιρήσῃ may have special meaning. Just as οὗ ἐὰν
πορεύωμαι (*v.* 6) suggests, 'It depends upon you whether I go
to Jerusalem or not,' so this might suggest, 'It depends upon
you whether he comes soon or not.' The proper καιρός rests
with the Corinthians; Apollos will not come while there is an
Apollos party in opposition to the Apostle. The ἦν implies
that Apollos is not with St Paul at the time of writing: 'when
I spoke to him, there was no wish at all to come now.' But
εὐκαιρήσῃ (Mark vi. 31; Acts xvii. 21; not in LXX) need not
imply more than that Apollos was at present not free to come;
for which meaning εὖ σχολῆς ἔχειν would be better Greek.
On the work of Apollos at Corinth see Knowling on Acts
xviii. 24, 25.

Before πολλὰ παρεκάλεσα, ℵ* D* E F G, Latt. Goth. insert δηλῶ ὑμῖν
ὅτι, *vobis notum facio quoniam*: A B C K L M P, Syrr. Copt. Aeth. Arm.
omit.

For πολλά, adverbial, comp. *v.* 19; Rom. xvi. 6, 12; it is frequent in
Mark (v. 10, 23, 38, 43, etc.).

13, 14. There is probably no thought of Apollos in this abrupt
transition, such as, 'Do not put your trust in any teacher, however competent; you must look to your own conduct.' St Paul
means to bring the letter to a close and begins his final exhortations. In five clear and crisp charges he gathers together the
duties which he has been inculcating, the duties of a Christian
soldier. Four of these have reference to spiritual foes and perils,
while the last sums up their duty to one another. They are an
army in the field, and they must be alert, steadfast, courageous,
strong; and in all things united. "The four imperatives are
directed respectively against the heedlessness, fickleness, child-
ishness, and moral enervation of the Corinthians" (Findlay).
Comp. vii. 29–31, x. 12, 13, xv. 1, xiv. 20, ix. 24, xiii.

13. Γρηγορεῖτε. This charge seems to have been often given
by our Lord, especially at the close of His ministry; Mark xiii.
34, 35, 37, xiv. 34, 37, 38, and parallels; and μακάριος ὁ
γρηγορῶν is one of the seven Beatitudes in Revelation (xvi. 15;
comp. iii. 2, 3; Matt. xxiv. 42). For its use as a military charge
see 1 Macc. xii. 27 of Jonathan the high priest to his men, and
for its metaphorical use, as here, γρηγόρει, ἀκοίμητον πνεῦμα κεκτη

μένος (Ign. *Polyc.* 1) : comp. 1 Thess. v. 6, 10 ; Col. iv. 2 ; 1 Pet.
v. 8. The verb is a late formation from ἐγρήγορα, and is found
in the later books of the LXX, in the Psalms of Solomon, and in
the Testaments of the XII. Patriarchs. Watchfulness against
various enemies and dangers and watchfulness for the coming of
Christ are specially meant here.

στήκετε ἐν τῇ πίστει. The warning in x. 12 unites this
charge with the preceding one : comp. Rom. v. 2, xi. 20 ; Eph.
iv. 13 ; 2 Thess. ii. 15. 'The faith' means belief in the Gospel
as a whole, and especially in the atonement won by Christ's
death on the Cross (i.) and in the life guaranteed by His
Resurrection (xv.). There must be no desertion, no λειποταξία,
with regard to that. These first two charges have reference to
the Christian warrior awaiting attack ; the next two refer to the
actual combat.

ἀνδρίζεσθε. 'Play the man,' 'act like men,' *viriliter agite*
(Vulg.). The verb occurs here only in N.T., but is common in
LXX in exhortations ; Deut. xxxi. 6, 7, 23 ; Josh. i. 6, 7, 9, 18,
etc. In 2 Sam. x. 12 and Ps. xxvii. 14, xxxi. 25, it is combined
with κραταιοῦσθαι, as here. Comp. the dying charge of
Mattathias to his sons ; 'And ye, my children, be strong, and
show yourselves men in behalf of the law' (1 Macc. ii. 64).
Arist. *Eth Nic.* III. vi. 12 and other illustrations in Wetstein.

κραταιοῦσθε. 'Be not only manly but mighty ; gain the
mastery' (Eph. iii. 16) : κραταιός (1 Pet. v. 6) and κράτος (Eph. i.
19, vi. 10 ; Col. i. 11 ; 1 Tim. vi. 16) are uniformly used of God.

14. πάντα ὑμῶν ἐν ἀγάπῃ γινέσθω. He is glancing back at
the party-divisions, at the selfish disorder at the Lord's Supper,
and at their jealousy in the possession of special charismata,
and is recalling xiii. Chrysostom has μετὰ ἀγάπης for ἐν ἀγάπῃ,
probably through inadvertence ; there seems to be no such
reading. The change is for the worse.* St Paul says more
than that everything they do must be accompanied with love :
love must be very atmosphere in which their lives move. This
love is the affection which all Christians are bound to cherish for
one another and all mankind. The phrase ἐν ἀγάπῃ is specially
frequent in Ephesians (i. 4, iii. 18, iv. 2, 15, 16, v. 2) and
always in this sense rather than in that of our love to God or of
His to us.

15-18. He remembers some other directions which must
be given before he concludes : comp. Rom. xvi. 17. He has
spoken of his own fellow-workers, Timothy and Apollos, who are
to visit them. He now says a word in commendation of some

* The AV. has the same weak rendering ; 'with charity,' following
Beza's *cum charitate.*

among themselves whose services to the Church ought to command esteem and deference as well as love. Perhaps he had heard that those whom he mentions had been treated with disrespect. Dobschütz, *Probleme*, pp. 66, 69.

15. Παρακαλῶ δὲ ὑμᾶς, ἀδελφοί. 'Now I beseech you, my brothers,'—and then he breaks off in order to mention something which will induce them to grant his request. Dionysius the Areopagite, Damaris, and possibly others (Acts xvii. 33) had been won over before Stephanas, but his was the first Christian household, and as such was the foundation of the Church in those parts. It began with 'the Church in his house.' In a similar sense Epaenetus was ἀπαρχὴ τῆς 'Ασίας (Rom. xvi. 5). It was no doubt on account of this important fact that St Paul made an exception in his usual practice and baptized Stephanas and his household (i. 16). What follows shows their devotion to the cause. Clement of Rome (*Cor.* 42), speaking of the Apostles, says: "So preaching everywhere in country and town, they appointed their firstfruits, when they had proved them by the Spirit, to be bishops and deacons unto them that should believe"; where τὰς ἀπαρχὰς αὐτῶν seems to mean the firstfruits of the country districts and towns, χώρας κ. πόλεις. But here it is evident that the Apostle had not appointed Stephanas and his household to any διακονία. They had spontaneously taken this service upon themselves. Just as the brethren appointed (ἔταξαν) that Paul and Barnabas and others should go to Jerusalem about the question of circumcision (Acts xv. 2), so Stephanas and his household appointed *themselves* (ἔταξαν ἑαυτούς) to the service of their fellow-Christians. It was a self-imposed duty.* 'The saints' does not mean the poor at Jerusalem, but believers generally,—the sick and needy, travellers, etc. In class. Grk. τάσσειν ἑαυτόν is common.

16. ἵνα καὶ ὑμεῖς ὑποτάσσησθε τοῖς τοιούτοις. 'That ye also be in subjection to such men as these'—to such excellent Christians. The AV. ignores the καί, which has special point; 'that you also do your duty to them as they do to all.' And perhaps ὑποτάσσεσθαι is chosen with special reference to ἔταξαν ἑαυτούς. 'They have taken the lead in good works; do you also follow such leadership.'

καὶ παντὶ τῷ συνεργοῦντι καὶ κοπιῶντι. 'And to every

---

* The AV. is not an improvement on earlier versions, with 'They have addicted themselves.' The Genevan is better, with 'They have given themselves'; and Tyndale still better, with 'They have appoynted them selves.' For the kind of διακονία see Rom. xv. 25, 31; 2 Cor. viii. 4, ix. 1; Heb. vi. 10; also Hort, *Christian Ecclesia*, pp. 206 f.

fellow-labourer and hard worker.'* The σύν in συνεργοῦντι is
indefinite and comprehensive; neither 'with us' (AV.) in
particular, nor 'with them,' but *omni co-operanti* (Vulg.), *omnibus
operam suam conferentibus* (Beza); every one who lends a
helping hand and works hard (Rom. xvi. 6, 12).

17. χαίρω δὲ ἐπὶ τῇ παρουσίᾳ Σ. κ.τ.λ. 'And it is a joy to
me to have Stephanas and Fortunatus and Achaicus here.'
They had probably brought the Corinthian letter and were
waiting to take this letter in reply to it. They were a little bit of
Corinth, and as such a delight to the Apostle. That Fortunatus
and Achaicus were members of the οἰκία Στεφανᾶ is unlikely;
they would have been mentioned in a different way, if they had
been; and it is improbable that all the delegates would be taken
from one household. Lightfoot thinks that there is no improbability in identifying Fortunatus with the Fortunatus mentioned
by Clem. Rom. (*Cor.* 65): but the identification is precarious,
for that Fortunatus may have been a Roman, and the name is
not at all rare.† It is possible that the use of παρουσία implies
that the visit of the delegates was official; see on xv. 23.

τὸ ὑμέτερον ὑστέρημα. Does this mean 'my want of you,'
or 'your want of me'? Both are possible, and each makes
good sense. 'I am deprived of you; but they compensate for
your absence'; which is a pleasing way of expressing his affection
for the Corinthians and his joy at having some of them with him.
On the other hand; 'You cannot all of you come to me; but
these excellent delegates will do quite as well.' The latter is
perhaps a little more probable. In the other case, would he
have said ἀνεπλήρωσαν? that these three men quite made up for
their absence (Phil. ii. 30)? But, as regards answering the
Corinthians' questions, these delegates were an adequate
substitute for the whole community; there was no need for the
whole community to interview the Apostle.

אAKL, Chrys. have ὑμῶν τὸ ὑστέρημα: BCDEFGMP read τὸ
ὑμέτερον ὑστέρημα, which is more likely to be right. For οὗτοι
(אBCKLP, Copt. Arm. Aeth. Goth.), ADEFGM, Vulg. Syrr. read
αὐτοί, which Lachmann and Alford uncritically prefer.

18. ἀνέπαυσαν γὰρ τὸ ἐμὸν πνεῦμα καὶ τὸ ὑμῶν. 'For they
refreshed (2 Cor. vii. 13; Philem. 7, 20) my spirit—and yours';
explaining how these three men were sufficiently representative

* In κοπιᾶν we perhaps have one of St Paul's athletic metaphors. It
seems to refer to laborious training for a contest; Phil. ii. 16; Col. i. 29;
1 Tim. iv. 10; [Clem. Rom.] ii. 7, οἱ πολλὰ κοπιάσαντες καὶ καλῶς ἀγωνισά-
μενοι, where see Lightfoot; also on Ign. *Polyc.* 6, συγκοπιᾶτε ἀλλήλοις,
συναθλεῖτε συντρέχετε.

† The names of Corinthian Christians that are known to us are mostly of
Roman or servile origin: see on i. 14; also Hastings, *DB.* Art. 'Achaicus.'

of the Corinthian Church. It was a great comfort to him to learn from their delegates how anxious they were for his direction and advice, and to have their assurance about matters which had greatly disturbed him respecting his 'brothers' in Corinth. And it is in the highest element of his being (πνεῦμα, not ψυχή) that he has this consolation. He adds καὶ τὸ ὑμῶν with affectionate after-thought : they are sure to feel the same. This may look backward to the relief with which the perplexed Corinthians sent representatives to consult the Apostle, or forward to the time of the representatives' return, when the Corinthians would be tranquillized by their report and this letter. The latter is better ; it will be a great consolation to the Corinthians to learn what a comfort their delegates have been to St Paul.

ἐπιγινώσκετε οὖν τοὺς τοιούτους. 'Acknowledge therefore such men as these': *cognoscite ergo qui hujusmodi sunt* (Vulg.); *agnoscite igitur qui sunt hujusmodi* (Beza). 'Such services as theirs ought to meet with a generous recognition. They have undertaken a long and perilous journey on your behalf, and they have brought great relief and refreshment to me as well as to you.' In 1 Thess. v. 12, St Paul uses εἰδέναι for 'know' in the sense of 'appreciate.' It would seem from these exhortations (15–18) that the Corinthians were wanting in respect for those whose work or position gave them a claim to reverence and submission. Clement of Rome finds similar fault in them.

19–24. Solemn conclusion to the Epistle with Salutations, Warning, and Benediction. The collective salutations are in three groups. First, those of all the Churches in the proconsular province of Asia, with which St Paul was constantly in touch. Then, from Ephesus in particular, a specially affectionate one from Prisca and Aquila and their household ; and finally, a more general one from all the Christians in Ephesus. To these, with his own hand, St Paul adds his own personal salutation, with a farewell warning and blessing.*

19. Elsewhere the Apostle mentions 'Asia' thrice (2 Cor. i. 8 ; Rom. xvi. 5 ; 2 Tim. i. 15), and in all places it is the Roman province that is meant ; but the Roman province was not always accurately defined and was used in more than one sense. Here the district of which Ephesus was the capital is probably intended. See Artt. 'Asia' in *DB.* and *Enc. Bibl.* ; Knowling on Acts ii. 9 ; Hort on 1 Peter i. 2, pp. 157 f.; Harnack, *Acts of the Apostles,* pp. 102 f. ; Swete on Rev. i. 4.

ἀσπάζεται ὑμᾶς ἐν Κυρίῳ πολλὰ Ἀκύλας καὶ Πρίσκα. Both ἐν

---

* In the papyri, ἀσπάζεσθαι is frequently used in salutations at the close of letters ; *e.g.* ἀσπάζου Ἐπαγαθὸν καὶ τοὺς φιλοῦντας ἡμᾶς πρὸς ἀληθίαν. See Milligan on 1 Thess. v. 26 ; Deissmann, *Bible Studies,* p. 257

Κυρίῳ and πολλά add to the impressiveness of the salutation: it is sent in a devout spirit of fellowship in Christ, and in affectionate earnestness. Ἐν Κυρίῳ, of the sphere or element in which anything exists or takes place, is frequent in all groups of the Pauline Epistles, except the Pastorals, and is specially frequent in the salutations in Rom. xvi. (2, 8, 11, 12, 13). It sometimes means 'in God' (i. 31; 2 Cor. x. 17), but generally means 'in Christ,' to which, however, it is not always equivalent; see J. A. Robinson on Eph. ii. 21, p. 72. For the adv. πολλά see on v. 12; also Milligan, Greek Papyri, p. 91.

Prisca would hardly be mentioned as well as her husband, if she were not a prominent Christian; and this prominence is still more marked in Rom. xvi. 3 and 2 Tim. iv. 19. "Plainly the woman was the leading figure of the two, so far as regards Christian activity at least. She was a fellow-labourer of St Paul, i.e. a missionary, and she could not take part in missionary work or in teaching, unless she had been inspired and set apart by the Spirit. Otherwise, St Paul would not have recognized her. She may be claimed as ἡ ἀπόστολος, although St Paul has not given her this title" (Harnack, The Mission and Expansion of Christianity, ii. p. 66). Harnack thinks it probable that either Prisca or Aquila wrote the Epistle to the Hebrews (Ibid. i. p. 79; Zeitschrift für die neutest. Wissenschaft, 1900, i. pp. 16 f.). In Acts xviii. 18, 26 the wife is placed first; in Acts xviii. 2, the husband, as here. In Acts she is always called by the diminutive form of the name, Priscilla, which St Paul, according to the best texts, never uses. They were evidently great travellers, according to the nomadic habits of many of the Jews (Sanday and Headlam on Rom. xvi. 3; Deissmann, Light, pp. 119, 170, 278; Renan, S. Paul, pp. 96, 97; Lightfoot, Biblical Essay, p. 299).

σὺν τῇ κατ' οἶκον αὐτῶν ἐκκλησίᾳ. At Rome, as at Ephesus, the house of this devoted pair was a centre of Christian activity (Rom. xvi. 3), and was probably used for common worship (Col. iv. 15; Philem. 2). Hort, The Christian Ecclesia, pp. 117, 118 122. We need increased information about this primitive arrangement.

A 34 omit this verse, doubtless through homoeoteleuton. After αἱ ἐκκλησίαι. C P 47, Chrys. insert πᾶσαι. For ἀσπάζεται (א C D E K P, Goth.), B F G L M, Vulg. have ἀσπάζονται, an obvious correction. For Πρίσκα (א B M P 17, Copt. Arm. Goth.), A C D E F G K L, Syrr. Aeth. have Πρίσκιλλα, which AV., Lachm. and Alford adopt.

20. ἀσπάζονται ὑμᾶς οἱ ἀδελφοὶ πάντες. 'All the brethren salute you,' with some emphasis on 'all' as in xv. 7. He means all the members of the Church in Ephesus. The Corinthians are not to think that only Aquila and Priscilla with their circle

take an interest in them.   St Paul can answer for every Christian
at Ephesus.   "One feels, in reading such salutations, that the
history of nations is coming to an end, and that of a new nation
of a wholly different kind is beginning" (Godet).   Comp. 2 Cor.
xiii. 13.

ἀσπάσασθε ἀλλήλους ἐν φιλήματι ἀγίῳ.   'The affection
which the Christians in Ephesus and Asia manifest towards
you must kindle in all of you affection for one another, which
should be expressed by a hallowed use of the common mark of
affection.'   Like *v.* 14, this is an exhortation to get rid of their
unhappy divisions and jealousies.   The solemn kiss was a token
of the love for one another which all Christians ought to regard
as a debt (Rom. xiii. 8).   This φίλημα ἅγιον (1 Thess. v. 26 ;
Rom. xvi. 16), or ἅγιον φίλημα (2 Cor. xiii. 12), or φίλημα
ἀγάπης (1 Pet. v. 14), very soon became part of the ritual of
public worship.   Justin (*Apol.* i. 65) calls it simply φίλημα.
Tertullian (*De Orat.* 14) calls it *osculum pacis*, and also *signac-
ulum orationis* (18), and asks whether any prayer can be complete
cum divortio sancti osculi.   Later he calls it *pax*, and in the
Church Order known as *The Testament of the Lord* (i. 23, 30 ;
ii. 4, 9) it is simply 'the Peace.'   But in the East the more
common term was ἀσπασμός.   Conybeare (*Expositor*, 1894
i. 461) shows that the 'kiss of peace' may have been customary
among the Jews.   If so, it is unlikely that the kiss was ever pro-
miscuous in Christian worship, for in the synagogue men would
kiss men and women women; and this was certainly the custom
at a later date in the Church (*Const. Apost.* ii. 57, viii. 11 ;
Canons of Laodicea, 19 ; comp. Athenagoras *Legat.* 32 ; Clem.
Alex. *Paed.* iii. 11, p. 301 ed. Potter).   See Suicer, ἀσπασμός
and φίλημα ; *D. Chr. Ant.* p. 902 ; Kraus, *Real-Ency. d. Chr.
Alt.* i. p. 543.   It is said that in some parts of Greece a kiss
is still given with the Paschal Salutation, "Christ is risen."
Chrysostom (on 2 Cor. xiii. 13) compares the later custom of
kissing the entrances of Churches ; "We are the temple of
Christ.   We kiss the porch and entrance of the temple in
kissing one another " ; and he contrasts the kiss of Judas, which
was not ἅγιον.   From England the custom spread in the
thirteenth century of passing round a tablet (*pax, instrumentum
pacis, tabella pacis, asser ad pacem, oculatorium*) to be kissed as
a substitute for the kiss of peace.   The passing of this through
the congregation led to so much confusion that at last it was
confined to the clergy (Kraus, ii. p. 602).

21. Ὁ ἀσπασμὸς τῇ ἐμῇ χειρὶ Παύλου.   'The salutation
with my own hand of me Paul.'   The Apostle takes the pen
from his amanuensis and himself finishes the letter, to authenti-

cate it as coming from him: it must not be possible for his
opponents in Corinth to question whether this letter is really
St Paul's: 2 Thess. iii. 17; Col. iv. 18. Up to this point he
had been dictating (Rom. xvi. 22), but he finishes the letter
himself. In the papyri, the signature is sometimes in quite
a different hand from the rest of the writing (Milligan, *Thessalonians*, p. 125). The Apostle's handwriting would be known
at Corinth; but we cannot safely infer from Gal. vi. 11 that
it was unusually large: like other people, he sometimes wrote
large, as we use large type, for emphasis (Ramsay, *Galatians*,
p. 466; Deissmann, *Light*, pp. 153, 158). Παύλου is in apposition with the gen. implied in ἐμῇ.*

εἴ τις οὐ φιλεῖ τὸν Κ., ἤτω ἀνάθεμα. We might have expected
ἀγαπᾷ, but the previous φιλήματι may have suggested the lower
word. Or St Paul may have purposely chosen it, to indicate
the poor character of the love indicated; 'If anyone does
not have even as much affection as φιλεῖν'; and those who
were uncharitable to one another could not have this. For the
difference between the two verbs see Trench, *Syn.* § 12; Cremer,
pp. 9 f.; comm. on John xxi. 15–17; Swete on Rev. iii. 19.
Nowhere else, excepting the somewhat similar Tit. iii. 15, does
St Paul use φιλεῖν, which is rare in the N.T. outside the Gospels.
The negative almost forms one word with φιλεῖ, 'if anyone has no
affection for Christ,' is heartless towards Him. As a matter of
fact, this was the case with some: comp. vii. 9, xi. 6. For ἤτω,
a later form of ἔστω, see Jas. v. 12; also ἤτω ἡ δόξα Κυρίου εἰς
τὸν αἰῶνα, Ps. civ. 31; Ἰερουσαλὴμ ἤτω ἁγία, 1 Macc. x. 31. It
may have been common in adjurations and curses. J. B. Mayor
quotes two inscriptions; εἰ δέ τις κακουργήσει, ἤτω ἔνοχος Ἡλίῳ
Σελήνῃ, and κατηραμένος ἤτω αὐτὸς καὶ τὰ τέκνα αὐτοῦ (*St James*,
p. 155). Gal. i. 8, 9, we have ἀνάθεμα ἔστω: see on xii. 3. See
Enc. Bibl. ii. 1432.

Μαρὰν ἀθά. Perhaps the most curious mistake in the
English Versions is that which attaches these words, combined
into one, to the preceding 'Anathema,' as if they formed part
of a formula of malediction, 'be Anathema Maranatha.' Coverdale has 'be Anathema Maharan Matha,' which has perhaps
been influenced by Shammatha, the highest form of Jewish
excommunication, like Luther's 'Maharam Motha.' The
Genevan *translates* the words; 'let him be had in execration,
yea excommunicate to death.' But the error is far older than
any English Version, and perhaps may be traced back to the

---

* In none of the Epistles which have come down to us does he call
himself Saul. Possibly, if he had to write to Jews, he would do so (ix. 20).
See Deissmann, *Bible Studies*, pp. 316 f.; Ramsay, *St Paul*, pp. 81 f.;
Schiller-Szinessy, *Expositor*, 3rd series, iv. p. 324   See also on xv. 9.

fifth century. Down to the seventeenth century it was accepted as correct by many scholars; and although abandoned by scholars now, it survives here and there in popular literature, and in the Second Lesson one may still sometimes hear 'Anathema Maranatha' read as one expression. Scholars, however, are not agreed as to the exact meaning of Maranatha; as to whether it means 'The Lord has come,' or 'Our Lord has come,'* or 'Our Lord cometh,' or 'Our Lord, come.' The last would resemble 'Amen; come Lord Jesus' (Rev. xxii. 20). Yet another interpretation is, 'Our Lord is the sign' (Abbott, *The Son of Man*, p. 465; *Ency. Bibl.* iii. 2935, from Klostermann, *Probleme im Aposteltexte*, pp. 220–246), but it is not likely to be right. With 'Our Lord cometh' compare Phil. iv. 5; Jas. v. 8; Rev. i. 7, iii. 11; and this agrees with the context and the substance of the Epistle. If it be right, the saying, though in no way a malediction, is monitory in tone. It warns them that at any moment they may have to answer for their shortcomings. Why St Paul gives this warning in Aramaic rather than in Greek, is unknown. The most probable conjecture is that in this language it had become a sort of motto or password among Christians, and familiar in that shape, like 'Alleluia' with ourselves. See Hastings, *DB.* iii. pp. 241 f.; Findlay *ad loc.*; Dalman, *Words*, p. 328. Zahn thinks that the Apostle uses "the language of the Palestinian Jews" because "the persons whom he has in mind are Christians who had come from Palestine" (*Introd. to N.T.*, i. p. 288).

ℵ* A B C* M 17 have τὸν Κύριον, without addition; D E F G K L P, Vulg. Syrr. Copt. Goth., Chrys. add ἡμῶν Ἰησοῦν Χριστόν, as in AV. F G have μαρανναθά, which g renders *in adventu domini*.

23. ἡ χάρις τοῦ Κυρίου Ἰησοῦ μεθ' ὑμῶν. The Apostle will not end with a word of warning or severity, but adds the usual benediction. Like a true teacher, as Chrysostom says, he helps not only with counsels, but with prayers.

The shortest of the Pauline benedictions is that in Col. iv. 18; 1 Tim. vi. 21, ἡ χάρις μεθ' ὑμῶν. This one is shorter than usual. Sometimes ἡμῶν is inserted after Κυρίου (Rom. xvi. 20, 24; Gal. vi. 18; 1 Thess. v. 28; 2 Thess. iii. 18), and A L P Vulg. add it here. Sometimes Χριστοῦ is inserted after Ἰησοῦ (Rom. xvi. 24; 2 Cor. xiii. 13; Gal. vi. 18; Phil. iv. 23; 1 Thess. v. 28; 2 Thess. iii. 18; Philem. 25), and A C D E F G

---

* Chrysostom renders it, Ὁ Κύριος ἡμῶν ἦλθε, and interprets it of the Incarnation: "as if the Apostle said, The common Lord and Ruler of all condescended to come down so low, and you remain unchanged and persist in sinning." The thought of the Incarnation incites to virtue and extinguishes the desire to sin. The *Didache* has the expression in the invitation to the Holy Communion; εἴ τις ἅγιός ἐστιν, ἐρχέσθω· εἴ τις οὐκ ἔστι, μετανοείτω μαραναθά. Ἀμήν (x. 6). See Schaff's note, p. 198; also Field, *Otium Norvic.* iii. p. 110; Deissmann, *Light*, pp. 305, 354.

K L M P, Syrr. Copt. Arm. Aeth. add it here, while א* B 17, Am. Goth. omit. Sometimes πάντων (2 Cor. xiii. 13 ; 2 Thess. iii. 18), sometimes τοῦ πνεύματος (Gal. vi. 18 ; Phil. iv. 23 ; Philem. 25), is inserted before ὑμῶν. The fullest form of all is 2 Cor. xiii. 13. In spite of the strong evidence for Χριστοῦ here, it is not to be accepted ; the probability of insertion, either deliberately or mechanically, is great. The evidence against Χριστόν in *v.* 22 is stronger, and if that is not genuine, Χριστοῦ is not likely to be genuine here.

24. To make his farewell words still more tender, he adds to the Apostolic Benediction a message of personal affection. The verb to be supplied is probably the same in both cases, εἴη, 'be,' as in AV. and RV. ; εἴη must be understood in *v.* 23, and is more probable than ἐστί in *v.* 24. He sends his love in the form of a blessing, to help them to correct what he has blamed, and to prove to them that, as regards his attitude towards them, ἡ ἀγάπη οὐδέποτε πίπτει. It embraces all of them, even the most faulty, for it is ἐν Χριστῷ ᾽Ιησοῦ, the 'bond of perfectness' and the 'bond of peace.' * He would not have said πάντων, if ἐστί were understood, for some offenders were too flagrant to be at present included ; but as a wish, an aspiration and a prayer, his message may embrace all. And, being 'in Christ Jesus,' it has nothing of the partiality or fickleness of human affection. It is, as Chrysostom says, πνευματική τις· διὸ καὶ σφόδρα γνησία.

The final ἀμήν (א A C D K L P, Versions) is, as usual, a liturgical addition : B F M 17 and some Latt. omit. The ἀμήν at the end of Galatians, Romans, and Jude is genuine ; that at the end of 2 Peter is possibly genuine. See Introduction, § 'Text.'

As already pointed out on *v.* 5, the note in K L and some Latin texts, stating that the letter was written from Philippi, is based on a misapprehension. P and some other texts say correctly that it was written 'from Ephesus' or 'from Asia,' while א B* C D* F 17 make no statement about the place of writing.

---

* See Deissmann, *Die neutestamentliche Formel " in Christo Jesu "* ; also Sanday and Headlam on Rom. vi. 11, pp. 160, 161.

INDEXES

INDEX I. GENERAL.

INDEX II. GREEK WORDS.

συνέρχομαι, xi. 17–20, 33, 34, xiv. 23, 26.
συνεσθίω, v. 11.
συνεσις, i. 19.
συνετός, i. 19.
συνευδοκέω, vii. 12, 13.
συνζητητής, i. 20.
συνήθεια, viii. 7, xi. 16.
συνκεράννυμι, xii. 24.
συνκοινωνός, ix. 23.
συνκρίνω, ii. 13.
συνμερίζομαι, ix. 13.
σύνοιδα, iv. 4.
συνπάσχω, xii. 26.
συνστέλλω, vii. 29.
συνχαίρω, xii. 26, xiii. 6.
σφραγίς, ix. 2.
σχῆμα, vii. 31.
σχίσμα, i. 10, xi. 18, xii. 25.
σχολάζω, vii. 5.
σώζω, i. 18, 21, iii. 15, v. 5, vii. 16, etc.
σῶμα, v. 3, vi. 13–20, vii. 4, ix. 27, x. 16, 17, xi. 24–29, xii. 12–27, xv. 35, etc.
Σωσθένης, i. 1.

τάγμα, xv. 23.
τάξις, xiv. 40.
τάσσω, xvi. 5.
ταχέως, iv. 19.
τέλειος, ii. 6, xiii. 10, xiv. 20.
τέλος, i. 8, x. 11, xv. 24.
τηρέω, vii. 37.
τήρησις, vii. 19.
τιμή, vi. 20, vii. 23, xii. 23, 24.
τίμιος, iii. 12.
Τιμόθεος, iv. 17, xvi. 10.
τί οὖν, iii. 5, x. 19, xiv. 15, 26.
τί ἐστιν, x. 19.
τοίνυν, ix. 26.
τοιοῦτος, v. 1, 5, 11, vii. 15, xv. 48, etc.
τολμᾷ, vi. 1.
τόπος, i. 2, xiv. 16.
τότε, iv. 5, xiii. 12, xv. 28, 54, xvi. 2.
τράπεζα, x. 21.
τρεῖς, x. 8, xiii. 13, xiv. 27, 29.
τρέχω, ix. 24, 26.
τρίτη, τ. ἡμέρα τ., xv. 4.
τρόμος, ii. 3.
τυγχανω, xiv. 10, xv. 37, xvi. 6.

τυπικῶς, x. 11.
τύποι, x. 6.
τύπτω, viii. 12.

υἱός, ὁ, i. 9, xv. 28.
ὑμέτερος, xv. 31, xvi. 17?.
ὑπάρχω, vii. 26, xi. 7, 18, xii. 22, xiii. 3.
ὑπέρ c. gen., i. 13?, iv. 6, x. 30, xi. 24, xii. 25, xv. 3, 29.
ὑπέρ c. acc., iv. 6, x. 13.
ὑπέρακμος, vii. 36.
ὑπερβολή, xii. 31.
ὑπεροχή, ii. 1.
ὑπηρέτης, iv. 1.
ὑπό c. acc., x. 1, xv. 25, 27.
ὑπὸ νόμον, ix. 20.
ὑποτάσσω, xiv. 32, 34, xv. 27, 28, xvi. 16.
ὑποφέρω, x. 13.
ὑπωπιάζω, ix. 27.
ὑστερέω, i. 7, viii. 8, xii. 24.
ὑστέρημα, xvi. 17.

φανερός, iii. 13, xi. 19, xiv. 25.
φανερόω, iv. 5.
φανέρωσις, xii. 7.
φείδομαι, vii. 28.
φεύγω, vi. 18, x. 14.
φημί, vii. 29, x. 15, 19, xv. 50.
φησίν, vi. 16.
φθαρτός, ix. 25, xv. 53, 54.
φθείρω, iii. 17, xv. 33.
φθόγγος, xiv. 7.
φθορά, xv. 42, 50.
φιλέω, xvi. 22.
φίλημα, xvi. 20.
φιλόνεικος, xi. 16.
φιμόω, ix. 9?.
φόβος, ii. 3.
φορέω, xv. 49.
Φορτοῦνατος, xvi. 17.
φρήν, xiv. 20.
φρονέω, xiii. 11.
φρόνιμος, iv. 10, x. 15.
φύραμα, v. 6, 7.
φυσιόω, iv. 6, 18, 19, v. 2, viii. 1, xiii. 4.
φύσις, xi. 14.
φυτεύω, iii. 6–8, ix. 7.
φωνή, xiv. 7–11.
φωτίζω, iv. 5.

Index III. Latin and English Words.